THE HARVEY LECTURES

From the engraving by Jacobus Houbraken

WILLIAM HARVEY

BORN APRIL 1, 1578 - DIED JUNE 3, 1657

THE HARVEY LECTURES

DELIVERED UNDER THE AUSPICES OF

The HARVEY SOCIETY of NEW YORK

1972–1973

UNDER THE PATRONAGE OF THE NEW YORK
ACADEMY OF MEDICINE

BY

LEO SACHS   GERALD M. EDELMAN
GORDON M. TOMKINS   DONALD S. FREDRICKSON
HOWARD K. SCHACHMAN   H. SHERWOOD LAWRENCE
GEORGE C. COTZIAS   JEROME GROSS

SERIES 68

1974

ACADEMIC PRESS   New York   San Francisco   London
A Subsidiary of Harcourt Brace Jovanovich, Publishers

ACADEMIC PRESS, INC.
111 Fifth Avenue, New York, New York 10003

United Kingdom Edition published by
ACADEMIC PRESS, INC. (LONDON) LTD.
24/28 Oval Road, London NW1

LIBRARY OF CONGRESS CATALOG CARD NUMBER: 7-2726

ISBN 0-12-312068-3

PRINTED IN THE UNITED STATES OF AMERICA

CONTENTS

HARVEY LECTURES 1972–1973

THE HARVEY SOCIETY*

A SOCIETY FOR THE DIFFUSION OF KNOWLEDGE OF THE MEDICAL SCIENCES

CONSTITUTION

I

This Society shall be named the Harvey Society.

II

The object of this Society shall be the diffusion of scientific knowledge in selected chapters in anatomy, physiology, pathology, bacteriology, pharmacology, and physiological and pathological chemistry, through the medium of public lectures by men who are workers in the subjects presented.

III

The members of the Society shall constitute two classes: Active and Honorary members. Active members shall be workers in the medical or biological sciences, residing in the metropolitan New York area, who have personally contributed to the advancement of these sciences. Active members who leave New York to reside elsewhere may retain their membership. Honorary members shall be those who have delivered lectures before the Society and who are not Active members. Honorary members shall not be eligible to office, nor shall they be entitled to a vote.

Active members shall be elected by ballot. They shall be nominated to the Executive Committee and the names of the nominees shall accompany the notice of the meeting at which the vote for their election will be taken.

---

* The Constitution is reprinted here for historical interest only; its essential features have been included in the Articles of Incorporation and By-Laws.

IV

The management of the Society shall be vested in an Executive Committee to consist of a President, a Vice-President, a Secretary, a Treasurer, and three other members, these officers to be elected by ballot at each annual meeting of the Society to serve one year.

V

The Annual Meeting of the Society shall be held at a stated date in January of each year at a time and place to be determined by the Executive Committee. Special meetings may be held at such times and places as the Executive Committee may determine. At all meetings ten members shall constitute a quorum.

VI

Changes in the Constitution may be made at any meeting of the Society by a majority vote of those present after previous notification to the members in writing.

THE HARVEY SOCIETY, INC.

A SOCIETY FOR THE DIFFUSION OF KNOWLEDGE OF THE MEDICAL SCIENCES

BY-LAWS

ARTICLE I

Name and Purposes of the Society

SECTION 1. The name of the Society as recorded in the Constitution at the time of its founding in 1905 was the Harvey Society. In 1955, it was incorporated in the State of New York as The Harvey Society, Inc.

SECTION 2. The purposes for which this Society is formed are those set forth in its original Constitution and modified in its Certificate of Incorporation as from time to time amended. The purposes of the Society shall be to foster the diffusion of scientific knowledge in selected chapters of the biological sciences and related areas of knowledge through the medium of public delivery and printed publication of lectures by men and women who are workers in the subjects presented, and to promote the development of these sciences.

It is not organized for pecuniary profit, and no part of the net earnings, contributions, or other corporate funds of the Society shall inure to the benefit of any private member or individual, and no substantial part of its activities shall be carrying on propaganda, or otherwise attempting, to influence legislation.

ARTICLE II

Offices of the Society

SECTION 1. The main office and place of business of the Society shall be in the City and County of New York. The Board of Directors may designate additional offices.

Article III

Members

Section 1. The members of the Society shall consist of the incorporators, members of the hitherto unincorporated Harvey Society, and persons elected from time to time. The members of the Society shall constitute two classes: Active and Honorary Members. Active members shall be individuals with either the Ph.D. or the M.D. degree or its equivalent, residing or carrying on a major part of their work in the New York metropolitan area at the time of their election, who are personally making original contributions to the literature of the medical or biological sciences. Honorary members shall be those who have delivered a lecture before the Society and who are not Active members. Honorary members shall be exempted from the payment of dues. Active members who have remained in good standing for 35 years or who have reached the age of 65 and have remained in good standing for 25 years shall be designated Life members. They shall retain all the privileges of their class of membership without further payment of dues. Honorary members shall not be eligible to office, nor shall they be entitled to participate by voting in the affairs of the Society. Volumes of The Harvey Lectures will be circulated only to Active and Life members. Honorary members will receive only the volume containing their lecture. New Active members shall be nominated in writing to the Board of Directors by an Active member and seconded by another Active member. They shall be elected at the Annual Meeting of the Society by a vote of the majority of the Active members present at the meeting. Members who leave New York to reside elsewhere may retain their membership. Active members who have given a Harvey Lecture and who have moved out of the New York metropolitan area may, if they wish, become Honorary members. Membership in the Society shall terminate on the death, resignation, or removal of the member.

Section 2. Members may be suspended or expelled from the Society by the vote of a majority of the members present at any meeting of members at which a quorum is present, for refusing or failing to comply with the By-Laws, or for other good and sufficient cause.

Section 3. Members may resign from the Society by written declaration, which shall take effect upon the filing thereof with the Secretary.

Article IV

Meetings of the Members of the Society

Section 1. The Society shall hold its annual meeting of Active members for the election of officers and directors, and for the transaction of such other business as may come before the meeting in the month of January or February in each year, at a place within the City of New York, and on a date and at an hour to be specified in the notice of such meeting.

Section 2. Special meetings of members shall be called by the Secretary upon the request of the President or Vice-President or of the Board of Directors, or on written request of twenty-five of the Active members.

Section 3. Notice of all meetings of Active members shall be mailed or delivered personally to each member not less than ten nor more than sixty days before the meeting. Like notice shall be given with respect to lectures.

Section 4. At all meetings of Active members of the Society ten Active members, present in person, shall constitute a quorum, but less than a quorum shall have power to adjourn from time to time until a quorum be present.

Article V

Board of Directors

Section 1. The number of directors constituting The Board of Directors shall be seven: the President, the Vice-President, the Secretary, and the Treasurer of the Society, and the three members of the Council. The number of directors may be increased or reduced by amendments of the By-Laws as hereinafter provided, within the maximum and minimum numbers fixed in the Certificate of Incorporation or any amendment thereto.

SECTION 2. The Board of Directors shall hold an annual meeting shortly before the annual meeting of the Society.

Special meetings of the Board of Directors shall be called at any time by the Secretary upon the request of the President or Vice-President or of one-fourth of the directors then in office.

SECTION 3. Notice of all regular annual meetings of the Board shall be given to each director at least seven days before the meeting and notice of special meetings, at least one day before. Meetings may be held at any place within the City of New York designated in the notice of the meeting.

SECTION 4. The Board of Directors shall have the immediate charge, management, and control of the activities and affairs of the Society, and it shall have full power, in the intervals between the annual meetings of the Active members, to do any and all things in relation to the affairs of the Society.

SECTION 5. Council members shall be elected by the members of the Society at the Annual Meeting. One Council member is elected each year to serve for three years, there being three Council members at all times. Vacancies occurring on the Council for any cause may be filled for the unexpired term by the majority vote of the directors present at any meeting at which a quorum is present. Only Active members of the Society shall be eligible for membership on the Council.

SECTION 6. A majority of the Board as from time to time constituted shall be necessary to constitute a quorum, but less than a quorum shall have power to adjourn from time to time until a quorum be present.

SECTION 7. The Board shall have power to appoint individual or corporate trustees and their successors of any or all of the property of the Society, and to confer upon them such of the powers, duties, or obligations of the directors in relation to the care, custody, or management of such property as may be deemed advisable.

SECTION 8. The directors shall present at the Annual Meeting a report, verified by the President and Treasurer, or by a majority of the directors, showing the whole amount of real and personal property owned by the Society, where located, and where and how invested, the amount and nature of the property acquired during the year immediately preceding the date of the report and the manner of the acquisition; the amount applied, appropriated, or expended during the year immediately preceding such date, and the purposes, objects, or persons to or for which such applications, appropriations, or expenditures have been made; and the names of the persons who have been admitted to membership in the Society during such year, which report shall be filed with the records of the Society and an abstract thereof entered in the minutes of the proceedings of the Annual Meeting.

Article VI

Committees

Section 1. The Board of Directors may appoint from time to time such committees as it deems advisable, and each such committee shall exercise such powers and perform such duties as may be conferred upon it by the Board of Directors subject to its continuing direction and control.

Article VII

Officers

Section 1. The officers of the Society shall consist of a President, a Vice-President, a Secretary, and a Treasurer, and such other officers as the Board of Directors may from time to time determine. All of the officers of the Society shall be members of the Board of Directors.

Section 2. The President shall be the chief executive officer of the Society and shall be in charge of the direction of its affairs, acting with the advice of the Board of Directors. The other officers of the Society shall have the powers and perform the duties that usually pertain to their respective offices, or as may from time to time be prescribed by the Board of Directors.

Section 3. The officers and the directors shall not receive, directly or indirectly, any salary or other compensation from the Society, unless authorized by the concurring vote of two-thirds of all the directors.

SECTION 4. The officers shall be elected at the Annual Meeting of the Active members. All officers shall hold office until the next Annual Meeting and until their successors are elected or until removed by vote of a majority vote of the directors. Vacancies occurring among the officers for any cause may be filled for the unexpired term by the majority vote of the directors present at any meeting at which a quorum is present. Officers must be Active members of the Society.

ARTICLE VIII

Fiscal Year—Seal

SECTION 1. The fiscal year of the Society shall be the calendar year.

SECTION 2. The seal of the Society shall be circular in form and shall bear the words "The Harvey Society, Inc., New York, New York, Corporate Seal."

ARTICLE IX

Amendments

SECTION 1. These By-Laws may be added to, amended, or repealed, in whole or in part, by the Active members or by the Board of Directors, in each case by a majority vote at any meeting at which a quorum is present, provided that notice of the proposed addition, amendment, or repeal has been given to each member or director, as the case may be, in the notice of such meeting.

REGULATION OF MEMBRANE CHANGES, DIFFERENTIATION, AND MALIGNANCY IN CARCINOGENESIS*

LEO SACHS

Department of Genetics, Weizmann Institute of Science, Rehovot, Israel

THE normal functioning of a multicellular organism requires that cells stop multiplying when there are enough cells in the body and that they differentiate to perform their specific functions. These essential properties of normal cells break down in carcinogenesis, when normal cells are transformed to malignant cells. In tumor cells, to various degrees depending on the kind of tumor, cell multiplication is no longer inhibited by the control mechanisms that inhibit the multiplication of normal cells. In many and perhaps all malignancies, the cells also no longer differentiate normally.

I have tried to understand the control of growth and differentiation in normal mammalian cells and the change in these controls in carcinogenesis, by developing and using *in vitro* systems to study cells that form a solid tissue and cells that are in suspension *in vivo*. For cells that form a solid tissue, I have used normal and malignant transformed fibroblasts; and for cells in suspension, normal lymphocytes, mast cells, macrophages and granulocytes, and leukemic cells. I would like to summarize in the present lecture, my studies on the regulation of growth and differentiation in normal and malignant cells with particular reference to: (I) changes in the cell surface membrane; (II) control of growth and differentiation in normal hematopoietic and leukemic cells; and (III) reversion of the malignant phenotype and the genetic control of malignancy.

---

* Lecture delivered September 21, 1972.

I. CHANGES IN THE CELL SURFACE MEMBRANE

The changes in cell regulation that are produced by malignant cell transformation can be associated with changes in the cell surface (Sachs, 1965, 1967). Lectins are proteins that bind to specific carbohydrates, and we have used lectins as probes to elucidate these changes in the cell surface membrane. We started these experiments with concanavalin A (Con A) (Sumner and Howell, 1936) a lectin that binds to glucose or mannose like sites on the cell surface membrane (Inbar and Sachs 1969a,b). Incubation of normal and transformed cells with Con A has shown that cells transformed by viral or nonviral carcinogens (Sachs and Medina, 1961; Sachs *et al.,* 1962; Berwald and Sachs, 1963, 1965) were agglutinated by Con A (Fig. 1) whereas normal cells were not agglutinated unless they had been treated with a proteolytic enzyme, such as trypsin (Inbar and Sachs, 1969a,b). Infection of normal fibroblasts with polyoma virus or simian virus 40 has indicated that both hereditarily transformed and abortively transformed cells (Medina and Sachs, 1961; Stoker, 1968) showed this gain of Con A-induced agglutinability and that it required at least one cell replication after virus infection and a certain cell density (Inbar and Sachs, 1969b; Ben-Bassat *et al.,*

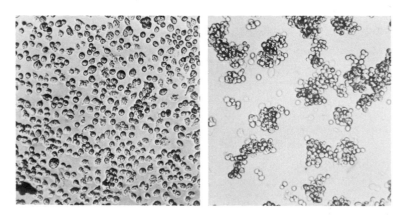

FIG. 1.   Normal hamster cells (left) and hamster cells transformed by polyoma virus (right) after incubation with Con A. From Sachs (1972).

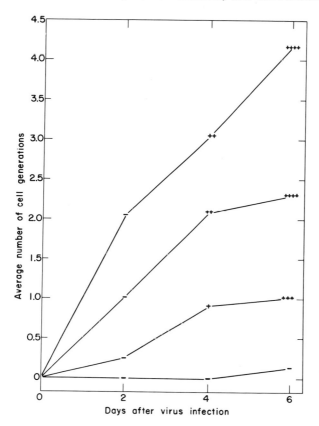

FIG. 2. Average number of cell generations and Con A agglutinability after infection of mouse cells with simian virus 40. Cells were seeded at different seeding levels and agglutination scored in a scale from − to ++++. From Ben-Bassat et al. (1970).

1970) (Fig. 2). The degree of agglutinability of transformed cells by Con A was related to their degree of malignancy *in vivo* (Inbar et al., 1972a).

Con A contains metal ions that are required for carbohydrate binding; the dimer has a molecular weight of 54,000 and 2 carbohydrate binding sites (Kalb and Levitzki, 1968; Edelman et al., 1972). We labeled the protein by substituting the metal ions in the native protein by [63]Ni (Inbar and Sachs, 1969a), or by

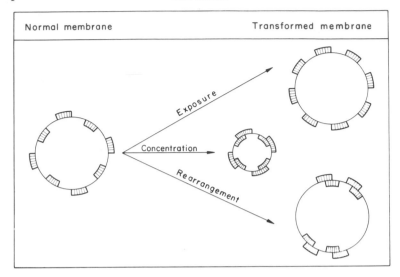

Normal membrane   Transformed membrane

FIG. 3. Model of the three types of changes of Con A binding sites in cell transformation, based on the results of binding of radioactively labeled Con A. From Ben-Bassat *et al.* (1971).

acetylation (Inbar *et al.*, 1973a). Measurements of the binding of radioactively labeled Con A molecules to the cell surface have indicated, that there can be 3 types of changes in the Con A binding sites on the surface membrane associated with cell transformation. Depending on the culture conditions of the cells, there can be an exposure of cryptic sites, a concentration of exposed sites by a decrease in cell size, or a rearrangement of exposed sites without a decrease in cell size resulting in a clustering of sites (Fig. 3) (Inbar and Sachs, 1969a; Ben-Bassat *et al.*, 1971). It was suggested from these results, that the changes in Con A binding sites result in regions with a greater density of sites on the transformed than on the normal cells (Ben-Bassat *et al.*, 1971). This was also indicated from studies with the electron microscope (Nicolson, 1972).

The study of Con A binding and agglutination at different temperatures has shown, that Con A-induced agglutinability of cells is temperature sensitive (Fig. 4) and that binding of Con A

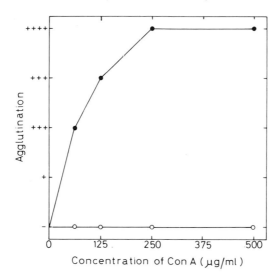

FIG. 4. Con Λ agglutinability of simian virus 40-transformed hamster cells at 4°C (O——O) and 24°C (●——●). From Inbar et al. (1971a).

molecules to the cell surface is by itself not sufficient to induce agglutination. This suggested that, in addition to Con A binding, a temperature-sensitive activity on the surface membrane was required for cell agglutinability (Inbar et al., 1971a). It was subsequently found that the temperature-sensitive activity required for agglutinability appears to be associated with mobility of the Con A binding sites (Inbar and Sachs, 1973; Sachs et al., 1973).

Changes in the distribution of Con A binding sites (Ben-Bassat et al., 1971; Inbar and Sachs, 1973) and the movement of antigens on the cell surface (Taylor et al., 1971; Loor et al., 1972; Yahara and Edelman, 1972; Edidin and Weiss, 1972) have indicated, that receptors can be mobile in a fluid surface membrane (Singer and Nicolson, 1972). The results indicate that all the types of cells studied have a more or less random distribution of Con A binding sites before Con A is bound to these sites. In cells with the appropriate site mobility, this distribution can be changed by cross-linking of Con A binding sites by Con A. Studies on the microscopic distribution of fluorescent Con A on the cell surface have indicated that there was the smallest amount

6 LEO SACHS

TABLE I

FINAL DISTRIBUTION OF CON A BINDING SITES AFTER
CON A BINDING, AND CELL AGGLUTINATION[a]

Cell type	Final distribution of Con A binding sites	Agglutination by Con A
Normal fibroblasts	Semirandom	−
Transformed fibroblasts and lymphoma cells	Many clusters	+ + + +
Normal lymphocytes	Caps	±

[a] From Sachs *et al.* (1973).

of such a redistribution in normal fibroblasts, the formation of large numbers of clusters of sites in transformed fibroblasts and lymphoma cells, and a redistribution of sites to one pole of the cell to form a cap in normal lymphocytes. Using these differences in final distribution after Con A binding as indicators of the mobility of Con A binding sites, this indicates that normal and transformed cells have different degrees of mobility of the Con A binding sites (Inbar and Sachs, 1973; Sachs *et al.*, 1973; Inbar *et al.*, 1973b). The transformation of normal to transformed fibroblasts was associated with an increase in the mobility of Con A binding sites, whereas the transformation of normal lymphocytes to lymphoma cells was associated with a decrease in the mobility of these sites. The transformed fibroblasts and lymphoma cells with a high degree of cluster formation after binding of Con A had a high degree of agglutinability (Table I). The agglutinability of transformed fibroblasts was associated with their content of ATP, and we have suggested that changes in the ATP content in these cells may change the mobility of Con A binding sites (Vlodavsky *et al.*, 1973).

Differences in the rotational mobility of Con A sites in normal and transformed cells and an increase in this mobility after treatment of the cells with trypsin, have been shown by fluorescent polarization analysis (Inbar *et al.*, 1973c; Sachs *et al.*, 1973). The lymphoma cells, with a decreased mobility of Con A sites compared to normal lymphocytes, showed by fluorescent polarization, an increased fluidity of the lipids in the surface membrane

(Inbar *et al.*, 1974). The lower fluidity of the surface membrane lipids of normal lymphocytes is due to a higher cholesterol-to-phospholipid ratio (Vlodavsky and Sachs, 1974).

The long-term binding of Con A to cells produces an inhibition of cell multiplication and cell killing, presumably due to cross-linking by Con A of the Con A binding sites. Treatment of normal and transformed fibroblasts with different concentrations of Con A for various periods of time has shown that, with the appropriate concentration and time of treatment, there is a greater cytotoxic effect on the transformed than on the normal cells (Shoham *et al.*, 1970) (Fig. 5). This was associated with a greater inhibitory effect in the transformed cells on the transport of amino

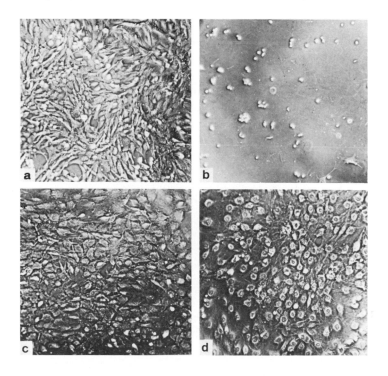

FIG. 5. Cultures of normal and simian virus 40-transformed mouse cells, 2 days after treatment with Con A. Untreated transformed cells (a), Con A-treated transformed cells (b), untreated normal cells (c), and Con A-treated normal cells (d). From Shoham *et al.* (1970).

acids, D-glucose, and D-galactose (Inbar *et al.*, 1971b). Treatment of tumors with Con A resulted in an inhibition of tumor development *in vivo* (Shoham *et al.*, 1970; Inbar *et al.*, 1972b). Variants resistant to Con A have been selected from transformed fibroblasts. These variants showed a decreased agglutinability by Con A and a reversion of the transformed phenotype (Wollman and Sachs, 1972).

In addition to Con A which shows specific binding to glucose- or mannose-like sites on the surface membrane, other lectins can be used to study sites with other carbohydrates. We have used the lectin from wheat germ that binds to N-acetyl-D-glucosamine-like sites (Burger, 1969), a soybean lectin that binds to N-acetyl-D-galactosamine-like sites (Sela *et al.,* 1970, 1971), and lectins from *Lotus tetragonolobus* and wax bean, which bind to L-fucose- (Vlodavsky *et al.*, 1972) and fetuin-like sites (Sela *et al.*, 1973), respectively. These lectins, except the one from *Lotus* which did not agglutinate fibroblasts, all showed a greater agglutinability of transformed than of normal mouse fibroblasts. The marked cell cytotoxicity shown by Con A was not found with the lectins from wheat germ and soybean (Inbar *et al.*, 1972b, 1973a).

Incubation of normal lymphocytes with different lectins has shown, that although these cells can be activated to undergo DNA synthesis and form blast cells by phytohemagglutinin (PHA) (Nowell, 1960) and Con A (Powell and Leon, 1970), there was no such activation by the lectins from wheatgerm and soybean (Inbar *et al.*, 1973a) (Fig. 6). Cell agglutinability by these lectins was temperature sensitive for Con A and PHA, but not for the lectins from wheat germ and soybean. This suggested that activation of lymphocytes is associated with a temperature-sensitive activity on the surface membrane. Studies with fluorescent lectins have shown that Con A, but not the lectins from wheatgerm or soybean, formed caps on normal lymphocytes and that the rotational mobility of the binding sites measured by fluorescent polarization analysis, was higher for the Con A binding sites than for the sites for the other two lectins (Shinitzky *et al.*, 1973). These data support the assumption that lectin activation of lymphocytes is associated with a redistribution of specific membrane components after binding of the lectin.

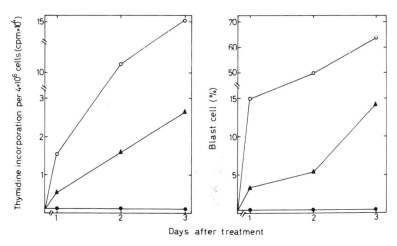

FIG. 6. Differences in the activation of normal lymphocytes, resulting in DNA synthesis and the formation of blast cells, by Con A (O———O), phytohemagglutinin (▲———▲), and the lectins from wheat germ and soybean (●———●). From Inbar *et al.* (1973a).

To determine possible changes in the cell cycle, normal and transformed fibroblasts have been studied in interphase and mitosis. The results indicate that, regarding the agglutinability by Con A and percentage of cells with surface fluorescence at non-saturation concentrations of fluorescent Con A, normal mitotic cells resemble transformed interphase cells, and normal interphase cells resemble transformed mitotic cells (Shoham and Sachs, 1972, 1974). This indicates that normal and transformed fibroblasts have different cyclic changes in the mobility of Con A sites on their surface membrane.

The use of lectins as probes has thus shown that changes in the dynamics of specific surface membrane sites are associated with changes in the control of cell growth and the cell cycle. These changes may result in differences in the transport and internal concentration of specific chemicals that regulate growth and the cell cycle. As will be described in the next section, these probes have also shown an association between the dynamics of specific surface membrane sites and the differentiation of myeloid leukemic cells.

10 LEO SACHS

II. CONTROL OF GROWTH AND DIFFERENTIATION IN NORMAL HEMATOPOIETIC AND LEUKEMIC CELLS

Studies on the mechanism that controls the growth and differentiation of normal hematopoietic cells can be of value in elucidating the blocks in cell differentiation that occur during leukemogenesis. We have, therefore, developed a tissue culture system in which the growth and differentiation of normal lymphocytes involved in the homograft reaction, mast cells, granulocytes, and macrophages can be studied in mass culture (Ginsburg and Sachs, 1963, 1965; Sachs, 1964). Colony formation was obtained with granulocytes and mast cells in liquid medium (Ginsburg and Sachs, 1963). We also developed a tissue culture cloning assay in semisolid medium for two types of these normal hematopoietic cells: macrophages and granulocytes in rodents (Pluznik and Sachs, 1965; 1966; Ichikawa *et al.*, 1966), and granulocytes in humans (Paran *et al.*, 1970). Our system was then also used by others for the cloning of these rodent (Metcalf *et al.*, 1967; Worton *et al.*, 1969) and human cells (Pike and Robinson, 1970).

In the cloning procedure in semisolid medium that was developed, normal hematopoietic cells were cloned in soft agar (Pluznik and Sachs, 1965) or methyl cellulose (Ichikawa *et al.*, 1966). The formation of colonies by normal hematopoietic cells required the presence of an inducer that can be produced by various types of cells, including fibroblasts. We now call this inducer MGI (macrophage and granulocyte inducer) (Landau and Sachs, 1971a). In the first experiments (Ginsburg and Sachs, 1963; Sachs, 1964; Pluznik and Sachs, 1965) MGI was supplied by a feeder layer of fibroblasts from mixed embryo cells. A study of the types of hematopoietic cell colonies obtained with such a feeder layer underneath the agar or methyl cellulose, showed that there were colonies of macrophages, granulocytes (Fig. 7), blast cells, or colonies with both macrophages and granulocytes (Fig. 8).

The macrophages in these colonies contained metochromatic granules when grown in agar, but not when the cells were grown in methyl cellulose (Ichikawa *et al.*, 1966), and they were also identified as macrophages by electron microscopy (Lagunoff *et*

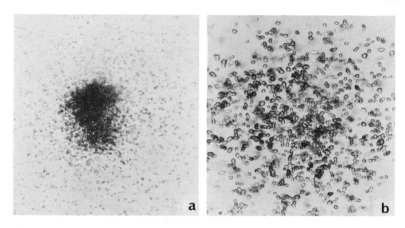

Fig. 7. Granulocyte colony (a) and macrophage colony (b) from normal mouse hematopoietic cells cloned in agar. From Ichikawa *et al.* (1966).

al., 1966). The granulocyte colonies contained cells in various stages of differentiation from myeloblasts to mature neutrophil granulocytes (Fig. 9). The blast cell colonies either degenerated without further differentiation or differentiated to granulocytes. The granulocyte colonies from human hematopoietic cells (Paran *et al.,* 1970) survived longer than those from rodents. Studies on the cloning efficiency of different mouse organs have shown that embryo liver and adult bone marrow had a higher cloning efficiency than adult spleen cells, and that no colonies were obtained from thymus or lymph node cells (Pluznik and Sachs, 1965; Sachs, 1970).

The relationship between the number of cells seeded and number of colonies has indicated that macrophage (Pluznik and Sachs, 1965) and granulocyte colonies (Ichikawa *et al.,* 1966) can be initiated from single colony-forming-units. The recloning of colonies has shown that macrophage (Pluznik and Sachs, 1966) and granulocyte colonies (Paran and Sachs, 1969) can originate from single cells and can therefore be classified as clones. When cells were washed at various times after the initiation of colony formation, there was no further development of either macrophage or granulocyte colonies unless the inducer was again added

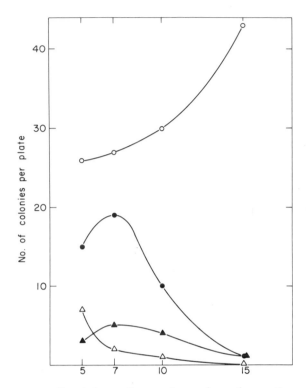

FIG. 8. Number of macrophage (○——○), granulocyte (●——●), mixed macrophage and granulocyte (▲——▲), and blast cell (△——△) colonies, at different times after seeding normal mouse hematopoietic cells in agar. From Ichikawa *et al.* (1966).

(Paran and Sachs, 1968). This indicates, that the development of colonies with differentiated cells requires both an initial and a continued supply of MGI.

MGI can be produced *in vitro* by various normal and neoplastic cells. The normal cells include embryo fibroblasts (Ginsburg and Sachs, 1963; Pluznik and Sachs, 1965, 1966), kidneys from young and adult animals and adult spleen cells (Ichikawa *et al.*, 1966). Studies with cells that are no longer normal have shown that

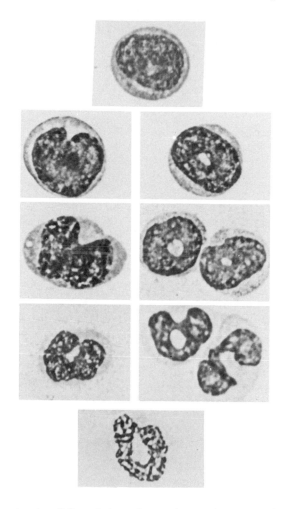

FIG. 9. Some stages in the differentiation of granulocytes in a normal granulocyte colony in agar. From Sachs (1968).

MGI was produced by a cell line derived from embryo fibroblasts, cell lines from polyoma virus- and methylcholanthrene-induced sarcomas, and from erythroid and lymphoid leukemia (Ichikawa *et al.*, 1966; Paran *et al.*, 1968). MGI has also been obtained from *in vivo* sources, and in humans it has been found in urine

and serum (Stanley and Metcalf, 1969; Mintz and Sachs, 1973a).
MGI has some species specificity. Conditioned medium containing
MGI from mouse spleen induces colony formation with mouse
or rat hematopoietic cells, but no colonies with human hematopoietic cells (Paran *et al.*, 1970) and human serum containing
MGI induces efficient colony formation with human, but not with
mouse or rat cells (Mintz and Sachs, 1973a). MGI has been
referred to by others as colony-stimulating factor (CSF) or colony-
stimulating activity (CSA) (Metcalf *et al.*, 1967; Worton *et al.*,
1969). The terminology of CSF and CSA, however, implies that
this inducer can induce colony formation without any specificity
of the cell types affected. Since there are other substances that
can induce colony formation nonspecifically and this inducer specifically induces the formation of colonies with differentiation
to macrophages and granulocytes, we prefer to use the term MGI
so as to indicate this specificity of cell types.

The finding that MGI was required for the differentiation of
normal granulocytes and macrophages made it possible to study
whether the blocks in cell differentiation that occur in myeloid
leukemia can be overcome by adding MGI. The results have
shown that some, but not all, myeloid leukemic cells from humans
(Paran *et al.*, 1970) and mice (Fibach *et al.*, 1972, 1973; Sachs,
1973) can be induced by MGI to undergo normal cell differentiation *in vitro*. Our studies with humans have also shown that
MGI can induce normal granulocyte differentiation *in vitro* in
blast cells from patients with infantile genetic agranulocytosis
(Paran *et al.*, 1970; Barak *et al.*, 1971) and genetic neutropenia
(Mintz and Sachs, 1973b).

Our experiments with mouse leukemia were carried out with
a tissue culture line of myeloblastic leukemic cells (Ichikawa,
1969) that we found to contain two types of clones. One type
(D+) could be induced to undergo normal cell differentiation
by MGI, whereas the other type (D−) could not be induced to
differentiate. After the addition of MGI, the D− clones were compact and contained only undifferentiated blast cells, whereas the
D+ clones contained a dispersed periphery of differentiated cells
(Fibach *et al.,* 1972, 1973) (Fig. 10). Both D+ and D− blast cells
were leukemic in mice, and the difference in the ability to

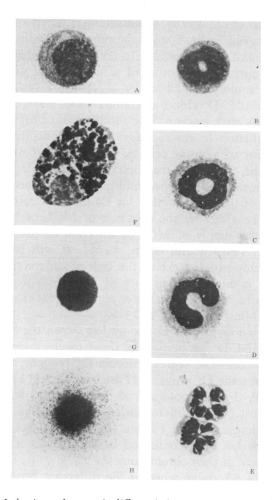

FIG. 10. Induction of normal differentiation to mature granulocytes and macrophages in mouse myeloid leukemic cells. Undifferentiated leukemic blast cell (A), stages in the differentiation to mature granulocytes (B–E), mature macrophage (F), D⁻ colony with no induction of differentiation (G), and D⁺ colony with induction of differentiation (H). From Fibach et al. (1973).

differentiate was not associated with a difference in the growth rate of the blast cells.

In the presence of MGI from conditioned medium from fibro-

cells with the lectins from wheat germ and soybean. The results show a difference in the mobility of Con A binding sites in these two types of cells and suggest a difference in the fluid state of these carbohydrate-containing structures on the surface membrane. This suggests that a gain of the ability to undergo normal cell differentiation is associated with an increase in the fluidity of structures on the surface membrane where the Con A sites are located. It will be of interest to determine whether the difference between D^+ and D^- cells is due to a difference in the membrane or intracellular receptors for MGI.

MGI can be released by cells in culture into the tissue culture medium (Pluznik and Sachs, 1966), so that conditioned medium from cultured cells can be used as a source for purification and characterization of MGI. We have purified MGI from serum-free conditioned medium from a cloned line of mouse cells to homogeneity in SDS polyacrylamide gel electrophoresis (Landau and Sachs, 1971a; Guez and Sachs, 1973). MGI is a protein whose mobility in SDS polyacrylamide gel electrophoresis indicates that it has a molecular weight of 68,000 (Guez and Sachs, 1973) (Fig. 12). The protein contained no detectable cystine or cysteine. The yield of purified protein was about 0.5 mg from 10 liters of conditioned medium.

Purification of the protein resulted in loss of biological activity (Landau and Sachs, 1971a). Activity was regained by addition

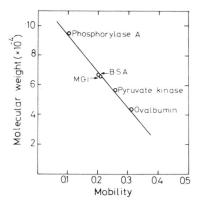

FIG. 12. Molecular weight determination of purified MGI by polyacrylamide gel electrophoresis with SDS. From Guez and Sachs (1973).

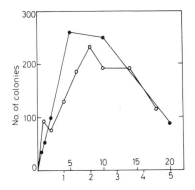

FIG. 13. Induction of colony formation by normal mouse hematopoietic cells in agar by MGI in the presence of the cofactor in conditioned medium (ml) (○———○) or adenine (μg) (●———●). From Guez and Sachs (1973).

of a low molecular weight cofactor that was also present in conditioned medium. The cofactor can be substituted by adenine containing nucleotides or by adenine (Landau and Sachs, 1971a,b; Guez and Sachs, 1973)(Fig. 13). The purified protein induced the development of both macrophage and granulocyte colonies from normal bone marrow cells. At optimum concentration of the natural cofactor or adenine, the purified MGI has an inducing activity of 0.5 ng protein per colony. The D^+ mouse myeloid leukemic cells produced their own cofactor and can be made to differentiate by purified MGI without adding the cofactor or adenine (Fibach et al., 1972).

Purified MGI can be labeled without loss of biological activity (Guez and Sachs, 1973). The availability of purified labeled MGI now makes it possible to determine the location of MGI binding sites on the target and other cells and its mode of action. With the availability of purified MGI from other sources, it will be of interest to compare this purified MGI in conditioned medium from mouse cells with MGI that is active on human cells and to determine what part of the protein carries the biological activity. Erythropoietin cannot substitute for MGI (Paran and Sachs, 1968). It will also be of interest to determine how MGI differs from the proteins erythropoietin, which effects erythrocytes (Goldwasser and Kung, 1972), and thymosin, which affects lymphocytes (Goldstein *et al.*, 1972), and to find such substances for other types of cells.

III.   REVERSION OF THE MALIGNANT PHENOTYPE AND THE GENETIC CONTROL OF MALIGNANCY

The results obtained with D^+ leukemic cells have shown that these leukemic cells can be induced by MGI to revert from the malignant phenotype to cells with the phenotypic properties of normal granulocytes and macrophages, even though they no longer contain a completely normal diploid chromosome complement. We have also studied sarcoma cells for reversion of the malignant phenotype to a phenotype with the growth control of normal fibroblasts. These studies have included an analysis of the chromosomes of the malignant and revertant cells, in order to obtain evidence for a genetic control of malignancy. Normal rodent fibroblasts, such as those from golden hamster embryos, can be transformed *in vitro* to cells with abnormal growth properties by infection with a virus such as polyoma virus (Vogt and Dulbecco, 1960; Sachs and Medina, 1961; Medina and Sachs 1961; Sachs, *et al.*, 1962; Sachs, 1962), by treatment with chemical carcinogens (Berwald and Sachs, 1963, 1965; Huberman and Sach, 1966) or by X-irradiation (Borek and Sachs, 1966a, 1968). The cells can then acquire the ability to multiply *in vitro* under conditions that inhibit the multiplication of normal fibroblasts and to form sarcomas in animals. The term transformation will be used for the acquisition of abnormal growth properties *in vitro,* and the term malignancy will be used for the ability to form tumors *in vivo.*

Our results have shown that clones of transformed hamster cells can produce progeny cells which have hereditarily reverted from the transformed and malignant phenotype to cells that again have a normal growth control. This can occur in cells transformed by polyoma virus, simian virus 40, chemical carcinogens, and X-irradiation. It was also shown that a high frequency of reversion can be experimentally induced by culturing cells at low cell density (Rabinowitz and Sachs, 1968, 1969a,b; 1970a,b,c; 1972a,b; Sachs, 1972).

Among the properties of transformed fibroblasts that can be

scored for reversion are a random growth and the pattern of contact inhibition of cell replication (Borek and Sachs, 1966b), high saturation density, high cloning efficiency at 37°C, the ability to form colonies in semisolid agar (MacPherson and Montagnier, 1964), the absence of a limited life-span (Hayflick, 1965) and agglutinability by a lectin such as Con A (Inbar and Sachs, 1969b). With cells transformed by a virus such as polyoma virus, the transformed also differ from the normal fibroblasts in that they can grow at 41°C (Ossovski and Sachs, 1967), contain a virus specific transplantation antigen (Sjögren et al., 1961; Habel, 1961), nuclear T-antigen (Fogel and Defendi, 1967), virus-specific RNA (Benjamin, 1966; Aloni et al., 1968), and virus-specific DNA (Sambrook et al., 1968; Shani et al., 1972).

In cells transformed after infection with polyoma virus there was a reversion of all the abnormal growth properties *in vitro* and *in vivo*, except the limited life-span shown by normal cells (Fig. 14, Table III). Revertants also showed no detectable virus-specific transplantation antigen (Rabinowitz and Sachs, 1970b).

Reversion in the polyoma-transformed cells was, however, not associated with a loss of the virus genome as measured by the presence of virus-specific RNA, T-antigen (Rabinowitz and Sachs, 1968) and virus-specific DNA (Shani et al., 1972) (Table III). Reversion was also not associated with either a decrease in the number of virus DNA copies per cell, or with a lack of integration of the virus DNA into chromosomal DNA (Shani et al., 1972). The hereditary integration of polyoma virus DNA into chromosomal DNA is therefore, by itself, not sufficient for expression of the abnormal growth properties found in transformed cells. The polyoma-transformed cells used in these experiments could not be induced to synthesize infection virus. It will be of interest to determine the inducibility of plaque-forming virus (Winocour and Sachs, 1969) in revertants from the polyoma-transformed cells in which the synthesis of infectious virus can be induced by irradiation or chemicals (Fogel and Sachs, 1969, 1970) and in which virus DNA is also integrated into chromosomal DNA (Manor et al., 1973).

In cells transformed after treatment with benzo[a]pyrene (Berwald and Sachs, 1963, 1965), dimethylnitrosamine (Huberman et al., 1968), or X-irradiation (Borek and Sachs, 1966a),

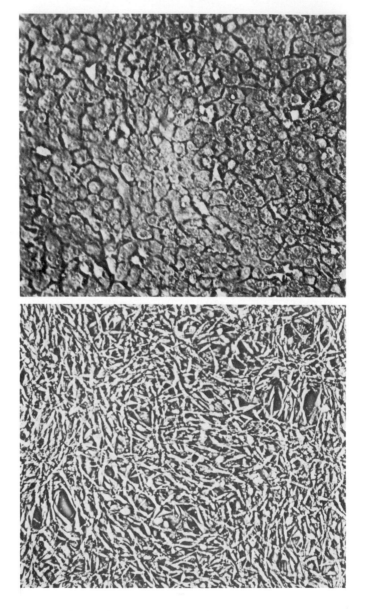

FIG. 14. Cultures of hamster cells transformed by polyoma virus (bottom) and a revertant (top). From Rabinowitz and Sachs (1968).

TABLE III

PROPERTIES OF NORMAL, REVERTANT, AND TRANSFORMED CELLS. TRANSFORMATION BY POLYOMA VIRUS[a]

Cell type	Growth pattern	Contact inhibition of cell replication	Saturation density	Cloning efficiency at 37°C	Growth at 41°C	Growth in soft agar	Agglutination by Con A	Transplantation antigen	Tumorogenicity	Virus DNA and RNA	T antigen
Normal	Regular	Normal	Low	Low	−	−	−	−	−	−	−
Revertant	Regular	Normal	Low	Low	−	−	−	−	−	+	+
Transformed	Random	Transformed	High	High	+	+	+	+	+	+	+

[a] From Sachs (1972).

LEO SACHS

TABLE IV

PROPERTIES OF NORMAL, REVERTANT AND TRANSFORMED CELLS. TRANSFORMATION BY CHEMICAL CARCINOGEN[a]

Cell type	Growth pattern	Contact inhibition of cell replication	Saturation density	Cloning efficiency at 37°C	Growth in soft agar	Limited life-span in vitro	Tumor-ogenicity
Normal	Regular	Normal	Low	Low	−	+	−
Revertant	Regular	Normal	Low	Low	−	+	−
Transformed	Random	Transformed	High	High	+	−	+

[a] From Sachs (1972).

there can be a reversion to all the normal properties including a limited life-span (Rabinowitz and Sachs, 1970c, 1972b) (Table IV). Persistence of the viral genome in revertants from the polyoma-transformed cells thus seemed to prevent reversion to a limited life-span.

Revertants from transformed cells can again re-revert to the transformed state. In the case of revertants with a limited life-span, these re-reverted cells (Rabinowitz and Sachs, 1970c, 1972b) (Fig. 15) no longer have a limited life-span. Different clones of revertants from polyoma transformed cells can re-revert with different frequencies, and re-reversion for one transformed

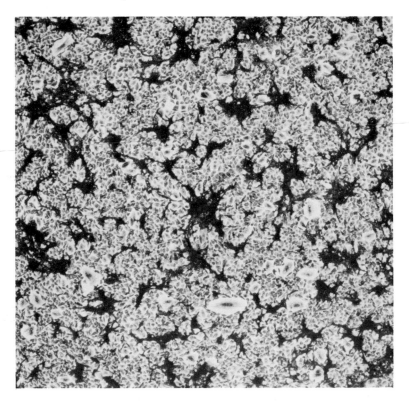

FIG. 15. Foci of re-revertant cells in a revertant from cells transformed after treatment with a chemical carcinogen. From Rabinowitz and Sachs (1970c).

property was not necessarily associated with re-reversion for another transformed property (Rabinowitz and Sachs, 1972a). There can also be reversion for *in vitro* transformed properties without reversion for malignancy (Rabinowitz and Sachs, 1969a, 1972b). This indicates that *in vivo* and *in vitro* properties of abnormal growth can be experimentally separated.

In order to obtain evidence for a genetic control of the transformed properties and malignancy, we have analyzed the chromosomes of normal, transformed, revertant and re-revertant golden hamster cells. Normal golden hamster cells have a diploid number of 44 chromosomes (Sachs, 1952). We found that reversion of all the transformed properties and malignancy was not associated with reversion to the normal diploid chromosome complement. Compared to the transformed cells from which they were derived, the revertants showed either an increase (Rabinowitz and Sachs, 1970a) or a decrease in the total chromosome number (Hitotsumachi *et al.,* 1971). This has been confirmed with mouse cells (Pollack *et al.,* 1970; Mondal *et al.,* 1971). It was also found that induction of reversion by culturing transformed cells at a low cell density was associated with the induction of polyploidy and the formation of aneuploid cells (Bloch-Shtacher *et al.,* 1972).

Our results on reversion, re-reversion, a lack of the normal diploid chromosome complement in revertants, and the association of reversion with changes in the total chromosome number led us to propose a model for the genetic control of malignancy and cell transformation (Rabinowitz and Sachs, 1970a) (Fig. 16) According to this model, malignancy and its reversion are controlled by the balance between genes for expression (E) and for suppression (S) of malignancy and these genes may be located on different chromosomes. When there is enough S to neutralize E, malignancy is suppressed, and when the amount of S is not sufficient to neutralize E, malignancy is expressed. E may exist in normal cells, where it is neutralized by S (Rabinowitz and Sachs, 1970a), or it may not exist in normal cells and be produced by carcinogen-induced mutation or introduced by a virus. It was also suggested (Rabinowitz and Sachs, 1970a) that there may be different E and S for different properties. This can explain the experimental dissociation of *in vitro* transformed properties and the dissociation of these properties from malignancy.

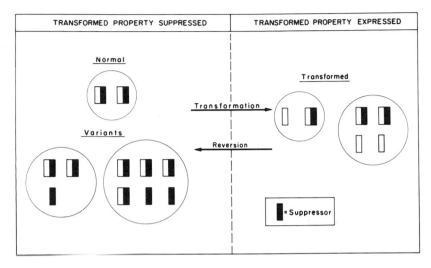

FIG. 16. Model for the genetic control of expression and suppression of malignancy and cell transformation. From Rabinowitz and Sachs (1970a).

According to our model, carcinogens induce malignancy by producing genetic changes that result in a change in the balance between E and S. Reversion to normal growth control can then be achieved without reversion to a normal diploid genotype, provided that the reverted cells contain sufficient S to neutralize E. Tumor viruses may acquire E by incorporation of cellular DNA into viral DNA (Aloni et al., 1969), or when their nucleic acid is integrated into cellular chromosomes (Sambrook et al., 1968; Shani et al., 1972; Temin, 1972; Todaro and Huebner, 1972), they may produce changes that result in mutation or amplification of E genes. Chemical carcinogens, including the carcinogenic hydrocarbons that have to be metabolically activated by cellular enzymes to exert their biological effects (Gelboin et al., 1969), can induce mutations in mammalian cells (Huberman and Sachs, 1974). Some of these mutations presumably include the genes that control malignancy and transformation. The delay in expression of transformed properties and malignancy after treatment of cells with carcinogens (Huberman et al., 1968; Huberman and Sachs, 1968) may be due to the time required to obtain the appropriate mutations and change in gene balance. The change in gene balance may be induced directly by the carcinogen, or it may be induced by extending the life-span of normal cells so as to increase the probability of such a change.

The chromosome analyses of normal and abnormal golden hamster fibroblasts (Hitotsumachi *et al.*, 1971, 1972; Yamamoto *et al.*, 1973a,b) has included the Giemsa chromosome banding technique (Sumner *et al.*, 1971) to identify the normal 44 chromosomes (Sachs, 1952) of the golden hamster and chromosome rearrangements (Fig. 17). The cells studied included cells transformed after treatment with the chemical carcinogen dimethylnitrosamine, revertants with a complete suppression of malignancy and transformed properties, re-revertants produced *in vitro,* and tumors derived from these cells. The chromosome banding pattern of these cell types (Yamamoto *et al.*, 1973a) (Fig. 18), has sup-

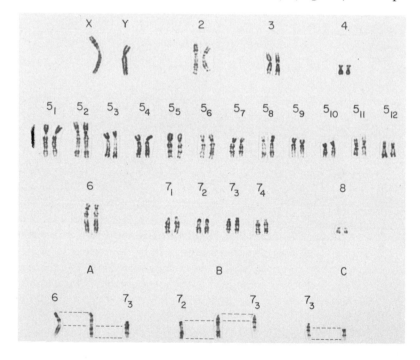

FIG. 17. Giemsa banding pattern of golden hamster chromosomes. Normal cells contain the chromosomes from X to 8. A, B, and C are examples of some chromosome rearrangements. From Yamamoto *et al.* (1973a).

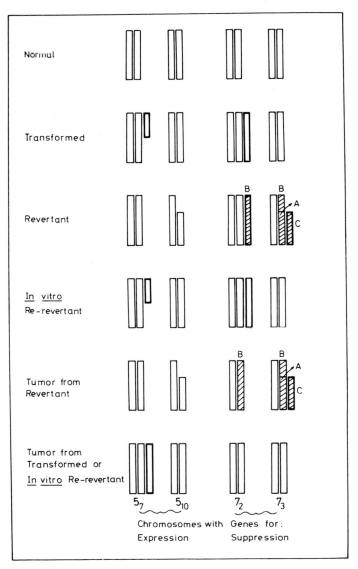

FIG. 18. Identification of hamster chromosomes with genes for expression and suppression of malignancy and cell transformation. Chromosomes in normal cells □, additional chromosome or chromosome piece ▯, rearranged chromosome ▨. A, B, and C are chromosome rearrangements shown in Fig. 17. From Yamamoto *et al.* (1973a).

ported our model of gene balance and identified chromosomes that carry E and S. Our data also indicate that the genes for malignancy and cell transformation need not necessarily be located on the same chromosomes. The chromosome banding pattern of polyoma transformed cells and their tumors has further supported the model of gene balance (Yamamoto *et al.*, 1973b).

The suppression of malignancy has also been obtained in the progeny of cell hybrids obtained by fusing malignant and non-malignant cells, and re-reversion in the progeny of the fused cells was associated with chromosome loss (Harris *et al.*, 1969). This suppression and re-expression of malignancy was presumably also produced by changes in the balance between chromosomes with E and S. It will be of interest to determine the chromosome location of E and S in tumors induced by different carcinogens, whether all changes in E and S can be identified by such obvious chromosome changes as those shown in Fig. 18, and whether there are nonchromosomal E and S. Differences between transformed cells and revertants (Hitotsumachi *et al.*, 1971, 1972) in the susceptibility to treatment with 5-bromodeoxyuridine and visible light (Puck and Kao, 1967) have indicated that cellular properties other than malignancy and cell transformation may be regulated by the balance between E and S.

Reversion of malignancy and cell transformation was obtained without reversion to a normal diploid genotype. The study of blocks in the hydrolysis of sugar nucleotides has shown (Sela *et al.*, 1972; Sela and Sachs, 1973), that there are genetic changes common to transformed cells and their revertants, that are not found in normal diploid cells. These results can explain why revertants can more readily produce malignant segregants than normal diploid cells (Yamamoto *et al.*, 1973a).

IV. Conclusions

I have studied the control of cell growth and differentiation in normal mammalian cells, and the change in this control in carcinogenesis, by developing and using *in vitro* systems. The use of lectins as probes for the behavior of membrane sites has shown the significance of changes in the dynamics of specific surface membrane sites in the control of growth and differentiation. These changes may result in differences in the transport and internal concentration of specific chemicals that regulate growth and differentiation. The development of an *in vitro* system for the study of growth and differentiation of hematopoietic cells has shown that the protein MGI is required for the differentiation of normal granulocytes and macrophages and that this protein can also induce normal differentiation in some myeloid leukemic cells. The findings that some, but not all, myeloid leukemic cells can be induced to differentiate normally and that there can be a segregation from one cell type to the other, has provided a system for further studies on the genetic and chemical control of normal differentiation in myeloid leukemic cells.

A hereditary reversion of the malignant phenotype to a phenotype with normal growth control, has also been found with sarcoma cells transformed by tumor viruses, chemical carcinogens, or X-irradiation. Reversion of the malignant phenotype in the virus transformed cells, was not associated with a loss of the virus genome. The induction of normal differentiation in myeloid leukemic cells and the phenotypic reversion of sarcoma cells, occurred in cells that no longer contained the normal diploid genotype. It has been proposed that malignant cell transformation and its reversion are controlled by the balance between genes for expression and suppression of malignancy, and chromosome data have been presented in support of this hypothesis. I have included in these studies fibroblasts as examples of cells that form a solid tissue *in vivo* and hematopoietic cells as examples of cells that are in suspension *in vivo*. I trust that the conclusions derived from the studies with these cells will also be of value in elucidating the control of growth and differentiation in other types of normal and malignant cells.

REFERENCES

Aloni, Y., Winocour, E., and Sachs, L. (1968). *J. Mol. Biol.* **31**, 415.
Aloni, Y., Winocour, E., Sachs, L., and Torten, J. (1969). *J. Mol. Biol.* **44**, 333.
Barak, Y., Paran, M., Levin, S., and Sachs, L. (1971). *Blood* **38**, 74.
Ben-Bassat, H., Inbar, M., and Sachs, L. (1970). *Virology* **40**, 854.

Ben-Bassat, H., Inbar, M., and Sachs, L. (1971). *J. Membrane Biol.* **6**, 183.
Benjamin, T. L. (1966). *J. Mol. Biol.* **16**, 359.
Berwald, Y., and Sachs, L. (1963). *Nature (London)* **200**, 1182.
Berwald, Y., and Sachs, L. (1965). *J. Nat. Cancer Inst.* **35**, 641.
Bloch-Shtacher, N., Rabinowitz, Z., and Sachs, L. (1972). *Int. J. Cancer* **9**, 632.
Borek, C., and Sachs, L. (1966a). *Nature (London)* **210**, 276.
Borek, C., and Sachs, L. (1966b). *Proc. Nat. Acad. Sci. U.S.* **56**, 1705.
Borek, C., and Sachs, L. (1968). *Proc. Nat. Acad. Sci. U.S.* **59**, 83.
Burger, M. M. (1969). *Proc. Nat. Acad. Sci. U.S.* **62**, 994.
Edelman, G. M., Cunningham, B. A., Reeke, G. N., Becker, J. W., Waxdal, M. J., and Wang, J. L. (1972). *Proc. Nat. Acad. Sci. U.S.* **69**, 2456.
Edidin, M., and Weiss, A. (1971). *Proc. Nat. Acad. Sci. U.S.* **70**, 343.
Fibach, E., and Sachs, L. (1974). *J. Cell. Physiol.* **83**, 177.
Fibach, E., Landau, T., and Sachs, L. (1972). *Nature (London) New Biol.* **237**, 276.
Fibach, E., Hayashi, M., and Sachs, L. (1973). *Proc. Nat. Acad. Sci. U.S.* **70**, 343.
Fogel, M., and Defendi, V. (1967). *Proc. Nat. Acad. Sci. U.S.* **58**, 967.
Fogel, M., and Sachs, L. (1969). *Virology* **37**, 327.
Fogel, M., and Sachs, L. (1970). *Virology* **40**, 174.
Gelboin, H., Huberman, E., and Sachs, L. (1969). *Proc. Nat. Acad. Sci. U.S.* **64**, 1188.
Ginsburg, H., and Sachs, L. (1963). *J. Nat. Cancer Inst.* **31**, 1.
Ginsburg, H., and Sachs, L. (1965). *J. Cell. Comp. Physiol.* **66**, 199.
Goldstein, A. L., Guha, A., Zatz, M. M., Hardy, M. A., and White, A. (1972). *Proc. Nat. Acad. Sci. U.S.* **69**, 1800.
Goldwasser, E., and Kung, C. K. (1972). *J. Biol. Chem.* **247**, 5159.
Guez, M., and Sachs, L. (1973). *FEBS (Fed. Eur. Biochem. Soc.) Lett.* **37**, 149.
Habel, K. (1961). *Proc. Soc. Exp. Biol.* **106**, 722.
Harris, H., Miller, O. J., Klein, G., Worst, P., and Tachibana, T. (1969). *Nature (London)* **223**, 363.
Hayflick, L. (1965). *Exp. Cell Res.* **37**, 614.
Hitotsumachi, S., Rabinowitz, Z., and Sachs, L. (1971). *Nature (London)* **231**, 511.
Hitotsumachi, S., Rabinowitz, Z., and Sachs, L. (1972). *Int. J. Cancer* **9**, 305.
Huberman, E., and Sachs, L. (1966). *Proc. Nat. Acad. Sci. U.S.* **56**, 1123.
Huberman, E., and Sachs, L. (1968). *J. Nat. Cancer Inst.* **40**, 329.
Huberman, E., and Sachs, L. (1974). *Int. J. Cancer* **13**, 326.
Huberman, E., Salzberg, S., and Sachs, L. (1968). *Proc. Nat. Acad. Sci. U.S.* **59**, 77.
Ichikawa, Y. (1969). *J. Cell. Physiol.* **74**, 223.
Ichikawa, Y., Pluznik, D. H., and Sachs, L. (1966). *Proc. Nat. Acad. Sci. U.S.* **56**, 488.

Inbar, M., and Sachs, L. (1969a). *Nature* **223**, 710.

Inbar, M., and Sachs, L. (1969b). *Proc. Nat. Acad. Sci. U.S.* **63**, 1418.

Inbar, M., and Sachs, L. (1973). *FEBS (Fed. Eur. Biochem. Soc.) Lett.* **32**, 124.

Inbar, M., Ben-Bassat, H., and Sachs, L. (1971a). *Proc. Nat. Acad. Sci. U.S.* **68**, 2748.

Inbar, M., Ben-Bassat, H., and Sachs, L. (1971b). *J. Membrane Biol.* **6**, 195.

Inbar, M., Ben-Bassat, H., and Sachs, L. (1972a). *Nature (London) New Biol.* **236**, 3, 16.

Inbar, M., Ben-Bassat, H., and Sachs, L. (1972b). *Int. J. Cancer* **9**, 143.

Inbar, M., Ben-Bassat, H., and Sachs, L. (1973a). *Exp. Cell. Res.* **76**, 143.

Inbar, M., Ben-Bassat, H., and Sachs, L. (1973b). *Int. J. Cancer* **12**, 93.

Inbar, M., Shinitzky, M., and Sachs, L. (1973c). *J. Mol. Biol.* **81**, 245.

Inbar, M., Shinitzky, M., and Sachs, L. (1974). *FEBS (Fed. Eur. Biochem. Soc.) Lett.* **38**, 268.

Inbar, M., Ben-Bassat, H., Fibach, E., and Sachs, L. (1973d). *Proc. Nat. Acad. Sci. U.S.* **70**, 2577.

Kalb, A. J., and Levitzki, A. (1968). *Biochem. J.* **109**, 669.

Lagunoff, D., Pluznik, D. H., and Sachs, L. (1966). *J. Cell. Physiol.* **68**, 385.

Landau, T., and Sachs, L. (1971a). *Proc. Nat. Acad. Sci. U.S.* **68**, 2540.

Landau, T., and Sachs, L. (1971b). *FEBS (Fed. Eur. Biochem. Soc.) Lett.* **17**, 339.

Loor, F., Forni, L., and Pernis, B. (1972). *Eur. J. Immunol.* **2**, 203.

MacPherson, I., and Montagnier, L. (1964). *Virology* **23**, 291.

Manor, H., Fogel, M., and Sachs, L. (1973). *Virology* **53**, 174.

Medina, D., and Sachs, L. (1961). *Brit. J. Cancer* **15**, 885.

Metcalf, D., Bradley, T. R., and Robinson, W. (1967). *J. Cell. Physiol.* **69**, 93.

Mintz, U., and Sachs, L. (1973a). *Blood* **42**, 331.

Mintz, U., and Sachs, L. (1973b). *Blood* **41**, 745.

Mondal, S., Embleton, M. J., Marquardt, H., and Heidelberger, C. (1971). *Int. J. Cancer* **8**, 410.

Nicolson, G. L. (1972). *Nature (London) New Biol.* **239**, 193.

Nowell, P. C. (1960). *Cancer Res.* **20**, 462.

Ossovski, L., and Sachs, L. (1967). *Proc. Nat. Acad. Sci. U.S.* **58**, 1938.

Paran, M., and Sachs, L. (1968). *J. Cell. Physiol.* **72**, 247.

Paran, M., and Sachs, L. (1969). *J. Cell. Physiol.* **73**, 91.

Paran, M., Ichikawa, Y., and Sachs, L. (1968). *J. Cell. Physiol.* **72**, 251.

Paran, M., Ichikawa, Y., and Sachs, L. (1969). *Proc. Nat. Acad. Sci. U.S.* **62**, 81.

Paran, M., Sachs, L., Barak, Y., and Resnitzky, P. (1970). *Proc. Nat. Acad. Sci. U.S.* **67**, 1542.

Pike, B. L., and Robinson, W. (1970). *J. Cell. Physiol.* **76**, 77.

Pluznik, D. H., and Sachs, L. (1965). *J. Cell. Comp. Physiol.* **66**, 319.

Pluznik, D. H., and Sachs, L. (1966). *Exp. Cell. Res.* **43**, 554.

Pollack, R., Wolman, S., and Vogel, A. (1970). *Nature (London)* **228**, 938.

Powell, A. E., and Leon, M. A. (1970). *Exp. Cell Res.* **62**, 315.

Puck, T. T., and Kao, F. (1967). *Proc. Nat. Acad. Sci. U.S.* **58**, 1227.

Rabinowitz, Z., and Sachs, L. (1968). *Nature (London)* **220**, 1203.

Rabinowitz, Z., and Sachs, L. (1969a). *Virology* **38**, 336.

Rabinowitz, Z., and Sachs, L. (1969b). *Virology* **38**, 343.

Rabinowitz, Z., and Sachs, L. (1970a). *Nature (London)* **225**, 136.

Rabinowitz, Z., and Sachs, L. (1970b). *Virology* **40**, 193.

Rabinowitz, Z., and Sachs, L. (1970c). *Int. J. Cancer* **6**, 388.

Rabinowitz, Z., and Sachs, L. (1972a). *Int. J. Cancer* **9**, 334.

Rabinowitz, Z., and Sachs, L. (1972b). *Int. J. Cancer* **10**, 607.

Sachs, L. (1952). *Heredity* **6**, 357.

Sachs, L. (1962). *Tumor Viruses Murine Origin, Ciba Found. Symp., 1962* p. 380.

Sachs, L. (1964). In "New Perspectives in Biology" (M. Sela, ed.), p. 246. Elsevier, Amsterdam.

Sachs, L. (1965). *Nature* **207**, 1272.

Sachs, L. (1967). *Curr. Top. Develop. Biol.* **2**, 129.

Sachs, L. (1968). In "Perspectives in Leukemia," (W. Damashek and R. M. Dutcher, eds.), p. 81, Grune & Stratton, New York.

Sachs, L. (1970). In "Regulation of Hematopoiesis," (A. S. Gordon, ed.), Vol. 1, p. 217. Appleton, New York.

Sachs, L. (1972). In "Molecular Bioenergetics and Macromolecular Biochemistry" (H. H. Weber, ed.), p. 118. Springer-Verlag, Berlin and New York.

Sachs, L. (1973). In "Control of Proliferation in Animal Cells." (B. Clarkson and R. Baserga, eds.). Cold Spring Harbor Laboratory, Cold Spring Harbor, New York, in press.

Sachs, L., and Medina, D. (1961). *Nature (London)* **189**, 457.

Sachs, L., Medina, D., and Berwald, Y. (1962). *Virology* **17**, 491.

Sachs, L., Inbar, M., and Shinitzky, M. (1973). In "Control of Proliferation in Animal Cells" (B. Clarkson and R. Baserga, eds.), Cold Spring Harbor Laboratory, Cold Spring Harbor, New York, in press.

Sambrook, J., Westphal, H., Srinivasan, P. R., and Dulbecco, R. (1968). *Proc. Nat. Acad. Sci. U.S.* **60**, 1288.

Sela, B., and Sachs, L. (1973). *FEBS (Fed. Eur. Biochem. Soc.) Lett.* **30**, 100.

Sela, B., Lis, H., Sharon, N., and Sachs, L. (1970). *J. Membrane Biol.* **3**, 267.

Sela, B., Lis, H., Sharon, N., and Sachs, L. (1971). *Biochim. Biophys. Acta* **249**, 564.

Sela, B., Lis, H., and Sachs, L. (1972). *J. Biol. Chem.* **247**, 7585.

Sela, B., Lis, H., Sharon, N., and Sachs, L. (1973). *Biochim. Biophys. Acta* **310**, 273.

Shani, M., Rabinowitz, Z., and Sachs, L. (1972). *J. Virol.* **10**, 456.

Shinitzky, M., Inbar, M., and Sachs, L. (1973). *FEBS (Fed. Eur. Biochem. Soc.) Lett.* **34**, 247.

Shoham, J., and Sachs, L. (1972). *Proc. Nat. Acad. Sci. U.S.* **69**, 2479.

Shoham, H., and Sachs, L. (1974). *Exp. Cell. Res.* **85**, 8.

Shoham, J., Inbar, M., and Sachs, L. (1970). *Nature (London)* **227**, 1244.

Singer, S. H., and Nicolson, G. L. (1972). *Science* **175**, 720.

Sjögren, H. O., Hellström, I., and Klein, G. (1961). *Cancer Res.* **21**, 329.

Stanley, E. R., and Metcalf, D. (1969). *Aust. J. Exp. Biol. Med.* **47**, 467.

Stoker, M. (1968). *Nature (London)* **218**, 234.

Sumner, A. T., Evans, H. J., and Buckland, R. A. (1971). *Nature (London) New Biol.* **232**, 31.

Sumner, J. B., and Howell, S. F. (1936). *J. Bacteriol.* **32**, 227–237.

Taylor, R. B., Duffus, W. P. H., Raff, M. C., and De Petris, S. (1971). *Nature (London) New Biol.* **233**, 225.

Temin, H. (1972). *Proc. Nat. Acad. Sci. U.S.* **69**, 1016.

Todaro, G., and Huebner, R. (1972). *Proc. Nat. Acad. Sci. U.S.* **69**, 1009.

Vlodavsky, I., and Sachs, L. (1974). *Nature (London)* in press.

Vlodavsky, I., Inbar, M., and Sachs, L. (1972). *Biochim. Biophys. Acta* **274**, 364.

Vlodavsky, I., Inbar, M., and Sachs, L. (1973). *Proc. Nat. Acad. Sci. U.S.* **70**, 1780.

Vogt, M., and Dulbecco, R. (1960). *Proc. Nat. Acad. Sci. U.S.* **46**, 365.

Winocour, E., and Sachs, L. (1959). *Virology* **8**, 397.

Wollman, Y., and Sachs, L. (1972). *J. Membrane Biol.* **10**, 1.

Worton, R. G., McCulloch, E. A., and Till, J. E. (1969). *J. Cell. Physiol.* **74**, 171.

Yahara, I., and Edelman, G. M. (1972). *Proc. Nat. Acad. Sci. U.S.* **69**, 608.

Yamamoto, T., Rabinowitz, Z., and Sachs, L. (1973a). *Nature (London) New Biol.* **243**, 247.

Yamamoto, T., Hayashi, M., Rabinowitz Z., and Sachs, L. (1973b). *Int. J. Cancer* **11**, 555.

REGULATION OF GENE EXPRESSION IN MAMMALIAN CELLS*

GORDON M. TOMKINS

Department of Biochemistry and Biophysics, University of California, San Francisco, San Francisco, California

I. GLUCOCORTICOID MEDIATED ENZYME INDUCTION

ALTHOUGH hormonal steroids control sexual differentiation in water fungi (1) and development in insects (2), the glucocorticoids appear first in evolution in the vertebrates (3). Most physiological and biochemical studies on their action, however, have been carried out in mammals, where these steroids mediate adaption to long-term stress. In this context, their role in promoting gluconeogenesis from amino acid precursors is well known (4). On the other hand, the corticoids influence the behavior of a number of cells and tissues in many seemingly unrelated ways [see (5) for references]. Although it is not presently possible to formulate entirely satisfactory generalizations about these aspects of their action, I would suggest that a fundamental role of the glucocorticoids is to promote development. For instance, these hormones stimulate maturation of the pancreas (6), nervous system (7), female genital tract (8), intestine (9), lung (10), liver (11), and a number of other organ systems (12). Viewed in this light, the metabolic aspects of glucocorticoid action in adult organisms might merely be reflections of the primary developmental role of these steroids.

In any event, glucocorticoids clearly play an extremely broad role in mammalian physiology. To assess how general, we have surveyed a number of tissues for the specific cytoplasmic glucocorticoid receptors which mediate the intracellular actions of the hormone (13). Receptor activity was found in virtually every tissue tested (except the immature uterus and the prostate) con-

---

* Lecture delivered Oct. 19, 1972.

TABLE I

JUVENILE BUFFALO RAT[a]

Tissue	Cytoplasmic receptor site concentration		Equilibrium dissociation constant (dexamethasone) (nM)
	Pmoles/mg DNA	Pmoles/mg protein	
Liver	10.62–4.1	0.64–0.24	13.6–7.9
Skeletal muscle	3.14–1.62	0.06–0.01	3.2–0.9
Heart	2.91–0.85	0.26–0.5	8.4–4.1
Brain	2.53–0.02	0.19–0.01	7.2–2.8
Kidney	1.38	0.23–0.05	6.6–1.0
Testis	1.23–0.49	0.15–0.05	3.0–0.7
Thymus	0.95–0.05	0.45–0.05	13.8–1.8
Stomach	0.56–0.03	0.08–0.01	31.0–9.0
Spleen	0.26–0.03	0.07–0.01	18.0–0.5
Lung	0.09–0.02	0.02–0.005	12.6–4.8
Jejunum	0	0	—
Adipose	0	0	—
Bladder	0	0	—
Seminal vesicle	0	0	—
Prostate	0	0	—
Uterus	0	0	—

[a] From Ballard et al. (13).

firming the idea that the glucocorticoids regulate the activities of many types of cells (Table I).

Among the best characterized glucocorticoid target cells are the cultured rat hepatoma (HTC) cells derived from Morris hepatoma 7288c (14). These cells grow in suspension or monolayer culture with a generation time of approximately 24 hours. They contain 60–70 chromosomes and, like other transformed cells, clone with high efficiency either in agar or attached to a glass or plastic substrate. HTC cells are easily synchronized by standard techniques using mitotic "shake-off" or double-thymidine block (see 15).

Another glucocorticoid-sensitive cell line which has become increasingly useful in our work is derived from a Balb/c mouse lymphoma induced with mineral oil and designated S49 (16). These pseudo-diploid cells grow in suspension or soft agar with a generation time of 16–18 hours. As evidence of their thymic origin, they contain θ antigen and are also TL-positive. Physiological concentrations of the glucocorticoids induce growth inhibition, followed 12–20 hours later by cell death. Steroid-resistant variants arise with a frequency of about 3×10^{-6} per cell per generation; the transition from steroid-sensitivity to steroid-resistance is stochastic and is enhanced by a variety of mutagens including alkylating and intercalating agents and gamma irradiation (17).

II. Early Steps in Hormone Action

Studies in cultured mouse L cells (18) suggest that there may be a selective uptake of the steroids by an active transport mechanism. Our own experiments, however, indicate that in HTC and lymphoma cells, at least, steroids enter cells passively and associate with highly specific receptor proteins in the cytoplasm (19). Cell-free binding experiments have shown that glucocorticoid–receptor associations are noncovalent, but of high affinity (with affinity constants in the range of 10^9) (20, 21). The receptors appear to be allosteric proteins, equilibrating between "active" and inactive" forms (22). Biologically active steroids are thought to associate with an "active" form whereas glucocorticoid antagonists such as progesterone would interact with an "inactive" conformation. This two-state model explains the action of "suboptimal inducers" (e.g., deoxycorticosterone) which produce submaximal biological effects even at very high concentrations.

HTC cells contain approximately 18,000 receptor sites per cell (23). In velocity sedimentation experiments in sucrose or glycerol gradients, these molecules sediment at 6 S in low salt (0.05 M), and 4 S at higher ionic strengths (21). The latter form has a molecular weight of about 60,000, estimated from gel filtration experiments (Wong, unpublished). Receptor–glucocorticoid complexes can be purified by conventional techniques 500- to 1000-fold in 30–50% yield, and preliminary experiments suggest that

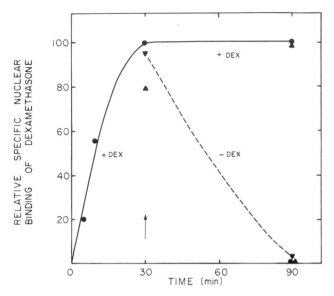

FIG. 1. Reversible nuclear binding of receptor–dexamethasone complex in intact HTC cells. Hepatoma cells were incubated at $37°C$ with 2×10^{-8} M dexamethasone-^{3}H without (●) and with 10^{-4} M cycloheximide (▲) or 5 μg of actinomycin D per milliliter (▼). Background cultures were incubated in parallel. Each culture was divided (↑) after 30 minutes, and part was kept in the presence of dexamethasone while the steroid was removed from the remainder. Data are expressed as percentage of the maximum binding at 30–90 minutes in two experiments. From Rousseau et al. (23).

using affinity chromatography significantly higher purifications can be obtained.

Following association of the receptors with glucocorticoids in the cytosol, the receptor–steroid complexes localize in the nucleus (Fig. 1)(23). Consequently there is a stoichiometric relationship between the number of receptor molecules that leave the cytosol and those that appear as complexes in the nucleus (Fig. 2). When steroids are removed from cultures of HTC cells, the receptor–steroid complex in the cytosol dissociates, liberating free receptor, and nuclear bound complexes leave the nucleus, allowing free receptor to reappear in the cytosol (Fig. 3). Thus, the entire sequence is readily reversible. Furthermore, the movement of re-

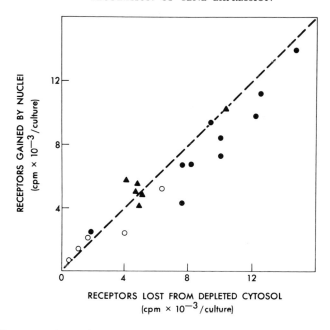

FIG. 2. Relation between nuclear binding of dexamethasone and depletion of cytoplasmic receptors in HTC cells. From Rousseau *et al.* (23).

ceptor from one cell compartment to another does not depend on macromolecular synthesis, since it occurs normally even when protein or RNA synthesis are inhibited (23). In whole cells, the number of steroid molecules localized in the nucleus is limited by the availability of cytoplasmic receptors. For example, in intact HTC cells approximately 13,000 nuclear sites are occupied at steroid levels that saturate the cytoplasmic receptors. Under these conditions approximately 70% of the specifically bound glucocorticoid is localized in the nucleus. The remaining 30% of the cellular hormone remains in the cytosol, presumably associated with the receptor (Table II).

These experiments suggest that there are a large but limited number of acceptor sites in the nucleus which bind the receptor–glucocorticoid complexes. This idea has been explored in cell-free experiments where receptor–steroid complexes are added in

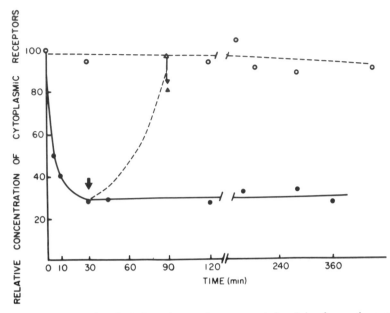

FIG. 3.   Reversible depletion of cytosol receptors induced by dexamethasone in intact HTC cells. At (↓) radioactive steroid was removed from the cultures marked ▲ and ▼ but retained in those marked ●. From Rousseau *et al.* (23).

TABLE II

CONCENTRATION OF SPECIFIC GLUCOCORTICOID RECEPTORS IN
CULTURED RAT HEPATOMA TARGET CELLS[a]

Site	Number/cell	Pmoles/mg protein	Pmoles/mg DNA
Steroid receptor sites	17,900 ± 1000	0.41 ± 0.02	1.85 ± 0.1
Nuclear acceptor sites occupied	12,400 ± 1900	—	1.29 ± 0.2
	12,900 ± 700		

[a] From Rousseau *et al.* (23).

increasing concentrations to isolated nuclei (24–26) (Fig. 4). The results illustrate two important features of the complex–nucleus interaction. First, receptor–glucocorticoid complexes bind specifically to nuclei in low ionic strength at 0° only after they have

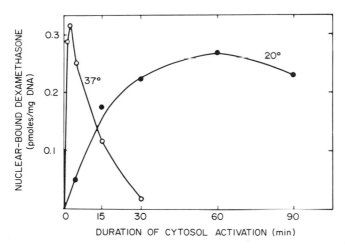

Fig. 4. Kinetics of temperature-dependent activation of cytosol. Cytosols containing dexamethasone-³H with and without competing nonradioactive dexamethasone were incubated at 37° (○) or 20° (●) for the time indicated. After cooling to 0°, duplicate samples (0.2 ml) were exposed to nuclei (1.0 mg of DNA) for 1 hour at 0° and the receptor-dexamethasone-³H bound was determined. From Higgins *et al.* (25).

been "activated" either by heating transiently to 20° or by being exposed temporarily to ionic strengths of 0.15 M. After either of these "activating" procedures, receptor–dexamethasone complexes bind to a limited number of specific nuclear sites. HTC cell nuclei contain about 12,000 such sites which interact with receptor–steroid complexes with an affinity of approximately 3×10^{10} M.

A second feature of the nuclear sites is revealed by experiments in which isolated nuclei are treated with pancreatic DNase (24) (Table III). This procedure completely prevents glucocorticoid–receptor complexes from binding to isolated nuclei, despite the fact that nuclear morphology is undisturbed, and that there is only a small loss of nuclear protein. These results suggest that DNA plays a role in the nuclear binding reaction, an impression which is strengthened by further experiments indicating that receptor–steroid complexes bind to both double- and single-stranded DNA, but not to RNA (24, 27) (Fig. 5).

TABLE III

EFFECT OF DEOXYRIBONUCLEASE TREATMENT OF HTC
CELL NUCLEI ON NUCLEAR BINDING[a]

Incubation conditions	Specific nuclear binding (% of control)	Percent of nuclear DNA released
Digestion (1 hour) followed by binding	8 (0–17)	33
Digestion (24 hours) followed by binding	11 (8–12)	38
Binding followed by digestion (1 hour)	75 (67, 83)	60

[a] From Baxter *et al.* (24).

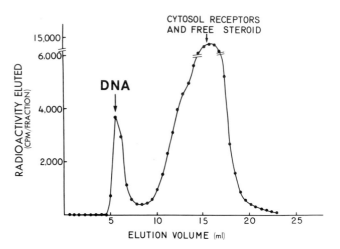

FIG. 5.   Agarose gel filtration of cytosol-bound dexamethasone-^{3}H incubated with HTC cell DNA. Modified from Baxter *et al.* (24).

To gain further information about the nuclear sites, we have inquired whether they recognize only particular steroid–receptor complexes (26). These experiments were based on observations that uterine nuclei can bind specifically, and with high affinity, both receptor–glucocorticoid and receptor–estradiol complexes (Figs. 6 and 7). (The receptor proteins themselves are quite

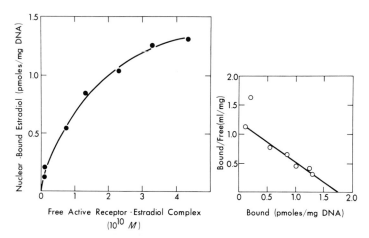

FIG. 6. Binding of active receptor-estradiol complex to uterine nuclei. From Higgins *et al.* (26).

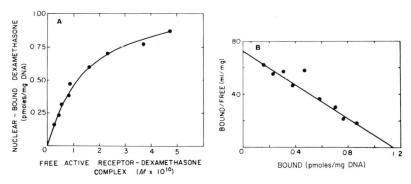

FIG. 7. Binding of active glucocorticoid receptor complex to uterine nuclei. HTC cell cytosol containing dexamethasone-^{3}H was used. (A) Effect of complex concentration. (B) Scatchard analysis of data. Modified from Higgins *et al.* (26).

distinct from one another.) In competition experiments, receptor–glucocorticoid complexes have no influence on receptor–estradiol complex binding or vice versa (Fig. 8). Furthermore, whereas receptor–glucocorticoid complex binding is abolished by DNase treatment of the uterine nuclei, the association of receptor–estradiol complexes is not diminished (Table IV). Therefore,

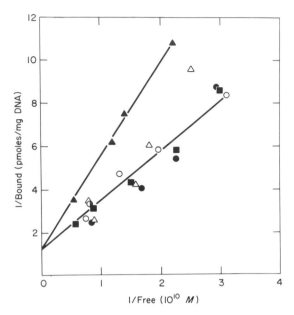

FIG. 8. Binding of active receptor estradiol-³H complex to uterine nuclei: effect of active glucocorticoid receptor bound with nonradioactive dexamethasone. The effects are shown of binding of active uterine receptor estradiol-³H complex to uterine nuclei (■) and of adding 0.35 ml of HTC cell cytosol with (●) or without (○) nonradioactive dexamethasone. Also shown are the effects of adding 0.35 ml of uterine cytosol with (▲) or without (△) nonradioactive estradiol. All cytosols were activated in the same way as the tritiated cytosol. From Higgins *et al.* (26).

nuclear acceptor sites not only bind specific receptor–steroid complexes with high affinity but discriminate between different receptor–steroid complexes.

Although it seems reasonable that the nuclear acceptor sites detected in cell-free binding experiments play a role in the biological actions of the glucocorticoids, this conclusion is weakened somewhat by other recent experiments (28). Intact HTC cells were exposed to sufficient dexamethasone (a synthetic glucocorticoid) to saturate the nuclear acceptor sites with receptor–glucocorticoid complexes. "Prebound" nuclei were isolated from these cells and exposed, under cell-free conditions, to additional incre-

TABLE IV

BINDING OF RECEPTOR–STEROID COMPLEXES TO
NUCLEI TREATED WITH DNASE[a]

Cytosol	Nucleus	Receptor–steroid complex bound by nuclei		
		Control	Treated	Treated (% of control)
HTC + dexamethasone	HTC	3,886	1,167	30
HTC + dexamethasone	Uterus	1,159	487	42
Uterus + estradiol	Uterus	15,864	25,073	158
HTC + dexamethasone	HTC	4,327	1,132	26
HTC + dexamethasone	Uterus	1,391	414	30
Uterus + estradiol	Uterus	19,144	29,498	154

[a] From Higgins *et al.* (26).

ments of receptor–steroid complexes. Surprisingly, prebound nuclei took up as much additional receptor–dexamethasone complex as did "naive" nuclei isolated from cells never exposed to dexamethasone. These results imply that the nuclear sites occupied by receptor–steroid complexes in intact cells are different from those detected in cell-free binding experiments.

To define the relation between the sites occupied *in vivo* and in cell-free experiments, elution studies were carried out comparing the quantity of receptor–steroid complex extracted by salt solutions of various ionic strengths. Nuclei were isolated either from steroid-treated cells or from untreated cells, then incubated with preformed receptor–steroid complexes. The extraction characteristics were the same in both cases.

Nevertheless, there is excellent correlation between the extent of a biological response to dexamethasone [for example, tyrosine aminotransferase (TAT) induction in HTC cells] and the number of steroid molecules bound to the nuclei *in vivo,* indicating that at least some of the nuclear sites occupied *in vivo* are involved in enzyme induction. However, the number of such sites and how they act remains to be determined.

III.   MECHANISMS OF ENZYME INDUCTION AND DEINDUCTION

After nuclear binding of receptor–steroid complexes, the capacity to synthesize TAT in cultured hepatoma cells increases (29)(Fig. 9) even if protein synthesis is blocked (30). These experiments suggest that the glucocorticoids increase the concentration of active messenger RNA coding for the inducible enzyme. Supporting this idea, induced cells contain more polyribosomes synthesizing the induced enzyme than do uninduced cells (29). Furthermore, cell-free extracts prepared from dexamethasone-treated HTC cells synthesize the inducible enzyme at an increased rate compared to uninduced cells (31), and the enhancement resides in the polyribosome fraction (32)(Table V).

When induced cells are resuspended in steroid-free medium, the rate of TAT synthesis declines with a half-time of 1–1.5 hours (Fig. 9) coincident with the disappearance of enzyme-specific polyribosomes (33); this finding suggests that the messenger

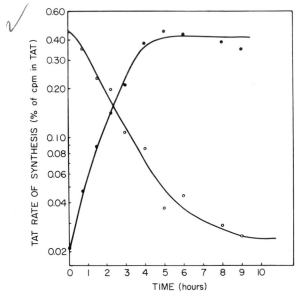

FIG. 9.   The effects of glucocorticoid induction (●) and deinduction (○) on the rates of tyrosine aminotransferase (TAT) synthesis. From Steinberg et al. (33).

TABLE V

FRACTION OF S-30[a]

Cellular components of the incubation mixture	TAT[b] enzymatic activity in the S-100 (milliunits/ mg protein)	Radioactivity in released polypeptides (cpm/mg protein $\times 10^{-4}$)	Corrected radioactivity in TAT (cpm)	Percent total released radioactivity in TAT (cpm in TAT $\times$ 100/cpm in total released protein)
S-30 (induced)	180	3.5	1300 ± 20	0.14
S-30 (uninduced)	26	3.8	160 ± 30	0.016
P_iS_i	183	1.8	790 ± 20	0.078
P_uS_u	20	2.3	80 ± 10	0.0079
P_iS_u	25	2.2	940 ± 20	0.094
P_uS_i	180	2.1	110 ± 10	0.011

[a] Extracts from dexamethasone-induced or control cells were centrifuged at 100,000 g for 90 minutes. The resulting polyribosome fractions were rinsed once with 0.4 ml TMK buffer and resuspended in 0.5 ml of buffer. Half of the polyribosome suspension from induced cells was added to 2.5 ml of the supernatant layer from induced cells (P_iS_i) and half of the supernatant layer from uninduced cells (P_iS_u). The same was done with the fractions from uninduced cells (P_uS_i, P_uS_u). From Klein (32).

[b] Tyrosine aminotransferase.

RNA (mRNA) for tyrosine aminotransferase is much less stable than most messengers [estimated to have turnover times of 8–20 hours (34, 35)]. Inactivation of TAT mRNA is regulated, as well. A number of experiments have shown that the decrease in the rate of enzyme synthesis following removal of the inducer ("deinduction") requires macromolecular synthesis: inhibitors of RNA formation effectively block deinduction (Fig. 10) (36), as does the trapping of HTC cells in certain portions of the cell cycle (G_2, M, early G_1) where the synthesis of the putative regulatory molecules cannot take place (37, 38).

Since messenger inactivation is controlled, we have questioned whether the receptor–steroid complexes, by associating with nuclei,

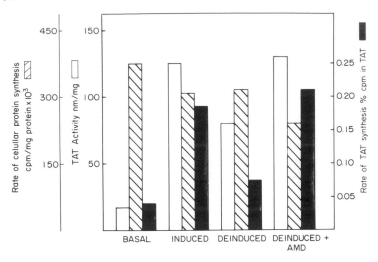

FIG. 10. Rates of general cell protein and tyrosine aminotransferase (TAT) synthesis in different experimental conditions. From Tomkins *et al.* (36).

prevent the formation of the molecules involved in messenger inactivation (39) or whether the complexes promote steps leading to the production of active mRNA. To distinguish between these two modes of inducer action, experiments were done comparing changes in the rates of TAT synthesis (assuming that this quantity is proportional to the concentration of its mRNA) under conditions of induction, and after steroid removal (Fig. 9). The rates of messenger inactivation calculated in both induced and deinduced states were indistinguishable, indicating that, in all likelihood, the hormones only accelerate steps in the production of TAT-specific mRNA. Since the appearance of an active cytoplasmic messenger is preceded by many complex steps involving DNA transcription, processing, and the addition of polyadenylic acid residues (see 40), it is not yet clear which reactions are directly under hormonal control.

IV. CONTROL OF ENZYME TURNOVER

Another means by which the expression of the TAT gene is modulated is through control of the intracellular lability of the

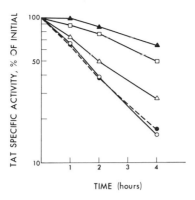

TIME (hours)

FIG. 11. Effect of the components of the growth medium on the degradation of induced tyrosine aminotransferase (TAT) in HTC cells. ▲, Serum + amino acids; ☐, serum; △, amino acids; ●, vitamins; ○, control. From Hershko and Tomkins (42).

enzyme molecules themselves. Under active growth conditions, the turnover time of TAT is 4–7 hours. However, in media deficient in sera or amino acids, the degradation rate is increased (41). This "enhanced degradation" is blocked by inhibitors of protein synthesis, although these agents do not interfere with the slower TAT inactivation in actively growing cells (Fig. 11). Furthermore, as has been observed with generally labeled intracellular proteins, the degradation of TAT requires ATP (42)(Fig. 12).

V. OTHER INDUCIBLE FUNCTIONS IN HTC CELLS

Several other specific phenotypic characteristics are altered on exposure of HTC cells to glucocorticoids. One is a surface modification detected as an increase in the adherence of cells to surfaces and to one another (43) and characterized by a change in cell surface antigenicity and surface change (43, 44). The inducible surface changes are blocked by inhibitors of RNA and protein synthesis, implying an alteration in the macromolecular composition of the cell membrane. Its chemical nature, however, has not as yet been elucidated.

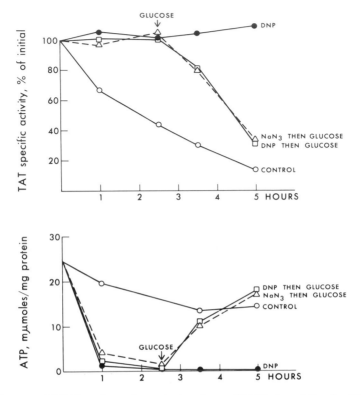

Fɪɢ. 12. Inhibition of tyrosine aminotransferase (TAT) degradation by ATP depletion.

Furthermore, certain clones of HTC cells (selected for their relative independence of glutamine in the growth medium) contain glutamine synthetase activity which is induced by the glucocorticoids (45). Like TAT, both induction and deinduction are inhibited by actinomycin D (46). Steroid dose-response curves for the induction of TAT and glutamine synthetase (as well as for the surface change) are very similar, suggesting that the same receptor mediates all three phenomena. The intracellular concentration of glutamine synthetase activity in HTC cells is also determined by the glutamine concentration in the media (45), but the relationships between hormonal control and the effect of exogenous glutamine are not yet clear.

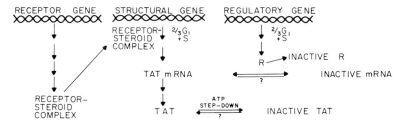

FIG. 13. Regulation of the expression of the tyrosine aminotransferase (TAT) gene in cultured HTC cells.

The processes known to regulate overall expression of genes in HTC cells are illustrated in Fig. 13.

VI. Hormonal Mechanisms of Growth Control

A second interest, developed more recently in our laboratory, concerns the hormonal control of cellular growth. The questions in this area are less well focused than those discussed above, since they deal not only with specific molecular mechanisms, but also with higher-order organizations of regulatory processes. In this work we are attempting to relate hormonal regulation in intact animals, growth control in cultured cells, and the process of malignant transformation.

Nongrowing differentiated cells generally contain the diploid complement of DNA and may thus be regarded as blocked in a G_0 phase of the cell cycle prior to the DNA synthetic S period. A number of cell types can enter the cycle in response to specific physiological stimuli; for example, in liver regeneration and during the mitogen- or antigen-stimulated transformation of immunocytes. In conventional target cells, specific hormones can also promote DNA synthesis and cell division in previously resting cells [see (47) for references].

Untransformed cultured fibroblasts have often been used as models for growth control in intact organisms (48). Thus, feeding serum-starved cells or adding fresh medium to confluent cultures initiates DNA synthesis and cell division (48). Crystalline insulin can replace serum in promoting DNA synthesis (47, 49, 50), and certain clones of 3T3 mouse embryo fibroblasts can grow in media in which serum is largely replaced by a gulcocorticoid, insulin, and a partially purified pituitary extract (51, 52). Therefore, the growth of cultured fibroblasts is regulated by the same hormones which affect cells *in situ*.

Moreover, malignantly transformed fibroblasts require less serum for growth than their untransformed counterparts (53), and there are qualitative differences as well between the serum fractions required for the growth of transformed and untransformed cells (54). The malignant process therefore produces a diminution in the hormone requirements of the transformed cells.

For our studies we have concentrated on a coordinated group of reactions, defined as part of a "pleiotypic" program, which responds when cells enter the cell cycle from G_0, or vice versa (47). The same reactions appear to be involved in growth control in many kinds of cells; typically, for example, when serum-starved fibroblasts are stimulated by the readdition of serum (47). Some of the processes in the response are the uptake of leucine, uridine, and 2-deoxyglucose, the synthesis of bulk RNA and protein, and overall intracellular proteolysis (Fig. 14).

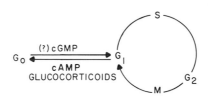

DECREASED TRANSPORT OF :   INCREASED TRANSPORT
   URIDINE
   LEUCINE
   2-DEOXYGLUCOSE
DECREASED SYNTHESIS OF :   INCREASED   SYNTHESIS
   RNA
   PROTEIN
INCREASED DEGRADATION OF :   DECREASED   DEGRADATION
   PROTEIN
INCREASED EXPRESSION OF :   DECREASED   EXPRESSION
   DIFFERENTIATED FUNCTIONS

FIG. 14.   Pleiotypic mechanisms in growth control.

Since all these reactions respond more readily to serum starvation and readdition in untransformed than in transformed fibroblasts, we proposed that they might all be controlled by a common intracellular effector termed the "pleiotypic mediator." This substance, in principle, is generated at the surface of untransformed cells when their membranes assume a hypothetical "no-growth" configuration. We presume that the interaction of specific membrane sites with the growth-promoting effectors in serum would alter this conformation, thereby decreasing the formation of the putative inhibitory pleiotypic mediator. According to this model, malignant transformation locks the membrane in the "growth" conformation. Therefore, transformed cells should be deficient in the inhibitory mediator and, as a consequence, should require little or no serum for growth (47).

Our first attempts to identify the pleiotypic mediator were based on the resemblance between the reactions coordinated under pleiotypic control and the adaptive changes that take place when bacteria under stringent control are deprived of an essential amino acid (55). This mechanism is mediated by ppGpp (56) which is made on ribosomes of stringent (rel^+) amino acid-starved organisms (57). Although not understood in detail, this novel nucleotide governs, directly or indirectly, the multiple responses to amino acid starvation. So-called "relaxed" mutants (rel^-) do not form adequate quantities of ppGpp, and therefore cannot adapt physiologically to amino acid starvation. The differences between rel^+ and rel^- microorganisms are reminiscent of the differences between untransformed and transformed cultured fibroblasts, and we therefore searched for ppGpp in cultured mammalian cells, but were unable to detect it (58).

Meanwhile, however, a host of studies were published showing that the cyclic nucleotides are important in growth control, which suggested that these substances might be pleiotypic mediators. Thus, exogenous cyclic adenosine monophosphate (cAMP) slows cell growth and restores the morphology of transformed cells toward normal (59–61). Moreover, transformed cells contain lower cAMP concentrations than their normal counterparts (62), and growth rates and intracellular cAMP concentrations are reciprocally related in a variety of cell types (63). We therefore

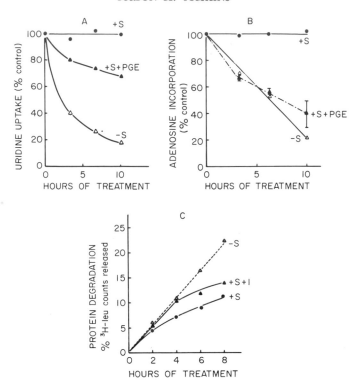

FIG. 15. The effect of prostaglandin E_1 (PGE_1) on the rates of uridine uptake (A), adenosine incorporation (B), and protein degradation (C). ^{3}H-leu = leucine-^{3}H. From Kram et al. (64).

investigated whether cAMP could act as a "negative pleiotypic mediator"; and in cultured 3T3 cells at least, our results were consistent with this idea. For example, serum starvation increases the cellular levels of the cyclic nucleotide and exogenous dibutyryl cAMP or prostaglandin E_1 (which stimulates adenylate cyclase) decrease the uptake of glucose, leucine, and uridine, slow RNA and protein synthesis and enhance protein degradation (64) (Fig. 15).

In the same series of experiments, evidence was obtained for a "positive mediator" as well. Thus cGMP was found to overcome many of the inhibitory effects of cAMP (65) (Fig. 16) suggesting

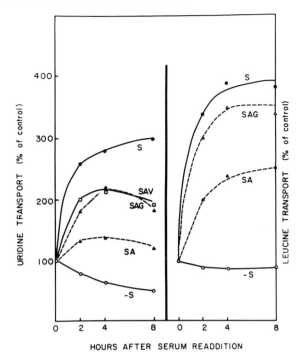

FIG. 16. Effect of dibutyryl cAMP, cGMP, and vinblastine on the serum-stimulated rates of uridine and leucine transport in 3T3 cells. After serum deprivation of 16 hours, the cells were, from time 0, further incubated in either fresh MEM (−S) or MEM plus 10% calf serum (S; control), with or without the following additions symbolized in the figures as follows: A = (Bu)₂cAMP (0.2 mM) + theophylline (1 mm); G = cGMP (1 mM); V = vinblastine (10 pg/ml). From Kram and Tomkins (65).

that cellular growth rates might depend on the ratio of the concentrations of the two "opposing" cyclic nucleotides.

Although rather unlikely, growth control in all cells could in principle be based entirely on these two nucleotides, particularly since their occurrence is extremely widespread. At first glance, this possibility would appear to be excluded since the steroid hormones [which do not act directly through adenylate cyclase (66)] also play a role in general growth regulation. Obvious examples of this control occur in tissues such as the oviduct, uterus, and breast, the proliferation of which is stimulated by the female sex hormones. The glucocorticoids also influence DNA synthesis and cell multiplication, but, interestingly enough, depending on the tissue, these steroids exert either inhibitory or stimulatory effects. For example, glucocorticoids block DNA synthesis in growing liver (67) and inhibit liver regeneration, slow the growth of cultured mouse L cells (68) and immunocytes and, in certain instances, cause cell death (69). Curiously, other lines of cultured mouse fibroblasts are stimulated by these hormones (70), as are certain complex tissues, such as the breast, in organ culture (71). To investigate the molecular basis of the growth control exerted by the glucocorticoids, we have taken advantage of the observations that these hormones inhibit the growth of S49 cultured mouse lymphoma cells and, ultimately cause their death. These facts have allowed us to isolate a number of mutant clones, resistant to the killing actions of the steroids (Fig. 17). Based on our experience with HTC cells, we presumed that the initial steps in glucocorticoid action in S49 cells would involve first, binding of the steroid to the cytoplasmic receptors; second, association of the receptor-steroid complex with specific nuclear sites; and third, consequent alteration in gene expression leading to cell death. In keeping with this formulation, we have indeed found the three expected classes of steroid-resistant variants; r⁻, lacking cytoplasmic steroid-binding activity; nt⁻, in which nuclear transfer of the receptor–steroid complex does not take place; and d⁻, ("deathless") in which, despite nuclear binding of the complex, cell killing does not result (72).

Therefore, like TAT induction, growth inhibition mediated by the glucocorticoids is very probably the result of alterations in macromolecular synthesis. To determine whether the inhibitory response is the result of an enhanced formation of inhibitory molecules or an inhibition of the synthesis of essential molecules, cell hybridization studies were carried out (73). In these experiments, "deathless" mouse lymphoma cells of the EL 4 line were hybridized with steroid-sensitive mouse myeloma cells of the CL 4 line.

If glucocorticoids kill cells by blocking the synthesis of essential macromolecules, then the hybrid should be steroid resistant since

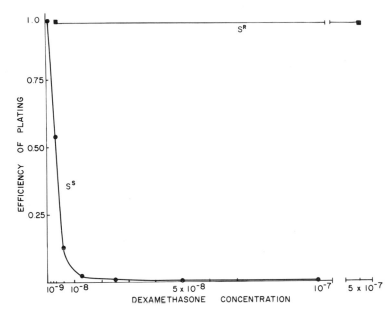

FIG. 17. Growth response of steroid-sensitive and resistant clones to dexamethasone. Appropriate dilutions of sensitive (●) and resistant (■) clones were plated in the presence of the indicated concentrations of dexamethasone. The number of clones per plate was counted at the end of 10 days. The efficiency of plating shown is the average of five identical plates. From Sibley *et al.* (78).

the d⁻ chromosomes, inherited from the EL 4 parent would continue to manufacture these molecules in the steroid-treated hybrid. On the other hand, should death result from the formation of lethal molecules, then the hybrid should be steroid-sensitive because the ability to form such molecules would be inherited from the wild-type (CL 4) parent.

These experiments showed (Fig. 18) that several independently isolated hybrid clones apparently containing the full chromosome complements from both parents were killed by the steroids (73). These results strongly suggest that the actions of the glucocorticoids result from the induced synthesis of inhibitory molecules.

Because of the growth-inhibitory properties of cAMP cited

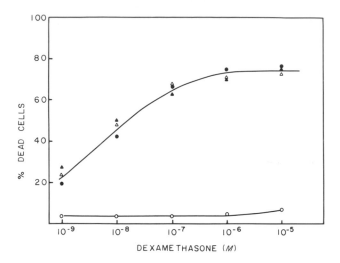

FIG. 18. Killing effect of dexamethasone. Cells were seeded at a density of 3×10^5/ml onto 5-cm Nunclon plastic petri dishes in 4 ml of medium to which dexamethasone (Sigma) has been added at various concentrations. After 48 hours at 37°C, cell viability was determined by trypan blue exclusion in triplicate cultures. ●, CL-4; ○, EL-4; ▲, N5; △, N6. From Gehring et al. (73).

above, we reexamined the question of whether a glucocorticoid-mediated increase in cAMP concentrations might not, after all, be the cause of S49 cell death. Since the steroids do not directly stimulate adenylate cyclase, they would have to increase cAMP indirectly, for example, by lowering the level of the specific phosphodiesterase which hydrolyzes cAMP (74).

Consistent with this possibility, we have found that, like the glucocortocoids, exogenous dibutyryl cAMP inhibits the growth of S49 cells and is ultimately lethal (Fig. 19). We have isolated a series of S49 cells resistant to these actions of cAMP (75). Like steroid resistance, cAMP resistance arises stochastically at low frequency (e.g., about 10^{-7} per cell per generation). Although several phenotypes could in principle result in cAMP resistance, only one has yet been found (75–77). These cells (called "violet" mutants) are deficient in both cAMP-binding activity and in the associated cAMP-stimulated protein kinase (75).

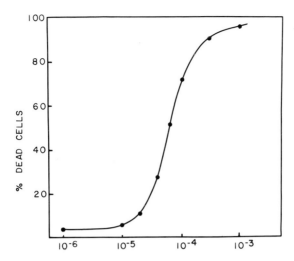

FIG. 19. Effect of dibutyryl cyclic AMP on S49 lymphoma cells. Cells were seeded at a density of 3×10^5/ml in 5 ml medium containing 5×10^{-4} M theophylline to which dibutyryl cyclic AMP had been added at various concentrations. After 48 hours, cell viability was determined by trypan blue exclusion in triplicate cultures. From Sibley *et al.* (78).

Exogenous dibutyryl cAMP does not inhibit the uptake of macromolecular precursors by violet mutants, although these processes are blocked in wild-type cells. Likewise, neither dibutyryl cAMP nor isoproterenol enhance the synthesis of cAMP phosphodiesterase in mutant cells whereas both compounds induce the enzyme in the wild-type (77) (Fig. 20).

These experiments imply that violet variants are resistant to most or all of the intracellular effects of cAMP. Using them it became possible to test whether growth inhibition by the glucocorticoids is indeed exerted via the cyclic nucleotide. Growth rate and viability studies showed that violet mutants and wild-type S49 cells are equally sensitive to killing by dexamethasone. The glucocorticoids must therefore inhibit by a cAMP-independent mechanism (78).

We conclude that cAMP and the glucocorticoids exert independent pleiotypic effects on S49 cells. The molecular mechanisms involved in these actions and their significance for the con-

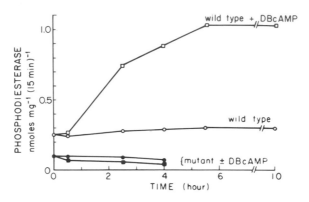

FIG. 20. Cyclic AMP phosphodiesterase in sensitive and resistant cells. From Bourne *et al.* (77). Copyright 1973 by the American Association for the Advancement of Science.

trol of cellular growth and differentiation remain to be investigated.

VII. CONCLUSIONS

Our studies on TAT induction in cultured hepatoma cells have revealed that specific gene expression is regulated at many levels. The glucocorticoids, acting through specific receptor proteins, control the formation of active mRNA for the inducible enzyme. A labile process, which acts only at certain times in the cell cycle and which requires continued RNA synthesis for its operation, is involved in the inactivation of the mRNA for TAT. Finally, the enzyme molecules themselves undergo rapid turnover, the rate of which is determined by the composition of the culture medium.

In addition, we have initiated studies on glucocorticoid-mediated growth control. These steroids inhibit the growth, and ultimately cause the death, of cultured lymphoma cells. Exogenously added or endogenously generated cAMP has rather similar effects. However, the isolation and study of a variety of regulatory mutants has led to the conclusions that the steroids induce macromolecules that impair cell growth and viability by mechanisms independent of the cyclic nucleotides.

REFERENCES

1. Kane, B. E., Reiskind, J. B., and Mullins, J. T., *Science* **180**, 1192 (1973).
2. Ashburner, M., *Exp. Cell. Res.* **71**, 433 (1972).
3. "Steroids in Non-Mammalian Vertebrates" (D. R. Idler, ed.). Academic Press, New York, 1972.
4. Ashmore, J., and Morgan, D., *in* "The Adrenal Cortex" (A. B. Eisenstein, ed.), p. 249. Little, Brown, Boston, Massachusetts, 1967.
5. Baxter, J. D., and Forsham, P., *Amer. J. Med.* **53**, 573 (1972).
6. Yalovsky, U., Zelikson, R., and Kulka, R. G., *FEBS* (*Fed. Eur. Biochem. Soc.*) *Lett.* **2**, 323 (1969).
7. Moscona, A. A., and Piddington, R., *Biochim. Biophys. Acta* **121**, 409 (1966).
8. Ramaley, J. A., *Endocrinology* **92**, 881 (1973).
9. Furihata, C., Kawachi, T., and Sugimura, T., *Biochem. Biophys. Res. Commun.* **47**, 705 (1972).
10. deLemos, R. A., Shermeta, D. W., Knelson, J. H., Kotas, R., and Avery, M. E., *Amer. Rev. Resp. Dis.* **102**, 459 (1970)
11. Greengard, O., and Dewey, H. K., *Proc. Nat. Acad. Sci. U.S.* **68**, 1698 (1971).
12. "Hormones in Development" (M. Hamburgh and E. J. W. Barrington, eds.), Appleton, New York, 1971.
13. Ballard, P. L., Baxter, J. D., Higgins, S. J., Rousseau, G. G., and Tomkins, G. M., *Endocrinology* **94**, 998 (1974).
14. Thompson, E. B., Tomkins, G. M., and Curran, J. F., *Proc. Nat. Acad. Sci. U.S.* **56**, 296 (1966).
15. Martin, D. W., Jr., Tomkins, G. M., and Granner, D. K., *Proc. Nat. Acad. Sci. U.S.* **62**, 248 (1969).
16. Horibata, K., and Harris, A. W., *Exp. Cell Res.* **60**, 61 (1970).
17. Sibley, C. H., and Tomkins, G. M., *Genetics* **74**, S 253 (1973).
18. Gross, S. R., Aronow, L., and Pratt, W. B., *J. Cell Biol.* **44**, 103 (1970).
19. Levinson, B. B., Baxter, J. D., Rousseau, G. G., and Tomkins, G. M. *Science* **175**, 189 (1972).
20. Baxter, J. D., and Tomkins, G. M., *Proc. Nat. Acad. Sci. U.S.* **65**, 709 (1970).
21. Baxter, J. D., and Tomkins, G. M., *Proc. Nat. Acad. Sci. U.S.* **68**, 932 (1971).
22. Rousseau, G. G., Baxter, J. D., and Tomkins, G. M., *J. Mol. Biol.* **67**, 99 (1972).
23. Rousseau, G. G., Baxter, J. D., Higgins, S. J., and Tomkins, G. M., *J. Mol. Biol.* **79**, 539 (1973).
24. Baxter, J. D., Rousseau, G. G., Benson, M. C., Garcea, R. L., Ito, J., and Tomkins, G. M., *Proc. Nat. Acad. Sci. U.S.* **69**, 1892 (1972).
25. Higgins, S. J., Rousseau, G. G., Baxter, J. D., and Tomkins, G. M., *J. Biol. Chem.* **248**, 5866 (1973).

26. Higgins, S. J., Rousseau, G. G., Baxter, J. D., and Tomkins, G. M., *J. Biol. Chem.* **248,** 5873 (1973).
27. Rousseau, G. G., personal communication.
28. Higgins, S. J., Rousseau, G. G., Baxter, J. D., and Tomkins, G. M., *Proc. Nat. Acad. Sci. U.S.* **70,** 3415 (1973).
29. Scott, W. A., Shields, R., and Tomkins, G. M., *Proc. Nat. Acad. Sci. U.S.* **69,** 2937 (1972).
30. Peterkofsky, B. and Tomkins, G. M., *Proc. Nat. Acad. Sci. U.S.* **60,** 222 (1968).
31. Beck, J. P., Beck, G., Wong, K. Y., and Tomkins, G. M., *Proc. Nat. Acad. Sci. U.S.* **69,** 3615 (1972).
32. Klein, C., personal communication.
33. Steinberg, R., personal communication.
34. Greenberg, J., and Perry, R., *Nature (London)* **240,** 102 (1972).
35. Singer, R. H., and Penman, S., *J. Mol. Biol.* **78,** 321 (1973).
36. Tomkins, G. M., Levinson, B. B., Baxter, J. D., and Dethlefsen, L., *Nature (London) New Biol.* **239,** 9 (1972).
37. Martin, D. W., Jr., Tomkins, G. M., and Bresler, M., *Proc. Nat. Acad. Sci. U.S.* **63,** 842 (1969).
38. Martin, D. W., Jr., and Tomkins, G. M., *Proc. Nat. Acad. Sci. U.S.* **65,** 1064 (1970).
39. Tomkins, G. M., Gelehrter, T. D., Granner, D. K., Martin, D. W., Jr., Samuels, H. H., and Thompson, E. B., *Science* **166,** 1474 (1969).
40. Mathews, M. B., *Essays in Biochemistry* **9,** 59 (1973).
41. Auricchio, F., Martin, D. W., Jr., and Tomkins, G. M., *Nature (London)* **224,** 806 (1969).
42. Hershko, A., and Tomkins, G. M., *J. Biol. Chem.* **246,** 710 (1971).
43. Ballard, P. L., and Tomkins, G. M., *Nature (London)* **224,** 344 (1969).
44. Ballard, P. L., and Tomkins, G. M., *J. Cell. Biol.* **47,** 222 (1970).
45. Kulka, R. G., Tomkins, G. M., and Crook, R. B., *J. Cell Biol.* **54,** 175 (1972).
46. Kulka, R. G., and Cohen, H., *J. Biol. Chem.* **248,** 6738 (1973).
47. Hershko, A., Mamont, P., Shields, R., and Tomkins, G. M., *Nature (London) New Biol.* **232,** 206 (1971).
48. Dulbecco, R., *Nature (London)* **227,** 802 (1970).
49. Temin, H. M., *J. Cell. Physiol.* **69,** 167 (1967).
50. Temin, H. M., Pierson, R. R., and Dulak, N. C., *in* "Growth, Nutrition, and Metabolism of Cells in Culture" (G. H. Rothblatt and V. J. Cristofalo, eds.) Vol. 1, p. 49. Academic Press, New York, 1972.
51. R. Holley, personal communication.
52. Armelin, H. A., *Proc. Nat. Acad. Sci. U.S.* **70,** 2702 (1973).
53. Jainchill, J., and Todaro, G. J., *Exp. Cell Res.* **59,** 137 (1970).
54. Holley, R. W., and Kiernan, J. A., *in* "Growth Control in Cell Cultures" (G. E. W. Wolstenholme and J. Knight, eds.), p. 3. Churchill, London, 1971.

55. Edlin, G., and Broda, P., *Bacteriol. Rev.* **32**, 206 (1968).
56. Cashel, M., and Gallant, T. J., *Nature (London)* **221**, 838 (1969).
57. Haseltine, W. A., Block, R., Gilbert, W., and Weber, K., *Nature (London)* **238**, 381 (1972).
58. Mamont, P., Hershko, A., Kram, R., Schacter, L., Lust, J., and Tomkins, G. M., *Biochem. Biophys. Res. Commun.* **48**, 1378 (1972).
59. Shapiro, D. L., *Nature (London)* **241**, 203 (1973).
60. Hsie, A. W., and Puck, T. T., *Proc. Nat. Acad. Sci. U.S.* **68**, 358 (1971).
61. Johnson, G., Friedman, R., and Pastan, I., *Proc. Nat. Acad. Sci. U.S.* **68**, 425 (1971).
62. Sheppard, J. R., *Nature (London) New Biol.* **236**, 14 (1972).
63. Otten, J., Johnson, G. S., and Pastan, I., *Biochem. Biophys. Res. Commun.* **44**, 1192 (1971).
64. Kram, R., Mamont, P., and Tomkins, G. M., *Proc. Nat. Acad. Sci. U.S.* **70**, 1432 (1973).
65. Kram, R., and Tomkins, G. M., *Proc. Nat. Acad. Sci. U.S.* **70**, 1659 (1973).
66. Granner, D., Chase, L. R., Aurbach, G. D., and Tomkins, G. M. *Science* **162**, 1018 (1968).
67. Henderson, I. C., and Loeb, J. N., *Nature (London)* **228**, 556 (1970).
68. Hackney, J. F., Gross, S. R., Aronow, L., and Pratt, W. B., *Mol. Pharmacol.* **6**, 500 (1970).
69. Dougherty, T. F., *Physiol. Rev.* **32**, 379 (1952).
70. Thrash, C. R., and Cunningham, D. D., *Nature (London)* **242**, 399 (1973).
71. Topper, Y. J., and Oka, T., *in* "Effects of Drugs on Cellular Control Mechanisms" (B. R. Rabin and R. B. Freedman, eds.), p. 131. Macmillan, New York, 1971.
72. Sibley, C. H., and Tomkins, G. M., *Cell* in press (1974).
73. Gehring, U., Mohit, B., and Tomkins, G. M., *Proc. Nat. Acad. Sci. U.S.* **69**, 3124 (1972).
74. Manganiello, V., and Vaughan, M., *J. Clin. Invest.* **51**, 2763 (1972).
75. Daniel, V., Litwack, G., and Tomkins, G. M., *Proc. Nat. Acad. Sci. U.S.* **70**, 76 (1973).
76. Daniel, V., Bourne, H. R., and Tomkins, G. M., *Nature (London) New Biol.* **244**, 167 (1973).
77. Bourne, H. R., Tomkins, G. M., and Dion, S., *Science* **181**, 952–954. September 7 (1973).
78. Sibley, C. H., Gehring, U., Bourne, H., and Tomkins, G. M., *in* "Control of Proliferation in Animal Cells" (B. Clarkson and R. Baserga, eds.) Cold Spring Harbor Laboratory, Cold Spring Harbor, New York, 1974.

ANATOMY AND PHYSIOLOGY OF A REGULATORY ENZYME—ASPARTATE TRANSCARBAMYLASE*

HOWARD K. SCHACHMAN

Department of Molecular Biology and Virus Laboratory, Wendell M. Stanley Hall, University of California, Berkeley, California

I. INTRODUCTION

DURING the past decade there have been remarkable advances in our understanding of the structure and dynamics of many proteins. Particularly noteworthy was the recognition of the special advantages which arise from subunit interactions in multichain proteins. Through these interactions, oligomeric proteins have acquired unique abilities to respond specifically and differently to a variety of metabolites. In this way certain proteins, such as regulatory enzymes, can serve to link diverse metabolic pathways. Among oligomeric proteins hemoglobin is preeminent not only because we know more about it than any other subunit containing protein, but also because of its crucial homeostatic role in the transport of oxygen in blood. The sigmoidal saturation curve for oxygen exhibited by hemoglobin and the effect of carbon dioxide on the dissociation of oxygen from the protein have been known for about 70 years (Bohr *et al.,* 1904). But only recently have we achieved an understanding of this behavior at the molecular level through the dramatic demonstration of the detailed changes in the hemoglobin structure under different physiological conditions (Perutz, 1970, 1972). By comparison our knowledge of other multichain proteins it still in its infancy. My goal in this lecture is to summarize our studies on the anatomy and physiology of one regulatory enzyme, aspartate transcarbamylase (ATCase), in terms of some of the basic concepts developed through the research on hemoglobin. The work presented here was performed largely by J. A. Cohlberg, M. W. Kirschner, G. M. Nagel, V. P. Pigiet,

* Lecture delivered on November 16, 1972.

J. M. Syvanen, and Y. Yang. Their innumerable and invaluable contributions have led to the formulation of a structural model which serves as a basis for speculation about the functional behavior of the enzyme. All the research stems directly from the pioneering studies of J. C. Gerhart, whose continued interest, suggestions, criticisms, and collaboration have been indispensable.

In several crucial ways hemoglobin is the prototype of regulatory enzymes which interlock degradative and biosynthetic pathways to produce the proper balance of metabolites needed for a cell's growth. The sigmoidal oxygen dissociation curve exhibited by hemoglobin, which accounts for the extremely efficient release of oxygen from the protein as the gas pressure falls, is one of the features defining a regulatory protein. This characteristic behavior was attributed very early to heme–heme interactions in the binding of oxygen as though the reactivity of the free sites is affected by the presence of oxygen molecules at other sites in the same hemoglobin molecule (Douglas et al., 1912; Hill, 1913; Adair, 1925; Roughton et al., 1955). Such interactions involving the multiple binding of identical ligands are now termed homotropic effects and are exhibited by many regulatory enzymes (Monod et al., 1965). Clearly, homotropic effects provide for much more efficient control than is obtained with proteins that show hyperbolic dissociation curves. Just as oxygen binding at the four hemes in hemoglobin is affected markedly by other ligands, such as hydrogen ions, which bind at different types of sites in the oligomeric protein (Christiansen et al., 1914), so the catalytic activity of regulatory enzymes is influenced by the binding of ligands, such as activators or inhibitors, at remote sites in these protein molecules. This type of interaction between different ligands is known as the heterotropic effect (Monod et al., 1965).

Both the homotropic and the heterotropic effects are now known to be mediated by oligomeric proteins through conformational changes affecting their tertiary and quaternary structures. Hence much effort is being devoted toward answering a variety of questions about the subunit structure and interactions in these proteins. Are the polpeptide chains in an oligomeric protein identical? Are these chains assembled into discrete functional subunits within the intact protein molecules? What groups are involved in the bonding domains within and between subunits? What forces hold the structure together, and how strong are they? Can active site regions be differentiated from intersubunit bonding domains? To what extent are the secondary and tertiary structures of the individual polypeptide chains altered when these chains are assembled into oligomers? Upon the interaction of the oligomers with ligands such as substrates and inhibitors, are there local conformational changes in the polypeptide chains? Are there also gross changes in the quaternary structures of oligomeric proteins upon the addition of specific ligands? Are these local and gross changes coordinated? If so, how are they linked? How are these conformational changes mediated? What is the role of the bonding domains between subunits? Do the subunits within each protein molecule isomerize in unison when a ligand is bound to only one subunit (Monod et al., 1965); i.e., is the transition from one state to another concerted as in a two-state model? Alternatively, do some subunits within an oligomer change their conformations sequentially while others in the same molecule remain unchanged (Koshland et al., 1966); i.e., are there intermediate states? In enzymes having multiple functions, like catalysis and regulation, can the cooperative (homotropic) and the inhibitory or activating (heterotropic) effects be separated by chemical modification of the different subunits? In hybrid molecules are conformational changes due to the binding of ligands to one subunit accompanied by conformational changes in the other subunits which, because of chemical modification, do not interact directly with the ligand?

Answers to most of the questions posed above are available only for hemoglobin. But partial answers are now available for other oligomeric proteins as well, and I welcome this opportunity to summarize our groping with these questions as they pertain to the regulatory enzyme, aspartate transcarbamylase.

II. PHYSIOLOGICAL ROLE OF ATCASE

The production of metabolites is frequently regulated by feedback inhibition of the first enzyme in a biosynthetic pathway so that the rate of formation of the final product is matched to the rate of its consumption for another pathway (Umbarger,

1961). This type of control is evident in pyrimidine biosynthesis in *Escherichia coli*. It is achieved in part through the mediation of ACTase which catalyzes the formation of the first compound unique to this pathway and which is inhibited by the end product, cytidine triphosphate (CTP). The operation of feedback inhibition in the pyrimidine pathway was shown by Gerhart and Pardee (1964) through experiments with intact cells of a mutant of *E. coli*. Such an experiment is illustrated in Fig. 1 which shows

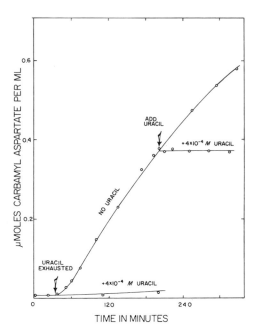

FIG. 1.   Feedback inhibition in the pyrimidine pathway in intact *Escherichia coli*. The *E. coli* mutant lacking dihydroorotase, the enzyme succeeding aspartate transcarbamylase (ATCase) in the pyrimidine pathway, was grown in a medium with sufficient uracil to support the growth of about 10^9 cells/ml. Just prior to the time expected for uracil exhaustion, the culture was divided into two portions, one of which was supplemented with uracil (4×10^{-4} M) and allowed to grow as a control. In the other aliquot, growth soon ceased due to uracil starvation and carbamyl aspartate accumulated in the cells and the medium. After 160 minutes of uracil starvation, a portion of this culture was removed and supplemented with uracil (4×10^{-4} M) and allowed to grow. From Gerhart and Pardee (1964).

the rate of production of carbamyl aspartate (the first product in the pathway) when the intact cells were grown under different conditions. By selecting a mutant which lacked dihydroorotase, the second enzyme in the pathway, Gerhart and Pardee were able to demonstrate that carbamyl aspartate accumulated as a result of the uncontrolled catalytic activity of ATCase. When the mutant was grown in the absence of uracil there was a very great synthesis of this compound. This synthesis was so extensive in cells grown under these conditions that carbamyl aspartate amounted to about one-half of the dry weight of the cells after 4 hours. Upon the addition of uracil (an exogenous pyrimidine source which is rapidly converted to CTP), the formation of carbamyl aspartate ceased within a few minutes, apparently as a result of the inhibition of ACTase activity. Other *in vivo* experiments suggested that the true inhibitor of ATCase was a cytosine derivative (Gerhart and Pardee, 1964), and studies with the purified enzyme indicated that CTP was the likely feedback inhibitor of the ACTase step in the biosynthesis of pyrimidines (Gerhart and Pardee, 1962). Figure 2 shows that the pyrimidine pathway and its regulatory circuits involve other enzymes, such as carbamyl phosphate synthetase and cytidine triphosphate synthetase. Although many features of the overall regulation have not yet been evaluated fully, the role of ATCase in this pathway has been established and certain aspects of its functional behavior can now be explained in terms of its structure.

All research on ATCase as an allosteric protein stems from the demonstration of its unusual kinetic behavior (Gerhart and Pardee, 1962). As seen in Fig. 3 the velocity of the enzymatic reaction varies in a sigmoidal fashion as the substrate concentration is increased. This striking departure from the hyperbolic behavior characteristic of most enzymes was first observed by Gerhart and Pardee (1962), who pointed out that the unusual kinetic properties could be interpreted in terms of cooperative binding of ligands to ATCase. The homotropic effect shown in Fig. 3 for aspartate saturation has also been observed recently for the other substrate, carbamyl phosphate (Bethell et al., 1968). Figure 3 also shows that the substrate saturation curves are shifted significantly by the nucleotide effectors, CTP and ATP. Inhibition by

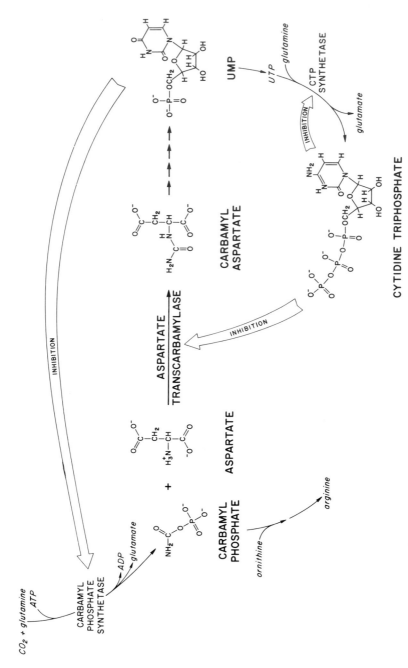

FIG. 2. Regulatory circuits governing pyrimidine biosynthesis at the level of enzyme activity in *Escherichia coli*. Heavy open arrows signify the inhibitory action of a specific metabolite on one of the enzymes of the pathway. From Gerhart (1970).

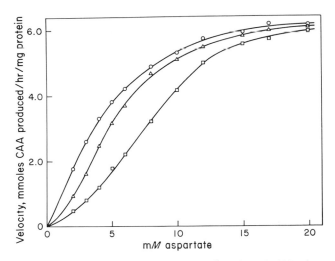

FIG. 3. Kinetic behavior of aspartate transcarbamylase (ATCase) as a function of aspartate concentration. All reaction mixtures contained 3.6 mM carbamyl phosphate, 50 mM imidazole acetate at pH 7.0, and 1.0 μg of ACTase per milliliter. The various concentrations of aspartate are indicated on the abscissa, and the velocity of formation of carbamyl aspartate in millimoles per hour per milligram of protein is shown on the ordinate. The heterotropic effects caused by the inhibitor (+0.5 mM CTP, □——□) and the activator (+2.0 mM ATP, ○——○) are shown in relation to the control (△——△). These nucleotides were present at concentrations sufficient to produce their maximal effects. In the presence of CTP the saturation curve was more sigmoidal than the control; in contrast the curve is less sigmoidal when ATP is added. From V. P. Pigiet, Jr., Y. Yang and H. K. Schachman, unpublished observations.

CTP leads to a reduction in the velocity of the enzymatic reaction at any aspartate concentration below about 20 mM. This inhibition is not complete, however, even at very high concentrations of nucleotides, and can be overcome by increasing the substrate concentration. Gerhart and Pardee concluded from their detailed kinetic studies that the inhibitory effect of CTP was not exerted directly as a competition with the substrate for binding at the active sites, but rather as an indirect effect due to binding at different types of sites. This heterotropic effect exhibited by CTP which caused inhibition has its counterpart in the activation caused by ATP.

The homotropic and heterotropic effects exhibited by ATCase in its kinetic behavior are similar to those shown by hemoglobin in its sigmoidal binding of oxygen (Bohr *et al.*, 1904) and in the shift of its saturation curve due to the binding of hydrogen ions at different sites (Christiansen *et al.*, 1914).

III.   Discrete Subunits in ATCase for Catalysis and Regulation

Early studies by Gerhart and Pardee (1962) showed that ATCase could be rendered insensitive to inhibition by CTP as a result of treatment of the enzyme with mercurials or mild heating. In the case of the heat treatment the sedimentation coefficient decreased from 11.7 S for the native enzyme to about 6 S. This observation constituted the first evidence for the existence of subunits in ATCase. Treatment with mercurials such as *p*-hydroxy-mercuribenzoate (PMB) proved to be a more gentle method of dissociating the native enzyme without destroying the various ligand binding sites (Gerhart and Schachman, 1965). As seen in Fig. 4 the addition of increasing amounts of PMB to ATCase led progressively to the conversion of the intact enzyme into two different types of subunits with sedimentation coefficients of 2.8 S and 5.8 S. In effect, Fig. 4 represents a titration experiment in which the amount of ATCase dissociated can be related to the number of PMB molecules reacting per intact enzyme molecule. The relative amounts of the two types of subunits were found to be independent of the amount of ATCase dissociated, and the reaction of PMB with the sulfhydryl groups of the enzyme was all-or-none in that no partially reacted intact ATCase molecules could be detected (Gerhart and Schachman, 1968). When fewer than 24 PMB molecules per molecule of ATCase were added, significant quantities of intact ATCase were observed, but these molecules contained no mercurial. The dissociation products, in contrast, had their full complement of bound mercurial even when only a small amount of PMB had been added. Subsequent work has shown that ATCase contains 30 sulfhydryl groups of which 24 react readily with mercurials like PMB. The ultracentrifuge experiments analogous to those illustrated in Fig. 4 revealed that the mercurial was bound exclusively to the smaller subunits

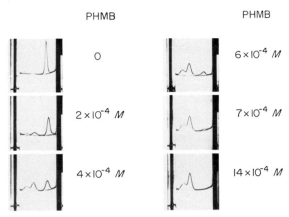

FIG. 4. Dissociation of aspartate transcarbamylase (ATCase) by mercurials. Samples were prepared at room temperature and contained 0.04 M potassium phosphate at pH 7.0, 8.7 mg of ATCase per milliliter (2.9×10^{-5} M), and p-hydroxymercuribenzoate (PMB) at the concentrations indicated. The ATCase preparation was dialyzed previously to remove mercaptoethanol and EDTA. All samples were incubated for about 40 minutes after mixing, and the ultracentrifuge patterns shown above were taken about 50 minutes after the rotor attained a speed of 60,000 rpm. Menisci are on the left. The angle of the phase plate in the schlieren optical system was 50°. Temperature was maintained at approximately 20° during centrifugation. The sedimentation coefficient of the most rapidly migrating component was 11.3 S, the intermediate component was 5.6 S, and the slow component was 2.8 S. From Gerhart and Schachman (1965).

which represented 32% of the total weight of the enzyme (Gerhart and Schachman, 1968; Cohlberg *et al.*, 1972).

Direct evidence for the independent nature of the subunits came from fractionation experiments of the dissociation mixture by zone centrifugation in a sucrose gradient. After separation the subunits were characterized in terms of molecular weight, electrophoretic mobility, chemical composition, enzyme activity, and their ability to bind CTP. These experiments demonstrated that the larger component of molecular weight, 1×10^5, possessed all of the catalytic activity and the smaller component of molecular weight about 3×10^4 possessed the binding sites for CTP (Gerhart and Schachman, 1965).

Although the 5.8 subunit was catalytically active, it was not

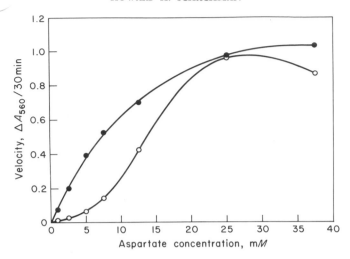

FIG. 5.   Kinetic behavior of aspartate transcarbamylase ATCase (○——○, 0.030 μg/ml) and the isolated catalytic subunit (●——●, 0.019 μg/ml). On the ordinate (in arbitrary units) is given the velocity of the production of carbamyl aspartate, and the abscissa gives the concentration of aspartate. Carbamyl phosphate was present at a concentration of 3.6 mM. The kinetic experiments at pH 8.5 and 28° involved concentrations of ATCase and catalytic subunits adjusted to give equal concentrations of active sites. From Changeux and Gerhart (1968).

inhibited by CTP. Moreover, its enzymatic activity varied in a hyperbolic fashion as a function of aspartate concentration. This is illustrated in Fig. 5, which shows that the isolated catalytic subunits do not exhibit the homotropic effects characteristics of native ATCase. In order to test whether the capacity for inhibition resides in the 2.8 S subunit, reconstitution was performed with the purified 5.8 S and 2.8 S components (Gerhart and Schachman, 1965). This experiment yielded an enzymatically active 11.8 S component (and larger aggregates), which was inhibited by about 60% in the presence of CTP. Thus the 2.8 S subunit, though devoid of enzymatic activity, was essential for inhibition (Gerhart and Schachman, 1965).

Through these experiments we showed conclusively that ATCase was composed of discrete catalytic and regulatory subunits and that the intact structure comprising both types of subunits was required for the existence of homotropic and heterotropic effects.

IV. Organization of Polypeptide Chains within Subunits in ATCase

Early experimental evidence from the subunit composition (Gerhart and Schachman, 1965), from molecular weight determinations on ATCase, its subunits and polypeptide chains (Gerhart and Schachman, 1965; Weber, 1968a), from amino-terminal analyses (Weber, 1968a; Hervé and Stark, 1967), from ligand binding studies (Changeux et al., 1968), and from X-ray diffraction analysis (Steitz et al., 1967) were all consistent with our proposed tetrameric model for ATCase (Changeux et al., 1967). Subsequent investigations (Weber, 1968b; Wiley and Lipscomb, 1968; Meighen et al., 1970; Wiley et al., 1971; Rosenbusch and Weber, 1971a,b; Cohlberg et al., 1972), however, indicated that ATCase is a hexamer composed of six pairs of regulatory and catalytic polypeptide chains. Supporting evidence for this model is shown in Table I which summarizes Cholberg's data for the structure of ATCase in terms of its constituent subunits and polypeptide chains (Cohlberg, 1972; Cohlberg et al., 1972). The

TABLE I

Subunit Composition of Aspartate Transcarbamylase (ATCase)[a]

	ATCase	Catalytic subunit	Regulatory subunit
Mol. wt. $\times 10^{-5}$	3.07 ± 0.03	1.03 ± 0.02	0.337 ± 0.004
Percent by weight	—	68	32
Weight in daltons per ATCase molecule $\times 10^{-5}$	3.07	2.09	0.98
Subunits/ATCase molecule	—	2.0	2.9
Mol. wt. of polypeptide chains $\times 10^{-4}$	—	3.2 ± 0.1	1.72 ± 0.04
Polypeptide chains per subunit	—	3.2	2.0
Polypeptide chains per ATCase molecule	—	6.4	5.8

[a] These results are taken from Cohlberg et al. (1972).

molecular weights for ATCase, 3.07×10^5, and the catalytic subunit, 1.03×10^5, are in excellent agreement with those reported earlier (Gerhart and Schachman, 1965; Rosenbusch and Weber, 1971a). In contrast, the value, 3.37×10^4, for the regulatory subunit is higher than the previously reported values (Gerhart and Schachman, 1965; Rosenbusch and Weber, 1971a). Taken in conjunction with the composition of ATCase in terms of weight percent of the two types of subunits, these results show that an ATCase molecule contains two catalytic and three regulatory subunits. Previous evidence regarding the number of regulatory subunits per ATCase molecule has been inconclusive because the observed molecular weights for the regulatory subunit were intermediate between the values expected for a single polypeptide chain (Weber, 1968b) and a dimer of such chains. Sedimentation equilibrium studies of the subunits in guanidine hydrochloride gave molecular weights for the catalytic polypeptide chains, 3.2×10^4, and for the regulatory chains, 1.72×10^4, which are in good agreement with those reported elsewhere (Weber, 1968b; Cohlberg et al., 1972). It follows that the catalytic subunits contain three polypeptide chains and that the regulatory subunits comprise two chains; hence there are six catalytic chains and six regulatory chains per ATCase molecule.

Although the isolated catalytic and regulatory subunits were found to exist as trimers and dimers, respectively, these observations do not constitute evidence that the trimers and dimers are structural entities within the native enzyme molecules. The respective polypeptide chains could have been spatially separated from one another in the native enzyme and association of them to form the distinct oligomers could have occurred subsequent to the disruption of the ATCase molecules upon treatment with mercurials. For proof of the existence of these discrete subunits as structural entities within the intact ATCase molecules we turn to other approaches.

A. Catalytic Polypeptide Chains and Subunits

In order to determine the organization of the catalytic polypeptide chains at both the intra- and intersubunit levels, we attempted to exploit hybridization techniques which have proved so useful in elucidating the subunit structures of oligomeric enzymes and clarifying the nature of isozymes (Markert and Møller, 1959; Markert and Apella, 1961; Kaplan, 1964; Penhoet et al., 1966, 1967). Unfortunately mutant enzymes in purified form were not available, so we resorted to chemical modification to produce a variant that would be suitable for hybridization with native enzyme. The procedure used for chemical modification required that the altered species be homogeneous, have an electrophoretic mobility distinctly different from that of the native material, be dissociable into subunits, be reconstitutable after denaturation, and preferably be inactive. For several enzymes we found that controlled modification by treatment with succinic anhydride produced variants that satisfied these criteria (Meighen and Schachman, 1970). Hence we were encouraged to apply this technique for the investigation of both the intra- and intersubunit structures of ATCase.

The approach we followed is shown schematically in Fig. 6. Our starting point was the treatment of the isolated, native catalytic subunits with succinic anhydride to give a relatively homogeneous, inactive electrophoretic variant with about 50% of the lysyl residues converted to succinyl-lysyl groups. This derivative had a sedimentation coefficient of 5.8 S, similar to that of the unmodified catalytic subunit. Treatment of the succinylated catalytic subunit, C_S, with guanidine hydrochloride (2 M) caused dissociation to material with a sedimentation coefficient of 1.9 S. Subsequent removal of the denaturant by dialysis gave a component with the same sedimentation coefficient, 5.8 S, as the unmodified catalytic subunit. Similar treatment of the native catalytic subunit, C_N, showed that it could be dissociated into unfolded polypeptide chains and then reconsituted to give active subunits having the same electrophoretic mobility and sedimentation coefficient as C_N. Hence hybridization experiments were conducted, as outlined in the lower part of Fig. 6. The resulting hybrid set contained four members, as seen in Fig. 7. These different species were readily detected by cellulose acetate electrophoresis (Meighen et al., 1970), and Pigiet subsequently separated and purified them by DEAE-Sephadex chromatography (Pigiet, 1971). The number,

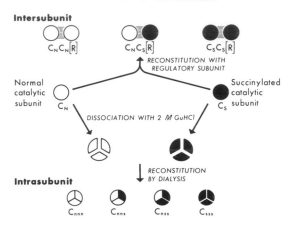

FIG. 6. Intra- and intersubunit hybridization scheme for the catalytic polypeptide chains of aspartate transcarbamylase (ATCase). Hybridization was performed with mixtures of native and succinylated protein. Intrasubunit hybridization was effected by dissociating a mixture of the two preparations with 2 M guanidine hydrochloride followed by reconstitution through dialysis. Intersubunit hybridization was accomplished by mixing the native and succinylated catalytic subunits and adding native regulatory subunits to form reconstituted ATCase-like molecules. The various types of hybrids are depicted with lower-case letters corresponding to the types of polypeptide chains, n for native and s for succinylated. Upper-case letters represent subunits with N corresponding to native and S to succinylated subunits.

relative mobilities, and enzyme activities of the intermediate bands in the hybrid set corresponded to those expected from the hybridization of two molecules each composed of three similar polypeptide chains. These four members of the hybrid set can be depicted as C_{nnn}, C_{nns}, C_{nss}, and C_{sss}, where n and s refer to native and succinylated polypeptide chains, respectivley. When C_N and C_S were incubated for long periods of time in the absence of a denaturing agent, no hybrids were detected. This finding, coupled with the observation that the catalytic subunit at a concentration as low as 1 $\mu g/ml$ had a sedimentation coefficient of 5.8 S (M. Springer, Y. Yang, and H. K. Schachman, unpublished results), shows that the catalytic subunits exist as stable trimers with virtually no dissociation into single polypeptide chains.

Hybridization was also achieved at the intersubunit level as

⊖
origin
↓

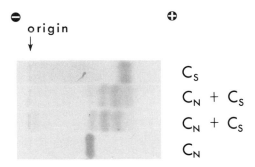

C_S

$C_N + C_S$

$C_N + C_S$

C_N

FIG. 7. Intrasubunit hybridization of native and succinylated catalytic sub-units. All samples were dissociated in 2 M guanidine hydrochloride and then reconstituted by dialysis. The top and bottom patterns were controls of succinylated catalytic subunit, C_S, and native protein, C_N. The intermediate patterns ($C_N + C_S$) represent the hybrid sets obtained with C_N and C_S at ratios of 0.6 and 0.9 for the upper and lower samples, respectively. The electrophoresis experiments were performed with cellulose polyacetate strips. From Meighen et al. (1970).

shown in Fig. 6. For this experiment C_N and C_S were mixed and regulatory subunits were then added to permit reconstitution to ATCase-like molecules. A three-membered hybrid set was produced (Meighen et al., 1970), and the three components were readily separated by chromatography on DEAE-Sephadex as shown in Fig. 8. From the number, position, expected elution order, and the relative specific activities, Pigiet (1971) was able to identify the components in the hybrid set as $(C_N)_2[R]$, $C_N C_S[R]$, and $(C_S)_2[R]$. We can conclude, therefore, that there are two catalytic subunits in each ATCase molecule.

The characteristics of both the intra- and the intersubunit hybridization reactions and the stability and properties of the various hybrids, C_{nns}, C_{nss}, and $C_N C_S[R]$ indicate that each of the catalytic subunits exists as a tightly folded trimer within the ATCase molecules. Had there been dissociation of the trimers into single polypeptide chains during the reconstitution process, a total of seven electrophoretic species would have been observed instead of three. These hybridization experiments thus provide conclusive evidence that the six catalytic chains exist in the form of two trimers within ATCase molecules (Meighen et al., 1970).

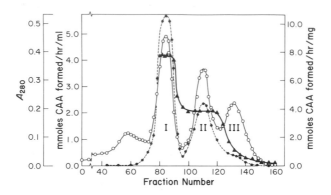

FIG. 8. Intersubunit hybridization of aspartate transcarbamylase (ATCase) with native regulatory subunits and a mixture of native and succinylated catalytic subunits. Separation was performed by DEAE-Sephadex chromatography. The hybrid set was produced by the addition of a small excess of regulatory subunits to a solution containing equal amounts of C_N and C_S. Reconstitution was performed for 0.5 hour in a phosphate buffer (0.04 M) at pH 7.0 containing 0.2 mM DTT and 0.2 mM EDTA. Fractions of 0.5 ml were collected and analyzed for absorbance at 280 nm (○), enzyme activity (●, units/ml) and specific activity (▲, units/mg). The various fractions were pooled to give samples I (fractions 79–88), II (fractions 107–116), and III (fractions 131–140). From Pigiet (1971).

Independent proof of the existence of catalytic trimers was obtained from the elegant cross-linking studies of Davies and Stark (1970).

B. Regulatory Chains and Subunits

Inasmuch as ATCase could be reconstituted in good yield from the isolated catalytic and regulatory subunits (Gerhart and Schachman, 1965), we tacitly assumed that protein–protein interactions alone were responsible for the stability of ATCase. However several puzzling observations during our early work indicated that other constituents, particularly metal ions, were involved in stabilizing ATCase. First, in all preparations of the regulatory subunit a substantial fraction of the protein did not reconstitute into ACTase. Second, the reconsituted enzyme differed detectably from the native enzyme in its sensitivity to inhibition by CTP. Third, the preparations of the regulatory subunit had a much greater ultraviolet absorbance than calculated on the basis of the spectra of native ATCase and the purified catalytic subunit. Fourth, the reconstituted ATCase had an absorption spectrum markedly different from that of the native enzyme. These observations prompted a search for metal ions which revealed that ATCase contains six atoms of zinc per molecule of protein (Nelbach *et al.*, 1972; Rosenbusch and Weber, 1971b). The zinc ions appear to be very strongly bound to the intact enzyme, and no exchange was detected when the native enzyme was exposed to free $^{65}Zn^{2+}$ for 40 days. However, treatment of purified ATCase with PMB to produce catalytic and regulatory subunits caused the zinc ions to become easily removable by dialysis against chelating agents. In this way metal-free catalytic subunits were obtained with full enzymatic activity. The regulatory subunits, however, were found to contain variable amounts of mercuric ions which, though tightly bound, could be removed to give aporegulatory subunits. These aporegulatory subunits when mixed with catalytic subunits yielded no reconstituted ATCase (Nelbach *et al.*, 1972). Upon the addition of zinc ions to such mixtures, reconstitution was effected in high yield and the zinc ions were then very firmly bound (Nelbach *et al.*, 1972). As a result of this study, which demonstrated the crucial role of metal ions, a modified procedure was devised for the preparation of regulatory subunits containing approximately one zinc ion per polypeptide chain. These preparations had a reproducible and low extinction coefficient in the ultraviolet region of the spectrum and showed complete competence in forming ATCase when mixed with catalytic subunits (Nelbach *et al.*, 1972). Moreover, this reconstituted ATCase, unlike that formed with mercury-containing regulatory subunits, had the spectrum, enzymatic behavior, and inhibition characteristic of the native enzyme (Pigiet, 1971; Nelbach *et al.*, 1972). These experiments showed that zinc ions were essential for the *in vitro* assembly of ATCase from the separate subunits. Other related studies (Nelbach *et al.*, 1972) demonstrated the requirement of zinc ions for the *in vivo* formation of ATCase under conditions of derepression in which pyrimidine biosynthesis is growth limiting.

Sedimentation velocity and equilibrium studies conducted by Cohlberg on the mercury-containing regulatory subunits gave varying results depending upon the protein concentration and the amount of mercuric ions in the preparation (Cohlberg, 1972). As seen in Fig. 9 the sedimentation coefficient of these preparations decreased markedly at protein concentrations below 1 mg/ml. Such behavior is characteristic of a rapidly reversible associating-dissociating system such as a monomer–dimer equilibrium (Gilbert, 1955). Additional evidence that the mercury-containing regulatory subunits existed as an associating-dissociating system came from sedimentation equilibrium experiments (Cohlberg, 1972). The plots of ln c vs r^2, one of which is presented in Fig. 10A, showed upward curvature as expected for an interacting system. Curve fitting of the experimental data showed that the concentration distribution could be satisfactorily fit by assuming that the bulk of the protein existed in a monomer–dimer equilibrium with a small amount of aggregated species (Cohlberg et al., 1972). In contrast, as seen in Fig. 9, Cohlberg found that the sedimentation coefficient of the Zn-regulatory subunits decreased slightly and linearly with increasing concentration; this behavior is characteristic of noninteracting globular proteins.

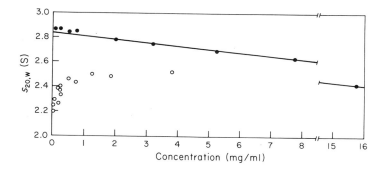

FIG. 9. Dependence of the sedimentation coefficient of the regulatory subunit on protein concentration. Data for the Zn-regulatory subunit are designated by ●, and the symbol ○ represents the mercury-containing regulatory subunit. Schlieren optics were used for protein concentrations above 2 mg/ml and the photoelectric scanner was used for lower concentrations. From Cohlberg et al. (1972).

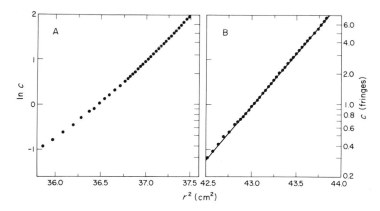

Fig. 10. Sedimentation equilibrium of the mercury-containing and Zn-regulatory subunits. The data are shown as plots of the natural logarithm of the concentration in fringes vs the square of the radial distance in square centimeters. For the mercury-containing regulatory subunits (A) the buffer was 0.04 M potassium phosphate at pH 7.0 containing 10 mM mercaptoethanol and 0.2 mM EDTA. The buffer for the Zn-regulatory subunits (B) contained in addition 10 mM mercaptoethanol and 0.2 mM ZnCl₂. The concentration (c) scale, in fringes, is shown on the right. From Cohlberg (1972).

Moreover, as shown in Fig. 10B, the plot of ln c vs r^2 was linear, corresponding to a molecular weight of 3.38×10^4 (Cohlberg *et al.*, 1972). This finding, taken in conjunction with the amino acid sequence of the regulatory chains (Weber, 1968b), demonstrates that the Zn-regulatory subunits exist as dimers. Although no dissocation of the Zn-regulatory subunit was detected in the sedimentation experiments and these subunits appeared as stable dimers at pH values from 7 to 10, it should be recognized that no special efforts were made to look for dissociation in very dilute solutions. Indeed other results presented later show that such an association–dissociation equilibrium does exist.

In the light of these observations on the regulatory subunits it seemed of interest to determine the nature of the regulatory combining units in reconstitution experiments. Preliminary attempts to prepare a suitable electrophoretic variant of the isolated regulatory subunit by treating it with succinic anhydride led to a derivative which did not form ATCase-like molecules upon the addition of native catalytic subunits (Meighen *et al.*, 1970). Hence Nagel performed the succinylation on native ATCase molecules (Nagel *et al.*, 1972), which were then treated with mercurial to cause dissociation into modified regulatory and catalytic subunits. These were separated by chromatography on DEAE-cellulose to give purified succinylated regulatory subunits, R_S, which were capable of combining in excellent yield with native catalytic subunits, C_N. With these modified regulatory subunits and native regulatory subunits, R_N, Nagel was able to prepare a hybrid set of reconstituted ATCase-like molecules upon the addition of catalytic subunits. As shown schematically in Fig. 11, a four-membered hybrid set would be obtained if there were three regulatory combining units in the reconstitution process. Rapid mixing of R_S, R_N, and C_N did, in fact, give a hybrid set of four equally spaced electrophoretic species on cellulose acetate membranes (Nagel and Schachman, in preparation). This result indicates that there are three regulatory combining units in the reconstitution process and that the six regulatory polypeptide chains in ATCase must exist as three dimers. When R_S and R_N were mixed for brief periods

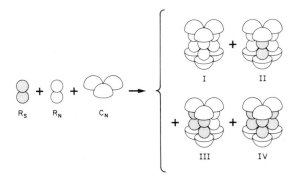

FIG. 11. Hybridization scheme for the formation of aspartate transcarbamylase (ATCase)-like molecules from native catalytic subunits (C_N) and a mixture of native (R_N) and succinylated (R_S) regulatory subunits. On the right are shown the four members of the hybrid set which would be expected if there were three regulatory combining units in an ATCase molecule. This scheme is based on the assumption that the regulatory subunits are preserved as dimers which function as recombining units. From G. M. Nagel and H. K. Schachman, unpublished observations.

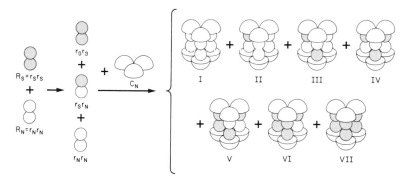

FIG. 12.   Hybridization scheme involving regulatory subunits which exist in a monomer–dimer equilibrium. The native and succinylated regulatory subunits are designated as R_N and R_S, or $r_S r_S$ and $r_N r_N$, respectively. The hybrid dimer of the regulatory subunit is represented by $r_S r_N$, and the catalytic subunit is indicated by C_N. On the right are shown the seven different hybrids that could be formed from two identical trimeric catalytic subunits and the three different dimeric regulatory subunits. From G. M. Nagel and H. K. Schachman, unpublished observations.

(20 seconds) prior to the addition of C_N, Nagel observed a complex hybrid set of unresolved bands. How can this be explained? If the regulatory dimers dissociate reversibly into monomers, then the mixtures of R_S and R_N would contain the dimeric species: $r_S r_S$, $r_N r_N$, and $r_S r_N$, where the symbol r represents a regulatory polypeptide chain. Reconstitution of ATCase-like molecules with such a mixture can be visualized schematically as shown in Fig. 12. Hence seven components would be expected in the hybrid set. The results of the experiment are shown in Fig. 13. If the addition of R_N and R_S to C_N is very rapid, four components are observed electrophoretically. However, prior mixing of R_N and R_S for only 20 seconds before the addition of C_N led to hybridization of the regulatory dimers which, upon subsequent addition of catalytic subunits, yielded a complex hybrid set composed presumably of seven species which differed so little in electrophoretic mobility that resolution of the bands was not achieved. This finding, in conjunction with the sedimentation equilibrium experiments on different types of regulatory subunit preparations, indicates that the

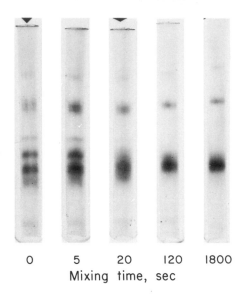

0   5   20   120   1800

Mixing time, sec

FIG. 13. Kinetics of formation of the complex hybrid set from native catalytic (C_N) subunits and a mixture of native (R_N) and succinylated (R_S) regulatory subunits. Reconstitution was performed in a Tris buffer containing zinc ions. The times indicate the periods of prior mixing of R_N and R_S before the addition of C_N. Electrophoresis was conducted on polyacrylamide disc gels, 10 cm in length, with migration (toward the anode) from top to bottom. The bands near the top of the gels are due to aggregated material forming during the reconstitution. From G. M. Nagel and H. K. Schachman, in preparation.

Zn-regulatory subunits exist in a rapidly reversible monomer–dimer equilibrium.

Additional evidence that the regulatory dimers existed as structural entities within ATCase molecules came from reconstitution experiments involving native catalytic subunits and regulatory subunits in which the two polypeptide chains in each dimer were covalently cross-linked to each other (Cohlberg et al., 1972; Cohlberg, 1972). Cross-linking was achieved by reacting the Zn-regulatory subunits with the bifunctional reagent dimethyl pimelimidate (Davies and Stark, 1970). Since this reaction, under the conditions employed, led to the formation of aggregates, Cohlberg fractionated the modified regulatory subunit preparation by chromatography on Sephadex G-100; in this way he obtained a derivative consisting predominantly of cross-linked dimers which were then used with native catalytic subunits for reconstitution of ATCase-like molecules (Cohlberg, 1972). The resulting material, formed in good yield, had the same size and electrophoretic mobility as the native enzyme (Cohlberg *et al.*, 1972). This result, like that from the hybridization experiments, provides conclusive evidence that the regulatory polypeptide chains in each Zn-regulatory dimer remain associated upon incorporation with ATCase and that the dimers of the regulatory chains are integral structural entities of the ATCase molecules (Cohlberg *et al.*, 1972; Cohlberg, 1972).

One other approach has led to the same conclusion about the relationship between the regulatory polypeptide chains within ATCase. Cross-linking native ATCase followed by SDS-polyacrylamide electrophoresis produced a major band corresponding to cross-linked regulatory dimers (Davies and Stark, 1972). Hence the regulatory chains must have been located so closely topographically in intact ATCase molecules as to permit cross-linking by a relatively small bifunctional reagent.

V. A Model of ATCase

We now proceed to consider the arrangement of the six catalytic and six regulatory polypeptide chains within ATCase in the form of two trimers and three dimers, respectively. This arrangement must be such that the ATCase complex possesses both 3-fold and 2-fold axes of symmetry as observed in crystallographic studies of ATCase and its derivatives (Wiley and Lipscomb, 1968; Wiley *et al.*, 1971).

Stable regulatory dimers are formed readily by isologous association of asymmetric polypeptide chains; such dimeric structures would have a 2-fold axis of symmetry (Monod *et al.*, 1965). In such an arrangement, illustrated by the smaller tailless monkeys (Green, 1968) in Fig. 14, the regions of bonding involve identical sets of residues (left hand to left hand in the model) on the two polypeptide chains. These contacts are designated as the r:r bonding domains. Closed stable trimers can be formed with all the intrasubunit bonding domains satisfied by heterologous

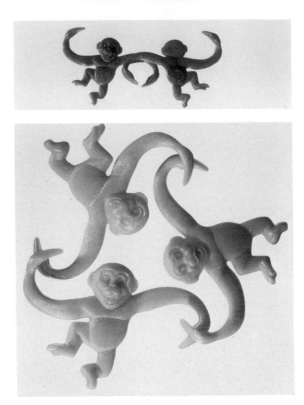

FIG. 14. Schematic model showing the bonding domains within the regulatory and catalytic subunits of aspartate transcarbamylase (ATCase). At the top are shown small tailless monkeys that illustrate individual regulatory polypeptide chains. The individual chains in these dimers are related to each other through a 2-fold rotation axis by an isologous association made up of identical contributions from each polypeptide chain of the pair. This is illustrated by having the monkeys bonded through their left arms. In the lower diagram is shown the corresponding representation of the catalytic chains that are related through a 3-fold symmetry axis. The bonding domains here are illustrated schematically as a heterologous association by bonding between left and right arms. From Pigiet (1971).

association among the c:c bonding domains (Monod *et al.*, 1965). A structure of this type, illustrated schematically in Fig. 14 by the larger tailless monkeys with bonding between left and right hands, would have a 3-fold axis of symmetry.

Since the catalytic subunits show little tendency to aggregate and the addition of Zn-regulatory subunits leads rapidly to reconsitution of ATCase, we can conclude that the regulatory subunits serve as cross-bridges between the two catalytic subunits. The bonding between the different types of polypeptide chains, designated r:c domains, can be visualized in our model as a link between the right hand of a small monkey and the right armpit of a large monkey. A partially assembled model of ATCase is shown in Fig. 15 with three such r:c bonding domains. Each regulatory dimer in the model would have a free right hand having an affinity for an armpit of a larger monkey; thus the completion of the assembly requires only the addition of a second trimer of large tailless monkeys. Symmetry considerations dictate an isologous association of catalytic subunits; hence the two trimers must face each other. Once again the association between

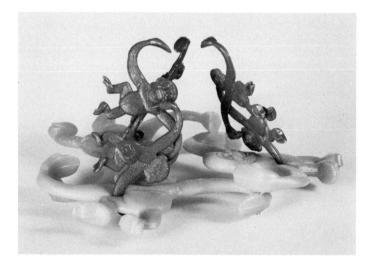

Fig. 15. Schematic representation of the domains of bonding between the catalytic and regulatory subunits in native aspartate transcarbamylase (ATCase). In this partially assembled schematic model of ATCase, the bonding domains between regulatory and catalytic chains are illustrated by having the right arm of a smaller monkey linked to the right armpit of a larger monkey. From Pigiet (1971).

a regulatory and a catalytic chain involves a right hand and a right armpit. In the assembled model we would have six c:c heterologous bonding domains within the two catalytic trimers, three isologous r:r bonding domains within the three regulatory dimers, and six r:c bonding domains linking the 12 polypeptide chains.

Although the monkey model is entertaining and useful in highlighting the symmetry of ATCase and in delineating the various types of bonding domains, it is too superficial to provide answers to a series of questions about the real structure of the native enzyme. Are the two catalytic trimers in an eclipsed or staggered arrangement relative to each other? Are the regulatory subunits sandwiched between the two catalytic subunits, or do they extend to the outside of the molecule? Is there direct physical contact between the two catalytic trimers and among the three regulatory dimers? Does each regulatory dimer link two catalytic chains which are directly under one another or does a regulatory dimer link catalytic chains which are 120° apart?

Partial answers to most of these questions come from recent electron micrographs of the catalytic subunit and ATCase (Richards and Williams, 1972). Negatively stained preparations of the catalytic subunit showed a structure with a contour close to that of an equilateral triangle with edge lengths of 90–95 Å. As seen in Fig. 16 the micrographs of ATCase showed a structure composed of an inner, solid equilateral triangle (appearing identical in size and form to the catalytic subunit) and a circumscribing triangle rotated by 60°. These micrographs of the intact enzyme dried in a very thin stain showed the 3-fold axis of symmetry normal to the plane of the specimen film. When, however, the enzyme was dried in thick stain it exhibited two prominent halves (with shapes somewhat like segments of a circle), indicating that the enzyme dried with its 3-fold axis parallel to the specimen film. There was a space, estimated to be in the range of 20–40 Å, between the two segments. In addition, some of the particles showed faint extensions of material beyond the ends of the segments. This material, which probably serves to connect the two segments, appears to correspond to the arms of the outer triangle and is thought to represent the regulatory subunits.

On the basis of the electron micrographs and a variety of physi-

FIG. 16. Electron micrographs of aspartate transcarbamylase (ATCase). At the top are shown the molecules oriented to illustrate the 3-fold axis of symmetry. On the right are selected particles that illustrate a solid triangular structure within a larger triangle which is delineated by its edges. Four composite views representing a photographic montage of the images of five particles are shown on the right. At the bottom are shown the ATCase molecules disposed in such a way to illustrate their 2-fold symmetry. Selected particles are shown on the right. From Richards and Williams (1972).

cal chemical data, we have constructed a model of ATCase which is shown in Fig. 17 (Cohlberg et al., 1972). Each catalytic subunit is represented as a slightly oblate structure having a triangular arrangement of the three asymmetrically shaped polypeptide chains. The heterologous association of the polypeptide chains through c:c bonding domains within the subunits is indicated

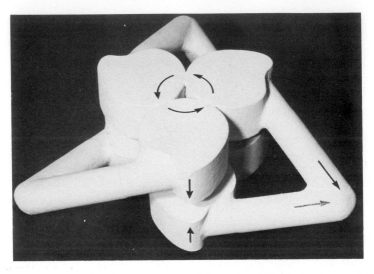

FIG. 17. Model for the arrangement of the polypeptide chains in aspartate transcarbamylase (ATCase). Each catalytic subunit is shown as a triangular array of three asymmetrically shaped catalytic polypeptide chains. Arrows on the upper face indicate the heterologous association of these chains through the c:c bonding domains; arrows on the side faces of the catalytic chains indicate the isologous relationship between the two catalytic trimers. Each regulatory subunit is shown as a pair of cylindrical regulatory chains oriented relative to one another at an acute angle; arrows on the cylinders illustrate the isologous association of these chains through the r:r bonding domains. From Cohlberg *et al.* (1972).

by the arrows on the upper face of one catalytic subunit. Arrows pointing toward each other on the side faces of the catalytic subunits illustrate the isologous relationship between the two catalytic trimers. Each regulatory subunit is shown as a pair of long cylinders each of which represents a regulatory polypeptide chain; the arrows pointing toward each other illustrate the isologous association at the r:r bonding domains. As shown in Fig. 17, one regulatory chain in each dimer bonds to one of the upper catalytic chains, the other regulatory chain in the same dimer being bonded to a lower catalytic chain displaced by 120°. In this way identical sets of amino acid residues in the two catalytic chains are involved in the r:c bonding domains; i.e., the residues located on the left-hand side of each chain in the upper trimer are identical to those on the right-hand side of each catalytic chain in the lower trimer.

The model shown in Fig. 17 is particularly interesting in terms of recent X-ray diffraction studies on ATCase which have led to an electron density map at 5.5 Å resolution (Wiley *et al.*, 1971; Warren *et al.*, 1973; Evans *et al.*, 1973). From these investigations it appears that the catalytic subunits exist as a stack of eclipsed triangles when viewed down the 3-fold axis. In contrast the regulatory chains are not in the eclipsed form; instead they appear to be rotated about the dimer axis. There is a central cavity between the catalytic subunits as indicated by the electron micrographs and illustrated by the model in Fig. 17. The overall dimensions deduced from the X-ray diffraction studies are in good agreement with those estimated from the electron micrographs. In constructing the model shown in Fig. 17, we have deliberately used two cylindrical particles in a V-shaped arrangement to represent the regulatory subunits. In this way we have only one r:c bonding domain between a single regulatory polypeptide chain and a single catalytic chain. The cork ball model (Wiley *et al.*, 1971) proposed on the basis of the X-ray diffraction studies, though having many of the same characteristics as that shown in Fig. 17, is not as definitive as the wooden model in showing only a single r:c domain between each regulatory and each catalytic chain. We, of course, do not know the exact size and shape of each regulatory cylinder in the V-shaped dimers and their rodlike shape and the resulting open space (between catalytic and regulatory chains) may be exaggerated. Indeed Evans *et al.* (1973) recently have suggested that the regulatory dimers are nearly globular in shape.

VI. Bonding Domains in ATCase

As yet we have no knowledge about the amino acid side chains involved in the three types of bonding domains responsible for the architecture and stability of ATCase. Even our information about the strengths of the various interactions is woefully inadequate. The c:c bonding domains implicated in the trimeric catalytic subunits are clearly very strong with the result that no dissociation into single chains has been detected unless strong denaturants like urea or guanidine hydrochloride are added to the protein. In addition no exchange of polypeptide chains was observed when solutions of C_N and C_S are incubated at neutral pH for long periods. It is clear that the zinc ions are not implicated in either the enzyme activity or the stability of the isolated catalytic subunits. In contrast the metal ions are essential for the formation and stabilization of the quaternary structure of the intact enzyme (Nelbach et al., 1972; Cohlberg et al., 1972), and they may be involved, directly or indirectly, in either the r:r or the r:c bonding domains (or both). The isolated regulatory subunits bind zinc and other metal ions strongly (Rosenbusch and Weber, 1971b; Nelbach et al., 1972). Accompanying the binding of zinc ions to the aporegulatory (metal-free) subunits is a marked alteration in the circular dichroism spectrum (Cohlberg et al., 1972). Hence there may be a conformational change in the aporegulatory subunits upon the addition of zinc ions with a consequent effect on the bonding domains between two regulatory chains and between a regulatory and a catalytic chain. As shown by Cohlberg (1972), the addition of zinc ions led to a large enhancement in the free energy of association of the regulatory chains of −4 to −10 kcal/mole. With three such r:r bonding domains in the intact enzyme this enhancement at each domain would constitute a major stabilizing influence. Analogous quantitative data for the r:c domains are lacking since, on the one hand, the aporegulatory subunits show little or no tendency to associate with catalytic subunits and, on the other hand, ATCase (containing six zinc ions) shows no tendency to dissociate into subunits even at very low concentrations. These observations, although not warranting any quantitative estimates of the strength of the r:c domains in the absence and presence of zinc ions, provide some indication that the zinc ions contribute to the strengthening of these domains (Cohlberg et al., 1972).

Additional evidence illustrating the strength of the r:r and r:c bonding domains comes from the recent discovery of an ATCase-like molecule lacking one regulatory subunit (Jacobson and Stark, 1973a; Yang et al., 1974). This regulatory subunit-deficient molecule is found in small amounts in most preparations of ATCase and it is formed in appreciable yield when reconstitution of ATCase is performed from mixtures of regulatory and catalytic subunits with the latter in large excess. The "incomplete" ATCase-like molecule has been purified from such a reconstitution experiment, and the available evidence indicates that it is composed of two catalytic subunits and only two regulatory subunits. Storage of it for several days leads apparently to disproportionation with the formation of ATCase and catalytic subunit. Although much additional study of this interesting molecule is clearly required, it does appear that four r:c domains (instead of six) are sufficient to produce a reasonably stable complex of catalytic and regulatory subunits. It is worth noting that this regulatory subunit-deficient ATCase molecule exhibits both the homotropic and heterotropic effects characteristic of the native enzyme (Jacobson and Stark, 1973a; Yang et al., 1974).

The arrangement of the subunits in the organized structure illustrated by the model in Fig. 17 is especially provocative in the light of the evidence that the isolated regulatory dimers dissociate readily into monomers. It might be expected, therefore, that we could detect half-molecules consisting of three catalytic and three regulatory polypeptide chains. Thus far such a symmetric dissociation of ATCase has not been observed. Success in this effort would depend on the relative strength of the r:r and the r:c bonding domains. Preliminary studies (Nagel and Schachman, in preparation) have shown that an ATCase-like molecule containing succinylated regulatory subunits undergoes some exchange when it is incubated with native regulatory subunits. Further experiments of this type, along with analogous studies of the exchange of catalytic subunits, may provide valuable data regarding the various bonding domains.

VII. Effect of Ligands on the Quaternary Structure of ATCase

All models that have been proposed to account for the cooperative behavior of oligomeric proteins are based on the postulate that the protein molecules can exist in different conformational states and that the relative populations of these states are influenced by the absence or the presence of stereospecific ligands (Monod *et al.*, 1965; Koshland *et al.*, 1966). Hence it is relevant to examine the physical properties of ATCase with techniques that are sensitive to different conformations. Many such techniques have now been exploited in a search for conformational changes in ATCase, and a wealth of information has been accumulated (Gerhart and Schachman, 1968; McClintock and Markus, 1968, 1969; Gerhart, 1970; Buckman, 1970; Eckfeldt *et al.*, 1970; Pigiet, 1971, Markus *et al.*, 1971; Hammes and Wu, 1971a–c) Griffin *et al.*, 1972; Schachman, 1972; Harrison and Hammes, 1973; Wu and Hammes, 1973; Jacobson and Stark, 1973). As yet it is not possible to integrate all the findings into a coherent picture, but it seems likely that neither the "two-state" nor the "intermediate-state" models in the simple forms originally proposed (Monod *et al.*, 1965; Koshland *et al.*, 1966) will account for all the experimental observations. Some limited conclusions can be drawn from our studies, and the following discussion will be restricted, therefore, to them and the supporting evidence. First, those ligands that bind to catalytic subunits affect the chemical reactivity of groups in the regulatory subunits. Second, there is a significant change in the quaternary structure of the intact enzyme upon the addition of ligands that bind to the catalytic subunits. Third, the binding of these ligands is accompanied by gross and opposite changes in ATCase and the isolated catalytic subunits. Fourth, there are local changes in the conformation of the catalytic subunits within ATCase molecules which resemble those in the isolated subunits. Fifth, the binding of CTP to the regulatory subunits in ATCase has an effect on the conformation of the enzyme which is partially antagonistic to that caused by the binding of ligands to the catalytic subunits within the intact ATCase molecules. Sixth, the local and gross conformational changes in ATCase are distinguishable and separable in the sense that the former is sequential and strongly linked to the binding of ligands and the latter is concerted and linked to only partial occupancy (and perhaps the first) of the available sites.

As pointed out in the discussion of Fig. 4 which shows the dissociation of ATCase by the mercurial PMB, the reaction in-

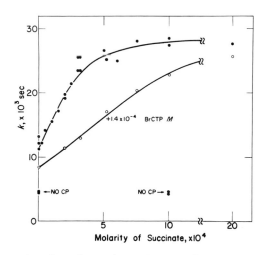

FIG. 18. The effect of ligands on the rate of reaction of aspartate transcarbamylase (ATCase) with PMB. Rate constants (k) for the pseudo-first-order reaction of ATCase with the mercurial were determined from spectrophotometric measurements with light at 250 nm. The curve represented by ● gives the results for solutions containing 1.8 mM dilithium carbamyl phosphate and various concentrations of succinate. The curve represented by ○ gives the results for solutions containing 1.8 mM dilithium carbamyl phosphate, 0.14 mM BrCTP, and various concentrations of succinate as indicated on the abscissa. In a few experiments, indicated by the pairs of points near the bottom, the measurements of reaction velocity constants were made on solutions that did not contain carbamyl phosphate (CP). From Gerhart and Schachman (1968).

volved the all-or-none formation of about 24 PMB-mercaptide bonds with the six regulatory polypeptide chains. The rate of reaction of these sulfhydryl groups is markedly influenced by the presence of carbamyl phosphate and succinate which bind to the catalytic subunits (Gerhart and Schachman, 1968). This enhancement of the rate of reaction of ATCase with PMB was almost 6-fold, as shown in Fig. 18. The effect of carbamyl phosphate and succinate is especially noteworthy since these ligands cause diminished reactivity of the isolated catalytic subunits toward PMB. This interesting change in reactivity of the intact enzyme must arise in an indirect manner through a change in the quaternary structure of the intact enzyme. Binding of ligands to the catalytic subunits of the intact enzyme is apparently accompanied by a conformational change in the whole molecule which is revealed by the marked increase in reactivity of the sulfhydryl groups of the regulatory chains. Figure 18 also shows the partial antagonism of this enhancement caused by the inhibitor, 5-bromo-cytidine triphosphate (BrCTP). A more complete representation of this antagonism is presented in Fig. 19. Excess BrCTP reduces the rate of the reaction of the sulfhydryl groups only partially, and this reduction is itself affected by the concentration of the substrate analog, succinate. At high concentrations of succinate the effect of BrCTP is almost completely obliterated. Figure 19 also shows the results obtained from kinetic studies of the enzymatic behavior (Gerhart and Pardee, 1964). The close parallelism of these sets of data indicates that the conformational changes in the enzyme which influence the reactivity of the sulfhydryl groups are intimately related to those structural changes responsi-

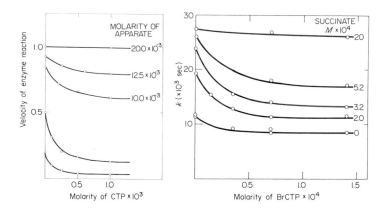

FIG. 19. The partial antagonism by cytidine triphosphate (CTP) (or BrCTP) of the effect of aspartate (or succinate) on the enzyme kinetics of aspartate transcarbamylase (ATCase) and on its reaction with PMB. On the left is the velocity of the enzymatic reaction, expressed as a fraction of V_{max}, plotted as a function of the concentration of CTP. The concentrations of aspartate are indicated with carbamyl phosphate maintained at 3.6 mM in all experiments. At the right are the pseudo-first-order velocity constants for the reaction of the sulfhydryl groups of ATCase with p-hydroxymercuribenzoate (PMB). In these experiments BrCTP was used in place of CTP and succinate instead of aspartate. The carbamyl phosphate concentration was 1.8 mM. From Gerhart and Pardee (1964) and Gerhart and Schachman (1968).

ble for mediating the heterotropic effect between inhibitor and substrate.

The results cited above show how chemical reactivity of groups on one type of subunit is influenced by the binding of ligands at sites on the other subunits. It is as if the enzyme can exist in two (or more) forms with differing reactivities of the sulfhydryl groups. In addition we can infer that the populations of molecules in the different states are influenced both by substrates (and analogs) which favor the reactive form and by the inhibitor which stabilizes the unreactive form. How else can we demonstrate the existence of these different conformational states and the conversion of one to another? To answer this question we turn to another technique which is sensitive to the size and shape of the enzyme molecules in solution.

Since ATCase shows so little tendency to dissociate into sub-units (unless treated with certain mercurials or denaturing agents) a change in its sedimentation coefficient upon the addition of ligands is indicative of alterations in its gross morphology, such as a change in the shape or volume (or both) of the protein molecule in solution. Although large changes are not expected it seemed worthwhile, nonetheless, to study ATCase (with and without ligands) by the sedimentation velocity technique because of the recent improvements in its sensitivity (Kirschner and Schachman, 1971a). The results justified the effort. Succinate alone had no effect on the sedimentation coefficient of ATCase just as it did not influence the reactivity of the sulfhydryl groups (see Fig. 18). In contrast, the addition of carbamyl phosphate caused a reduction of 0.5% in the sedimentation coefficient of ATCase; it also markedly affected the reactivity of the sulfhydryl groups of the regulatory chains of the intact enzyme. When both succinate and carbamyl phosphate were present there was a much larger change (-3.6%) in the sedimentation coefficient of the intact enzyme. Figure 20 shows the titration of the conformational change of the enzyme as revealed by the sedimentation coefficient. At approximately 2×10^{-4} M succinate the decrease in the sedimentation coefficient was half the limiting value obtained at 10-fold higher levels of succinate. This level of 2×10^{-4} M succinate is virtually identical with that required for half-completion of the enhancement of the reactivity of the sulfhydryl groups of ATCase (see Fig. 18).

The decrease in the sedimentation coefficient of ATCase upon the addition of both carbamyl phosphate and succinate is indicative of profound alterations in the structure of the protein such as a "swelling" of the molecules in solution. Alternatively we could interpret this result as indicating that the protein molecules in the presence of the ligands are more elongated (or flattened) relative to the enzyme in the absence of ligands. Thus we can visualize at least two different conformational states of the enzyme. One, at very low concentrations of ligands (which bind to the catalytic subunits), is taut or compact with a relatively low reactivity for its sulfhydryl groups and the other, at saturating concentrations of carbamyl phosphate and succinate, is relaxed or swollen (or more anisometric) with a markedly enhanced reactivity toward PMB (Gerhart and Schachman, 1968). This transition in the quaternary structure of the intact enzyme, revealed by the changes in its physical properties, is likely to be responsible for mediating the marked change in catalytic activity as well.

VIII. Linkage between Local and Gross Conformational Changes in ATCase

Studies on the isolated catalytic subunits of ATCase have shown that they undergo conformational changes upon the addition of carbamyl phosphate and succinate (Gerhart and Schachman, 1968; Collins and Stark, 1969; Kirschner and Schachman, 1971b). As seen in Fig. 20, these ligands promote a 1.0% increase in the sedimentation coefficient of the isolated subunits (Kirschner and Schachman, 1971b). Thus there is a contraction of the isolated subunits upon the addition of the same ligands which promote a swelling of the intact ATCase molecules. Just as the enzymatic behavior of the intact enzyme is not merely the sum of the activities of its parts, so the conformational change in ATCase does not correspond to the changes in the various isolated parts. However, it is not known whether, and to what extent, the catalytic subunits within the intact enzyme molecules change upon the addition of ligands. On the one hand, we might visualize a model

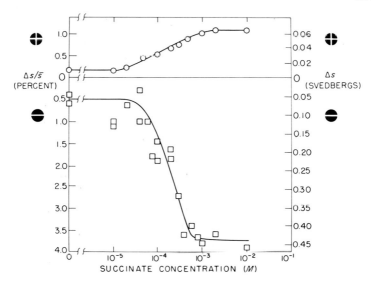

FIG. 20. Conformational titration of the change in sedimentation coefficient of aspartate transcarbamylase (ATCase) and the catalytic subunit as a function of ligand concentration. The change in quaternary structure is revealed as the difference in sedimentation coefficient, $\Delta s/\bar{s}$ in percent, plotted on the ordinate vs succinate concentration on the abscissa. The right-hand scale gives the measured values of Δs in Svedberg units. The data on ATCase, obtained from simultaneous experiments with schlieren optics using wedge and plain window cells, are illustrated by □. Each point represents the difference in sedimentation rate between the sample and reference solution. The sample contained 1.8 mM carbamyl phosphate and the various concentrations of succinate as indicated on the abscissa. These components were replaced in the reference solution by 1.8 mM phosphate and varying amounts of the noninteracting compound, glutarate. The ATCase concentration was 4.2 mg/ml in 0.04 M phosphate buffer at pH 7. In the presence of the interacting ligands the values for $\Delta s/\bar{s}$ for ATCase were negative. Data for the catalytic subunit, obtained by difference sedimentation with Rayleigh optics, are represented by ○. The two compartments of the double-sector cells were filled with sample and reference with each solution composed as described above except that the catalytic subunit was at a concentration of· 8 mg/ml. All values of $\Delta s/\bar{s}$ for the sample compared to the reference were positive. From Kirschner and Schachman (1971b).

in which the local changes in the catalytic subunits within the intact enzyme are similar to those observed in the isolated subunits and are linked to gross and different transitions in the enzyme complex. Such a model could account for the hydrodynamic results shown in Fig. 20 where the ligand-promoted change in the sedimentation coefficient of the isolated catalytic subunits was opposite in direction (and smaller in magnitude) to that of the intact enzyme. According to this model there would be a contraction of each catalytic subunit upon the binding of ligands and an expansion of the whole enzyme resulting from a change in packing or orientation of the subunits within it. On the other hand, we might consider a model in which the quaternary structure of ATCase constraints the catalytic subunits into a conformation different from that of the isolated subunits. With this model the conformational transition of the intact enzyme could represent merely the sum of the changes experienced by the individual subunits which differ from those observed with the isolated subunits. In order to distinguish between these two alternative models we required a technique that could be employed selectively on both the isolated catalytic subunits and on these same subunits within intact enzyme molecules. For this purpose we employed spectrophotometric methods sensitive to only one type of chromophore, which was known to be located only on the catalytic polypeptide chains (Kirschner and Schachman, 1973a).

By treating the catalytic subunit with tetranitromethane in the presence of the substrates, Kirschner (1971) obtained an enzymatically active derivative containing about one nitrotyrosyl group per polypeptide chain. This derivative had a maximum in its absorption spectrum at 430 nm. Succinate alone had no effect on the spectrum at pH 7, and there was only a slight change in the spectrum when carbamyl phosphate was added. In contrast, upon the addition of both carbamyl phosphate (4 mM) and succinate (2 mM) there was a 14% decrease in the absorbance at 430 nm and an increase in absorption at 360 nm with an isosbestic point at 390 nm. Spectrophotometric titration of the unliganded species gave a pK of 6.25, which was raised to 6.62 upon the addition of the ligands. Studies with a variety of different ligands (in pairs and singly) showed that the absorbance at 430 nm, the absorption in the ultraviolet region of the spectrum (Collins and Stark, 1969), and the sedimentation coefficient changed in a parallel fashion. As seen in the titration curve of the spectral change (Fig. 21), saturation was achieved at a relatively low concentration of succinate and the curve was readily fit by a Michaelis-Menten type function with a dissociation constant of 3.7×10^{-4} M (Kirschner and Schachman, 1973a). Similar values were obtained from titration of the change in sedimentation coefficient (Fig. 20), titration of the change in the optical rotatory dispersion (Pigiet, 1971), direct binding experiments by equilibrium dialysis, and enzyme kinetic studies which yielded the inhibition constant for succinate under the same conditions (buffer and temperature) (Kirschner, 1971). Hence the conformational changes in the isolated catalytic subunits seem to be closely linked to binding. Although it is possible that the actual spectral change in the nitrotyrosyl chromophore is caused by a direct effect of the bound dicarboxylic acid, succinate, the evidence at hand suggests that upon binding there is a conformational change in

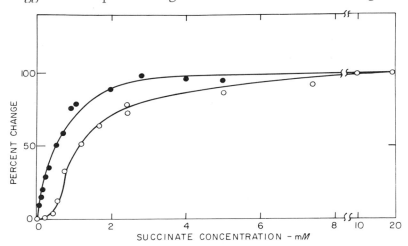

FIG. 21. Succinate titration of spectral change of nitrated catalytic subunit (C^N, ●——●) and of nitrated aspartate transcarbamylase (ATCase) ($C^N R$, ○——○). All measurements were made by difference spectroscopy, and the results are plotted on the ordinate as the percent of maximal change in the difference absorbance measurement vs succinate concentration on the abscissa. The maximal change in absorbance at 430 nm was 15% for C^N and 16% for $C^N R$. The buffer in both cases was 0.04 M phosphate containing 2 mM MET, 0.2 mM EDTA, and 4 mM carbamyl phosphate. From Kirschner and Schachman (1973b).

the secondary or tertiary structure of the catalytic subunit. In either case the chromophore serves as a probe for monitoring local effects in the protein.

When the nitrated catalytic subunits were mixed with native regulatory subunits, Kirschner (1971) obtained reconstituted ATCase-like molecules, $C^N R$, which exhibited properties similar to those of native ATCase. Although the maximum velocity of the enzymatic reaction, the inhibition by CTP, the Hill coefficient, and the value of $\Delta s / \bar{s}$ upon the addition of ligands were all slightly less for $C^N R$ than for the native enzyme, the principal allosteric phenomena (cooperativity and feedback inhibition) were preserved. Hence studies were conducted to determine the effect of ligands on the spectral response of the nitrotyrosyl groups within the ATCase-like molecules. As with C^N, the addition of both carbamyl phosphate and succinate to $C^N R$ caused a 13% decrease in the absorbance at 430 nm (some change in the absorbance occurred upon reconstitution due to the altered environment of the chromophore in $C^N R$ as compared to C^N). Unlike C^N, which responded in a hyperbolic fashion to varying concentrations of succinate (at a constant level of 4 mM carbamyl phosphate), $C^N R$ showed distinctly sigmoidal behavior with a Hill coefficient of 1.68. As seen in Fig. 21, the half-titration level for $C^N R$ was shifted to a higher succinate concentration compared to that for C^N. Thus the incorporation of the nitrated catalytic subunits into ATCase led to an alteration in the nature and extent of the response of the chromophore to varying ligand concentration. This sigmoidal dependence of the absorbance of $C^N R$ on succinate concentration is very similar to the ligand binding curve for ATCase (Changeux et al., 1968). Moreover, they both resemble the sigmoidal response of enzyme activity to substrate concentration (Fig. 5). In a similar vein, the hyperbolic titration curve for the absorbance of C^N as a function of succinate concentration is directly analogous to the ligand saturation curve for the catalytic subunit and to the dependence of enzyme activity on substrate concentration (Fig. 5).

Upon their incoporation into ATCase-like molecules the nitrated catalytic subunits exhibit a decreased response of their chromophores to low concentrations of succinate. Increasing the ligand concentration leads to parallel effects on enzymatic activity, saturation of binding sites, and local conformational changes. These results suggest that the conformational changes within the catalytic subunits in intact ATCase molecules are sequential and that the binding of each succinate molecule makes a separate and equivalent contribution to the conformational change of each catalytic chain. However, as seen in Fig. 22, the sedimentation coefficient of $C^N R$ changed at a much lower concentration of succinate than was required to produce an equivalent percentage change in the spectrum of the nitrotyrosyl chromophores. At a succinate concentration corresponding to a 50% change in $\Delta s/\bar{s}$, there was only 7% of the maximal change in absorbance at 430 nm (Kirschner and Schachman, 1973b). There was also a marked difference in the shapes of the curves describing the change in the physical properties of $C^N R$ as a function of succinate concentration. It thus appears from these studies on the nitrated derivative of ATCase that binding of ligands is accompanied by sequential, local changes in the conformation of the catalytic chains which are weakly linked with a concerted, gross change in the

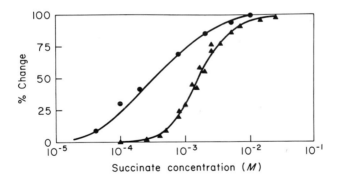

FIG. 22. Effect of succinate on the sedimentation coefficient and spectrum of nitrated aspartate transcarbamylase (ATCase). Difference sedimentation data are represented by ● and changes in absorbance at 430 nm are represented by ▲. In each experiment the concentration of carbamyl phosphate was 2 mM in one sector plus a given concentration of succinate; the other sector contained 2 mM phosphate and a corresponding concentration of glutarate. The data are plotted as percent maximal change on the ordinate vs succinate concentration on the abscissa. From Kirschner and Schachman (1973b).

quaternary structure of the intact molecules. This gross change in conformation, corresponding to a swelling (or loosening) of the structure, may involve alterations in the packing or orientation of the catalytic subunits relative to each other and the regulatory subunits as in the model proposed by Gerhart (1970). As indicated above in the discussion of Fig. 20, the gross conformational change in ATCase is not merely the sum of the changes in the constituent catalytic subunits. In contrast, the local conformational changes revealed by the spectral measurements are additive and seem to be related to the saturation of the binding sites (Kirschner and Schachman, 1973b).

This proposed weak linkage of two different levels (local and gross) of conformational change in an oligomeric protein is very similar to that described recently for hemoglobin (Perutz, 1970, 1972). Our interpretation of the available evidence for ATCase embraces the principal elements of the models of Monod *et al.* (1965) and of Koshland *et al.* (1966). There seem to be both a concerted conformational change in the gross structure which occurs when only a fraction of the binding sites are occupied and local conformational changes which are sequential and intimately linked to the binding of ligands. The major change in the affinity for ligands apparently stems from the transition between the taut, compact form of the enzyme to the relaxed, swollen conformation.

IX. CONCLUDING REMARKS

I hope that this summary has conveyed our excitement about ATCase and has illustrated our efforts to obtain some understanding of its structure and dynamics. Developments from other laboratories engaged in research on this enzyme are discussed in an excellent review by Jacobson and Stark (1973). We have come a long way since the original, bold proposal of Gerhart and Pardee (1962) that ATCase possessed an exclusive regulatory site for the inhibitor, CTP, and was designed in a special way in order to achieve feedback inhibition. Many of the questions posed in the introduction have been answered in the decade following their pioneering kinetic studies of the behavior of this regulatory enzyme. Nonetheless our knowledge of the anatomy of ATCase in the form of two catalytic trimers and three regulatory dimers must be considered still as rather crude. Thus we await with optimism the results of further X-ray diffraction studies which should provide much-needed information about the folding of the polypeptide chains, the location of the six metal ions, and the nature of the crucial bonding domains. Similarly we anticipate eagerly additional studies on the conformational changes whereby the enzyme mediates both the homotropic and heterotropic effects.

As yet we have no direct evidence that the binding of ligands to one catalytic subunit can promote local conformational changes in the other. Presumably this occurs through linkage between the gross and local conformational changes, but thus far there is no conclusive experimental proof demonstrating the interdependence of local conformational changes in the two catalytic subunits. It should be possible to obtain such evidence from studies on ATCase-like molecules containing a chromophore which is sensitive to ligand-promoted conformational changes. The appropriate molecule would contain one native catalytic subunit and a second, inactive subunit which, by suitable chemical modification, is rendered incapable of binding ligands but has incorporated covalently the needed spectral probe. With such a molecule it should be possible to determine whether the absorption spectrum of the chromophore is altered as a consequence of binding ligands to the active catalytic subunit. Preliminary studies on hybrids of this general type (Pigiet, 1971; Schachman, 1972) showed that cooperativity could be achieved even when one catalytic subunit in the ATCase-like molecule was inactive. However, more extensive investigations have cast doubt on this observation since the hybrids were found to be contaminated with other types of molecular species including undefined aggregates. In these experiments the isolated catalytic subunits were succinylated directly (as illustrated schematically in Fig. 6) and it is possible that the treatment led to alteration of sensitive groups near the bonding domains between the catalytic and regulatory chains. Hence the entire procedure must be changed so as to protect these groups during the chemical treatment. This can be accomplished by subjecting the intact ATCase molecule to the chemical modification followed by isolation of the derivatized catalytic subunits. In addition, other types of chemical modification must be explored since the large increase in the negative charge of the protein due to the introduction of succinyl groups may prevent the allosteric transition required for cooperativity. Such chemical reactions must not only lead specifically to inactivation of the catalytic subunit but also they must introduce sufficient charges to permit resolution of the hybrid set after reconstitution of ATCase-like molecules. Perhaps a combination of reactions will prove necessary. In particular, the use of anhydrides other than succinic anhydride seems promising since some of them can be used for reversible modification of amino groups. Such experiments are now being initiated by Gibbons and Yang in our laboratory using the inactive catalytic subunit produced by its reaction with pyridoxal 5'-phosphate followed by reduction with sodium borohydride (Greenwell et al., 1973).

Analogous studies with hybrid molecules containing native and chemically modified (and presumably nonfunctional) regulatory subunits have proved rewarding. These hybrids exhibit both homotropic and heterotropic effects. Such molecules appear similar in their behavior to the "incomplete" ATCase-like molecules lacking a regulatory subunit. On the basis of these experiments we are tempted to propose that a cooperative unit requires a combination of at least four functionally active catalytic and regulatory polypeptide chains bonded to each other from one catalytic subunit to that beneath it. The means to test this hypothesis are at hand since ATCase-like molecules containing three active catalytic chains in one subunit and three inactive chains in the other can be constructed by suitable hybridization techniques. Soon we should know the properties of such species; until this type of information is available speculations about the minimal structural features required for cooperativity are bound to be hazardous.

It is obvious that during the next decade we will witness research aimed at answering a host of new questions about ATCase. Can half molecules be produced? Will such molecules exhibit inhibition when CTP is added? Can homotropic and heterotropic effects be separated in an ATCase-like molecule or are they inextricably linked? What role does the metal play? Can we have stable ATCase molecules lacking metal ions? How is ATCase assembled? What type of intermediates can be detected? How stable are they? What are their properties? What are the structural features in mutants which are responsible for the differences in their regulatory behavior? Answering these and related questions will not only prove a challenge to the research worker but will also be rewarding in enhancing our understanding of the mechanisms of the regulation of enzyme activity.

ACKNOWLEDGMENTS

This work was supported by Public Health Service Research Grant GM 12159 from the National Institute of General Medical Sciences, and National Science Foundation Research Grant GB 4810X.

REFERENCES

Adair, G. S. (1925). *J. Biol. Chem.* **63**, 493.

Bethell, M. R., Smith, K. E., White, J. S., and Jones, M. E. (1968). *Proc. Nat. Acad. Sci. U.S.* **60**, 1442.

Bohr, C., Hasselbalch, K. A., and Krogh, A. (1904). *Skand. Arch. Physiol.* **16**, 401.

Buckman, T. (1970). *Biochemistry* **9**, 3255.

Changeux, J.-P., and Gerhart, J. C. (1968). *In* "The Regulation of Enzyme Activity and Allosteric Interactions" (E. Kvamme and A. Pihl, eds.), Vol. 1, p. 13 (Fed. Eur. Biochem. Soc., 4th Meeting). Academic Press, New York.

Changeux, J.-P., Gerhart, J. C., and Schachman, H. K. (1967). *In* "Regulatory Mechanisms in Nucleic Acid and Protein Biosynthesis" (V. V. Koningsberger and L. Bosch, eds.), *Biochim. Biophys. Acta Libr.* **10**, 344.

Changeux, J.-P., Gerhart, J. C., and Schachman, H. K. (1968). *Biochemistry* **7**, 531.

Christiansen, J., Douglas, C. G., and Haldane, J. S. (1914). *J. Physiol. (London)* **48**, 244.

Cohlberg, J. A. (1972). Ph.D. Thesis, University of California, Berkeley.

Cohlberg, J. A., Pigiet, V. P., Jr., and Schachman, H. K. (1972). *Biochemistry* **11**, 3396.

Collins, K. D., and Stark, G. R. (1969). *J. Biol. Chem.* **244**, 1869.

Davies, G. E., and Stark, G. R. (1970). *Proc. Nat. Acad. Sci. U.S.* **66**, 651.

Davies, G. E., and Stark, G. R. (1972). Private communication.

Douglas, C. G., Haldane, J. S., and Haldane, J. B. S. (1912). *J. Physiol. (London)* **44**, 275.

Eckfeldt, J., Hammes, G. G., Mohr, S. C., nad Wu, C.-W. (1970). *Biochemistry* **9**, 3353.

Ebans, D. R., Warren, S. G., Edwards, B. F. P., McMurray, C. H., Bethge, P. H., Wiley, D. C., and Lipscomb, W. N. (1973). *Science* **179**, 683.

Gerhart, J. C. (1970). *Curr. Top. Cell. Regul.* **2**, 275.

Gerhart, J. C., and Pardee, A. B. (1962). *J. Biol. Chem.* **237**, 891.

Gerhart, J. C., and Pardee, A. B. (1964). *Fed. Proc., Fed. Amer. Soc. Exp. Biol.* **23**, 727.

Gerhart, J. C., and Schachman, H. K. (1965). *Biochemistry* **4**, 1054.

Gerhart, J. C., and Schachman, H. K. (1968). *Biochemistry* **7**, 538.

Gilbert, G. A. (1955). *Discuss. Faraday Soc.* **20**, 68.

Green, N. M. (1968). *Nature (London)* **219**, 413.

Greenwell, P., Jewett, S. L., and Stark, G. R. (1973). J. Biol. Chem. **248**, 5994.

Griffin, J. H., Rosenbusch, J. P., Weber, K. K., and Blout, E. R. (1972). *J. Biol. Chem.* **247**, 6482.

Hammes, G. G., and Wu, C.-W. (1971a). *Biochemistry* **10**, 1051.

Hammes, G. G., and Wu, C.-W. (1971b). *Biochemistry* **10**, 2150.

Hammes, G. G., and Wu, C.-W. (1971c). *Science* **172**, 1205.

Harrison, L. W., and Hammes, G. G. (1973). *Biochemistry* **12**, 1395.

Hervé, G. L., and Stark, G. R. (1967). *Biochemistry* **6**, 3743.

Hill, A. V. (1913). *Biochem. J.* **7**, 471.

Jacobson, G. R., and Stark, G. R. (1973). *In* "The Enzymes" (P. Boyer, ed), Vol. 9, p. 225. Academic Press, New York.

Jacobson, G. R., and Stark, G. R. (1973a). *J. Biol. Chem.* **248**, 8003.

Kaplan, N. O. (1964). *Brookhaven Symp. Biol.* **17**, 131.

Kirschner, M. W. (1971). Ph.D. Thesis, University of California, Berkeley.

Kirschner, M. W., and Schachman, H. K. (1971a). *Biochemistry* **10**, 1900.

Kirschner, M. W., and Schachman, H. K. (1971b). *Biochemistry* **10**, 1919.

Kirschner, M. W., and Schachman, H. K. (1973a). *Biochemistry* **12**, 2987.

Kirschner, M. W., and Schachman, H. K. (1973b). *Biochemistry* **12**, 2997.

Koshland, D. E., Jr., Nemethy, G., and Filmer, D. (1966). *Biochemistry* **5**, 365.

McClintock, D. K., and Markus, G. (1968). *J. Biol. Chem.* **243**, 2855.

McClintock, D. K., and Markus, G. (1969). *J. Biol. Chem.* **244**, 36.

Markert, C. L., and Apella, E. (1961). *Ann. N.Y. Acad. Sci.* **94**, 678.

Markert, C. L., and Møller, F. (1959). *Proc. Nat. Acad. Sci. U.S.* **45**, 753.

Markus, G., McClintock, D. K., and Bussel, J. B. (1971). *J. Biol. Chem.* **246**, 762.

Meighen, E. A., and Schachman, H. K. (1970). *Biochemistry* **9**, 1163.

Meighen, E. A., Pigiet, V., and Schachman, H. K. (1970). *Proc. Nat. Acad. Sci. U.S.* **65**, 234.

Monod, J., Wyman, J., and Changeux, J.-P. (1965). *J. Mol. Biol.* **12**, 88.

Nagel, G. M., and Schachman, H. K. In preparation.

Nagel, G. M., Schachman, H. K., and Gerhart, J. C. (1972). *Fed. Proc.,* *Fed. Amer. Soc. Exp. Biol.* **31**, 423 Abs.

Nelbach, M. E., Pigiet, V. P., Jr., Gerhart, J. C., and Schachman, H. K. (1972). *Biochemistry* **11**, 315.

Penhoet, E., Rajkumar, T., and Rutter, W. J. (1966). *Proc. Nat. Acad. Sci. U.S.* **56**, 1275.

Penhoet, E., Kochman, M., Valentine, R., and Rutter, W. J. (1967). *Biochemistry* **6**, 2940.

Perutz, M. F. (1970). *Nature (London)* **228**, 726.

Perutz, M. F. (1972). *Nature (London)* **237**, 495.

Pigiet, V. P., Jr. (1971). Ph.D. Thesis, University of California, Berkeley.

Richards, K. E., and Williams, R. C. (1972). *Biochemistry* **11**, 3393.

Rosenbusch, J. P., and Weber, K. (1972a). *J. Biol. Chem.* **246**, 1644.

Rosenbusch, J. P., and Weber, K. (1971b). *Proc. Nat. Acad. Sci. U.S.* **68**, 1019.

Roughton, F. J. W., Otis, A. B., and Lyster, R. L. J. (1955). *Proc. Roy. Soc. Ser. B* **144**, 29.

Schachman, H. K. (1972). In "Protein-Protein Interactions" (R. Jaenicke and E. Helmreich, eds.), p. 17. Springer-Verlag, Berlin.

Steitz, T. A., Wiley, D. C., and Lipscomb, W. N. (1967). *Proc. Nat. Acad. Sci. U.S.* **58**, 1859.

Umbarger, H. E. (1961). *Cold Spring Harbor Symp. Quant. Biol.* **26**, 301.

Warren, S. G., Edwards, B. F. P., Evans, D. R., Wiley, D. C., and Lipscomb, W. N. (1973). *Proc. Nat. Acad. Sci. U.S.* **70**, 1117.

Weber, K. (1968a). *J. Biol. Chem.* **243**, 543.

Weber, K. (1968b). *Nature (London)* **218**, 1116.

Wiley, D. C., and Lipscomb, W. N. (1968). *Nature (London)* **218**, 1119.

Wiley, D. C., Evans, D. R., Warren, S. G., McMurray, C. H., Edwards, B. F. P., Franks, W. A., and Lipscomb, W. N. (1971). *Cold Spring Harbor. Symp. Quant. Biol.* **36**, 285.

Wu, C.-W., and Hammes, G. G. (1973). *Biochemistry* **12**, 1400.

Yang, Y., Syvanen, J. M., Nagel, G. M., and Schachman, H. K. (1974). *Proc. Nat. Acad. Sci. U.S.* **71**, 918.

LEVODOPA, MANGANESE, AND
DEGENERATIONS OF THE BRAIN* †

GEORGE C. COTZIAS

*The Medical Research Center, Brookhaven National Laboratory,
a Clinical Campus, University of the State of New York at
Stony Brook, Upton, New York*

I. INTRODUCTION

SOME gifts of science to humanity, like quinine, digitalis, and penicillin, are admittedly consequences of collisions between a biological accident and an alert observer. Other great drugs, like the steroids and the insulins, are, however, consequences of making, testing, rephrasing, and retesting scientific hypotheses. The first process appears to be inhibited by direct promotion. The second is eminently responsive to changing social and scientific needs; it can proceed with equal validity on the wards and in the laboratory; its excitement and pace are heightened if it proceeds in both; and it spawns rather than inhibits happy accidents.

These points illustrate perhaps the method, the outlook, and the spirit of the work to be presented in tonight's personal, discursive account. The historical part of the account ends with the acceptance of levodopa as an official treatment for two hitherto unmanageable types of brain degeneration. Levodopa brought the challenges with which we deal under "Present Developments" (Section IV) and which include the following. Treating idiopathic psychoses could induce pharmacological parkinsonism, which eventually was used as a biochemical model in the evolution of treatment for idiopathic Parkinson's disease. Treating idiopathic parkinsonism with levodopa has induced pharmacological

* Lecture delivered December 14, 1972.

† This work was supported by the U.S. Atomic Energy Commission and the National Institutes of Health (Grant No. NS 09492-03), No. OH 00313-08 coordinated by Pan American Health Organization, Project AMRO-4618, the Charles E. Merrill Trust, and Mrs. Katherine Rodgers Denckla.

psychoses, studies of which may have similar consequences for treatment of idiopathic psychoses. This account therefore concludes with preliminary experiments on some psychoses.

It is an omen of good luck that this talk is given at the Rockefeller University, since it was here that our story began with Vincent Dole as my mentor, and this I gratefully acknowledge. It is an honor to present it as a Harvey Lecture, since, to paraphrase a quotation attributed to Sir Francis Bacon, the Harvey Society "rings the bell that calls the wits together."

II. BACKGROUND

A. Manganese versus Catecholamines

Before our investigation of treatments of parkinsonism or chronic manganese poisoning, we had guessed that essential connections must exist between the metabolism of manganese and that of biogenic amines. This guess was based on the following: (a) Catecholamines were metal binding agents. (b) They became deaminated after entering the mitochondria (9, 10, 44) in which manganese accumulated also (34). (c) Polymelanosomes (43), which outnumbered mitochondria in some melanocytes (45) deaminated catecholamines while accumulating manganese. (d) The pathway of manganese through the organs of the body was specific for that metal (12). (e) The transport of manganese and that of some catecholamines were linked *in vivo* by cyclic AMP (42). (4) The syndromes of manganese deficiency in animals and of chronic manganese poisoning in man seemed compatible with defects of cerebral catecholamine metabolism (11). (g) Chronic manganese poisoning (manganism) displayed clinical similarities to parkinsonism, while pharmacological parkinsonism (induced by reserpine or phenothiazine drugs) has been linked by others to defective cerebral metabolism of catecholamines (see ref. 19). These points argued in favor of studying in parallel parkinsonism and manganism as well as catecholamines and manganese. Before starting clinical studies, however, we developed both some methodology and some physiological insight.

B. Neutron Activation Analysis and Manganese Radioisotopes

On the technical level Dr. Paul S. Papavasiliou and I found that manganese, a scarce trace metal, can be determined accurately in small tissue samples without either loss or exogenous contamination by first rendering the metal radioactive *in situ* (15, 39) and then measuring the radioactivity (^{56}Mn) and comparing it with that of similarly treated standards. Initially the measurement involved a separation of the radionuclide ^{56}Mn, causing destruction of the tissue. With a later nondestructive method, brain tissue is kept frozen while being bombarded in the reactor and while some trace metals are measured; it is later destroyed in the course of catecholamine analyses. Since the required samples are small, one might persuade neurosurgeons that they could be obtained with impunity at operation.

On the physiological level, radioisotopes were applied to the study of some dynamic and homeostatic mechanisms in the metabolism of manganese (3, 4, 8, 16, 20, 32, 33, 41); its incorporation in heme (5) and in melanins (21); into some other biological complexes (30); and in short-lived complexes with phenothiazine drugs which yielded semiquinone free radicals by interacting with the trivalent metal (16).

C. Initial Clinical Findings

At this juncture, Dr. Ismael Mena and I proposed to the National Institutes of Health and the World Health Organization that we might treat Chilean victims of manganism by removing the excess metal, since both the removal of manganese and the postulated clinical improvement were now amenable to measurement. We studied appropriate groups of Chilean subjects consisting of pensioned miners with chronic manganese poisoning, of healthy, working manganese miners, and of nonexposed Chilean controls (13, 36, 38). Two different methods showed the existence of a group with excessive tissue manganese, but this group represented the vigorous, healthy miners. The pensioned-off victims of manganism, whom we were proposing to treat, had cleared these excesses via homeostatic mechanisms which we had described, without clearing their neurological disease.

We observed, thereafter that the neurological deficit of these patients showed short-lived spontaneous improvement in an episodic manner, which suggested substitution of another myth for the one which had led us astray. The new myth was that manganese poisoning had injured some nerve cells (later identified by others as nigral) regulating nerve centers (striatal) which must have remained intact in view of the subtle remissions. A method for potentiating these remissions in manganism was initially precluded by the absence of studies of brains from its victims. This was in contrast with parkinsonism, which also shows episodic remissions, but in which brains had been studied to some extent (22).

D. Correlations with Work by Others

Studies of brains from patients with parkinsonism had shown low melanin concentrations in the substantia nigra, often associated with death of the nigral cells (see ref. 19). Reserpine had been found to induce parkinsonism in psyhotic patients and to deplete animal brains of serotonin while rendering the animals immobile.

Carlsson discovered dopamine (3,4-dihydroxyphenylethylamine) in mouse brains and found that it too was diminished by reserpine. Since he could not replenish brain dopamine in reserpinized mice by administering dopamine, he assumed that dopamine fails to cross the blood–brain barrier (see below), and he therefore administered its precursor amino acid, dopa (3,4-dihydroxyphenylalanine). Dopa increased cerebral dopamine and reversed the immobility of these animals whereas serotonin precursors did not (see Ref. 19).

In their now classical experiments Ehringer and Hornykiewicz (see ref. 19) reported low concentrations of dopamine and of serotonin in the corpus striatum of patients with idiopathic parkinsonism. Several subsequent investigators injected dopa into parkinsonian patients and some gave it orally, but these clinical efforts led to disillusionment with dopa as a drug. In a recent review (19) we have not stated that we were essentially ignorant of these developments at the outset, and did not not know that levodopa had been abandoned by the profession as a drug.

III. PAST HISTORY

A. DL-*Dopa*

We hypothesized initially that we might remelanize the substantia nigra with the melanophore-stimulating hormone β-MSH, thus ameliorating the symptoms of parkinsonism (26). The hormone, however, darkened the skin and aggravated the symptoms; this led to the alternate hypothesis that under the influence of the hormone, the skin, a large organ, might be sequestering melanin precursors away from the brain and thus causing the aggravation. We therefore had to test the effects of such precursors, particularly since they can be precursors also of catecholamines. The first precursor we administered was phenylalanine; this either was ineffective or aggravated the symptoms. We opined arbitrarily that phenylalanine was not becoming sufficiently hydroxylated in the brains of these patients. We skipped the singly hydroxylated tyrosine and studied instead 3,4-dihydroxyphenylalanine, i.e., dopa (26). This was a serendipitous compromise, because on later trials neither L-*o*-tyrosine nor L-*m*-tyrosine improved the symptoms of parkinsonism, although the latter was pushed to the limits of toxicity.

The only preparation of dopa available to us in sufficient quantities was the racemic DL form. We knew that it had to be given orally, but not in what doses or how many times a day. Its beneficial effects, if any, had to result from its enzymatic conversion into metabolites, among which only melanin and dopamine were known to us. It appeared that beneficial effects would be induced by saturating these and other enzymatic pathways, but without causing toxicity to the patients. A "controlled" double-blind study could therefore be neither safe nor conclusive, since it would preclude our being alert for signs of toxicity. Instead, we kept increasing the doses of levodopa slowly and waited for improvement or toxicity to emerge.

The main message from the trials with DL-dopa was that the

nausea, the vomiting, the fainting, the cardiac arrhythmia, the renal effects, and hypertension induced in animals by acute administration of DL-dopa or of dopamine could be easily circumvented by our slow administration of DL-dopa (26). This permitted us to treat the brain, which had remained reactive indeed. The maximal doses of DL-dopa necessary for symptomatic control were literally enormous: 16 g/day. This clearly meant that tachyphylaxis (tolerance) had been induced against dopamine in receptors located within peripheral tissues but not in the central receptors to which we were addressing the treatment. Thus a seminal concept for our work emerged, which we used thereafter with several kinds of neuroactive drugs: Timing is of the essence.

DL-Dopa improved all cardinal symptoms of parkinsonism among responding patients, albeit not to the same extent in each. Since minor involuntary movements had constituted its only cerebral side effect, DL-dopa looked like a good option for treatment until the following complications emerged. Four of the 16 treated patients developed a drug-dependent, reversible depression of their circulating granulocytes accompanied by severe vacuolization of the corresponding bone marrow cells. This complication argued for the study of L-dopa (levodopa) which could probably be used in doses about one-half those of the racemic DL compound, since the D compound had been inactive in our experimental animals.

B.   Levodopa in Parkinsonism

Levodopa at that time was extremely expensive and scarce, but the U.S. Atomic Energy Commission was willing to defray the cost for the Nutritional Biochemicals Corporation to provide it. The initial studies (18) showed that, if the patients were treated slowly and meticulously, only a small number would fail to derive benefit; indeed it is doubtful that all nonresponders have parkinsonism.

The neurological symptoms of parkinsonism were improved by levodopa in roughly the following sequence: first akinesia (slowness), then rigidity, and finally tremor—last and sometimes least (Fig. 1). This sequence became one of the several reasons

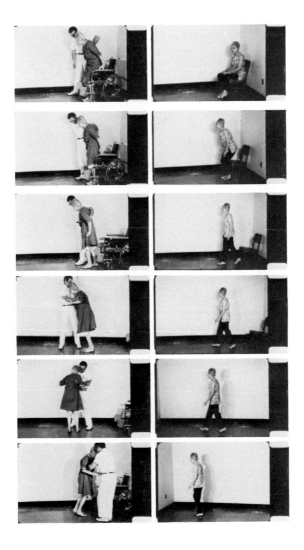

FIG. 1.   A patient with parkinsonism before (left) and during (right) treatment with levodopa (clippings from moving pictures of an excellent therapeutic response).

for our interest in apomorphine, which improves the neurological symptoms in roughly the reverse order, as discussed later.

Correction of the neurological deficit by levodopa was often accompanied by striking mental improvement early in the treatment. Late during therapy, however, some patients have shown adverse but reversible mental reactions of great interest to us. These psychoses consisted of hallucinations, delusions, agitation, and paranoia. When the idiopathic forms of these psychoses had been treated with reserpine or some other major tranquilizers, there had emerged pharmacological parkinsonism, a chemical model for idiopathic parkinsonism. We seem therefore to have closed a cycle: treating idiopathic psychoses has induced pharmacological parkinsonism whereas treating idiopathic parkinsonism had induced pharmacological psychoses. Since pharmacological parkinsonism had led to treatment of parkinsonism we considered that treating pharmacological psychoses might lead to treatment of psychoses, as discussed at the end of this talk.

Hypotension has occurred in few patients. It is puzzling that it should disappear with passing time although it is primarily central in origin: other cerebral effects of levodopa have either remained steady or have increased with time. Involuntary movements of the lips, the face, or the tongue are relatively common side effects of levodopa whereas movements involving the head, the extremities, or the trunk are less frequent. These adventitous movements occur at the peak of the symptomatic control of parkinsonism and remain drug dependent, intermittent, and of variable severity; they disappear after the drug is stopped. They are baffling because they emerge usually after long therapy; because they are readily induced in normal animals; and because they can be controlled in the extremities of some patients by injected apomorphine, namely another dopaminergic drug. This is discussed later along with management of the last limitation of levodopa, which is the episodic, intermittent, often diurnal loss of symptomatic control occurring late in treatment. Many other side effects attributed to levodopa are difficult to separate from consequences of aging and must be dealt with in standard ways.

On the credit side, the levodopa regimen is more effective for treating parkinsonism than any previous one. This drug differs from earlier ones by the virtual absence of the "falloff" phenomenon, that is, the progressive decline of therapeutic effects. Since levodopa can maintain therapeutic effects for a very much longer time than was possible earlier, this drug has extended significantly both the self-sufficiency and the life expectancy of many parkinsonian patients. It is a great drug because it has induced neither permanent damage nor death, by contrast to penicillin, steroids, etc. Even under rather limited supervision, others have found that about 60% of the patients experience at least a 50% improvement in their disability. We are uncertain whether or not this prolongation of life and improvement of function expresses a slowdown in the rate of degeneration of the afflicted cerebral neurons.

C. Levodopa in Chronic Manganese Poisoning

In chronic manganese poisoning, worsening of the symptoms occurs only early during the neurological phase of the disease. This neurological phase is almost always preceded by a psychiatric phase (38) characterized by delusions, hallucinations, and psychomotor excitement, but with full insight into the nature of the disease. Interestingly, the psychiatric phase of chronic manganese poisoning (which lasts for about a month) is recognized in the Chilean mining districts as "locura manganica," namely, manganese madness (38). It is challenging to us that mental aberrations have been restricted to the "locura manganica," being notably absent during the several years of treating the neurological phase of manganism with levodopa (35). In further contrast to parkinsonism, involuntary movements have also been absent in manganism treated with levodopa. The only limitation shared in the treatment of the two diseases remains the episodic, intermittent loss of symptomatic control, which has occurred among members of both groups. As shown below, this intermittent loss of function is due primarily to metabolic vagaries within peripheral tissues, intercepting levodopa on its way to the brain. It appears therefore that these diseases have similar peripheral metabolism of levodopa whereas their respective cerebral metabolism differs (Fig. 2).

A striking similarity between parkinsonism and manganism

FIG. 2. Dystonic victim of chronic manganism. He represents 10% of the population, the others being Parkinson's-like. Dystonic victim of manganism before (on left) and during (on right) L-dopa therapy. For both pictures, the patient was asked to lift arms and extend fingers. Note reversal of muscular hypertrophy. (Copyright, *Journal of the American Medical Association*.)

is the great individual variation among patients in both the symptoms and their control. Whether this divergence indicates a spectrum of genetic substrata (with different susceptibilities to both disease and drug) is a cardinal question indeed. This question caused us to study the mouse mutant *pallid,* in which cerebral reactivity to levodopa can be judged by studying the absorption and elimination of radiomanganese (^{54}Mn), as will be seen below.

Levodopa is now an official drug and therefore, as a drug, past history for us. To date, however, we have largely failed to communicate the two fundamental considerations for treating patients with levodopa: (a) One must start with small multiple doses, given from small capsules and increase them gradually thereafter, until the patient's requirements are met. Otherwise one is merely conducting an experiment in the survival of the fittest which is still the practice in several quarters. (b) Levodopa, being a large neutral amino acid, has features both of a nutrient and of a drug (19). The fraction that enters the brain depends upon factors affecting the catabolism, the transport, and the competition among amino acids on their way to the brain. Therefore periodic readjustments of the dose of levodopa and of its scheduling are required. These readjustments are often in the direction of diminishing the dose and increasing the frequency of administration. To facilitate the practical use of levodopa we have engaged in studies of the peripheral inhibitor of L-amino acid decarboxylases discussed below, which is not an official drug as yet.

IV. PRESENT DEVELOPMENTS

A. *Inhibition of Peripheral Catabolism of Levodopa*

Hypotheses formulated on the wards were tested either there or in the laboratory. The two processes were firmly integrated, and we must therefore intersperse clinical and laboratory experiments.

Some of our patients reported that their temporary losses of the therapeutic effects of levodopa occurred after a single high-protein meal. This negative effect occurred in coincidence with the meal, 3–7 hours after it, or both. Since, as will be seen, we could reverse these episodes with apomorphine injections, we assumed that the brain was failing to receive levodopa during these episodes rather than failing to react with it. This could be due to (a) excessive catabolism of levodopa within peripheral tissues, or (b) competition of alimentary amino acids with levodopa for absorption (which would occur in coincidence with the meals) or for entrance into the brain (which would occur during the height of the postprandial amino acidemia, 3–7 hours later). These two alternatives were studied separately as follows.

Our first attempt was directed at blocking the peripheral catabolism of levodopa, without interfering with its cerebral metabolism. Decarboxylation of levodopa into dopamine is one of its two major catabolic pathways, the other being catechol O-methylation, alluded to later. We blocked the peripheral decarboxylations of aromatic amino acids including levodopa by coadministering (with levodopa) L-α-methyldopa hydrazine (MK-486, Merck Sharp & Dohme) (40). This L-aromatic amino acid decarboxylase inhibitor has remained exclusively outside the brain regardless of dose, in contrast to another such inhibitor used in Europe (2). Our clinical studies (40) yielded the following results. (a) This inhibitor is remarkably nontoxic, despite being a hydrazine, despite being administered chronically to aging populations, and despite its coadministration with other drugs including levodopa. (b) It has markedly diminished the production of dopamine in peripheral tissues, the ectopic production of which could be noxious when induced quickly. (c) It has almost eliminated the necessity of first inducing tachyphylaxis against dopamine in peripheral tissues before imposing therapeutic effects, thus permitting more rapid induction of treatment. (d) It has diminished or eliminated effects of levodopa on the heart and other peripheral tissues. Since nausea and vomiting were almost eliminated even during rapid treatment, the inhibitor must have acted on the respective chemoreceptors which are located outside the blood-brain barrier. (e) It has permitted the coadministration with levodopa of vitamin B_6 (pyridoxine) in large doses, a salutary development because (i) before the advent of levodopa, massive and prolonged administration of pyridoxine had improved parkinsonism, possibly by activating the cerebral decarboxylases that produce dopamine from endogenous dopa (40); and (ii) without this inhibitor, pyridoxine had been canceling the effects of levodopa, which necessitated marketing of the pyridoxine-free vitamin preparation, Larobec, for the use of patients with parkinsonism (19). (f) It has permitted recognition of the site of origin of several effects of levodopa, by eliminating others. Hypotension, for example, could be potentiated, as could involuntary movements and mental aberrations, which indicated beyond dispute the cerebral origin of hypotension. (g) It has diminished the daily doses of levodopa by 70–80% without, however, diminishing the necessity for adjusting the dose to each patient's differing needs and for frequent administration. (h) It has been eminently compatible with other antiparkinsonian drugs. (i) Its judicious use has allowed stabilization of the diurnal performance of some symptomatically unstable parkinsonian patients, leading to the theoretical considerations and metabolic explorations which follow.

B. Further Metabolic Considerations

Theoretically, the following appeared relevant: (a) This inhibitor can block decarboxylation of many alimentary amino acids, including tyrosine, which yields the short-lived tyramine in large amounts. The inhibitor could perhaps help determine the consequences of inhibiting tyramine production and thus elucidate its physiological role. Tyramine might be functioning like some other aliphatic mono- and diamines, which have regulatory effects on various steps of protein synthesis, including Wurtman's deaggregation of cerebral polyribosomes by dopamine (see ref. 19). (b) Blocking only decarboxylases cannot be the culmination of our efforts to block peripheral catabolism of catecholamine precursors, such as levodopa, because catechol O-methyltransferases constitute another major catabolic pathway, which has remained unaffected by this inhibitor. We proved this by measuring the production of HVA, an O-methylated derivative of 3,4-dihydroxyphenylacetic acid (dopac) in patients by blocking O-methyltransferases exclusively in peripheral tissues and administering dopac (40). One might therefore further potentiate the milligram potencies of levodopa and of other amino acid precursors of biogenic amines by using catechol O-methyltransferase inhibitors. Although this premise is generally conceded, the choice of a blocking agent is a matter of confusion. One should not use a competitive substrate like the several already proposed. Substrates become methylated and thus sequester methyl groups essential to several cellular functions. One needs instead to curtail losses of methyl groups, which are already excessive due to various methylations of levodopa and its metabolites (18). A true inhibitor, furthermore, might be synthesized in such a manner that it does not enter the brain. Dr. James Z. Ginos is therefore attempting to synthesize the compounds shown together with the formula of our present decarboxylase inhibitor in Fig. 3. The aliphatic chain (which should block decarboxylations) and the hydrazine moiety (which should stop these compounds from crossing the blood–brain barrier) will be attached to the seven-carbon tropolone moiety (instead of the six-carbon catechol one), which can inhibit catechol O-methyltransferases (19). Tropolones are well established catechol O-methyltransferase inhibitors (19).

Further application of these notions prerequired a demonstration of whether or not the metabolites that we had diminished by applying the peripheral decarboxylase inhibitor could them-

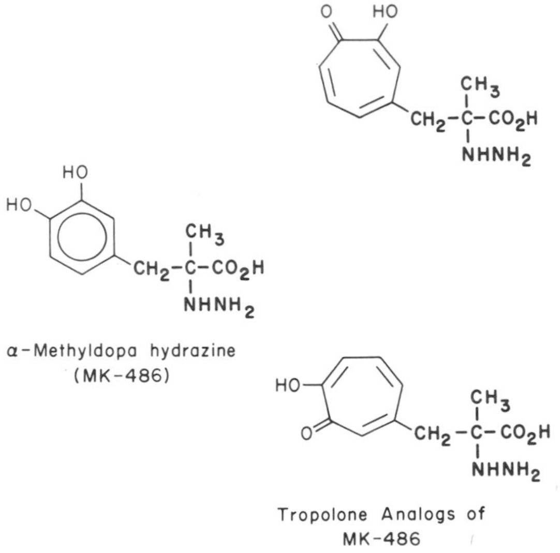

FIG. 3. Structural formulas of L-α-methyl dopa (MK-486) and its proposed tropolone analogs. The former acts only peripherally and only to block decarboxylation of L-aromatic amino acids. The latter should also act only peripherally but should block catechol O-methylation in addition to decarboxylation.

selves affect the cerebral actions of levodopa. Studies were therefore conducted on mice (23) in which levodopa was administered after pretreatment with either water or with various metabolites of levodopa. These experiments showed that nonmethylated metabolites (dopamine and 3,4-dihydroxyphenylacetic acid) blocked the cerebral effects of levodopa whereas methylated analogs did not. Blocking could be induced also with nicotinamide, but not with N-methyl nicotinamide; this finding suggests that methylation of a methyl-acceptor substance can abolish its blocking effects. Blocking of the cerebral actions was accompanied by diminution of the cerebral dopamine generated from levodopa.

Since the inhibitor of L-aromatic amino acid decarboxylases had stabilized the diurnal control of the symptoms in patients receiving levodopa, we thought that changing the dietary intake of L-aromatic amino acids might change the "on-and-off" phenomenon encountered during treatment with levodopa. This phenomenon, however, can be rapid indeed. Dr. Ismael Mena and I therefore needed a rapid but accurate method for quantifying changes in neurological state without conducting a time-consuming neurological examination. In a study to be presented elsewhere we showed that changes in output of work correlate with changing neurological status in parkinsonism. We have developed therefore an automated ergometer that provides a quantitative method of recording and computing diurnal changes in performance that is simple enough to be used by inexpert personnel or by the patient himself (Fig. 4).

C. Protein Intake and Control of Parkinsonism

In a hitherto unpublished study, neurological examinations plus ergometric measurements were performed repetitively on 8 patients with parkinsonism who were participating in a dietary study covering two 5-week periods. During the first period, the patients received only levodopa, in optimal and steady doses given 6 times a day. During the second period, the dopa decarboxylase inhibitor discussed above was coadministered in order to diminish the optimal dose of levodopa to about 20% of that given during the first period. During each period, the number and composition of isocaloric meals were changed 5 times, each regimen lasting for about a week. The protein intake was varied between 10 g per patient per day and 2 g per kilogram per patient per day, and the number of meals between 3 and 8 per day. The amino

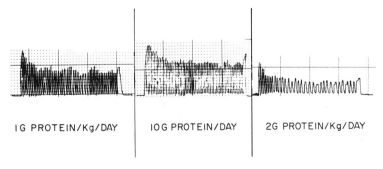

IG PROTEIN/Kg/DAY   IOG PROTEIN/DAY   2G PROTEIN/Kg/DAY

FIG. 4. Tracings obtained by an ergometer while the dietary intake of protein was varied. Levodopa dosage, 3.0 g per day. Note that the output of work depended upon the protein intake. (Reprinted by permission from the *Journal of the American Dietetic Association,* in press, 1973.)

acid and fat composition of the meals was constant, and the diets were kept isocaloric by varying carbohydrate intake.

While the patients received only levodopa, the following findings emerged: (a) The symptoms of the 5 unstable patients were very responsive to changes in protein intake, whereas the symptoms of the three stable ones were not changed as the diet was changed. (b) In the unstable ones, increasing the intake of protein tended to cancel the effects of levodopa and to increase both severity and incidence of the diurnal "on and off" phenomenon. (c) Low-protein diets potentiated both the cerebral effects of levodopa and the diurnal stability of the symptomatic control. (d) More frequent meals induced more stability, and vice versa.

These experiments led us to assume that the "on-and-off" phenomenon was due to competition of alimentary amino acids against levodopa, first for absorption by the intestinal mucosa and then for crossing the blood–brain barrier. If this hypothesis were valid, diminishing the doses of levodopa by using the inhibitor would increase the competition of alimentary amino acids and thus increase the "on-and-off" phenomenon during high protein intakes. Yet, diminution of levodopa by coadministration of our inhibitor eliminated the statistical significance of the diurnal changes in symptomatic control, even with the most adverse of our diets, 2.0 g of protein per kilogram per day given in three daily meals (Fig. 5). This was incompatible with the "competition" hypothesis. It called for a new hypothesis, the formulation of which required some animal experimentation.

D. Growth Hormone

We wondered whether the "on-and-off" phenomenon might not be related somehow to the release of growth hormone by levodopa (7) for the following reason: Our experiments on mice (24) showed that pretreatment with either bovine or porcine growth hormone promoted, prolonged and intensified the cerebral effects not only of levodopa, but also of apomorphine (another dopaminergic drug) as well as of cholinergic agents like oxotremorine, physostigmine, and nicotine. A reverse effect, namely a reduction of cerebral reactivity, was induced by using a series

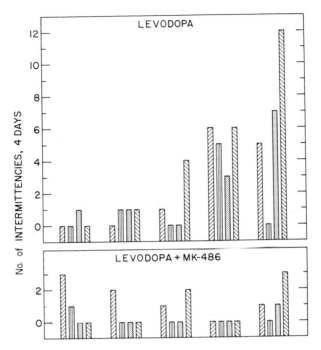

FIG. 5. Episodes of losing more than 50% of the optimal performance were counted over each 4-day period and recorded as "intermittencies." Note that despite the marked diminution of the intake of levodopa by MK-486 the "intermittencies" diminished. Protein: ▨, 1 g/kg per day; ▥, 1 g/kg per day, 8 meals; ▦, 10 g/day; ◨, 2 g/kg per day. Reprinted by permission from the Parkinson's Disease Foundation and Merck Sharp & Dohme.

of inhibitors of protein synthesis, acting by different molecular mechanisms. These diminished the cerebral effects of levodopa, apomorphine, and oxotremorine. The fact that most of these inhibitors of protein synthesis rapidly affected the cerebral responses to such a wide range of neuroactive drugs suggested that proteins having a rapid turnover were critical to the functions of the corresponding receptors.

Prior to applying the results of these animal experiments to man, we thought that we must study the release of growth hormone through the day and the night in untreated patients with parkinsonism and then in some receiving levodopa. In preliminary experiments, Dr. Ismael Mena and I have found only minor circadian output of growth hormone in untreated patients with parkinsonism, by contrast to "normals," in whom large pulses of hormone are released several times a day. The relative inability of these patients to release growth hormone beyond the steady basal levels was readily corrected by levodopa. Diets which have increased the therapeutic effects of levodopa have also increased the diurnal output of circulating growth hormone and vice versa, in preliminary experiments.

E. Injected Apomorphine

None of the above pertained to whether or not dopamine is necessary for the various effects that we have induced with levodopa in parkinsonism or in chronic manganese poisoning. This question could not be answered by administering dopamine to humans in lieu of levodopa. The reason for this is not, as is generally assumed, that dopamine cannot cross the blood–brain barrier. It is that dopamine, a primary amine, is degraded extensively by monoamine oxidase. Given in large doses, it will cause toxicity before some of it can trickle into the brain, as shown below. We therefore sought an analog of dopamine that can be injected into humans and would enter the brain. Others, whom we have quoted elsewhere (19), had shown that apomorphine evokes some of the characteristic responses of levodopa in experimental animals, although it also evokes some responses of its own. When we injected apomorphine into patients with parkinsonism (17) we reversed the symptoms for about an hour (Fig. 6); this reversal suggested that cerebral dopamine production had been instrumental in the therapy with levodopa. We could now determine by injecting apomorphine whether the intermittent episodic loss of symptomatic control exhibited by some patients receiving levodopa meant that their cerebral neurons had become refractory to dopamine or whether some other explanation might be sought. Since we did abort the episodic emergence of "freezing," slowness and tremor by injecting apomorphine (27), we became convinced that the neurons to which the drug was ad-

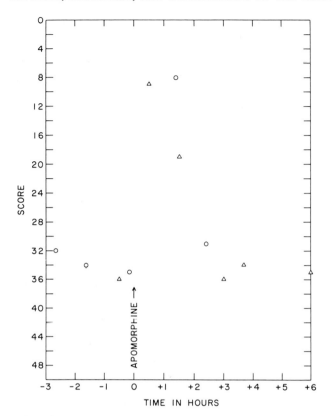

FIG. 6. Effect of injected apomorphine HCl (Δ, 1.0 mg; ◯, 2.0 mg) on the neurological scores of a patient with parkinsonism. A lower score indicated less neurological deficit. From Cotzias *et al.* (17); reprinted by permission of the *New England Journal of Medicine*.

dressed had remained responsive. The story was therefore pat until some curious findings developed (27).

Apomorphine induced less total improvement in patients who had never received levodopa than in those in whom chronic treatment had been discontinued for at least a week, an observation which suggested that chronic treatment with levodopa had tended to increase the responses of some cerebral neurons to dopaminergic drugs. During chronic oral administration of levodopa, furthermore, the adverse reactions to injected apomorphine have been

134 GEORGE C. COTZIAS

TABLE I

CHIEF SIDE EFFECTS OF INJECTED APOMORPHINE[a,b]

Side effect	Off levodopa (17 patients) %	On levodopa (20 patients) %
Sedation (sleepiness and/or yawning)	100.0	90.0
Orthostatic hypotension	85.7	44.4
Supine blood pressure fall (≥ 20 mm Hg)	80.0	26.7
Nausea	70.6	55.0
Vomiting	29.4	10.0
Pallor and/or sweating	52.9	40.0
Bradycardia	52.9	55.0
Weak feeling and/or dizziness	29.4	30.0
Lacrimation and/or salivation	29.4	20.0

[a] From Duby et al. (27). Reprinted by permission of the Archives of Neurology and the copyright owner, the American Medical Association.
[b] These side effects of injected apomorphine were not present when the drug was given orally despite its improving the symptoms of parkinsonism.

less severe and less frequent (Table I). The therapeutic effects of these two drugs were additive whereas several respective side effects tended to cancel each other out (27). Nausea induced by levodopa, for example, was sometimes counteracted by injecting apomorphine. Involuntary movements of the extremities induced by levodopa were reduced in several patients by apomorphine injections (Fig. 7). The sedation of apomorphine was antagonized by levodopa, whereas the awakening effect of levodopa (18) was antagonized by apomorphine. Apomorphine given alone induced hypotension, but when it was injected in patients receiving levodopa, hypotension was mild or absent. Even given alone, apomorphine had some paradoxic effects, namely emesis or antiemesis and increased or decreased salivation. Study of these paradoxes was kept in abeyance until we could test whether oral administration of apomorphine is a promising treatment for parkinsonism. For this we had to test first whether we could induce tachyphylaxis (tolerance) to apomorphine in peripheral tissue while remitting the symptoms of the disease. As with DL and L-dopa, evidence in favor of tachyphylaxis would be the diminu-

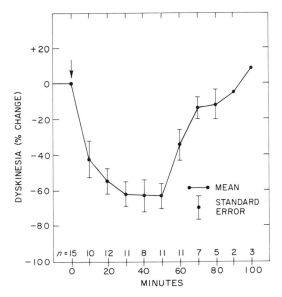

FIG. 7. Percentile changes in the arbitrary scores of dyskinesia (involuntary movements) in 11 patients with parkinsonism under treatment with oral levodopa from subcutaneously injected apomorphine. A lower score indicates less dyskinesia. Note that the duration of this antagonism of an effect of levodopa is approximately the same as the effect on the symptoms of parkinsonism shown on Fig. 5. From Duby *et al.* (27). Reprinted by permission of the *Archives of Neurology* and the copyright owner, the American Medical Association.

tion or absence of the side effects evoked by acute injection of apomorphine (Table I) whereas evidence for control of parkinsonism would be gathered by double-blind scoring of the symptoms (17).

F. Oral Apomorphine

The fourteen patients participating in the oral tests of apomorphine (14) included two who were also receiving levodopa and during the tests required much less levodopa for symptomatic control. Among the others, five showed steady improvement with regard to tremor, rigidity, and akinesia, with a total improvement in their disability scores of at least 50%. Some of the less improved ones had lost their tremor. The lowest doses at which clinical improvement emerged ranged between 160 and 600 mg per day, compared with the maximal 10 mg recommended for the emetic use of parenteral apomorphine in the U.S. Pharmacopeia. Although oral apomorphine was not given during the night, the rate of improvement continued to be progressive, in contrast to its short-lived effects when it was being injected. Maximal doses ranged between 660 and 1440 mg per day in the markedly improved patients. Only one patient showed involuntary movements, and even these were mild. All side effects shown in Table I were totally absent, except for rare, mild, transitory nausea. Not one episode of vomiting occurred with this classical emetic drug. Oral apomorphine, therefore, might have turned out to be a plausible alternative to levodopa for treating parkinsonism and chronic manganese poisoning, if the following unexpected complications had not emerged.

Three of the patients developed marked elevations of blood urea nitrogen and blood creatinine, essentially without changes in urine analyses or serum electrolytes (Fig. 8). The azotemia (14) progressed for 7–10 days, reaching 32–136 mg/100 ml for BUN and 2.3–9.5 mg/100 ml for creatinine, and declined spontaneously thereafter (Fig. 8). Since some minor elevations of BUN and creatinine were found in some of the other patients, this azotemia appeared to be dose-dependent and extrarenal in origin.

The azotemic patients showed clear reemergence of parkinsonism prior to their azotemia starting its spontaneous decline. About a week after discontinuation of apomorphine, one nonazotemic patient showed marked aggravation of his symptoms, beyond the level prevailing prior to treatment. These findings indicated that trials must be conducted with N-propylnorapomorphine which is 50 times as potent as apomorphine, so that one-fiftieth of the dose might suffice and thus azotemia might be avoided.

Despite our interest in these findings, our most notable experience with oral apomorphine was the following. A man and a woman who had developed garrulity, hallucinations, paranoia, and delusions on levodopa failed to show mental aberrations while

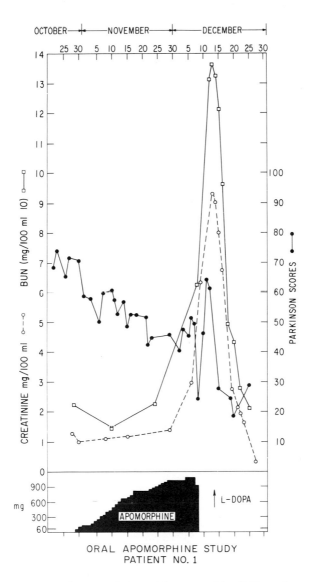

FIG. 8. Effects of orally administered apomorphine HCl on the neurological deficit (scores) and the blood creatinine and blood urea nitrogen (BUN) levels of a patient with parkinsonism.

receiving apomorphine, although their parkinsonism was corrected to an equivalent degree (Fig. 8).

G. *Structural Components of Apomorphine*

In view of these paradoxic effects of apomorphine, we examined its structural formula for the presence of neuroactive moieties. Three such moieties are evident (see Fig. 9): (a) A dopaminelike moiety. Since dopamine is a known neurotransmitter, this moiety might perhaps be responsible for the therapeutic activation of dopaminergic receptors. (b) A phenylethylamine-like moiety. Since phenylethylamine is known to displace neuro-

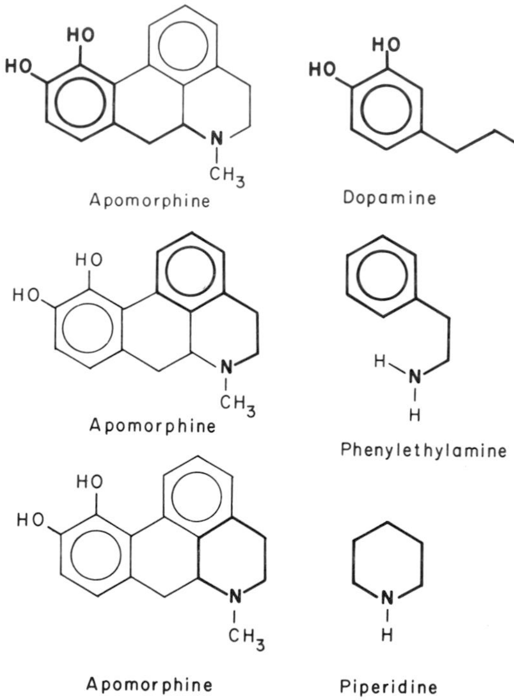

FIG. 9. Neuroactive substances in apomorphine. The structure of the almost planar apomorphine molecule is depicted on the left. Note the similarities between the heavily drawn segments of this molecule and the substances shown on the right.

transmitters from cellular sites (see ref. 27) this moiety might be responsible for the antagonistic effects between levodopa and apomorphine. (c) A piperidine-like moiety. Since piperidine has improved psychotic patients (1), this moiety might account for the absence of mental aberrations in the two patients mentioned above. If apomorphine is indeed acting like a hybrid drug, we should be able to duplicate its behavioral effects on mice with a mixture of drugs which imitates its composition. An equimolar mixture of dopamine, phenylethylamine, and piperidine does imitate the composition of apomorphine, although it provides three moles of nitrogen to the one provided by apomorphine, without providing the N-methyl group (Fig. 9). Furthermore, both the amines included in this mixture are primary and are therefore substrates for monoamine oxidases, whereas apomorphine is a tertiary amine that cannot be attacked by these enzymes. Therefore, if dopamine in particular must enter the brain, we thought one must protect it from deamination by using a monoamine oxidase inhibitor. The equimolar mixture as well as each of its ingredients was given to animals pretreated with the monoamine oxidase inhibitor, nialamide (0.25/mg per gram of mouse) in hitherto unpublished experiments conducted with Mrs. Lily C. Tang. With such a pretreatment, both of the amines induced measurable cerebral effects. The behaviorial effects of dopamine administration imitated closely those of levodopa; and phenylethylamine induced head-shaking and jerky movements; whereas piperidine induced sedation. Administration of their equimolar mixture, however, duplicated the behavioral effects of apomorphine, which showed that the sum of the parts can imitate effects of the whole. The effective doses of apomorphine were much smaller than those of the mixture; the respective responses being similar when 2 μg of apomorphine versus 13 μg of the mixture per gram were injected intraperitoneally.

H. Carbon-11 Dopamine

Our having made possible the cerebral uptake of injected dopamine has opened up the possibility of delivering carbon-11-labeled dopamine to the brain and scanning for the visualization of intracerebral structures. The short-lived ^{11}C, by contrast to all other isotopes of carbon, emits powerful gamma rays and positrons, thus being ideally suitable for external scanning. This isotope has been incorporated into dopamine by Dr. Alfred P. Wolf and his colleagues of the Chemistry Department at Brookhaven. This labeled dopamine, has now been used by Dr. Harold L. Atkins for the visualization of the adrenal medulla in experimental animals. Dopamine-^{11}C might be useful in the study of parkinsonism since in some cases extrapyramidal structures were found at autopsy to be atrophic. These might be now visualized.

I. Tritiated and Modified Apomorphine

In other unpublished experiments, Dr. James Z. Ginos has synthesized and characterized twelve compounds in which neuroactive moieties like those in apomorphine were combined in various permutations. Tests of these agents on mice showed the following: (a) Both an N-methyl group and a catechol (or an equivalent) configuration are necessary for dopaminergic action. (b) The optimal distance between these two groups is the one depicted in apomorphine (Fig. 9).

To investigate the underlying reasons for the short-lived versus the long-lived effects of apomorphine, the following procedures were developed: (a) A spectrofluorimetric method for measuring apomorphine in biological materials, one version of which capitalized on the potentiation of its fluorescence by boric acid. (b) Synthesis of tritiated apomorphine (31) having different labeled sites, starting either with morphine or with apomorphine itself. The compounds, mentioned above as unpublished, have shown absence of significant exchange of the tritium both in vivo and in vitro. Therefore, mice were given tritiated apomorphine orally, reactions to it were scored, and tissues were analyzed periodically for apomorphine by both fluorimetry and scintillation counting. The behavioral scores correlated with the concentration of apomorphine in the brain, which was in apparent equilibrium with storage sites located in the liver and the gut. Other mice, which had been injected intraperitoneally with tritiated apomorphine, were homogenized in perchloric acid together with their excreta, and the total body apomorphine was separated on alumina (to eliminate its metabolites). Measurements by spectrofluorimetry and by scintillation counting had a high coefficient of correlation (0.99). Kinetic analysis of the latter data showed that the drug became catabolized at three distinct half-times, the longest being about an hour and a half. Thus both stored and metabolically long-lived components were found for apomorphine.

J. Genetic Considerations

In the behavioral experiments, the cerebral effects of apomorphine varied among individual mice; this finding suggested that our colony was genetically heterogenous. If genetic factors were determinants of cerebral reactivity to this or other receptor-stimulating drugs, one might find differences in reactivity between some well-defined animal mutant and its control. Such a mutant would be more serviceable to us if it also displayed some abnormality in the metabolism of manganese, in view of the guess we indicated in Section II,A. A well-defined "manganese" mutant is the mouse mutant *pallid*, which differs presumably only by one gene from its control C57 B1/6J (or black). This mutant (*pa/pa*) is called a "manganese mutant" because it has been shown by others (see ref. 25) to produce young with a neurological syndrome that can be prevented for one generation by feeding pallid mothers excess manganese early in pregnancy. We interbred pallids with blacks (25) and obtained homozygote pallids (*Pa/Pa*), heterozygotes (*Pa/pa*), and homozygote blacks (*Pa/Pa*). After injecting radiomanganese ($^{54}Mn^{2+}$) intraperitoneally, we showed that pallids eliminated the metal from their whole bodies at a significantly slower rate than blacks. This slow elimination (as well as the distribution of this radioisotope among the organs of pallid mice) was similar to that encountered earlier in manganese-deficient mice. To rule out the possibility of nutritional manganese deficiency, we conducted some dietary experiments which showed that these differences in eliminating radiomanganese could be abolished only be administering toxic excesses of manganese to both pallids and blacks. Thus it appeared that even adult pallids in which the neurological syndrome had been prevented in the fetal state displayed signs of manganese deficiency in the midst of plenty (20). Furthermore, analyses of tissues for manganese showed significantly smaller concentrations of the natural metal (^{55}Mn) in the bones and brains of pallids than of blacks. Low concentrations might have little biological meaning unless accompanied by well recognized functional changes characteristic of manganese deficiency. The disease perosis, caused by manganese deficiency, induces high fragility, low density, and low nitrogen concentration in the afflicted bones. After we showed that bones from pallid mice displayed these functional changes of perosis, we thought that the low manganese concentration in brain might also have functional meaning. Our preoccupation with catecholamines and manganese led us to administer standardized doses of levodopa to representative animals and study their reactions. The pallids were remarkably resistant to levodopa in comparison to blacks (see Fig. 10). Analyses of whole brains for dopa and dopamine showed that the intrinsic levels were similar in pallids and in blacks, whereas the levels following administration of extrinsic levodopa were lower in pallids. Since tryptophan, the precursor of serotonin, is, like levodopa, a large neutral amino acid, we administered tryptophan to mice and analyzed their brains. Again, the intrinsic levels of serotonin were similar in

FIG. 10. Sequential photographs of a pallid mouse and its control a black (see text) both of which had received levodopa (0.4 mg per gram of mouse) 1 half hour before the picture was taken (2).

pallids and blacks, but those accruing from administered tryptophan were lower in pallids. These experiments led us to believe that the pallid gene imposes a slow transportation of manganese, of levodopa, and of tryptophan. Furthermore, we found later that the reactivity of either individual pallids or individual blacks to levodopa could be predicted, double-blind, from the individual whole body turnover rates of [54]Mn, determined before levodopa administration. It is therefore conceivable that this radionuclide might be developed into a clinical marker for cerebral reactivity to levodopa.

These studies on pallids and blacks had two consequences. (a) We decided to capitalize on the nondestructive feature of neutron activation analysis so that we could determine the concentration in the same small sample of brain first of manganese and then of some catecholamines. In unpublished experiments conducted with Mr. Samuel T. Miller, we showed the feasibility of this combined analysis as well as some correlations between the levels of manganese and those of dopamine in the hypothalamus and the caudate nucleus of cats receiving levodopa. (b) Dr. Ismael Mena and his colleagues (37) discovered that administration of levodopa to pregnant rats resulted in production of young that had hemorrhages in their brown fat (which is the thermogenic organ of their postnatal life) and increased susceptibility to cold and were subject to selective cannibalism by their mothers or foster mothers. Coadministration of manganous chloride with levodopa during pregnancy markedly reduced these levodopa-dependent effects on offspring. Manganous chloride was chosen because of the correlations described above.

K. Pharmacological Psychoses

One issue not directly involved in any of the foregoing experiments is the induction of psychotic states during treatment of parkinsonism with levodopa. It must be emphasized again that (a) treatment of idiopathic psychoses with reserpine (and later with the other major tranquilizers) had induced pharmacological parkinsonism; (b) pharmacological parkinsonism became a biochemical model which has served in devising treatment for idio-

pathic parkinsonism; and (c) The treatment of idiopathic parkinsonism has closed the cycle by inducing pharmacological psychoses. This therapeutic dilemma could reflect disturbance of the
balance between dopaminergic and cholinergic neurons by the respective drugs (19). Therefore, we might address ourselves phar-
macologically to both dopaminergic and cholinergic receptors in
order to achieve willful control of both. The fact that two patients
who were highly prone to develop pharmacological psychoses
from levodopa had not done so under treatment with apomorphine had led us to the considerations of the structure of apomorphine discussed earlier (see Fig. 9). Since piperidine is a weak
cholinergic agent, it was possible that stronger cholinergic agents,
given together with levodopa might modify pharmacological
psychoses without compromising the control of parkinsonism, thus
solving a therapeutic dilemma. These postulations appeared important enough to warrant some experimental effort.

One of the most accessible and best established cholinergic
agents is physostigmine, an acetylcholinesterase inhibitor listed
in the U.S. Pharmacopeia as a drug. Although it is not a direct
stimulator of cholinergic receptors and tends to lose its potency
with passing time, it was chosen for preliminary studies in view
of the following. Duvoisin (29) has shown that physostigmine
can reverse psychoses induced by anticholinergic drugs in parkinsonian patients, whereas it may aggravate parkinsonism in otherwise untreated patients. If physostigmine were administered (together with probanthine, which blocks its peripheral effects) it
might ameliorate levodopa-induced psychoses without necessarily
jeopardizing the control of parkinsonian symptoms. We therefore
injected milligram quantities of physostigmine salicylate into 5
patients while they were exhibiting garrulity, agitation, hallucinations, delusions, and paranoid interpretations of innocuous events
under the influence of levodopa. In these preliminary demonstrations the injections of physostigmine were followed by alleviation
or disappearance first of garrulity and agitation and next of hallucinations and delusions, paranoia being the last to respond and
the one to respond the least.

These preliminary pharmacological demonstrations do not constitute a treatment. If, however, pharmacological parkinsonism

had not been considered as a pharmacological demonstration, the current treatment of idiopathic parkinsonism might have been delayed. Therefore, it behooves us to follow this precedent by studying pharmacological psychoses as possible models for their idiopathic equivalents. In unpublished experiments with mice, we have induced tolerance to oxotremorine (a potent, direct stimulator of muscarinic cholinergic receptors) without causing a loss of cerebral reactivity. These experiments might be useful if we should decide to conduct human experiments with oxotremorine, particularly since physostigmine is acting erratically as of this writing.

V. Conclusion

The results of testing and rephrasing hypotheses about the diseased human brain can be useful, while the process itself is stimulating, exciting, and fun.

Acknowledgments

I have recognized the scientific contributions of my colleagues in the text and the references. Above and beyond such contributions, however, I herewith express deep gratitude to my friend Dr. Paul S. Papavasiliou for his intelligent, perceptive, and loyal support during most phases of this work. I must also thank Mrs. Geraldine Callister, whose efficient performance of wide-ranging secretarial assignments is, in no small way, responsible for the efficient functioning of our group.

REFERENCES

1. Abood, L. C., Ostfeld, A., and Biel, J. H. *Arch. Int. Pharmacodyn.* **120**, 186 (1959).
2. Bartholini, G., Burkard, W. P. and Pletscher, A., *Nature (London)* **215**, 852 (1967).
3. Bertinchamps, A. J., Miller, S. T., and Cotzias, G. C., *Amer. J. Physiol.* **211**, 217 (1966).
4. Borg, D. C., and Cotzias, G. C., *J. Clin. Invest.* **37**, 1269 (1958a).
5. Borg, D. C., and Cotzias, G. C., *Nature (London)* **182**, 1677 (1958b).
6. Borg, D. C., and Cotzias, G. C., *Proc. Nat. Acad. Sci. U.S.* **48**, 617 (1962).
7. Boyd, A. E., III, Lebovitz, H. E., and Pfeiffer, J. B., *N. Engl. J. Med.* **283**, 1425 (1970).
8. Britton, A. A., and Cotzias, G. C., *Amer. J. Physiol.* **211**, 203 (1966).

9. Cotzias, G. C., and Dole, V. P., *J. Biol. Chem.* **190**, 665 (1951a).
10. Cotzias, G. C., and Dole, V. P., *Proc. Soc. Exp. Biol. Med.* **78**, 157 (1951b).
11. Cotzias, G. C., and Foradori, A. C., *In* "The Biological Basis of Medicine" (E. E. and N. Bittar, eds.), Vol. I, p. 105. Academic Press, New York, 1968.
12. Cotzias, G. C., and Greenough, J. J., *J. Clin. Invest.* **37**, 1298 (1958).
13. Cotzias, G. C., Horiuchi, K., Fuenzalida, S., and Mena, I., *Neurology* **18**, 376 (1968).
14. Cotzias, G. C., Lawrence, W. H., Papavasiliou, P. S., Duby, S. E., and Mena, I., *Trans. Amer. Neurol. Ass.* in press, (1972).
15. Cotzias, G. C., Miller, S. T., and Edwards, J., *J. Lab. Clin. Med.* **67**, 836 (1966).
16. Cotzias, G. C. and Papavasiliou, P. S., *Nature (London)* **195**, 823, (1962).
17. Cotzias, G. C., Papavasiliou, P. S., Fehling, C., Kaufman, B. and Mena, I., *N. Engl. J. Med.* **282**, 31 (1970).
18. Cotzias, G. C., Papavasiliou, P. S., and Gellene, R., *N. Engl. J. Med.* **280**, 337 (1969).
19. Cotzias, G. C., Papavasiliou, P. S., Ginos, J. Z., Steck, A., and Duby, S., *Annu. Rev. Med.* **22**, 305 (1971).
20. Cotzias, G. C., Papavasiliou, P. S., Hughes, E. R., Tang, L., and Borg, D. C., *J. Clin. Invest.* **47**, 992 (1968).
21. Cotzias, G. C., Papavasiliou, P. S., and Miller, S. T., *Nature (London)* **201**, 1228 (1964).
22. Cotzias, G. C., Papavasiliou, P. S., Van Woert, M. H., and Sakamoto, A., *Fed. Proc., Fed. Amer. Soc. Exp. Biol.* **23**, Part I, 713 (1964).
23. Cotzias, G. C., Tang, L., Ginos, J. Z., Nicholson, A. R., and Papavasiliou, P. S., *Nature (London)* **231**, 533 (1971).
24. Cotzias, G. C., Tang, L. C., and Mena, I., *Neurosci. Res.* **5**, 97 (1972).
25. Cotzias, G. C., Tang, L. C., Miller, S. T., Sladic-Simic, D., and Hurley, L. S., *Science* **176**, 410 (1972).
26. Cotzias, G. C., Van Woert, M. H., and Schiffer, L., *N. Engl. J. Med.* **276**, 374 (1967).
27. Duby, S. E., Cotzias, G. C., Papavasiliou, P. S., and Lawrence, W. H., *Arch. Neurol.* **27**, 474 (1972).
28. Duvoisin, R. C., *Arch. Neurol.* **17**, 124 (1967).
29. Duvoisin, R. C., and Katz, R., *J. Amer. Med. Ass.* **206**(9), 1963 (1968).
30. Foradori, A. C., Bertinchamps, A., Gulibon, J. M., and Cotzias, G. C., *J. Gen. Physiol.* **50**(9), 2255 (1967).
31. Ginos, J. Z., LoMonte, A., Cotzias, G. C., Bose, A. K., and Brambilla, R. J., *J. Amer. Chem. Soc.* **95**, 2991 (1973).
32. Hughes, E. R., and Cotzias, G. C., *Amer. J. Physiol.* **201**, 1061 (1961).
33. Hughes, E. R., Miller, S. T., and Cotzias, G. C., *Amer. J. Physiol.* **211**, 207 (1966).
34. Maynard, L. S., and Cotzias, G. C., *J. Biol. Chem.* **214**, 489 (1955).

35. Mena, I., Court, J., Fuenzalida, S., Papavasiliou, P. S., and Cotzias, G. C., *N. Engl. J. Med.* **282**, 5 (1970).
36. Mena, I., Horiuchi, K., Burke, K., and Cotzias, G. C., *Neurology* **19**, 1000 (1969).
37. Mena, I., Lopez, G., Horiuchi, K., and Croxatto Jr., H., *Nature (London)* **239**, 285 (1972).
38. Mena, I., Marin, O., Fuenzalida, S., and Cotzias, G. C., *Neurology* **17**, 128 (1967).
39. Papavasiliou, P. S., and Cotzias, G. C., *J. Biol. Chem.* **236**, 2365 (1961).
40. Papavasiliou, P. S., Cotzias, G. C., Duby, S. E., Steck, A. J., Fehling, C., and Bell, M. A., *N. Engl. J. Med.* **286**, 8 (1972).
41. Papavasiliou, P. S., Miller, S. T., and Cotzias, G. C., *Amer. J. Physiol.* **211**, 211 (1966).
42. Papavasiliou, P. S., Miller, S. T., and Cotzias, G. C., *Nature (London)* **220**, 74 (1968).
43. Prasad, K. N., Johnson, H. A., and Cotzias, G. C., *Nature (London)* **205**, 525 (1965).
44. Van Woert, M. H., and Cotzias, G. C., *Biochem. Pharmacol.* **15**, 275 (1966).
45. Van Woert, M. H., Nicholson, A., and Cotzias, G. C., *Comp. Biochem. Physiol.* **22**, 477 (1967).

ANTIBODY STRUCTURE AND CELLULAR SPECIFICITY IN THE IMMUNE RESPONSE*

GERALD M. EDELMAN

The Rockefeller University, New York, New York

I. INTRODUCTION

THE idea of immunological specificity was first formulated in molecular terms as a result of the work of Landsteiner (1945). His research on artificial hapten antigens served to ally immunology to chemistry and provided the operational tools necessary for the precise thermodynamic analysis of antigen–antibody reactions. From this analysis, it became clear that immunological specificity results from molecular complementarity between the antigenic determinant group and the antigen-combining site of the antibody molecule. Landsteiner's work was carried out on humoral antibodies against a general background of belief in instructive theories of antibody formation. It has now become apparent, however, that the notion of immunological specificity must be revised and broadened, largely because of two developments: the clonal selection theory of immunity and the detailed analysis of antibody structure.

In this lecture, I shall consider several ideas that have emerged from the structural analysis of antibodies and attempt to relate them to the framework of the theory of clonal selection and to several problems of cellular immunology at the molecular level. The analysis of antibodies can be considered as the first of the projects of molecular immunology, the task of which is to interpret the properties of the immune system in terms of molecular structure. Before this task can be considered complete, however, our knowledge of immunoglobulin molecules must be matched by a comparably detailed knowledge of the cellular and genetic events underlying their synthesis. Although I shall not hesitate

* Lecture delivered January 18, 1973.

149

to put forth working hypotheses on these events, my main purpose is to consider some experimental approaches which, however incomplete, suggest that these events are susceptible to chemical and structural analysis.

According to the theory of clonal selection (Jerne, 1955; Burnet, 1959) molecular recognition of antigens occurs by selection among different lymphoid cells already committed to producing surface antibodies prior to contact with the antigen (Fig. 1). Interaction of the antigen with an appropriately complementary antibody on the cell surface results in clonal expansion, i.e., maturation, mitosis, and increased production of the same kind of antibodies by daughter cells.

For such a system to function effectively, there are two major requirements. First, a sufficient diversity of antibodies with different combining sites must be synthesized by the cell population,

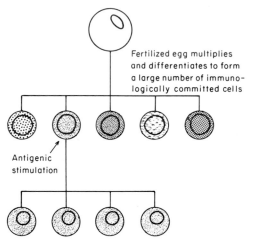

FIG. 1. A diagram illustrating the basic features of the clonal selection theory. The stippling and shading indicate that different cells have antibody receptors of different specificities, although the specificity of all receptors on a given cell is the same. Stimulation by an antigen results in clonal expansion (maturation, mitosis, and antibody production) of those cells having receptors complementary to the antigen.

each cell making surface antibodies of a single specificity that must, in general, be different than that of antibodies on other cells. Second, interaction with an antigen must either specifically trigger or specifically inhibit clonal expansion. Corresponding to these requirements are several fundamental problems of molecular immunology: (1) What is the origin of antibody diversity? (2) What is the mechanism of lymphocyte stimulation or suppression? Although these problems are far from being solved, their consideration in molecular terms, particularly in terms of antibody structure, sheds new light on the nature of immunological specificity.

II. Antibody Structure, Function, and Evolution

Antibodies carry out two main functions in the immune response: antigen binding functions and biologically important effector functions such as interaction with complement. Although antibodies occur in different immunoglobulin classes that mediate different effector functions (Table I), within each class, the immunoglobulins are still enormously heterogeneous and reflect the diversity required for the antigen-binding function. Immunoglobulins in all classes are multichain structures, consisting of either κ or λ light chains and a class-distinctive heavy chain. The most prevalent class in mammals is IgG; detailed structural work indicates that molecules within this class are sufficiently representative to illustrate the basic features of the relationship between antibody structure and function (for reviews, see Cold Spring Harbor Symposium, 1967; Nobel Symposium, 1967; Edelman and Gall, 1969).

Analysis of the complete amino acid sequence of an IgG molecule (Edelman et al., 1969) and comparison with other partial structures (Cunningham et al., 1971) reveals a particularly simple differentiation of the structure to carry out antigen-binding and effector functions (Fig. 2). Both the light and the heavy chains contain variable regions consisting of the first 110–120 amino acid residues, having sequences that differ from molecule to molecule. This observation was first made on light chains from Bence-Jones proteins by Hilschmann and Craig (1965). The remaining portions of the chains are called constant regions because, with

TABLE I

HUMAN IMMUNOGLOBULIN CLASSES

Class	Physiological properties	Heavy chain[a]	Light chains	Molecular formula[b]	Molecular weight ($\times 10^{-3}$) and sedimentation constant	Carbo-hydrate content (%)
IgG	Complement fixation; placental transfer	γ	κ or λ	$(\gamma_2\kappa_2)$ or $(\gamma_2\lambda_2)$	143–149; 6.7 S	2.5
IgA	Localized protection in external secretions	α	κ or λ	$(\alpha_2\kappa_2)$ or $(\alpha_2\lambda_2)$	158–162; 6.8–11.4 S	5–10
IgM	Complement fixation; early immune response	μ	κ or λ	$(\mu_2\kappa_2)_5$ or $(\mu_2\lambda_2)_5$	800–950; 19.0 S	5–10
IgD	Unknown	δ	κ or λ	$(\delta_2\kappa_2)$ or $(\delta_2\lambda_2)$	175–180; 6.6 S	10
IgE	Reagin activity; mast cell fixation	ϵ	κ or λ	$(\epsilon_2\kappa_2)$ or $(\epsilon_2\lambda_2)$	185–190; 8.0 S	12

[a] The class distinctive features of these chains are in their constant regions.

[b] IgA can have additional unrelated chains called SC and J; J chains are also found in IgM. For nomenclature, see World Health Organization, 1964.

the exception of certain genetic polymorphisms, they are the same in molecules of a given class and subclass. Experiments on the reconstitution of antibodies from their separate chains (Franěk and Nezlin, 1963; Edelman et al., 1963; Olins and Edelman, 1964) and their completely denatured chains (Haber, 1964) as well as experiments on affinity labeling (Singer and Doolittle, 1966) and on the isolation of antigen-binding fragments consisting of variable regions (Inbar et al., 1972) all indicate that both V_H and V_L regions mediate the antigen-binding function. The effector functions are carried out by constant regions.

Additional hints about the evolutionary origin and functional differentiation of immunoglobulins have emerged from a detailed analysis of their primary structure (Edelman, 1970). A considera-

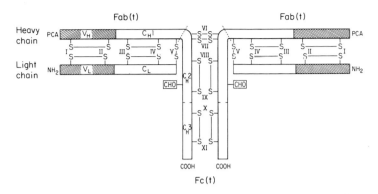

FIG. 2. Overall arrangement of chains and disulfide bonds of the human γG₁ immunoglobulin Eu. Half-cystinyl residues are I–XI; I–V designate corresponding half-cystinyl residues in light and heavy chains. PCA, pyrrolidonecarboxylic acid; CHO, carbohydrate. Fab(t) and Fc(t) refer to fragments produced by trypsin, which cleaves the heavy chain as indicated by dashed lines above half-cystinyl residues VI. Variable regions, V_H and V_L, are homologous. The constant region of the heavy chain (C_H) is divided into three regions, C_H1, C_H2, and C_H3, that are homologous to each other and to the C region of the light chain. The variable regions carry out antigen-binding functions and the constant region the effector functions of the molecule.

tion of the amino acid sequences of immunoglobulin G (Figs. 3 and 4) supports the following conclusions:

1. V_H and V_L regions are homologous to each other but are not obviously homologous to C_H or C_L regions. V regions from the same molecule appear to be no more closely related than V regions from different molecules.

2. The constant region of the heavy chain consists of three homology regions, C_H1, C_H2, and C_H3, each of which is closely homologous to the others and to C_L.

3. Each variable region and each constant homology region contains one disulfide bond, and as a result the intrachain disulfide bonds are linearly and periodically distributed in the structure.

4. The region containing all the interchain disulfide bonds is in the middle of the linear sequence of the heavy chain and has no homologous counterpart in other portions of the heavy or the light chains.

These observations are consistent with the hypothesis of Hill

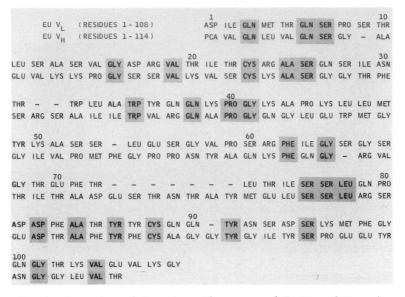

FIG. 3. Comparison of the amino acid sequences of the V_H and V_L regions of protein Eu. Identical residues are shaded. Deletions indicated by dashes are introduced to maximize the homology.

et al. (1966) and Singer and Doolittle (1966) that immunoglobulin chains arose by duplication of a precursor gene about 330 nucleotides in length. Because there is no clear-cut evidence of homology between V and C regions, however, it is somewhat harder to decide whether V and C regions evolved from a single gene. The alternative is that there were two precursor genes for V and C which were originally unrelated but were brought together because of the selective advantages of combining their functions in a single product molecule (Edelman, 1970).

The unusual homology relationships and arrangement of disulfide bonds prompted my colleagues and me to suggest that the molecule is folded in a congeries of compact domains (Edelman, 1970; Cunningham *et al.*, 1971), each formed by separate V homology regions or C homology regions (Fig. 5). In such an arrangement, each domain is stabilized by a single intrachain disulfide bond and is linked to neighboring domains by less tightly folded stretches of the polypeptide chains. A 2-fold pseudosym-

```
                                    110                                       120
EU C_L  (RESIDUES 109-214)  THR VAL ALA ALA PRO SER VAL PHE ILE PHE PRO PRO SER
EU C_H1 (RESIDUES 119-220)  SER THR LYS GLY PRO SER VAL PHE PRO LEU ALA PRO SER
EU C_H2 (RESIDUES 234-341)  LEU LEU GLY GLY PRO SER VAL PHE LEU PHE PRO PRO LYS
EU C_H3 (RESIDUES 342-446)  GLN PRO ARG GLU PRO GLN VAL TYR THR LEU PRO PRO SER


                                            130
ASP GLU GLN  -   -  LEU LYS SER GLY THR ALA SER VAL VAL CYS LEU LEU ASN ASN PHE
SER LYS SER  -   -  THR SER GLY GLY THR ALA ALA LEU GLY CYS LEU VAL LYS ASP TYR
PRO LYS ASP THR LEU MET ILE SER ARG THR PRO GLU VAL THR CYS VAL VAL VAL ASP VAL
ARG GLU GLU  -   -  MET THR LYS ASN GLN VAL SER LEU THR CYS LEU VAL LYS GLY PHE


140                                  150
TYR PRO ARG GLU ALA LYS VAL  -   -  GLN TRP LYS VAL ASP ASN ALA LEU GLN SER GLY
PHE PRO GLU PRO VAL THR VAL  -   -  SER TRP ASN SER  -  GLY ALA LEU THR SER GLY
SER HIS GLU ASP PRO GLN VAL LYS PHE ASN TRP TYR VAL ASP GLY  -  VAL GLN VAL HIS
TYR PRO SER ASP ILE ALA VAL  -   -  GLU TRP GLU SER ASN ASP  -  GLY GLU PRO GLU


160                                  170
ASN SER GLN GLU SER VAL THR GLU GLN ASP SER LYS ASP SER THR TYR SER LEU SER SER
 -  VAL HIS THR PHE PRO ALA VAL LEU GLN SER  -  SER GLY LEU TYR SER LEU SER SER
ASN ALA LYS THR LYS PRO ARG GLU GLN GLN TYR  -  ASP SER THR TYR ARG VAL VAL SER
ASN TYR LYS THR THR PRO PRO VAL LEU ASP SER  -  ASP GLY SER PHE PHE LEU TYR SER


180                                  190
THR LEU THR LEU SER LYS ALA ASP TYR GLU LYS HIS LYS VAL TYR ALA CYS GLU VAL THR
VAL VAL THR VAL PRO SER SER SER LEU GLY THR GLN  -  THR TYR ILE CYS ASN VAL ASN
VAL LEU THR VAL LEU HIS GLN ASN TRP LEU ASP GLY LYS GLU TYR LYS CYS LYS VAL SER
LYS LEU THR VAL ASP LYS SER ARG TRP GLN GLU GLY ASN VAL PHE SER CYS SER VAL MET


200                                  210
HIS GLN GLY LEU SER SER PRO VAL THR  -  LYS SER PHE  -   -  ASN ARG GLY GLU CYS
HIS LYS PRO SER ASN THR LYS VAL  -  ASP LYS ARG VAL  -   -  GLU PRO LYS SER CYS
ASN LYS ALA LEU PRO ALA PRO ILE  -  GLU LYS THR ILE SER LYS ALA LYS GLY
HIS GLU ALA LEU HIS ASN HIS TYR THR GLN LYS SER LEU SER LEU SER PRO GLY
```

FIG. 4. Comparison of the amino acid sequences of C_H, C_H1, C_H2, and C_H3 regions. Deletions, indicated by dashes, have been introduced to maximize homologies. Identical residues are darkly shaded; both light and dark shadings are used to indicate identities that occur in pairs in the same position.

metry axis relates the V_LC_L to the V_HC_H1 domains, and a true dyad axis through the disulfide bonds connecting the heavy chains relates the C_H2-C_H3 domains. The tertiary structure within each of the homologous domains is assumed to be quite similar to that in the others. Moreover, each domain is assumed to contribute to at least one active site mediating a function of the immuno-globulin molecule.

As I have already mentioned, the V domains have been shown to mediate the antigen-binding function. The proposed similarities in tertiary structure among C domains have not been established,

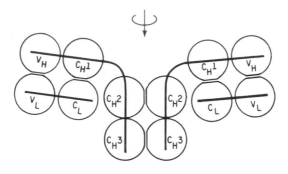

FIG. 5. The domain hypothesis. Diagrammatic arrangement of domains in the free immunoglobulin G molecule. The arrow refers to a dyad axis of symmetry. Homology regions (see Figs. 2–4) which constitute each domain are indicated: V_L, V_H—domains made up of variable homology regions; C_L, C_H1, C_H2, and C_H3—domains made up of constant homology regions. Within each of these groups, domains are assumed to have similar three-dimensional structures and each is assumed to contribute to an active site. The V domain sites contribute to antigen recognition functions, and the C domain sites to effector functions.

however, nor have the various effector functions of the different C domains been fully determined. There is a suggestion that C_H2 may play a role in complement fixation (Kehoe and Fougereau, 1970). A good candidate for binding to the lymphocyte cell membrane is C_H3, the function of which may be concerned with the mechanism of lymphocyte triggering following the binding of antigen by V domains. The C_H3 domain has already been found to bind to macrophage membranes (Yasmeen *et al.*, 1973).

There is now some evidence that lymphocytes can synthesize isolated domains similar to C_H3 as separate molecules. Berggård and Bearn (1968) first isolated a urinary protein called β_2-microglobulin from patients with renal tubular insufficiency. On the basis of the sequence analysis of the first 41 residues of this protein, Smithies and Poulik (1972) suggested that this protein was homologous to immunoglobulins. Work by Peterson *et al* (1972) and Cunningham *et al.* (1973) in my laboratory has defined the complete amino acid sequence of this protein (Fig. 6), strongly confirming the homology. It appears, therefore, that

```
                                          1                           10
β₂-MICROGLOBULIN                ILE GLN [ARG] THR [PRO] LYS ILE [GLN VAL] [TYR] SER
EU C_L  (RESIDUES 109-214)      THR VAL ALA ALA [PRO]  -   -  SER [VAL] PHE ILE
EU C_H1 (RESIDUES 119-220)      SER THR LYS GLY [PRO]  -   -  SER [VAL] PHE PRO
EU C_H2 (RESIDUES 234-341)      LEU LEU GLY GLY [PRO]  -   -  SER [VAL] PHE LEU
EU C_H3 (RESIDUES 342-446)      GLN PRO [ARG] GLU [PRO] -   -  [GLN VAL] [TYR] THR


                                                  20
ARG HIS [PRO] ALA  -  [GLU]  -   -   -   -  ASX [GLY] LYS SER ASX PHE [LEU] ASN [CYS] TYR [VAL]
PHE PRO [PRO] SER ASP [GLU] GLN  -   -  LEU LYS SER GLY THR ALA SER VAL VAL [CYS] LEU LEU
LEU ALA [PRO] SER SER LYS SER  -   -  THR SER [GLY] GLY THR ALA ALA [LEU] GLY [CYS] LEU [VAL]
PHE PRO [PRO] LYS PRO LYS ASP THR LEU MET ILE SER ARG THR PRO GLU VAL THR [CYS] VAL [VAL]
LEU PRO [PRO] SER ARG [GLU] GLU  -   -  MET THR LYS ASN GLN VAL SER [LEU] THR [CYS] LEU [VAL]


             30                                    40
SER [GLY PHE] HIS [PRO SER ASP ILE] GLU [VAL]  -   -  ASP LEU LEU LYS [ASP GLY] GLU ARG ILE
ASN ASN [PHE] TYR [PRO] ARG GLU ALA LYS [VAL]  -   -  GLN TRP LYS VAL [ASP] ASN  -  ALA LEU
LYS ASP TYR PHE [PRO] GLU PRO VAL THR [VAL]  -   -  SER TRP ASN SER  -  [GLY]  -  ALA LEU
VAL ASP VAL SER HIS GLU [ASP] PRO GLU VAL [VAL] LYS PHE ASN TRP TYR VAL [ASP] GLY  -   -  VAL
LYS [GLY PHE] TYR [PRO SER ASP ILE] ALA [VAL]  -   -  GLU TRP GLU SER ASN ASP  -   -  GLY


             50                                    60
[GLX] LYS VAL [ASX]  -  [HIS] SER GLX LEU SER PHE SER LYS ASN  -  [SER] TRP PHE [TYR] LEU [LEU]
[GLN] SER GLY [ASN] SER GLN GLU SER VAL THR GLU GLN ASP SER LYS ASP SER THR [TYR] SER [LEU]
THR SER GLY  -  VAL [HIS] THR PHE PRO ALA VAL LEU GLN SER  -  [SER] GLY LEU [TYR] SER [LEU]
[GLN] VAL HIS [ASN] ALA LYS THR LYS PRO ARG GLU GLN GLN TYR  -  ASP SER THR [TYR] ARG VAL
[GLU] PRO GLU [ASN] TYR LYS THR THR PRO PRO VAL LEU ASP SER  -  ASP GLY SER PHE PHE [LEU]


         70                              80
[TYR SER] TYR  -  [THR] GLU PHE THR PRO THR  -  [GLU LYS]  -  ASP [GLU] TYR ALA [CYS] ARG [VAL]
SER SER THR LEU [THR] LEU SER LYS ALA ASP TYR [GLU LYS] HIS LYS VAL [TYR ALA] [CYS] GLU [VAL]
SER SER VAL VAL [THR] VAL PRO SER SER SER LEU GLY THR GLN  -  THR [TYR] ILE [CYS] ASN [VAL]
VAL SER VAL LEU [THR] VAL LEU HIS GLN ASN TRP LEU ASP GLY LYS [GLU] TYR LYS [CYS] LYS [VAL]
[TYR SER] LYS LEU [THR] VAL ASP LYS SER ARG TRP GLN GLN GLY ASN VAL PHE SER [CYS] SER [VAL]


                 90                                      100
ASX [HIS] VAL THR [LEU SER] GLX [PRO]  -   -   -  [LYS] ILE [VAL]  -  [LYS] TRP ASP ARG ASP MET
THR [HIS] GLN GLY [LEU SER] SER [PRO] VAL THR  -  [LYS] SER PHE  -   -  ASN ARG GLY GLU CYS
ASN [HIS] LYS PRO SER ASN THR LYS VAL  -  ASP [LYS] ARG [VAL]  -   -  GLU PRO LYS SER CYS
SER ASN LYS ALA [LEU] PRO ALA [PRO] ILE  -  GLU [LYS] THR ILE SER [LYS] ALA LYS GLY
MET [HIS] GLU ALA [LEU] HIS ASN HIS TYR THR GLN [LYS] SER LEU SER LEU SER PRO GLY
```

FIG. 6. Comparison of the amino acid sequence of β₂-microglobulin with the homology regions C_L, C_H1, C_H2, and C_H3 of the γG₁ immunoglobulin Eu. Deletions, indicated by dashes, have been inserted to maximize homologies. Identical residues are enclosed in boxes. Numbers are for β₂-microglobulin.

this protein is a free immunoglobulin domain, and indeed there is now evidence that it is synthesized by lymphocytes (Bernier and Fanger, 1972). Even more exciting is the recent observation (Nakamuro *et al.*, 1973; Peterson *et al.*, 1974) that this protein is the light polypeptide chain of the histocompatibility (HL-A) antigen. This tends to support the hypothesis (Gally and Edelman, 1972) that immunoglobulin genes have arisen in evolution from those specifying the histocompatibility system.

Although many details still are lacking, the gross structural aspects of the domain hypothesis have received direct support from X-ray crystallographic analyses of Fab fragments (Poljak *et al.*, 1972) and whole molecules (Davies *et al.*, 1971), in which separate domains were clearly discerned. Indirect support for the hypothesis has also come from experiments on proteolytic cleavage of regions between domains (Gall and D'Eustachio, 1972; D. Inbar *et al.*, 1972). Whatever the selective advantages of the domain arrangement, it is clear that gene duplication would permit the modular alteration of immunological function by addition or deletion of domains during evolution.

III. The Origin of Diversity and the Arrangement of Immunoglobulin Genes

One of the most satisfying conclusions that emerged from the structural analysis of antibodies is that the diversity of the V regions of antibody chains is sufficient to satisfy the requirements of clonal selection theories.

Comparisons of the primary structures of a great variety of immunoglobulins shows that the diversity of V regions has several distinct features. The fact that V regions fall into subgroups of related sequences was first pointed out for light chains by Milstein (1967) and Hood *et al.* (1967) and is illustrated for heavy chains (Cunningham *et al.*, 1969; Press and Hogg, 1969; Wikler *et al.*, 1969) in Figs. 7 and 8. The sequences of the different V region subgroups are sufficiently different to warrant the conclusion that the subgroups are specified by different genes. Within a subgroup, the amino acid sequence variations may be accounted for by single base substitutions in the genetic code. Moreover,

FIG. 7.   Comparison of V_H regions of protein Eu (subgroup V_{HI}) and protein He (subgroup V_{HIII}). V_H regions within each subgroup are more closely similar in sequence than proteins belonging to different subgroups.

certain positions show many substitutions (the so-called hypervariable regions; see Wu and Kabat, 1970) whereas others, such as the half-cystine residues at positions 23 and 88 of kappa chains, have never been observed to vary at all and may play a role in stabilizing the antigen combining site (Edelman, 1971). This set of observations indicates that both mutation and selection have operated to yield variable region structure.

The ultimate origin of the mutation and selection is one of the two outstanding large problems of molecular immunology. Although this problem is not solved, it is understood that the diversity arises at three levels of structural or genetic organization:

1. Association of various V_H with various V_L regions; i.e., inasmuch as V regions from both heavy and light chains contribute to the antigen-binding site, the number of possible antibodies may be as great as the product of the number of different V_L and V_H regions (Edelman, 1971).

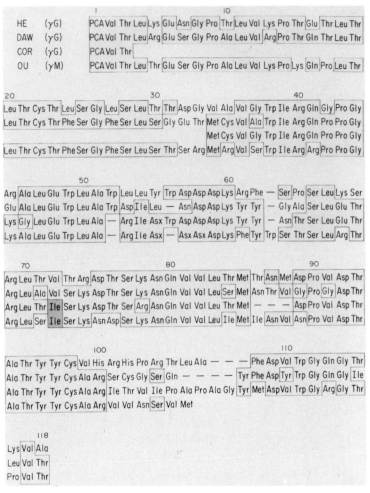

FIG. 8. Comparison of V_{HII} regions showing variations within a single heavy-chain subgroup. Proteins Daw and Cor are described by Press and Hogg (1969) and protein Ou is from μ chains (Wikler *et al.*, 1969). Copyright 1969 by the American Association for the Advancement of Science.

2. The existence of V region subgroups, each specified by at least one separate germ line gene which must have been selected during evolution (Milstein, 1967; Hood *et al.*, 1967).

3. Intrasubgroup variation of unknown origin.

The key problem of the generation of antibody diversity has been converted by the work on immunoglobulin chains and V region subgroups to the problem of the origin of sequence variations within each subgroup. It is still not known whether there is a germ line gene for each V region within a subgroup or whether each subgroup contains only a few genes, and intrasubgroup variation arises by somatic genetic rearrangements within precursors of antibody-forming cells. The various theories supporting one or the other of these alternatives have been discussed elsewhere (Gally and Edelman, 1970). At this time, therefore, we can conclude that only the basis, but not the ultimate origin, of diversity has been adequately explained by the work on structure.

Although the work on the structure of antibodies has not fully resolved the problem of the origin of diversity, it has contributed much to an understanding of the nature of the structural genes for immunoglobulins. There is now considerable evidence to suggest that the arrangement of these genes is unusual, and it may in fact turn out that this arrangement reflects the unusual requirements for the generation of diversity. Briefly, the facts leading to the conclusion that structural genes for immunoglobulins are special are as follows: whereas different V region subgroups are specified by a number of nonallelic genes (Milstein, 1967), the analysis of genetic or allotypic markers suggests that C regions of a given immunoglobulin class are specified by no more than one or two genes. These allotypic markers, first described by Grubb (1956, 1970) and Oudin (1956), provide a means in addition to sequence analysis for understanding the genetic basis of immunoglobulin synthesis. It has been found that V regions specified by a number of different genes can occur in different chains, each of which may have the same C region specified by a single gene. This leads to the remarkable conclusion that each immunoglobulin chain is specified by two genes, a V gene and a C gene (Milstein, 1967; Hood et al., 1967).

Work in a number of laboratories (reviewed by Gally and Edelman, 1972) has shown that genetic markers on the two types of light chains are not linked to those of the heavy chains or to each other. These findings, and the conclusion that there are separate V and C genes, led Gally and me (1970, 1972) to suggest that immunoglobulins are specified by three unlinked gene clusters (Fig. 9). The clusters have been named translocons to emphasize the fact that a mechanism must be provided to combine genetic information from V region loci with information from C region loci to make complete V-C structural genes. According to this hypothesis, the translocon is the basic unit of immunoglobulin evolution, different groups of immunoglobulin chains having arisen by duplication and various chromosomal rearrangements of a precursor gene cluster. Presumably, gene duplication during evolution also led to the appearance of V region subgroups within each translocon.

In this cursory discussion, I have attempted to show that the work on antibody structure carried out in a number of laboratories has not only satisfied certain basic requirements of the theory of clonal selection, but has also sharpened certain remaining questions. We now understand that the heterogeneity of antibodies is the result of sequence diversity of V regions as well as sequence differences in C_H regions specifying the different immunoglobulin classes. The structure–function problem has been neatly resolved: V domains carry out antigen-binding functions and C domains

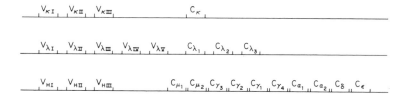

Fig. 9. A diagrammatic representation of the proposed arrangement in mammalian germ cells of antibody genes in three unlinked clusters termed translocons. κ and λ chains are each specified by separate translocons, and heavy chains are specified by a third translocon. The exact number and arrangement of V and C genes within a translocon is not known. Each variable region subgroup (designated by a subscript corresponding to chain group and subgroup) must be coded by at least one separate germ line V gene. The number of V genes within each subgroup is unknown, however, as is the origin of intrasubgroup diversity of V regions. A special event is required to link the information from a particular V gene to that of a given C gene. The properties of the classes and subclasses (see Table I) are conferred on the constant regions by C genes.

mediate effector functions. Furthermore, the evidence suggests that the genes for classes and domains almost certainly arose by gene duplication and chromosomal rearrangements during evolution. As a result of these processes, it appears that separate V and C genes occur in clusters, each cluster specifying a given kind of chain.

Practically all these conclusions and the formulation of the major problem of the origin of diversity have come from work on humoral antibodies. This work is just a beginning, however, for the subject of antibodies on cells and the nature of the specific triggering of these cells comprise a second major problem of molecular immunology. Much less is known in this area of study, but there are some hints that it may be approached at the molecular level.

IV. Cellular Specificity and Cell Surface Antibodies

What is the mechanism by which a particular antigen induces clonal proliferation or immune tolerance in certain populations of lymphoid cells? Although many means are being used by cellular immunologists to study this question, two approaches seem to be particularly suitable for its analysis at the molecular level. The first and most direct approach is to fractionate lymphocytes according to the specificity of their receptor antibodies both for subsequent studies of these antibodies and of the cellular response to antigens of known molecular geometry. The second approach is to analyze the structure and activity of molecules, such as lectins, that can stimulate lymphocytes regardless of their antigen-binding specificity. I shall discuss below some experiments, admittedly preliminary, that my colleagues and I have recently carried out using each of these approaches.

In the attempt to understand cellular specificity, it is particularly important to distinguish between antigen-binding and antigen-reactive cells (Fig. 10). The work of Nossal and Mäkelä (see Mäkelä and Cross, 1970) showed that each antibody secreting cell makes antibodies of a different specificity and the work of Ada and Nossal and others (see Nossal and Ada, 1971) has

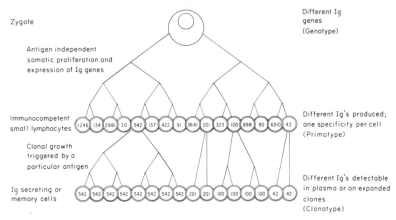

Zygote

Antigen independent
somatic proliferation and
expression of Ig genes

Immunocompetent
small lymphocytes

Clonal growth
triggered by a
particular antigen

Ig secreting or
memory cells

Different Ig
genes
(Genotype)

Different Ig's produced;
one specificity per cell
(Primotype)

Different Ig's detectable
in plasma or on expanded
clones
(Clonotype)

FIG. 10. A model of the somatic differentiation of antibody-producing cells according to the clonal selection theory. The number of immunoglobulin genes may increase during somatic growth so that, in the immunologically mature animal, different lymphoid cells are formed, each committed to the synthesis of a structurally distinct receptor antibody (indicated by an arabic number). A small proportion of these cells proliferate upon antigenic stimulation to form different clones of cells, each clone producing a different antibody. This model represents bone marrow-derived (B) cells, but with minor modifications it is also applicable to thymus-derived (T) cells.

demonstrated the existence of antigen binding cells of different specificities.

Inasmuch as an animal is capable of responding specifically to an enormous number of antigens to which it is usually never exposed, it must contain genetic information for synthesizing a much larger number of different immunoglobulin molecules on cells than actually appear in detectable amounts in the bloodstream. One may therefore distinguish two levels of expression in the synthesis of immunoglobulins that Gally and I (1972) have termed for convenience the *primotype* and the *clonotype* (Fig. 10). The primotype consists of the sum total of structurally different immunoglobulin molecules generated within an organism during its lifetime. The clonotype consists of those immunoglobulin molecules synthesized as a result of antigenic stimulation and clonal expansion. These molecules can be detected and classified according to antigen-binding specificity, class, antigenic determinants, primary structure, allotype, or a variety of other experimentally measurable molecular properties. As a class, the clonotype is smaller than the primotype and is wholly contained within it (Fig. 10).

Although a view of the clonotype is afforded by the analysis of humoral antibodies, we know very little about the primotype. In our laboratory, we have been attempting to approach the problem of the specific fractionation of lymphocytes expressing the primotype by using nylon fibers to which antigens have been covalently coupled (Edelman *et al.*, 1971; Rutishauser *et al.*, 1972). The derivatized fibers are strung tautly in a tissue culture dish (Fig. 11) so that cells shaken in suspension may collide with them. Some of the cells colliding with the fibers are specifically bound to the covalently coupled antigens by means of their surface receptors. Bound cells may be counted microscopically

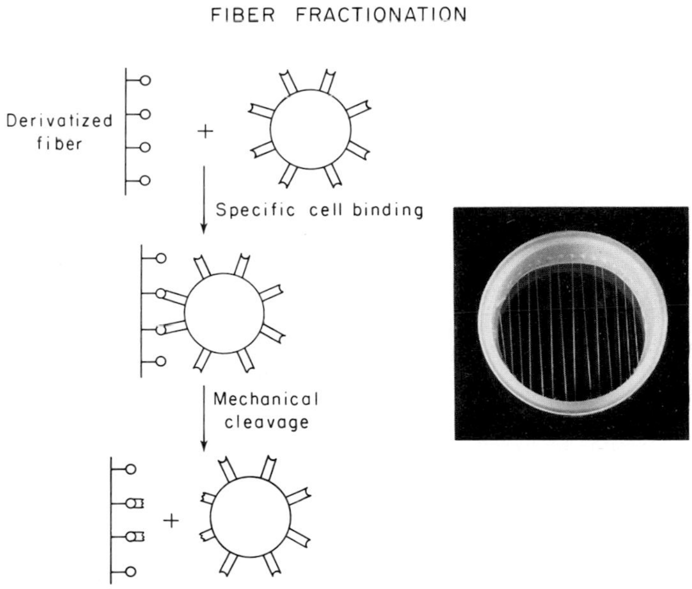

FIBER FRACTIONATION

FIG. 11. General scheme for fiber fractionation of cells. Inset shows a tissue culture dish with nylon fibers held under tension in a polyethylene frame.

in situ by focusing on the edge of the fiber (Fig. 12). After washing away unbound cells, the specifically bound cells may be removed by plucking the fibers and shearing the cells quantitatively from their sites of attachment. The removed cells retain their viability provided that the tissue culture medium contains serum.

Derivatized nylon fibers have the ability to bind both thymus-derived lymphocytes (T cells) and bone marrow-derived lymphocytes (B cells) (Gowans *et al.*, 1971) according to the specificity

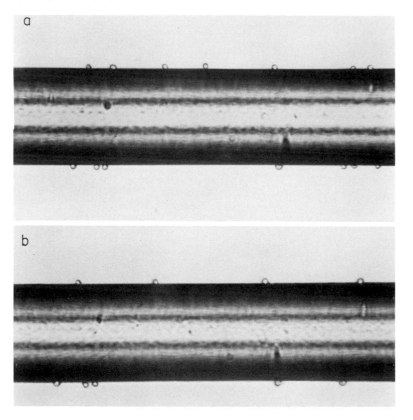

FIG. 12. Lymphoid cells from the mouse spleen bound by their antigen-specific receptors to a nylon fiber to which dinitrophenyl bovine serum albumin has been coupled. Treatment of bound cells in (a) with antiserum to the T cell surface antigen θ and with serum complement destroys the T cells, leaving B cells still viable and attached (b). See Table II. ×130.

of their receptors for a given antigen (Rutishauser and Edelman, 1972) (Fig. 12, Table II). About 60% of spleen cells specifically isolated are B cells, and the remainder are T cells. By the use of appropriate antisera to cell surface receptors, the cells of each

TABLE II

CHARACTERIZATION OF MOUSE LYMPHOID CELLS FRACTIONATED ACCORDING TO THEIR ANTIGEN-BINDING SPECIFICITIES[a]

Antigen on Fiber	Dnp NO$_2$ / NO$_2$	Dnp	Tosyl CH$_3$ / SO$_2$	Tosyl
Immunization	none	Dnp	none	Tosyl
Cells Bound to Fiber (per cm)	1200	4000	800	2000
% Inhibition of Binding by:				
Dnp	90	95	5	10
Tosyl	1	2	75	87
Anti-Ig	85	93	73	90
High Avidity Cells (per cm)	<100	2800	—	—
Low Avidity Cells (per cm)	1200	1200	—	—
% T Cells	41	39	43	—
% B Cells	59	56	54	—

[a] Nylon fibers were derivatized with hapten conjugates of bovine serum albumin, and mice were immunized with each of the designated haptens coupled to hemocyanin. Inhibition of binding was achieved by addition of hapten-protein conjugates (250 μg/ml) or rabbit antimouse immunoglobulin (Ig) (250 μg/ml) to the cell suspension. High avidity cells are defined as those prevented from binding by concentrations of DNP-bovine serum albumin of less than 4 μg/ml in the cell suspensions. Cells inhibited by higher concentrations are defined as low avidity cells. Virtually complete inhibition occurs at levels of homologous hapten greater than 100 μg/ml.

type can be counted on the fibers and most of the cells of one type or the other may then be destroyed by the subsequent addition of serum complement. In this way, one can obtain populations of either T or B cells that are highly enriched in their capacity to bind a given antigen.

Cells of either kind may be further fractionated according to the relative affinity of their receptors. This can be accomplished by prior addition of a chosen amount of the free antigen, which serves to inhibit specific attachment of subpopulations of cells to the antigen-derivatized fibers by binding to their receptors. As defined by this technique, cells capable of binding specifically to a particular antigen constitute as much as 1% of a mouse spleen cell population. Very few of these original antigen-binding cells appear to increase in number after immunization, however (Rutishauser et al., 1972), and the cells that do respond are those having receptors of higher relative affinities (Fig. 13a). This is in agreement with the conclusions reached by Siskind and Benacerraf (1969) in their analysis of the humoral antibody response.

Using this method together with serological means of distinguishing T and B cells, the cells may be compared for their range of antigen-binding specificities and avidities for antigens. Our studies suggest that T and B cells do not differ in their antigen-binding specificities, at least for several hapten and protein antigens (Rutishauser and Edelman, 1972). A comparison of the avidities of T and B cells for the DNP hapten showed that the avidities of T and B cells were the same for the monovalent ε-DNP-lysine (Fig. 13b,c). In contrast, T cells showed a consistently higher apparent avidity for multivalent DNP-bovine serum albumin containing an average of 10 DNP groups per molecule. This suggests the possibility that the receptors of T cells may be arranged or are arrangeable on the cell surface in clusters that differ from those of B cells.

Whether these cell populations correspond to the cells expressing the primotype remains to be determined. It is significant, however, that fiber-binding cells do not include plaque-forming cells (Jerne et al., 1963), and it is therefore possible to fractionate antigen-binding cells from cells that are already actively secreting

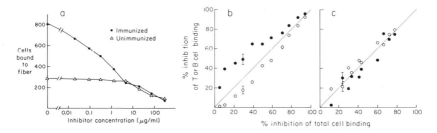

FIG. 13.   (a) Inhibition by free DNP-BSA of spleen cell binding to DNP-BSA derivatized fibers. Cell numbers represent fiber edge counts for a 2.5 cm fiber segment. Spleens from immunized mice were removed at the height of a secondary response to DNP-BGG, and cells from several mice were pooled. ●——●, immunized; △——△, unimmunized.

(b and c) Percent inhibition of T cell (●) and B cell (○) binding to DNP-BSA-derivatized fibers as a function of the percent inhibition of total cell binding. Inhibition was obtained with different amounts of (b) DNP-BSA or (c) ε-DNP-lysine. As described (Rutishauser *et al*, 1972), the percent inhibition of total cell binding increased from 0 to 90% as the concentrations of either inhibitor increased from 0 to 300 μg/ml. T and B cells were identified by cytolytic treatment of the total bound cell population with anti-θ or antimouse immunoglobulin sera. The cells were obtained from the spleens of mice 5 days after secondary immunization with DNP-hemocyanin. Error bars represent the standard deviation from the average values obtained in four experiments. If there were no differences in the binding behavior of T and B cells, the points would fall on the 45° line.

antibodies. Our recent experiments indicate that the antigen-binding cells isolated by this method may be transferred to irradiated animals to reconstitute a response to the antigen used to isolate them. Moreover, they are capable of secondary immune responses in tissue culture. These findings suggest that the antigen-specific population of cells removed from the fibers contains at least some of the precursors of plaque-forming cells. Although these results are encouraging, a number of questions remain to be answered concerning the specificity and function of lymphoid cells isolated by fiber fractionation. In addition, the method must be compared and combined with other means of cell fractionation. This approach should be useful for the isolation of surface antibodies as well as for analysis of populations of lymphoid cells in both developing and adult animals.

The comparison of the distribution of the relative affinities of antigen-binding cells before and after immunization (Fig. 13a) suggests that the concept of immunological specificity must be reexamined. Diversification of receptor antibodies may to a certain extent have been a result of selective pressure resulting from exposure to certain classes of antigens during evolution. But according to the theory of clonal selection, it is impossible for each cell receptor to have been selected for or against during evolution. Instead, a great number of antibody variants have been generated (by whatever process, germ line or somatic) many of which will never be selected during the lifetime of the organism. Under these circumstances how specific can such a system be? This question can be posed in the following terms: Is the probability of cross-reactivity with various antigens the same in the primotype and the clonotype?

The evidence on antigen-binding and antigen-reactive cells suggests that the degree of cross-reactivity may be much greater in the primotype. If this is the case, selection for specificity cannot merely be the result of antigen-binding, but must also depend on a second factor. The most likely candidate is the triggering threshold for stimulation of the cell carrying the antibody receptor. If, for example, a cell population contains cells that can bind two different antigens, specificity could be lost. It would be preserved, however, if a particular cell capable of binding both antigens is more likely to be triggered by only one of them. The trigger threshold might depend on the state of the cell but might also depend particularly on steric factors (reflected in the free energy of binding for each particular antigen) as well as on the surface density of the antigen molecules leading to changes in the avidity of the binding.

Whatever the detailed mechanism of triggering, the implication of this two-factor hypothesis is that variation at the level of the primotype leads to a relatively nonspecific set of immunoglobulin molecules, many of which are capable of binding various antigens with relatively low specificity. According to this idea, the selective forces that yield specificity are a product of both the probability of binding and the probability of lymphocyte stimulation above a certain triggering threshold.

V. The Use of Lectins for the Analysis of Lymphocyte Stimulation

Antigens are not the only means by which lymphocytes can be stimulated. It has been found that certain plant proteins called lectins can bind to glycoprotein receptors on the lymphocyte surface and induce blast transformation, mitosis, and immunoglobulin production (see Sharon and Lis, 1972, for a review). Although their mitogenic properties can be quite similar, different lectins have different specificities for cell surface glycoproteins as well as different molecular structures. In addition, they have a variety of effects on cell metabolism and transport. Such effects are independent of the antigen-binding specificity of the cell, and they may therefore be studied prior to specific cell fractionation.

The fact that antigens and lectins of different specificity and structure may stimulate lymphocytes suggests that the induction of mitosis is a property of membrane-associated structures on the lymphocyte that can respond to a variety of receptors. The process of stimulation appears to be independent of the specificity of these receptors for their various ligands. This implies that the triggering threshold may depend upon the affinity of a receptor, as well as upon its distribution and mode of attachment to the cell membrane in a given type of T or B cell. To understand mitogenesis, it is therefore necessary to solve two problems. The first, to determine in molecular detail how the lectin binds to the cell surface and to compare it to the binding of antigens. The second is to determine how the binding induces metabolic changes necessary for the initiation of cell division. These changes are likely to include the production or release of a messenger which acts as a final common pathway for the stimulation of the cell by any particular lectin or antigen.

In attempting to solve these problems, it would be valuable to know the complete structure of several different mitogenic lectins. This structural information is particularly useful in trying to understand the molecular transformation at the lymphocyte surface required for stimulation. With the knowledge of the three-dimensional structure of a lectin, for example, various amino acid side chains at the surface of the molecule may be modified by group reagents, which also may be used to change the valence of the molecule. The activities of the modified lectin derivatives may then be observed in various assays of their effects on cell surfaces and cell functions.

My colleagues and I (Edelman *et al.*, 1972) have recently determined both the amino acid sequence and three-dimensional structure (Fig. 14) of the lectin concanavalin A (Con A). This lectin has specificity for glucopyranosides, mannopyranosides, and fructofuranosides, and it binds to glycoproteins and possibly glycolipids on a variety of cell surfaces. Our studies were aimed at determining the exact size and shape of the molecule, its valence, and the structure and distribution of its binding sites.

With this knowledge in hand, we have been attempting to modify the structure and to determine the effects of that modification on various biological activities of the lymphocyte. So far, there are several findings suggesting that such alterations of the structure have distinct effects. Con A in free solution stimulates thymus-derived lymphocytes (T cells) but not bone marrow-derived lymphocytes (B cells) (Andersson *et al.*, 1972a,b). This stimulation leads to increased uptake of thymidine by the cells and to blast transformation. The dose response curve of stimulation of T cells by native Con A shows a rising limb of thymidine uptake and a falling limb (Fig. 15) that probably reflects cellular inhibition and death. The fact that the mitogenic effect and the killing effect are dose dependent suggests an analogy to stimulation and tolerance induction by antigens.

Derivatization of a lectin can alter the dose response curve. When Con A is succinylated, for example, it dissociates from a tetramer to a dimer without alteration of its carbohydrate binding specificity (Gunther *et al.*, 1973). Although succinylated Con A is just as mitogenic as native Con A, the falling limb is not seen until much higher doses are reached (Fig. 15). The dose response curve for this derivative indicates that the mitogenic response approaches saturation at high doses of the lectin.

Succinylation of Con A also alters another effect of this lectin on cell surfaces. Taylor *et al.* (1971) have demonstrated that immunoglobulin receptors are mobile and that they form "patches" and "caps" after addition of divalent antibodies

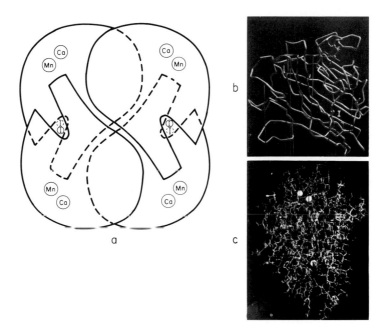

FIG. 14. Three-dimensional structure of concanavalin A, a lectin mitogenic for lymphocytes. (a) Schematic representation of the tetrameric structure of Con A viewed down the z axis. The proposed binding site for transition metals, calcium, and the iodine atom of the labeled inhibitor β-(o-iodophenyl)-D glucopyranoside (β-IPG) are indicated by Mn, Ca, and I, respectively. The monomers on top (solid lines) are related by 2-fold axis, as are those below. The two dimers are paired across an axis of D_2 symmetry to form the tetramer. (b) Wire model of the polypeptide backbone of the concanavalin A monomer oriented approximately to correspond to the monomer on the upper right of the diagram in (a). The two balls at the top represent the Ca and Mn atoms and the ball in the center (marked I) is the position of an iodine atom in the sugar derivative, β-IPG, which is bound in the crystal. Four such monomers are joined to form the tetramer as shown in (a). (c) A view of the Kendrew model of the Con A monomer rotated to show the deep pocket formed by the binding site. (The white ball at the bottom of the figure is at the position of the iodine atom of β-iodophenyl glucoside.) The two white balls at the top represent the metal atoms.

GERALD M. EDELMAN

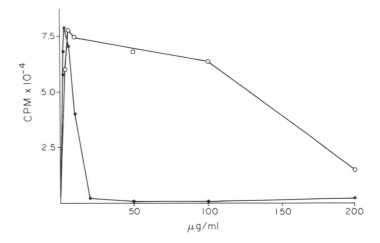

FIG. 15. Stimulation of uptake of radioactive thymidine by mouse spleen cells after addition of concanavalin A (●——●) and succinylated concanavalin A (○——○) in increasing doses (μg/ml).

directed against immunoglobulin receptors (Fig. 16). Yahara and I (1972) have found that, at certain concentrations, the binding of Con A to the cell surface restricts the movement of immuno-globulin receptors, preventing both cap and patch formation (Fig. 16). This suggests that Con A somehow changes the fluidity of the cell membrane, resulting in reduction of the relative mo-bility of these receptors. In contrast, succinylated Con A has no such effect, although it binds to lymphocytes to the same extent as native Con A molecules and it can also compete with Con A for binding sites.

If Con A is added to cells at 4°C, and the cells with bound Con A are brought to 37° after washing away free Con A, the Con A receptors themselves will form caps. If the Con A is not washed away or if the experiment is carried out at 37°, how-ever, cap formation is inhibited. Succinyl-Con A does not itself form caps under any of these conditions nor does it inhibit cap formation as I have already pointed out. Even more striking is the observation (Gunther *et al.*, 1973) that the addition of diva-lent antibodies against Con A to cells that have already bound

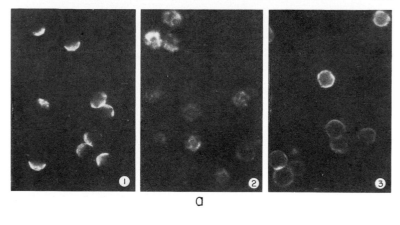

a

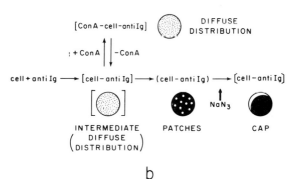

b

FIG. 16. Patch and cap formation in mouse spleen cells and its inhibition by Con A. (a) Patterns of caps (1); patches obtained after addition of fluorescein-labeled antiimmunoglobulin (2); and diffuse distribution of fluorescence when cells are first treated with Con A (3). (b) A model for patch and cap formation and its inhibition by Con A.

succinylated Con A results again in restriction of immunoglobulin receptor mobility.

All these findings (summarized in Table 3 and Fig. 17) suggest that Con A has two antagonistic actions that depend both on the state of the lectin and on the state of the cell. These actions are the induction of cap formation by the Con A receptors themselves and the inhibition of the mobility of Con A receptors as well as other cell receptors. The results appear to be compatible

176   GERALD M. EDELMAN

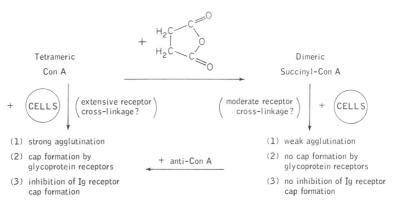

FIG. 17. Schematic comparison of the biological properties of native Con A and succinyl-Con A. The activities listed include the immediate cellular reactions mediated by the lectin.

TABLE III

COMPARISON OF THE BIOLOGICAL ACTIVITIES OF CON A AND SUCCINYL-CON A

Properties	Con A	Succinyl-Con A
No. of binding sites per cell		
Sheep erythrocytes	1.1×10^6	2.8×10^6
Mouse spleen cells	1.4×10^6	4.4×10^6
Percent inhibition of anti-Ig capping		
Lectin (100 µg/ml)	100	0
Lectin (50 µg/ml) + anti-Con A (100 µg/ml)	100	40
Percent of cells forming lectin receptor caps		
Lectin (5 µg/ml, 37°)	0.2–2	0
Lectin (100 µg/ml, 37°)	≤ 0.2	0
Lectin (170 µg/ml), preincubated in ice bath, washed, then brought to 37°	62	—
Lectin (20 µg/ml) + anti-Con A (100 µg/ml)	18	82
Mitogenesis		
Lectin (5 µg/ml)	Positive	Positive
Lectin (50 µg/ml)	Negative	Positive

with the hypothesis that there are at least two states or types of Con A receptors. According to this hypothesis, attachment of Con A to one type of receptor has no effect on the mobility of other receptors, but attachment to the other type inhibits the mobility of the other receptors. These findings may be related to those of Sachs and his co-workers (M. Inbar *et al.*, 1972) on the agglutination of cells by Con A.

What is the major factor in the alteration of Con A activity by succinylation? The abolition of the inhibition effect in mitogenic assays (Fig. 15) and the failure to inhibit receptor mobility may be the result of a change in valence or a change in the surface charge of the molecule. The restoration of the Con A effects after addition of antibodies against Con A (Fig. 17) suggests that the valence is the major factor. Nonetheless, alteration of side chains certainly has some influence, for the acetyl derivative of Con A is also divalent at pH 7.4 and although it has no effect on membrane mobility, it sharply inhibits thymidine uptake at doses above 5 μg/ml (Gunther *et al.*, 1973). Examination of other derivatives and localization of the substituted side chains in the three-dimensional structure should help to determine the exact causes of these alterations.

In addition to modifications that lead to structures of lower valence, Con A may also be modified by chemically cross-linking several molecules. A very striking effect is seen if the surface density of the Con A molecules presented to the lymphocyte is increased by cross-linking them at solid surfaces (Andersson *et al.*, 1972a). As I have indicated, Con A in free solution stimulates mouse T cells, with resultant increased incorporation of radioactive thymidine, but it has no effect on B cells. When cross-linked at a solid surface, however, it stimulates mainly mouse B cells, although both T and B cells have approximately the same number of Con A receptors. Similar results have been obtained with other lectins (Greaves and Bauminger, 1972). A reasonable interpretation of these phenomena (although not the only one) is that the lectin acts at the cell surface, that the surface density of mitogen binding sites is an important variable in exceeding the threshold for the lymphocyte stimulation, and that this threshold differs in the two kinds of lymphocytes.

VI. A Working Hypothesis to Account for
Lectin Activity

Before a detailed model of lymphocyte stimulation can be for-mulated, much more must be known about the structure and movements of the cell membrane and the chemistry and attach-ment of the cell surface receptors. Nevertheless, the experiments that I have described and those of other workers do suggest a working hypothesis which may serve to consolidate the disparate findings on lectin activity. This working hypothesis deliberately excludes consideration of the important but complex mass of data on T cell–B cell cooperation after antigenic stimulation as well as the important information on nonspecific factors involved in the immune response (Andersson *et al.*, 1972b). Instead, the hypothesis focuses on the necessary first step of mitogenesis, i.e., the nature and immediate consequences of lectin and antigen binding.

One of the key assumptions made in formulating this hypothe-sis is that both lectin-induced triggering and antigen-mediated triggering share the same mechanism as well as a final common pathway for surface nuclear interaction. A number of observations suggest that antigens and lectins stimulate lymphoid cells in the same way (Greaves and Janossy, 1972) providing indirect support for the assumption of a shared pathway of stimulation. These observations include the similarity of the time course in culture, the indication that high doses of either lectins or antigens inhibit the response, and the similarity of blast formation and immuno-globulin production. Moreover, as is the case with antigens, the available data suggest that stimulation by lectins is mediated at the cell surface; suppression may be mediated at the cell surface but also by endocytosis of the lectin–receptor complex. Although T and B cells have different thresholds for stimulation and sup-pression, it is assumed here that the same basic mechanism of stimulation and suppression applies to both cell types.

The assumption that there is a common pathway of stimulation implies that both the mode of attachment of antibody and lectin receptors to the membrane and their perturbation by cross-linkage at the cell surface may be similar, despite the difference in their specificities and molecular structures. It also implies that triggering or suppression of clonal proliferation is specifically related to the mode of anchorage of the antibody molecule to the cell membrane. The experiments on succinyl-Con A indicate that suppression by this lectin is related to the valence and the state of aggregation of the molecule, but they do not as yet indicate whether these factors are important in stimulation. There are two points to decide: (1) Is intermolecular interaction among receptors in the same cell a necessary and sufficient condition for stimulation or is attachment to single receptors sufficient? (2) Are stimulation and suppression related or are they caused by different mechanisms?

In the present hypothesis, I assume that the necessary and sufficient first step in triggering is the formation of cross-linked aggregates of certain of the cell surface glycoprotein receptors to form a *micropatch*. Such a micropatch would consist of as few as two or as many as 100 receptor molecules; after adequate stimulation, the membrane of a given lymphocyte could therefore have as many as 100–500 micropatches. These micropatches must remain stable (i.e., neither increase nor decrease greatly in size) for sufficient periods of time (up to hours) and diffusion of receptors into and out of a micropatch must therefore be balanced. The formation of a micropatch requires multivalence of the antigen or lectin. Therefore, the formation of a micropatch of proper size and stability depends upon the binding constant, the valence of the lectin or antigen as well as upon its specificity for the proper cell surface receptors. Antigenic determinants or lectin molecules need not, however, be presented in a *regular* array to provide an adequate stimulus; the only requirement is that a sufficient surface density of receptor-lectin or receptor-antigen complexes (Fanger *et al.*, 1970) be maintained.

Formation of larger aggregates would lead to patches, cap formation, and interruption of the stimulation cycle. Failure to form micropatches rapidly enough after binding low doses of antigen or lectin would lead to blockade of stimulation. As I have said, B cells are assumed to have a different threshold of response to micropatches than T cells, and it is likely that their thresholds for patch and cap formation also differ (Yahara and Edelman, unpublished observations).

In the absence of further experimental tests of these ideas, little can be said in detail about the coupling of micropatch formation to metabolic events initiating cell division. The data indicate that irreversible changes *in vitro* require as long as 12–24 hours of exposure to lectins, and it is likely that a whole series of enzymatic reactions are involved. The assumption that there is a final common pathway for the mitogenic stimulus, however, would suggest a single mediator such as cyclic AMP or cyclic GMP, and there is some evidence that the latter is involved (Hadden *et al.*, 1972). A possible means of coupling micropatch formation to metabolic changes is via interaction with enzymes such as adenyl cyclase or phosphodiesterase. One plausible hypothesis is that the formation of stable micropatches allows interaction of intramembranous particles to which such enzymes might be linked. Such interactions could result in induction of enzymatic action via allosteric or other conformational changes. An alternative mode in which receptor aggregation may be coupled to metabolic events is by means of transport defects, induced after perturbation of the alignment of the phospholipid head groups by the micropatches in the membrane. Movements of ions or small molecules in or out of the cell might then provide the necessary stimulus. Finally, lectin effects may be indirect and require the induction in one cell type of stimulatory or inhibitory factors, which then act on target cells, i.e., two cell types may be required (Andersson *et al.*, 1972b).

The foregoing hypothesis on the necessary initial conditions for stimulation and suppression is compatible with any one of these subsequent metabolic events and it leads to a number of predictions: (1) the valence, state of aggregation, specificity, and binding constant for carbohydrate on the appropriate receptors are overriding in stimulation; the detailed structure of a particular mitogenic lectin plays only a minor role in mitogenic activity. Only certain cell receptors are linked to the mitogenic pathway; some lectins will be nonmitogenic because they bind to receptors that are not so linked. (2) If lectins that are multivalent are made univalent, mitogenesis will be blocked (an exception to this prediction might conceivably occur if univalent lectins aggregated *after* binding to the cell surface). (3) Lectins that are not mitogenic for B cells but are mitogenic for T cells may be made mitogenic for B cells by cross-linking (this has already received support in two cases, as I have already indicated). (4) Some lectins that are not mitogenic may become mitogenic by cross-linking them to themselves or to other lectins, or after coupling them to Fab fragments of anti-immunoglobulins. (5) In a purified cell population specific for binding to a given antigen, stimulation by an antigen in the proper form should be additive with stimulation by a mitogenic lectin.

Now that fractionated populations of lymphocytes specific for particular antigens are available, it should be possible to determine the connection between lectin-induced and antigen-induced changes by comparing responses to molecular variants of both agents on the same cells and to test various hypotheses on the mechanisms of lymphocyte stimulation. Ultimately, of course, we must return to the cell surface antibody itself and relate its mode of attachment and function at the cell surface to our knowledge of antibody structure.

VII. Conclusion

Our understanding of the origin of immunoglobulin diversity and of the molecular mechanisms of lymphocyte stimulation is in a very early stage. Experiments stemming from the analysis of antibody structure suggest, however, that these two outstanding problems of immunology can be profitably attacked at a molecular level. The results of the experiments on antibody structure provide a basis for studying antibodies on lymphoid cells as well as a molecular framework for the understanding of cellular specificity in the immune response. It appears that immunological specificity results from the interaction of a number of factors including the specificity of the initial binding of the antigen, the affinity and avidity of the antibody receptors and the cellular threshold for stimulation and clonal expansion. In order to understand this interaction in detail, it is necessary to study the structure of the lymphoid cell membrane and particularly the mode of attachment of its antibody and lectin receptors. Recent developments in the specific fractionation of lymphocytes and in the analysis of the structure and function of membrane probes such as lectins should help to ease this task.

A fuller understanding of the behavior and specificity of lymphocyte receptors and the mechanism of mitogenesis may not only help to solve one of the central problems of immunology, but also be of great importance for a general understanding of growth control and cellular interactions in other areas of cell biology. The pace of recent developments both in this field and in molecular immunology suggests that we can look forward to an exciting decade of research.

ACKNOWLEDGMENT

The work described here has been carried out largely by my colleagues, whose names will be found in association with mine in the references cited. I am grateful for the privilege of that association. Much of the work has received support from the National Institute of Health and the National Science Foundation. Portions of this lecture were presented in a Nobel Lecture, 1972, to be published under copyright by the Nobel Foundation.

REFERENCES

Andersson, J., Edelman, G. M., Möller, G., and Sjöberg, O. (1972a). *Eur. J. Immunol.* **2**, 233.

Andersson, J., Möller, G. and Sjöberg, O. (1972b). *Cellular Immunol.* **4**, 381.

Berggård, I., and Bearn, A. G. (1968). *J. Biol. Chem.* **243**, 4095.

Bernier, G. M. and Fanger, M. W. (1972). *J. Immunol.* **109**, 407.

Burnet, F. M. (1959). "The Clonal Selection Theory of Acquired Immunity." Vanderbilt Univ. Press, Nashville, Tennessee.

Cold Spring Harbor Symposium (1967). *Antibodies, Cold Spring Harbor Symp. Quant. Biol.* **32**.

Cunningham, B. A., Pflumm, M. N., Rutishauser, U., and Edelman, G. M. (1969). *Proc. Nat. Acad. Sci. U.S.* **64**, 997.

Cunningham, B. A., Gottlieb, P. D., Pflumm, M. N., and Edelman, G. M. (1971). *In* "Progress in Immunology" (B. Amos, ed.), p. 3. Academic Press, New York.

Cunningham, B. A., Wang, J. L., Berggård, I., and Peterson, P. A. (1973). *Biochemistry* **12**, 4811.

Davies, D. R., Sarma, V. R., Labaw, L. W., Silverton, E. W., and Terry, W. D. (1971). In "Progress in Immunology" (B. Amos, ed.), p. 25. Academic Press, New York.

Edelman, G. M. (1970). *Biochemistry* **9**, 3197.

Edelman, G. M. (1971). *Ann. N.Y. Acad. Sci.* **190**, 5.

Edelman, G. M., and Gall, W. E. (1969). *Annu. Rev. Biochem.* **38**, 415.

Edelman, G. M., Olins, D. E., Gally, J. A., and Zinder, N. D. (1963). *Proc. Nat. Acad. Sci. U.S.* **50**, 753.

Edelman, G. M., Cunningham, B. A., Gall, W. E., Gottlieb, P. D., Rutishauser, U., and Waxdal, M. J. (1969). *Proc. Nat. Acad. Sci. U.S.* **63**, 78.

Edelman, G. M., Rutishauser, U., and Millette, C. F. (1971). *Proc. Nat. Acad. Sci. U.S.* **68**, 2153.

Edelman, G. M., Cunningham, B. A., Reeke, G. N., Jr., Becker, J. W., Waxdal, M. J., and Wang, J. L. (1972). *Proc. Nat. Acad. Sci. U.S.* **69**, 2580.

Franěk, F., and Nezlin, R. S. (1963). *Biokhimia* **28**, 193.

Fanger, M. W., Hart, D. A., Wells, J. V., and Nisonoff, A. (1970). *J. Immunol.* **105**, 1484.

Gall, W. E., and D'Eustachio, P. G. (1972). *Biochemistry* **11**, 4621.

Gally, J. A., and Edelman, G. M. (1970). *Nature (London)* **227**, 341.

Gally, J. A., and Edelman, G. M. (1972). *Annu. Rev. Genet.* **6**, 1.

Gowans, J. L., Humphrey, J. H., and Mitchison, N. A. (1971). *Proc. Roy. Soc. Ser. B* **176**, No. 1045, 369.

Greaves, M. F., and Bauminger, S. (1972). *Nature (London) New Biol.* **235**, 67.

Greaves, M. F., and Janossy, G. (1972). *In* "Cell Interactions," Proc. Third Lepetit Colloquium (L. G. Silvestri, ed.), p. 143. North-Holland Publ., Amsterdam.

Grubb, R. (1956). *Acta Pathol. Microbiol. Scand.* **39**, 195.

Grubb, R. (1970). "The Genetic Markers of Human Immunoglobulins." Springer-Verlag, Berlin, Heidelberg, and New York.

Gunther, G. R., Wang, J. L., Yahara, I., Cunningham, B. A., and Edelman, G. M. (1973). *Proc. Nat. Acad. Sci. U.S.* **70**, 1012.

Haber, E. (1964). *Proc. Nat. Acad. Sci. U.S.* **52**, 1099.

Hadden, J. W., Hadden, E. M., Haddox, M. K., and Goldberg N. D. (1972). *Proc. Nat. Acad. Sci. U.S.* **69**, 3024.

Hill, R. L., Delaney, R., Fellows, R. R., Jr., and Lebovitz, H. E. (1966). *Proc. Nat. Acad. Sci. U.S.* **56**, 1762.

Hilschmann, N., and Craig, L. C. (1965). *Proc. Nat. Acad. Sci. U.S.* **53**, 1403.

Hood, L., Gray, W. R., Sanders, B. G., and Dreyer, W. J. (1967). *Cold Spring Harbor Symp. Quant. Biol.* **32**, 133.

Inbar, D., Hachman, J., and Givol, D. (1972). *Proc. Nat. Acad. Sci. U.S.* **69**, 2659.

Inbar, M., Ben-Bassat, H., and Sachs, L. (1972). *Proc. Nat. Acad. Sci. U.S.* **68**, 2748.

Jerne, N. K. (1955). *Proc. Nat. Acad. Sci. U.S.* **41**, 849.

Jerne, N. K., Nordin, A. A., and Henry, C. (1963). *In* "Cell Bound Antibodies" (B. Amos and H. Koprowski, eds.), p. 109. Wistar Inst. Press, Philadelphia, Pennsylvania.

184   GERALD M. EDELMAN

Kehoe, J. M., and Fougereau, M. (1970). *Nature* (*London*) **224**, 1212.
Landsteiner, K. (1945). "The Specificity of Serological Reactions," 2nd ed. Harvard Univ. Press, Cambridge, Massachusetts.
Mäkelä, O., and Cross, A. W. (1970). *Progr. Allergy* **14**, 145.
Milstein, C. (1967). *Nature* (*London*) **216**, 330.
Nobel Symposium (1967). *Gamma Globulins, Proc. Nobel Symp. 3rd 1967.*
Nakamuro, K., Tanigaki, N., and Pressman, D. (1973). *Proc. Nat. Acad. Sci. U.S.* **70**, 2863.
Nossal, G. J. V., and Ada, G. L. (1971). "Antigens, Lymphoid Cells and the Immune Response." Academic Press, New York.
Olins, D. E., and Edelman, G. M. (1964). *J. Exp. Med.* **119**, 789.
Oudin, J. (1956). *C. R. Acad. Sci.* **242**, 2489, 2606.
Oudin, J. (1960). *J. Exp. Med.* **112**, 125.
Peterson, P. A., Cunningham, B. A., Berggård, I., and Edelman, G. M. (1972). *Proc. Nat. Acad. Sci. U.S.* **69**, 1697.
Peterson, P. A., Rask, L., and Lindblom, J. B. (1974). *Proc. Nat. Acad. Sci. U.S.* **71**, 35.
Poljak, R. J., Amzel, L. M., Avey, H. P., Becka, L. N., and Nisonoff, A. (1972). *Nature* (*London*) *New Biol.* **235**, 137.
Press, E. M., and Hogg, N. M. (1969). *Nature* (*London*) **223**, 807.
Rutishauser, U., and Edelman, G. M. (1972). *Proc. Nat. Acad. Sci. U.S.* **69**, 3774.
Rutishauser, U., Millette, C. F., and Edelman, G. M. (1972). *Proc. Nat. Acad. Sci. U.S.* **69**, 1596.
Sharon, N., and Lis, H. (1972). *Science* **177**, 949.
Singer, S. J., and Doolittle, R. E. (1966). *Science* **153**, 13.
Siskind, G. P. and Benacerraf, B. (1969). *Advan. Immunol.* **10**, 1.
Smithies, O., and Poulik, M. D. (1972). *Science* **175**, 187.
Taylor, R. B., Duffus, P. H., Raff, M. C., and DePetris, S. (1971). *Nature* (*London*) *New Biol.* **233**, 225.
Wikler, M., Kohler, H., Shinoda, T., and Putnam, F. W. (1969). *Science* **163**, 75.
World Health Organization (1964). *Bull. W.H.O.,* **30**, 447.
Wu, T. T., and Kabat, E. A. (1970). *J. Exp. Med.* **132**, 211.
Yahara, I., and Edelman, G. M. (1972). *Proc. Nat. Acad. Sci. U.S.* **69**, 608.
Yasmeen, D., Ellerson, J. R., Dorrington, K. J., and Painter, R. H. (1973). *J. Immunol.* **110**, 1706.

PLASMA LIPOPROTEINS AND APOLIPOPROTEINS*

DONALD S. FREDRICKSON

Public Health Service, National Institutes of Health, Bethesda, Maryland

I. INTRODUCTION

THE plasma lipoproteins have been dealt with previously in the Harvey Lectures. Tiselius made passing reference to them in 1939 as vaguely defined substances that could be partially separated by electrophoresis (164). Fifteen years later Oncley described some of the studies at Harvard on these macromolecular systems (119). This work, combined with contemporary achievements at Berkeley (57), were to lay down the nomenclature and basic definitions that have structured further exploration until today. In this period of the early 1950's there was considerable perception of the physical properties and lipid composition of the plasma lipoproteins, but not yet an inkling of the number and nature of the proteins that afford them at least stability, if not solubility, in water. Detailed knowledge of the *apolipoproteins,* or protein constituents of plasma lipoproteins, is both relatively recent and rapidly increasing. This lecture will be built about some of this information.

It is my intent to lay out the scattered knowledge of plasma apolipoproteins and try to reconstruct some of the grand design by which they have evolved to effect lipid transport in extracellular fluid. Some of the information that I will describe in more detail has been obtained in Bethesda by a group of talented associates with whom it has been an immeasurable pleasure to collabo-

---

* Lecture delivered February 15, 1973.

rate.* These contributions obtain their meaning only when inter-
woven with the much greater, but quite incomplete, fabric that
has been developed by a large number of workers in many laboratories (49, 113, 114, 134, 143).

Studies of the plasma apolipoproteins hold considerable promise. One suspects that they will someday provide valuable infer-
ences to the structure and function of other lipoproteins that
carry out exclusively intracellular functions, including the maintenance of integrity of membranes and the regulation of activity
of certain enzymes. This possibility enhances the value of studying
plasma lipoproteins as models of other less accessible lipid–protein
associations. Presently, data on apoproteins are having heavy impact on research in plasma lipoproteins. They have created a small
crisis in nomenclature. More importantly, they have forced
changes in the traditional ways of thinking about lipoproteins.
For years it has been customary to begin lectures on the subject
with a serene landscape composed of the four lipoprotein classes
of chylomicrons, VLDL,† LDL,† and HDL.† The heterogeneity
of these family lines is now beyond dispute, and arguments have
been advanced for reclassification of lipoproteins in terms of their
apoproteins (2–4). There is much that argues for this point of
view; some modifications are due. What is lacking today is enough
information to establish new conventions that are certain to
endure.

The Secretion and Transport of Triglycerides in Relation to Plasma Lipoproteins

The plasma lipoprotein pattern in man at birth is much like
that of fasting adults in most other mammalian species (44).
There is mainly HDL, lesser amounts of LDL, and little VLDL.

---

* This includes particularly the work of the following present and past
members of the Molecular Disease Branch, NHLI: Drs. Thomas Bersot, David
W. Bilheimer, H. Bryan Brewer, W. Virgil Brown, Schlomo Eisenberg, Antonio
M. Gotto, Peter N. Herbert, Ronald M. Krauss, John C LaRosa, Robert I.
Levy, Samuel E. Lux, Robert W. Mahley, Richard S. Shulman, and Ms.
Kathryn John.

† VLDL, very low density or pre-β lipoproteins; LDL, low density or β-lipo-
proteins; HDL, high density or α-lipoproteins.

Beginning at birth a dramatic transformation occurs over the next month of life. HDL concentrations rise somewhat, but LDL greatly increase to become the dominant lipoprotein class; VLDL increase and, transiently after fat feedings, chylomicrons also are present in appreciable quantities. A portion of the postnatal rise in LDL is regulated by the amount of sterol and saturated fat in the infant diet (56). But the major influence on the changes in lipoprotein pattern appears to be a great increase in triglyceride transport. This begins at the moment of extrauterine existence (endogenous triglyceride transport in VLDL) and is soon augmented with each feeding of fat (exogenous triglyceride transport in chylomicrons).

Triglyceride transport is not the only function of plasma lipoproteins, but these esters represent the bulk of cargo transferred through human plasma in the course of a day. I will center most of my discussion and speculations around this process.

Schumaker and Adams have called the chylomicrons and VLDL *micellar* lipoproteins (<30% protein), and LDL and HDL *pseudomolecular* lipoproteins. X-ray diffraction studies have suggested, however, that HDL may also be micelles. The chylomicrons and VLDL are particles of a diameter ranging from about 300 Å to more than 1000 Å. They are quite arbitrarily separated in the ultracentrifuge by differences in flotation rate (the traditional boundary between VLDL and chylomicrons being S_f 400), and can also be partly distinguished by electrophoretic migration (97) and flocculation techniques (17, 31). The physiologist's operational distinction is to take all fat away from the diet for a few days. The resulting plasma or lymph lipoproteins having density <1.006 are considered to be transporting only endogenous glycerides and are called VLDL.

The apoproteins of the lipoproteins defined as VLDL have been the subject of intensive study. Only a single published study of chylomicron apoproteins, by Kostner and Holasek, has appeared (86). It contains no certain qualitative differences between chylomicron and VLDL apoproteins, but I will deal only with VLDL apoproteins about which much more is known. Endogenous glyceride secretion is known to occur from both the liver and the small intestine (118, 169). The processes involved, in-

cluding their regulation, may not be identical in both organs
(167).

II. Very Low Density Lipoproteins

We may begin the life-story of VLDL by panning in, through
the lens of the electron microscope, on the Golgi apparatus in
the hepatocyte (Fig. 1). Under appropriate conditions, one can
see here lipid-rich particles, having a diameter of 300–1000 Å,
filling the tubules and vesicles (65, 109, 110). These are VLDL,
or their most proximate precursors, that shortly will be secreted
into the circulation (65, 80, 108, 109, 163). The particles have
been assembled to remove triglycerides that would otherwise
burden the liver. Their major destination is the adipose tissue.
The triglycerides are accumulating as the result of net synthesis
controlled by a number of operators, some of which are also
illustrated in Fig. 1. A major determinant is the metabolism of
free fatty acids (FFA) (45, 69). When FFA are delivered to

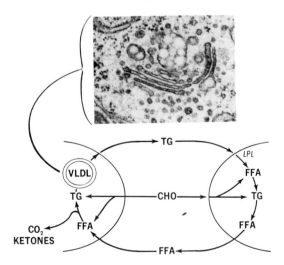

Fig. 1. Schematic representation of some elements related to endogenous
triglyceride metabolism. TG, triglycerides; FFA, free fatty acids; LPL, lipoprotein lipase; CHO, carbohydrate. Photograph of very low density lipoproteins
(VLDL) in liver Golgi apparatus by courtesy of Dr. R. W. Mahley.

the liver in amounts greater than the capacity for their oxidation, the excess is mainly returned to adipose tissue storage sites as "endogenous" triglycerides. Glucose, in excess of that required to meet oxidative demand or to maintain the hepatic supply of glycogen, is also converted to triglycerides and similarly transshipped. VLDL therefore represent an important system for maintenance of *caloric homeostasis*. VLDL particles may also be observed in the Golgi apparatus of the epithelial cells in the small intestine (107). Within the intestinal Golgi apparatus two populations of different-sized lipoproteins are visible (107). One of about 250–800 Å in diameter, presumably VLDL, is usually kept well segregated from particles greater than 800 Å, which sccm to represent chylomicrons. These latter will bear dietary glycerides into the intestinal lymph and, from there, to the systemic circulation.

The packing of triglycerides for transport is complex. The materials include free and esterified cholesterol, several phospholipid classes, and traces of other lipids. At least four proteins, and perhaps many others in small quantities, form part of the "envelope." We do not really know whether all these components represent one complex aggregation of proteins and lipids or clusters of different and independent lipoproteins, how they are held together, or what regulates their supply and assemblage under the variable scheduling that characterizes triglyceride transport. The collection of Golgi bodies being an arduous task, and thus far impossible in man, the answers to some of these questions have been sought mainly in the plasma. Here large amounts of lipoproteins can be collected, taken apart, and, with some success, partially reassembled.

A. Plasma VLDL

Particles in the Golgi apparatus bear strong physical (65, 109, 110) and chemical (110) resemblance to plasma VLDL (Fig. 2), but perhaps we should insert a caveat or two at this point. "Normal VLDL" have been little studied in man. Hyperlipoproteinemic patients, who have something wrong with delivery or removal of lipoproteins, make more efficient donors for collection

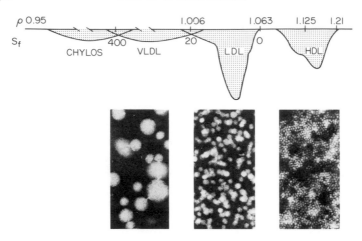

FIG. 2. Schematic representation of the four major plasma lipoprotein families, visualized as schlieren patterns obtained in the analytical ultracentrifuge, and the appearance of negatively stained very low density, (VLDL), low density (LDL), and high density (HDL) lipoproteins under the electron microscope. Chylos = chylomicrons. Micrographs by courtesy of Dr. R. W. Mahley.

of these particles. Some of them may have contributed abnormal VLDL to the pools that have been characterized and the "standards" may be biased. Indeed, chemical differences in apoproteins from different donors have been reported (140, 152), and we have seen much variation in their quantity, but it will take some time to straighten out differences between people and artifacts of analysis. It also may be important that most VLDL and other lipoproteins captured for chemical characterization have been "washed" by repeated ultracentrifugation after their initial isolation. Dr. Herbert in our laboratory has been assiduously examining the effects of washing VLDL from plasma. His results suggest that their textbook composition may deviate significantly from that of the "native" micelles. (75).

Whatever the vagaries introduced during their characterization, VLDL represent a collection of particles differing in flotation rates from S_f 20 to >400 and having molecular weights in the millions of daltons (113). When negatively stained, they appear spherical and vary greatly in size from about 300 to 1000 Å. The VLDL spectrum appears continuous in the analytical ultracentrifuge, but actually consists of many discrete and different-sized subpopulations. The larger particles (S_f 100–400) contain relatively more triglyceride and less protein than the smaller particles (68, 100, 101, 130). The triglyceride:protein ratio (w/w) in VLDL of S_f 100–400 is about 20:1, whereas it is about 5:1 in the molecules of S_f interval 20–60. The proportions of glycerides and protein change much more radically over the whole VLDL range than do the proportions of phospholipid to protein; the molar ratio of free cholesterol to phospholipid remains relatively constant (130). These differences will become more meaningful when VLDL catabolism is discussed later.

The "typical" composition of VLDL as shown in Fig. 3, therefore, represent an average for the collective content of all "endogenous" plasma lipoproteins which do not sediment at density 1.006 and which remain in flotation after repeated washing to eliminate "contaminants." Since we are primarily concerned with

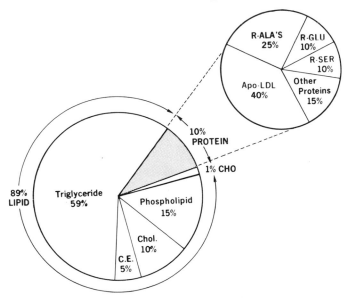

FIG. 3. Composition of very low density lipoproteins (VLDL) expressed in percentage of anhydrous weight. For fuller explanation, see text. C.E., cholesteryl esters; Chol., unesterified cholesterol; CHO, carbohydrate.

the VLDL apoproteins, it should be kept in mind that the relative proportions of those proteins shown in Fig. 3 also vary markedly from one end of the VLDL spectrum to the other (35).

B. VLDL Apoproteins (ApoVLDL)

Until about 15 years ago the chemical information about any of the apolipoproteins was limited to differences in immunochemical reactivity between LDL and HDL and different amino-terminal residues in the proteins isolated from them. In the late 1950's, several additional amino-terminal residues were detected in proteins isolated from VLDL (11, 127, 147, 148). Between 1964 and 1966 Gustafson et al. (62, 63) isolated three phospholipid-protein complexes from human VLDL and concluded that three different proteins were present. Two of these resembled, respectively, the protein moieties of HDL and LDL, which they called "apolipoproteins A and B." The third they called "apolipoprotein C." Between 1966 and 1969, Virgil Brown in our laboratory set out to purify "apoprotein C." He succeeded in isolating and partially characterizing three new apoproteins (24–26). One of these was also independently identified by Shore and Shore at the same time (150). The work of Gustafson et al. (63) was confirmed to the extent that the apoprotein characteristic of LDL was found to be the largest single component of apoVLDL (Fig. 3). However, only trace amounts of the major HDL or "A" apoprotein—at that time still considered to be a single polypeptide—were found (24).

1. Isolation of Apoproteins

Lipoproteins contain very little covalently bound lipid (38), and they can be delipidated fairly easily by exposing them to organic solvents. Polar solvents, such as mixtures of chloroform–methanol or ethanol–diethyl ether, are required to remove phospholipids, which are the most tenaciously bound. Most of the resulting apoproteins are soluble in aqueous buffers at or near neutral pH. The delipidated protein characteristic of LDL (called apoLDL or apo-B, see below), which is an important part of apoVLDL, is relatively insoluble. A variety of techniques are used to effect its solution (49); we routinely use a detergent (0.1 M sodium decyl sulfate) to dissolve all of the lipid-free apoproteins of VLDL in preparation for further purification.

2. Nomenclature of Apolipoproteins

It is necessary at this point to introduce some explanation of present-day nomenclature of the apoproteins. The Shores and ourselves have preferred to identify them according to their carboxy-terminal residues, hence the appellations apoLP-Glu, R-Glu, or apo-Glu, etc. (Table I). This system has been justifiably criticized. Mistakes have been made in assignment of carboxy-terminal residues (77, 85, 106). Two apoproteins have turned out to have the same terminal amino acid and must be called apo-Gln-I and apo-Gln-II. Perhaps polymorphic forms with different ultimate residues will be identified. Clearly a better permanent naming system will be required. Scanu proposes calling the apoproteins fractions III, IV, V, etc. (Table I) (142). This is a less committed method, but an oblique way to designate a protein like

TABLE I

THE APOLIPOPROTEINS

Nomenclature[a]	Special functions
Apo-Gln-I (apo A-I, R-Gln I, fraction III)	Activation of LCAT[b] (37)
Apo-Gln II (apo A-II, R-Gln II, fraction IV)	—
ApoLDL (apo B)	Essential for triglyceride secretion: (60)
ApoLP-Ser (apo C-I, fraction V)	Activation of LCAT? (53), activation of post-heparin LPL (51)
ApoLP-Glu (apo C-II, fraction V)	Activation of adipose tissue, postheparin and human milk LPL (51, 72, 92)
ApoLP-Ala (apo C-III, fraction V)	Activation of human milk LPL? (51, 72)

[a] For more complete listing of different terms that have been employed, see (49).
[b] LCAT, lecithin: cholesterol acyl transferase.

fraction IV, which is now generally agreed to be homogeneous (103, 139) and has already been sequenced (20). Fraction V, moreover (Table I), is at least 3 proteins, which at times require individual designation.

Potentially the best solution, because it uses the simplest designations, is that contained in the suggestions of Alaupovic and co-workers (4, 5). Adopting a historical viewpoint, they propose to identify "A, B, and C apoplipoproteins." "Apolipoprotein A" consists of two proteins called A-I and A-II; and "apolipoprotein C" consists of three proteins, C-I, C-II, C-III (Table I). There is present danger, too, in the adoption of this particular convention. As its authors have been among the first to point out (2), apoproteins may form independent lipoproteins. And lipoproteins which have the same density may not necessarily be intimately related in a genetic, or functional sense. I will later mention some evidence concerning possible infidelity, in genetic terms, of the A and C groupings. More importantly, some apoproteins remain to be identified, and it may prove difficult to fit them into a prematurely rigid framework. It behooves us to avoid, if we can, a repetition of the minor tragedies of nomenclatural sequence that make it difficult to remember the complement system or the blood-clotting factors.

For these reasons, I will continue here a habit of referring to the apolipoproteins mainly by their carboxy-terminal residues, as in Table I. The C-terminal residue(s) of the characteristic apoproteins in LDL are unknown, and hence the simple collective term, apoLDL or apoB will be used.

3.   Human ApoVLDL's

There is now general agreement that human VLDL contains at least four apoproteins (Fig. 3). The separation of VLDL apoproteins represented in Figs. 4 and 5 is similar to that reported by Brown et al. (24–26). The first fraction obtained in the void volume upon gel filtration in Sephadex G-100 or G-150 contains protein that is immunochemically identical to apoLDL (24, 58) (Fig. 5). The second and minor fraction is inhomogeneous and incompletely characterized. The third fraction contains three major proteins of relatively low molecular weight. They can be

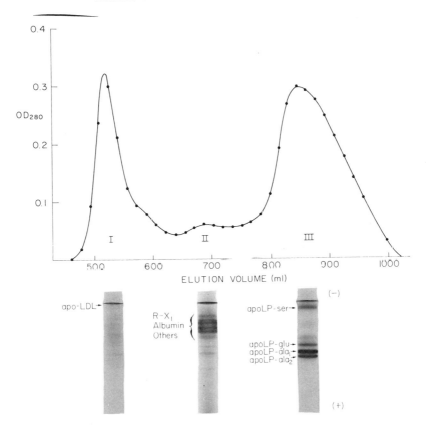

FIG. 4. Preliminary separation (Sephadex G-200) of delipidated (VLDL) apoproteins from human plasma similar to that described elsewhere (24–26). The contents of fractions I, II, and III are illustrated in the polyacrylamide gels displayed below them. In this and subsequent figures, the electrophoreses were carried out at pH 9.4 in 10% gels containing urea.

separated into five major peaks on ion exchange chromatography (Fig. 5). Optimal separation is obtained in the presence of urea.

a. *ApoLP-Ser.* The first peak eluted from DEAE represents apo-Ser, a protein having a molecular weight of 6550 (26, 157). We made an error in the original assignment (24, 77) of its carboxyl-terminal residue, and apo-Ser (77) also appears in the literature variously as R-Val or apoLP-Val or, in the original

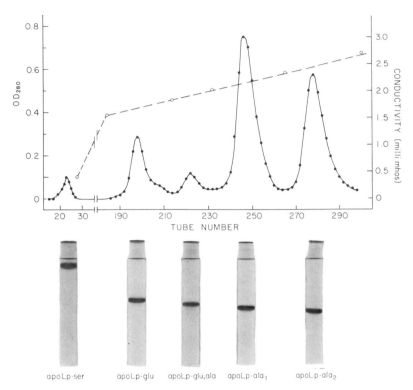

FIG. 5. Purification of fraction III (Fig. 4) by DEAE chromatography, as modified after Brown *et al.* (24, 25). Polyacrylamide gels run as in Fig. 4. The broken line indicates the elution gradient.

report as Dl (24). It contains threonine at the amino terminus. Apo-Ser contains a high content of lysine (16 moles percent) (Table II), which doubtless accounts for its relatively high solubility at acid pH and little mobility on alkaline polyacrylamide gel electrophoresis (Fig. 5). It contains no histidine, tyrosine, or cysteine (Table II); no carbohydrate has been obtained on fairly exhaustive analyses. At pH 7.5, the lipid-free protein appears to contain a relatively large amount of helical configuration (26).

 b. ApoLP-Ala. The last two peaks from the DEAE column (Fig. 5) contain a protein having alanine as the carboxy-terminal residue. Its polymorphism is due to differences in sialic acid con-

TABLE II

AMINO ACID COMPOSITION[a] OF THE APOLIPOPROTEINS

Amino acid	Apo-Gln-I A-I	Apo-Gln-II A-II	ApoLDL B	Ap-Ser C-I	Apo-Glu C-II	Apo-Ala C-III
Lys	9	12	8	16	7	8
His	2	0	2	0	0	1
Arg	7	0	3	5	1	3
Asp/Asn	9	4	11	9	7	9
Thr	4	8	7	5	10	6
Ser	6	8	9	12	11	14
Glu/Gln	20	19	12	16	17	13
Pro	4	5	5	2	5	3
Gly	4	4	5	2	3	4
Ala	8	6	6	5	8	12
1/2-Cys	0	1	1	0	0	0
Val	5	8	5	4	5	8
Met	1	1	2	2	2	3
Ile	0	1	5	5	1	0
Leu	17	10	12	11	10	6
Tyr	3	5	3	0	6	3
Phe	3	5	5	5	3	3
Trp	2	0	N.D.	2	3	4
PCA	—	1	—	—	—	—
Glu/Gln	—	8/7	—	7/2	—	5/5
Asp/Asn	—	2/1	—	4/1	—	7/0
MW	28,000	17,380	?	6,550	9,000	8,764

[a] Moles percent.

tent (26). The first eluted peak, apo-Ala$_1$ (apoC-III-1) contains 1 mole of sialic acid per mole of protein. The second peak, apo-Ala$_2$ (apoC-III-2), migrates faster on polyacrylamide and contains 2 moles of sialic acid per mole of protein. Isolation of an asialo form of apo-Ala (apo-Ala$_0$) from plasma VLDL has been reported (9). The sialic acid is probably the terminal member of a short glycosidic chain which also contains equimolar amounts of galactose and galactosamine (74). This single chain is attached to a threonine six residues removed from the carboxyl-terminal amino acid. Apo-Ala contains no cysteine, and we find no isoleucine, although a "polymorphic form" containing the latter amino acid has been reported (151). The secondary structure of delipidated apo-Ala is primarily random coil with a small contribution of α-helix (26, 156). Its anhydrous molecular weight is 8764 (22). VLDL samples usually contain about three times as much apo-Ala as apo-Ser. Apo-Ala, in its several polymorphic forms, constitutes the fourth most abundant apolipoprotein in human plasma, but ranks in amount far below apoLDL and the two major HDL apoproteins.

     c. Primary Structure of Apo-Ala and Apo-Ser. Completion of the covalent structural analysis of apo-Ala was reported by Brewer *et al.* in 1971 (22) and that of apo-Ser by Shulman *et al.* (157) in 1972. These were the first two among the apolipoproteins to have been so analyzed. Their amino acid sequences are illustrated in Fig. 6. Admittedly, we hoped that, as each partial sequence was revealed, it would include segments notably rich in aromatic or other less polar residues that were obvious sites of hydrophobic bonding with the aliphatic chains of the phospholipids or neutral esters, presumably the raison d'être of an apolipoprotein. Earlier analyses had shown that plasma apolipoproteins contained an amino acid composition which was not less polar in the aggregate than those of other plasma proteins, and more polar than in some cellular proteins (67, 111). These comparisons had two weaknesses. The number of "glutamic acids" that were actually amides was not known, and the massed data could conceal selective alignments of special importance. Exposure of the entire chains, however, has not given away the secret of lipid binding. One feature of the chains early interested us. This was the prominence of acid-base pairs, viz. adjacent pairing of Lys and Glu. Such pairs could form points of attachments for the basic and acidic components on a phospholipid such as phosphatidylcholine. The actual number of acid-base conjunctions in either apo-Ser or apo-Ala is not significantly different from the number expected from random distribution within chains having their amino acid compositions (Table III). Acid-base pairing of the degree observed is also not unique to apolipoproteins (21). Failure to perceive obvious bases for lipid binding in the primary structure of apoproteins may mean that their conformation provides the

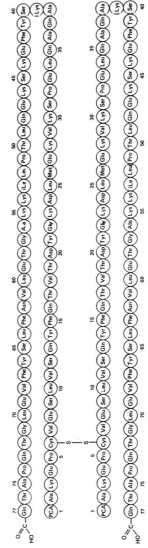
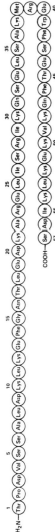

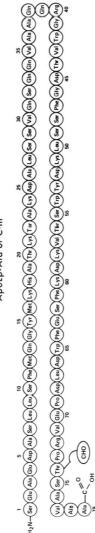

FIG. 6. The amino acid sequences of human apo-Ser (157), apo-Ala (22), and apo-Gln-II (20).

TABLE III

PAIRING OF ACIDIC AND BASIC RESIDUES IN APOLIPOPROTEINS[a]

	Apo-Ala	Apo-Ser	Apo-Gln-II
Total residues	79	57	77
Acidic	11	11	10
Basic	8	12	9
Other	60	34	58
Expected conjunctions ± SD	2.2 ± 2.0	4.6 ± 1.9	2.1 ± 2.4
Observed conjunctions	4	7	5

[a] Analyses by Dr. R. S. Shulman and Dr. M. Gail of data available in Table II and Fig. 6.

hydrophobic or hydrophilic surfaces important for binding to lipids.

d. Relationship of Apo-Ser and Apo-Ala. The availability of the primary structures of the apoproteins permits other comparisons that may shed light on their relationships and evolution. A number of computer methods have been developed for detection of relationships between proteins from their amino acid sequences. Barker and Dayhoff have quite recently examined the available sequences of the apolipoproteins, using their "mutation matrix," which scores the amino acid alignments of different chains, taking into account the nature of the genetic code, the rates of mutation at the nucleotide level, and natural selection (14). The method determines the highest possible score for any alignment (including gaps) of two protein sequences. This score is then compared with the highest possible scores obtained by aligning pairs of randomized sequences having the same amino acid composition as the two real sequences. The alignment score is expressed in units of standard deviation from the mean of random scores.

By this technique, apo-Ser and the first portion (residues 1–59) of apo-Ala appear very probably to be distantly related (13) (Table IV). This strongly implies that they have arisen from a common ancestral gene. Possibly they began as proteins of similar length and during their divergent evolution apo-Ala was elon-

TABLE IV

RELATIONSHIPS OF HUMAN APOLIPOPROTEINS

Sequence 1	Sequence 2	Alignment score[a]	p
Apo-Ser	Apo-Ala (1–59)	4.56	$<10^{-5}$
Apo-Ser	Apo-Gln-II (1–59)	4.66	$<10^{-5}$
Apo-Gln-II (1–59)	Apo-Ala (1–59)	3.66	$<10^{-3}$
Apo-Gln-II	Apo-Ala	3.46	$<10^{-3}$

[a] Alignment scores (in SD units) were obtained using the mutation data matrix of Barker and Dayhoff (14) for comparison of complete sequence of apo-Ser and shortened or complete sequences of apo-Ala and apo-Gln-II. The p value (derived from 270 random runs in each comparison) is the calculated probability that the similarities in amino acid sequence would occur by chance. Data were kindly supplied by Dr. Winona Barker (13).

gated and acquired a glycosidyl side chain near its carboxyl terminus. The alignment score for apo-Ser and the last 59 residues of apo-Ala is not different from that expected from random distribution of the amino acids present (13).

Thus, these two apoproteins, considered in the conceptual scheme of Alaupovic et al. to be two of a special group of "C-apoproteins" (4), have a probable genetic relationship consistent with their appearance together in common portions of the density spectrum of plasma lipoproteins. How closely they may be related functionally remains to be determined.

e. *Apo-Glu.* The primary structure of the third protein isolated in fraction III obtained by Sephadex chromatography of apoVLDL (Fig. 5) has not yet been reported. Because there is evidence that it may have an important and possibly unique function, and yet seems to be a fairly constant companion of the other two proteins of lower molecular weight, the sequence of apo-Glu [apo C-II (4)] will afford opportunity for some further interesting comparisons.

Apo-Glu is similar to apo-Ala in molecular weight ($\sim$9000) (26); they have the same amino-terminal residue (serine), and similar proportions of lysine and aromatic amino acids (Table II). Like both apo-Ser and apo-Ala, apo-Glu contains no cysteine, and is relatively rich in serine and glutamic acid/glutamine residues. Apo-Glu is difficult to purify (77), but we have not detected any glycosidic residues in the molecule. Optical measurements of lipid-free apo-Glu do not suggest much ordered secondary structure (151).

f. The ApoLDL in VLDL. The largest single protein component of apoVLDL is called "apoLDL" in Fig. 3 and related illustrations. ApoLDL is the only (66), or almost the only (5, 93), apoprotein in the LDL class of lipoproteins, the bulk of which are normally isolated between the densities of 1.019 and 1.063 (S_f 0–12). In the adult human male, the high concentration of LDL alone is sufficient to make apoLDL the commonest apoprotein in plasma.

Through its prominence among the apoproteins, and its relative insolubility after delipidation and resistance to characterization, its homogeneity are subjects of disagreement. The chemical nature of apoLDL has been probed in many studies, summarized elsewhere (5, 49, 59, 81, 111, 140, 141, 150, 161); it will not serve my purpose to expand much upon them here. The size of the protein and its homogeneity remain in disagreement. Tanford and co-workers have recently concluded that apoLDL is a single protein having a minimal molecular weight of about 300,000 (161). To others it has appeared to be an associating system of monomers and polymers of the same basic subunit with molecular weight of about 30,000 (121, 141). Still others have concluded that apoLDL may be a heterogeneous complex of several proteins (30, 81, 150, 151). ApoLDL is a glycoprotein (111); its glycosidic residue(s) includes sialic acid (160). All in all, what is known about apoLDL suggests that it is a membrane protein being extruded from the cell with triglycerides and other lipids.

As isolated in the LDL class over the S_f interval of 0–20, apoLDL exists in lipoproteins having molecular weights of from 2 to over 3×10^6 (100). The proportion of protein to lipid varies inversely with the S_f value. In LDL of S_f 3.5–4.5, which represent the subpopulation near the maximum of total LDL concentration, the apoprotein constitutes about 25% of the dry weight of these lipoproteins. Compared to VLDL, the lipid present includes much less glyceride (about 8% of total lipids) and somewhat more cholesteryl esters. The ratio of total cholesterol to phospholipids increases going from VLDL to LDL owing to a disproportionate increase in esterified cholesterol (114). Small amounts of the "C-apoproteins" have been reported to be present in isolates of LDL (5, 93).

g. *Other VLDL Apoproteins.* In Fig. 3, about 15% of the VLDL complement of apoproteins is left unassigned. Part of this represents still poorly characterized proteins first reported by Shore and Shore (151, 155). Their "R-X₁" is contained mainly in the fraction II obtained by gel filtration (Fig. 4) and is known to be unusually rich in arginine and glutamic acid. A second "R-X₂" is believed to contain high proportions of serine, glycine, and glutamic acid. No other nomenclature has been assigned to these proteins.

One of the older theories about the triglyceride-rich lipoproteins is that they also contain significant amounts of major HDL apoproteins (apoLP-A). This has been based on peptide fingerprints identified as apoA in VLDL (63) and immunochemical recognition of HDL apoproteins in partially delipidated VLDL (83, 95, 120). In much earlier work (49) and in one quite recent study (86) major HDL apoproteins have similarly been identified in chylomicrons. The conventional methods for isolating VLDL apoproteins employed today yield a small amount of reactivity to antiserums directed against major HDL apoproteins (5). It is mainly located in the Sephadex fraction II (Fig. 4), but only traces of these antigens are recovered. It may be that there is selective loss of HDL-apoproteins from VLDL as they are washed in the ultracentrifuge. Herbert (75) has obtained evidence that this is so, although there is proportionally a much greater loss of apoLDL (ApoB) from VLDL as such washing proceeds. I will have occasion to refer again to the question of the HDL apoproteins in connection with VLDL. Rephrased, the question becomes: Which of the proteins of lipoprotein complexes that become associated with VLDL or chylomicrons during their residence in the cell or passage through the lymph or plasma are essential for transport and metabolism of triglyceride, and which may simply be "going along for the ride?" What is known of the comparative biochemistry of VLDL suggests that apoLDL and the "C-proteins" have always had a function in triglyceride transport.

4. ApoVLDL in Other Species

Plasma VLDL from the rat (16) and dog have a complement of apoproteins very similar to that in man (Fig. 7). All contain

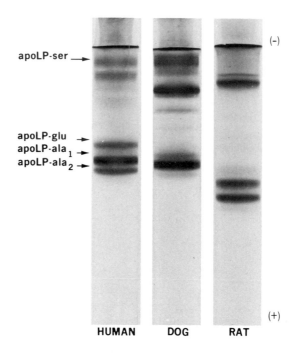

apoLP-ser

apoLP-glu
apoLP-ala$_1$
apoLP-ala$_2$

(-)

(+)

HUMAN   DOG   RAT

FIG. 7.   Polyacrylamide gel patterns of very low density lipoprotein apoproteins in man, dog, and the rat. In the rat, the equivalent of apo-Ser is not stained well, but is in the same position as in man; the first two well-stained bands correspond to "fraction II" proteins (Fig. 4); the lower two heavy bands are homologs of human apo-Ala, and the equivalent of apo-Glu (the lipase activator) comigrates with the uppermost of these bands.

apoLDL as a major fraction, and the equivalents of apo-Ser, the several forms of apo-Ala, and apo-Glu are all recognizable. So is a band on polyacrylamide gel tentatively identified as "R-X$_1$." Comparisons of patterns suggest that "R-X$_1$" may be the apoprotein described by Eder, Rombauer, and Roheim (33) as capable of promoting triglyceride release from the rat liver.

At least three of the low molecular weight apoproteins and the apoLDL in rat plasma VLDL have also been identified in VLDL obtained from rat liver Golgi apparatus (108), in "liposomes" obtained from rat liver (122), and in VLDL released from rat liver or small intestine during perfusion of the isolated organs (167) (Fig. 8).

When provided with labeled amino acid, the isolated liver releases into a perfusate (containing plasma) lipoproteins in the VLDL, LDL, and HDL density classes that contain labeled apoproteins (167). More recently Windmueller and Spaeth have developed a perfused small intestine system which emits lymph containing chylomicrons, VLDL, and HDL (170). These preparations have been used to advantage in exploring the synthesis or appearance of apoproteins during secretion of VLDL (167). Rat liver appears to be capable of synthesizing all the apoproteins in VLDL and HDL. However, during VLDL formation the liver more actively synthesizes apoLDL and the fraction II apoproteins (Fig. 4) than it does the rat equivalents of the "C-proteins." The rat small intestine produces VLDL that contain newly synthesized apoLDL and fraction II apoprotein(s), but the "C-proteins" do not appear to be made at this site. In the rat, at least, the VLDL secreted into intestinal lymph thus appear to obtain their complement of apo-Ser, -Glu and -Ala equivalents from HDL after the VLDL particles have emerged from the cell (167).

C. *Apoproteins in Metabolism of VLDL*

There have been other studies suggesting that protein synthesis is required for triglyceride secretion (129, 168, 169). Among the apoproteins that seem to be cellular or intravascular companions in HDL, at least two have been suggested to have important and special functions.

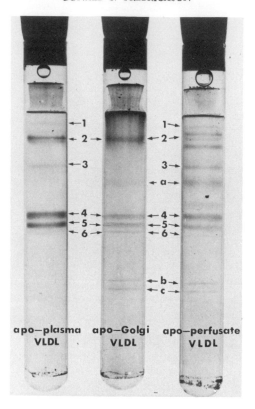

FIG. 8. Apoproteins in very low density lipoproteins (VLDL) from plasma, hepatocyte Golgi apparatus and perfusates of liver, all in the rat. Reprinted from Mahley *et al.* (108) with the permission of *Science*. The numbered bands correspond to the following homologs of human apolipoproteins: 1, apo-Ser; 2, R-X$_1$; 3, unassigned; 4 and 5, apo-Ala; and 6, unassigned. Copyright 1970 by the American Association for the Advancement of Science.

1. Essentiality of ApoLDL

Despite its resistance to full characterization, apoLDL has been the subject of many clinical or physiological experiments. Some of these take advantage of the fact that LDL is a powerful antigen, provoking antibodies that are directed to apoLDL and do not cross-react with any of the other major apoproteins (59). Thus there exist sensitive immunochemical techniques for detecting the presence of apoLDL in body fluids and tissues. One study conducted in a rare human mutant, abetalipoproteinemia, has permitted some theorizing concerning relative importance of the apoproteins in enabling triglycerides to be secreted from the intestine and liver (60).

In abetalipoproteinemia there is a life-long absence of plasma lipoproteins meeting the usual definitions of chylomicrons, VLDL, and LDL (46). The triglyceride content of plasma is thus vanishingly small, and ingested glycerides are stagnated in the villi of the small intestine. The remaining lipoproteins in the plasma in this disease have been shown to contain apo-Ser, apo-Glu, apo-Ala$_2$, and the two major HDL apoproteins. No trace of immunochemically reactive apoLDL was found (60). We have concluded that apoLDL is either not synthesized or not utilized in abetalipoproteinemia and that apoLDL must be elaborated anew with intracellular formation of each triglyceride particle. Someday this theory must be further tested by identification of "R-X$_1$" and some of the other vague fraction II apoproteins synthesized during VLDL secretion (167). It also remains to be determined whether the tissues contain apoLDL which is not being utilized, for when apoLDL is provided to patients with abetalipoproteinemia in infusions of plasma, it fails to stimulate triglyceride secretion (50, 96).

2. Apoproteins in VLDL Catabolism. Triglyceride Hydrolysis

The mechanisms whereby the triglyceride-rich particles are metabolized are the subject of a literature rich in detail and uncertainty. I will generalize what others have better summarized (69, 70, 145), only to provide a framework for present speculations about the participation and fate of the apoproteins in the process. First it will be useful to assume that the glycerides in chylomicrons and VLDL are removed by similar mechanisms, the rate processes probably being related rather to the size of the particles (124) than to the origin of the glyceride fatty acids. As the particles or micelles course through the capillary beds, their triglycerides are subject to attack by lipase(s) near the surface of the endothelial cells. Ester bonds are hydrolyzed and some products, including partial glycerides, are passed beyond into the tissues. Free fatty acids, glycerol, and "remnant lipoproteins" poorer in triglyceride content and altered in both lipid and apoprotein composition, continue on in the blood to other fates at different organ sites.

3. Lipoprotein Lipase "Activation"

The principal enzyme catalyzing triglyceride hydrolysis is lipoprotein lipase (EC 3.1.1.3). It is obtainable in high concentration in extracts of adipose tissue and also appears briefly in plasma when displaced by heparin. The postheparin lipase(s) in plasma are derived from both the plasma membrane of the liver and from extrahepatic sources (10, 89). The latter represents mainly lipoprotein lipase located in the capillary bed of adipose tissue. Korn showed many years ago that lipase extracted from adipose tissue was not able to hydrolyze triglyceride in artificial emulsions unless a small amount of plasma or plasma lipoproteins was present (84). Recently it has been demonstrated (51, 72, 92) that this requirement for lipoprotein lipase "activation" can be fulfilled by apo-Glu provided phospholipid is also present. Typical evidence of the enhancement of lipolysis by this apoprotein is shown in Fig. 9. Similar enhancement of lipolysis attributed to apo-Ala (72, 92) is, in our opinion, most likely due to contamination of apoprotein preparations with apo-Glu (23). Brown *et al.* have recently suggested that apo-Ala might selectively inhibit lipase activity and perhaps be a negative regulator of hydrolysis (23). We have found that many other lipoproteins diminish the stimulatory effect of apo-Glu (88). Ganesan *et al.* reported that apo-Ser is also an activator of lipolysis catalyzed by a partially purified fraction of lipase from postheparin plasma (51). This is contrary to our experience with either lipoprotein lipase (Fig. 9) or with the lipase released by heparin from the liver (10). In fact, we have not been able to demonstrate a stimulatory effect of any of the apoproteins on the hydrolysis of triglycerides by hepatic lipase (87).

Ganesan and co-workers also have described a separation of hyperglyceridemic patients into several groups on the basis of deficiency of an apo-Glu activated lipase and of an apo-Ser activated lipase (51). Some discrepancies in apoprotein-activation experiments will have to be cleared up before these results can

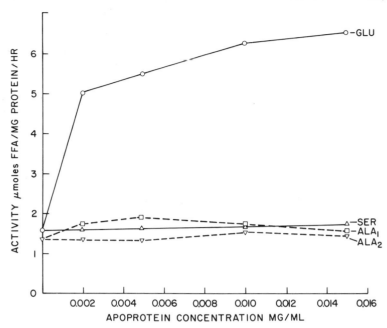

FIG. 9. The effect of various apoproteins on the hydrolysis of ^{14}C-labeled triolein by adipose tissue extracts of lipoprotein lipase. FFA, free fatty acids. Methodology described in (88).

be placed in perspective. We have examined the plasma lipoproteins of patients with familial hyperchylomicronemia (type I hyperlipoproteinemia) to determine whether this apoprotein might be missing or inactive; in this disease the heparin-releasable lipoprotein lipase activity is severely deficient and leads to massive hyperglyceridemia. It was found (76) (Fig. 10) that the chylomicron–VLDL fraction of plasma contained the usual VLDL apoproteins, and they proved to be capable of the usual activation of triglyceride hydrolysis *in vitro*. Apo-Ser (53) and one of the major HDL apoproteins (37) also appear to activate another enzyme (lecithin:cholesterol acyltransferase) whose functions I will mention further on.

It is reasonable that some apoproteins should have special functions in the metabolism of their lipid companions, but it is possi-

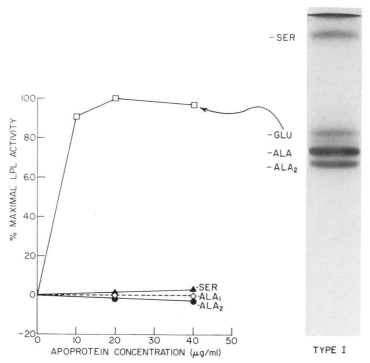

FIG. 10. Demonstration of the presence of the different "C-proteins" in the chylomicrons obtained from a patient with familial type I hyperlipoproteinemia and the capability of purified apo-Glu from this patient to activate lipoprotein lipase (LPL). Methods and results as described in (88) and (76).

ble, of course, that the intriguing "activation" of lipid hydrolases demonstrated *in vitro* is the nonspecific effect of a good emulsifier.

4. *Apoproteins and Lipoprotein Interconversions*

Useful information about lipoprotein metabolism can be obtained by labeling the apoproteins in lipoproteins and observing their behavior after reinjection in plasma. In our laboratory the metabolism of both LDL (90) and VLDL have been extensively studied in this way (18, 34, 35). Several phenomena of particular importance to this discussion have been dealt with. Foremost is the confirmation and refinement of other observations (36, 54,

116, 123, 166) that plasma LDL or lipoproteins of intermediate density arise from VLDL. Whether all LDL must originate as VLDL (and chylomicrons) is not yet known, but a sizable fraction of these lipoproteins appear to do so. Eisenberg *et al.* (35) have recently interpreted the sum of their labeling experiments added to older data as showing that essentially one VLDL molecule is converted to one LDL molecule. By the time a molecule of S_f 400 has been transformed to one having an S_f between 20 and 60 (a change in molecular weight from over 100×10^6 to a few million daltons) it has lost $>95\%$ of its glyceride complement and $>80\%$ of the associated cholesterol, phospholipids and apo-Ser, apo-Glu, and apo-Ala. Essentially all the apoLDL arrives at this "intermediate" stage, and all of it will progress to become LDL, through subsequent loss of some cholesterol and phospholipids and perhaps enrichment of the esterified sterol content at the expense of both phospholipid and free cholesterol. Normally, the intermediates (of density 1.006–1.019) seem to be in plasma for only a short time compared to the longer stay of the final LDL product of density 1.019 to 1.063.

5. Apoprotein Transfers

The other occurrence handily demonstrated with the labeled lipoproteins is the ready transfer from VLDL of the apoproteins -Glu, -Ala$_1$, -Ala$_2$, and probably apo-Ser (which, lacking tyrosine, is often poorly labeled with ^{125}I) to lipoproteins in the HDL density class (18, 34). This transfer also occurs *in vitro* at low temperatures, when it probably represents primarily exchange. During VLDL catabolism, there is net transfer of the "C proteins," probably with some cholesterol and phospholipid, to HDL. This is in accord with other evidence that the net amounts of HDL (71) and of the quantity of apo-Ala in HDL increase as triglycerides are removed from plasma (91). There is also net movement of the "C proteins" in the other direction (71). Havel *et al.* (71) have used the activation of lipoprotein lipase to quantify net transfer of apo-Glu from HDL to chylomicrons and VLDL during alimentary lipemia in man. Examination of polyacrylamide gel patterns of either triglyceride-rich lipoproteins or fat emulsions after incubation with HDL suggests that all

of the "C-apoproteins," migrate together during this exchange
(71). The evidence suggests therefore that HDL may assist in
conservation of the "C proteins," to permit them to be used more
than once in synthesis (167) and catabolism (70) of triglyceride-
rich lipoproteins.

6. Type III and Other Concepts

Such observations have added new dimensions to older theories
about the places of LDL and HDL in triglyceride metabolism.
That VLDL secretion may have major control over input into
the plasma pool of LDL has far-reaching clinical implications,
particularly in hyperlipoproteinemic states. One ill-defined genetic
abnormality in man, type III hyperlipoproteinemia (47), appears
to be due to mutation(s) involving the transformation of VLDL
to LDL. There is a topsy-turvy inversion of the usual concentrations of lipoproteins of S_f 0–12 (LDL) and S_f 12–60 (48).
In the normal state, the latter group of lipoproteins presumably
include the "intermediate" lipoproteins derived from VLDL (34,
35). In the patient with type III hyperlipoproteinemia, these intermediate lipoproteins have a high ratio of cholesterol to triglycerides and VLDL apoproteins in addition to apoLDL (73, 125).
This disease suggests that one or more unique steps govern the
conversion of "intermediates" to LDL. The search for the defect
in type III has ranged from deficient activity of a lipase of hereto-
fore unsuspected specificity (52) to a functionally defective apoprotein. The apoLDL in type III thus far appears to be identical
to the normal form (58).

III. High Density Lipoproteins

Revelation of the behavior of the VLDL apoproteins has
focused attention on the lipoproteins collectively called HDL or
α_1 lipoproteins, whose origins and functions have long been obscure. While it is now inferred that the HDL density class as
a whole provides a reservoir for VLDL apoproteins, the reasons
why there is such a large bulk of HDL, with a complex protein
moiety, have not yet been convincingly set forth.

The HDL are lipoproteins that float between d 1.063 and 1.210

g/ml. They are spherical macromolecules of a diameter that ranges between 40 and 140 Å (40, 42). When negatively stained they appear under the electron microscope like those shown in Fig. 2. Some have interpreted the micrographs as showing the existence of substructure, possibly representing aggregation of four or five or more subunits (40, 42). The calculated molecular weights of HDL range from about 170,000 to 400,000 (100). From the early days of ultracentrifugal fractionation, it has been conventional to divide HDL into two major subclasses: HDL_2 (mean hydrated density 1.09, $F_{1.20}$ 3.5–9) and HDL_3 (mean hydrated density 1.14 and $F_{1.20}$ 0–3.5) (100). A small HDL_1 fraction with a mean hydrated density of 1.05 g/ml is poorly understood and usually avoided in both collections and discussion of HDL. Beyond the traditional density limits of HDL, small amounts of lipoprotein are isolable, usually between densities 1.210 and 1.215 g/ml. These have been called very high density lipoproteins (VHDL) (6). Extensive studies (57) have indicated that the amounts of HDL_2 and HDL_3 vary independently, suggesting mixed populations under diverse control. Any division between these density subclasses is obviously arbitrary, however, and significant chemical differences are most likely to be perceptible at the outer extremes of the HDL distribution. Much of the work carried out relative to the HDL apoproteins has been carried out in pools containing both HDL_2 and HDL_3.

The composition of HDL shown in Fig. 11 is a rough average for human $HDL_2 + HDL_3$. The molecules of greater density will have proportionately more protein and less lipid. Extensive analyses of relatively minor variations in lipid composition of HDL fractions have been summarized elsewhere (113). The apoproteins are associated mainly with phospholipids and cholesterol; the content of glyceride is low.

A. HDL Apoproteins

Until relatively recently it was assumed that apoHDL consisted of a single protein subunit of molecular weight 21,000–31,000 that contained amino-terminal aspartic acid and carboxyl-terminal threonine (132, 147, 153). Heterogeneity had been suggested

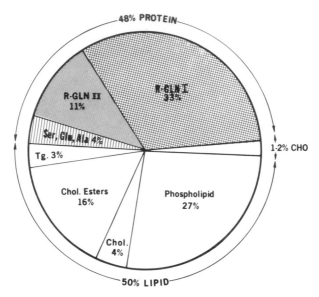

Fig. 11. Representation of the "average" composition of HDL. Chol. Esters, cholesteryl esters; CHO, carbohydrate; Chol., unesterified cholesterol; Tg., triglycerides.

by immunochemical studies (1, 12, 27, 94) and partial fractions (29, 94, 131, 138) but was difficult to confirm. In 1968, the Shores reported the purification and partial characterization of two different principal apoHDL components (149, 154). Using carboxypeptidase, they reported that one protein contained carboxy-terminal threonine, and the other carboxy-terminal glutamine. The latter had apparently been consistently overlooked by prior reliance on the technique of hydrazinolysis, which does not readily permit the identification of the amide. The presence of two major apoproteins was confirmed shortly thereafter by Scanu (142), Rudman (128), and Camejo (28) and their co-workers. It now appears, however, that the first of these apoproteins does not contain C-terminal threonine, but glutamine (85). The frequent references to "apoHDL-Thr" or "R-thr" in the literature therefore should now read apo-Gln-I, or apo-A-I (2), or fraction III (142). The more recently discovered apoprotein is called apo-Gln-II, apo-A-II (2) or fraction IV (142).

A wide variety of methods has been used in different laboratories for the isolation of apoproteins in HDL (49). In our experience satisfactory preparation of the largest number of components is best achieved by the combined use of gel filtration and ion exchange chromatography (Fig. 12). By this means, the yield of proteins from delipidated human HDL (HDL$_2$ + HDL$_3$) is roughly as follows. The largest component (65–75%) is apo-Gln-I; apo-Gln-II represents about 20–25%, and 5–10% are accounted for by apo-Ser, apo-Glu, and apo-Ala. It has not been demonstrated that the relative proportions of the C-proteins in HDL are the same as in VLDL. Both the mono- and disialylated forms of apo-Ala are present. There remains a small percentage of poorly characterized proteins, some of which have been described by Shore and Shore (151, 155). These include "R-X$_2$," the arginine-rich protein, and other minor proteins (150).

1. Apo-Gln-II

The smaller of what are called the "two major" HDL apo-proteins is better characterized despite its obscurity for so many years. Apo-Gln-II has a "blocked" amino terminus, insusceptible to attack by either the dansylation procedure or the Edman technique. After digestion with pyrrolidonecarboxylyl peptidase, pyrrolidone carboxylic acid (pyroglutamic acid) is recovered (PCA in Fig. 6).

The structure of human apo-Gln-II is unusual, perhaps unique, and was difficult to establish. As isolated from HDL, the protein appears to be about 17,000 molecular weight and contains two half-cystines. Lux et al. (103) consistently found that after reduction and treatment with iodoacetic acid a single protein is obtained which appears to be homogeneous by polyacrylamide gel electrophoresis, analytical gel-isoelectric focussing, or ion exchange chromatography. Multiple forms once obtained by Scanu et al. (135, 137) appear now to have been most likely due to carbamylation (139). The reduced and alkylated "monomer" contains one carboxymethyl cystine residue (20, 103, 139) and is immunochemically distinct from any of the other known apoproteins. Although it is difficult to rule out all possibility that sulfhydryl bonding occurs during purification procedures, it is highly probable that the basic subunit of apo-Gln-II in circulating HDL consists of

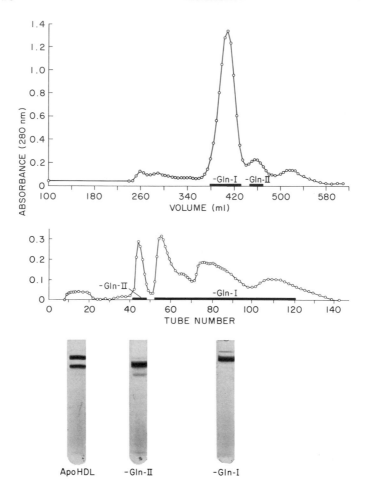

FIG. 12. Separation of delipidated high density lipoprotein (HDL) apoproteins by gel filtration (Sephadex G-200) (top) or by DEAE ion exchange chromatography (middle). The multiple peaks containing apo-Gln-I on DEAE all migrate to the same position after polyacrylamide gel electrophoresis (below). The peak following -Gln-II on Sephadex contains the "C-proteins." Techniques similar to those described by Lux *et al.* (103).

two identical monomers joined by a single disulfide bond (Fig. 6). On the basis of experiments in which the reduced and alkylated monomer has been subsequently cross-linked by treatment with dimethyl suberimidate, Scanu *et al.* have speculated that apo-Gln-II is present in circulating HDL as an aggregate of 4 protomeres with a molecular weight totaling about 32,000 (139). *a. Comparisons with Other Apoproteins.* The complete amino acid sequence of the monomer (calculated molecular weight 8690) was determined in Bethesda a few months ago by Brewer, Lux, Ronan, and John (20) (Fig. 6). Apo-Gln-II contains no carbohydrate; it also lacks histidine, arginine, and tryptophan (Table II). Like apo-Ser, it is relatively rich in lysine (9/77 residues). Other frequently occurring amino acids are glutamic acid and glutamine (7 each) and threonine. As with the other two apoproteins whose covalent structure has been determined (Fig. 6), inspection does not reveal especially hydrophobic segments. In five positions along the monomer chain, lysine is adjacent to a dicarboxylic amino acid, but the frequency of such acid-base conjunctions is perhaps not significantly greater than that expected in random association with a chain of the same amino acid content (Table III). It is probable that the higher order of structure of the apoproteins will have influence on their lipid-binding and other functions. The moderate amount of α-helix in delipidated apo-Gln-II (61, 102, 142) is decreased by reduction and alkylation (133). This has no obvious effect on its capacity to bind lipid (104), however, and the importance of the sulfhydryl bridge is not known.

b. Genetic Relationships. As recently reported by Barker and Dayhoff (15), their comparisons of the primary structures of apo-Gln-II and apo-Ala indicate a high probability that they are distantly related (Table IV). When the entire sequence of the shorter protein, apo-Ser, is compared with the first 59 residues of these two other apoproteins, it is of great interest that the genetic relationship of apo-Ser to apo-Gln-II is at least as strong as that previously described between apo-Ser and apo-Ala. In fact, the data in Table IV raise a question about whether apo-Ser and apo-Gln-II will properly be separated into "A" and "C" apolipoproteins (2–4), when their genetic and functional relationships have been better sorted out.

2. *Apo-Gln-I*

The first major peak obtained when apoHDL is separated by gel filtration (Fig. 12) contains apo-Gln-I (the old "R-Thr"),

218   DONALD S. FREDRICKSON

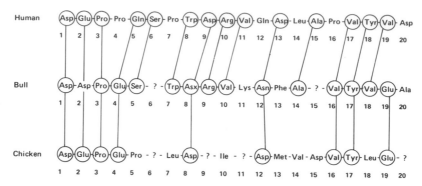

FIG. 13. Comparison of the reported sequences of the first 20 amino acids in human apo-Gln-I (151) and homologous proteins in the bull and the chicken (98, 99).

an apoprotein for which no complete amino acid sequence has yet been published. There are also some unresolved questions concerning its homogeneity. The protein can be isolated by gel filtration free of any contamination with apo-Gln-II and the "C-apoproteins" (Fig. 12) (32, 103). This protein gives a single broad band on polyacrylamide gel electrophoresis at alkaline and acid pH (103, 128, 142). Rechromatography on DEAE permits separation of multiple "polymorphic forms" of apo-Gln-I (32, 103, 111, 150). Similar findings are obtained with isoelectric focusing (7, 32, 142). Albers et al. (7) and Lux et al. (103) have found these different proteins to have the same amino acid composition and none have significant amounts of isoleucine. Shore and Shore (151) and Scanu et al. (32) reported that some peaks have isoleucine. There is no significant content of cysteine or cystine in these proteins (103). All the forms of apoGln-I are immunochemically identical, have the same migration on poly-acrylamide gel and the same molecular weight (about 27,000) (32, 103). Trace quantities of phospholipids (<1%) are found in all the fractions and probably are not responsible for the poly-morphism. There appears to be no sialic acid or hexosamines in any form of apo-Gln-I (32); some still undefined neutral sugars may be present. It is possible that the microheterogeneity of Apo-Glu-I is due to carbamylation or to changes in amide content occurring during fraction. Evidence for the latter has been reported (32), but this is a technically difficult point to prove beyond all doubt.

Partial Sequence. Partial sequences of proteins analogous to apo-Gln-I derived from man, bull, and chicken are available in preliminary form. These include the first 39 amino acids of the human apoprotein reported by the Shores (151, 155). Analyses of material from the bull and the chicken, reported by Levy *et al.* (98, 99) were performed on partially fractionated apoHDL. Judged from the available data, the first portions of apo-Gln-I from the three species appear to be homologous (Fig. 13). This comparison is a hazardously incomplete venture into the comparative biochemistry of apoHDL. We are impressed, nonetheless, with the apparent homology of the major HDL apoproteins in the rat, human and dog suggested by polyacrylamide gel patterns and other data (16, 82, 167). It all implies that the structure and presumably function of HDL were well established many millions of years prior to man's appearance.

B. *Apoprotein Separatism*

One uncertain piece of information can be added to reflections on the evolution of HDL. Comparisons made between the partial amino acid sequence of human apo-Gln-I and similar portions of apo-Ser, apo-Ala, or apo-Gln-II suggest that the relationships of these three apoproteins to each other are closer than the relationship any bears to apo-Gln-I (13). It is possible, then, that the two major apoproteins of HDL have come to rest in a common lipoprotein class by an accidental similarity in the density of their usual combinations with lipid. On the other hand, the relative constancy of proportion between apo-Gln I and apo-Gln II in HDL argues for an interdependence which serves some useful function. Alaupovic and co-workers favor such interdependence, and "regard the apo A peptides [apo-Gln-I and Gln-II] and apo C peptides [apo-Ser, -Glu, -Ala] as constitutive components of the quaternary structure of apolipoprotein A and C" (5). I presume the authors mean by this that apo-Gln-I and apo-Gln-II, for example, are likely integral parts of an HDL particle.

Although we cannot test this hypothesis adequately at present, there are interesting data that argue for and against it. The first have to do with other immunological experiments, the second with the reassembly of lipoproteins in the test tube, and the third with some abnormal disease states.

1. *Immunochemical Separations*

Using specific antiserums to the apoproteins, Alaupovic, Lee, and McConathy (5) have shown that the collective apolipoproteins A, B, and C are detectable throughout the lipoprotein spectrum. Trace amounts of "apolipoprotein A" were found in VLDL and LDL. They could not detect any separatism of apo-A-I and -A-II (-Gln-I and -Gln-II) in HDL preparations. Albers and Aladjem, however, have selectively precipitated lipoproteins by specific antisera made to either apo-Gln-I or apo-Gln-II with somewhat different results. They find that about 90% of lipoproteins in the broad $HDL_2 + HDL_3$ density class seem to contain both apo-Glu-I and apo-Glu-II; 10% contain Gln-I, but not Glu-II (8). There is a progressive enhancement of the ratio apo-Gln-I:apo-Gln-II with increasing HDL particle density, and only Gln-I is present in VHDL. As they recognized, there is the possibility of artifact. Years ago, Levy and I found that immunochemical heterogeneity could be detected in HDL exposed to repeated ultracentrifugation or freezing and thawing (94). Only one immunochemical form appeared in VHDL and increased in quantity with increasing manipulation of the lipoproteins. When the existence of two major HDL apoproteins became known and specific antibodies to them became available, Borut and Aladjem (19) and Nichols *et al.* (115) showed that this phenomenon could be attributed to (artificial) production of very high density lipoproteins containing only apo-Glu-I.

2. *Lipoprotein Recombination*

Recombination of apoproteins with lipids has been demonstrated in several ways. The most common procedure has been to sonify lipids, incubate them with apoproteins, and isolate protein–lipid complexes in the ultracentrifuge (34, 41, 78, 79, 102, 104, 136). Usually the density range of 1.063–1.21 has been selected for isolation of the complexes. In this way the uncombined lipids can be removed by flotation ($d < 1.063$) and the uncombined proteins be sedimented at $d > 1.21$. A second technique is measurement of changes in circular dichroism induced by recombination. It has been suggested that α-helical conformation may provide hydrophobic surfaces necessary for interaction between proteins and lipids (102, 159), and the helicity of apoproteins does tend to increase when they bind phospholipids. Yet another method is to allow the apoprotein to compete with delipidated mitochondrial β-hydroxybutyrate dehydrogenase, which has an absolute requirement for lecithin for enzymatic activity (104). By one or more of these techniques, all of the five better characterized apoproteins have been shown to recombine *in vitro* with phospholipids. Various soluble plasma proteins, including albumin, fail to demonstrate the avidity for lipid that is typical of the apoproteins (136, 162).

Further insight has been provided by electron micrographic examination of the recombinants isolated by ultracentrifugation. Forte of the Donner Laboratory, in collaboration with others, has probably had the most extensive experience in studying the results of recombination in this way (39, 41). Dr. Forte has kindly supplied Fig. 14 and allowed me to summarize some of her impressions. Upon recombination of any of the apoproteins with phospholipid, one obtains rouleaux of discs that appear to consist of a single bilayer (Fig. 14). When cholesteryl esters or triglycerides are added, many of the complexes now form spherical particles that closely resemble the morphology of intact lipoproteins. The behavior of apo-Gln-I and apo-Gln-II is similar. When these proteins, singly or in combination, are added to phospholipid and cholesteryl esters, the recombined complexes have the same appearance.

The addition of phospholipid to apo-Ser or apo-Glu also produces discs, which become spherical particles when either cholesteryl esters or triglycerides are also added (39). As isolated between densities 1.063 and 1.21 (the HDL range) these spheres have a diameter of 60–130 Å. Recombination also produces larger particles of lower density. Both apo-Ala$_1$ and -Ala$_2$ behave like apo-Glu and apo-Ser. Apo-Ala will form spherical structures with addition of triglyceride alone, but it has not yet been shown

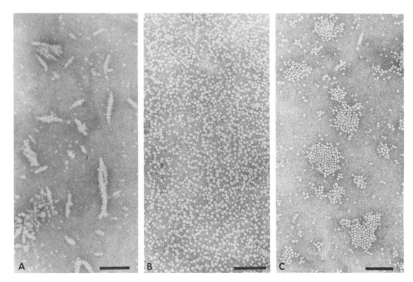

FIG. 14. Electron micrographs of negatively stained (1% sodium phosphotungstate, pH 7.4) fractions of density 1.063–1.21 g/ml isolated from sonicated mixtures including apo-Ser and various lipids. (A) Apo-Ser and lecithin (1.0 and 1.5 mg/ml, respectively). The predominant morphological entities are rouleaux with a periodicity of 50–60 Å. Individual members of the rouleaux are presumed to be disc-shaped and have diameters of 110–220 Å. Occasional small particles which are 40–70 Å in size are also present. (B) Apo-Ser + lecithin + cholesteryl ester (1.0, 1.13, and 0.37 mg/ml, respectively). The reassembled lipoprotein consists of small particles with diameters of 90–110 Å. (C) Apo-Ser + lecithin + triglyceride (1.0, 1.13, and 0.37 mg/ml, respectively). These lipoprotein structures are similar to those seen in (B). The particles are round and range in diameter from 100 to 115 Å. In some areas where the particles are close-packed they form hexagonal arrays, a configuration which one might expect if the particles are spherical and of uniform size. The bar markers represent 1000 Å. Kindly supplied by Dr. G. Forte.

whether this is a unique property of this apoprotein. When other soluble plasma proteins are recombined with high density lipoprotein lipids, discoidal bilayers may be formed, but spherical "lipoproteins" are not obtained (39).

3. Lipid-Binding by Apoprotein Fragments

Apo-Gln-II contains a single methionine, at position 26, which permits cleavage into two fragments by cyanogen bromide. The

carboxy-terminal two-thirds of the molecule binds sonically prepared dispersions of egg lecithin (104). Very little lipid-binding
activity is retained by the amino-terminal third of the molecule.
The delipidated whole apo-Gln-II contains about 35% helix
(102), and the amount of helicity increases upon binding with
lecithin. There is little evidence of helicity in either of the CNBr
pices of apo-Gln-II. There is a marked increase in helical content
of the carboxyl-terminal fragment when it is incubated with
lecithin (104). Similar experiments have been performed with
fragments of apo-Gln-I by Jackson et al. (79). This apoprotein
contains 3 methionines and yields 4 CNBr peptides. Of these,
the piece representing the last 92 residues also binds lecithin.
This fragment contributes to (79) the unusually high α-helical
conformation found in apo-Gln-I (61, 102). Apo-Ala also binds
phospholipid (112). Shulman et al. have found that when whole
apo-Ala is incubated with lecithin, the carboxyl-terminal half of
the molecule resists cleavage with trypsin. Recombination experiments with tryptic fragments of apo-Ala suggest that the major
binding site for phospholipid is located in the middle or carboxy-
terminal third of the molecule (158).

C. HDL Deficiency (Tangier Disease)

We have been following patients with Tangier disease since
its discovery over 10 years ago (46). There are 15 patients from
11 families known to have this syndrome. All are severely deficient in circulating HDL; if any HDL is present it is abnormal
in composition and immunochemical behavior (HDL$_T$) (46,
105). The heterozygote's plasma contains HDL$_T$ and about half
of the normal concentration of HDL. Recently we have collected
from one homozygote sufficient Tangier HDL for fractionation
of the apoproteins (105). As shown in Fig. 15, this HDL is
relatively very deficient in apoLP-Gln-I. The proportion of apo-
Gln-I to apo-Gln-II is about 1:12 (w/w) instead of the normal
3:1. The "minor protein" peak in Fig. 15 contains apo-Ser, -Glu,
-Ala$_1$, and -Ala$_2$ in amounts that are in proportion to their usual
contribution to total HDL proteins (5–7%) but in absolute quantities that are greatly reduced. We are now attempting to deter-

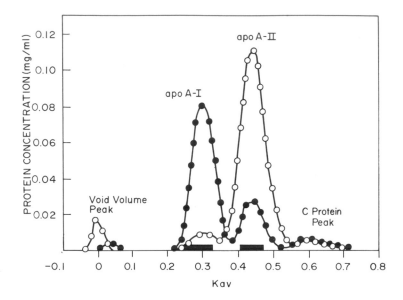

FIG. 15.   Sephadex chromatography of equal amounts of high density lipoprotein (HDL) apoproteins from normal subject (●——●) and patient with
Tangier disease (○——○). See text for explanation. Reprinted from Lux *et al.*
(105) with permission of *Journal of Clinical Investigation.*

mine whether the small amounts of the apo-Gln-I and -Gln-II
in Tangier plasma are identical to their normal counterparts.

We have suggested that the genetic error in Tangier disease
is most likely one limiting synthesis of apo-Gln-I or producing
a mutant protein incapable of participating in formation of HDL.
If this is correct, it would appear that both apo-Gln-I and apo-
Gln-II are essential contributors to the quaternary structure of
a common HDL particle. The available data, of course, do not
provide alternatives, such as the normal existence of each major
apoprotein in a separate lipoprotein, but some important interdependence that sustains a normal concentration of total "HDL."

The reduction of the "C-apoproteins" in Tangier plasma merits
further comment. The chemical composition of chylomicrons and
VLDL and the metabolism of plasma triglycerides are also not
normal in Tangier homozygotes (43). All of the "C-apoproteins"
seem to be present, but their reservoir in HDL is gone. This

attests to the importance of the HDL complexes in holding the C-proteins in the high-density range when they are not in triglyceride-rich particles. There may be other functions of HDL in triglyceride transport that are not met in Tangier disease.

To round out the discussion of confusing abnormal states, I should mention the human mutants who have diminished activity of the enzyme lecithin:cholesterol acyl transferase (LCAT) and thus little capability to esterify their plasma cholesterol (117). In these patients the major HDL apoproteins circulate in discs, analogous to the lipoprotein recombinants *without* cholesteryl ester shown in Fig. 14 (42). Rouleaux of discs that are similar, but not identical to these, are also seen in patients who have biliary obstruction and low levels of esterified cholesterol (Lp-X lipoproteins) (64, 146). It is noteworthy that patients with Tangier disease, who are truly deficient in the apo's-Gln, store extraordinary quantities of cholesteryl esters in their reticuloendothelial cells. Patients with familial LCAT deficiency, who lack normal HDL but have ample quantities of the major HDL apoproteins in plasma, store some free cholesterol but no sterol esters in tissues. There seems to be something about these HDL apoproteins that helps maintain lipid transfer between plasma and cell membranes. The Shores have briefly described a single patient whose HDL is "grossly deficient" in apo-Gln-II (151), but specific consequences of this deficiency are not known.

LCAT: A Function for Apo-Gln-I? Apo-Gln-I has been shown by Fielding to activate the LCAT enzyme *in vitro* (37). The importance of cholesteryl esters in maintaining a healthy well-rounded shape to lipoproteins has made it appear that LCAT has an important role in lipoprotein metabolism, one that has recently been summarized by Glomset (55, 117). I will return to those functions, as I move now to sum up for the apoproteins and their place in the scheme of lipid (triglyceride) transport.

IV. Summing Up

In higher forms of life, specialized systems exist for the inter-organ transportation of lipids, substances which share a general property of relative insolubility in water. For those organisms which maintain appreciable quantities of energy in reserve, the movement of combustible fats has become particularly important in keeping caloric economy in balance. In these animals, readily oxidizable fats are mainly stored in adipose tissue and transported from there as long-chain fatty acid anions bound to albumin. However, when fatty acids move from the intestine or liver to the adipose tissue stores, and perhaps to depots in other organs, they do so mainly in the form of glyceryl esters. The triglycerides in plasma thus come both from outside (the diet) and from synthesis within. They are packaged for export in combination with phospholipid, cholesterol, and certain proteins (apolipoproteins) in a manner providing dispersions in water that are at once stable and yet easily handled at their destination. The plasma apolipoproteins seem to be peculiarly well adapted for this purpose, and, although comparisons between species have been limited, it is evident that the homologs of the human apolipoproteins must have appeared fairly early in evolution. Having relevance to many disciplines and possibly to several important diseases in man, the properties, functions, and interactions of apolipoproteins have been subjects of much recent research and speculation. What I have reconstructed here concerning them is both tentative and flawed, for there are many gaps in essential knowledge. I have also ignored most of the other aspects of lipid transport to concentrate on the secretion of endogenous triglycerides and events that follow soon after their release into the blood.

We have considered as the first model the liver parenchymal cell. Here, when net synthesis of glyceride begins, or when these lipids have accumulated in some critical amount, the elaboration of several apoproteins also takes place. One of these is apoLDL, a protein whose size and structure are still uncertain. Lipid-free apoLDL is probably insoluble in intracellular fluids and we may guess that it is synthesized in close proximity to phospholipids and cholesterol. [With an appropriate combination of these lipids this apoprotein forms "soluble" low density lipoproteins (LDL) in plasma.] Conceivably, apoLDL may be intimately involved in regulation of lipid synthesis itself; it may also be a membrane protein. It has been suggested that apoLDL is the "sterol carrier

protein" known to facilitate the conversion of squalene to cholesterol (126), although another apoprotein has been also mentioned
as possibly serving this purpose (144). In any event, it is likely
that as soon as apoLDL leaves the polyribosomes it accumulates
lipids that help maintain its solubility or state of disaggregation
as it migrates through the channels of the endoplasmic reticulum
to the Golgi apparatus.

Concomitant with the production of apo-LDL, several other
apoproteins are newly synthesized in the liver. Three of these
have been relatively well defined. They are much smaller than
apoLDL, having molecular weights of from 7 to 10,000, and
in the nomenclature I have chosen to employ for this discussion
are known as apo-Ser, apo-Glu, and apo-Ala. The trio is usually
found together in plasma and is sometimes referred to collectively
as the "C-proteins." The primary structures of apo-Ser and apo-
Ala bear similarities that suggest derivation from a common ancestral gene. The sequence of apo-Glu has not been determined.
Like apoLDL, the "C-proteins" probably always exist in the cell
in the company of lipids. Each alone, in the presence of phospholipid, forms a bilayer, which assumes the spherical structure of
a lipoprotein when triglyceride or cholesteryl esters are added.
It is not yet known whether, as they migrate to the Golgi apparatus, the "C-proteins" complex with lipid in unison or whether
they independently stabilize different packets of triglyceride. In
addition to apoLDL and the "C-proteins," small quantities of
other newly synthesized apoproteins are found in the triglyceride
rich particles. Sometimes called the "fraction II proteins," these
have not been adequately characterized.

In the Golgi bodies, lipoprotein assembly appears to be complete, and one can discern droplets of lipoproteins, 300–800 Å
in diameter, that chemically resemble plasma very low density
lipoproteins (VLDL). Both apoLDL and apoAla are notable for
the presence of sialic acid-containing glycosidic residues. It is
likely that these are affixed by glycosyl transferases within the
Golgi bodies. It could be that this is a final step in the assembly
of lipoproteins, for beyond the Golgi storage area, the next destination of the "VLDL" will be either the lymph or blood stream.

In the mucosal cells located in the villi of the small intestine, the processing of glycerides occurs in a similar fashion, but there are important differences. In the intestinal Golgi apparatus, two populations of triglyceride-rich particles are visible. One of these consists of droplets that are about the same size and have a composition very much like the VLDL in liver Golgi bodies. Not far from these, but discretely apart, stand other groups of larger particles (>1000 Å) awaiting shipment. These are chylomicrons, containers of newly reassembled glycerides and small portions of phospholipids, cholesterol, and other fat-soluble substances, that have recently arrived from the intestinal lumen. ApoLDL is present in both VLDL and chylomicrons. As judged from chylomicrons and larger VLDL isolated in plasma, the quantity of protein per mass of glyceride, and the proportion of the total protein represented by apoLDL, are less than in smaller VLDL particles. There is something else that is different about the manner in which the intestinal cell is packaging triglycerides and proteins. ApoLDL is synthesized by the intestinal cell—as are some of the "fraction II" apoproteins—but the "C-proteins" are neither being synthesized nor do they appear in any quantity in the lipoproteins being formed. It is suspected that the "C-proteins" found in chylomicrons or the VLDL are acquired by these particles as they exit from the cell into the intestinal lymph. If we add this suspicion to other evidence derived from a disease (abetalipoproteinemia) in which apoLDL is selectively missing and all triglyceride transport is abolished, we come to the tentative but important conclusion that apoLDL is essential for triglyceride secretion from the cell.

Moving now with the chylomicrons and VLDL out of the Golgi into the blood stream, we can discern some interesting events that transpire in delivery of triglyceride to its destination. Some, if not all, of these particles immediately acquire a richer complement of "C-proteins," borrowed from the pool maintained by HDL. There is something purposeful in this welcoming embrace, for at least one of the "C-proteins," apo-Glu, is an "activator" of the enzyme lipoprotein lipase. As the particles come in contact with this enzyme in the endothelial wall of capillaries, the triglyceride is progressively stripped away. Shortly, the VLDL and chylomicrons, some of them originally >1000 Å in diameter and over 100 million daltons are reduced to "remnants" of <200 Å diameter and of $1-3 \times 10^6$ molecular weight. The ultimate residuals are LDL which contain only apoLDL and a fairly constant proportion of phospholipids and cholesterol, most of the latter being esterified. Gone is nearly all of the original triglyceride, most of it "absorbed" by cells near the site where lipolysis occurred. Gone is most of the original free cholesterol and phospholipid. Some of these lipids have been retained in LDL and, perhaps, HDL, but most of them probably disappear in unstable remnants taken up by the liver and other organs. Some of the original C-proteins are not gone, but have transferred to the HDL, and will apparently spend some time equilibrating between the protective bulk of these lipoproteins and new triglyceride-rich lipoproteins entering the plasma to proceed through the same catabolic cycle.

The image, conveyed by this reconstruction, of plasma LDL as a slag pile of debris accumulating from triglyceride transport is probably too narrow, if not badly distorted. Possibly LDL are derived from several other pathways as well, but there is no evidence that LDL or their constituent apoLDL reenter the cycle of triglyceride transport. The sites of LDL disposal and the methods of disassembly employed are not known. It is apparent that the rate of disposal is relatively limited. Man, whose LDL concentration exceeds that of all other species, operates dangerously close to the margin, for LDL is an important atherogenic factor. One would like to know more about possible differences in demand for triglyceride transport, or of alternate routes of LDL production, in man compared to other animals, as this may relate to LDL accumulation or to apoprotein metabolism in general.

The conversion of VLDL to LDL passes through successive stages in which lipoproteins of intermediate density and composition are transiently produced. One human genetic abnormality, type III hyperlipoproteinemia, exists in which "intermediates" accumulate in plasma even though lipoprotein lipase activity is not obviously deficient. This disorder suggests that other discrete mechanisms are operative during the dissolution of triglyceride-rich particles.

Among the possibly complex operations which must accompany the lipolysis of triglyceride in lipoproteins is a replacement reaction. Nonpolar lipids like triglycerides help maintain the spherical form and stability of lipoproteins. Cholesteryl esters can also serve this function. Cholesterol is esterified in plasma by an enzyme, lecithin:cholesterol acyltransferase (LCAT), and it has been suggested that this reaction proceeds in step with lipolysis to assure the continued stability of the lipoproteins produced. HDL may both activate LCAT and provide some of the lecithin required as acyl donor in the reaction this enzyme controls.

HDL are a mystery not yet fathomed. This is true even though we have assigned them the role of conservator of the peripatetic "C proteins" and believe they are the source of activator(s) for LCAT. It is still true even though we know much about the chemistry of the "major" HDL apoproteins. Known as apo-Gln-I and apo-Gln-II, their names may mislead, for they are not identical twins. Apo-Gln-II is a distant cousin of apo-Ser, to judge from their primary structures. Apo-Gln-I is much larger and present in higher concentrations in plasma. It apparently is the activator of LCAT. We are not sure whether the apo's-Gln may be secreted together or separately, and with or without accompanying "C-proteins." As is the case with the other apoproteins, we know they can separately recombine with lipid in the test tube, but not whether they can form independent lipoproteins in plasma. From one mutation, Tangier disease, we surmise that when one of them (probably apo-Gln-I) is not available or structurally altered, the other cannot form a lipid complex capable of survival in plasma. The absence of normal HDL leaves the "C-proteins" without their convenient "sink" for storage. Large amounts of cholesteryl esters also accumulate intracellularly, and there is strong suspicion that the functions served by the major apoproteins of HDL include one of "sweeping" excess cholesterol from cells to the liver or other sites.

I think it is likely that mutations involving deletions of each of the apoproteins will have to be discovered before the reason for its selection in evolution will become apparent. Thus far, the rate of identification of new apoproteins has exceeded that of the discovery of new mutants. We have had to make up for the lag by employing generous amounts of conjecture.

REFERENCES

1. Aladjem, F., Lieberman, M., and Gofman, J. W., *J. Exp. Med.* **105**, 49 (1957).
2. Alaupovic, P., *Atherosclerosis* **13**, 141 (1971).
3. Alaupovic, P., "Proceedings of the XIX Annual Colloquium on Peptides of the Biological Fluids" (Bruges), p. 9. Pergamon, Oxford, 1971.
4. Alaupovic, P., Kostner, G., Lee, D. M., McConathy, W. J., and Magnani, H. N., *Exposes Annu. Biochim. Med.* **31**, 145 (1972).
5. Alaupovic, P., Lee, D. M., and McConathy, W. J., *Biochim. Biophys. Acta* **260**, 689 (1972).
6. Alaupovic, P., Sanbar, S. S., Furman, R. H., Sullivan, M. L., and Walraven, S. L., *Biochemistry* **5**, 4044 (1966).
7. Albers, J. J., Albers, L. V., and Aladjem, F., *Biochem. Med.* **5**, 48 (1971).
8. Albers, J. J., and Aladjem, F., *Biochemistry* **10**, 3436 (1971).
9. Albers, J. J., and Scanu, A. M., *Biochim. Biophys. Acta* **236**, 29 (1971).
10. Assmann, G., Krauss, R. M., Fredrickson, D. S., and Levy, R. I. *J. Biol. Chem.* **248**, 7184 (1973).
11. Avigan, J., Redfield, R., and Steinberg, D., *Biochim. Biophys. Acta* **20**, 557 (1956).
12. Ayrault-Jarrier, M., Levy, G., and Polonovski, J., *Bull. Soc. Chim. Biol.* **45**, 703 (1963).
13. Barker, W. C., and Dayhoff, M. O. Personal communication
14. Barker, W. C., and Dayhoff, M. O., *in* "Atlas of Protein Sequence and Structure" (M. O. Dayhoff, ed.), Vol. 5, p. 101. The National Bio-Chemical Research Foundation, Silver Spring, Maryland, 1972.
15. Barker, W. C., and Dayhoff, M. O., Abstracts Meeting, Spring, *Biophys. J.*, p. 205a (1973).
16. Bersot, T. P., Brown, W. V., Levy, R. I., Windmueller, H. G., Fredrickson, D. S., and LeQuire, V. S., *Biochemistry* **9**, 3427 (1970).
17. Bierman, E. L., Porte, D., Jr., O'Hara, D. D., Schwartz, M., and Wood, F. C., Jr., *J. Clin. Invest.* **44**, 261 (1965).
18. Bilheimer, D. W., Eisenberg, S., and Levy, R. I., *Biochim. Biophys. Acta* **260**, 212 (1972).
19. Borut, T. C., and Aladjem, F., *Immunochemistry* **8**, 851 (1971).
20. Brewer, H. B., Jr., Lux, S. E., Ronan, R., and John, K. M., *Proc. Nat. Acad. Sci. U.S.* **69**, 1304 (1972).
21. Brewer, H. B., Jr., and Ronan, R., *Proc. Nat. Acad. Sci. U.S.* **67**, 1862 (1970).

22. Brewer, H. B., Jr., Shulman, R., Herbert, P., Ronan, R., and Wehrly, K., *Advan. Exp. Biol. Med.* **26**, 280 (1972).
23. Brown, W. V., and Baginsky, M. L., *Biochem. Biophys. Res. Commun.* **46**, 375 (1972).
24. Brown, W. V., Levy, R. I., and Fredrickson, D. S., *J. Biol. Chem.* **244**, 5687 (1969).
25. Brown, W. V., Levy, R. I., and Fredrickson, D. S., *Biochim. Biophys. Acta* **200**, 573 (1970).
26. Brown, W. V., Levy, R. I., and Fredrickson, D. S., *J. Biol. Chem.* **245**, 6588 (1970).
27. Burstein, M., and Fine, J.-M., *Rev. Fr. Etud. Clin. Biol.* **9**, 105 (1964).
28. Camejo, G., Suarez, Z. M., and Munoz, V., *Biochim. Biophys Acta* **218**, 155 (1970).
29. Cohen, L., and Djordjevich, J., *J. Clin. Invest.* **45**, 996 (1966).
30. Day, C. E., and Levy, R. S., *J. Lipid Res.* **9**, 789 (1968).
31. Dole, V. P., and Hamlin, J. T. III, *Physiol. Rev.* **42**, 674 (1962).
32. Edelstein, C., Lim, C. T., and Scanu, A. M., *J. Biol. Chem.* **247**, 5842 (1972).
33. Eder, H. A., Rombauer, R. B., and Roheim, P. S., *Exposes Annu. Rev. Biochem.* **47**, 53 (1972).
34. Eisenberg, S., Bilheimer, D. W., and Levy, R. I., *Biochim. Biophys. Acta* **280**, 94 (1972).
35. Eisenberg, S., Bilheimer, D., Lindgren, F., and Levy, R. I., *Biochim. Biophys. Acta* **260**, 329 (1972).
36. Fidge, N. H., and Foxman, C. J., *Aust. J. Exp. Biol. Med. Sci.* **49**, 581 (1971).
37. Fielding, C. J., Shore, V. G., and Fielding, P. E., *Biochem. Biophys. Res. Commun.* **46**, 1493 (1972).
38. Fisher, W. R., and Gurin, S., *Science* **143**, 362 (1964).
39. Forte, G. M. Personal communication.
40. Forte, G. M., Nichols, A. V., and Glaeser, R. M., *Chem. Phys. Lipids* **2**, 396 (1968).
41. Forte, G. M., Nichols, A. V., Gong, E. L., Lux, S., and Levy, R. I., *Biochim. Biophys Acta* **248**, 381 (1971).
42. Forte, G., Norum, K. R., Glomset, F. A., and Nichols, A. V., *J. Clin. Invest.* **50**, 1141 (1971).
43. Fredrickson, D. S., *in* "The Metabolic Basis of Inherited Disease" (J. B. Stanbury, J. B. Wyngaarden, and D. S. Fredrickson, eds.), 2nd ed., p. 486. McGraw-Hill, New York, 1966.
44. Fredrickson, D. S., and Breslow, J., *Annu. Rev. Med.* **24**, 315 (1973).
45. Fredrickson, D. S., and Gordon, R. S., Jr., *Physiol. Rev.* **38**, 585 (1958).
46. Fredrickson, D. S., Gotto, A. M., and Levy, R. I., *in* "The Metabolic Basis of Inherited Disease, 3rd ed. (J. B. Stanbury, J. B. Wyngaarden, and D. S. Fredrickson, eds.) p. 493. McGraw-Hill, New York, 1972.
47. Fredrickson, D. S., Levy, R. I., and Lees, R. S. (1967). *N. Engl. J. Med.* **276**, 34, 94, 148, 215, 273.

48. Fredrickson, D. S., Levy, R. I., and Lindgren, F. T., *J. Clin. Invest.* **47,** 2446 (1968).
49. Fredrickson, D. S., Lux, S. E., and Herbert, P. N., *Advan. Exp. Med. Biol.* **26,** 25 (1972).
50. Frezal, J., Rey, J., Polonovski, J., et al., *Rev. Fr. Clin. Biol.* **6,** 677 (1961).
51. Ganesan, D., Bradford, R. H., Alaupovic, P., and McConathy, W. J., *FEBS Lett.* **15,** 205 (1971).
52. Ganesan, D., Bradford, R. H., Ganesan, G., McConathy, W. F., Alaupovic, P., and Hazzard, W. R., *Circulation* **46,** II-248 (1972).
53. Garner, C. W., Jr., Smith, L. C., Jackson, R. L., and Gotto, A. M., Jr., *Circulation* **46,** II-246 (1972).
54. Gitlin, D., Cornwell, D. G., Nakasato, D., Oncley, F. L., Hughes, W. L., Jr., and Janeway, C. A., *J. Clin. Invest.* **37,** 172 (1958).
55. Glomset, J. A., in "Atlas of Protein Sequence and Structure" (M. O. Dayhoff, ed.), Vol. 5, Chap. 14, p. 745 (1972). National Biomedical Research Foundation, Georgetown University Medical Center, Washington, D.C.
56. Goalwin, A., and Pomeranze, J., *Arch. Paediat.* **79,** 58 (1962).
57. Gofman, J. W., deLalla, O., Glazier, F., Freeman, N. K., Lindgren, F. T., Nichols, A. V., Strisower, B., and Tamplin, A. R., *Plasma* **2,** 413 (1954).
58. Gotto, A. M., Brown, V. W., Levy, R. I., Birnbaumer, M. E., and Fredrickson, D. S., *J. Clin. Invest.* **51,** 1486 (1972).
59. Gotto, A. M., Levy, R. I., Birnbaumer, M. E., and Fredrickson, D. S., *Nature (London)* **223,** 835 (1969).
60. Gotto, A. M., Levy, R. I., John, K., and Fredrickson, D. S., *N. Engl. J. Med.* **284,** 813 (1971).
61. Gotto, A. M., and Shore B., *Nature (London)* **224,** 69 (1969).
62. Gustafson, A., Alaupovic, P., and Furman, R. H., *Biochim. Biophys. Acta* **84,** 767 (1964).
63. Gustafson, A., Alaupovic, P., and Furman, R. H., *Biochemistry* **5,** 632 (1966).
64. Hamilton, R. L., Havel, R. F., Kane, F. P., Beaurock, A. E., and Sato, T., *Science* **172,** 475 (1971).
65. Hamilton, R. L., Regen, D. M., Gray, M. E., and LeQuire, V. S., *Lab. Invest.* **16,** 305 (1967).
66. Hammond, M. G., and Fisher, W. R., *J. Biol. Chem.* **246,** 5454 (1971).
67. Hatch, F. T., and Bruce, A. L., *Nature (London)* **218,** 1166 (1968).
68. Hatch, F. T., Freeman, N. K., Jensen, L. C., Stevens, G. R., and Lindgren, F. T., *Lipids* **2,** 183 (1967).
69. Havel, R. J., *N. Engl. J. Med.* **287,** 1186 (1972).
70. Havel, R. J., *Advan. Exp. Med. Biol.* **26,** 57 (1972).
71. Havel, R. J., Kane, J. P., and Kashyap, M. L., *J. Clin. Invest.* **52,** 32 (1973).
72. Havel, R. J., Shore, V. G., Shore, B., and Bier, D. M., *Circ. Res.* **27,** 595 (1970).

73. Hazzard, W. R., Porte, D. Jr., and Bierman, E. L., *J. Clin. Invest.* **49**, 1853 (1970).
74. Herbert, P. N. Personal communication.
75. Herbert, P. N., Forte, G. M., Shulman, R. S., Gong, E. L., LaPiana, M. J., Nichols, A. V., Levy, R. I., and Fredrickson, D. S., *Fed. Proc., Fed. Amer. Soc. Exp. Biol.* **32**, 1862, 1973.
76. Herbert P., LaRosa, J., Krauss, R., Lux, S., Levy, R. I., and Fredrickson, D. S., *J. Clin. Invest.* **50**, 44a (1971).
77. Herbert, P., Levy, R. I., and Fredrickson, D. S., *J. Biol. Chem.* **246**, 7068 (1971).
78. Hirz, R., and Scanu, A., *Biochim. Biophys. Acta* **207**, 364 (1970).
79. Jackson, R. L., Baker, H. N., David, J. S. K., and Gotto, A. M., *Biochem. Biophys. Res. Commun.* **49**, 1444 (1972).
80. Jones, A. L., Rudermann, N. B., and Herrera, M. G., Jr., *J. Lipid Res.* **8**, 429 (1967).
81. Kane, J. P., Richards, E. G., and Havel, R. J., *Proc. Nat. Acad. Sci. U.S.* **66**, 1075 (1970).
82. Koga, S., Bolis, L., and Scanu, A. M., *Biochim. Biophys. Acta* **236**, 416 (1971).
83. Kook, A. I., Eckhaus, A. S., and Rubinstein, D., *Can. J. Biochem.* **48**, 649 (1970).
84. Korn, E. D., *J. Biol. Chem.* **215**, 15 (1955).
85. Kostner, G., and Alaupovic, P., *FEBS Lett.* **15**, 320 (1971).
86. Kostner, G., and Holasek, A., *Biochemistry* **7**, 1217 (1972).
87. Krauss, R. M. Personal communication.
88. Krauss, R. M., Herbert, P. N., Levy, R. I., and Fredrickson, D. S. *Circ. Res.* **33**, 403 (1973).
89. Krauss, R. M., Windmueller, H. G., Levy, R. I., and Fredrickson, D. S. *J. Lipid Res.* **14**, 286 (1973).
90. Langer, T., Strober, W., and Levy, R. I., *J. Clin. Invest.* **51**, 1528 (1972).
91. LaRosa, J. C., Levy, R. I., Brown, W. V., and Fredrickson, D. S., *Amer. J. Physiol.* **220**, 785 (1971).
92. LaRosa, J. C., Levy, R. I., Herbert, P., Lux, S. E., and Fredrickson, D. S., *Biochem. Biophys. Res. Commun.* **41**, 57 (1970).
93. Lee, D. M., and Alaupovic, P., *Biochemistry* **9**, 2244 (1970).
94. Levy, R. I., and Fredrickson, D. S., *J. Clin. Invest.* **44**, 426 (1965).
95. Levy, R. I., Lees, R. S., and Fredrickson, D. S., *J. Clin. Invest.* **45**, 63 (1966).
96. Lees, R. S., and Ahrens, E. H., Jr., *N. Engl. J. Med.* **280**, 1261 (1969).
97. Lees, R. S., and Fredrickson, D. S., *J. Clin. Invest.* **44**, 1968 (1965).
98. Levy, R. S., and Martin, M. V., *Fed. Proc., Fed. Amer. Soc. Exp. Biol.* **30**, 1187 (1971).
99. Levy, R. S., Martin, M. V., van Remortel, H., and Harbaugh, J. F., *Fed. Proc., Fed. Amer. Soc. Exp. Biol.* **31**, 3776 (1972).
100. Lindgren, F. T., Jensen, L. C., and Hatch, F. T., *in* "Blood Lipids and Lipoproteins: Quantitation, Composition, and Metabolism (G. J. Nelson, ed.), p. 181. Wiley (Interscience), New York, 1972.

101. Lossow, W. J., Lindgren, F. T., Murchio, J. C., Stevens, G. R., and Jensen, L. C., *J. Lipid Res.* **10**, 68 (1969).
102. Lux, S. E., Hirz, R., Shrager, R. I., and Gotto, A. M., *J. Biol. Chem.* **247**, 2598 (1972).
103. Lux, S. E., John, K. M., and Brewer, H. B., Jr., *J. Biol. Chem.* **247**, 7510 (1972).
104. Lux, S. E., John, K. M., Fleischer, S., Jackson, R. L., and Gotto, A. M., Jr., *Biochem. Biophys. Res. Commun.* **49**, 23 (1972).
105. Lux, S. E., Levy, R. I., Gotto, A. M., and Fredrickson, D. S., *J. Clin. Invest.* **51**, 2505 (1972).
106. McConathy, W. J., Quiroga, C., and Alaupovic, P., *FEBS (Fed. Eur. Biochem. Soc.) Lett.* **19**, 323 (1972).
107. Mahley, R. W., Bennett, B. D., Morre, J., Gray, M. E., Thistlethwaite, W., and LeQuire, V. S., *Lab. Invest.* **25**, 435 (1971).
108. Mahley, R. W., Bersot, T. P., LeQuire, V. S., Levy, R. I., Windmueller, H. G., and Brown, W. V., *Science* **168**, 380 (1970).
109. Mahley, R. W., Gray, M. E., Hamilton, R. L., and LeQuire, V. S., *Lab. Invest.* **19**, 358 (1968).
110. Mahley, R. W., Hamilton, R. L., and LeQuire, V. S., *J. Lipid Res.* **10**, 433 (1969).
111. Margolis, S., and Langdon, R. G., *J. Biol. Chem.* **241**, 469 (1966).
112. Morrisett, F. D., David, F. S. K., Pownall, H. F., and Gotto, A. M., *Circulation* **46**, II-246 (1972).
113. Nelson, G. J., "Blood Lipids and Lipoproteins: Quantitation, Composition, and Metabolism" Wiley (Interscience), New York, 1972.
114. Nichols, A. V., *Advan. Biol. Med. Phys.* **11**, 109 (1967).
115. Nichols, A. V., Lux, S., Forte, G., Gong, E., and Levy, R. I., *Biochim. Biophys. Acta* **270**, 132 (1972).
116. Nichols, A. V., Strisower, E. H., Lindgren, F. T., Adamson, G. L., and Coggiola, E. L., *Clin. Chem. Acta* **20**, 277 (1968).
117. Norum, K. R., Glomset, J. A., and Gjone, E., *in* "The Metabolic Basis of Inherited Disease" (J. B. Stanbury, J. B. Wyngaarden, and D. S. Fredrickson, eds.), 3rd ed. p. 531. McGraw-Hill, New York, 1972.
118. Ockner, R. K., Hughes, F. B., and Isselbacher, K. J., *J. Clin. Invest.* **48**, 2079 (1969).
119. Oncley, J. L., *Harvey Lect.* **50**, 71 (1956).
120. Pearlstein, E., Eggena, P., and Aladjem, F., *Immunochemistry* **8**, 865 (1971).
121. Pollard, H., Scanu, A. M., and Taylor, E. W., *Proc. Nat. Acad. Sci. U.S.* **64**, 304 (1969).
122. Pottenger, L. A., and Getz, G. S., *J. Lipid Res.* **12**, 450 (1971).
123. Quarfordt, S. H., Frank, A., Shames, D. M., Berman, M., and Steinberg, D., *J. Clin. Invest.* **49**, 2281 (1970).
124. Quarfordt, S. H., and Goodman, DeW. S., *Biochim. Biophys. Acta* **116**, 382 (1966).

125. Quarfordt, S. H., Levy, R. I., and Fredrickson, D. S., *J. Clin. Invest.* **50,** 754 (1971).
126. Ritter, M. C., and Dempsey, M. E., *Circulation* **46,** II-235 (1972).
127. Rodbell, M., *Science* **127,** 701 (1958).
128. Rudman, D., Garcia, L. A., and Howard, C. H., *J. Clin. Invest.* **49,** 365 (1970).
129. Sabesin, S. M., and Isselbacher, K. J., *Science* **147,** 1149 (1965).
130. Sata, T., Havel, R. J., and Jones, A. L., *J. Lipid Res.* **13,** 757 (1972).
131. Scanu, A., *Nature (London)* **207,** 528 (1965).
132. Scanu, A., *J. Lipid Res.* **7,** 295 (1966).
133. Scanu, A. M., *Biochim. Biophys. Acta* **200,** 570 (1970).
134. Scanu, A. M., *in* "Plasma Lipoproteins (R. M. S. Smellie, ed.), p. 29. Academic Press, New York, 1971.
135. Scanu, A., *Fed. Proc., Fed. Amer. Soc. Exp. Biol.* **31,** 3471 (1972).
136. Scanu, A., Cump, E., Toth, J., Koga, S., Stiller, E., and Albers, L., *Biochemistry* **9,** 1327 (1970).
137. Scanu, A. M., Edelstein, C., and Lim, C. T., *FEBS (Fed. Eur. Biochem. Soc.) Lett.* **18,** 305 (1971).
138. Scanu, A., and Granda, J. L., *Biochemistry* **5,** 446 (1966).
139. Scanu, A. M., Lim, C. T., and Edelstein, C., *J. Biol. Chem.* **247,** 5850 (1972).
140. Scanu, A., Pollard, H., Hirz, R., and Kothary, K., *Proc. Nat. Acad. Sci. U.S.* **62,** 171 (1969).
141. Scanu, A., Pollard, H., and Reader, W., *J. Lipid Res.* **9,** 342 (1968).
142. Scanu, A., Toth, J., Edelstein, C., Koga, S., and Stiller, E., *Biochemistry* **8,** 3309 (1969).
143. Schumaker, V. N., and Adams, G. H., *Annu. Rev. Biochem.* **38,** 113 (1969).
144. Scallen, T. J., Srikantaiah, M. V., Skrdlant, H. B., and Hansburg, E., *Circulation* **46,** II-245 (1972).
145. Scow, R. O., Hamosh, M., Blanchette-Mackie, E. J., and Evans, A. J., *Lipids* **7,** 497 (1972).
146. Seidel, D., Agostini, B., and Müller, P., *Biochim. Biophys. Acta* **260,** 146 (1972).
147. Shore, B., *Arch Biochem. Biophys.* **71,** 1 (1957).
148. Shore, B., and Shore, V., *J. Atheroscler. Res.* **2,** 104 (1962).
149. Shore, B., and Shore, V., *Biochemistry* **7,** 2773 (1968).
150. Shore, B., and Shore, V., *Biochemistry* **8,** 4510 (1969).
151. Shore, B., and Shore, V., *in* "Atherosclerosis: Proceedings of the 2nd Intl. Symposium" (Richard J. Jones, ed.), p. 144. Springer-Verlag, New York, 1970.
152. Shore, B., and Shore, V., *Exposes Annu. Biochem. Med.* **31,** 3 (1972).
153. Shore, V., and Shore, B., *Biochemistry* **6,** 1962 (1967).
154. Shore, V., and Shore, B., *Biochemistry* **7,** 3396 (1968).
155. Shore, V. G., and Shore, B., *in* "Blood Lipids and Lipoproteins: Quantitation Composition, and Metabolism, (G. J. Nelson, ed.), Chap. 15, p. 789, Wiley (Interscience), New York, 1972.

156. Shulman, R., Herbert, P., and Brewer, H. B., *Fed. Proc., Fed. Amer. Soc. Exp. Biol.* **30**, 1187 (1971).
157. Shulman, R., Herbert, P., Wehrly, K., Chesebro, B., Levy, R. I., and Fredrickson, D. S., *Circulation* **46**, *II* 246 (Abstr.) (1972).
158. Shulman, R. S., Herbert, P. N., Witters, L. A., Qucker, T., Wehrly, K. A., Fredrickson, D. S., and Levy, R. I., *Fed. Proc., Fed. Amer. Soc. Exp. Biol.* **32**, 1858 (1973).
159. Singer, S. J., *in* "Structure and Function of Biological Membranes" (L. I. Rothfield, ed.), p. 145. Academic Press, New York, 1971.
160. Sloan, H. R., Kwiterovich, P. O., Levy, R. I., and Fredrickson, D. S., *Circulation* **42**, III-8 (1970).
161. Smith, R., Dawson, J. R., and Tanford, C., *J. Biol. Chem.* **247**, 3376 (1972).
162. Sodhi, H. S., and Gould, P. G., *J. Biol. Chem.* **242**, 1205 (1967).
163. Stein, O., and Stein, Y., *J. Cell Biol.* **33**, 319 (1967).
164. Tiselius, A., *Harvey Lect.* **35**, 37 (1941).
165. Torsvik, H., *Clin. Genet.* **3**, 188 (1972).
166. Walton, K. W., Scott, P. J., Jones, J. V., Fletcher, R. F., and Whithead, T., *J. Atheroscler. Res.* **3**, 396 (1963).
167. Windmueller, H. G., Herbert, P. N., and Levy, R. I., *J. Lipid Res.* **14**, 215 (1973).
168. Windmueller, H. G., and Levy, R. I., *J. Biol. Chem.* **242**, 2246 (1967).
169. Windmueller, H. G., and Levy, R. I. *J. Biol. Chem.* **243**, 4878 (1968).
170. Windmueller, H. G., and Spaeth, A. E., *J. Lipid Res.* **13**, 92 (1972).

TRANSFER FACTOR IN
CELLULAR IMMUNITY*

H. SHERWOOD LAWRENCE

*Infectious Disease and Immunology Division,
Department of Medicine,
New York University School of Medicine,
New York, New York*

I. INTRODUCTION

IT is now commonplace to find that investigations initiated as pure basic science have a way of evolving to converge ultimately upon the *in vivo* realities of the human condition and either provide lucid insights into the pathogenesis of disease or a potent means of restoring health. Transfer factor affords a cogent example of such practical dividends that can arise from the pursuit of an idea. There is a twinge of irony in the fact that the branch of immunology concerned with delayed-type hypersensitivity was not regarded in itself as a very promising area of investigation when this work was begun. The discovery of transfer factor initially seemed to compound this bleak outlook, yet recent developments would suggest instead that the whole problem has finally moved into the mainstream of modern molecular biology and clinical practice.

It is perhaps no accident that early studies on transfer factor were fated to retrace the vicissitudes that had dogged work on delayed-type hypersensitivity (DTH) and cell-mediated immunity (CMI). When viewed with detachment, it is understandable that the whole crude enterprise provoked either heated controversy or studied neglect. To begin with, DTH and CMI immune responses were tied to immunology proper by only a slender thread woven around the specificity of the response that required one to meet and recognize the tubercle bacillus in order to express

* Lecture delivered March 15, 1973.

tuberculin sensitivity. Moreover, the ambiguity surrounding the transaction was accentuated by the fact that the appearance of an indolent red spot in the skin was the sole end point of the reaction until the recent availability of *in vitro* assays (Lawrence and Landy, 1969; Bloom and Glade, 1971). Further difficulties arose from the lack of a reagent to quantitate *in vitro,* akin to an immunoglobulin, for example, that did so much to enlarge our understanding of humoral immune responses. And the gulf was widened by the fact that DTH and CMI responses persisted in evading fashionable central dogma and fastidious theories of antibody formation that held sway at any given moment.

It was thus that matters stood a captive of the past until rescued by the discovery of cellular transfer of DTH in the guinea pig by Landsteiner and Chase (1942), subsequently pioneered and developed to perfection by Chase (1945, 1953, 1954, 1959, 1965a,b, 1966, 1967). This finding resulted in a clear separation of the class of immune responses initiated by cells from those mediated by circulating immunoglobulins and at the same time provided an immune reagent to permit quantitation and analysis of the origins and consequences of DTH and CMI.

Our work began with the observation that cellular transfer of cutaneous DTH could be accomplished in man using viable blood leukocytes (Lawrence, 1949). This demonstration led in turn to the observation that leukocyte extracts were as effective as viable cells in the transfer of DTH resulting in the concept of transfer factor (Lawrence, 1955). The term transfer factor (TF) was coined as a convenient, operational shorthand designation of the material or materials present in viable cells or extracts of immune leukocytes responsible for the transfer of DTH and CMI to nonimmune recipients. Moreover, the possibility that more than one factor may be involved in the effects achieved was ackowledged (Lawrence, 1960b).

The finding of TF activity in leukocyte extracts permitted the beginning of attempts to identify and characterize the active material(s) and led to the partial purification of TF as a dialyzable, nonimmunoglobulin moiety of >10,000 MW, composed of peptide-nucleotide residues and possessed of the immunological activities of the cells that bear it (Lawrence *et al.,* 1963).

The principal long-term goal of our work has been to purify and characterize biochemically the molecule(s) responsible for this potent biological activity and to delineate the mechanism(s) whereby such effects are achieved, while continuing to broaden the scope of the biological functions of TF *in vivo* and *in vitro*. In pursuit of this goal our laboratory has made sporadic forays into the design and perfection of *in vitro* assays of DTH and CMI which have yielded techniques and reagents that are now in widespread use (Lawrence and Pappenheimer 1956, 1957; Lawrence, 1963, 1968b; David *et al.*, 1964a–d; Al-Askari *et al.*, 1965a,b; Lebowitz and Lawrence, 1969a,b; Valentine and Lawrence, 1968b, 1969; Marshall *et al.*, 1969; Holzman *et al.*, 1973a,b; Ascher *et al.*, 1973). And along the way, attention has been called to the possible role of TF in the pathogenesis of disease (Lawrence, 1956, 1959c, 1965b, 1969a, 1970a; Solowey *et al.*, 1967; Lawrence and Zweiman, 1968) as well as its potential clinical application in immunotherapy (Editorial, 1968; Lawrence 1969b,c, 1970a, 1971, 1972a,b,c; Oettgen *et al.*, 1971 1974).

II. Early Beginnings—Transfer with Viable Cells

This phase of our work on TF is worth reviewing briefly since much of the structure of later work derives from the findings secured using viable leukocytes and since viable leukocytes or concentrated lymphocyte suspensions are still employed by some investigators in the immunotherapy of disease (Lawrence, 1959a,b). In interpretation of the effects achieved with such preparations containing transfer factor, it is critical to emphasize at the outset that whenever histoincompatible viable cells are employed for transfer they are rejected via an allograft response when the host is immunocompetent. Thus although the cellular vehicle of TF is rejected, TF is not itself rejected since it is separable from histocompatibility antigens and the immunocompetent host in rejecting the transferred cells liberates TF *in vivo* (Rapaport *et al.*, 1965a). The only other outcome possible in this situation occurs in T-cell-deficient, incompetent individuals, where the transferred cells initiate an allograft reaction against his tissue antigens and produce graft vs. host disease. The latter end point is difficult to overlook and poses grave problems, as evidenced by the experience with incompatible bone marrow transplantation in humans.

A. Qualitative and Quantitative Determinants of Successful Transfer and the Origins of the Concept of Specificity

The results secured using viable blood leukocytes as vehicles for TF have also been demonstrated to apply with equal force in later experiments when leukocyte extracts or partially purified preparations of dialyzable transfer factor (TF_D) were used. The original studies in man employed peripheral blood leukocytes and demonstrated that successful transfer of cutaneous DTH to tuberculin was possible (Lawrence, 1949). These results are of interest in that they established the fact that the capacity to transfer DTH to nonimmune recipients resided only in the cells of leukocyte series, not in erythrocytes or serum obtained from the same immune donor. It became evident early that the transfer of cutaneous DTH was an all-or-none phenomenon; and, despite gradations in the individual recipient's response, the skin test following transfer either remained negative or became positive. Moreover, there also emerged stringent dual qualitative and quatitative requirements that exerted a direct effect on the outcome. Stated simply, the transfer of DTH was successful only when the leukocyte donors expressed exquisite cutaneous reactivity to the antigen, (e.g., purified protein derivative PPD), under study and when an adequate volume of leukocytes was injected. For example, 0.05 ml (4.2×10^6) white blood cells (WBC) from a donor with marked cutaneous tuberculin (PPD) sensitivity failed to transfer DTH to each of 2 tuberculin-negative recipients whereas 0.1 ml of WBC (85×10^6) obtained from the same donor and given subsequently to the same two recipients did transfer tuberculin sensitivity. It should be noted that this effect occurred despite the prior induction of allograft sensitization in both recipients to the transferred leukocytes. Other studies showed that 0.2 ml of WBC (170×10^6) obtained from a tuberculin-negative donor had no effect on the cutaneous DTH of a tuberculin-negative recipient whereas 0.2 ml of WBC (170×10^6) obtained from a tuberculin-positive donor and subsequently given to the same tuberculin-negative recipient resulted in the transfer of marked cutaneous tuberculin sensitivity (Lawrence, 1949, 1959, 1969). Identical findings were obtained in a subsequent study when streptococcal materials were used as test antigens; namely, only leukocytes obtained from donors with marked cutaneous DTH were capable of transferring that reactivity to recipients, and leukocytes obtained from negative reactors were not capable of producing a positive result (Lawrence, 1952).

Of interest was the prompt appearance of the transferred DTH as early as 4–6 hours after transfer as evidenced by the triggering of negative screening skin test sites (PPD; diphtheria toxoid) that had been applied 3–4 days earlier (Lawrence, 1949; Lawrence and Pappenheimer, 1956). An analogous systemic effect was also evidenced by a flare-up of quiescent intradermal leukocyte depots in the shoulder of a recipient with transferred DTH to streptococcal M-substance coincident with maximum cutaneous reactivity to antigen placed in the forearm (Lawrence, 1952). It was also noted that the transferred DTH persisted for prolonged periods in humans compared to the guinea pig model. The consequences of this observation will be discussed below.

From the results of these initial studies it became imperative to recognize that for continued operational successful transfer at the most pragmatic level the quality and intensity of the immune status of the leukocyte donor is a paramount consideration. Although transfer of DTH could occasionally be achieved using donors with lesser degrees of sensitivity by increasing the quantity of leukocytes transferred, such transfers when they do occur are usually feeble and evanescent. Thus a successful transfer of DTH can be expected if the donor expresses an exquisite degree of cutaneous reactivity to the antigen under study and an adequate quantity of cells are transferred. Moreover, diminishing the quantity of cells transferred even when obtained from such suitable donors can result in failure to transfer DTH.

These results using viable leukocyte populations for the transfer of DTH have been repeatedly confirmed and extended by a number of investigators using a vast array of antigenic systems for DTH, and their cumulative experience has been reviewed in detail elsewhere (Lawrence, 1959a, 1969a,b). We will consider a few of these studies here, however, since they have a particular bearing on interpretation of the phenomenon.

B. Transfer of DTH via Blood Transfusions or via Renal Transplantation

As might be anticipated from the foregoing discussion, ordinary transfusions of 1 unit of blood obtained from tuberculin-sensitive donors has been shown to transfer tuberculin sensitivity in humans (Mohr et al., 1969). The authors suggested that this possibility should be queried when conversion of tuberculin skin reactivity occurs since the transferred reactivity is indistinguishable from the natural state and may persist for a year.

Similarly, patients with renal disease were studied and found to acquire cutaneous DTH following renal transplantation (Kirkpatrick et al., 1964). Of considerable interest, the allograft recipients developed DTH only to the antigens (mumps, candida, trichophytin) to which the individual kidney donor reacted, not to antigens that elicited no response in the donor; and the transfer of reactivity was not affected by the fact that the recipients were on immunosuppressive drugs (6M-P). In this study also, the transferred DTH was enduring and persisted despite rejection of the transplanted kidney by some recipients. Although these results raise the possibility that cells other than leukocytes may bear TF, the more likely explanation of the transfer of DTH implicates passenger leukocytes and lymphoid cells transplanted en bloc with the renal allograft.

C. Transfer with Nonadherent "Lymphocyte" Populations

In an attempt to delineate which blood cell type in whole buffy coat contains the biological activity, Slavin and Garvin (1964) found that granulocytes or glass-adherent cells alone were not effective whereas nonadherent populations of mononuclear cells, predominantly lymphocytes, were obligatory for transfer of DTH to occur. These experiments used glass to separate the adherent and nonadherent populations.

The lymphocyte or mononuclear cell was further confirmed to possess TF activity when buffy coat preparations that had been passed through nylon filters and cleared of granulocytes were also found to transfer DTH (Hattler and Amos, 1965). The multiple specificities transferred to recipients in these experiments were concordant with those possessed by the donor (i.e., mumps, trichophytin, candida, tuberculin, histoplasmin), and no DTH was transferred to antigens to which the donor was unreactive.

These studies suggest that the cellular vehicles of TF are a nonadherent mononuclear subpopulation of lymphoid cells. This conclusion has been reinforced by recent studies using Ficoll-Hypaque purified cell populations (ca, 98% lymphocytes and 2% monocytes) to prepare dialyzable TF. Nevertheless, the precise cell that yields TF and the particular cell engaged by it remains to be defined.

D. Comparison of Human vs Animal Models

In these early studies using viable leukocytes, most of the findings in humans paralleled those obtained in guinea pigs. These similarities included the requirement for donors with marked degrees of cutaneous DTH to the particular antigen under study as well as the use of an optimal quantity of cells. However, striking qualitative and quantitative species differences soon began to emerge which revealed humans to be infinitely more responsive to the effects of TF. For example, to achieve transfer of DTH between outbred guinea pigs, pooled-cell populations from 5–7 donors were required to sensitize 1 recipient animal and the transferred DTH endured for only 5–7 days after transfer. In the transfer of DTH between outbred humans, cells from 1 donor could transfer DTH to 5 recipients and the transferred sensitivity persists for 6 months to 1 year. Thus smaller quantities of cells produced more intense and enduring effects in humans. The effects produced in animal species were also found to depend upon viable cells, and transfer of DTH could not be achieved if killed cell populations were employed (Bloom and Chase, 1967).

Moreover, the DTH is terminated in outbred guinea pig recipients when the transferred cells are rejected via an allograft response at 7 days (Harris and Harris, 1960). This type of observation has been extended to demonstrate that pretreatment of prospective recipient animals with cells from the prospective donor, results in a state of heightened allograft immunity that results in accelerated rejection of that donor's cells and abrogates the transfer of DTH entirely (Warwick et al., 1962).

We have indicated above the prompt onset (hours to days) and long duration (months to 2 years) of the transferred DTH in humans. Moreoever, pretreatment of prospective human recipients with cells from the prospective donor did not abolish or affect the subsequent transfer of DTH to the recipient despite the induction of allograft immunity to the transferred cells (Lawrence, 1949). These observations would suggest that when viable cells are transferred to immunocompetent humans they are rejected via an allograft response yet this event does not interfere with the transfer of DTH even in recipients that have been presensitized to allograft antigens.

In subsequent collaborative studies that we undertook to define the subcellular locus of human histocompatibility antigens, it was shown that such antigens are closely associated with the endoplasmic reticulum of blood leukocyte fractions and are nondialyzable (Rapaport et al., 1965a). Conversely, pretreatment of individuals with dialyzates, prepared from the same leukocyte extracts that had demonstrable HL-A antigenic potency, failed to cause allograft immunity to skin grafts obtained from the leukocyte donors that were subsequentially applied. Since TF is a dialyzable, nonantigenic moiety, we conclude from these results that although the cellular vehicles of TF are rejected via an allograft response, TF itself is separable from histocompatibility antigens and liberated *in vivo* in the rejection process. Thus, the prolonged duration of transferred DTH in humans following the use of viable cells provided clues to the possibility that the viability of the cells transferred was not an obligatory requirement for successful transfer of DTH.

This brings us to the most significant departure from the animal model where leukocyte extracts in humans were found to be as effective as viable cells in the transfer of DTH. (Lawrence 1954b, 1955). We discuss, in a later section, new evidence for the existence of TF in animal-to-animal and human-to-animal transfers of DTH and CMI (see Table VIII).

III. Transfers of DTH with Leukocyte Extracts

A. Tuberculin and Streptococcal M-Substance

Because of the species differences in the cellular transfer system discussed above it became possible to think of attempts at transfer in humans with subcellular components. In our initial approach to this problem, buffy coat leukocytes were totally disrupted by osmotic lysis following incubation in distilled water at 37°C for 4–6 hours. The resultant leukocyte lysate was found to be capable of transferring DTH to streptococcal M-substance, as were the centrifuged fractions of such lysates comprised of Feulgen-positive nucleoprotein sediment resuspended in 2 ml of cytoplasmic supernatants or the Feulgen-negative cytoplasmic supernatant solution alone. Transfer of DTH to streptococcal M-substance was also achieved when leukocytes were alternatively frozen (alcohol–dry ice) and thawed (37°C) through 7–10 cycles (Lawrence 1954b, 1955).

Here again we evaluated the contribution of the intensity of donor's cutaneous reactivity and the quantity of cells lysed to the success of transfer. In one instance, lysate from 0.5 ml of WBC (425×10^6) obtained from a door with 3+ cutaneous reactivity failed to transfer DTH to M-substance whereas lysate prepared from fewer WBC (0.3 ml or 255×20^6) from another donor with marked (4+) cutaneous reactivity and given to the same recipient resulted in a positive transfer.

In another instance, the quantity of cells used to prepare lysate from a markedly sensitive donor was deliberately reduced to 0.08 ml (68×10^6). This reduced dosage failed to transfer DTH to M-substance to a negative recipient whereas when the dosage of WBC lysate, obtained from the same donor and given to the same recipient, was increased to 0.4 ml (340×10^6) prompt transfer of a marked degree of M-substance reactivity resulted. It should be noted that repeated testing with antigen alone did not result in a positive DTH response until after these recipients had received an adequate quantity of TF obtained from a markedly sensitive donor. The findings with frozen and thawed leukocyte extracts using M-substance as the test antigen were confirmed when tuberculin (OT, PPD) was used as the antigen. Leukocyte extracts obtained from tuberculin-negative individuals failed to transfer DTH to tuberculin despite repeated tuberculin testing of the recipients (Lawrence, 1955).

Thus, the results achieved using extracts of leukocytes prepared by two different techniques and assessed using two different antigenic systems were identical to those obtained using viable cells. The similarities observed included the same requirements for adequate intensity of antigen-specific donor reactivity and adequate quantities of cells used; as well as the prompt appearance of DTH after transfer (18 hours) and its prolonged duration (>10 months) when these conditions are adhered to.

B.   Serial Transfer of Cutaneous DTH

Thus we observed extensive and enduring alterations in specific immunological reactivity following the introduction of minuscule quantities of nonliving fragments of leukocytes relative to the surface area and the dilutional capacities of the adult human recipient. This raised the question whether TF functioned as merely a signal to initiate the changes encountered; or alternatively, whether the recipient, in responding to this stimulus, replicated the active moiety in his circulating lymphocytes and made more TF of the same immunologic specificity. To test this question we made two attempts at serial passage of TF from individual A to B to C using two different antigens and two modes of leukocyte extract preparation as shown in Table I.

As may be seen, leukocyte extract prepared by osmotic lysis from an M-positive donor transferred DTH to an M-negative recipient, and on day 3 after transfer, at the height of the response, leukocyte extract prepared from this recipient transferred

TABLE I

SERIAL TRANSFER OF DELAYED HYPERSENSITIVITY[a,b]

Sensitive donor, A	Transfer factor preparation	Reaction 1st recipient, B	Time bled after 1st transfer	Transfer factor preparation	Reaction 2nd recipient, C
Streptococcal M-substance positive 4+	Water lysis, 0.5 ml WBC	4+	Day 3	Water lysis, 0.5 ml WBC	2+
Tuberculin positive 4+	Freeze-thaw, 0.2 ml WBC	4+	Week 3	Freeze-thaw, 0.5 ml WBC	2+

[a] From Lawrence (1955).
[b] Each 0.1 ml of packed wet buffy coat leukocytes (WBC) ca. 85×10^6 cells; each "+" = 10×10 mm of induration and erythema.

M-substance reactivity to a secondary negative recipient. In a companion experiment leukocyte extract obtained from a tuberculin-positive donor and prepared by freezing and thawing transferred tuberculin sensitivity to a primary tuberculin-negative recipient; at the third week after transfer, leukocyte extract prepared from this recipient transferred tuberculin reactivity to a secondary negative recipient.

Although limited to only two attempts, these results of serial transfer suggested at the very least that TF in addition to conferring DTH *in vivo* causes a new population of leukocytes to appear in the circulation of the recipient; these leukocytes have a newly acquired capacity to transfer the reactivity to the antigen under study. Moreover, this new population of cells was detected as early as day 3 after transfer and as late as the third week; and it is probable that such cells could be detected in the primary recipient's circulation for as long as the state of transferred DTH endures in force. These results by virtue of the serial dilutional considerations alone also tended to weaken the notion that TF is a "superantigen" or a unique type of antibody.

The results of serial transfer evoked a healthy skepticism at that time (Lawrence, 1955). Nevertheless, subsequent studies using dialyzable TF have repeatedly documented the *de novo* appearance of a new clone of specific antigen-responsive lymphocytes in the circulation of recipients that was not present before TF administration. This observation was made initially in a cancer patient (Lawrence, 1969a,b) and subsequently confirmed in patients with disseminated infections or immunodeficiency disease (Levin *et al.*, 1970; Kirkpatrick *et al.*, 1972; LoBuglio *et al.*, 1973; Graybill *et al.*, 1973; Griscelli *et al.*, 1973; Hitzig, *et al.*, 1972; Moulias *et al.*, 1973; Pabst and Swanson, 1972; Valdimarsson *et al.*, 1972; Whitcomb and Rocklin, 1973).

In these studies also (see Tables X–XII), the circulating lymphocytes of recipients following TF administration will respond *in vitro* to the appropriate antigen with lymphocyte proliferation and/or mediator (MIF, lymphotoxin, interferon) production. The antigenic specificities to which the recipient's lymphocytes do respond are usually concordant with the pattern of cutaneous DTH expressed by the donor of TF.

The early results of serial transfer thus appeared to favor the interpretation that TF was replicated by the recipient, and therefore we looked into the possibility that we might be dealing with a mammalian type of transforming or transducing agent such as existed in microbial species. To test this question further, we treated frozen and thawed leukocyte extracts from sensitive donors of known potency alternatively with pancreatic DNase and pancreatic RNase, respectively. These enzymatic treatments did not abolish or diminish the capacity of such preparations to transfer intense and enduring DTH when compared to untreated controls. Additionally, treatment of such leukocyte extracts with DNase plus trypsin also had no effect on the capacity to transfer DTH. From these results we concluded that the active moiety in leukocyte extracts was not dependent for its function upon highly polymerized DNA or RNA, nor upon proteins that are susceptible to tryptic digestion. Nevertheless, our main goal had been achieved in that we provided a preparation that would allow further attempts at the purification and chemical characterization of TF as a step toward the ultimate elucidation of its mechanism of action.

C. Transfer of DTH to Diphtheria Toxoid

To pursue this problem further, it became of considerable interest to attempt to relate TF to conventional immunology and subject its *in vivo* activities to precise immunochemical analysis. For this purpose the diphtheria toxin/toxoid-antitoxin system was selected as an ideal model. In earlier studies with Pappenheimer (Pappenheimer and Lawrence, 1948a,b) we had isolated highly purified diphtheria toxin and had shown in a large series of naturally sensitive individuals that minute quantities of toxoid elicited intense cutaneous DTH reactions and the delayed response was always accompanied by high levels of circulating antitoxin.

This antigenic system afforded the additional advantages of working with (1) a well-characterized and highly purified protein antigen (ca. 95% pure toxoid); and (2) a most sensitive biological neutralization test for the detection of antitoxin even when present in minute quantity (>0.01 μg/ml). Thus, if TF functioned as a superantigen or antigen fragment sufficient to induce DTH to toxoid, it was reasonable to expect the stimulation of antibody production and to detect antitoxin in recipients of TF obtained from hyperimmune donors with exquisite DTH to toxoid.

We found that transfer of DTH both to diphtheria toxoid and to tuberculin was readily accomplished using DNase-treated leukocyte extracts obtained from donors with intense DTH to toxoid and only moderate DTH to tuberculin. Yet no antitoxin was detected in the sera of such recipients at the time of maximum DTH response to toxoid following transfer. It was possible that the local DTH inflammatory reaction evoked by skin test with toxoid in the TF recipient may contain reactive cells containing or secreting antitoxin, hence toxin was injected into nascent DTH skin test sites initiated several hours earlier by injection with toxoid: the toxin was not neutralized and the cutaneous DTH response was superseded at 4 days by the classical dermonecrotic reaction to toxin that is characteristic of Shick-positive individuals who do not possess antitoxin.

Since diphtheria toxoid, even in minute skin test doses, is such a potent antigen special precautions were taken in the testing of TF recipients. The donors were selected for reactivity to both tuberculin (PPD) and toxoid to which the recipients were negative, and the latter were tested only with tuberculin (PPD) as a marker to determine the onset and peak of transferred DTH reactivity, while the test with toxoid was withheld at will. We found that withholding the first test with toxoid for as long as 19 days after transfer had no effect on the quality or intensity of the transferred DTH to toxoid. This response was comparable to that of other recipients tested with toxoid at 19 days who had also responded with DTH to prior tests with toxoid at 4 and again at 11 days after transfer. We also documented that the screening test with toxoid to select negative recipients had no effect on the quality of the transferred DTH whether the recipient had been tested as long as 2 years or as little as 3 days before transfer.

These results obtained with a potent antigen, toxoid, suggest that skin testing before and immediately after transfer appears to have no detectable preparative or conditioning effect on the recipients response to TF *in vivo*. This conclusion was reinforced in later studies on the transfer of skin graft rejection where prior testing of the recipient is unnecessary (Lawrence *et al.*, 1960). From this study of TF in the diphtheria toxoid system, it was concluded that, despite the ease of transfer of cutaneous DTH by means of leukocyte extracts from toxoid-sensitive donors, it was not possible to transfer either a primary or secondary antibody response to the same antigenic determinants. Viewed in this light the recipient of TF, unlike the native donor, can only express pure DTH responses, and this expression occurs in the absence of any contribution from circulating or cell-bound immunoglobulin of the same specificity. These results showing lack of antibody transfer by blood leukocyte preparations of TF were subsequently confirmed by Good *et al.* (1957) in agammaglobulinemic children where transfer of viable leukocytes from SK-SD sensitive donors conferred only DTH responses to SK-SD and no secondary antibody response to typhoid-parathyphoid A-B antigens, despite vigorous priming of the donors. We also subsequently failed to transfer coccidioidal complement-fixing antibody responses to recipients of DNase-treated leukocyte extracts from coccidioidin-sensitive donors despite the transfer of intense DTH to coccidioidin (Rapaport *et al.*, 1960b). This has also been the recent experience where TF has been used to treat children with combined immunodeficiency syndromes where only cellular immunity is restored and replacement therapy with gamma globulin is still required (Hitzig *et al.*, 1972).

D. Attempts to Neutralize TF with Antigen (PPD, Toxoid)

Having failed to detect an antibody response following transfer, we attempted to neutralize or block TF activity by incubating sensitive leukocyte populations with corresponding antigen (Lawrence and Pappenheimer, 1956). Viable leukocytes were isolated from donors expressing the respective sensitivity and resuspended in recipient serum to which either tuberculin PPD (25 μg) or purified diphtheria toxoid (3 μg) was added. After incubation in a rotary water bath for 0.5 to 1 hour at 37°C, both the cell pellet extract and the cell-free supernatant solution were assayed for TF activity by *in vivo* transfer. When toxoid was used as antigen, an equivalent amount of toxoid-TF activity was found in the cells and in the supernatant; whereas incubation with tuberculin PPD caused 3 times the tuberculin TF activity to be liberated into the supernatant versus 1$\times$ tuberculin TF activity remaining in the cell pellet. It was also observed that TF activity could leak out of leukocyte suspensions into the supernatant merely upon standing such suspensions at 37°C for 1 hour in the absence of added antigen.

We concluded from such *in vitro* results that TF activity can be rapidly liberated from sensitive cells following interaction with the corresponding antigen and that antigen did not block TF activity. These observations suggested that TF interacted with antigen, but, unlike the usual behavior of an antibody, even a cell-bound antibody, it was not neutralized by antigen.

Subsequent studies of this *in vitro* system attempted to evaluate the specificity of the interaction of TF and antigen (Lawrence and Pappenheimer, 1957). Our earliest results showed that special precautions must be taken to minimize damage to the cells during the incubation period, or TF could leak out whether antigen was present or absent. Therefore care was taken to employ in the isolation and culture of leukocytes optimal conditions to ensure their viability and health. The results of one such experiment done under these conditions is shown in Fig. 1. Blood leukocyte populations taken from a donor sensitive to tuberculin (PPD) and to diphtheria toxoid when incubated with 25 μg PPD for 1 hour at 37°C resulted in the liberation only of TF activity for tuberculin, not for toxoid, into the cell-free supernatant solution; the TF activity for toxoid, however, remained in the cell pellet, which had lost its tuberculin TF as measured by *in vivo* transfer. Control cells incubated without antigen retained the equivalent TF activity for both tuberculin and toxoid whereas neither activity was detected in that supernatant solution after *in vivo* transfer. These results suggested that the interaction with TF and antigen is specific, resulting in the liberation of the corresponding TF into the supernatant while the cells that bear it

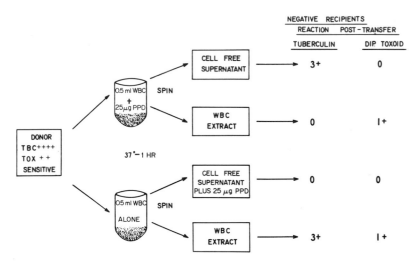

FIG. 1. *In vivo* specificity of transfer factor liberated from sensitive cell population within 1 hour of incubation with antigen *in vitro*. Each "+" = 10 × mm of induration and erythema. Data from Lawrence and Pappenheimer (1957); the figure is reproduced from Lawrence (1969a). DIP, diphtheria; PPD, purified protein derivative tuberculin; TBC, tuberculin; TOX, toxoid.

have become "desensitized" and lose the capacity to transfer. Since techniques for prolonged lymphocyte culture were not available at the time of these experiments and since an extract of the cell pellet was made promptly for *in vivo* transfer, we do not know whether the loss of TF by such "desensitized" cells was temporary or whether on continued culture of such cells more tuberculin TF may be synthesized.

Similar results were obtained when the principle derived from these *in vitro* results was applied to the *in vivo* transfer system by Oliveira-Lima (1958). He showed that leukocytes obtained from 6 donors sensitive to both tuberculin and streptococcal antigens transferred both reactivities to 6 correspondingly negative recipients. The following desensitization of the same 6 donors to tuberculin to the point of negative cutaneous reactivity, he showed that only streptococcal, but not tuberculin, sensitivity could be transferred to 6 additional recipients negative to both antigens. In retrospect one would now have looked at the time of desensitization for the tuberculin TF in the donor's serum or, since it is a small molecule, in donor urine.

The preparation of antigen-liberated TF holds great promise as a technique for providing a pure monospecific TF for biochemical analysis or therapeutic use by incubating sensitive lymphocytes with the desired antigen and leaving behind in the cell pellet the myraids of TF specificities, known and unknown, possessed by most normal donors. Recently, Graybill *et al.* (1973) have applied this technique to prepare a monospecific coccidioidin TF for the treatment of disseminated coccidiodomycosis. They found that incubation of lymphocytes from coccidioidin-sensitive donors with coccidioidin resulted in the liberation of coccidioidin TF into the supernatant. This antigen-liberated, monospecific TF was also found to be dialyzable and as potent clinically and immunologically as that prepared from leukocyte extracts directly.

E.   Transfer of DTH to Coccidioidin

The results of transfer using antigens that are ubiquitous in the environment (e.g., tuberculin, streptococcal proteins, diphtheria toxoid) may be interpreted as arising from the elevation of a latent sensitivity by means of TF rather than conferring a *de novo* state (Bloom and Chase, 1967; Turk 1967). This possibility is difficult to exclude with certainty for microbiol antigens despite accrual of the cumulative experimental evidence pointing to the quality and intensity of the immunological experience of the TF donor rather than that of the recipient as a critical determinant of the outcome of transfer (reviewed in Lawrence 1969a,b). To clarify this problem further, we sought to exclude elevation of latent sensitivity by selecting coccidioidin as an antigen, since exposure to this fungus is limited to the western portions of this country. The one fungal antigen with which coccidioidin may cross-react is histoplasmin, and this fungus is also restricted in distribution to southern and central geographic areas of this country with an incidence of 1.4% positive reactors of 11,000 residents of New York City tested. Therefore, TF was prepared from DNase-treated leukocyte extracts obtained from coccidioidin-sensitive donors living in California; the TF was frozen for the flight to New York and transferred to coccidioidin-negative recipients who had resided exclusively on the Eastern Seaboard (Rapaport *et al.,* 1960a,b). These studies showed that transfer of DTH to coccidioidin was possible in 23 of 27 consecutive attempts with preparations of TF obtained from moderately to markedly sensitive donors; in 5 of 8 consecutive attempts when obtained from minimally to moderately sensitive donors; and in 1 of 9 consecutive attempts when obtained from a single negative donor. Transferred coccidioidin sensitivity was observed to persist for >16 months in the absence of repeated skin tests or environmental exposure to coccidioides and the prolonged duration of such transferred sensitivity appeared to be correlated with the intensity of the cutaneous DTH initially transferred.

Thus a group of 12 recipients was tested 1 week after transfer and again 1+ years later. We found that the 6 recipients who had developed only moderate DTH to coccidioidin (2+) at 1 week had reverted to negative at the end of 1 year, whereas the 6 recipients who had developed marked coccidioidin sensitivity (4+) at 1 week were still reactive a year later. It was also noted that injections of incubated mixtures of coccidioidin-negative leukocyte extracts plus coccidioidin failed to transfer sensitivity in 8 of 9 attempts. Additionally, repeated testing of these 8 recipients with coccidioidin failed to cause the appearance of DTH to this antigen. These results yielded suggestive but not conclusive evidence for the transfer of *de novo* sensitivity. Although skin test with antigen was obligatory to reveal the state of transferred sensitivity, such tests did not appear to cause the sensitive state nor contribute to its intensity or duration. This is also illustrated in the feeble intensity and transient duration of transferred DTH in individuals who then revert to a negative state in a matter of weeks and who do not reacquire DTH despite subsequent application of repeated skin tests. Some of the properties of transfer factor as detailed up to this point are briefly set out in Table II.

Thus it was demonstrated that minute quantities of nonliving fragments of leukocyte extracts as well as cell-free supernatants prepared to contain TF were found to be as effective as viable cells in the transfer of DTH in man. Moreover, the results achieved with such subcellular preparations paralleled those initially secured with viable cells, namely, documentation of early onset (hours to days) and long duration (months to 2 years) of the transferred DTH and confirmation of the critical role of intensity of donor sensitivity as well as an optimum quantity of cells to ensure successful transfer of DTH.

These findings represented a radical departure from prior experiences in the guinea pig system and reopened the whole question of transfer with cell-free materials in a species which had served as a paradigm for the study of DTH. Extensive additional studies in the guinea pig during that period failed to confirm the observations secured in humans using cell-free or subcellular preparations (cf. Bloom and Chase, 1967; Turk, 1967). In this climate attempts at confirmation in man of the efficiency of leukocyte extracts by other investigators was naturally delayed. Nevertheless, when the transfer with leukocyte extracts was finally repeated in humans the original observations were confirmed in precise detail by several laboratories. (Maurer, 1961; Baram and Mosko, 1962; Brown and Katz, 1967). The results of Maurer (1961) are of particular theoretical interest in that he employed a neoantigen (ethylene oxide-treated human serum albumin) to which

TABLE II

SOME PROPERTIES OF TRANSFER FACTOR (TF)[a]

Biological	Biochemical, TF unaffected by:	Immunological[b]
Endows recipient with specific sensitivity of donor	25°C or 37°C—6 hours	Interacts with but is not neutralized by antigen
Sensitivity is systemic	Distilled-water lysis	WBC desensitized by antigen
Onset early (hours)	Freeze-thaw, 10 cycles	Neg. WBC + antigen → no transfer
Duration long (months → >1 year)		
Minute dosage WBC effective:	Deep freeze, 5 months	No detectable AB in donor WBC extract
As little as 0.01 ml → local transfer	DNase	No detectable AB in skin or serum of recipient of transferred sensitivity
As little as 0.1 ml → systemic transfer		
Capacity for transfer parallels donor sensitivity and dosage WBC	RNase	Not active sensitization, early onset
Negative donors incapable	Lysosomal hydrolases	Not passive sensitization, long duration
Extracts or cell-free supernatants as effective as viable cells	DNase + trypsin	Repeated test with antigen may increase intensity and duration of transferred sensitivity— yet is not necessarily its cause

[a] From Lawrence (1960b).
[b] AB, antibody; WBC, buffy coat leukocytes.

neither donors nor recipients had been previously exposed. He induced intense cutaneous DTH to this neoantigen without concomitant antibody formation in prospective TF donors. Prior skin testing of prospective recipients of TF was thereby avoided since they had not been exposed to the neoantigen. Frozen and thawed leukocyte extracts obtained from such sensitive donors were found to transfer intense (35 mm) DTH to the neoantigen to five consecutive recipients. Three recipients who served as controls received viable cells, obtained from the same donors, and each developed DTH comparable to that observed in the recipients of leukocyte extracts. All of the recipients received only one skin test with neoantigen after transfer; this was repeated 1 year later at which time all recipients were still sensitive. This last result is of particular interest and paralleled our experience with coccidioidin, where the transferred DTH was found to persist for >1 year in the absence of repeated application of skin tests or environmental exposure to antigen (Rapaport *et al.*, 1960b). Maurer's results are more incisive, however, in consequence of the selection of an antigen that can only be prepared in the laboratory and in the avoidance of a screening skin test before transfer.

It was not deliberately demonstrated by Maurer (1961) that the donors lacked a TF for the neoantigen before being sensitized to it. Nevertheless, we would conclude that a TF with that specificity was raised *de novo* in the donors who lacked it before their exposure to the neoantigen. This conclusion is based on our detection of the *de novo* appearance of histocompatible specific TF's in donors actively sensitized to skin allografts (Lawrence *et al.*, 1960, 1962).

The confirmation of TF in leukocyte extracts by Jensen *et al.* (1962) is also of interest with regard to immunological specificity of transfer to cross-reactive antigens. Twenty-six donors were selected with variable reactivity to human (PPD-S), Battey (PPD-B), and avian (PPD-A) tuberculin, and various doses of frozen leukocytes (0.1–0.65 ml) were used for transfer. DTH to one or more tuberculin preparations was transferred to 18 of 26 negative receipients, while 8 recipients remained negative to all three tuberculins. Six recipients were given preparations obtained from negative donors, 4 remained negative, and 2 developed positive reactions. Upon retesting one of the negative donors, he was found to react to PPD-B.

The latter finding is in keeping with our own experience over the years; we have found that a putatively "negative" donor who does transfer DTH will respond upon retesting with a higher concentration of antigen and is actually a positive reactor (cf. Table V in Rapaport *et al.*, 1960b). Nevertheless there are two exceptions where truly skin test negative individuals in our experience have transferred DTH once to streptococcal M-substance (cf Table III in Lawrence, 1955) and once to coccidioidin (cf Table VI in Rapaport 1960b). We have no explanation for these exceptions to the general experience.

F. Raising TF de novo and Transfer of Specific Allograft Immunity

At this time we undertook studies of allograft immunity in man in an attempt to extend the biological functions of TF and explore a possible mechanism involved in allograft rejection (Lawrence et al., 1960). We viewed the allografted host as being infected with cells possessed of metabolic properties and antigen mosaics that differed from microbial cells and yet utilized the same pathways of immunological recognition and disposal (Lawrence, 1957).

In all of our prior studies of TF using microbial antigens, we selected leukocyte donors with the most intense naturally acquired cutaneous DTH reactions. Since exposure to allograft antigens is not a natural environmental event, we had to depart from the usual protocol and actively immunize normal individuals in order that they could serve as TF donors. Preliminary studies in genetically dissimilar human subjects had shown that in response to the initial exposure to 11-mm orthotopic skin allografts, the graft becomes vascularized by the third day and lives for 8–10 days, at which time rejection occurs—the "first-set reaction" of nonimmune subjects. Upon subsequent reexposure to another skin graft from the same individual, the host responds with a "second-set reaction," where the graft becomes vascularized on the third day and is rejected in an accelerated fashion within the fourth to sixth day. This reaction of accelerated rejection was thus shown to be a hallmark of prior exposure or immunity to skin allografts (Lawrence et al., 1960). The end point selected for detection of the effects of allograft-specific TF was to cause the nonimmune recipient to respond to a first-set skin graft with a second-set reaction of accelerated rejection, i.e. as though he had been presensitized. To accomplish this, TF was raised in individual B after repeated exposure to 11-mm orthotopic skin grafts from individual A. The anti-A TF prepared from leukocyte extracts was then injected into a third individual, C, either 8 days prior to or 3 days after the target graft from A and control grafts from other individuals (D, E or F) were placed *in situ*.

We found that if the TF donor was immunized with only one exposure to A's skin no transfer of accelerated rejection occurred. Similarly leukocyte extracts taken from the TF donor at the time of a first-set rejection and pooled with those taken following a second exposure and rejection of A's skin also failed to transfer systemic allograft immunity. Thus, on four successive occasions transfer into C had no effect on 8 target grafts which survived 10–12 days and were accorded a first-set rejection identical to that of control grafts (cf. Table II, Lawrence *et al.*, 1960). These consistently negative findings established the absence of an allograft specific TF in the nonimmune donor and suggested that neither one exposure nor even two sequential exposures to skin grafts were sufficient antigenic stimuli to raise a new TF.

Since the technique of systemic transfer (i.e., injection of WBC extract into the shoulder and skin grafts applied to the forearm) was used in the above experiments, we next employed the technique of local transfer (i.e., injection of WBC extract around the graft in halo fashion where the target and TF are placed in close proximity) (Lawrence, 1959a,b). The local juxtaposition of TF and antigen had been shown to magnify the effects of TF both locally and systematically and permit a 10-fold reduction in the quantity of cells required compared to systemic transfer (Lawrence, 1949, 1959a).

When this technique was adopted in the allograft system we observed that two sequential graft exposures provided an antigenic stimulus adequate to cause the appearance in donor leukocyte extracts of a quantity of allograft-specific TF only sufficient to allow for local but not systemic transfer of accelerated rejection of target grafts. Additionally, controls for this observation included infiltration of nonimmune leukocyte extracts as well as immune serum locally around target grafts and were without effect. The results of this approach are summarized in Table III.

In order to accomplish systemic transfer of allograft rejection it was found that the TF donor must be exposed to a series

TABLE III

SPECIFICITY OF TRANSFER FACTOR FOR HISTOCOMPATIBILITY ANTIGENS. PART A.
LOCAL TRANSFER DONE 3 DAYS AFTER GRAFTS IN RESIDENCE[a,b]

Donor	Status	Material transferred	Recipient	Target, A	Control, D	Score
D4	Sens. vs A	0.2 ml WBC Ext.	R5	4/5	8	Positive
		1.0 ml Serum	R5	10	8	Negative
D5	Sens. vs A	0.2 ml WBC Ext.	R7	4	10	Positive
		1.0 ml Serum	R7	10	—	Negative
Normal	Not Sens.	0.2 ml WBC Ext.	R7	10	—	Negative
D6	Sens. vs A	0.17 ml WBC Ext.	R8	5/6	10	Positive
		0.17 ml WBC Ext.	R9	5/6	10	Positive
D6	Sens. vs A	1.0 ml Serum	R10	10	—	Negative
Normal	Not sens.	0.2 ml WBC Ext.	R10	10	—	Negative

The "Day of graft rejection" header spans the Target, A and Control, D columns.

[a] From Lawrence et al. (1960).

[b] The shorter period of sensitization (Sens.) of the transfer factor donor (e.g., 2 sequential exposures to 11-mm skin grafts) and the lower dosages of transfer factor used to achieve local transfer (e.g., 0.2 ml of packed WBC $\approx 170 \times 10^6$ cells) were insufficient to cause systemic sensitization of the recipient. Therefore target grafts not in juxtaposition to transfer factor were unaffected. WBC Ext., buffy coat leukocyte extract.

of 4 sequential skin grafts with a latent period of 2–3 weeks between each graft application. When these conditions are followed, systemic tranfer of specific allograft immunity is observed regularly as summarized in Table IV. It may be seen that additional control observations were afforded by Donor 7, whose leukocyte extracts were able to transfer accelerated rejection at the height of his immunization schedule but not 11 days later at a time when donor 7 had lost his earlier immunity to A's skin. Finally, attempts to speed up the long period required for donor sensitization resulted in the finding that second-, third-, and fourth-set skin grafts applied at weekly intervals after the

TABLE IV

SPECIFICITY OF TRANSFER FACTOR FOR HISTOCOMPATIBILITY ANTIGENS. PART B
SYSTEMIC TRANSFER EFFECTIVE WITH SENSITIZED BUT NOT
DENSENSITIZED TRANSFER FACTOR DONOR[a,b]

Donor	Status	Material transferred	Recipient	Transfer in relation to skin grafting	Day of graft rejection Target, A	Day of graft rejection Control, D	Score
D7	Sens. vs A	0.52 ml WBC Ext.[c]	R11	8 Days before	4	11	Positive
		0.52 ml WBC Ext.	R12	3 Days after	4/5	8	Positive
D7	Desens. vs A	0.50 ml WBC Ext.	R13	11 Days before	8	8	Negative
		0.50 ml WBC Ext.	R14	11 Days before	9	9	Negative
		0.5 ml WBC Ext.	R15	3 Days after	10	14	Negative
		0.5 ml WBC Ext.	R16	3 Days after	8	15	Negative
D9	Sens. vs A	0.7 ml WBC Ext.	R22	8 Days before	4	11	Positive
		0.7 ml WBC Ext.	R23	8 Days before	4	8	Positive
D10	Sens. vs A	0.9 ml WBC Ext.	R24	8 Days before	4	13	Positive
		0.9 ml WBC Ext.	R25	8 Days before	4	7	Positive

[a] From Lawrence et al. (1960).

[b] Donor 7 exhibited a "recall flare" at each previous skin graft site coincident with the rejection of second-, third-, and fourth-set A grafts used to sensitize him. His leukocyte extracts taken at the height of the fourth set rejection transferred accelerated rejection of target but not control grafts to each of 2 recipients. However, leukocyte extracts in the same dosage obtained from Donor 7 (11 days after the above bleeding) failed to transfer accelerated graft rejection to each of 4 additional recipients. Following this unexpected result, Donor 7 received a fifth-set of A skin 80 days after his first exposure and now accorded it a first-set reaction with a survival time of 9–10 days (Lawrence et al., 1962). It is a pity his serum was not tested at the time his leukocyte extracts failed to transfer, since we have shown that incubation of sensitive leukocytes with specific antigen results in the liberation of transfer factor into the supernatant which now can transfer delayed sensitivity whereas the cells have become desensitized and lose this capacity (Lawrence and Pappenheimer, 1957).

[c] Transfer factor donors for purposes of systemic transfer were exposed to four sequential applications of 11-mm skin grafts, and larger dosages of transfer factor were used (e.g., 0.5 ml to 0.9 ml packed WBC $\simeq$ 425 to 765 $\times$ 10^6 cells).

first set, resulted in the phenomenon of "white graft" rejection. When leukocyte extracts were obtained from a donor immunized in this fashion, they failed to transfer allograft rejection to four consecutive recipients.

These results afford the most comprehensive and strongest critical evidence for the specificity of TF. The observations demonstrate the following findings: (1) Normal individuals do not naturally possess an allograft-specific TF directed vs other individuals' HL-A antigens, yet do acquire that TF following precise conditions of immunization. (2) Such allograft-specific TF can only cause accelerated rejection of the target graft used to immunize and it has no affect on control grafts even when both are placed in close proximity (3) TF obtained from nonimmune donors cannot cause the accelerated rejection of either target or control grafts. (4) Serum from immune donors is also without effect on graft survival. In avoiding the necessity for prior screening of recipients by test with antigen and in showing that the allograft-specific TF was equally active when administered either 11 days before or 3 days after the target graft was applied, this study also served to provide hard data for the conclusion that it is the immune status of the TF donor rather than that of the recipient which is the critical determinant of the success of transfer. An example of the results discussed above is illustrated in Fig. 2.

The results also delineated clearly at least one mechanism concerned with the initiation of allograft rejection and suggested that it is the particular subpopulation of lymphocytes bearing a specific TF directed vs the transplanted organ that should afford a more precise target of immunosuppression.

Subsequent extension of this work evaluated the subcellular locus of allograft antigens in leukocyte fractions and found the antigenic activity that was able to immunize an individual to respond with accelerated rejection or white graft rejection of the leukocyte donor's skin resided in the endoplasmic reticulum (Rapaport et al., 1965a,b). It was also observed that allograft antigens are nondialyzable and that dialyzates prepared from active preparations were unable to immunize subjects to the leukocyte donor's skin graft. Therefore, in this system of immunity,

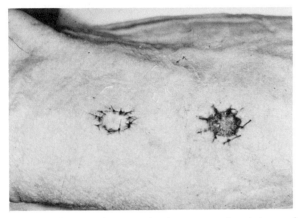

FIG. 2. Transfer of allograft immunity by means of anti-A transfer factor (TF). Photo taken 4 days after application of test and control skin grafts and 12 days after transfer. The graft from individual (A) is a black eschar; control graft from unrelated individual (C) is unaffected by anti-A TF and survived 11 days. From Lawrence *et al.* (1960).

TF which is dialyzable is readily separable from allograft antigens.

The observations secured in studying the transfer of allograft rejection combined with the finding that allograft antigens are not dialyzable has come to have a particular meaning for patients with organ transplants who develop disseminated infections while on immunosuppressive drugs. Dialyzable TF can be used to treat such infections since the normal donor will not possess a TF vs the alloantigens of the patient nor of his organ transplant and since dialysis frees TF of all allograft antigens. This application of the use of TF in the treatment of an immunosuppressed renal transplant recipient suffering from mycobacteriosis has been attempted recently (Graybill *et al.*, 1974). There were no adverse effects on the renal transplant function following administration of TF.

Finally, it is now well established that the principles learned from allograft immunity are generally applicable to tumor immunity. However, certain distinctions arise in the tumor system by virtue of weaker antigenic differences between the tumor and its host coupled with the potential for antigenic modulation inherent in a replicating, metastasizing population of tumor cells. Within the limits imposed by the latter distinctions, the principles elucidated in respect of allograft-specific TF in the initiation of allograft rejection are also broadly applicable to the tumor-bearing host, as will be detailed below.

IV. FURTHER PURIFICATION AND CHARACTERIZATION— STUDIES WITH DIALYZABLE TRANSFER FACTOR (TF$_D$)

Having evaluated in some depth the phenomenological aspects of TF and extended the scope of its biological functions, the time had come to return to the more demanding task of further purification and biochemical characterization of the active moiety as a prelude to a precise understanding of its mechanism of action. Progress toward this goal was greatly facilitated by our finding that TF passes through a Visking cellulose dialysis sac (Lawrence et al., 1963). With this one simple maneuver, TF is separated from all of the macromolecules of the leukocyte extract, assorted passenger virions, and histocompatibility antigens which are left behind inside the sac. The dialyzate containing TF is then concentrated by lyophilization and may be stored as a lyophilized powder that is stable for as long as 5 years at ordinary refrigerator temperatures (4°C) without loss of in vivo potency (Lawrence, 1969a). For this study, DNase-treated frozen and thawed leukocyte extracts were placed in a Visking cellulose dialysis sac and dialyzed vs equal volumes of distilled water for 18 hours in the cold room on a shaker. In our initial studies the ratio of dialyzant:dialyzate was 1:1 with 4 ml WBC extract inside to 4 ml H$_2$O outside the bag in order to limit the volume injected into recipients. After 18 hours of dialysis, the dialyzate was filtered through a Swinney or Millipore filter and injected into the shoulder of tuberculin-negative or coccidioidin-negative recipients, and the related skin tests were made in the forearm.

It was observed that TF$_D$ prepared from a single tuberculin-sensitive donor (Jos.) transferred systemic tuberculin sensitivity to 11 tuberculin-negative recipients. The intensity of the cutaneous DTH reactions was marked in 7 recipients (4+) and moderate in 4 recipients (2+). The findings secured with dialyzable TF using tuberculin as antigen were confirmed when coccidioidin was used as antigen: 11 coccidioidin negative recipients of coccidioidin-positive TF$_D$ developed sensitivity; of these, 7 developed marked (4+) and 4 developed moderate (2+) DTH to coccidioidin.

To monitor the integrity of the dialysis sac, either Bence-Jones protein or papain-digested γ-globulin fragments were added to the inside of the sac, and these molecules were not detected in dialyzates containing TF by immunological tests. Moreover, the dialyzate contained no protein detectable by addition of 10% trichloroacetic acid; and no albumin, α_2-globulin or γ-globulin were detected by immunodiffusion tests in agar gel. The materials in the dialyzate gave positive orcinol and biuret tests. Prior treatment of the dialyzate with 50 mg of pancreatic RNase *in vitro* did not abolish nor diminish TF$_D$ activity *in vivo* when given to 8 individual recipients. As an additional control to exclude enzyme inhibitors, we demonstrated that authentic RNA and DNA substrate added to dialyzates containing active TF were broken down by treatment with RNase or DNase, respectively.

It was then determined that dialyzates containing TF can be lyophilized and the lyophilized powder redissolved in water without loss of biological activity. This allowed the preparation of more potent aliquotes of TF by virtue of increasing the ratio of dialyzant:dialyzate from 1:1 to 1:50 (e.g., 4 ml of WBC extract inside the sac to 200 ml of water outside). Increasing the volume of dialyzate was observed to result in the diffusion of greater quantities of TF into dialyzates prepared from equivalent volumes of extracted leukocytes as determined by the increased intensity of DTH to coccidioidin transferred.

Dialysis and lyophilization also allowed further attempts at purification by passage of reconstituted lyophilized dialyzate through Sephadex G-25. For example dialyzate of 7 ml of DNase-treated leukocyte extracts vs 200 ml of distilled water for 18 hours was lyophilized, reconstituted, and passed through a Sephadex G-25 column. The total eluate was pooled, lyophilized, redissolved, and injected into negative recipients. On three consecutive occasions this resulted in the transfer of marked degrees (4+)

of cutaneous DTH to coccidioidin to negative recipients of coc-cidioidin-positive TF prepared in this fashion. A more precise separation of activity into two peaks on Sephadex G-25 is, illustrated in Fig. 3, where optical density at 260 nm/280 nm is plotted vs tube number. The fractions collected under peak I (tubes 9–12) where molecules of >10,000 MW appear, failed to transfer coccidioidin sensitivity *in vivo* to one negative recipient whereas fractions collected under the broad peak II (tubes 19–37) where molecules <10,000 MW appear, transferred marked (3+) cutaneous DTH to coccidioidin to another negative recipient. Upon retesting, the recipient of peak I developed minimal but definite (1+) DTH to coccidioidin probably due to contamination of peak I with minute quantities of TF.

TF_D was found to exhibit most of the biological properties of the parent leukocytes or leukocyte extracts from which it was prepared—namely, the initiation of cutaneous DTH in recipients promptly (1 day to 1 week) and the prolonged duration of the transferred DTH (months to >1 year). Quantitative considerations of the requirements for intense donor cutaneous DTH as well as use of adequate amounts of TF_D were also evident. For

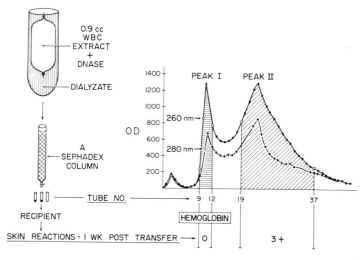

FIG. 3. Transfer of coccidioidin sensitivity with active transfer factor fraction (peak II < 10,000 MW) isolated from raw dialyzate of immune leukocyte extract after passage through Sephadex G-25. From Lawrence *et al.* (1963).

example, in early attempts at transfer using 1:1 ratios of dialyzant:dialyzate, occasional failures occurred when inadequate amounts of TF_D appeared in the dialyzate. It is of interest that repeated skin tests with tuberculin or coccidioidin, respectively, in 6 such recipients in whom transfer failed to occur, did not by itself cause the appearance of DTH to either tuberculin or coccidioidin.

Attempts to prepare an antibody to TF_D injected in Freund's adjuvant into rabbits were unsuccessful (Lawrence *et al.*, 1963; unpublished observations). More recent efforts by Plescia (personal communication) have been successful in raising antibody to TF_D when it is coupled to methylated bovine serum albumin. This approach affords promise for raising a neutralizing antibody for adaptation to immunofluorescence and for the development of a radioimmunoassay of TF_D.

In additional studies that we undertook to identify and characterize human HL-A antigens, we observed that dialyzates of leukocyte extracts were incapable of immunizing recipients to reject skin allografts from the leukocyte donor upon subsequent transplantation (Rapaport *et al.*, 1965a,b). Thus dialysis separates histocompatibility antigens from TF_D which can only transfer allograft rejection but is incapable of active immunization to subsequent allografts.

These experiments represent a critical *in vivo* attempt to detect a "superantigen" function of TF using a sensitive biological test system and were without success. This finding was subsequently confirmed in our failure to find antibodies to numerous HL-A antigens in cancer patients receiving massive doses of TF_D repeatedly for about a year (Oettgen *et al.*, 1971, 1974). Of additional interest for clinical applications of TF_D in immunotherapy, Prince *et al.* (personal communication) have shown that both the large and small Au antigen is nondialyzable. Some properties of TF_D as delineated up to that time are summarized in Table V.

The dialyzable nature of TF, its low molecular weight, polypeptide-polynucleotide composition, and absoprtion spectra on Sephadex G-25 were rapidly confirmed in precise detail by several investigators (Baram and Mosko, 1965; Baram *et al.*, 1966; Arala-Chaves *et al.*, 1967; Fireman *et al.*, 1967, 1968; Brandriss, 1968).

TABLE V

SOME PROPERTIES OF DIALYZABLE TRANSFER FACTOR[a]

Biological	Biochemical	Immunological
Properties of WBC extract: prompt onset (hours), long duration (>1 year), equal intensity	Soluble, dialyzable, lyophilizable	Not immunoglobulin
	<10,000 MW	Not immunogenic
	No protein, albumin, α- or γ-globulin	Immunologically specific
Dissociable from transplantation antigens	Orcinol positive, biuret positive	Converts normal lymphocytes *in vitro* and *in vivo* to antigen-responsive state
	Polypeptide/polynucleotide composition	Transformation and clonal proliferation of converted lymphocytes exposed to antigen
Small quantities → magnified effects	Inactivated 56°C, 30 minutes	
	Resists pancreatic RNase	Informational molecule/ derepressor/receptor site?
	Retains potency 5 years	

[a] From Lawrence (1969a).

Baram and co-workers (Baram *et al.,* 1966; Baram and Mosko, 1965) found that TF$_D$ from tuberculin-positive donors was capable of transferring DTH to tuberculin-negative recipients whereas tuberculin-negative TF$_D$ was without this activity; the transferred DTH appeared promptly (3 days) and endured >6 months; equilibrium dialysis failed to detect mycobacterial antigens in the dialyzate; TF$_D$ activity was concentrated under one peak following passage of raw dialyzate through Sephadex G-25; the peak was comprised of polynucleotides lacking uracil and contained no immunoglobulin or leukocyte antigens. These studies also revealed residual TF activity to be present in the nondialyzable fraction. Arala-Chaves *et al.* (1967) also showed that tuberculin-positive TF$_D$ transferred DTH to tuberculin-negative recipients whereas tuberculin-negative TF_D failed to do so; TF_D activity could be concentrated under one peak after passage of raw dialyzate through Sephadex G-25; TF_D was of polypeptide-polynucleotide composition with an estimated 5000–15,000 molecular weight, and no immunoglobulins were detected in the dialyzate. Fireman et al. (1967, 1968) also showed: that tuberculin-positive TF_D transferred DTH to negative recipients where tuberculin-negative TF_D did not; TF_D activity could be concentrated in one fraction after passage of dialyzate through Sephadex G-25; this active fraction was purified further after its passage through Sephadex G-10 and was eluted in the region for materials of 700–4000 MW. Brandriss (1968) found that tuberculin-sensitive donors that had undergone active sensitization to dinitrochlorobenzene (DNCB) yielded TF_D capable of transferring DTH to tuberculin but not to DNCB to negative recipients. When this raw dialyzate was passed through Sephadex G-25 and optical density was plotted vs tube number, two peaks were recorded at 260 and 280 nm with patterns very similar to those we obtained (see Fig. 3) (Lawrence et al., 1963).

We also continued studies on TF_D and, using the technique of "local" transfer, took advantage of the sarcoid patient's inability to respond to TF with the development of systemic sensitization (Urbach et al., 1952). This permitted an internally controlled in vivo assay to compare the effects of various treatments on equivalent quantities of TF_D (40×10^6 WBC) obtained from the same tuberculin-sensitive donor and given to the same negative recipient (Lawrence and Zweiman, 1968). We observed that 5 of 7 consecutive anergic sarcoid recipients acquired local cutaneous DTH to tuberculin injected atop the TF_D site, and 2 of these 5 recipients also developed systemic DTH when tested at remote sites. The systemic sensitivity although weak (1+) persisted for a year. Two of the 7 sarcoid recipients failed to develop either local or systemic sensitivity whereas 5 of 5 normal individuals developed both local and systemic sensitivity following local transfer using equivalent aliquots of TF_D. It was also confirmed again that treatment of TF_D with 5, 50, or 500 μg of pancreatic ribonuclease did not diminish or abolish TF_D activity. Yet heating the dialyzate for 56°C or 100°C for 30 minutes and rapid cooling abolished the capacity of TF_D to transfer local sensitivity in this system. We also observed, as had Baram and Mosko (1965), that when TF_D was prepared at a 1:1 ratio of dialyzant:dialyzate, as in these experiments, a variable amount of TF_D activity was detected in the undialyzed residue. In addition to the interesting data in respect of comparative behavior of various TF preparations in an internally controlled *in vivo* assay this study provided some clues concerning the origins of anergy encountered in sarcoidosis.

We had also utilized this method of local transfer to study patients with advanced metastatic cancer who were anergic to a battery of antigens (Solowey *et al.*, 1967). Skin sites were prepared with SK-SD positive TF_D in 10 such cancer patients, and 24 hours later the TF_D site and a remote unprepared skin site were injected with SK-SD. Each of the 10 anergic cancer patients developed both local and systemic cutaneous DTH to SK-SD. The reaction to SK-SD were intense (4+) at the TF_D sites and minimal (1+) at the remote sites in each instance. Moreover, the feeble systemic DTH transferred was not as enduring as that observed in normal recipients of TF_D.

Recent attempts at further purification and characterization of TF_D have successfully extended Sephadex column fractionation techniques and have carefully demonstrated the immunologic specificity of the active fractions eluted. Neidhart *et al.* (1973) upon passage of raw dialyzate through Sephadex G-25 have isolated a single fraction which they proved to be active by local and systemic transfer of specific immunity present in the donor. The active fraction of TF_D was found only in peak 4 which had the highest 260:280 ratio, and no activity was detected in peaks 1, 2, 3, 5, 6, which had been pooled, lyophilized, and reconstituted for transfer. It was also observed that fraction 4 conferred more intense reactivity than the raw TF_D. The authors question the possibility that an inhibitor is present in the raw dialyzate and it had been excluded by fractionation. They found the active components of TF_D absorbs to Sephadex and caution against estimates of molecular weight based on this technique alone. They also found both raw TF_D and the purified TF fraction 4 to be immunologically specific as judged by local and systemic transfer of DTH only to those antigens to which the donor expressed reactivity. In no case was there transfer of sensitivity to antigens to which the donor was unreactive, nor was there observed any nonspecific enhancement of skin reactivity to other antigens to which the recipients had been sensitive prior to transfer.

In further extension of this precise approach to the purification of TF_D LoBuglio's group (personal communication) have sensitized donors to keyhole limpet hemocyanin (KLH) and transferred cutaneous reactivity to KLH to 15 of 15 negative recipients using the purified TF fraction 4. An additional group of 8 KLH-negative recipients served to control the specificity of TF and received TF fraction 4 prepared from 8 KLH-negative donors. None of the 8 recipients of KLH-negative TF developed reactivity to KLH. The use of KLH as antigen in this system, like the use of HL-A antigens, may represent another example of raising TF *de novo* and then demonstrating its specificity *in vivo*.

Gottlieb *et al.* (1973) have also used the technique of local transfer to study the activity of raw TF_D and fractions A, B, and C prepared after passage of TF_D through Sephadex G-10. Using TF_D from a candida-positive, histoplasmin-negative donor, they demonstrated only raw TF_D and its fraction B, but not fraction A or C, transferred reactivity to candida. Additionally TF fraction B, but not A or C, transferred reactivity to candida (15×12 mm) and slight reactivity to histoplasmin (6×6 mm). The authors noted raw TF_D as well as A and C fractions, but not fraction B, when challenged locally with antigen could result in erythema without induration, and they raise the question of the nonspecific inflammatory contribution of the family of molecules present in the raw dialyzate in addition to TF. They also noted the greater intensity of transferred DTH caused by fraction B compared to that caused by TF_D and postulate the presence of an inhibitor in raw dialyzates. Finally cells were labeled with 35 S, and most of the label appeared in fraction B, which when subjected in ultracentrifugation in $CsSO_4$ had a density of 1.47. This coupled with the gel-filtration data suggest molecular weights for fraction B to be in the range of 2000–4000.

Gallin and Kirkpatrick (1974) have also studied the biological activities of Sephadex G-25 chromatographed fractions of human TF_D assayed *in vivo* in rhesus monkeys. The human TF_D donors expressed varying patterns of cutaneous DTH reactivity to one or two of several antigens (e.g., PPD, SK-SD, mumps, candida) to which monkey recipients were nonreactive. It was observed that TF$_D$ transferred cutaneous DTH to mumps, SK-SD, or candida concordant with donor reactivity. In no case did reactions to antigens not present in the human TF$_D$ donor appear in recipient monkeys. The raw TF$_D$ preparations were also found to have potent chemotactic activity *in vitro* and *in vivo* for human granulocytes and weaker chemotactic activity for human mononuclear cells. When TF$_D$ was passed through Sephadex G-25, the fraction that contained the chemotactic activity was also shown to contain TF activity *in vivo*. Here also, there were no DTH reactions observed in the recipient of purified TF fractions to which the donor was not reactive. The chemotactic activity of the TF fractions was labile when stored at 4°C for 2 weeks or heated at 56°C for 30 minutes, but unaffected by goat antibody to human C3 and C5.

The foregoing series of publications provided extensive detailed confirmation of our original report on TF$_D$ as a dialyzable, lyophilizable, nonantigenic, nonimmunoglobulin moiety of <10,000 MW that is of peptide-nucleotide composition and resistant to treatment with pancreatic RNase (Lawrence *et al.*, 1963). Where specificty controls were deliberately tested, the results summarized above also document repeatedly the immunologic specificity of TF$_D$. TF has the unique property of selectively conferring and/or elevating cellular immunity without concomitant production of immunoglobulin to the antigenic determinants of DTH transferred. The active moiety can be further purified on Sephadex chromatography, and TF fractions can be isolated that possess more potent biological activity than the raw dialyzate, which may contain inhibitors. Our early caution in the designation of "transfer factor" as a convenient shorthand descriptive term that allows for the presence of more than one factor with immunological activity in raw dialyzates still applies until the precise moiety is isolated and characterized biochemically.

V. The Search for an *in Vitro* Assay of TF—Disappointments and Consolations

It was apparent from the beginning of this work that the chief impediment to the isolation and characterization of TF was the

TABLE VI

THE SEARCH FOR TRANSFER FACTOR (TF) *in Vitro*—DISAPPOINTMENTS
AND CONSOLATIONS

In vitro test	Intent	Result	Unanticipated development
1. Immune WBC + antigen	Neutralize TF	Negative	Antigen-liberated mono-specific TF
2. Macrophage migra-tion	Find guinea pig TF	Negative	Migration inhibitory factor (MIF)
3. Immune lympho-cytes + antigen	More potent TF	Negative	Lymphocyte transforming factor (LTF)
4. Lymphocyte trans formation cine-matography	Recruitment by TF or LTF	Negative	Clonal proliferation of lymphocytes
5. Cloning of HeLa cells	TF assay	Negative	Cloning inhbitory factor (CIF)
6. TF_D + naive lymphocytes	Conversion	Positive, 23%	Inhibitor of lymphocyte proliferation
7. TF_{DM} + naive lymphocytes	Conversion	Positive, 50%	To be detected

lack of an animal model and/or an *in vitro* assay system. Our efforts to develop an *in vitro* assay for TF over the years have been notable, until recently, for consistent failure to achieve this primary goal. However, the unanticipated success in developing other *in vitro* assays of DTH and CMI, which have found wide application (Bloom, 1971; David and David, 1972), mitigated the failures and ultimately led to the crude beginnings of a proper *in vitro* assay system for TF (Lawrence and Valentine, 1970a,b; Ascher *et al.*, 1973, 1974). These approaches are summarized in Table VI.

A.   Assay Systems

1.   Antigen-Liberated "Monospecific" TF

The earliest *in vitro* attempt along these lines was undertaken with Pappenheimer as outlined in detail above (see Fig. 1). Our aim was to neutralize or block TF by incubation of sensitive blood cells wih antigen (PPD; toxoid) *in vitro*. We failed to block such activity, yet succeeded in liberating TF from the cells that bear it (Lawrence and Pappenheimer, 1956, 1957, cf. Muftuoglu and Yalcin, 1973). When these experiments were performed with especial care, it could be shown in a mixed cell population containing two markers (tuberculin-diphtheria toxoid) that the liberation of TF was antigen-specific whereby PPD released tuberculin-TF into the supernatant leaving the toxoid-TF in the cell pellet. This approach is of considerable interest in that it provides a means of preparing a monospecific TF corresponding to the antigen used for incubation while leaving behind in the cell pellet the myriads of other TF's of different specificities possessed by the donor. This approach to the liberation and concentration of a monospecific TF should be of value as a starting point for further purification and biochemical analysis.

This technique has been recently adapted to prepare coccidioidin-positive TF for the immunotherapy of coccidioidomycosis by incubating sensitive leukocytes with coccidioidin and preparing TF_D from the supernatant solution (Graybill *et al*, 1973). This monospecific antigen-liberated TF, was found to exhibit equal potency when compared to raw TF_D prepared from leukocyte extracts as measured by the immunological responses (cutaneous DTH, MIF) and clinical improvement of the patients who received it.

2. *Macrophage Migration Inhibition*

We next turned to the evaluation of other *in vitro* techniques for possible adaptation to TF assay. The capillary migration technique described by George and Vaughn (1962) was studied extensively in our laboratory in collaboration with David, Al-Askari, and Thomas (David *et al.*, 1964a–d). This technique was shown in the guinea pig to be a sensitive and reproducible indicator of cellular immunity and DTH induced by bacteria (PPD, toxoid), proteins (BSA) and exhibited carrier specificity for simple chemical compounds (DNP-GPA). Macrophage migration inhibition was also readily shown to be an *in vitro* correlate of allograft immunity (Al-Askari *et al.*, 1965a,b; Al-Askari and Lawrence 1969, 1973) as well as analogous states of cellular immunity to altered histocompatibility antigens, such as immunity to autologous tissues seen in allergic encephalomyelitis (David and Paterson, 1965) and later in immunity to tumor-specific antigens (Bloom *et al.,* 1969).

Our initial results using this technique showed that as few as 2.5% of immune peritoneal exudate cells could be seeded into a population of nonimmune cells and cause the entire population to be inhibited from migration in the presence of the appropriate antigen (David *et al.,* 1964b). This finding suggested that a transfer of information and or a signal from cell to cell might occur and made the prospect of searching for a guinea pig TF a feasible undertaking in this sensitive system. It was also anticipated that the migration assay might be amenable to adaptation to human blood cell populations. Yet, Dr. David and I were unable to find evidence for TF activity in the guinea pig system and encountered technical difficulties in adapting the assay to human blood leukocyte populations. However, this did not deflect my colleague David from finding out why so few immune cells caused so many nonimmune cells to respond to antigen. Subsequent studies by Bloom and Bennett (1966, 1968) and independently by David (1966, 1967, 1968) led to the discovery of migration inhibitory factor (MIF)—a heat stable, nondialyzable, nonimmunoglobulin protein product of lymphocytes activated by antigen which causes macrophages to adhere to each other. Both Dr. Bloom and Dr. David have become leading investigators in this field, and the impact of their discovery on the basic science as well as the clinical applications of cellular immunity has been recently ably reviewed in critical perspective (Bloom, 1971; David and David, 1972).

Successful adaptation of this system to human leukocyte populations was subsequently achieved, using lymph node cells, by Thor and Dray (1968a,b), who also reported on the transfer of migration inhibition *in vitro* to nonimmune cell populations by means of RNA prepared from immune lymphocytes. Soberg (1967) was also successful in adapting the migration inhibition assay of CMI using human buffy coat leukocytes and thus provided a model that has been extensively applied to a variety of diseases. Additionally, Thor and Dray (1968a,b) showed that human immune lymphocytes incubated with antigen elaborated MIF which is active vs guinea pig macrophages and provided another approach to study of the human condition.

3. *Lymphocyte Transformation*

    a. *Conversion of Nonimmune Lymphocytes with* TF_D. With the establishment of the lymphocyte transformation test as a reproducible *in vitro* correlate of DTH and cellular immune responses *in vivo* it became possible to consider adding TF_D to this system. Since TF_D is not immunogenic in rabbits (Lawrence 1969a,b) and the dialyzate is freed of histocompatibility antigens (Rapaport *et al.*, 1965a,b), it can be added to lymphocytes in culture without activating or stimulating such cells to transform. The goal of these experiments was therefore conversion of nonimmune lymphocytes to an antigen-responsive state by means of TF_D as measured by increased thymidine incorporation. The few times Valentine and I initially tried this experiment it worked, but the results were not very convincing because the responses, although selective, were feeble in intensity. A single experiment of this type is illustrated in Fig. 4, where tuberculin-positive, diphtheria toxoid-negative TF_D from donor Jos. is incubated with

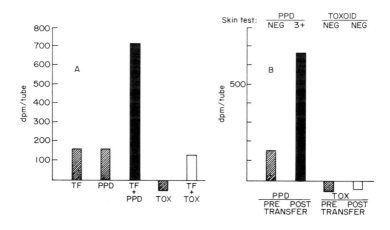

FIG. 4.   Specificity of (A) *in vitro* sensitization of normal blood lymphocytes with dialyzable transfer factor (tuberculin positive, toxoid negative) compared to (B) *in vivo* transfer factor conversion of cutaneous reactivity as well as blood lymphocyte response of recipient to tuberculin but not to toxoid. From Lawrence (1969b).

lymphocytes that are nonreactive to both antigens *in vitro* shown on the left-hand side of the figure. It may be seen that increased thymidine incorporation occurred only in tubes containing TF_D plus tuberculin (PPD) but not in those containing TF_D plus toxoid, nor in those containing either antigen alone (see also Fig. 11).

An aliquot of this same TF_D was injected into a tuberculin-negative, toxoid-negative recipient *in vivo* (who had supplied the negative cells for the *in vitro* experiment above) and caused conversion of cutaneous DTH to tuberculin (0 to 3+) while the reaction to toxoid remained negative. After this *in vivo* transfer, the recipients lymphocytes underwent transformation and incorporated thymidine *in vitro* only when cultured in the presence of tuberculin (PPD), but not in the presence of toxoid, as is shown in the right-hand Fig. 4, which compares the pre- and post-transfer response to these antigens. Of additional interest for the *in vivo* specificity of TF_D, donor Jos. was also reactive to SK-SD but not to coccidioidin, and the recipient developed cutaneous DTH to SK-SD but not to coccidioidin following injection of TF_D.

b. *Lymphocyte Transforming Factor (LTF)*. In an attempt to increase the magnitude of this interesting response Valentine and I recalled the *in vitro* experiments that yielded a monospecific antigen-liberated TF (Lawrence and Pappenheimer, 1956, 1957) and by this means tried to produce a more potent TF preparation for further *in vitro* study. When we incubated tuberculin-sensitive lymphocytes with tuberculin (PPD) for 24–36 hours and added the cell-free supernatant to tuberculin-negative lymphocytes, we found a striking increase in thymidine incorporation in the presence of added tuberculin (PPD) (Valentine and Lawrence 1968a, 1969). Moreover, we observed a 4–5 times increase in thymidine incorporation caused by such supernatants (2400–3000 dpm) when compared to TF_D cultured in the presence of nonimmune lymphocytes plus PPD (600 dpm) and a 3 times increase in the number of lymphoblasts detected (i.e., 3% blasts on day 7 with TF_D + PPD vs 10% blasts on day 6 with LTF).

Additional studies revealed that this supernatant activity is nondialyzable, inactivated by heating at 56°C for 30 minutes, not sedimented at 100,000 g, and antigen-dose dependent. The finding that such activity is nondialyzable suggested that it is a moiety distinct from TF$_D$, a conclusion reinforced by the recent finding of Graybill *et al.* (1973) showing that antigen-liberated monospecific TF is dialyzable.

Valentine and I named this material lymphocyte transforming factor (LTF) to distinguish it from TF$_D$ particularly since the activity of each material was so similar in end point, namely the engagement of nonimmune lymphocytes to respond to antigen with transformation and proliferation. In additional studies with Spitler, we were able to demonstrate the preparation of an LTF with similar properties in guinea pigs (Spitler and Lawrence, 1969). Independently, Maini *et al.* (1969) described identical results using antigen-stimulated human lymphocytes. Dumonde *et al.* (1969) also independently demonstrated this activity in the guinea pig, giving the generic name "lymphokines" to embrace all the products of activated lymphocytes. Lymphocyte transforming factor (LTF) in its form and functions has many properties in common with similar preparations that have been studied by others and called blastogenic factor (BF) or mitogenic factor (MF). By whatever name, a lymphocyte product with the propensity for calling other idle lymphocytes into an antigen-driven proliferative response is a most welcome recruiting agent to help explain the amplification of so few antigen-responsive cells into a rapidly proliferating clone when confronted with antigen.

In any event we had failed in our goal to prepare a more potent TF for *in vitro* conversion of nonimmune lymphocyte and succeeded in uncovering a new mediator of CMI that did just that, and with far greater efficiency than TF$_D$ itself. Dr. Valentine has continued to study this material with great effectiveness (Valentine, 1971a,b, 1972). A comparison between the *in vivo* and *in vitro* activities of TF$_D$ is diagrammed in the upper portion of Fig. 5, and the *in vitro* activities of LTF and *in vivo* activity of antigen-liberated TF are shown in the lower portion.

4. Amplification of CMI—Recruitment vs Clonal Proliferation

Thus we had isolated and identified two distinctive products from immune lymphocytes that convert nonimmune lymphocytes to an antigen-responsive state. One of the products, TF$_D$ is detected as a preexistent moiety that is dialyzable and the other, LTF, makes its appearance after a 24–36-hour latent period fol-

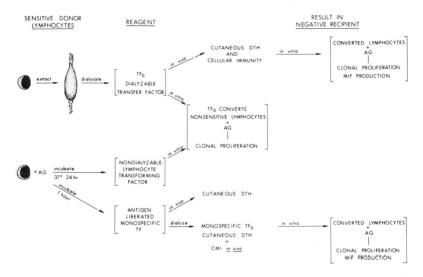

FIG. 5. Diagrammatic comparison of *in vivo* and *in vitro* activities of dialyzable transfer factor (TF_D), antigen-liberated transfer factor, and lymphocyte transforming factor. AG, antigen; CMI, cell-mediated immunity; DTH, delayed-type hypersensitivity; MIF, migration inhibitory factor. From Lawrence (1969a).

lowing contact of cells with antigen and is nondialyzable. Hence we began to view the cumulative antigen-triggered proliferative response of immune lymphocytes as arising from stimulation of only a very few primary reactive cells. We postulated that the TF liberated and the LTF production that ensued could result in the recruitment of uncommitted cells by conversion to immune activity and thus amplify the total proliferative response with a subpopulation of secondary reactive cells. This postulate in respect of TF had been proposed earlier by Pappenheimer (1956).

With Marshall and Valentine, we set out to examine this question by continuous time-lapse cinematography of a captive population of cultured immune human lymphocytes stimulated with PPD or with SK-SD, respectively, and of rat lymphocytes responding to alloantigens in a mixed leukocyte culture (MLC) system (Marshall *et al.*, 1968a,b, 1969). These studies revealed that the large numbers of lymphoblasts (20–30%) at the end of 7 days' culture arose from an initial population estimated at <2%, of antigen-reactive cells by a process of repeated cell division.

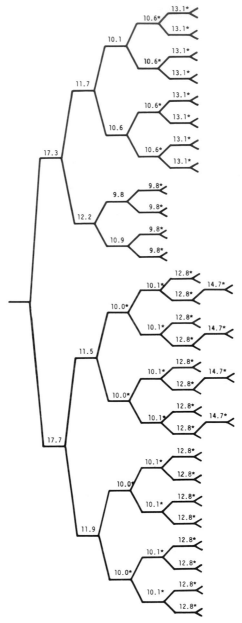

FIG. 6. A diagram to represent the development of a single lymphoblast into a clone that went through to the seventh, and in a few cases, the eighth generation

Where it was possible to trace antigen-stimulated cells through a series of divisions, large clones were observed to arise from a single cell as diagrammed in Fig. 6. A representative sequence of still photos illustrating the development of such a clone is shown in Fig. 7. Thus we found no evidence for the type of recruitment that we had postulated, and the demonstration that lymphoblasts divide and redivide argued strongly for clonal proliferation as the major mechanism by which antigen-reactive lymphocytes are increased. The only reservation that remained arose from the design of the experiments whereby lymphoblasts could be selected for observation only 48–72 hours after contact with antigen. There are no data available during this latent period where recruitment could indeed occur.

To evaluate this possibility further, we added LTF generated from immune lymphocytes activated with tuberculin to captive populations of nonimmune lymphocytes in culture and repeated the time-lapse cinematography observations as described above. Again, only a small population of cells ($<2\%$) were initially engaged by LTF and responded to tuberculin with transformation to lymphoblasts and repeated cell division to form a large clone of lymphoblasts (15–20%) by day 7 of culture. The entire cinematography sequence was qualitatively, quantitatively, and temporally identical to that observed using naturally sensitive cells stimulated with tuberculin. Thus, there still exists the possibility that recruitment of uncommitted cells does occur in nature and could occur in the first 48–82 hours after contact with antigen *in vitro* as demonstrated in the above experiment (F. T. Valentine, W. H. Marshall, and H. S. Lawrence, unpublished observations).

This approach to lymphocyte behavior yielded the first concrete visual evidence of clonal proliferation and documented the generation times of such cells. The methodology may have further use: for example—in distinguishing which cells are engaged by TF_D specifically (precommitted) and which by LTF nonspecifi-

after exposure of tuberculin-sensitive human lymphocytes to tuberculin. The line at the left represents the initial lymphoblast. Numbers over subsequent lines are generation times in hours. Asterisks indicate an average generation time as taken for the whole group of cells. From Marshall *et al.* (1969).

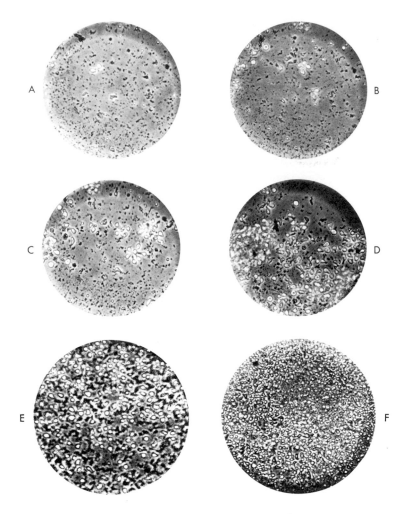

FIG. 7. An individual microchamber demonstrating tuberculin-stimulated cell proliferation, photographed on (A) day 3, (B) day 4, (C) day 5, and (D) day 6. Photographs E and F are two individual microchambers which were not followed by time-lapse but photographed to illustrate the magnitude the proliferating clones may reach by day 7 or 8. The proliferating lymphoblasts are seen as large, light-colored, refractile cells often connected in clusters. From Marshall *et al.* (1969).

cally (uncommitted); in providing a pure clone of large numbers of lymphoblasts that arise from a single antigen-stimulated progenitor; and in providing a pure clone arising from a single non-immune lymphocyte converted to an immune state by TF or by LTF. In any event, we sought recruitment in naturally sensitive cell populations triggered by antigen and found clonal proliferation instead; and since nature refused to cooperate with our preconceived notions, we manipulated the system artifically to show that recruitment does indeed occur, yet our work leaves open the question of whether or not it is a natural act.

5. *Target Cell Sickness or Death*

We turned next to a target-cell system with the goal of seeking a more sensitive and perhaps quantitative end point for TF assay *in vitro.* The initial idea derived from the "self + X" hypothesis where we had postulated earlier that all DTH and CMI reactions were virtually allograft rejection responses (Lawrence, 1959c, 1960a,b, 1967). This aberration we viewed as arising from prolonged amicable intracellular residence of microbes or virions (X) resulting in the alteration of host histocompatibility antigens (self) and thereby causing lymphocytes to acquire a TF vs self + X. To test this hypothesis *in vitro,* we incubated tuberculin-positive lymphocytes plus PPD with pulmonary tissue monolayers with variable results. Lebowitz and I abandoned this crude approach for the more precise indicator system afforded by the cloning of HeLa cells in culture (Lebowitz and Lawrence, 1969a,b, 1971). These studies revealed that sensitive lymphocytes stimulated wtih tuberculin *in vitro,* when cultured with HeLa cells for 12 days, resulted in a marked decrease in the number of clones of HeLa cells. Identical results were obtained when cell-free supernatants were prepared from antigen-stimulated sensitive lymphocytes and added to HeLa cell cultures. Neither unstimulated lymphocytes, nor tuberculin-sensitive lymphocytes incubated with histoplasmin generated in the supernatant the inhibitory factor for HeLa cell clones. This supernatant activity was found to be nondialyzable and inactivated by heating at 56°C for 30 minutes. Time-lapse cinematography studies of HeLa cells in the presence of such active supernatants revealed that target-cell sickness rather than target cell lysis occurred—the HeLa cells going through one or two divisions, rounding up, fusing to form giant cells, and finally cessation of division after a variable number of cell cycles (Lebowitz and Lawrence, 1969a,b; Holzman *et al.*, 1973a,b). The macroscopic

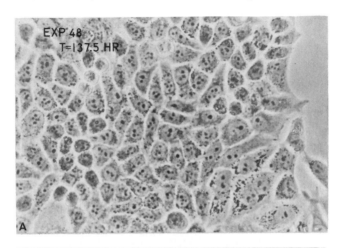

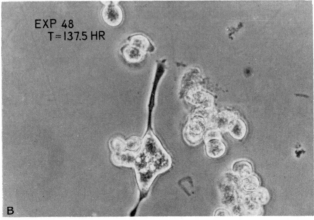

Fig. 8. Microscopic (A,B) and corresponding macroscopic (C,D) appearance of clones of HeLa cells grown for 6 days in medium containing supernatant from an unstimulated lymphocyte culture (control, labeled A and C) compared to effects of supernatant from a tuberculin-stimulated lymphocyte culture (experimental, labeled B and D). From Lawrence (1969b).

CONTROL

EXPERIMENT

FIG. 8.   (C) and (D). See legend on facing page.

and microscopic appearance of the effects of CIF upon HeLa cell cloning compared to untreated control supernatants of lymphocytes cultured in the absence of antigen is shown in Fig. 8.

At about this time Green *et al.* (1970) described independently a material in phytohemagglutinin (PHA)-stimulated lymphocyte culture supernatants with similar activity on HeLa cells in culture, which they named proliferation inhibitory factor (PIF). With Dr. Holzman, we have continued our analysis of this material, which we had named cloning inhibitory factor (CIF), and find that CIF shares many properties with and may be identical to PIF (Holzman *et al.,* 1973a,b).

Thus we failed in our original intent to demonstrate either the consequences of self + X *in vitro* or to perfect a direct assay of TF. Nevertheless, the detection of CIF activity uncovered yet another mediator of CMI concerned with target-cell sickness or death. In addition, a new regulatory mechanism controlling cell-division and cell growth was provided by these studies and the mediator CIF was shown to operate in a way distinctive from the direct cytolytic effects of lymphotoxin (LT) (Granger and Kolb, 1968).

The CIF assay system also gives promise of successful adaptation to an assay of TF either directly by detecting actual conversion of lymphocytes to specific target-cell recognition or indirectly by measuring antigen-stimulated CIF production following such conversion.

6.   In Vitro *Properties of Dialyzates Containing TF*

We continued to explore the reproducibility of the experimental model described above, whereby TF_D added to nonimmune lymphocytes *in vitro* resulted in their conversion to immune reactivity as measured by increased thymidine incorporation following exposure to antigen (Fireman *et al.,* 1967; Lawrence, 1969a,b; Lawrence and Valentine, 1970a,b; Adler *et al.,* 1970).

a.   Employing Water-Dialyzed Transfer Factor (TF_D). TF was obtained from senitive donors and prepared as for *in vivo* use, by dialysis vs large volumes of water (200 ml), lyophilization, and reconstitution before addition to nonimmune lymphocytes in culture (Lawrence *et al.,* 1963; Lawrence and Al-Askari, 1971). When such water-dialyzed TF (TF_D) was added to lymphocytes in the presence of antigen (PPD), enhancement of thymidine incorporation occurred. In extensive studies with this preparation the level of thymidine incorporation in cultures with TF_D plus antigen was usually only 1.5–3 times that of lymphocytes cultured with antigen alone and was not statistically significant. In 100 such consecutive experiments using TF_D and tuberculin (PPD) as antigen, only 23% were successful in achieving such limited increments of lymphocyte conversion to reactivity. Nevertheless, the preparations of TF_D that displayed this activity were obtained from only those donors with exquisite cutaneous DTH to tuberculin, suggesting that the minimal activity detected was not an artifact.

Additionally, TF_D alone or with added antigen resulted frequently in slight depression of lymphocyte transformation, suggesting the presence of an inhibitor. Since TF_D activity *in vivo* was separable from inactive components on Sephadex G-25 (Lawrence *et al.,* 1963), we applied this technique to two raw dialyzates that were inactive *in vitro* and retested the separate fractions. The excluded fraction of each sample contained the inhibitory material and the retarded fraction exhibited minimal activity. This clue suggested the introduction of a material toxic for lymphocytes in culture consequent to the method of preparation of TF_D (Ascher et al., 1973, 1974).

  b. *Employing Media-Dialyzed Transfer Factor* (TF_{DM}). In an attempt to diminish the toxicity and increase the activity of TF preparations *in vitro*, lyophilization was eliminated by dialysis of leukocyte lysates directly into a small volume of physiological tissue culture medium (MEM) (Ascher et al., 1973, 1974). Figure 9 outlines the response to antigen of TF_{DM} prepared from immune lymphocytes (6×10^6) and added to nonimmune lymphocytes (2×10^6), compared to the effect of water-dialyzed TF made in parallel from an equal aliquot (6×10^6) of the same cell lysate. It may be seen that TF_{DM} alone causes no stimulation and TF_{DM} plus toxoid resulted in a 30-fold increase in thymidine incorporation over toxoid alone. The failure of an equivalent aliquot of TF_D plus toxoid to increase thymidine incorporation is an indication that the TF activity preserved in TF_{DM} is diminished to suboptimal levels or can be lost entirely when lyophilized water-dialyzed preparations are assayed *in vitro*.

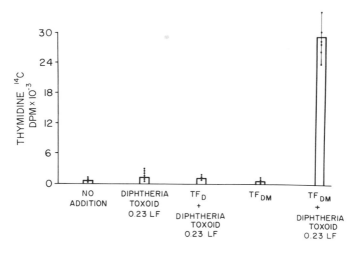

FIG. 9. Transfer factor (TF) *in vitro:* media-dialyzed TF (TF_{DM}) is active compared to water-dialyzed TF (TF_D). Each aliquot of TF = 6×10^6 lymphocytes. In this and all figures, bars represent means and dots represent individual replicate points. From Ascher et al. (1974).

Further studies revealed that increasing the quantities of TF_{DM} added to nonimmune lymphocytes in the presence of a constant amount of antigen (4 μg PPD) resulted in a proportionate increase in the increments of thymidine incorporation achieved. This effect is illustrated with tuberculin (PPD) as antigen in Fig. 10. We have also observed a comparable dose response effect of toxoid-positive TF_{DM} in the presence of constant amounts of diphtheria toxoid (0.23LF).

To assess the specificity of TF_{DM} *in vitro,* we utilized a transfer factor donor (Jos.) with marked DTH to SK-SD and PPD, but not to diphtheria toxoid, and known to transfer regularly reactivity to SK-SD and PPD, but not to toxoid, *in vivo.* TF_{DM} prepared from this donor (see also Fig. 4) was added to lymphocytes from an individual without reactivity to SK-SD, PPD, or toxoid and resulted in the finding that enhanced thymidine incorporation consequent to exposure of nonimmune lymphocytes to TF_{DM} occurs

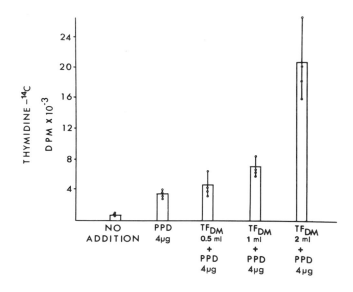

FIG. 10. Dose response to tuberculin-positive media-dialyzed transfer factor (TF_{DM}) in the presence of a constant concentration of tuberculin purified protein derivative (PPD). Each milliliter of TF = 6 × 10⁶ lymphocytes. From Ascher *et al.* (1974).

only in the presence of the two antigens (SK-SD, PPD) to which the TF donor is reactive, as shown in Fig. 11.

In searching for adjuvant effects we were unable to demonstrate an enhancement of thymidine incorporation by TF_{DM} in lymphocytes exposed to suboptimal PHA stimulation. Additionally, endotoxin was found to be unable to substitute for TF_{DM} in this system to achieve the enhanced stimulation of lymphocytes observed. Whether the activity of raw dialyzates we have described *in vitro* is an exclusive property of the same active moiety of TF that functions *in vivo* or is an expression of an additional immunologic phenomenon remains to be established. Nevertheless, the assay gives promise of further improvement and exploitation in the laboratory and at the bedside (Ascher *et al.*, 1973, 1974).

Similar results of TF_{DM} *in vitro* have been obtained by Arala-Chaves *et al.* (1974) and by A. S. Hamblin and D. C. Dumonde (personal communication). In addition these authors find that some preparations of TF_{DM} by itself may have variable blastogenic effects when cultured with lymphocytes (cf. Palmer and Smith, 1974b).

This *in vitro* assay of TF_{DM} activity is merely a crude beginning, and refinements leap to mind with its bare description. It is worth emphasizing that, although the end result of adding TF_{DM} *in vitro*

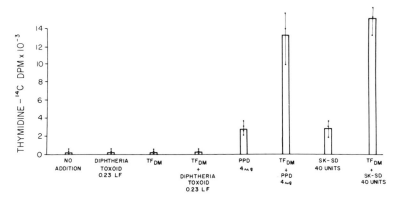

FIG. 11. Concordance of specificity of media-dialyzed transfer factor (TF_{DM}) *in vitro* with donor's cutaneous sensitivity and ability to transfer *in vivo*. Donor is tuberculin purified protein derivative (PPD) and SK-SD positive; toxoid negative. Each aliquot of TF = 6×10^6 lymphocytes. From Ascher *et al.* (1974).

is lymphocyte transformation (a proliferative event that can occur independent of mediator production), it is possible that TF_{DM} may either engage a proliferating cell type directly, or may as a primary event engage a distinct lymphocyte subpopulation concerned with lymphokine production and that in the presence of antigen a mitogenic mediator such as lymphocyte transforming factor (LTF) could secondarily trigger another lymphocyte subpopulation to undergo a proliferative response. In any event, this *in vitro* assay system can be manipulated to provide answers to these an other pressing questions.

Finally, it should be emphasized that the necessity for using TF_{DM} is a manuever primarily designed to satisfy the fastidious requirements of the lymphocyte culture system *in vitro* which are not encountered *in vivo* where TF_D is quite effective. This requirement also arises from the miniaturization of events in a closed system *in vitro* where minute losses of activity or the detection of inhibitors is greatly magnified.

7.   *Additional* In Vitro *Assays of TF*

Although this problem seemed so bleak and unpromising for so long, it is reassuring to observe a proliferation of other *in vitro* assays of TF from other laboratories at a time when the vagaries of the assay described above were just beginning to be resolved by dint of persistent effort.

a.   Macrophage Migration Inhibition. Paque *et al.* (1973) using immune leukocyte lysates were able to confer macrophage migration inhibition on nonsensitive cell populations in humans. This result was specific for only those antigens to which the leukocyte donor was reactive. Moreover, the result could be achieved only with the nondialyzable leukocyte lysate, not with the dialyzate itself. More recently, however, Baram and Condoulis (1973) have been able to demonstrate KLH-specific *in vitro* conversion of macrophage migration inhibition in monkeys using a single fraction of TF_D prepared from a raw dialyzate following passage through Sephadex G-25. However, these authors were unable to detect a parallel enhancement of thymidine incorporation in such lymphocyte populations. Whether the TF preparation used in these studies is a suitable preparation for the demanding conditions of the lymphocyte culture system that we have outlined above is not known.

b. *Inhibition of Leukocyte Migration—Man.* Zabriskie and his associates (Reed and Zabriskie, 1972; Utermohlen and Zabriskie, 1973) have adapted the leukocyte migration inhibition technique of Soberg (1967) to demonstrate conversion from negative to positive test by incubation of nonimmune cell populations with TF_D prepared from immune cells. This test employs human buffy coat leukocytes that are inhibited in their migration from capillaries when immune lymphocytes interact with specific antigen resulting in the production of an MIF that acts on polymorphonuclear cells. Reed and Zabriskie (1972) have shown that TF_D prepared by our standard method from tuberculin-sensitive donors when incubated with nonimmune cell populations causes the cells to respond to PPD with inhibition of migration. Additionally Utermohlen and Zabriskie (1973) extended these observations to show that TF_D prepared from measles-positive normal donors converts nonimmune cell populations from patients with multiple sclerosis to a positive response to measles antigen (i.e., inhibition of migration).

Very similar results have been obtained also by Brandes and Goldenberg (1973) in the Epstein-Barr (E-B) virus system using the Soberg leukocyte migration technique. Here TF_D is prepared by the standard method from E-B-positive normal individuals and converts the cell-populations of E-B-negative individuals to a positive response when exposed to antigen derived from nasopharyngeal carcinoma.

It is of interest that in each of the above studies the TF_D was prepared as for *in vivo* use without any particular precautions for *in vitro* usage, and was found to be quite effective. This precaution becomes unnecessary with the realization that both the macrophage and leukocyte migration systems are not as demanding as the lymphocyte culture system, which requires optimum initial conditions for the continued proliferation of lymphocytes without media change over a 7-day period. The leukocyte migration assays require only a 24-hour incubation period for the end point to occur via mediator production by antigen-stimulated lymphocytes that have been engaged by TF_D. Finally if the end point of lymphocyte proliferation that we measure (Ascher *et al.*, 1973, 1974) is a secondary event and the engagement of mediator producing lymphocytes by TF_{DM} the primary event, then our assay may burden the whole transaction with a more demanding sequence than merely lymphocyte activation and migration inhibition.

 c.   Chemotactic Assay of TF_D. Gallin and Kirkpatrick (1974), have recently described the *in vivo* transfer of specific DTH to rhesus monkeys using human TF_D. The recipient monkeys became reactive only to those antigens to which the individual donors responded (e.g., mumps and SK-SD or mumps and candida), but not to antigens to which the corresponding donors were unreactive (e.g., PPD or candida). These authors also found that TF_D was strongly chemotactic for granulocytes and weakly chemotactic for monocytes *in vitro* as well as *in vivo* in monkey skin. Of the multiple fractions with absorbency at 255 nm and 280 nm after passage of TF_D through Sephadex G-25 the fractions containing chemotactic activity *in vitro* were also active in the *in vivo* transfer of cutaneous DTH to monkeys. The chemotactic material had an estimated MW of 5000, and its activity was not abolished by goat antibody to human C_3 and C_5; it was labile on storage for 2 weeks at $-40°C$, and was variably inactivated by heating at $56°C$ for 30 minutes. This *in vitro* assay system that detects a chemotactic activity in Sephadex-purified fractions of TF_D gives promise of adaptation and further refinement as a possible *in vitro* assay of TF_D.

 d.   Potential for a Radioimmunoassay of TF_D. We have indicated that TF_D by itself is not immunogenic in rabbits even when incorporated in Freund's adjuvant (Lawrence *et al.*, 1963; and unpublished observations). This is not surprising behavior for such a small molecule and is a highly desirable property that allows repeated injections for immunotherapy without raising a neutralizing antibody to TF (Lawrence, 1969a,b,c).

However, Plescia (personal communication, 1972) has been able to raise antibody in animals to the polynucleotides present in the dialyzate by coupling known TF_D to methylated bovine serum albumin (MBSA). This finding gives promise of adaptation as a radioimmunoassay of TF and development of a fluorescent antibody to TF to light up the particular cell populations that donate and receive it *in vitro*. Additionally the potential for development of an immunological reagent that could block the activity of TF for experimental purposes *in vitro* and for therapeutic purposes *in vivo* is apparent. For example the development of a monospecific anti-TF antiserum directed only against those cells bearing TF vs an individual organ transplant may have advantages over the crude antilymphocyte serum (ALS) or the total immunosuppression achieved by drugs that are in current usage.

VI. COMPARISON OF TF AND MEDIATORS OF CELLULAR IMMUNITY

Since TF was the first cell-free reagent isolated from immunocompetent cells, it was initially regarded as a mediator of cellular immunity. It is now clear that TF is distinctive from the mediators or "lymphokines" both structurally and functionally. Some of these salient distinctions are summarized briefly in Table VII. (Lawrence 1969d, 1973).

One of the chief differences lies in the fact that TF operates as an initiator of cellular immunity converting naive lymphocytes to an antigen-responsive state—an event that allows all the rest, including mediator production, to happen. The role of TF as an initiator of DTH and CMI distinct from the effector arc of the response is also emphasized by the fact that the new clone of antigen-responsive lymphocytes induced by TF have the immunocompetence of natively sensitive cells *in vivo* and *in vitro* when confronted with antigen, including proliferation and mediator production (e.g., MIF, lymphotoxin, interferon). In this sense TF intervenes to correct a central deficit, and in so doing ensures the correction of the efferent arc of the response.

Other distinctive differences include chemical composition and immunological specificity. TF is a dialyzable, peptide-nucleotide moiety of $<10,000$ MW, whereas the mediators are nondialyzable macromolecules that migrate in the region of albumin and range from 12,000 to 80,000 MW. In its immunological activities TF exhibits specificity as well as causes nonspecific consequences of CMI while the mediators are largely nonspecific in their activities. Additionally, TF is a preexistent moiety in immune lympho-

TABLE VII

COMPARISON OF TRANSFER FACTOR WITH EFFECTOR MOLECULES[a]

	Transfer factor	Effector molecules
Activity	Initiator of cellular immunity converts lymphocytes to antigen-responsive state	Effectors of cellular immunity produced by antigen-stimulated lymphocytes
Latency	Preexistent "memory" moiety liberated promptly from sensitive cells by antigen or by extraction	Latent period required for production after contact o sensitive cells with antigen
Specificity	Immunologically specific	Nonspecific effects
Properties	Dialyzable; <10,000 MW	Nondialyzable ca. 80,000 MW (except interferon)
Composition	Polynucleotide and/or polypeptide	Nonimmunoglobulins, migrate with albumin
In vivo function	1. Initiates delayed cutaneous reactivity	1. Mediate delayed cutaneous reactivity (MIF, SRF)[b]
	2. Initiates homograft rejection	2. Inhibit viral replication (interferon)
	3. Reconstitution cellular immune deficiency disease	3. Others under study
	4. Recovery disseminated intracellular infection	
	5. Immunological surveillance?	

[a] From Lawrence (1970c).
[b] MIF, migration inhibitory factor; SRF, skin reactive factor.

cytes that can be liberated promptly by antigen (30 minutes) or extraction procedures, whereas mediator production by antigen-stimulated lymphocytes requires a variable latent period (6–36 hours) before detection in the supernatants. Finally, the most striking difference between TF and the mediators is the established *in vivo* potency of TF in the initiation, restoration, and augmentation of systemic DTH and CMI responses in health and disease. The *in vivo* activities of supernatants containing mediators have been thus far limited to local effects, such as the cutaneous reac-

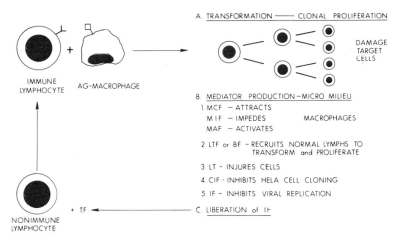

FIG. 12. The transfer factor (TF) shunt: Antigen-liberated TF engages non-immune lymphocytes, and proliferation plus mediator production ensues. AG, antigen; CIF, cloning inhibitory factor; IF, interferon; LT, lymphotoxin; LTF or BF, lymphocyte transforming factor or blastogenic factor; MAF, macrophage activating factor; MCF, macrophage chemotactic factor; MIF, migration inhibitory factor.

tions that resemble DTH responses (SRF) and the inhibition of tumor size upon local infiltration. Whether the *in vivo* activity of the mediators is restricted solely to a microenvironment or systemic concomitants also occur, is not yet clear.

It would appear that TF functions via a shunt that bypasses the stage of active immunization and converts naive lymphocytes to an antigen-responsive state. Once this event occurs, such naive cell populations acquire all the *in vivo* and *in vitro* capacities of natively immune cells. The descriptive aspects of the TF shunt are diagrammatically oversimplified in Fig. 12.

VII. NEWER ANIMAL MODELS FOR TF$_D$

One of the more hotly contested areas that TF research in man engendered, had its origin in the bleak and chequered history of attempts at adaptation of the findings in humans to animal species that were encountered. This aspect of work on TF has had its share of vicissitudes in claims for successful transfer in animal species with cell-free materials that until only recently, fell by the wayside one by one (Bloom and Chase, 1967). In this pervasive atmosphere of gloom and failure it is surprising that the whole enterprise did not languish and die. Nevertheless, work on the guinea pig model has been revived recently by Burger and his associates (1972) with reports on the successful transfer of DNCB sensitivity using TF_D prepared from supernatants of cultured peritoneal cells. Several investigators are currently engaged in attempts at duplication of these most interesting and potentially important findings. Additional work on this general problem has also been revitalized by the extension of the search for an animal TF_D to other species.

A.   Monkey-to-Monkey and Human-to-Monkey Transfer with TF_D

Maddison et al. (1972) showed that monkeys (Macaca mulatta) when infected with Schistosoma mansoni or various mycobacterial strains develop classical cutaneous DTH reactions as seen on skin biopsy when tested intradermally with an extract of S. mansoni adult worms or PPD, respectively. They prepared TF_D by the usual method from blood leukocytes of animals sensitive to mycobacterial antigens and transferred cutaneous reactivity to PPD but not to schistosomal antigens to nonimmune recipients. Conversely TF_D prepared from blood or lymph nodes of monkeys infected with schistosomes and reactive to schistosomal antigens transferred cutaneous reactivity to schistosomal antigens but not to PPD. Lymphocytes taken from two animals of the latter group following transfer responded to schistosomal antigen in vitro with transformation to lymphoblasts and thymidine incorporation.

These investigators also prepared TF_D from tuberculin-positive human donors who were unreactive to schistosomal antigens. The nonimmune monkey recipients of human TF_D developed biopsy-positive reactivity to PPD but not to schistosomal antigens. The recipient monkey lymphocytes also responded to PPD in vitro with transformation and proliferation. These in vitro and in vivo effects of TF_D are similar to those described following human-to-human transfers.

In each instance in these experiments the nondialyzable residue of leukocyte extract was compared to the corresponding TF_D for its capacity to transfer DTH *in vivo*. Both preparations were found effective, except that *in vivo* activity was lost when nondialyzable residue was exhaustively dialyzed. The latter finding agrees with our experience in humans discussed above and suggests an equilibrium between the concentration of TF_D inside and outside of the dialysis sac occurs under the usual conditions where the dialysis solution is not removed and replaced with fresh aliquots.

These experiments demonstrate the feasibility of monkey-to-monkey and human-to-monkey transfer of DTH *in vivo*. They also suggest the effects of TF_D are immunologically specific in this animal model with the exception that two putatively noninfected monkeys although incapable of transferring schistosomal sensitivity did transfer tuberculin sensitivity.

B. Human-to-Monkey Transfer with TF_D

Gallin and Kirkpatrick (1974) have also reported on successful transfer *in vivo* of cutaneous DTH from human to monkey (rhesus) using TF_D and determined by skin biopsy. These authors used human donors that expressed different patterns of cutaneous reactivity to mumps, SK-SD, candida, and PPD and found the monkey recipients acquired cutaneous reactivity only to those antigens to which the donor was reactive, not to those to which that he was unreactive. They also showed this activity in purified fractions of TF_D isolated by chromatography on Sephadex G-25. We have discussed about their finding that TF_D has chemotactic activity for polymorphonuclear cells and mononuclear cells *in vitro* and *in vivo*.

Zanelli, J. M., Wu, C. Y., Adler, W. H., Lance, E. M., and Medawar, P. B., (personal communication, workshop on TF-Tuscon, 1973) have successfully transferred cutaneous DTH to monkeys (rhesus) using TF_D from human donors reactive to tuberculin (PPD) or to keyhole limpet hemocyanin (KLH) or to both antigens. The results were determined by gross appearance and biopsy of skin test reactions which appeared within 48 hours of transfer and endured for at least 3 months with diminishing intensity. The results of transfer with human TF_D were immunologically specific, and recipient monkeys developed reactivity to PPD but not KLH when the donor was reactive to PPD only; and conversely to KLH but not PPD when tuberculin negative donors reactive to KLH were used to prepare TF_D. None of the monkey recipients developed a positive lymphocyte transformation test when their cells were exposed to the appropriate antigen.

Zanelli *et al.* also gave identical human TF_D preparations systematically to guinea pigs and did not detect cutaneous DTH to PPD or KLH. However, lymphocytes from recipients did transform and incorporate thymidine in the presence of KLH but not PPD. These are promising results and suggest that the feeble effects may be related to the quantity of TF_D and/or the intensity of the donors cutaneous DTH.

C. Rat-to-Rat Transfer with TF_D

An additional animal model for studies using TF_D has been reported by Liburd *et al.* (1972) in the rat. The end point measured in the rat following transfer is not cutaneous DTH, but immunity to infection with an intracellular protozoan parasite (*Eimeria neisulzi*). These investigators prepared TF_D from the lymphoid tissues of rats that had experienced coccidiosis infection and were immune to the parasite. Immune TF_D was given to nonimmune rats 48 hours before challenge with the infectious agent and the number of oocytes excreted in the stool was measured as an index of immunity. Rats given immune TF_D experience a 7-fold reduction of oocyte excretion (ca 5×10^6) compared either to untreated control animals (ca 35×10^6) or controls that had received nonimmune TF_D. The rats treated with immune TF_D before the primary challenge with *Eimeria* were completely immune to a second challenge with the parasite.

D. Guinea Pig-to-Guinea Pig Transfer with TF_D

In addition to Burger *et al.* (1972), Rosenfeld and Dressler (1974) have recently described a potent dialyzable TF_D preparation in guinea pigs which transfers immunologically specific cutaneous DTH to either Dinitrochlorbenzene (DNCB) or Orthochloro-benzoyl Chloride (OCBC) respectively corresponding to the immunological reactivity of the TF_D donor. TF_D obtained from non-immune donors failed to transfer DTH to either DNCB or OCBC. Further studies by Rosenfeld and Dressler (1974) on the chemical nature of TF_D in this animal model present data to indicate that the biological activity resides partly or entirely in low molecular weight double-stranded RNA molecules. This suggestion arises from their findings that TF_D activity *in vivo* is not affected by treatment with DNase, trypsin, pronase, pancreatic RNase or T_1 RNase but the activity is destroyed by treatment with RNase III and TF_D can be protected from this enzymatic digestion by addition of authentic double-stranded RNA (r A · r U and r I · r C) to the reaction mixture. Additional evidence presented indicates that TF_D is also inactivated by heating >90°C and exposure to Ultraviolet (U-V) light. Confirmation and extension of these important observations is awaited with great interest.

Thus animal models are becoming available not only for further characterization of the form and functions of TF_D, but also for the more precise analysis of mechanisms of CMI in experimentally induced intracellular infections (microbial, viral, parasitic). The animal models are readily adaptable to the study of neoplasia and autoimmune disease and to assess potential of TF_D as an immunizing agent for diseases for which no vaccine is available.

It is of considerable interest that where specificity controls were evaluated in the human-to-animal or animal-to-animal transfers of DTH, TF_D was found to possess immunological specificity (Burger *et al.*, 1972; Maddison *et al.*, 1972; Liburd *et al.*, 1972; Zanelli's group, personal communication; Gallin and Kirkpatrick, 1974; Rosenfeld and Dressler, 1974). The results of human-to-animal and animal-to-animal transfer of specific DTH and CMI using TF_D are summarized in Table VIII.

In any event, it appears that TF_D is operative in experimental animals and man is not so unique after all. The problem surrounding the reproducible demonstration of TF_D in laboratory rodents may prove to be more difficult than in primates but is not insoluble. The recent evidence for the existence of an inhibitor of TF_D activity *in vivo* in humans (Neidhart *et al.*, 1973; Gottlieb *et al.*, 1973) suggests a promising approach to reevaluation of TF_D in laboratory rodents. There is irony in the fact that if TF_D had been discovered in the experimental animal and brought to

TABLE VIII

$In \ Vivo$ Transfer of Delayed-Type Hypersensitivity (DTH) in Animals with Dialyzable Transfer Factor (TF_D)[a]

Reference	Species	Lymphocyte source	TF preparation	Immune response to transferred:				Immunological Specificity of TF_D
				Cutaneous DTH	Lymphocyte transformation	Other		
Liburd et al. (1972)	Rat–rat	Nodes, spleen	TF_D	ND	ND	Immunity to Eimeria, excretion coccidia		Yes
Maddison et al. (1972)	Monkey–monkey, (Macaca)	Blood	TF_D	PPD, schistosomal antigen	Positive			Yes
	Human–monkey	Blood	TF_D	PPD only	Positive			Yes
Gallin and Kirkpatrick (1974)	Human–monkey (rhesus)	Blood	TF_D, Sephadex G-25	SK-SD, candida	ND	Chemotactic for polys and monos		Yes
Zanelli, J. M., Wu, C. Y., Adler, W. H., Lance, E. M., and Medawar, P. B.	Human–monkey (rhesus)	Blood	TF_D	PPD, KLH	Negative			Yes
	Human–guinea pig	Blood	TF_D		Positive KLH			Yes

Reference	Species	Source		Antigen		Characteristics	
Hornung et al. (1973)	Chimp–chimp	Blood	TF$_D$	PPD	ND		ND
	Chimp–human	Blood	TF$_D$	PPD	ND		ND
Burger et al. (1972)	Guinea pig–guinea pig	PEC, nodes	TF$_D$	DNCB	ND		Yes
Rosenfeld and Dressler (1974)	Guinea pig–guinea pig	PEC, spleen, alveolar cells	TF$_D$	DNCB, OCB	ND	Double-stranded RNA nucleotide, sensitive to T3, heating 90°C, UV light	Yes
Adler et al. (1970); Palmer and Smith (1974)	Human–mouse in vitro	Blood	TF$_D$	ND	PPD positive		Yes

[a] ND, not done; PPD, tuberculin purified protein derivative; KLH, keyhole limpet hemocyanin; polys, polymorphonuclear cells; monos, mononuclear cells; DNCB, dinitrochlorobenzene; PEC, peritoneal exudate cells; OCB, orthochlorobenzoyl chloride; SK-SD, streptokinase-streptodornase.

its present stage of development, it would be just about ready to consider for exploration of its therapeutic possibilities in human disease. Instead, the reverse has occurred, but then one cannot quarrel with the manner in which nature chooses to reveal her secrets.

VIII. CLINICAL APPLICATIONS OF DIALYZABLE TRANSFER FACTOR (TF$_D$)

This is not the place to go into extensive clinical detail about immunotherapy with TF$_D$ since it has been covered elsewhere and the approaches are still empiric and largely anecdotal (Levin *et al.*, 1973; Lawrence, 1974). However, sufficient detail will be included in the discussion that follows to allow interpretation of the immunological activities that administration of TF$_D$ to diseased individuals has either newly uncovered or confirmed.

In the preceding sections we have outlined the two decades of carefully documented studies that have delineated the nature and extended the biological functions of TF as a potent moiety derived from immune leukocytes that can initiate as well as augment DTH and CMI responses of normal humans. This cumulative experience set the stage for the application of TF to the therapy of diseases either arising from or resulting in defects of cellular immunity (Lawrence, 1949, 1959a, 1969a, 1970a). The rapid transition to clinical usage was also greatly facilitated when TF$_D$ became available as a partially purified, nonantigenic product with potency equivalent to the viable cells or crude leukocyte extracts from which it is prepared (Lawrence *et al.*, 1963).

Interest in the nature and immunological significance of TF has been rekindled by a spate of recent literature confirming and documenting the effectiveness of this material in the initiation, restoration, or augmentation of cellular immunity in patients afflicted with congenital and acquired immunodeficiency syndromes, intracellular infections, and neoplastic diseases (Editorial, 1967, 1968, 1973, 1974; Grob *et al.*, 1973). These developments were an outgrowth of the gradual acceptance of the reality of TF coupled with the realization that the cellular immunity it conveys could exert a beneficial impact on so many of the disabling *in vivo* aberrations of immune function that result in disease (Lawrence, 1969a, 1970a; Lawrence and Fishman, 1971).

Initial clinical applications of this principle employed viable cells either as buffy coat leukocytes and more recently as concentrated lymphocyte preparations obtained from immune donors. These approaches to immunotherapy represented important preliminary steps and have been reviewed in detail elsewhere (Lawrence, 1969a, 1974).

The diseases that have responded to various TF preparations (either buffy coat leukocytes or lymphocytes as vehicles of TF or leukocyte extracts of TF_D) are outlined in Table IX. Disorders of this group are characterized by anergy that results from the primary disease process. Of interest for subsequent approaches to immunotherapy of cancer with TF is the general experience that cutaneous DTH to microbial antigens (PPD, SK-SD) can be transferred to patients with metastatic carcinoma, leukemia, and lymphosarcoma. These results suggested that such patients despite their anergic state are capable of responding to TF and mounting the immune responses to specific microbial antigens conferred by the normal donor.

The uniformly negative results of early attempts to transfer cutaneous DTH to patients with Hodgkins disease were secured using only one dose of viable cells and may reflect quantitative variables rather than absolute unresponsiveness. This interpretation is suggested by a recent report that TF_D, when given in a large dose repeatedly, resulted in the prompt termination of disseminated Herpes zoster in a patient with Hodgkins disease (Drew *et al.*, 1973).

It is of interest that, despite the vagaries of the disease under study and the individual experimental approaches to the problem, the incidence of successful transfer of DTH in these patients was 66 of 73, or 90%. This figure compares favorably with our own cumulative experience secured in normal subjects, where successful transfer was achieved in 143 of 152 consecutive attempts, an incidence of 94% (Lawrence, 1969a).

TABLE IX: TRANSFER FACTOR (TF)-RECONSTITUTION OF ACQUIRED CELLULAR IMMUNE DEFICIENCY STATES[a,b]

Disease	Reference	TF preparation	No. of patients	Specific DTH transferred		No. of patients reconstituted per No. treated
				Local	Systemic	
Sarcoid	Urbach et al. (1952)	WBC	6	6 (+++)	0	11/13
	Lawrence and Zweiman (1968)	TF$_D$	7	5 (+++)	2 (+)	
Lymphoma	Mufuoglu and Balkuv (1967)	WBC				
Acute leukemia			4		3 (+)	8/10
Chronic leukemia			2		2 (+)	
Lymphosarcoma			4		3 (+)	
Carcinoma	Hattler and Amos (1965)	Lymphs	18	17 (+++)	0	35/38
	Solowey et al. (1967)	TF$_D$	10	10 (+++)	10 (+)	
	Oettgen et al. (1971)	TF$_D$	5		3 (++++)	
	Klein (1968)	WBC	5		5	
Kwashiorkor, marasmus	Brown and Katz (1967)	TF$_{ext}$	12		12	12/12
						66/73 (90%)
Hodgkins	Fazio and Calciati (1962)	WBC	7	0	0	0/42[c]
	Good et al. (1962)	WBC	13	ND	0	
	Mufuoglu and Balkuv (1967)	WBC	22	ND	0	

[a] Reprinted with permission from Lawrence (1972a).

[b] WBC, buffy coat leukocytes; Lymphs, circulating lymphocytes; TF$_{ext}$, transfer factor WBC extracts; TF$_D$, transfer factor dialyzate; DTH, delayed-type hypersensitivity.

[c] Versus 41/43 transfers to normal controls.

A. Reconstitution of Congenital Immunaodeficiency Diseases with TF$_D$ Therapy

1. Wiskott-Aldrich Syndrome

Much of the current interest in TF as an immunological therapeutic agent has been stimulated by the reports of its beneficial effects achieved in the treatment of the Wiskott-Aldrich syndrome (Levin et al., 1970, 1973; Spitler et al., 1972c). This group of investigators have had the most extensive experience in the treatment of this T-cell deficiency syndrome with standardized preparations of TF$_D$ prepared by the same laboratory. Seven of 12 patients treated with TF$_D$ prepared from 250 ml of blood and given in one dose, acquired the same pattern of cutaneous DTH expressed by the donor, and their lymphocytes were converted to MIF production to the corresponding antigens. It was also observed that clinical improvement occurred in the 7/12 patients that exhibited an immunological response to TF$_D$; 6/10 patients recovered from infection and experienced regression of splenomegaly; 5/11 experienced clearing of their eczema; and 3/10 experienced rise in platelets and clearing of their bleeding tendency.

One dose of TF$_D$ from 250 ml of blood resulted in clinical and immunological remission sustained for about 6 months, when relapse occurred. Two patients in this series experienced four such remission—relapse cycles following TF$_D$ therapy with each relapse over a 2-year period carefully documented before the next dose of TF$_D$ was administered and produced clinical and immunological remission again (Fudenberg et al., 1974). The documentation of such episodes suggests a causal relationship between the administration of TF$_D$ and the clinical and immunological improvement observed, and that TF$_D$ at the doses employed is replacement therapy rather than curative in the Wiskott-Aldrich Syndrome. It is also of interest that the clone of lymphocytes with antigenic specificity that appear in the circulation of TF$_D$ recipients in this T-cell deficiency has a limited half-life and appears to be exhausted at the end of 6 months. This result stands in contrast to the response of normal individuals possessed of a full complement of T-cells, where the transferred cutaneous DTH can persist for 1–2 years following one miniscule dose of TF_D prepared from 85×10^6 leukocytes.

These initial results of TF_D therapy of the Wiskott-Aldrich syndrome reported by Levin *et al.* (1970, 1973) and Spitler *et al.* (1972c) have been confirmed in essential immunological and clinical detail by other groups of investigators. Griscelli *et al.* (1973) have reported clinical improvement in 2/4 Wiskott-Aldrich patients following treatment with TF_D. They also noted regression of infections, eczema, splenomegaly, and bleeding for a period of 3 months after 2 injections of TF_D, and this remission was followed by a relapse. The lymphocytes of one individual developed a response to PHA *in vitro,* and both patients developed the capacity to respond to DNCB *in vivo* during their clinical remission. One individual did not develop cutaneous DTH or respond clinically, yet his lymphocytes transformed upon exposure to antigen (SK-SD, candida) following TF_D.

Ballow *et al.* (1973) have also reported on TF_D administration to two patients with Wiskott-Aldrich syndrome. The first course of TF_D was without detectable effect in either patient; however, both responded clinically and immunologically after a second course. The clinical response consisted of clearing of eczema in both patients and decreased bruising in one. The immunological responses consisted of conversion of cutaneous DTH reactions *in vivo* and lymphocyte transformation *in vitro* to a number of specific antigens to which the TF_D donor was reactive. Most provocative, however, is the finding that the lymphocytes of both patients also acquired the capacity to react to allogeneic cells in the mixed leukocyte culture (MLC) test following TF_D administration (cf. Dupont *et al.* 1974).

One of the patients developed Coombs-positive hemolytic anemia associated with Coxsackie B5 viral pneumonitis during the course of therapy, and the authors consider TF to be a possible etiologic factor in the events leading to autoimmunity. These findings, as the authors discussed, raise the possibility that TF_D in elevating CMI also improves the helper function of T-cells and facilitates T-B cooperation in response to autoantigens. This effect is to be distinguished from the finding that the TF cannot transfer the capacity for a secondary antibody response to antigens experi-

enced by the donor (Lawrence and Pappenheimer, 1956; Good
et al., 1957).
These studies confirm the finding of Spitler et al. (1972) that
Wiskott-Aldrich patients who have abnormal monocyte IgG receptors show clinical improvement following TF$_D$ administration.
Unlike Spitler et al. (1972c), who could detect only MIF production, Ballow et al. (1973), like Griscelli et al. (1973), were able
to detect lymphocyte transformation in vitro to specific antigens
experienced by the TF$_D$ donor. They pointed out that this additional
increment of reactivity is very likely a result of the multiple doses
of TF$_D$ administered compared to the single-dose schedule employed by Spitler et al. (1972c).

2. Swiss-Type Agammaglobulinemia

It will be noted that 2 out of 3 patients with Swiss-type agamma-
globulinemia have responded to TF$_D$ administration with conversion of cutaneous DTH in vivo and MIF production in vitro and
sustained clinical improvement as well as clearing of candida infection. This response is of great interest since it would have been
considered impossible on purely theoretical grounds (Hitzig et al.,
1972).

3. Ataxia-Telangiectasia

In a series of various congenital immunodeficiency syndromes
studied by Griscelli et al. (1973), 4 of 5 patiens with ataxia-
telangiectasia responded to TF$_D$ administration with conversion
of cutaneous DTH reactivity in vivo. Three of these four patients
acquired concomitant lymphocyte transformation responses in
vitro—two to the corresponding antigens and one to PHA. Three
of the 4 patients that responded immunologically experienced
clinical improvement as well.

4. Combined Immunodeficiency

Montgomery et al. (1973) and Mogerman et al. (1973) have
each administered TF$_D$ to a single patient with combined immunodeficiency syndrome. Each of the 2 patients responded immunologically with conversion of cutaneous DTH reactivity in vivo and
either lymphocyte transformation or MIF production to the

corresponding antigens *in vitro*. Clinical improvement was also observed in each patient. This positive response is in contrast to the negative results that were observed by Griscelli *et al.* (1973) in their 2 patients with combined immunodeficiency that had received TF$_D$.

Gelfand *et al.* (1973) reported on immunoglobulin production *in vivo* and *in vitro* by a child with severe combined immunodeficiency direase folowing administration of TF$_D$. They observed no change in T-cell function, but rather an elevated leukocyte count and the appearance of primitive lymphoid cells and mature plasma cells in the bone marrow and peripheral blood. The lymphoid cells formed rosettes with complement-coated SRBC (S-sheep) and surface Ig was detected by immunofluroescence; serum IgM reached 2000 mg/100 ml and contained K and x chains and anti-A; anti-B, anti-I and anti-i antibodies were detected. A long-term culture of lymphoid cells from the patient's blood produced IgM with anti-i specificity, and B$_2$ microglobulin was detected. Although it is difficult to establish cause and effect, the authors postulated that the TF may have stimulated precursors of B-cells to differentiate in this patient in the absence of T-cell regulation (Polmar, 1973).

5. *Nezelof Syndrome*

None of 3 patients with a probable diagnosis of Nezelof syndrome responded either clinically or immunologically to TF$_D$ administration (Lawlor *et al.,* 1973).

6. *Variable Hypogammaglobulinemia*

Two patients with variable hypogammaglobulinemia responded to TF$_D$ administration with conversion of cutaneous DTH reactivity *in vivo* and lymphocyte transformation to the corresponding antigens *in vitro*. However, neither patient experienced a clinical response despite the immunological conversion (Griscelli *et al.,* 1973).

7. *Unclassified Immunodeficiency Syndromes*

A variety of patients with immunodeficiency syndromes that do not fall into one or another well established categories have been studied for their clinical and immunological response to TF_D. Amman *et al.* (1974) studied 6 patients in this category and observed conversion of cutaneous DTH reactivity *in vivo* in 3 of 6 patients. The transferred DTH endured for 9 months to a year in 2 patients and for only 2 weeks in a third patient. TF_D was specific and in each instance only those skin tests that were positive in the TF_D donor became positive in the recipient. There were no changes in antibody-mediated immunity detected; immunoglobulin levels remained unchanged; and immunization post-transfer produced no rise in antibody titer. No conversion of PHA responsiveness of each recipients lymphocytes *in vitro* was observed. Three of the 6 patients that responded immunologically to TF_D administration were also noted to experience clinical improvement. The patients who failed to respond had severely depressed CMI, and the authors suggested that a population of immunocompetent cells must be present for effective TF_D therapy.

Valdimarsson *et al.* (1974) have reported clinical and immunological improvement following TF_D administration to a child with defective T-cell function, recurrent skin ulcerations, and high fever. The patient had responded dramatically on two earlier occasions following blood transfusion with conversion of cutaneous DTH reactivity and acquisition of the capacity of his lymphocytes to respond to PHA with transformation and to SRBC with E-rosette formation. Each remission lasted 2 months and was followed by relapse associated with progressive loss of T-cell function. After three injections of TF_D given after the last relapse the patient improved and has remained well for the ensuing 9 months. The clinical improvement was noted to parallel the conversion of blood lymphocytes to *in vitro* responsiveness to PHA and SRBC.

Arala-Chaves *et al.* (1974) have also reported similar improvement following administration of TF_D in a young woman with unclassified complex immunodeficiency characterized by recurrent skin ulcerations. Conversion of cutaneous DTH *in vivo* to PPD, SK-SD, and candida occurred within 48 hours of administration of TF_D obtained from donors sensitive to these antigens. This result was associated with conversion of MIF production to the same antigens and conversion of lymphocyte transformation response to SK-SD and candida, but not to PPD. Additionally, although the TF_D donors lacked DNCB reactivity the patient developed the capacity to respond to DNCB, and her lymphocytes also acquired an increased responsiveness to PHA. The patient had been refractory to typhoid vaccine but did respond to a second immunization with antibody production 2 months after TF_D administration.

At 3 months, cutaneous reactivity and MIF production to PPD reverted to negative while remaining positive to SK-SD and candida, and at 4 months the skin ulcerations recurred and the patient experienced a relapse. A second dose of TF_D was followed by prompt reconversion of cutaneous reactivity and MIF production to PPD and gradual clearing of the skin ulcerations occurred over the next month; this remission has endured for longer than 4 months.

8. Comments

The details of the immunological responses *in vivo* and *in vitro* and the clinical improvement observed following TF_D therapy of the various categories of immunodeficiency syndromes are summarized in Table X.

The administration of TF_D to patients with congenital immunodeficiency syndromes has resulted in either initiation or restoration of cellular immunity in 24/36 (66%) individuals (i.e., conversion of cutaneous DTH, and/or MIF production and/or lymphocyte transformation responses to corresponding antigens). In addition, clinical improvement was observed in 16/36 (44%) patients who exhibited an immunological response to TF_D. There are many variables encountered in this broad spectrum of disease syndromes treated in a variety of clinics in this country and abroad (e.g., TF_D of variable dose and potency, one dose vs continued therapy, relapse rate, nature, severity, and complications of underlying disease). Nevertheless, a conservative estimate would suggest that more than mere coincidence is at work and that the effects achieved, like those ascribed to successful marrow transplantation, are related to the immunological reagent employed.

The opportunity to study these effects in congenital immunodeficiency syndromes has uncovered additional properties of TF_D

TABLE X: TF$_D$ IMMUNOTHERAPY OF CONGENITAL IMMUNODEFICIENCY DISEASE[a]

Disease	Responders	Immune conversion[b]			Clinical improvement	Reference
		DTH	MIF	Lymph		
Wiskott-Aldrich syndrome	7/12	+	+	–	7/12	Levin et al. (1970, 1973); Spitler et al. (1972c)
	4/4	+	ND	+ (1/4)	2/4	Griscelli et al. (1973)
	2/2	+	ND	+	0/2	S. P. Gotoff[c]
Swiss-type agamma-globulinemia	2/3	+	+	ND	1/3	Hitzig et al. (1972)
		+	ND	ND		B. Pirofsky[c]
		–	ND	ND		E. R. Stiehm[c]
Ataxia-telangiectasia	4/5	+	ND	+	3/5	Griscelli et al. (1973)
Combined deficiency	1/1	+	–	+	1/1	Montgomery et al. (1973)
	1/1	+	+	–	1/1	Mogerman et al. (1973)
	0/2	–	ND	–	0/2	Griscelli et al. (1973)
Dysgamma	1/1	+			1/1	Levin et al. (1970)
Nezelof syndrome	0/3	–	–	–	0/3	Lawlor et al. (1973)
Variable hypogamma-globulinemia	2/2	+	ND	+	0/2	Griscelli et al. (1973)
	24/36 (66%)				16/36 (44%)	

[a] TF$_D$, dialyzable transfer factor from normal donors; DTH, delayed skin reactivity; MIF, migration inhibitory factor; Lymph, lymphocyte transformation; ND, not done.

[b] Multiple specificites transferred (DTH, MIF, or lymphocyte transformation) were generally concordant with TF donor pattern of cutaneous reactions.

[c] Unpublished observations.

that were not detected when normal recipients were studied (Lawrence, 1969a,b). For example, administration of TF_D to immunodeficient patients has highlighted the contribution of a nonspecific increment of cellular immune responses in addition to the initiation or augmentation of specific cellular immunity. Where it has been documented carefully, the pattern of antigen-specific cutaneous DTH, MIF production, and/or lymphocyte transformation endowed on the recipient by TF_D is concordant with that of the TF_D donor (Spitler *et al.,* 1972c; Ballow *et al.,* 1973). Nevertheless no particular pattern of donor specificity is required, and the subset of TF's possessed by any one normal donor appear as effective as those of any other donor or donors. Moreover, in addition to the specific activities transferred, there appears to be a restoration of a general capacity to initiate and sustain cellular immune responses. This general "nonspecific" augmentation of CMI engendered by TF_D is evidenced by the acquisition of the capacity of such patients to recognize and respond to old and new antigens in their environment. Examples are seen in the capacity to respond *in vivo* to trichophytin (Spitler *et al.,* 1972c) or to be actively sensitized to DNCB (Griscelli *et al.,* 1973; Ballow *et al.,* 1973; Arala-Chaves *et al.,* 1974); and *in vitro* with conversion of the lymphocyte response to PHA; or to histocompatibility antigens in the MLC test (Ballow *et al.,* 1973), or to rosette formation with sheep RBC (Wybran *et al.,* 1973; Valdimarsson *et al.,* 1974).

The experience with TF_D administration to combined or dual immunodeficiency syndromes with inadequate T and B cell function has reemphasized earlier findings that demonstrated TF prepared from blood leukocytes can only transfer DTH and CMI, but not the capacity for Ig production to the same antigenic determinants (Lawrence and Pappenheimer, 1956). Patients with B-cell deficiencies (cf. Good *et al.,* 1957) as well as those with dual system disease continue to need prophylactic γ-globulin after TF_D administration despite selective elevation of CMI (Hitzig *et al.,* 1972).

Although the capacity for a secondary antibody response cannot be transferred with TF_D, recent clues suggest that the initiation or augmentation of CMI by TF may also facilitate T-B cell cooperation and Ig production to unrelated antigens in the recipient's environment. Examples of this possibility may be that of the Coombs-positive hemolytic anemia observed by Ballow *et al.* (1973); the IgM antibody response described by Gelfand *et al.* (1973); and the improved antibody response to typhoid vaccine described by Arala-Chaves *et al.* (1974). One may expect that the possibility of increased T-B cell cooperation following TF_D administration to immunodeficient children will be detected more frequently with increasing awareness of the problem. Finally, TF_D should provide a more sensitive probe to define the nature and extent of the precise mechanism underlying a particular immunodeficiency syndrome and enlarge our view of immunological homeostasis in health and disease. The ultimate place and clinical usefulness of this new modality of therapy is a matter for the future that will be determined by subsequent experience.

B. TF_D Immunotherapy of Disseminated Intracellular Infections

We have summarized in Table XI the cumulative specific immunological conversion to the related antigen (cutaneous DTH, MIF production, lymphocyte transformation) and clinical improvement (curtailment or eradication of the infective agent) following administration of TF_D to patients with refractory infections caused by obligatory or facultative intracellular microorganisms.

1.   Viral Infections

a.   Disseminated Vaccinia. The initial efforts at immunotherapy of viral infections employed viable leukocytes from vaccinia immune donors and were administered to 3 patients suffering from disseminated vaccinia. The patients responded promptly with acquisition of cutaneous DTH to vaccinia antigen and cessation of the viral infection (Kempe, 1960; O'Connell *et al.,* 1964; Hathaway *et al.,* 1965). TF_D has not been administered to such patients as yet, but these results suggest that it would be effective in initiating cellular immunity to vaccinia virus.

b.   Measles Pneumonia. Two children with "giant-cell' measles pneumonia were treated with TF_D from immune donors by Moulias

TABLE XI: DIALYZABLE TRANSFER FACTOR (TF$_D$) IMMUNOTHERAPY: INFECTIOUS DISEASE[a]

Disease	TF$_D$ source	Responders	Immune conversion			Clinical improvement	Reference
			DTH	MIF	Lymph		
Viral							
Measles	Rubeola +	2/2		+	0	2/2	Moulias et al. (1973)
SSPE	Rubeola +	5/7		+	0	2/7	Moulias et al. (1973)
Neonatal herpes	Herpes +	1/1				1/1	Moulias et al. (1973)
Herpes zoster	Herpes +	1/1				1/1	Drew et al. (1973)
SSPE	Rubeola +	2/2				2/2	Vandvik et al. (1973)
		11/13				8/13	
Mycobacterial							
Leprosy	Lepromin +	6/9	+	+	0	6/9 Reversal	Bullock et al. (1972)
Tuberculosis	Tubercle bacilli +	1/1	+	+	+	1/1	Whitcomb and Rocklin (1973)
Fungal							
Coccidioidomycosis	Coccidiocidin +	3/3	+	+	+	2/3	Graybill et al. (1973)
Candidiasis	Candida +	1/2	+	+		0/2	Rocklin et al. (1970)
		1/1	+	+		1/1	Schulkind et al. (1972)
		1/1	+		+	1/1	Pabst and Swanson (1972)
		4/5	+	+	+	2/5	Kirkpatrick et al. (1970, 1972)
		5/7	+	+		1/7	Spiler et al. (1972b)
		1/1	+	+	+	1/1	Valdimarsson et al. (1972)
		5/5	+	+	0	5/5	Hitzig et al. (1972)
		1/1	+		+	1/1	Griscelli et al. (1973)
		2/2	+			2/2	Bläker et al. (1973)
		21/25				14/25	
Total for infectious diseases:		42/51 (82%)				31/51 (62%)	

[a] DTH, delayed skin reactivity; MIF, migration inhibitory factor; lymph, lymphocyte transformation; SSPE, subacute sclerosing panencephalitis.

et al. (1973). Both patients responded with marked improvement and regression of pulmonary lesions after an initial inflammatory response occasioned by the acquisition of cellular immunity to the virus launched by TF_D. In each patient the *in vitro* leukocyte migration test (LMT) of Soberg (1967) converted to positive in the presence of measles viral antigens coincident with the clinical improvement observed.

    c. Subacute Sclerosing Panencephalitis (SSPE). This chronic degenerative disease has come to be regarded as a "slow-virus" infection of the brain caused by measles virus. Reinert *et al.* (1972) reported evidence to show that patients with SSPE had depressed or absent lymphocyte transformation responses and leukocyte migration responses (LMT) when tested *in vitro* with measles viral antigen. In their failure to respond to these *in vitro* tests the children with SSPE reacted like nonimmune infants rather than like children immune to measles who had served as controls. Reinert *et al.* found that, in children with SSPE given lymphocyte infusions or TF_D preparations from immune donors, there was restoration of CMI to measles viral antigen.

    These suggestive results led to a trial measles-positive TF_D administraiton to 7 children with SSPE by Moulias *et al* (1973). Although 5 of 7 patients responded to TF_D with conversion of the LMT test to measles antigen *in vitro,* only 2 of 7 responded clinically. In 2 of these children improvement in the clinical, electroencephalographic and cerebrospinal fluid findings occurred coincident with the conversion of the LMT test. One child with a consistently negative LMT test despite TF_D administration experienced a rapid worsening of the clinical parameters.

    Vandvik *et al.* (1973) have also reported similar clinical, neurological and immunological improvement in a 16-year-old boy with rapidly progressing SSPE following administration of measles immune TF_D on three separate occasions. In addition to improved specific CMI following TF_D there occurred a marked drop in the IgG content of the CSF and a selective drop in the measles antibody titer in the CSF and serum. The patient underwent marked mental and physical improvement and suffered no undesirable effects from TF_D injections. Of additional interest is the observation that the patient's serum interferon levels rose from 30 to 220 after the first injection of TF_D. The authors refer to a favorable response to TF_D administration in an additional patient; this was also associated with clinical improvement.

d. Herpetic Infections. A newborn infant with neonatal herpes was treated with TF_D from immune donors by Moulias *et al.* (1973) with disappearance of the herpetic eruption in the ensuing days.

Additionally, Drew *et al.* (1973) have reported on the containment and eradication of disseminated Herpes zoster following administration of TF_D from immune donors to a patient with Hodgkins disease. The acquisition of CMI promptly followed TF_D injection and was associated with fever, development of intense erythema around the vesicles, and conversion of lymphocyte responsiveness to varicella-zoster antigen and PHA. The viral cultures taken after TF_D administration had also become negative.

2. Mycobacterial Infections

a. Lepromatous Leprosy. The carefully controlled studies of Bullock *et al.* (1972) have documented that 6/9 lepromatous patients responded immunologically equally well to lepromin-positive viable lymphocytes or TF_D equivalents prepared from such cell populations. The 6 responders converted to lepromin-positive cutaneous DTH responses on microscopic and biopsy examination. Coincident with the acquisition of lepromin-sensitivity, the patients initiated DTH inflammatory responses in multiple local tissue depots of the previously tolerated lepra bacilli. The authors found that this type of systemic inflammatory response and its associated fever is readily controlled with small doses of prednisone. The appearance of this type of "reversal reaction" is usually considered a good clinical prognostic sign. None of the patients studied experienced any change in their clinical status over the ensuing year. We have discussed elsewhere that the administration of a single dose of TF_D to patients with defective CMI is probably insufficient to eradicate a widespread chronic infective disease (Lawrence, 1972a,b,c, 1974).

The suggestion that a multiple dose schedule for TF_D administration may also exert a beneficial clinical effect is supported by the recent experience of R. C. Hastings and his co-workers (personal communication, 1973). They treated an anergic patient with sulfone-resistant, polar lepromatous leprosy over a 3-month period with 37 divided doses of TF_D (equivalent to 7.44×10^9 lymphocytes) obtained from lepromin-positive normal donors. The patient experienced a "reversal reaction" after 15 injections of TF_D followed by clinical improvement, flattening of nodular skin lesions and a significant decrease in the bacillary counts detected in skin lesions. However, skin tests to lepromin remained negative in this patient.

   b. *Miliary Tuberculosis.* In many respects miliary tuberculosis and lepromatous leprosy share common features of a mycobacterial disease caused by organisms with similar properties and resulting in marked depression of CMI and cutaneous anergy in afflicted patients. Whitcomb and Rocklin (1973) have recently documented a sustained bacteriological and clinical remission in an anergic patient with miliary tuberculosis following repeated administration of TF_D. Of interest was the finding that the patient's tubercle bacillus remained susceptible *in vitro* to the antimicrobial agents used that were ineffective in eradicating the infection *in vivo*. The disease failed to respond to antibiotic therapy over many months until TF_D was added to the antimicrobal regimen and given in 6 doses over a 3-month period, when cellular immunity was restored (cutaneous DTH, MIF production, and lymphocyte transformation to PPD; negative cultures for tubercle bacilli) and sustained clinical recovery ensued.

3. *Fungal Infections*

   a. *Disseminated Mucocutaneous Candidiasis.* The largest numerical experience of immunological and clinical effect of TF_D in infectious disease has been accumulated in patients with chronic disseminated mucocutaneous candidiasis that have proved to be resistant to protracted amphotericin therapy. Of 25 anergic patients in this category treated with TF_D from immune donors, 14 have responded with eradication of the disease or sustained clinical improvement, an incidence of 52% of those treated. Immunological conversion of cutaneous DTH to candida antigen was observed in 21/25 patients (80%) after TF_D administration. The restoration of cutaneous DTH to candida was also accompanied in most patients by conversion to MIF production *in vitro,* whereas lymphocyte transformation and a proliferative response to candida appeared to occur with less regularity than MIF production and was detected in only 4 of 5 patients tested. The dissociation of MIF production and lymphocyte transformation in patients receiving TF_D therapy could be a result of the immunologic block consequent to the disease or could be an expression of quantitative variables related to dosage of TF_D and total duration of administration.

An example is shown in Fig. 13, which illustrates the favorable response of a child with amphotericin-resistant disseminated candidiasis treated with repeated administration of TF_D by Schulkind *et al.* (1972). Coincident with elevation of DTH and CMI to candida, the infection was slowly eradicated and a sustained recovery resulted with clearing of all lesions and only local recurrences in the ensuing 3 years.

b. Disseminated Coccidiodomycosis. Graybill *et al.* (1973) have administered TF_D to 3 patients with chronic disseminated coccidioidomycosis that was refractory to amphotericin therapy of several years duration. Following repeated injections of TF_D, 2 of

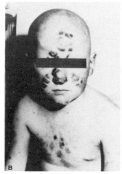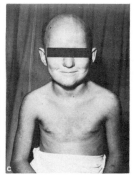

FIG. 13. Response of patient with amphotericin-resistant chronic mucocutaneous candidiasis to TF and amphotericin (A) at start of therapy, (B) after 120 days, and (C) after 265 days. Clearing of all lesions with only localized recurrences after 30 months. By courtesy of Schulkind *et al.* (1972) with permission of *Cellular Immunology.*

the 3 patients experienced prolonged clinical remissions of their infection. This was associated with the acquisition of MIF production to coccidiodin in all 3 patients, whereas conversion of cutaneous DTH occurred in 2 patients and conversion of lymphocyte transformation in only 1 patient.

These authors prepared TF_D from coccidioidin-positive normal donors either by the usual method of dialysis of leukocyte extracts (Lawrence et al., 1963) or by dialysis of supernatant solutions containing a single monospecific, antigen-liberated TF (Lawrence and Pappenheimer, 1956, 1957). The monospecific TF_D was prepared by incubating sensitive leukocytes with coccidioidin and dialysis of the cell-free supernatant. The antigen-liberated, monospecific TF_D appeared to be equally effective and of comparable potency in vivo. This is an interesting adaptation of experimental results to therapy, since it provides concentration of the specific TF_D related to the disease, leaving TF's with other specificities possessed by the donor in the cell pellet (e.g., tuberculin, SK-SD) which are all present in dialyzates of leukocyte extracts. Should administration of a specific TF prove to be either necessary or desirable for specific infections or tumors, this type of preparation may offer particular advantages.

Four additional patients with chronic disseminated coccidioidomycosis have been treated with TF_D by A. Catanzaro and L. E. Spitler (personal communication; cf. Spitler et al., 1974). Each of the four patients experienced clinical improvement although it was transient and additional administration of TF was required. Conversion of the lymphocyte transformation response and cutaneous DTH to coccidioidin was observed in all four patients while MIF production was detected in only three patients following administration of TF_D from immune donors.

4. General Comment

The results of TF_D therapy in these categories of infectious disease is summarized in Table XI above. It should be emphasized that in this cumulative experience an infinite number of variables are operative (e.g., varieties and stages of the diseases treated; the different regimens of TF_D administration employed; quantitative and qualitative variables of TF_D potency). The only constancy arises from the fact that diseases of this group were either refractory to the usual antimicrobial agents or no satisfactory therapy is available. Nevertheless, despite the anecdotal nature of the experience and the bleak outlook for success of any intervention in hosts compromised by such chronic disseminated infections, 42/51 (82%) of such patients responded to TF_D immunologically with conversion of cutaneous DTH and/or MIF production and/or lymphocyte transformation to the respective antigen specificities conferred by different donors. Additionally, 31/51 (62%) of this group of patients experienced clinical and microbial improvement and/or sustained remissions of their respective infectious disease.

Where successful eradication of the infection has occurred, TF_D has been administered repeatedly over several weeks. This strategy has proved effective in candidiasis (Schulkind et al., 1972; Valdimarsson et al., 1972; Pabst and Swanson, 1972) as well as in disseminated coccidioidomycosis (Graybill et al., 1973) and in miliary tuberculosis (Whitcomb and Rocklin, 1973).

Most patients with disseminated candidiasis who had been resistant to amphotericin therapy responded after TF_D administration and experienced clinical remissions. However, reinstitution of amphotericin therapy concurrent with TF_D appears to produce better clinical responses in some patients than when TF_D was given alone (Kirkpatrick et al., 1970, 1971, 1972). Nevertheless, exceptions to this experience have been reported by Pabst and Swanson (1972), Valdimarsson et al. (1972), and Graybill et al. (1973), who achieved clinical remissions in candidiasis and in coccidioidomycosis following administration of TF_D alone without concomitant amphotericin therapy.

It is of more than passing interest to comment on the question of whether DTH and cellular immunity is beneficial to the host infected with intracellular microbial agents despite the inflammatory concomitants that ensue. This dilemma had plagued investigators since Metchnikoff, Koch, and von Pirquet, and its resolution was initiated by the careful, quantitative studies Mackaness and his colleagues (Mackaness and Blanden, 1967). Their findings that DTH and cellular immunity exert a beneficial effect on the course such infective disease in experimental animals are amply confirmed by the favorable results of TF$_D$ administration to patients with such infections and the final resolution of the question may be at hand.

C. Transfer Factor and Cancer Immunotherapy

Extensive studies carried out in tumor-bearing patients and experimental animal models (Hellström and Hellström, 1970), have revealed that the host so afflicted usually does possess cellular immunity vs the specific antigens of the tumor (TSA). It has also been shown that such cellular immunity is either depressed or abrogated by serum "blocking factors," probably tumor anti-gen–antibody complexes, that appear to coat the reactive lympho-cytes of the host as well as the target cells of the tumor. The tumor-bearing host is therefore the only example in nature of a permanently successful allograft take—an irony made possible by serum "blocking factors" which serve as nature's immunosup-pressive device. The patient's tumor is the allograft that evades the usual cellular immune responses that would ordinarily result in rejection. Thus it appears that the tumor-bearing host has the normal immune responses to foreign cells, but these are over-whelmed by a replicating antigenic mass to which a vigorous but ineffective humoral response is made which is associated with a widespread depression of cellular immunity.

With this information concerning the plight of the tumor-bearing host evolving, the prospect of selectively elevating cellular immunity versus TSA with TF$_D$ afforded a safe and rational ap-proach to the problem. The application of TF$_D$ offers the additional advantage of augmenting CMI without a concomitant boost of immunoglobulin production to the same antigenic determinants. Early approaches to this problem evaluated the potential responsive-ness of tumor-bearing patients; viable cell transfers were used by Muftuoglu and Balkuv (1967), leukocyte extracts by Hattler and Amos (1965), or TF$_D$ by our laboratory (Solowey et al., 1967). As summarized above in Table IX, patients with a variety of metastatic neoplastic disease, although anergic, do possess cell populations that can respond to TF from normal donors with acquisition of cutaneous DTH to the corresponding microbial antigens (PPD, SK-SD). These results indicated that should a tumor-specific TF_D be administered, patients in this category, even those with advanced disease, do retain the capacity to make an appropriate immunological response. The fragmentary and inconclusive experience that has been secured with the beginning application of TF_D immunotherapy to a variety of cancers is outlined in Table XII.

1. Effects of "Nonspecific" Pooled TF_D on Breast Cancer

To assess the therapeutic potential and safety of TF_D in cancer patients, we undertook a collaborative study with colleagues at the Sloan-Kettering Institute (Oettgen *et al.*, 1971, 1974). The effects of pooled TF_D obtained from normal individuals upon the course of 5 patients with advanced metastatic breast cancer of the "inflammatory" type were evaluated. The basic assumption for this experimental protocol derived from the original suggestions of an immune surveillance mechanism for disposal of mutant neoplastic cells as proposed by Thomas (1959). We assumed that normal mature women who are free of breast cancer may have been exposed to and raised a specific TF vs neoplastic breast cells from puberty onward. Therefore, pooled TF_D was prepared from blood leukocytes of 177 normal women over 45 years of age. A dose of 1–4 ml of the TF_D was injected subcutaneously daily or thrice weekly into each patient with breast cancer for periods ranging from 21 to 310 days. The total TF_D given to individual patients was equivalent to from 17 to 217 billion cells. When cutaneous reactivity to PPD and SK-SD was used as a TF_D marker, these reactions were transferred to 3 patients, 1 of 5 patients experienced partial regression of the tumor which was sustained for 6 months before relapse. When the relapse was treated with a different pool of TF_D, it failed to respond.

In this study TF_D was administered repeatedly and in massive doses for the first time, and it was evaluated as if it were a new drug. In such large dosage TF_D did not cause any inflammatory or hypersensitivity reactions in the 5 patients studied. There were no hematological, immunological, biochemical, or enzymatic abnormalities detected, nor were any harmful side effects observed.

TABLE XII

DIALYZABLE TRANSFER FACTOR (TF$_D$) IMMUNOTHERAPY OF CANCER[a]

Disease	TF$_D$ source	Responders	Immune conversion	Clinical response	Reference
Breast cancer	Pooled "nonspecific"	3/5	+ DTH to PPD, SK-SD	Remission, 1/5	Oettgen et al. (1971, 1974)
Melanoma	Sens. donor-specific WBC Ext.	1/1	ND	Rejection of metastatic nodules, 1/1	Brandes et al. (1971)
	Family-specific	2/9	+ Lymph. trans. to TSTA	Regression of lesions, 2/9	Spitler et al. (1972a, 1973a)
	Sensitized-donor-specific	4/10	ND	Regression of lesions, 4/10	Morse et al. (1973)
Sarcoma					
Alveolar	Twin-specific	1/1	+ MIF to TSTA	0/1	LoBuglio et al. (1973)
Osteogenic	Family-specific	1/1	+ RFC	0/1	Levin et al. (1972)
Nasopharyngeal carcinoma	Infectious mononucleosis patients	2/2	Fall antibody titer to E-B virus antigen	Regression 2/2	Goldenberg and Brandes (1972)
Total		14/29 (48%)		10/29 (34%)	

[a] DTH, delayed-type hypersensitivity; Lymph. trans, lymphocyte transformation; WBC Ext., buffy coat leukocyte extract; ND, not done; MIF, migration inhibitory factor; PPD, purified protein derivative; RFC, rosette-forming cells; TSTA, tumor specific transplantation antigens.

Immunological studies revealed that IgM, IgA, and IgG were found in normal concentration in the patients' sera before TF$_D$ administration and no changes were detected after the full course of treatment. No antibodies to a broad range of human leukocyte antigens (1, 2, 3, 9, 10, 11, W19, W28 or 5, 7, 8, 12, 13, W10, W22, W27, W14, W15, W17, W5, W18, W21, W29, and Da) were detectable in the serum of 2 patients who had received TF$_D$ from an amount of leukocytes equivalent to 81 and 128 units of blood transfusions, respectively. In addition to the absence of immediate side effects, no evidence for transmission of hepatitis by pooled TF$_D$ was detected in recipients clinically or by hemagglutination-inhibition tests for Au antigen and hemagglutination tests for Au antibody.

Whether pooled "nonspecific" TF$_D$ holds promise for the immunotherapy of tumors cannot be decided from these limited observations. Nevertheless, we can conclude from this study that TF$_D$ can be given safely and in large doses (257 ml of TF$_D$ equivalent to 217 billion cells) repeatedly (125 injections) over a prolonged period (310 days). This dose range, repetitive nature, and duration of therapy with TF$_D$ far exceeds the dosage and duration of therapy that have been reported effective in the reconstitution of immunodeficiency or in the eradication of infectious disease. Our data in this regard give a clue to the margin of safety that is afforded by TF$_D$ under ordinary circumstances of its use.

2.   Effects of TF on Malignant Melanoma

Brandes et al. (1971) have reported on the effects of antimelanoma TF in leukocyte extracts prepared from the blood of a melanoma patient that had been sensitized to the prospective recipient patient's tumor antigens. After subcutaneous injection of TF in leukocyte extracts the patient initiated a prompt and vigorous response to the metastatic depots of tumor both locally and systemically. The local response was characterized by inflammation and rejection of tumor nodules in the skin and was of greater intensity in those nodules that had been infiltrated with leukocyte extract. Systemically the patient experienced a febrile response and the appearance of lymphoblasts in his circulation. He died subsequently of a cerebral hemorrhage.

Spitler *et al.* (1972a,b, 1973a,b) have made the interesting observation that family contacts of the index case of melanoma exhibit lymphocyte reactivity (transformation, MIF production) to the patient's tumor antigens. These authors prepared TF_D from such family contacts and administered it to 9 patients with metastatic malignant melanoma. Only 2 of the 9 patients responded immunologically with acquisition of lymphocyte transformation to their own tumor antigens and clinically with regression of tumor lesions. One of these patients remained free of new metastatic lesions for 7 months with continued TF_D administration. However new metastatic lesions developed 1.5 years later coincident with loss of lymphocyte transformation and MIF production to tumor antigens and in the face of TF_D therapy.

Morse *et al.* (1973) sensitized cancer patients versus the prospective recipient patient's killed tumor and prepared TF_D from their blood leukocytes. Morse *et al.* reported on 10 patients with malignant melanoma following administration of TF_D and noted regression of lesions and reactions of rejection in 4 patients.

3. Effects of TF_D on Sarcoma

Levin *et al.* (1972) have reported clinical improvement in a patient with osteogenic sarcoma. In this tumor, as in melanoma cited above, they found that the lymphocytes of a healthy family contact possessed CMI vs the patient's tumor antigens as determined by colony inhibition assay. Administration of this tumor-specific TF_D to the patient resulted in clinical improvement. The number of rosette-forming cells (RFC) detected when the patient's lymphocytes were exposed to sheep erythrocytes increased significantly within 48 hours after transfer. This response to TF_D is thought to be a T-cell function (Wybran *et al.*, 1973). The number of RFC were observed to correlate well with the clinical improvement detected in the patient. The clinical improvement associated with repeated administration of TF_D was sustained for 7 months before deterioration of the patient's status occurred. The healthy TF_D donor was retested at this time and his lymphocytes had lost reactivity to the patient's tumor in the interim. Fudenberg and his colleagues (1974) have recently updated and enlarged this experience and reported restoration of specific immunocompetence and clinical improvement in 8 of 12 patients with osteogenic sarcoma that have been treated with tumor-specific TF_D from 3 months to 1.5 years.

LoBuglio and his colleagues (LoBuglio *et al.,* 1973) studied a patient with alveolar sarcoma. They adapted an MIF assay and failed to detect lymphocyte reactivity of the patient to his own tumor antigens. Lymphocytes from the patient's healthy twin did, however, produce MIF when exposed to a homogenate of the patients tumor. TF_D was prepared from blood lymphocytes (15×10^8) of the healthy twin and administered to the patient on 3 occasions at 3-week intervals. The patient experienced a conversion of MIF production to his tumor antigens not after the first dose of TF_D and only transiently after the second dose. However, the MIF response became strongly positive at 3 days and 3 weeks after the third dose of TF_D. There was no change in the clinical course of the disease noted during the 6-month period of observation.

4. *Effects of E-B Virus-Positive TF_D on Nasopharyngeal Carcinoma*

Goldenberg and Brandes (1972) prepared TF_D from E-B virus-positive normal young adults who had recovered from infectious mononucleosis and administered it to 2 patients with nasopharyngeal carcinoma refractory to conventional therapy. Following administration of TF_D, slowing of tumor growth was observed in both patients. Tumor regression in one patient was associated with intense lymphocytic infiltration of the tumor on biopsy; with conversion of cutaneous DTH to PPD and *T. rubrum* used as markers of TF_D activity; and a fall of antibody titer to the viral capsid antigen (VCA) of the E-B virus. Tumor regression in the second patient was temporary. These results are of great interest not only in relation to TF_D therapy of tumors but also in respect of providing additional clues to the postulated relationship between E-B virus, infectious mononucleosis and nasopharyngeal carcinoma. The results also raise the obvious possibility that E-B virus-positive TF_D may have implications for Burkitt's lymphoma.

5. General Comment

The assessment of the effects of TF$_D$ on the responses of patients with metastatic cancer has only just begun. Although the augmentation of immunological responses ensues with regularity following TF$_D$ administration, clinical improvement when it occurs is transient and unpredictable. This is not surprising since the patients selected are those refractory to conventional therapy. The fact that such end-stage disease responds to TF$_D$ at all is unanticipated.

It would be premature to attempt to evaluate any advantage to the use of TF$_D$ alone or in combination with other immunological and conventional modalities of cancer therapy. The promise afforded by TF$_D$ lies in its capacity to selectively augment the host's specific CMI responses to tumor antigens without concomitant antibody production and with relative safety over a wide range of dosages (Oettgen et al., 1971, 1974).

D. Immunotherapy with TF$_D$—Prospects and Questions

This is not the place to go into extensive detail since the cumulative clinical experience with TF$_D$ is still at its most primitive, anecdotal level. Taken together, the beneficial results that have followed the administration of TF$_D$ in such a broad range of diseases under widely diverse conditions, in a variety of clinics would suggest that, at the very least, more than just the wild vagaries of coincidence are responsible for the beneficial effects observed. Such cumulative experience as exists is sufficiently promising to warrant a double-blind clinical trial of the type that any new drug or antibiotic regimen requires before any firm conclusions concerning efficacy can be reached. Since TF$_D$ is so easy to prepare and administer with safety, only the exercise of stringent requirements to determine its use and sophisticated immunobiology to monitor its effects will result in the development of an adequate rationale and critical proof of its effectiveness. Moreover, control of quantitative variables such as dosage and potency will have to await the final definition of the molecular species that constitutes TF as well as the precise subpopulation of cells that donate and accept it.

In Table XIII, we have summarized the variety of diseases in which patients have derived benefit following administration of TF$_D$. The general principle that begins to emerge from this experience would suggest that TF therapy may be expected to benefit those disease syndromes that arise from a result in absent or depressed cellular immunity.

The array of diseases responsive to TF administration that are listed in Table XIII may be expected to enlarge in scope and numbers as general appreciation of the principle involved becomes more widespread and our knowledge about TF more concrete. Further extensions of TF immunotherapy to diseases of unknown origin are on the horizon and have begun to be explored. These include Multiple Sclerosis (Jersild *et al.*, 1973; Utermohlen and Zabriskie, 1973); Behcet's Syndrome (Spitler *et al.*, 1974; Denman, 1974); Chronic Active Hepatitis (Spitler *et al.*, 1974); Chediak-

TABLE XIII

SUMMARY OF TF$_D$ IMMUNOTHERAPY

Congenital immunodeficiency	Acquired immunodeficiency	Infectious disease
Wiskott-Aldrich	Sarcoid	Vaccinia
Swiss-type	Metastatic cancer	Herpes
Ataxia-telangectasia	Kwashiorkor	Measles
X-linked variety	Marasmus	SSPE
Dysgammaglobulin, combined variety		
		Candidiasis
		Coccidioidomycosis
Breast cancer		
Melanoma		Leprosy
Sarcoma		Tuberculosis
Nasopharyngeal carcinoma		
		Coccidioides (rats)
		Schistosomiasis (monkeys)

TABLE XIV

Cutaneous Delayed Type Hypersensitivity (DTH) or Cell-Mediated
Immunity (CMI) Conferred by Transfer Factor
(TF) from Immune Donors[a]

Microbial antigens: Bacterial	Fungal	Viral	Parasitic
Tuberculin	Coccidioidin	Vaccinia	Schistosomal (monkey)
Streptococcal	Histoplasmin	Herpes	Coccidioides (rat)
Diphtheria toxoid	Candidin	Rubeola	
Lepromin	*Trichophyton*	Mumps	
Tularin	*T. rubrum*	E-B virus	
	Blastomycin		

Neoantigens: Ethylene-oxide human serum protein
Keyhole limpet hemocyanin
Histocompatibility antigens: HLA skin allograft specificities
Tumor antigens: Melanoma
Sarcoma
Nasopharyngeal carcinoma
Other antigens: Kviem antigen
"Cat-scratch" antigen

[a] Recipients express pure DTH or CMI in absence of antibody to same antigenic determinants.

Higashi Syndrome (Khan *et al.*, 1973); and Juvenile Rheumatoid Arthritis (Froland *et al.*, 1974). Although diverse in expression these disease syndromes share in common either an associated chronic infectious process and/or depressed cellular immune responses.

From a broader immunological perspective and scope of antigenic specificities to which cutaneous DTH or CMI has been conferred by various TF preparations obtained from immune donors is summarized in Table XIV.

IX. Specific Activities and "Nonspecific" Consequences of TF_D

We have detailed above the evidence collected to support the conclusion that TF exhibits immunological specificity in normal individuals (Lawrence, 1969a,b). The strongest evidence secured on this question was obtained from studies in normal individuals where a TF of a particular specificity did not preexist and had to be raised *de novo*. This type of induction of a new TF was achieved following active sensitization of prospective donors to alloantigens (Lawrence *et al.*, 1960) and then demonstrating that transfer only of the corresponding specificity did indeed occur. Additional controls showed that leukocyte extracts from nonimmune donors had neither systemic nor even local activity when placed in close juxtaposition to the target graft.

Our work since its inception would have been greatly facilitated if TF were really nonspecific and any donor would do as well as any other for the transfer of DTH to tuberculin or toxoid or SK-SD. The real test of specificity however, came with the discovery of TF_D as $<10,000$ MW. This brought the added embarrassment of trying to explain how such a small molecule could transmit so much information and still remain true to the macromolecular central dogma. Unhappily, there is still no easy explanation within the limits of current knowledge available. This vexing state of affairs has naturally led to alternative explanations that fit conventional pegs namely TF is specific because it is an immunogen or TF is nonspecific because it is an adjuvant. It is possible that TF_D may turn out to be neither or both.

Nevertheless where specificity controls have been deliberately assessed, our claim for the immunological specificity of TF has been confirmed over and over again. Although it makes for dull reading, it may be worth while to set the record straight and help to clarify this issue by listing the growing number of investigators who report on the immunological specificity of TF_D: Amman *et al.*, 1974; Arala-Chaves *et al.*, 1967, 1974; Ballow *et al.*, 1973; Baram and Mosko, 1965; Baram *et al.*, 1966; Baram and Condoulis, 1973; Fireman *et al.*, 1967; Fudenberg, *et al.*, 1974; Gallin and Kirkpatrick, 1974; Kirkpatrick *et al.*, 1972; Levin *et al.*, 1973; Liburd *et al.*, 1972; LeBuglio *et al.*, 1973; Maddison *et al.*, 1972; Neidhart *et al.*, 1973; Spitler *et al.*, 1972a,b,c,d; Zanelli's group (personal communication). It should be emphasized that the specificity detected extends over a wide range of antigens studied and has been shown for Sephadex-purified fractions of TF_D as well as the raw diazyzate.

The specific effects of TF, however, do not preclude the initiation of certain "nonspecific" consequences that will result from the augmentation of cellular immunity in general. Such general effects that can be anticipated are the concomitants that are currently known to accrue from the induction of DTH and CMI to antigenic determinants of any specificity, such as activation of macrophages for more efficient ingestion and disposal of foreign matter and increased efficiency of T-B cell cooperation. These nonspecific effects are yet to be documented deliberately in recipients of TF, but it is very likely that they do indeed occur, as Dienes and Freund discovered long ago and as Mackaness has so carefully documented.

The first clues to the operation of "nonspecific" consequences of TF$_D$ administration were detected in patients with T-cell immunodeficiency syndromes as part of the general restoration of cellular immune responsiveness that ensued. We have discussed above the initiation of the capacity to respond to DNCB sensitization *in vivo* and the acquisition of PHA, RFC, and MLC responsiveness *in vitro* following administration of TF$_D$ to immunodeficient children. These effects of TF$_D$ appear to be magnified in immunodeficiency syndromes since they are seen against a null background. It is quite likely that a similar augmentation of such "nonspecific" responses also occurs in normals, but the increment may be less striking in individuals already possessed of a full complement of T-cells and a normal repertoire of immune responsiveness.

Thus the question is not one of specificity vs nonspecificity of TF$_D$ since both specific activities and nonspecific consequences are transferred and both have a contribution to make to the overall augmentation of CMI responses. However, the current surge of interest in the therapeutic applications of TF$_D$ has brought resolution of a related question into sharp focus. The question is now whether a specific TF is either necessary or more beneficial than pooled normal TF, comprised of random subsets of specificities, for the recovery of patients with specific infections or specific tumors. Alternatively, will a specific TF confer any additional increment of responsiveness that will favor eradication of the infection or the tumor beyond that afforded by the "nonspecific" consequences that it may initiate? Thus, as Bloom (1973) has inidcated, the whole question transcends theoretical interest and has become a very practical matter. If a "universal" TF that is equally effective immunotherapy for all categories of disease were to evolve, it would provide a most satisfactory solution to the problem both for the clinical immunobiologist as well as for immunological theory.

To assess this question, a controlled, double-blind protocol has been suggested for a proposed field trial of TF_D immunotherapy of lepromatous leprosy by a World Health Organization panel (W.H.O. Expert Panel, 1974). It is planned to evaluate the effects of administration of lepromin-negative TF compared to lepromin-positive TF on the clinical and immunological responses of groups of patients with lepromatous leprosy. There are two other field trials in progress that may also help clarify this question: (1) E-B positive TF_D in the immunotherapy of nasopharyngeal carcinoma by Goldenberg and Brandes (1972) in Hong Kong, sponsored by the Canadian National Research Council; (2) schistosomal-positive TF_D as an immunizing agent and for therapy of schistosomiasis by Warren and his associates in Puerto Rico, sponsored by the Rockefeller Foundation.

It is only from such carefully controlled field trials in selected diseases that the effectiveness of TF_D alone or combined with conventional therapy can be evaluated properly and the superiority, if any, of specific vs nonspecific TF may emerge. In any event it is hoped that opinion, conjecture, and bias will be superseded by reliable data that are carefully collected. In Table XV, we have compared the known specific activities of TF with the "nonspecific" consequences of elevating CMI with this reagent.

X. TF_D Potential as an Immunizing Agent

We have seen that TF_D can initiate as well as augment sustained CMI responses that enable patients with overwhelming infection to eradicate the causative agent. These effects are achieved in a compromised host and suggest that administration of TF_D prior to exposure may also exert a beneficial effect on the individual's response to a subsequent infection. The potential usefulness of

TABLE XV

SPECIFIC ACTIVITIES AND "NONSPECIFIC" CONSEQUENCES OF
TRANSFER FACTOR (TF)[a]

Specific activities	"Nonspecific" consequences
1. Cutaneous DTH and CMI	1. General stimulus CMI
2. Homograft rejection	2. Transfer PHA-response
3. Lymphocyte transformation	3. Transfer E-rosette response
4. Mediator production	4. Transfer MLC response
5. New TF's raised de novo	5. Transfer capacity for DNCB
6. No transfer 2nd antibody response	6. Transfer polychemotaxis

Macrophage activation—probable
T-B cell facilitation—possible

Are "nonspecific" consequences of TF sufficient for effective immunotherapy?
or
What additional beneficial increment conferred by TF specific for related infection
or tumor?

[a] CMI, cell-mediated immunity; DTH, delayed-type hypersensitivity; MLC mixed leukocyte culture; PHA, phytohemagglutinin; DNCB, dinitrochlorobenzene

TF_D as a prophylactic immunizing agent for grave infections for which no effective vaccine is available has just begun to be recognized.

This approach to prevention of disease is likely to have limited application. However, among scientists who work with highly infective and potentially lethal microbes and viruses and among patients who are immunosuppressed as a consequence of therapy, organ transplantation or lymphomatous disease, such a need does exist. In one sense this approach may be currently under way in patients with Wiskott-Aldrich syndrome who have been successfully maintained with repeated injections of TF_D every 5–6 months (Spitler et al., 1972c; Levin et al., 1973; Fudenberg et al., 1974). These patients appear to contain a variety of infections that formerly threatened their survival, as a result of the restoration and maintenance of cellular immunity achieved by TF_D.

XI. The Form and Functions of TF

Thus we have seen that the facts are no longer in question and that TF does indeed selectively initiate and augment CMI under a wide variety of circumstances and in diverse conditions of health and disease. What remains a healthy matter of enquiry is the definition of the exact nature and biochemical structure of this small molecule(s) and the final documentation of how it functions to achieve the effects observed. Until such knowledge is available, considerations concerning possible mechanisms of action must remain operational and descriptive. It would appear that administration of TF confers on the recipient most of the specific memories and many of the nonspecific consequences of DTH and CMI experienced by the donor. Those specific responses that are remembered with the greatest intensity will be conveyed readily to the recipient. The memories of prior antigenic encounters that are weak or fading in the donor are likely to be expressed feebly or not at all in the recipient as well. The recurrent experience would suggest that recipients of TF are promptly endowed with highly sophisticated knowledge of antigens to which they may not have been exposed and are thus primed to respond with all of the *in vivo* and *in vitro* expressions of DTH and CMI of the natively immune donor.

Yet without exposure of the recipient or his circulating lymphocytes to the appropriate antigens, there is no apparent evidence that any such transaction had occurred. Additionally, within the descriptive limitations of our present knowledge, the cumulative data provided by earlier as well as current *in vivo* and *in vitro* results suggest that TF acts operationally as though it either uncovers or causes the *de novo* appearance of specific receptor sites on the recipient's circulating lymphocytes resulting in the generation of a new clone of antigen-reactive cells. Alternatively TF may activate a clone of cells already programmed to respond to a given antigen. The detection of receptor sites with other recognition units which are considered "nonspecific" is a recent finding uncovered in the circulating lymphocytes of immunodeficient children after TF administration. The latter include lymphocyte receptor sites for PHA that result in the acquisition of PHA responsiveness; receptor sites for sheep RBC that result in the capacity for E-rosette formation; and receptor sites for recognition of HL-A antigens that result in the acquisition of the capacity for an MLC response. It is of interest that the PHA response, the E-rosette response, and the MLC response are thought, but not yet proved, to be T-cell responses in humans.

Both the antigen-specific and the nonspecific lymphocyte reactivities detected after TF administration also suggest the possibility that TF may initiate the maturation of a primitive stem cell(s) concerned with T-cell functions. In any event, possibilities that remain to be explored are the intimation of subtle relationships that may exist between TF and the elusive T-cell receptor, between TF and thymosin, and between TF and the nonimmunoglobulin product of the *Ir* gene.

At a recent workshop on TF in Tucson (Kirkpatrick and Rifkind, 1974), most investigators working with partially purified fractions of chromatographed dialyzates reached a consensus that TF is immunologically specific and comprised of a peptide–RNA nucleotide complex of <10,000 MW that is resistant to DNase, pancreatic RNase, and T1 RNase. Evidence was presented by Spitler that heating of the dialyzate produced variable effects on function and treatment with Pronase abolished the capacity to transfer DTH to humans *in vivo*. Most investigators were also agreed that Sephadex-purified fractions of TF were more potent *in vivo* than the raw dialyzate, and Gottlieb had isolated a peptide inhibitor separable from the peptide–nucleotide complex that contained TF activity on Sephadex G-10 (Gottlieb *et al.,* 1973).

On earlier occasions we suggested that TF in its *in vivo* and *in vitro* behavior appeared to function as a de-repressor of lymphocytes (Lawrence 1969a,b). Although little has occurred in the interim either to strengthen or to weaken this interpretation, it remains more descriptive than revealing of the structure and function of TF.

Additionally we suggested that if the active moiety in the raw dialyzate TF_D turned out to be a polynucleotide, it shared in common properties of double-stranded RNA species, namely resistance to pancreatic RNase digestion and inactivation by heating to 56°C or 100°C for 0.5 hour and rapid cooling (Lawrence and Zweiman, 1968; Lawrence 1969a,b). This latter possibility may turn out to be correct in view of Rosenfeld and Dressler's (1974) recent finding that guinea pig TF_D resists digestion by pancreatic RNase but is inactivated by RNase III, heating to $>90°C$, and UV light—evidence for a double-stranded RNA moiety. Nevertheless, despite the attractiveness of a nucleotide as the active moiety of TF_D, most are agreed that it would be premature to abandon the peptides and other molecules with potential biological activity that are present in the raw dialyzate.

Thus the detailed biochemical and biophysical analysis of TF as a molecular species has just about begun and has underscored the pitfalls of ascribing all the biological activities induced by administration of raw dialyzates containing transfer factor to TF itself. This is a sensible precaution which our earlier studies had stressed when the term "transfer factor" was coined as a convenient, descriptive, shorthand expression that allowed for more than one factor to be present and contribute to the biological activities detected (Lawrence, 1960b).

It is also possible that TF itself may be comprised of a family of molecules. For example, if TF should turn out to be related to cellular immunity in a manner akin to which Ig is related to humoral immunity, then the additional possibility of subclasses of TF may exist and each subclass may be possessed of a pattern of distinctive specificities.

There are many more questions that remain to be clarified than there are answers available, and this narrative has been as much an attempt to highlight such questions as it is an assessment of the facts that are known about TF. It is apparent that much remains to be done before the final answers on TF are known. Nevertheless, the problem is a soluble one: the reagents and the techniques have been provided, and the necessary interest in this small molecule has been generated. Moreover, with the advent of new *in vitro* assay systems and new experimental animal models, the detours and roadblocks are cleared and progress toward the ultimate denouement cannot help but continue to accelerate at an exponential rate.

XII. TF AND IMMUNOLOGICAL HOMEOSTASIS

Although much of the discussion has been devoted to the effects of TF from an immune donor on a nonimmune recipient, it is worth emphasizing that the functions of TF revealed in such recipients are operative in all normal donors. It is the donor's own TF that contributes to his well being, and becomes operative following recognition of foreign antigenic mosaics. It is his own TF acquired by educated lymphocytes that initiates rejection of neoplastic cells or organ transplants and restrains the progress of infections with intracellular parasites. It is thus likely that in addition to the repertory of TF specificities that have been uncovered to date, there exist myriads of other specificities to infective agents known and unknown (e.g., assorted virions, Au-antigen, mycoplasma). Additionally it is possible as suggested earlier (Lawrence, 1970a) that upon exposure to mutant neoplastic cells from birth onward, normal individuals via immune surveillance may possess TF's to a variety of tumor antigens previously encountered. There is some recent evidence for this latter possibility in the finding of tumor-specific TF's for melanoma and for sarcoma in family contacts of the respective tumor patient (Levin et al., 1972; Spitler et al., 1973a,b; LoBuglio et al., 1973).

It would also appear that the common targets of TF that unify its diverse functions are foreign histocompatibility antigens. We have discussed elsewhere the fallacy of concluding that foreign histocompatibility antigens arise only in individuals other than the host (Lawrence, 1970a). In the self + X hypothesis we had suggested earlier that prolonged amicable intracellular residence of microbes and virions could produce subtle alterations in self-antigens on host cell surfaces resulting in the raising of a TF vs the self + X complex (Lawrence 1959c, 1960b). In this view, all responses of DTH and CMI were virtually identified as allograft responses and the consequences of prolonged intracellular microbial and viral parasitism was seen as an invitation to autoimmunity (Lawrence, 1974).

The reality of the type of self + X alterations that were postulated has been proved subsequently with the discovery of new

T-antigens and new membrane antigens in cells infected with either oncogenic or nononcogenic viruses and their demonstrable allograft function. It is further suggested by the spate of autoantibodies detected in patients with lepromatous leprosy in consequence of prolonged microbial parasitism of host cells (Lawrence, 1967, 1973). The self + X concept is diagrammatically oversimplified in Figs. 14 and 15, where the case for a preferential intracellular bacterium is given as an example. The principle proposed extends to all intracellular parasites (virions, fungi) and agents that result in alteration of the antigenic determinants on host cell surfaces. This proposal was further substantiated by dem-

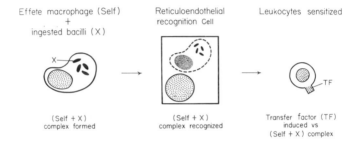

Effete macrophage (Self)
+
ingested bacilli (X)

Reticuloendothelial
recognition Cell

Leukocytes sensitized

(Self + X)
complex formed

(Self + X)
complex recognized

Transfer factor (TF)
induced vs
(Self + X) complex

FIG. 14. Induction of delayed-type hypersensitivity: a consequence of perpetual autophagocytosis, self + X recognition, and the generation of transfer factor by informed lmphocytes. From Lawrence (1959c).

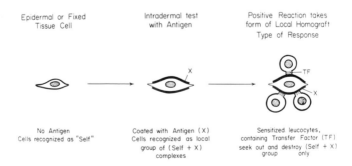

Epidermal or Fixed
Tissue Cell

Intradermal test
with Antigen

Positive Reaction takes
form of Local Homograft
Type of Response

No Antigen
Cells recognized as "Self"

Coated with Antigen (X)
Cells recognized as local
group of (Self + X)
complexes

Sensitized leucocytes,
containing Transfer Factor (TF)
seek out and destroy (Self + X)
group   only

FIG. 15. Manifestation of delayed-type hypersensitivity: immune surveillance of infectious self + X mosaics can inadvertently lead to autoimmunity. From Lawrence (1959c).

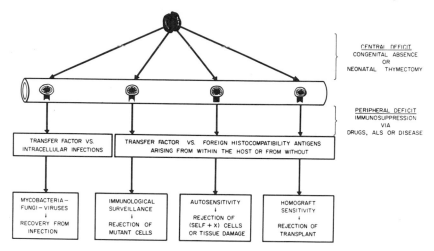

FIG. 16. Predilection and specificity of transfer factor for foreign histocompatibility mosaics arising from within and without the host. ALS, antilymphocyte serum. From Lawrence (1970a). Reprinted by permission from the New England Journal of Medicine **283**, 41 (1970).

onstration of the acquisition of foreign histocompatibility antigens that arise within the tumor-bearing host as neoantigens consequent to embryonal dedifferentiation or of oncogenic origin. We have also noted above the detection of tumor-specific TF's in family contacts of such patients as well.

Finally in this view it was anticipated that TF would converge on host cells in which microbes and virions take refuge, becoming coated with bits and pieces of HLA antigens or becoming incorporated into the host's genome in order to refrain from calling immunological attention to themselves (Lawrence, 1974). The scope and significance of such relationships is diagrammatically oversimplified in Fig. 16.

XIII. CONCLUSIONS

We have traced the history of TF from idea to concept to extensive factual documentation of the broad *in vivo* and *in vitro* functions of this product of immunocompetent cells. Thus TF has emerged as soluble cellular immunity, a moiety that converts the recipient and his circulating lymphocytes to an antigen-responsive state. After *in vitro* exposure to the corresponding antigen, such lymphocytes then undergo transformation and clonal proliferation as well as production of mediators of CMI, such as MIF, lymphotoxin, and interferon. The *in vivo* effects include cutaneous DTH, allograft and tumor rejection, and eradication of infectious agents (mycobacteria, fungi, viruses). The host's failure to make TF can result merely in cutaneous energy, or can ultimately lead to all of the grave consequences of cellular immunodeficiency.

In its recent development, TF is recognized as one of the most potent immunological reagents currently available for the initiation, restoration, or augmentation of cellular immunity. This small molecule(s) has moved into the privileged position of converging on the analysis and potential resolution of those aberrant *in vivo* realities to which we give a name and call disease. And suddenly a study that began as a basic investigation into the mechanisms of DTH and CMI may provide a critical key to understanding and effectively dealing with a broader range of problems that encompass allograft and tumor immunity; immunological surveillance of mutant neoplastic cells; autoimmunity; and adaptive host responses that ensure survival from the incessant incursions of microbial inhabitants of our internal and external milieu.

Two decades after its discovery, studies on this material are increasing at an exponential rate. Transfer factor has survived early adversities by virtue of careful documentation and modest claims for the scope and significance of the activities described. The problem has been served best by restraint and a reluctance to squeeze interpretation of the available facts into preconceived notions, current dogma, or fashionable trends.

For my own view, TF is trying to provide us with the key to a new general biological function of cells, which we happen to detect with immunological end-points, that we are still not yet fully prepared to understand. The next phase of its development gives promise of opening more new vistas and providing additional insights even more challenging than those catalogued here. The work has really only just begun, and this Harvey Lecture is an introduction to the scope and fascination of the problem.

Thus the field of DTH and CMI has evolved a long distance from its preoccupation with the contemplation of an indolent red spot in the skin. Happily, the outcome of investigative efforts on TF that once seemed so esoteric and obscure has assumed critical practical importance to patients brought low by disease as well as to immunological theory. Needless to say, not even those of us most deeply committed to the pursuit of this idea could have predicted such a felicitous outcome, and we owe much to those who preceded us along this path.

ACKNOWLEDGMENTS

It is always a privilege and a happy accident to come upon a new scientific finding. Much of the personal enjoyment that stems from the pursuit of this problem has arisen from the many fine associations with my teachers, colleagues, and students. I wish particularly to acknowledge a vast and continuing debt to my teachers: Tillett, Pappenheimer, MacLeod, and Medawar.

The individual contributions of former Fellows is acknowledged in their senior authorship of most of our collaborative efforts, and it gives particular pleasure to express my appreciation to each of them here also: Drs. S. Al-Askari, M. S. Ascher, J. R. David, D. C. Dumonde, R. S. Holzman, A. S. Lebowitz, P. Livingston, F. T. Rapaport, J. P. Revillard, W. Schneider, L. E. Spitler, F. T. Valentine, and B. Zweiman.

The sustained support of New York University and its Department of Medicine is gratefully acknowledged, as is the generous research and Training Grant support of the National Institute of Allergy and Infectious Diseases of the USPHS (AI-01254-16; AI-00005-15) and the Streptococcal and Staphylococcal Commission of the Armed Forces Epidemiological Board.

REFERENCES

Adler, W. H., Takiguchi, T., Marsh, B., and Smith, R. T. (1970). *J. Exp. Med.* **131**, 1049.

Al-Askari, S., and Lawrence, H. S. (1972). *Cell. Immunol.* **5**, 402.

Al-Askari, S., and Lawrence, H. S. (1969). *Transplant. Proc.* **1**, 400.

Al-Askari, S., and Lawrence, H. S. (1973). *Cell. Immunol.* **6**, 292.

Al-Askari, S., David, J. R., Lawrence, H. S., and Thomas, L. (1965a). *Nature (London)* **205**, 916.

Al-Askari, S., David, J. R., Lawrence, H. S., and Thomas, L. (1965b). *Nat. Acad. Sci., Nat. Res. Council. Publ.* **1229**, 17.

Ammann, A. J., Wara, D., and Salmon, S. (1974). *Cell. Immunol.* **12**, 94.

Arala-Chaves, M. P., Lebacq, E. G., and Heremans, J. F. (1967). *Int. Arch. Allergy Appl. Immunol.* **31**, 353.

Arala-Chaves, M. P., Proenca, R., and De Sousa, M. (1974a). *Cell. Immunol.* **10**, 371.

Arala-Chaves, M. P., Ramos, M. T. F., Rosado, R., and Branco, P. (1974b). *Int. Arch. Allergy Appl. Immunol.* **46**, 612.

Ascher, M. S., Schneider, W. J., Valentine, F. T., and Lawrence, H. S. (1973). *Fed. Proc., Fed. Amer. Soc. Exp. Biol.* **32**, 955.

Ascher, M. S., Schneider, W. J., Valentine, F. T., and Lawrence, H. S. (1974). *Proc. Nat. Acad. Sci. U.S.* **71,** 1178.

Ballow, M., Dupont, B., and Good, R. A. (1973). *J. Pediat.* **83,** 772.

Baram, P., and Condoulis, W. V. (1973). *Fed. Proc., Fed. Amer. Soc. Exp. Biol.* **32,** 955.

Baram, P., and Mosko, M. M. (1962). *J. Allergy* **33,** 498.

Baram, P., and Mosko, M. M. (1965). *Immunology* **8,** 461.

Baram, P., Yuan, L., and Mosko, M. M. (1966). *J. Immunol.* **97,** 407.

Bläker, F., Grob, P. J., Hellwege, H. H., and Schultz, K. H. (1973). *Deut. Med. Wochenschr.* **98,** 415.

Bloom, B. R. (1971). *Advan. Immunol.* **13,** 101.

Bloom, B. R. (1973). Editorial: Does Transfer Factor Act Specifically or as an Immunologic Adjuvant? *N. Engl. J. Med.* **288,** 908.

Bloom, B. R., and Bennett, B. (1966). *Science* **153,** 80.

Bloom, B. R., and Bennett, B. (1968). *Fed. Proc., Fed Amer. Soc. Exp. Biol.* **27,** 13.

Bloom, B. R., and Chase, M. W. (1967). *Progr. Allergy* **10,** 151.

Bloom, B. R., and Glade, P. R., Eds. (1971). *"In Vitro* Methods of Cell-Mediated Immunity." Academic Press, New York.

Bloom, B. R., Bennett, B., Oettgen, H. F., McClean, E. P., and Old, L. J. (1969). *Proc. Nat. Acad. Sci. U.S.* **64,** 1176.

Brandes, L., Galton, D. A. G., and Wiltshaw, E. (1971). *Lancet* **2,** 293.

Brandriss, M. W. (1968). *J. Clin. Invest.* **47,** 2152.

Brown, R. E., and Katz, M. (1967). *J. Pediat.* **70,** 126.

Burger, D. R., Vetto, R. M., and Malley, A. (1972). *Science* **175,** 1473.

Bullock, W. E., Fields, J. P., and Brandriss, M. W. (1972). *New Engl. J. Med.* **287,** 1053.

Chase, M. W. (1945). *Proc. Soc. Exp. Biol. Med.* **59,** 134.

Chase, M. W. (1953). *In* "The Nature and Significance of the Antibody Response" (A. M. Pappenheimer, Jr., ed.), p. 156. Columbia Univ. Press, New York.

Chase, M. W. (1954). *Int. Arch. Allergy Appl. Immunol.* **5,** 163.

Chase, M. W. (1959). *In* "Cellular and Humoral Aspects of the Hypersensitive States" (H. S. Lawrence, ed.), p. 251. Harper (Hoeber), New York.

Chase, M. W. (1965a). *In* "Bacterial and Mycotic Infections of Man" (R. J. Dubos and J. G. Hirsch, eds.), 4th ed., p. 238. Lippincott, Philadelphia, Pennsylvania.

Chase, M. W. (1965b). *Med. Clin. N. Amer.* **49,** 1613.

Chase, M. W. (1966). *Cancer Res.* **26,** 1097.

Chase, M. W. (1967). *Harvey Lect.* **61,** 169.

David, J. R. (1966). *Proc. Nat. Acad. Sci. U.S.* **56,** 72.

David, J. R. (1967). *In* "Immunopathology" (P. A. Miescher and P. Grabar, eds.), p. 253. Grune & Stratton, New York.

David, J. R. (1968). *Fed. Proc., Fed. Amer. Soc. Exp. Biol.* **27,** 6.

David, J. R., and David R. A. (1972). *Progr. Allergy* **16,** 300.

David, J. R., and Paterson, P. Y. (1965). *J. Exp. Med.* **122,** 1161.

David, J. R., Al-Askari, S., Lawrence, H. S., and Thomas, L. (1964a). *J. Immunol.* **93,** 264.

David, J. R., Lawrence, H. S., and Thomas, L. (1964b). *J. Immunol.* **93,** 274.

David, J. R., Lawrence, H. S., and Thomas, L. (1964c). *J. Immunol.* **93,** 279.

David, J. R., Lawrence, H. S., and Thomas, L. (1964d). *J. Exp. Med.* **120,** 1189.

Denman, A. M. (1974). *In* "Infectious Agents in Rheumatic Diseases" (D. C. Dumonde, ed.). Blackwell, Oxford, in press.

Drew, W. L., Blume, M. R., Miner, R. Silverberg, I., and Rosenbaum, E. H. (1973). *Ann. Int. Med.* **79,** 747.

Dumonde, D. C., Wolstencroft, R. A., Panayi, G. S., Matthew, M. Morlew, J., and Howson, W. T. (1969). *Nature, (London)* **224,** 38.

Dupont, B., Ballow, M., Hansen, J. A., Quick, C., Yunis, E. J., and Good, R. A. (1974). *Proc. Nat. Acad. Sci. U.S.* **71,** 867.

Editorial (1967). Transfer factor and Hodgkin's disease. *N. Engl. J. Med.* **277,** 158.

Editorial (1968). Transfer factor and leprosy. *N. Engl. J. Med.* **287,** 1092.

Editorial (1973). Transfer factor. *Lancet* **2,** 79.

Editorial (1974). Transfer factor. *Brit. Med. J.* **II,** 397.

Fazio, M., and Calciati, A. (1962). *Panminerva Med.* **4,** 164.

Fireman, P., Boesman, M., Haddad, Z. H., and Gitlin, D. (1967). *Science* **155,** 337.

Fireman, P., Boesman, M., Haddad, Z. H., and Gitlin, D. (1968). *Fed. Proc., Fed. Amer. Soc. Exp. Biol.* **27,** 29.

Froland, S. S., Natvig, J. B., Hoyeraal, H. M., and Kass, E. (1974). *Scand. J. Immunol.* **3,** 223.

Fudenberg, H. H., Levin, A. S., Spitler, L. E., Wybran, J., and Byers, V. (1974). *Hosp. Pract.* **9,** 95.

Gallin, J. I., and Kirkpatrick, C. H. (1974). *Proc. Nat. Acad. Sci. U.S.* **71,** 498.

Gelfand, E. W., Baumal, R., Huber, J., Crookston, M. C., and Shumak, K. H. (1973). *N. Engl. J. Med.* **289,** 1385.

George, M., and Vaughan, J. H. (1962). *Proc. Soc. Exp. Biol. Med.* **111,** 514.

Goldenberg, G., and Brandes, L. (1972). *Clin. Res.* **20,** 947.

Good, R. A. (1972). Editorial, Transfer Factor, *Cell. Immunol.* **3,** i.

Good, R. A., Varco, R. L., Aust. J. B., and Zak, S. J. (1957). *Ann. N.Y. Acad. Sci.* **64,** 882.

Good, R. A., Kelly, W. D., Rotstein, J., and Varco, R. L. (1962). *Progr. Allergy* **6,** 187.

Gottlieb, A. A., Foster, L. G., Waldman, S. R., and Lopez, M. (1973). *Lancet* **2,** 822.

Granger, G. A., and Kolb, W. P. (1968). *J. Immunol.* **101,** 11.

Graybill, J. R., Silva, J., Alford, R. H., and Thor, D. E. (1973). *Cell. Immunol.* **8,** 120.

Graybill, J. R., Silva, J., Fraser, D. W., Lordon, R., and Rogers, E. (1974). *Amer. Rev. Resp. Dis.* **109,** 4.

Green, J. A., Cooperband, S. R., Rutstein, J. A., and Kibrick, S. (1970). *J. Immunol,* **105,** 48.

Griscelli, C., Revillard, J. P., Beteul, H., Herzog, C., and Touraine, J. L. (1973). *Biomedicine* **18**, 220.

Grob, P. J., Bläker, F., and Schulz, K. H. (1973). *Deut. Med. Wochenschr.* **98**, 446.

Harris, T. N., and Harris, S. (1960). *Ann. N.Y. Acad. Sci.* **87**, 156.

Hathway, W. E., Githens, J. N., Blackburn, W. R., Fulginiti, V., and Kempe, C. H. (1965). *N. Engl. J. Med.* **273**, 953.

Hattler, B. G., Jr., and Amos, D. B. (1965). *J. Nat. Cancer Inst.* **35**, 927.

Hellström, K. E., and Hellström, I. (1970). *Annu. Rev. Microbiol.* **24**, 373.

Hitzig, W. H. (1973). *Blut* **27**, 145.

Hitzig, W. H., Fontanellaz, H. P., Muntener, U., Paul, S., Spitler, L. E., and Fudenberg, H. H. (1972). *Schweiz. Med. Wochenschr.* **102**, 1237.

Holzman, R. S., Lebowitz, A. S., Valentine, F. T., and Lawrence, H. S. (1973a). *Cell. Immunol.* **8**, 249.

Holzman, R. S., Valentine, F. T., and Lawrence H. S. (1973b). *Cell. Immunol.* **8**, 259.

Hornung, M. O., Pradel, P. and Krementz, E. (1973). *Clin. Research,* **32**, 1035.

Jensen, K., Patnode, R. A., Townsley, H. C., and Cummings, M. M. (1962). *Amer. Rev. Resp. Dis.* **85**, 373.

Jersild, C., Platz, P., Thomsen, M., Hansen, G. S., Svejgaard, A., Dupont, B., Fog, T., Ciongoli, A. K., and Grab, P. (1973). *Lancet ii,* 138.

Kahn, A., Hill, J. M., Loeb, E., Mac Lellan, A. and Hill, N. O. (1973). *Amer. J. Dis. Child.* **126**, 797.

Kempe, C. H. (1960). *Pediatrics* **26**, 176.

Kirkpatrick, C. H., and Rifkind, D. (1974). Meeting Report: Workshop on TF. *Cell. Immunol.* **10**, 165.

Kirkpatrick, C. H., Wilson, W. E. C., and Talmadge, D. W. (1964). *J. Exp. Med.* **119**, 727.

Kirkpatrick, C. H., Chandler, J. W., and Schimke, R. N. (1970). *Clin. Exp. Immunol.* **6**, 375.

Kirkpatrick, C. H., Rich, R. R., and Bennett, J. E. (1971). *Ann. Int. Med.* **74**, 955.

Kirkpatrick, C. H., Rich, R. R., and Smith, T. K. (1972). *J. Clin. Invest.* **51**, 2948.

Klein, E. (1968). *N.Y. State J. Med.* **68**, 900.

Landsteiner, K., and Chase, M. W. (1942). *Proc. Soc. Exp. Biol. Med.* **49**, 688.

Lawlor, G. J., Ammann, A. J., Wright, W. C., La Franchi, S. F., Bilstrom, D., and Stiehm, E. R. (1973). *Clin. Res.* **21**, 206.

Lawrence, H. S. (1949). *Proc. Soc. Exp. Biol. Med.* **71**, 516.

Lawrence, H. S. (1952). *J. Immunol.* **68**, 159.

Lawrence, H. S. (1954a). *In* "Streptococcal Infections" (M. McCarty, ed.), p. 143. Columbia Univ. Press, New York.

Lawrence, H. S. (1954b). *J. Clin. Invest.* **33**, 951.

Lawrence, H. S. (1955). *J. Clin. Invest.* **34**, 219.

Lawrence, H. S. (1956). *Amer. J. Med.* **20**, 428.

Lawrence, H. S. (1957). *Ann. N.Y. Acad. Sci* **64**, 826.

Lawrence, H. S. (1959a). *In* "Cellular and Humoral Aspects of the Hypersensitive States" (H. S. Lawrence, ed.), p. 279. Harper (Hoeber), New York.

Lawrence, H. S. (1956b). *In* "Mechanisms of Hypersensitivity" (J. H. Shaffer, G. A. LoGrippo, and M. W. Chase, eds.), p. 453. Little, Brown, Boston, Massachusetts.

Lawrence, H. S. (1959c). *Physiol. Rev.* **39**, 811.

Lawrence, H. S. (1960a). *Annu. Rev. Med.* **11**, 207.

Lawrence, H. S. (1960b). *Cell. Aspects Immunity Ciba Found. Symp. 1959*, p. 243.

Lawrence, H. S. (1963). *In* "Cell-Bound Antibodies" (B. Amos and H. Koprowski, eds.), p. 3. Wistar Inst. Press, Phildephia, Pennsylvania.

Lawrence, H. S. (1965a). *Ann. Int. Med.* **62**, 166.

Lawrence, H. S. (1965b). *Ann. N.Y. Acad. Sci.* **124**, 56.

Lawrence, H. S. (1965c). *Nat. Acad. Sci. Nat. Res. Council Publ.* **1229**, 141.

Lawrence, H. S. (1967). *In* "Cross-Reacting Antigens and Neoantigens" (J. J. Trenton, ed), p. 70. Williams & Wilkins, Baltimore, Maryland.

Lawrence, H. S. (1968a). *In* "Human Transplantation" (F. T. Rapaport and J. Dausset, eds.), p. 11. Grune & Stratton, New York.

Lawrence, H. S. (1968b). Introductory Remarks, Intersociety Symposium on "In Vitro Correlates of Delayed Hypersensitivity," *Fed. Proc., Fed. Amer. Soc. Exp. Biol.* **27**, 3.

Lawrence, H. S. (1969a). *Advan. Immunol.* **11**, 195.

Lawrence, H. S. (1969b). *In* "Mediators of Cellular Immunity" (H. S. Lawrence and M. Landy, eds.), p. 143. Academic Press, New York.

Lawrence, H. S. (1969c). *Hosp. Pract.* **4**, 40.

Lawrence, H. S. (1969d). *Transplant Proc.* **1**, 645.

Lawrence, H. S. (1970a). *N. Engl. J. Med.* **283**, 411.

Lawrence, H. S. (1970b). Editorial, Cellular Immunology, *Cell. Immunol.* **1**, 1.

Lawrence, H. S. (1970c). *In* "Proceedings of the Fifth Leukocyte Culture Conference (J. E. Harris, ed.), p. 551. Academic Press, New York.

Lawrence, H. S. (1970d). *In* "Immunological Surveillance" (R. T. Smith and M. Landy, eds.), p. 500. Academic Press, New York.

Lawrence, H. S. (1971). In "*In Vitro* Methods of Cell-Mediated Immunity" (B. R. Bloom and P. R. Glade, eds.), p. 95. Academic Press, New York.

Lawrence, H. S. (1972a). *In* "Immunological Intervention" (J. Uhr and M. Landy, eds.), p. 20. Academic Press, New York.

Lawrence, H. S. (1972b). Editorial: Immunotherapy with Transfer Factor. *N. Engl. J. Med.* **287**, 1092.

Lawrence, H. S. (1972c). *In* "Clinical Immunobiology" (F. H. Bach and R. A. Good, eds.), Vol. I, p. 48. Academic Press, New York.

Lawrence, H. S. (1973). *Transplant. Proc.* **5**, 49.

Lawrence, H. S. (1974). *In* "Clinical Immunobiology" (F. H. Bach and R. A. Good, eds.), Vol. II, p. 115. Academic Press, New York.

Lawrence, H. S., and Al-Askari, S. (1971). *In* "In Vitro Methods of Cell-Mediated Immunity" (B. R. Bloom and P. Glade, eds.), p. 531. Academic Press, New York.

Lawrence, H. S., and Fishman, M. (1971). In "Progress in Immunology" (B. Amos, ed.), p. 1395. Academic Press, New York.

Lawrence, H. S., and Landy, M., eds. (1969). "Mediators of Cellular Immunity." Academic Press, New York.

Lawrence, H. S., and Pappenheimer, A. M., Jr. (1956). J. Exp. Med. 104, 321.

Lawrence, H. S., and Pappenheimer, A. M., Jr. (1957). J. Clin. Invest. 36, 908.

Lawrence, H. S., and Valentine, F. T. (1970a). Ann. N.Y. Acad. Sci. 169, 269.

Lawrence, H. S., and Valentine, F. T. (1970b). Amer. J. Pathol. 60, 437.

Lawrence, H. S., and Zweiman, B. (1968). Trans. Ass. Amer. Physicians 81, 240.

Lawrence, H. S., Rapaport, F. T., Converse, J. M., and Tillett, W. S. (1960). J. Clin. Invest. 39, 185.

Lawrence, H. S., Rapaport, F. T., Converse, J. M., and Tillett, W. S. (1962). Ciba Found. Symp. Transplantation 1961, p. 271.

Lawrence, H. S., Al-Askari, S., David, J., Franklin, E. C., and Zweiman, B. (1963). Trans. Ass. Amer. Physicians 76, 84.

Lebowitz, A., and Lawrence, H. S. (1969a). Fed. Proc., Fed. Amer. Soc. Exp. Biol. 28, 630.

Lebowitz, A., and Lawrence, H. S. (1969b). In "Mediators of Cellular Immunity" (H. S. Lawrence and M. Landy, eds.), p. 354. Academic Press, New York.

Lebowitz, A., and Lawrence, H. S. (1971). In "In Vitro Methods of Cell-Mediated Immunity" (B. R. Bloom and P. R. Glade, eds.), p. 375, Academic Press, New York.

Levin, A. S., Spitler, L. E., Stites, D. P., and Fudenberg, H. H. (1970). Proc. Nat. Acad. Sci. U.S. 67, 821.

Levin, A. S., Spitler, L. E., Wybran, J., Fudenberg, H. H., Hellström, I., and Hellström, K. E. (1972). Clin. Res. 20, 568.

Levin, A. S., Spitler, L. E., and Fudenberg, H. H. (1973). Annu. Rev. Med. 24, 175.

Liburd, E. M., Pabst, H. F., and Armstrong, W. D. (1972). Cell. Immunol. 5, 487.

LoBuglio, A. F., Neidhart, J. A., Wilberg, R. W., Metz, E. N., and Balcerzak, S. P. (1973). Cell. Immunol. 7, 159.

Mackaness, G. N., and Blanden, R. V. (1967). Progr. Allergy 11, 89.

Maddison, S. E., Hicklin, M. D., Conway, B. P., and Kagan, I. G. (1972). Science 178, 757.

Maini, R. N., Bryceson, A. D. M., Wolstencroft, R. A., and Dumonde, D. C. (1969). Nature (London) 224, 43.

Marshall, W. H., Valentine, F. T., and Lawrence, H. S. (1968a). Clin. Res. 16, 322.

Marshall, W. H., Valentine, F. T., and Lawrence, H. S. (1968b). In "Leucocyte Culture Conference" (W. O. Rieke, ed.), p. 475. Appleton, New York.

Marshall, W. H., Valentine, F. T., and Lawrence, H. S. (1969). J. Exp. Med. 130, 227.

Maurer, P. H. (1961). J. Exp. Med. 113, 1029.

Mogerman, S. N., Levin, A. S., Spitler, L. E., Stites, D. P., Fudenberg, H. H., and Shinefield, H. R. (1973). Clin. Res. 21, 310.

Mohr, J. A., Killebrew, L., Muchmore, H. G., Felton, F. G., and Rhoades, E. R. (1969). J. Amer. Med. Ass. 207, 517.

Montgomery, J. R., South, M. A., Wilson, R., Richie, E., Heim, L. R., Criswell, S., and Trentin, J. J. (1973). *Clin. Res.* 21, 118.

Morse, P. A., Deraps, G. D., Smith, G. V., Raju, S., and Hardy, J. D. (1973). *Clin. Res.* 21, 71.

Moulias, R., Goust, J. M., Reinert, P., Fournel, J. J., Deville-Chabrolle, A., Duong, N., Muller-Berat, C. N., and Berthaux, P. (1973). *Nouv. Presse Med.* 2, 1341.

Muftuoglu, A. U., and Balkuv, S. (1967). *N. Engl. J. Med.* 277, 126.

Muftuoglu, A. U., and Yalcin, B. (1973). *Z. Immunitaetsforsch. Allerg. Klin. Immunol.* 145, 413.

Neidhart, J. A., Schwartz, R. S., Hurtubise, P. E., Murphy, S. G., Metz, E. N., Balcerzak, S. P., and LoBuglio, A. F. (1973). *Cell. Immunol.* 9, 319.

O'Connell, C. J., Karzon, D. T., Barron, A. L., Plaut, M. E., and Ali, V. M. (1964). *Ann. Int. Med.* 60, 282.

Oettgen, H. F., Old, L. J., Farrow, J. H., Valentine, F. T., Lawrence, H. S., and Thomas, L. (1971). *J. Clin. Invest.* 50, 71a.

Oettgen, H. F., Old, L. J., Farrow, J. H., Valentine, F. T., Lawrence, H. S., and Thomas, L. (1974). *Proc. Nat. Acad. Sci. U.S.* 71, in press.

Oliveira-Lima, O. (1958). *Amer. Rev. Tuberc.* 78, 346.

Pabst, H. F., and Swanson, R. (1972). *Brit. Med. J.* 2, 442.

Palmer, D. W., and Smith, R. T. (1974). *Cell. Immunol.* 13, 196.

Pappenheimer, A. M., Jr. (1956). *Harvey Lect.* 52, 100.

Pappenheimer, A. M., Jr., and Lawrence, H. S. (1948a). *Amer. J. Hyg.* 47, 233.

Pappenheimer, A. M., Jr., and Lawrence, H. S. (1948b). *Amer. J. Hyg.* 47, 241.

Paque, R. E., Dray, S., Kniskern, P. and Baram, P. (1973). *Cell. Immunol.* 6, 368.

Polmar, S. H. (1973). Editorial, Transfer Factor Therapy of Immunodeficiencies. *N. Eng. J. Med.* 289, 1420.

Rapaport, F. T., Lawrence, H. S., Millar, J. W., Pappagianis, D., and Smith, C. E. (1960a). *J. Immunol.* 84, 358.

Rapaport, F. T., Lawrence, H. S., Millar, J. W., Pappagianis, D., and Smith, C. E. (1960b). *J. Immunol.* 84, 368.

Rapaport, F. T., Dausset, J., Converse, J. M., and Lawrence, H. S. (1965a). *Transplantation* 3, 490.

Rapaport, F. T., Dausset, J., Converse, J. M., and Lawrence, H. S. (1965b). *Nat. Acad. Sci. Nat. Res. Council Publ.* 1229, 97.

Reed, S. E., and Zabriskie, J. (1972). *Transplant. Proc.* 4, 247.

Reinert, P., Moulias, R., Goust, J. M., Hors, J., Bussel, A. (1972). *Arch. Fr. Med.* 29, 655.

Rocklin, R. E., Chilgren, R. A., Hong, R., and David, J. R. (1970). *Cell. Immunol.* 1, 290.

Rosenfeld, S., and Dressler, D. (1974). *Proc. Nat. Acad. Sci. U.S.* 71, in press.

Schulkind, M. L., Adler, W. H., Altemeir, W. A., and Ayoub, E. M. (1972). *Cell. Immunol.* 3, 606.

Slavin, R. G., and Garvin, J. E. (1964). *Science* 145, 52.

Soberg, M. (1967). *Acta Med. Scand.* 182, 167.

Solowey, A. C., Rapaport, F. T., and Lawrence, H. S. (1967). *In* "Histocompatibility Testing," p. 75. Karger, Basel.

Spitler, L. E., and Lawrence, H. S. (1969). *J. Immunol.* **103**, 1072.

Spitler, L. E., Levin, A. S., Blois, M. S., Epstein, W., Fudenberg, H. H., Hellström, I., and Hellström, K. E. (1972a). *J. Clin. Invest.* **51**, 92a.

Spitler, L. E., Levin, A. S., Fudenberg, H. H., Pirofsky, B., Hitzig, W., and Feigin, R. (1972b). *Clin. Res.* **20**, 519.

Spitler, L. E., Levin, A. S., Stites, D. P., Fudenberg, H. H., Pirofsky, B., August, C. S., Stiehm, E. R., Hitzig, W. H., and Gatti, R. A. (1972c). *J. Clin. Invest.* **51**, 3216.

Spitler, L. E., Wybran, J., Fudenberg, H. H., Levin, A. S., and Lewis, M. (1973a). *Clin. Res.* **21**, 221.

Spitler, L. E., Levin, A. S., and Fudenberg, H. H. (1973b). *Methods Cancer Res.* **8**, 59.

Spitler, L. E., Levin, A. S., and Fudenberg, H. H. (1974). In "Immunologic Deficiency Diseases in Man" (R. A. Good and D. Bergsma, eds.). Sinauer Press, Stamford, Connecticut, in press.

Thomas, L. (1959). In "Cellular and Humoral Aspects of the Hypersensitive States" (H. S. Lawrence, ed.), p. 529. Harper (Hoeber), New York.

Thor, D. E., and Dray, S. (1968a). *J. Immunol.* **101**, 51.

Thor, D. E., and Dray, S. (1968b). *J. Immunol.* **101**, 469.

Turk, J. L. (1967). In "Frontiers of Biology" (A. Neuberger and E. L. Tatum, eds.) Vol. 4, p. 65. Wiley, New York.

Urbach, F., Sones, M., and Israel, W. L. (1952). *N. Engl. J. Med.* **247**, 794.

Utermohlen, V., and Zabriskie, J. (1973). *J. Exp. Med.* **138**, 159.

Valentine, F. T. (1971a). In "In Vitro Correlates of Cell-Mediated Immunity" (J. P. Revillard, ed.), p. 6. Karger, Basel.

Valentine, F. T. (1971b). In "In Vitro Methods of Cell-Mediated Immunity" (B. R. Bloom and P. R. Glade, eds.), p. 443. Academic Press, New York.

Valentine, F. T. (1972). In "Proceedings of the Sixth Leukocyte Culture Conference." (M. Roy Schwarz, ed.), p. 337. Academic Press, New York.

Valentine, F. T., and Lawrence, H. S. (1968a). *J. Clin. Invest.* **47**, 98a.

Valentine, F. T., and Lawrence, H. S. (1968b). *Fed. Proc., Fed. Amer. Soc. Exp. Biol.* **27**, 265.

Valentine, F. T., and Lawrence, H. S. (1969). *Science* **165**, 1014.

Valentine, F. T., and Lawrence, H. S., (1971). *Advan. Int. Med.* **17**, 51.

Vandvik, B., Froland, S. S., Hoyeraal, H. M., Stien, R., and Degre, M. (1973). *Scand. J. Immunol.* **2**, 367.

Valdimarsson, H., Wood, C. B. S., Hobbs, J. R., and Holt, P. J. L. (1972). *Clin. Exp. Immunol.* **11**, 151.

Valdimarsson, H., Hambleton, G., Henry, K., and McConnell, I. (1974). *Clin. Exp. Immunol.* **16**, 141.

Warwick, W. J., Archer, D. K., and Good, R. A. (1962). *Ann. N.Y. Acad. Sci.* **99**, 620.

Whitcomb, M. E., and Rocklin, R. E. (1973). *Ann. Int. Med.* **79**, 161.

W.H.O. Expert Panel (1974). Immunology of Leprosy. *Bull. W.H.O.*, in press.

Wybran, J., Levin, A. S., Spitler, L. E., and Fudenberg, H. H. (1973). *N. Engl. J. Med.* **288**, 710.

COLLAGEN BIOLOGY: STRUCTURE, DEGRADATION, AND DISEASE*

JEROME GROSS

The Developmental Biology Laboratory, Department of Medicine, Harvard Medical School at the Massachusetts General Hospital, Boston, Massachusetts

I. INTRODUCTION

IT was just 20 years ago that Dr. Paul Klemperer, the distinguished pathologist of Mt. Sinai Hospital in New York, delivered his Harvey Lecture (Klemperer, 1953) on the significance of connective tissue in human disease. Ten years previously Professor Francis O. Schmitt, head of the Department of Biology at MIT, also in a Harvey Lecture (Schmitt, 1945) had described the fresh discoveries made by himself and his colleagues, Hall and Jakus (Schmitt *et al.,* 1942), of the cross striations of collagen fibrils as seen in the electron microscope.† Paul Klemperer had whetted my interest in pathogenetic mechanisms, and Frank Schmitt, who had a considerable influence on my approach to scientific problems, gave me every reason to believe that "until we have progressed sufficiently with the difficult problem of molecular morphology it is unlikely that rapid advance will be made with those problems which involve far higher levels of organization" (Schmitt, 1960).

The concept of "collagen disease," which included rheumatic fever, rheumatoid arthritis, scleroderma, dermatomyositis, periarteritis nodosa, and almost all other obscure chronic debilitating disorders involving inflammatory processes, was originally proposed by Klinge (1933) and subsequently elaborated by Klem-

---

* Lecture delivered April 12, 1973.

† Wolpers (1943) in Germany had independently reported the same observation, and Schmitt's colleague, R. S. Bear (1942, 1944) and again, independently, Kratky and Sekora (1943) in Germany had found the axial period by low-angle X-ray diffraction.

perer *et al.* (1942). The term served a useful purpose in that it stimulated fundamental studies of connective tissue, but its limited usefulness in helping to understand the pathogenesis of these disorders soon became apparent. Klemperer (1961) himself clarified the issue by pointing out that the original definition of "collagen" had been used to encompass all the connective tissue and that he had not meant to imply that this great diversity of disease processes was based on any primary involvement of the protein, collagen. He also clearly recognized that cellular mechanisms were involved, that collagen might be affected as an innocent bystander in the arena of inflammation. At that time the only bona fide disease of collagen recognizable as such was scurvy, since it had been adequately demonstrated that in the absence of ascorbic acid, collagen formation stops, wound healing is inhibited, and tissue breakdown leads, through structural weaknesses, to rapidly increasing disability.

Although the term "collagen disease" fell into well deserved disrepute, this protein is known to be involved in a wide range of common medical problems. The ultimate crippling sequelae of many human ailments, from simple scars to the complex lesions of arteriosclerosis and the well known variety of common and less common fibrotic states, including postsurgical adhesions, cirrhosis of the liver, pulmonary fibrosis, all involve abnormal regulation of collagen metabolism. Intrinsic tissue destruction, from corneal ulceration to tumor invasion, involves the metabolism of this protein. Collagen as a major structural component of the body, provides tensile strength, flexibility, shape and form, and physical, possibly functional barriers between different cell and tissue types. It is also evident that both heritable and acquired birth defects causing skeletal, vascular, and skin deformities also involve aberrations in the biology of this protein. These defects may involve abnormalities in the primary structure of the collagen molecule, its synthesis, its mode of organization into fibrils, the pattern of its distribution in the tissues, its turnover, or the synchronization between the mechanism of biosynthesis and degradation. Since it is clear that such abnormalities on the molecular or tissue level are ascribable to cells, the ultimate purpose of defining in detail these molecular or tissue defects in collagen is to shed light on cellular regulatory mechanisms and to aid in understanding gross morphologic and functional defects.

In the two intervening decades, studies on collagen attracted a small but intensely interested group of investigators, who were intrigued by its unusual structural, chemical, and physical properties and, not the least, by its use as a tool for the study of molecular self-assembly processes. An early and important step toward understanding biological structure was our ability to reconstitute collagen molecules in solution to perfect replicas of the cross-striated native fibrils simply by manipulating salt concentrations, pH, and temperature.

In the last twenty years we have defined the molecule in terms of its primary, secondary, and tertiary structure, its range of variability and structural constraints, its specific modes of aggregation, and its possible role in embryogenesis. We have learned much concerning its biosynthesis and the enzyme systems that subsequently modify the polypeptide chains in order to make them functional, and their involvement in the heritable diseases of connective tissue. We are beginning to understand the enzymatic mechanisms involved in the removal of collagen from the tissue during growth, remodeling, and regeneration.

II. COLLAGEN STRUCTURE

(See Fig. 1 for summary diagram)

My studies on this protein began some 27 years ago in the Biology Department at MIT with the idea that electron microscopy and X-ray diffraction analyses of collagen in the rheumatic nodule would lead to important revelations regarding the pathogenesis of rheumatic fever. It rapidly became clear that, at least with regard to the pathology of human disease, one had to have good ideas—not just powerful techniques. After a frustrating year spent examining what William Astbury called "gubbins" in these bits of diseased tissues, my interest shifted to the mechanism of the reconstitution of striated collagen fibrils from a solution of its molecules and its implications for morphogenesis at the molecular level. By repeating the published experiments of Orekhovich et al. (1948), who extracted connective tissues with

354   JEROME GROSS

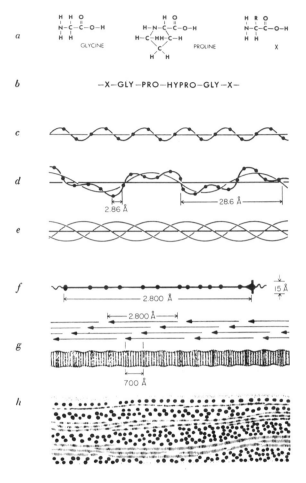

FIG. 1. Hierarchies of collagen structure: The amino acids (*a*) are incorporated in the polypeptide chain (*b*), after which some of the prolines and
lysines are hydroxylated to hydroxyproline and hydroxylysine. Each α chain
(*c*) is coiled in the form of a polyproline type II helix, three of which
(*d, e*) are wrapped around each other to form a superhelical rigid rod, 2800 Å
in length and about 15 Å wide, the tropocollagen molecule (*f*). Note the two
short nonhelical regions, telopeptides, at each end of the molecule. These molecules pack in a "quarter stagger" array polarized in one direction to give rise to
the striated collagen fibrils (*g*), which are found in geometrical patterns, parallel
in tendon, orthogonally arrayed as in plywood in the cornea, and in more
random bundles in mammalian skin. *c–e*, ×9,625,000; *f*, ×181,500; *g*,
×66,000; *h*, ×27,500.

citrate buffers and produced needlelike precipitates (seen in the light microscope) by dialysis against water, we discovered, using the electron microscope, a new highly ordered fibrillar structure with a repeating period of about 2800 Å, which we called "fibrous long spacing" or FLS (Highberger et al., 1951, 1952). We soon discovered that slightly alkaline extracts of connective tissues in cold phosphate buffer contained dissolved collagen and also had a very strong absorption peak at 260 nm, quite characteristic of nucleotides. Dialysis of these extracts against slightly acidified water produced a precipitate of another highly ordered structure, which we called "segment long spacing" (SLS), consisting of crystallites all about 2800 Å in length and of varying width, displaying a highly reproducible asymmetric band pattern from one end to the other (Fig. 2). The addition of adenosine triphosphoric acid to purified collagen in acid solution proved to be a more efficient way to make SLS (Schmitt et al., 1953). We demonstrated the quantitative interconvertibility of the three different forms of collagen structures, one into the other, and concluded that this phenomenon represented a remarkable morphogenetic potential of collagen molecules; from these data we deduced the dimensions of the molecule to be about 3000 Å in length and less than 20 Å wide. We named the particle "tropocollagen" (Gross et al., 1954). Boedtker and Doty (1956) using hydrodynamic methods on solutions of monodispersed purified collagen firmly established the dimensions of the molecule to be 2900×15 Å. We concluded (1) that the molecule was polarized, i.e., had to have an asymmetric primary structure; (2) that SLS represented an alignment of all the molecules in parallel array and in register, that FLS represented an antiparallel array of collagen molecules associated end-to-end to give rise to a fibril with periods representing the length of the individual molecules; and (3) that the native collagen fibrils with axial periods of about 640 Å, or one-quarter the length of the molecule must represent these molecules aligned in parallel order but staggered with respect to each other by one-fourth of their length, i.e. the "quarter stagger hypothesis" (Schmitt et al., 1955; Gross, 1956). This construct was elaborated and important new observations and deductions were added by Hodge and Schmitt (1960), who

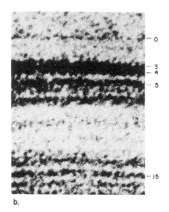

b.

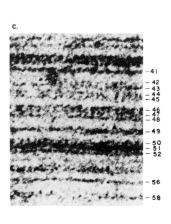

c.

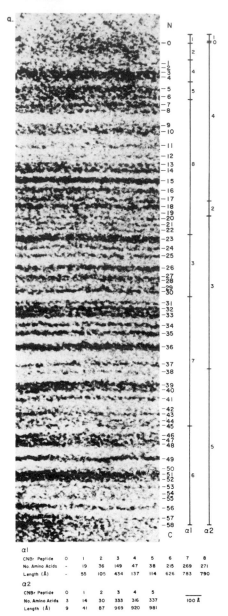

a.

αl

CNBr Peptide	0	1	2	3	4	5	6	7	8
No. Amino Acids	–	19	36	149	47	38	215	269	271
Length (Å)	–	55	105	434	137	114	626	783	790

α2

CNBr Peptide	0	1	2	3	4	5
No. Amino Acids	3	14	30	333	316	337
Length (Å)	9	41	87	969	920	981

100 Å

compared the pattern of quarter-staggered SLS, using "optical synthesis," with the axial band structure of the native fibril. Soon thereafter, Hodge and Petruska (1963) proposed that the quarter-stagger arrangement had to be modified by considering that the molecules interacted with each other in a manner which indicated that the length of the molecule is 4.4 times that of the native axial period (700 Å). In this model there is an overlap region of 0.4 of a period, and in addition there must be a "hole" region between the ends of linearly arranged molecules accounting for 0.6 of a period. Substantiating data came from careful quantitative measurements of the axial structure and also from negative staining and reconstitution experiments. Figure 3 illustrates three reconstituted native-type collagen fibrils, one stained positively with heavy metal stains and revealing the characteristic fine structure within each axial period; the adjacent fibril is negatively stained and shows the alternating light (hole) and dark (overlap) regions within a single period, and the third fibril is stained both positively and negatively. A schematic arrangement of these relationships is shown in Fig. 4, which also includes the location at the edges of the hole region, of certain structural features with known biologic significance. Although nearly all these studies were accomplished within the decade 1950–1960, these various structures and the model of the fibril have gathered increasing attention. The SLS form of collagen has played an important role in the sequencing of the polypeptide chains (see Traub and Piez, 1971, for review), in the location and characterization of the action of animal collagenases (Gross and Nagai, 1965) in-

---

FIG. 2. (a) Electron micrograph of a segment-long-spacing (SLS) crystallite, prepared from native, acid-soluble calf skin collagen, showing the location of 58 characteristic bands. The dark bands (stained) are numbered consecutively from the NH$_2$-terminal (N) to the COOH-terminal (C) end of the band pattern. The schematic diagrams of α1 and α2 chains illustrate the relation of individual peptides (isolated after specific cyanogen bromide cleavage of calf skin collagen) to bands of the segment-long-spacing crystallite. (b) Electron micrograph showing the NH$_2$-terminal end (0) of the band pattern (c) Electron micrograph of the COOH-terminal region of the pattern, showing several bands that are unresolved in (a). The specimens were stained with 0.1% phosphotungstic acid followed by 0.01% uranyl acetate. From Bruns and Gross (1973). ×428,350.

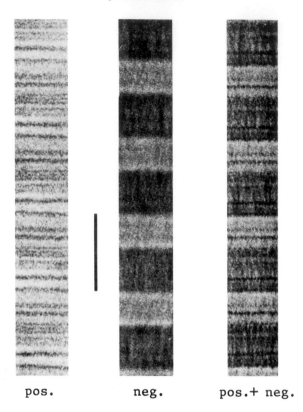

pos.   neg.   pos.+ neg.

FIG. 3. Electron micrographs of native collagen fibrils from chick skin:
Positive stain with uranyl nitrate showing loci of acidic residue concentrations.
Negative stain with neutral phosphotungstic acid, showing overlap region (dark)
and hole region (light). Combination staining, negative and positive. By
courtesy of Dr. R. Bruns.

volved in biological degradation of this protein, and in identifying
and characterizing the newly discovered procollagen (Lenaers *et
al.*, 1971; Stark *et al.*, 1971; Dehm *et al.*, 1972; Goldberg, 1974).

Although the structures produced by nearly all types of collagen
are remarkably similar in terms of position of bands and their
staining intensity, some reproducible differences have been seen
in the SLS (Fig. 5) and the fibrils reconstituted from cartilage
collagen. The reconstituted fibrils display a staggered, steplike

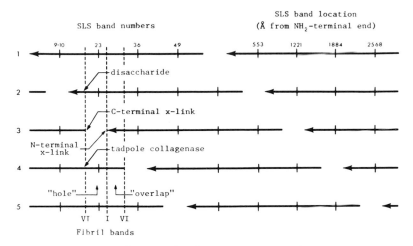

FIG. 4. Diagram of the modified quarter-stagger packing arrangement in a "5 molecule" collagen microfibril. The arrows represent collagen molecules. The SLS band numbers 9–10, 23, 36, and 49 follow the numbering system of Bruns and Gross (1973) and their location on the collagen molecule is shown at the upper right in the diagram. Note that the site where disaccharides are covalently· bound to the α1 chains (SLS band I-4, the interband region following band 4), the site where carboxyl-terminal cross-linking occurs and the site where the collagen molecule is cleaved by tadpole collagenase (SLS band I-41, fibril band V) all occur near the amino-terminal edge of the "hole zone"; and the site of amino-terminal cross-linking occurs near the carboxyl-terminal edge of the "hole zone." From Bruns and Gross (1974).

arrangement of subfibrillar units (Fig. 6), suggesting that the major helix in the molecule with a pitch of about 90 Å may reflect itself onto the next two levels of higher order, those of the microfibril and fibril (Bruns et al., 1973). Closer scrutiny of the quarter-stagger arrangement has led to the concept of a microfibril intermediate consisting of 4 or 5 (probably the latter) collagen molecules arranged in quarter-stagger array within an indefinitely long filament. These filaments when aligned laterally in specific associations with each other give rise to the characteristic fibril band pattern (Smith, 1965, 1968; Veis et al., 1967; Hulmes et al., 1973).

The most common collagen form seen in thin sections is the striated fibril with an axial period of about 640 Å. However,

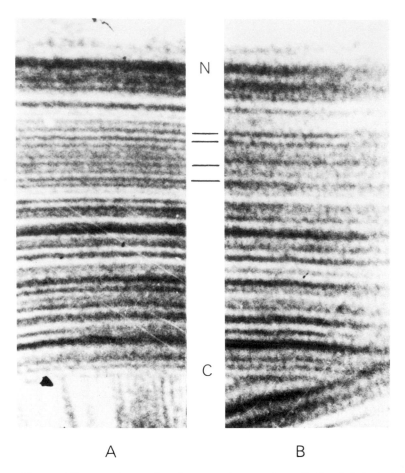

A   B

FIG. 5. Electron micrographs of segment-long-spacings (SLS) of (A) chick xiphoid cartilage collagen, and (B) chick skin collagen. Stained with 12 mM uranyl acetate, pH 3.8. Lines drawn between segments indicate the loci at which clear and reproducible band differences appear. Other differences in staining density elsewhere in the pattern may also be discerned but are not as sharply defined. N is the NH$_2$ terminus of the molecule, and C, the COOH terminus. From Trelstad et al. (1970). ×269,110.

there is a wide range of variability in fibril diameter, from less than 100 Å to two-dimensional sheets and three-dimensional nets of essentially indefinite dimensions. In addition, fibrillar structures

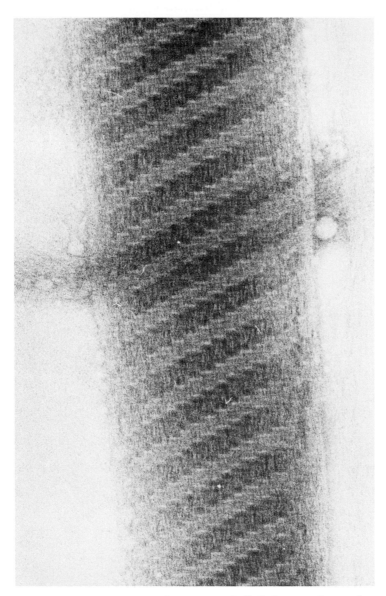

FIG. 6. Electron micrograph of reconstituted fibril from cartilage collagen shows the staggered arrangement of subfibrils regularly displaced by 89 Å from each other giving a stepwise appearance across the fibril. Negative staining. [Similar to micrograph of fibril published by Bruns, Trelstad, and Gross (1973).]

showing no striations in the electron microscope, and some showing unusual periodicities have been described in specialized tissues (reviewed by Banfield *et al.*, 1973). Identification of such fibrils simply on morphologic grounds is difficult and indeterminate and can be established only by isolation and molecular or biochemical definition.

It became clear a number of years ago that we were not going to get very far with structural and biological studies of collagen until we knew more about the amino acid sequence. The functional molecule in the fibril consists of three polypeptide chains, and each chain, except for two small regions at the end is twisted in the form of a polyproline type II helix (Ramachandran and Kartha, 1954, 1956; Rich and Crick, 1955) (Fig. 1). Each of these three helices are wrapped around each other in ropelike fashion to produce a higher order, rigid triple helix [see Gross (1961) for general structural description, and the recent reviews by Traub and Piez (1971) and Gallop *et al.* (1972) for detailed discussion of structural and chemical properties]. Although the helical characteristics of the collagen molecule depend crucially on the presence of glycine residues at every third position and the frequent presence of proline in the second position of the repeating triplets in the polypeptide, there is considerable latitude for variation in both number and position of every other amino acid. The collagens of mammalian skin, bone, and many viscera consist of two distinct gene products. Two of the chains ($\alpha 1$) are identical in composition and sequence, and the third, although equal in molecular weight and helical structure, has a different composition and sequence (more about this later). Characteristically, collagen contains a relatively large amount of the imino acids, proline and hydroxyproline (in variable proportions) and until very recently was thought to be totally deficient in cysteine and tryptophan. These properties are typical of all the known collagens in animals ranging from sponges and coelenterates to man (see review by Gross, 1963b).

Five laboratories, four in this country and one in Germany, have embarked on the arduous process of determining the complete primary structure of this molecule, consisting of about 3000 residues, from several different species. The task is formidable since there are no repeating subunits along the length of these very large polypeptides (ca. 1000 residues per α chain). Therefore the analysis of sequence required a highly reproducible method for dissecting the molecule into smaller manageable pieces. Through the use of cyanogen bromide (CNBr) cleavage of methionyl peptide bonds (E. Gross and Witkop, 1961), the α chains of rat skin were reduced to a smaller number of peptides, eight for α1 and five for α2, all different in size and composition but all reproducible and isolatable in pure form (Bornstein and Piez, 1965; Butler *et al.*, 1967). This has also been accomplished for rat skin, tendon, and bone, calf skin, chick skin and bone, human and guinea pig skin (see Traub and Piez, 1971, for review). By means of a combination of chemical overlapping and electron microscopy (utilizing the SLS band pattern of the renatured collagen fragments (Piez *et al.*, 1968; Rauterberg and Kühn, 1969, 1971; Igarashi *et al.*, 1970) (see Fig. 7) matching them up with the pattern of the intact SLS crystallite) and metabolic experiments using the time sequence of isotope incorporation into newly synthesized α chains (Vuust and Piez, 1970, 1972) by the method first applied by Dintzis (1961) to hemoglobin, it proved possible to decisively order the cyanogen bromide peptides in both chains. Both size and order of arrangement of the CNBr peptides in the α1 type I chain, characteristic of skin and bone, are essentially identical but very different from α2 (Fig. 8).

This has also been accomplished for cartilage collagen, which is a different gene product and has a different amino acid sequence, hence a different set of CNBr peptides (Fig. 8) (Miller and Lunde, 1973; Miller *et al.*, 1973). However, since the SLS band pattern of cartilage collagen is, with the exception of small but definite variations, the same as that for skin and bone (and indeed nearly identical for all the phylogenetically different collagens) and the banding depends on location of charged groups, there must be extensive sequence homology.

These peptides range in residue number from 3 to 337, and therefore they all lie within the present capability for determining amino acid sequence. In the past several years, it has been possible

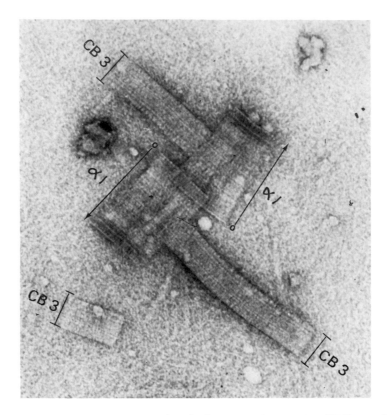

FIG. 7. Electron micrograph of "hybrid" segment-long-spacing (SLS) revealing locus of CNBr peptide α1-CB3: A mixture of denatured α1 chains of chick skin collagen and of isolated purified CNBr peptide α1-CB3 (see Fig. 2) were corenatured by temperature annealing, then precipitated with adenosine triphosphoric acid to form the SLS crystallites. SLS consisting of full length renatured molecules with the fragments formed from CB3 "hybridized" to it at the appropriate locus, thus precisely revealing the position of this peptide fragment along the length of the α chain. Negatively stained. From S. Igarashi, A. H. Kang, and J. Gross, unpublished.

to determine the complete sequence for the α1 chain (although it is a hybrid of bovine and rat skin fragments) (Fig. 9).

The sequence of the 16 residue nonhelical NH_2-terminal peptide and the next 123 residues of the adjacent helical region

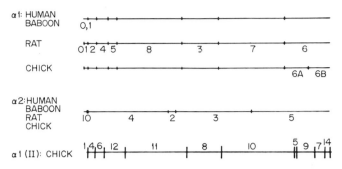

FIG. 8. Linear peptide maps of various types of α chains indicating the known linear order of all the peptides derived by cleavage of methionyl bonds by cyanogen bromide. The short crossbars indicate the positions of methionyl residues and the numbers identify the CNBr peptides. The number order relates to the order in which they elute from the CM cellulose column. Note the nearly perfect homology among the α1(I) chains of divergent species and the differences from α2 and α1(II). From Traub and Piez (1971) and Slavkin (1972).

of the α1 chain of rat skin and tendon collagen (the CNBr peptides α1-CB0, 1, 2, and 4) were described as Kang et al. (1967), Bornstein (1967), Butler (1970), and Butler and Ponds (1971). The large CNBr peptide α1-CB8, from residues 124–402, were sequenced by Balian et al. (1971, 1972) and the remainder of the helical region of the α1 chain including residues 403–1011 from calf skin collagen plus the 25 residues of the newly discovered COOH-terminal "nonhelical" peptide which covers α1-CB3, 7 and 6 from calf skin collagen was reported by Fietzek et al. (1972a,b; 1973), Wendt et al. (1972), and Rauterberg et al. (1972).

This sequence data has settled a number of long standing controversies, provided new insight into the relationship between primary structure and fibrillar structure (Balian et al., 1971, 1972; Fietzek et al., 1972a; Hulmes et al., 1973) and should go a long way to help us understand the regulatory mechanisms for post-translational modifications and degradation. The question of the presence or the absence of repeating subunits along the length of the α chain, or of the presence of non-α peptide bonds has been conclusively settled. There are none of either. It is firmly pGlu-Met-Ser-Tyr-Gly-Tyr-Asp-Glu-Lys-Ser-Ala-Gly-Val-Ser-Val-Pro-

```
   1  Gly-Pro-Met-Gly-Pro-Ser-Gly-Pro-Arg-Gly-Leu-Hyp-Gly-Pro-Hyp-Gly-Ala-Hyp-Gly-Pro-Gln-Gly-Phe-Gln-Gly-Pro-Hyp-
  28  Gly-Glu-Hyp-Gly-Glu-Hyp-Gly-Ala-Ser-Gly-Pro-Met-Gly-Pro-Arg-Gly-Pro-Hyp-Gly-Pro-Hyp-Gly-Lys-Asn-Gly-Asp-Asp-
  55  Gly-Glu-Ala-Gly-Lys-Pro-Gly-Arg-Hyp-Gly-Gln-Arg-Gly-Pro-Hyp-Gly-Pro-Gln-Gly-Ala-Arg-Gly-Leu-Hyp-Gly-Thr-Ala-
  82  Gly-Leu-Hyp-Gly-Met-Hyl-Gly-His-Arg-Gly-Phe-Ser-Gly-Leu-Asp-Gly-Ala-Lys-Gly-Asn-Thr-Gly-Pro-Ala-Gly-Pro-Lys-
 109  Gly-Glu-Hyp-Gly-Ser-Hyp-Gly-Glx-Asx-Gly-Ala-Hyp-Gly-Gln-Met-Gly-Pro-Arg-Gly-Leu-Hyp-Gly-Glu-Arg-Gly-Arg-Hyp-
 136  Gly-Pro-Hyp-Gly-Ser-Ala-Gly-Ala-Arg-Gly-Asp-Asp-Gly-Ala-Val-Gly-Ala-Ala-Gly-Pro-Hyp-Gly-Pro-Thr-Gly-Pro-Thr-
 163  Gly-Pro-Hyp-Gly-Phe-Hyp-Gly-Ala-Ala-Gly-Ala-Lys-Gly-Glu-Ala-Gly-Pro-Gln-Gly-Ala-Arg-Gly-Ser-Glu-Gly-Pro-Gln-
 190  Gly-Val-Arg-Gly-Glu-Hyp-Gly-Pro-Hyp-Gly-Pro-Ala-Gly-Ala-Ala-Gly-Pro-Ala-Gly-Asn-Hyp-Gly-Ala-Asp-Gly-Gln-Hyp-
 217  Gly-Ala-Lys-Gly-Ala-Asn-Gly-Ala-Hyp-Gly-Ile-Ala-Gly-Ala-Hyp-Gly-Phe-Hyp-Gly-Ala-Ala-Gly-Pro-Ser-Gly-Pro-Gln-
 244  Gly-Pro-Ser-Gly-Ala-Hyp-Gly-Pro-Lys-Gly-Asn-Ser-Gly-Glu-Hyp-Gly-Ala-Hyp-Gly-Asn-Lys-Gly-Asp-Thr-Gly-Ala-Lys-
 271  Gly-Glu-Hyp-Gly-Pro-Ala-Gly-Val-Gln-Gly-Pro-Hyp-Gly-Pro-Ala-Gly-Glu-Glu-Gly-Lys-Arg-Gly-Ala-Arg-Gly-Glu-Hyp-
 298  Gly-Pro-Ser-Gly-Leu-Hyp-Gly-Pro-Hyp-Gly-Glu-Arg-Gly-Gly-Hyp-Gly-Ser-Arg-Gly-Phe-Hyp-Gly-Ala-Asp-Gly-Val-Ala-
 325  Gly-Pro-Lys-Gly-Pro-Ala-Gly-Glu-Arg-Gly-Ser-Hyp-Gly-Pro-Ala-Gly-Pro-Lys-Gly-Ser-Hyp-Gly-Glu-Ala-Gly-Arg-Hyp-
 352  Gly-Glu-Ala-Gly-Leu-Hyp-Gly-Ala-Lys-Gly-Leu-Thr-Gly-Ser-Hyp-Gly-Ser-Hyp-Gly-Pro-Asp-Gly-Lys-Thr-Gly-Pro-Hyp-
 379  Gly-Pro-Ala-Gly-Gln-Asp-Gly-Arg-Hyp-Gly-Pro-Ala-Gly-Pro-Hyp-Gly-Pro-Ala-Arg-Gly-Gln-Ala-Gly-Val-Met-Gly-Phe-Hyp-
 406  Gly-Pro-Lys-Gly-Ala-Ala-Gly-Glu-Hyp-Gly-Lys-Ala-Gly-Glu-Arg-Gly-Val-Hyp-Gly-Pro-Hyp-Gly-Ala-Val-Gly-Pro-Ala-
 433  Gly-Lys-Asp-Gly-Glu-Ala-Gly-Ala-Gln-Gly-Pro-Hyp-Gly-Pro-Ala-Gly-Pro-Ala-Gly-Glu-Arg-Gly-Glu-Gln-Gly-Pro-Ala-
 460  Gly-Ser-Hyp-Gly-Phe-Gln-Gly-Leu-Hyp-Gly-Pro-Ala-Gly-Pro-Hyp-Gly-Glu-Ala-Gly-Lys-Hyp-Gly-Glu-Gln-Gly-Val-Hyp-
 487  Gly-Asp-Leu-Gly-Ala-Hyp-Gly-Pro-Ser-Gly-Ala-Arg-Gly-Glu-Arg-Gly-Phe-Hyp-Gly-Glu-Arg-Gly-Val-Glu-Gly-Pro-Hyp-
 514  Gly-Pro-Ala-Gly-Pro-Arg-Gly-Ala-Asn-Gly-Ala-Hyp-Gly-Asn-Asp-Gly-Ala-Lys-Gly-Asp-Ala-Gly-Ala-Hyp-Gly-Ala-Hyp-
 541  Gly-Ser-Gln-Gly-Ala-Hyp-Gly-Leu-Gln-Gly-Met-Hyp-Gly-Glu-Arg-Gly-Ala-Ala-Gly-Leu-Hyp-Gly-Pro-Lys-Gly-Asp-Arg-
 568  Gly-Asp-Ala-Gly-Pro-Lys-Gly-Ala-Asp-Gly-Ala-Pro-Gly-Lys-Asp-Gly-Val-Arg-Gly-Leu-Thr-Gly-Pro-Ile-Gly-Pro-Hyp-
 595  Gly-Pro-Ala-Gly-Ala-Hyp-Gly-Asp-Lys-Gly-Glu-Ala-Gly-Pro-Ser-Gly-Pro-Ala-Gly-Thr-Arg-Gly-Ala-Hyp-Gly-Asp-Arg-
 622  Gly-Glu-Hyp-Gly-Pro-Hyp-Gly-Pro-Ala-Gly-Phe-Ala-Gly-Pro-Pro-Gly-Ala-Asp-Gly-Gln-Hyp-Gly-Ala-Lys-Gly-Glu-Hyp-
 649  Gly-Asp-Ala-Gly-Ala-Lys-Gly-Asp-Ala-Gly-Pro-Hyp-Gly-Pro-Ala-Gly-Pro-Ala-Gly-Pro-Pro-Gly-Pro-Ile-Gly-Asn-Val-
 676  Gly-Ala-Hyp-Gly-Pro-Hyl-Gly-Ala-Arg-Gly-Ser-Ala-Gly-Pro-Hyp-Gly-Ala-Thr-Gly-Phe-Hyp-Gly-Ala-Ala-Gly-Arg-Val-
 703  Gly-Pro-Hyp-Gly-Pro-Ser-Gly-Asn-Ala-Gly-Pro-Hyp-Gly-Pro-Hyp-Gly-Pro-Ala-Gly-Lys-Glu-Gly-Ser-Lys-Gly-Pro-Arg-
 730  Gly-Glu-Thr-Gly-Pro-Ala-Gly-Arg-Hyp-Gly-Glu-Val-Gly-Pro-Hyp-Gly-Pro-Hyp-Gly-Pro-Ala-Gly-Glu-Lys-Gly-Ala-Hyp-
 757  Gly-Ala-Asp-Gly-Pro-Ala-Gly-Ala-Hyp-Gly-Thr-Pro-Gly-Pro-Gln-Gly-Ile-Ala-Gly-Gln-Arg-Gly-Val-Val-Gly-Leu-Hyp-
 784  Gly-Gln-Arg-Gly-Glu-Arg-Gly-Phe-Hyp-Gly-Leu-Hyp-Gly-Pro-Ser-Gly-Glu-Hyp-Gly-Lys-Gln-Gly-Pro-Ser-Gly-Ala-Ser-
 811  Gly-Glu-Arg-Gly-Pro-Hyp-Gly-Pro-Met-Gly-Pro-Hyp-Gly-Leu-Ala-Gly-Pro-Hyp-Gly-Glu-Ser-Gly-Arg-Glu-Gly-Ala-Hyp-
 838  Gly-Ala-Glu-Gly-Ser-Hyp-Gly-Arg-Asp-Gly-Ser-Hyp-Gly-Ala-Lys-Gly-Asp-Arg-Gly-Glu-Thr-Gly-Pro-Ala-Gly-Ala-Hyp-
 865  Gly-Pro-Hyp-Gly-Ala-Hyp-Gly-Ala-Hyp-Gly-Pro-Val-Gly-Pro-Ala-Gly-Lys-Ser-Gly-Asp-Arg-Gly-Glu-Thr-Gly-Pro-Ala-
 892  Gly-Pro-Ile-Gly-Pro-Val-Gly-Pro-Ala-Gly-Ala-Ala-Gly-Pro-Ala-Gly-Pro-Gln-Gly-Pro-Arg-Gly-Asx-Hyl-Gly-Glx-Thr-
 919  Gly-Glx-Glx-Gly-Asx-Arg-Gly-Ile-Hyl-Gly-His-Arg-Gly-Phe-Ser-Gly-Leu-Gln-Gly-Pro-Hyp-Gly-Pro-Hyp-Gly-Ser-Hyp-
 946  Gly-Glu-Gln-Gly-Pro-Ser-Gly-Ala-Ser-Gly-Pro-Ala-Gly-Pro-Arg-Gly-Pro-Hyp-Gly-Ser-Ala-Gly-Ser-Hyp-Gly-Lys-Asp-
 973  Gly-Leu-Asn-Gly-Leu-Hyp-Gly-Pro-Ile-Gly-Hyp-Hyp-Gly-Pro-Arg-Gly-Arg-Thr-Gly-Asp-Ala-Gly-Pro-Ala-Gly-Pro-Hyp-
1000  Gly-Pro-Hyp-Gly-Pro-Hyp-Gly-Pro-Hyp-Gly-Pro-Pro-
```

Ser-Gly-Gly-Tyr-Asp-Leu-Ser-Phe-Leu-Pro-Gln-Pro-Pro-Gln-Gln-Glx-Lys-Ala-His-Asp-Gly-Gly-Arg-Tyr-Tyr

FIG. 9. The complete amino acid sequence of the α1 chain: The peptides at top and bottom beyond the numbers, represent the sequences of the "non-helical" telopeptides attached at the NH₂ and COOH terminal regions, respectively. Composite of data from rat and calf skin. Reproduced from Hulmes *et al.* (1973).

established that glycine occupies every third residue as predicted from X-ray diffraction analysis and model building, and that the triplet types Gly·Pro·Y and Gly·X·Hyp occur in the proportions of 21.4 and 21.1%, respectively, of the total α1 triplets. Hydroxy-proline appears only in the Y position, and Gly·Pro·Hyp accounts for 10.1% of the triplets. The position of proline in the triplets has an important effect on stability, since Doyle *et al.* (1971) established through studies on synthetic polypeptides that order of thermal stability follows the pattern Gly·Pro·Pro(Hypro) > Gly·Pro·Y > Gly·X·Pro > Gly·X·Y.

There appears to be total asymmetry of distribution of charged residues along the α1 chain although they appear to be more concentrated in the SLS band regions (Chapman, 1974). There appears to be significant grouping of nonpolar residues at regular intervals of about 2/11 of the fibril axial period (Hulmes *et al.*, 1973).

Many of the lysine residues that are hydroxylated are only partially hydroxylated, and the same is true of some of the hydroxyproline residues, probably reflecting microheterogeneities in any proportion of collagen molecules. For the $\alpha1$ chain of extractable rat skin collagen, carbohydrate in the form of glucosylgalactose is located in only one position, namely on the first residue of the CNBr peptide $\alpha1$-CB5, which is near the NH_2-terminus of the chain. Some other hydroxylysine positions, however, carry residues of galactose only (Aguilar *et al.*, 1973). Cartilage collagen contains more sugar than does that of skin and bone, and invertebrate collagens are much more heavily glycosylated than are those of vertebrates. Thus far, the significance of glycosylation, remains obscure, owing largely to insufficient biological information.

There is no evidence that any regions of the normal $\alpha1$ chain are incompatible with the polyproline type II helix except for two short lengths of peptide, one at the NH_2-terminal end accounting for 16 residues (rat and chick), and 25 residues at the COOH-terminal end [for calf skin, the only collagen to date for which the COOH-terminal peptides have been sequenced (Rauterberg *et al.*, 1972)]. Both regions contain little glycine and no hydroxyproline. With regard to the types of amino acid substitutions comparing homologous regions of $\alpha1$ chains from several different species (rat, chick, and calf), all appear to represent not more than a single nucleotide substitution in the DNA codon triplet. The data are still fragmentary, and with further information this statement may need revision.

III. Molecular Heterogeneity and Embryology

We had assumed, since the characterization of the α chain structure of collagen in chemical terms by Piez and associates (1961, 1963), that among the vertebrates all collagens consisted of two $\alpha1$ chains and one $\alpha2$ with only minor variations in composition. With the report of Miller and Matukas (1969) of another type of collagen in cartilage, our horizons broadened again with the realization that there might be considerable molecular heterogeneity. We thought perhaps the story of hemoglobin and the various hemoglobinopathies might be recapitulated for collagen and the genetic diseases of connective tissues.

Although it was believed intuitively for many years that most, if not all, vertebrate collagens had the same primary structure, we were aware of amino acid composition differences among the tissues of one animal as well as among species (Gross, 1963b). We now know there is considerable heterogeneity in both chain distribution and sequence of the α chains.

In mature vertebrates the commonest form of collagen, typified by that found in skin and bone, consists of two $\alpha 1$ chains (identical in amino acid sequence), termed $\alpha 1(I)$, and a third chain, termed $\alpha 2$, differing from the other two in composition but identical in size and secondary structure. Symbolically the intact molecule is designated $[\alpha 1(I)]_2\alpha 2$, generally referred to as type I collagen. Miller and Matukas (1969) suspected the existence of another type of collagen in cartilage when they observed an abnormally high $\alpha 1:\alpha 2$ ratio in cartilage extracts. They found a new type of $\alpha 1$ chain eluting from carboxymethylcellulose columns in the same region as $\alpha 1$ from skin and bone but having a different amino acid composition and structure. They postulated a molecule consisting of three $\alpha 1$ chains—designated as $[\alpha 1(II)]_3$. Soon thereafter Trelstad and colleagues (1970) isolated this molecule intact from lathyritic chicks (cartilage collagen from normal animals is insoluble). The latter has now been obtained from many types of cartilage and extensively characterized in terms of composition (Miller, 1971, 1972; Trelstad *et al.,* 1970, 1972; Strawich and Nimni, 1971; Linsenmayer *et al.,* 1973a), physical properties (Miller, 1971; Igarashi *et al.,* 1973), SLS structure (Trelstad *et al.,* 1970; Stark *et al.,* 1972) and *in vitro* fibril formation (Bruns *et al.,* 1973). We have since become aware of the existence in the same animal of a number of different collagen gene products giving rise to molecules consisting of all one type of α chain. In embryonic skin (Chung and Miller, 1974), adult aorta (Trelstad, 1974), and uterine leiomyoma (Chung and Miller, 1974) a third type of $\alpha 1$ chain, termed $\alpha 1(III)$, has been identified and the molecule coded as $[\alpha 1(III)]_3$ (type III collagen). Basement membrane isolated from several mammalian tissues also consists, at least in part, of a single $\alpha 1$ type (Kefalides, 1971b, 1973), but again differing in composition and sequence from the others, coded as $[\alpha 1(IV)]_3$ or type IV collagen. The collagen of chick liver, spleen and lung (Trelstad, unpublished) are of the skin-bone type $[\alpha 1(I)]_2\alpha 2$. The human aorta collagen, however, is heterogeneous, again containing an excess of $\alpha 1$ chains suggesting a mixture of types; among these are two different molecules, which may be related to type IV of basement membrane and to type III of embryonic skin (Trelstad, 1974). The various chain types have been designated members of the $\alpha 1$ family because they fall within the same elution domain on carboxymethyl cellulose chromatography. The one exception is the $\alpha 3$ chain of codfish (Piez, 1965; Lazlo and Olsen, 1969), which needs further examination. Thus far, definite heterogeneity of the $\alpha 2$ chain has not been described, although we now suspect its existence. Of interest is the fact that the few collagens from invertebrates which have been analyzed to date are all $(\alpha 1)_3$ (Nordwig et al., 1973; Katzman and Kang, 1972), and we wonder whether the $\alpha 2$ chain represents a late vertebrate evolutionary development. In a detailed study of the chick eye, Trelstad and Kang (1974) have described five different collagen types, each possibly constituting a different gene product. Of importance is the very recent characterization of the type III collagen (Chung and Miller, 1974) found in unexpectedly high concentrations in a number of connective tissues and previously overlooked because its α chains are disulfide cross-linked and not readily extractable.

The discovery of primary structure heterogeneity of collagen immediately raised the question whether different cell types are responsible for the different types of collagen. It has been commonly considered that only cells of mesenchymal origin, fibrocytes, chondrocytes, osteocytes, were the sole sources of collagen; however as far back as 1897, von Ebner claimed that the notochord sheath collagen in lower fish was produced by nonmesenchymal cells. The opinion that nonmesenchymal cells would produce collagen was also held by Baitsell (1920, 1925) for certain tissues in both amphibian and chick, and by Giersberg (1921), who reported that the collagenous fibers of the reptile egg shell derived from epithelial oviduct cell secretions. Similarly the collagenous component of ovokeratin found in the egg capsule of selachian fishes appears to be derived from the secretory gland cells (see review by Bear, 1952). In recent years Hay and her associates (Hay and Revel, 1969; Dodson and Hay, 1971; Hay and Dodson, 1973) have provided strong evidence that isolated corneal epithelium in culture produces characteristic collagen fibrils. Since essentially all cell types, with the probable exception of fibroblasts, produce morphogenetically identifiable basement membranes, and since purified basement membrane material examined to date from a variety of tissues contains collagen as a major component (Kefalides, 1973; Spiro, 1972), one must assume widespread production of this protein by a number of nonmesenchymal cell types.

In the past few years direct demonstration of collagen production by a variety of epithelial cell types from the embryonic chick has been accomplished in cell and tissue cultures by the incorporation of labeled proline from the medium into hydroxyproline containing α chains of the correct molecular weight and hydroxyproline:proline ratio (measured isotopically). The product was characterized in terms of behavior on molecular sieve and carboxymethylcellulose chromatography, following the radioactivity profiles and their correspondence with known cold carrier α chains. To date the demonstration of collagen synthesis in epithelial type cells of the chick includes spinal cord, notochord, neural crest, retinal pigmented epithelium, lens, cornea, and epidermis. Simply by chromatographic profile it would appear that epidermis (Linsenmayer, unpublished), neural crest, and retinal pigmented epithelial cells (Newsome, Lichtenstein and Martin, personal communication) makes $(\alpha 1)_2\alpha 2$ and corneal epithelium (Trelstad et al., 1974); lens, Kefalides (1971a); notochord (Linsenmayer et al. 1973b); spinal cord (Trelstad et al., 1973) all make $(\alpha 1)_3$. Until we can obtain more precise characterization of these α chains, we will not know whether they are the same as any of the species isolated and characterized chemically from adult animals. This technique has been further refined to permit identification of the chain type by mapping cyanogen bromide peptides, again as radioactive profiles, in the presence of carrier. We hope to sharpen the identification even further by sequencing isotopically labeled proteins.

The question as to whether or not a single cell type may under different environmental stimuli produce genetically different types of collagen is being asked in several laboratories. Shiltz *et al.* (1973) have reported the effect of bromodeoxyuridine on cartilage cell cultures, presumably free of other cell types, whereby the normal production of type II collagen was converted to type I. Levitt and Dorfman (1974) briefly described similar unpublished experiments of B. D. Smith, G. R. Martin, and A. Dorfman to the effect that chick limb mesenchyme when grown in culture will produce cartilage type II collagen but in the presence of bromodeoxyuridine becomes irreversibly committed to the skin-bone type I. In the last situation there could easily be a selection of cell type from the heterogeneous, as yet uncommitted, mesenchymal cell population. The full significance of this seeming regulation of expression of differentiated properties awaits considerably more pointed experimentation.

Three questions are being asked with regard to developmental significance of collagen: (1) Is a single cell type capable of producing a range of different collagen gene products, or is cell selection in some subtle way at work here? We have a partial answer in that a single fibroblast of skin or bone produces both $\alpha 1$ and $\alpha 2$ chains. However, these are really different subunits of a single molecule.

The question might be more precisely asked: can a single cell produce genetically distinct molecular species, such as skin-bone and the cartilage type? (2) If so, what is the intracellular regulatory mechanism and what are the external "inducing" factors? (3) What is the functional significance of the different types of collagens? What roles do they play in morphogenesis?

The observations of Hauschka and Konigsberg (1966) and Hauschka and White (1971), that contact with extremely small quantities of collagen or certain of its fragments would greatly enhance the differentiation of myoblasts to myotubes, stimulated wide interest in the potential role of collagen in embryonic development. Bernfield and Wessells (1970) have concluded from experiments on *in vitro* development of embryonic salivary gland and lung anlage that morphogenesis, as indicated by lobulation of the epithelium, was modulated by deposition of collagen in very specific regions. Superimposed on studies such as these is the old puzzling question as to the difference between reticulin and collagen, reticulin accounting for nearly all the early embryonic extracellular fibrillar material and remaining in specific regions of the adult organs. The discovery of the molecular heterogeneity of collagen then raised the question whether there were clearly definable transitions from one type to another during embryonic growth in a manner analogous to the hemoglobin story. Do the different forms of collagen play significant and specific roles in morphogenesis, growth, and differentiation?

In an effort to test whether transitions from one collagen type to another occur during embryonic development, studies were initiated in our laboratory to determine the type of collagen synthesized at various stages during development of the embryonic chick limb. At about stage 22 (3 days of incubation) the essentially homogeneous mesenchyme of the chick limb condenses to form a distinguishable central core which soon takes on the histologic characteristics of cartilage. Then, linear and lateral growth of this cartilagelike structure occurs rapidly through 8 or 9 days of development, during which the distinguishing outlines of the femur and tibia begin to appear. Shortly thereafter, regions of calcification may be observed in the shaft, and with further development there appears to be a rapid transition of the diaphyses from a cartilaginous to bony structure with the epiphysis and articular surface remaining cartilaginous in appearance. Alpha chain analysis of the 8-day cartilaginous tibia, diaphysis, and vertebral bodies revealed the nearly exclusive presence of cartilage type collagen $[\alpha 1 (II)]_3$ (Linsenmayer *et al.*, 1973a). A more detailed examination of the various stages of development by Linsenmayer and colleagues (1973c) showed that the entire early limb collagen of the stage 23–24 embryos was $(\alpha 1)_2 \alpha 2$, and throughout development this type collagen remained the chief product of the outer, soft tissue region of the limb. In the precartilaginous core region, however, $(\alpha 1)_3$ began to appear at about

5 days and progressively increased in amount until by 8 days the diaphysial collagen was predominently if not exclusively $[\alpha 1(\text{II})]_3$, the cartilage type. Shortly thereafter typical bone type collagen $[\alpha 1(\text{I})]_2\alpha 2$ appeared in the diaphyseal region in increasing amounts until it replaced the cartilage type, the latter remaining the major, if not exclusive component of the epiphysis. Thus, in the developing limb there is a three-stage transition beginning in the early mesenchyme as $(\alpha 1)_2\alpha 2$ (which may or may not be the characteristic skin-bone prototype) followed by the appearance of cartilage type collagen consisting of exclusively $\alpha 1$ type II chains, followed finally by replacement with characteristic adult bone type collagen. Are these different types of collagens dependent upon the appearance and disappearance of different cell types, or do they represent an induced transition from one cell product to another in the same population? What are the stimuli for these transitions?

IV. Biosynthesis, Procollagen, and Dermatosparaxis

Metabolic studies on collagen turnover using isotopes began with the experiments of Orekhovich and colleagues (1948) from which they concluded that the collagen extracted with citrate buffers at acid pH was the earliest precursor of the extracellular fibrils. Several years later, however, Harkness et al. (1954) found a much more rapid turnover rate and higher specific activity in the collagen fraction extracted with slightly alkaline phosphate solutions. The discovery of collagen extractable in cold physiologic salt solutions, first reported by Gross and colleagues (1955) and Jackson and Fessler (1955) independently, followed by isotope incorporation studies on this fraction by Jackson and Bentley (1960) bestowed upon that collagen component the honor of being the earliest synthesized.

It was proposed by Gross (1956) and Jackson and Bentley (1960) that the fibroblast secreted collagen in molecular dispersion into the extracellular space, where it first aggregated into loose liquid crystal type structures. These could be dissociated readily with cold physiologic salt solutions but with time crystallized into more perfectly organized fibrils of decreasing solubility, represented by fractions progressively extractable at higher salt concentration, then in dilute acid. The end product of this time-dependent maturation process would be a cross-linked fabric of fibrils barely soluble in strong denaturing agents. Once the sequence of events in the extracellular deposition of collagen was described, the next obvious step was the exploration of intracellular synthesis. Goldberg and Green (1967), Manner *et al.* (1967), and Fernandez-Madrid (1967) made the first efforts with cultured fibroblasts exposed to labeled proline. From cell homogenates they isolated a collagen fraction which they considered to be polyribosome bound; however, there remained the indeterminacy of contamination from newly synthesized extracellular molecules. Resolution of this problem required the establishment of a cell-free system capable of synthesizing collagen. Early attempts at isolating polysomes containing nascent collagen chains were promising but were still subject to the problems of contamination with already secreted highly labeled collagen molecules. Lazarides and Lukens (1971; Lazarides *et al.,* 1971) reported the completion and release of unhydroxylated nascent chains from detergent-dispersed polysomes which required the addition of prolyl hydroxylase and essential cofactors for hydroxylation. Cochromatography of the completed chains with carrier confirmed their identity with both α1 and α2. Of interest was the fact that nascent chains obtained from polysomes which had been labeled *in vivo* prior to isolation were already partially hydroxylated without subsequent exposure to prolyl hydroxylase. Diegelman *et al.* (1973) added significantly to this bit of information by demonstrating that completely hydroxylated nascent chains could be obtained from cell-free systems if membrane-bound instead of free polysomes were used. They interpreted their data as indicating the presence of prolyl hydroxylase bound to the membrane in close association with collagen-synthesizing polysomes. In both these systems both α1 and α2 chains were produced. Benveniste and colleagues (1973) have isolated messenger RNA from mouse embryo calvaria, the cells of which devote 60% of their total protein-synthesizing apparatus to production of collagen. Crude total RNA extracts added to "alien" (Krebs II ascites cells) membrane bound polysomes with the appropriate "goodies" programmed the synthesis of characteristic α chains. Transfer RNA's from chick embryo skeletal tissues were much more effective in potentiating collagen synthesis than were tRNA's from liver. In contrast with earlier experiments, those of Benveniste and colleagues (1973) demonstrated *de novo* synthesis of polypeptide chains, not just the completion of already initiated polypeptides.

It is important to note that in all the reported instances of cell-free synthesis of collagen, none have successfully produced a native triple-stranded molecule. This limitation of the cell-free homogenate system may be telling us something important about the manner in which two α1 and one α2 chains locate each other. From the observation that a random solution of mammalian α chains may be renatured, slowly and incompletely, under specific and unnatural conditions—i.e., at acid pH in citrate buffer at temperatures below 30°—plus the observation that the molecules produced in a mixture of two parts α1 and one part α2 produce the characteristic hybrid, it might be concluded that the natural process is another example of simple self-assembly. The assumption is that there are twice as many messengers for α1 as there are for α2, and that the pro-α chains are synthesized and released randomly, then in solution they spontaneously assemble in the proper proportions. It should be noted that no one has as yet renatured the native molecule from solutions of either pro-α or α chains at neutral pH and 37°C. In addition we know that mixtures of varying concentrations of α1 and α2 chains when annealed will produce $(\alpha1)_3$, $(\alpha1)_2\alpha2$, $(\alpha1)(\alpha2)_2$, or $(\alpha2)_3$, depending on relative concentration of α1 and α2 in the original mixture (Nold, 1973.)

I might suggest an alternative possibility, to wit, the existence of a specifically structured group of three polysomes, two of which can translate the α1 messenger, and the third is specified in some manner for α2. The three nascent chains would synchronously spin out in close association permitting an immediate joining through disulfide bridges of the NH_2-terminal extension peptides (Fessler *et al.*, 1973; Harwood *et al.*, 1974). There is nothing yet in the available data that speaks against a highly structured grouping of selective polysomes for collagen synthesis; however, it must be noted that specificity of polysomes for different messengers has not as yet been reported. Failure to produce a triple helical molecule in currently used cell-free homogenates may reflect disarray of the hypothesized polysome complex.

Hyroxylation

Among the earliest studies of collagen biosynthesis were those of Stetten and Schoenheimer (1944) and Stetten (1949), who were intrigued with hydroxyproline as an amino acid unique to collagen. They observed that this hydroxylated amino acid was not directly incorporated into the protein, but proline was its precursor. Since then, several laboratories almost simultaneously had discovered that in an anaerobic atmosphere collagen producing tissues synthesized a proline-rich, hydroxyproline-poor polypeptide which became hydroxylated upon exposure to oxygen. Inhibitors of protein synthesis, while interfering with the production of a new collagen, would not block hydroxylation of a preformed precursor (only detected but not isolated at the time). It thus became apparent that hydroxylation of proline was a post-translational event which required molecular oxygen, a series of cofactors, and an enzyme system. Similar observations were made for hydroxylation of lysine and although the enzymes are different the cofactor requirements are the same. This intriguing story has been adequately reviewed by Grant and Prockop (1972) and Cardinale and Udenfriend (1974).

The observations of Hurych and Chvapil (1965) that the iron chelator, α,α-dipyridyl effectively blocks hydroxylation of nascent α chains and prevents their secretion led to the isolation of an unhydroxylated precursor called "protocollagen" by Prockop and colleagues (Prockop and Juva, 1965; Kivirikko and Prockop, 1967) which provided a natural substrate for the search for the hydroxylating enzymes. These unhydroxylated α chains, both $\alpha 1$ and $\alpha 2$, containing less than 2 hydroxyproline residues per 1000 residues could be extracted in triple helical form from chelator-treated tendon cells below 15°C, but not above 28°C, at which they denature (Berg and Prockop, 1973a). The specific enzymes, prolyl hydroxylase (Fig. 10, E_6) (Kivirikko and Prockop, 1967;

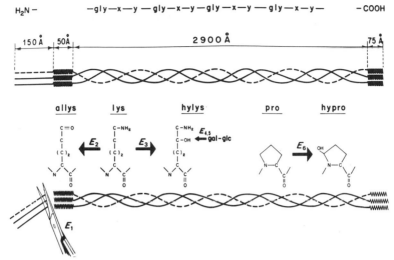

FIG. 10. Schematic representation of post-translational modifications of a collagen molecule: Top diagram, protocollagen, nonhydroxylated, nonglycosylated, and artificially "natured" into the triple helical form, still carries the registration peptide extension at the amino terminal end. The adjacent 50 Å region and the 75 Å piece at the NH_2-terminal end represents the telopeptides. The lower diagram shows the six different post-translational enzymatic modifications of the protocollagen precursor. E_1, procollagen peptidase; E_2, lysyl oxidase; E_3, lysyl hydroxylase. $E_{4,5}$, glucosyl and galactosyl transferases; E_6, prolyl hydroxylase.

Hutton *et al.*, 1967) and lysyl hydroxylase (Fig. 10, E_3) (R. L. Miller, 1971; Popenoe and Aronson, 1972; Kivirikko *et al.*, 1973), were isolated and purified, and their cofactors and functional kinetics were determined. Both enzymes require O_2, Fe^{2+}, α-ketoglutarate and a reducing agent, such as ascorbic acid. Both enzymes have specific steric requirements in their substrates as determined by studies using synthetic peptides analogous to known sequences of collagen. It is now clear, for example, that hydroxylation of proline can occur only on the third residue, in the triplet, $(Gly-X-Pro)_n$ where n is greater than 2 (Miller and Udenfriend, 1970) and that the enzyme works best, and perhaps only, on the totally randomized chain; it will not hydroxylate the polypeptide in helical configuration (Berg and Prockop, 1973b; see Grant and Prockop, 1972, for review).

The evidence is now strong that hydroxylation occurs intracellularly, probably close to the polyribosomes and on the membranes of the endoplasmic reticulum (Diegelman et al., 1973). Using ferritin-labeled antibodies to prolyl hydroxylase, Olsen et al. (1973) visualized the intracellular location of the enzyme by electron microscopy.

Less is known about lysyl hydroxylase. It would appear that the extent of hydroxylation of proline is much more rigidly fixed than that of lysine since considerable variation of the hydroxylysine:lysine ratio occurs between tissues (Spiro, 1969), within the same tissue during aging (Kivirikko et al., 1973) and in pathological conditions, such as in vitamin D deficiency rickets (Toole et al., 1972). In a case of fatal osteogenesis imperfecta in the newborn, we have found excessively high hydroxylation in skin and bone α chains as compared with age-matched controls (Trelstad and Gross, unpublished). Just as for prolyl hydroxylase, the lysine enzyme hydroxylates lysine only in the "Y" position in Gly-X-Y and only in peptides containing more than one triplet (Grant and Prockop, 1972). Again, similar to the behavior of prolyl hydroxylase, which can hydroxylate bradykinen (Rhoads and Udenfriend, 1969) lysyl hydroxylase will operate on substrates other than collagen, such as vasopressin, as long as they contain the appropriate triplet (Kivirikko et al., 1972).

Some of the hydroxylysine residues are specifically glycosylated; for example, the NH_2-terminal residue in α1 CB5 of rat skin and the adjacent regions of the α2 chain carry the disaccharide glycosyl galactose, glycosidically linked through the hydroxyl group. There appear to be four major sites of glycosylation along the α chains, and on other hydroxylysyl residues there may occur a single galactose (Aguilar et al., 1973). Cartilage collagen (type II) and basement membrane collagen (type IV) are highly glycosylated, 5% by weight for chick sternum cartilage, 11% for glomerular basement membrane (Spiro, 1972; Kefalides, 1973). Glycosylating enzymes for both galactose and glucose have been measured and isolated from a variety of tissues (Spiro and Spiro, 1971). Because interference by α,α-dipyridyl with hydroxylation of both proline and lysine, and consequently glycosylation of hydroxylysine, prevents the secretion of collagen, it was assumed that the secretory process requires both hydroxylation and glycosylation. With respect to hydroxylation of lysine, hence also glycosylation, we know now that this is not the case since in a recently discovered birth defect, hydroxylysine deficiency disease (Pinnell *et al.*, 1972), the protein is normally deposited in the extracellular space although lysine is largely unhydroxylated, compared to normal human skin and bone collagen in which about one third of the hydroxylysines are glycosylated (Pinnell *et al.*, 1971).

The function of hydroxyproline in collagen has always been a perplexing mystery, and the well known chemist the late K. H. Gustavson (1954) offered a reasonable hypothesis, namely, that hydrogen bonds form between the hydroxyl group of hydroxyproline in one of the three chains and the ketoimide of the peptide bond in an adjacent chain. Gustavson supported this hypothesis with a comparative analysis of the hydroxyproline content with shrinkage temperature for collagen from a wide range of animals (Gustavson, 1954, 1957). Subsequently, this hypothesis was modified when further analysis of the relationship between shrinkage temperature and total imino acid content, i.e., proline and hydroxyproline, showed an even better correlation, leading to the idea that the stability of the collagen, molecule was dependent upon total imino acids, rather than on hydroxyproline itself. Model building also suggested that the hydroxyl groups would point in the wrong direction for the type of hydrogen bonds Gustavson proposed. However, Gustavson's suggestion has recently been revived and supported on the basis of experiments in which the stability of extracted protocollagens (unhydroxylated α chains or molecules) varied directly and closely with the degree of hydroxylation experimentally produced (Jimenez *et al.*, 1973; Berg and Prockop, 1973b). Unexpectedly, this recent line of experimentation relating to the substrate requirements for proline and lysine hydroxylation is leading directly to the mechanism of triple helix formation.

Early experiments designed to test the question of whether or not hydroxylation of proline required the helical state (Nordwig and Pfab, 1968; Hutton *et al.*, 1967) did not take into account the fact that under the conditions of the incubation, the substrate would be partially renatured. Rhoads and colleagues (1971) found, however that only denatured protocollagen could be hydroxylated. Two laboratories (Jimenez *et al.*, 1973; Berg and Prockop, 1973b) simultaneously reexamined this question in greater depth. Protocollagen was extracted from chelator-inhibited fibroblasts, at 4°C, conditions under which unhydroxylated protocollagen is in the triple-helical state. Jimenez and associates, to monitor thermal stability, used the knowledge that pepsin at acid pH will not attack the triple helix but will degrade only nonhelical regions. Berg and Prockop (1973b) obtained chemical amounts of protocollagens and could monitor thermal stability directly by measuring optical rotation. Using substrates of different degrees of hydroxylation (produced by cell cultures treated with different concentrations of α,α-dipyridyl) they obtained direct correlation between denaturation temperature and the hydroxyproline:proline ratio (Berg and Prockop, 1973a). With a 4°C increment from 25°C the extent of hydroxylation increased about threefold. This could not simply be a temperature effect on enzyme activity; Murphy and Rosenbloom (1973) concluded that unhydroxylated protocollagen chains within the cell at body temperature must be in the nonhelical form, that extracting them at 4° causes formation of triple helix which, however, is unstable above 26°C. Since fully hydroxylated collagen in the helical state is stable at temperatures of 38°–39°C, and since the denaturation temperature is directly proportional to the degree of hydroxylation, they also concluded that hydroxyproline functions primarily to stabilize the triple helix. However, there is an alternative explanation, namely, that hydroxyproline is essential to *make* the triple helix and that if the molecule is not fully hydroxylated the helix is defective to that degree and therefore is unstable because of its defects. There may be enough helix under these circumstances to prevent further hydroxylation, but not enough perfection to permit full stability. The degree of perfection of helix could be measured by intrinsic viscosity and optical rotatory dispersion in the far ultraviolet. A further important suggestion by Murphy and Rosenbloom (1973) is that "the hydroxyproline content of collagen in different animals may in part be governed by the body temperature and not entirely by the primary amino acid sequence that is encoded genetically."

It is worthwhile to consider the implication of these experiments with respect to the possible regulatory interactions between two enzymes working on different parts of a macromolecular substrate mediated by substrate conformational change. At body temperature, underhydroxylated protocollagen chains will not form triple helix and are therefore in optimum configuration for hydroxylation of both proline and lysine. There fore it is likely that the rate (and extent) of hydroxylation of proline is rate limiting for triple helix formation, and conversely, this latter conformational change prevents further hydroxylation—a nice instance of feedback control of enzyme function by conformational change in the substrate. If hydroxylation of lysine occurs subsequent to that of proline, one can then visualize how the extent of the former process is regulated by the rate of the latter, the two enzymatic actions being coupled through substrate conformation. The faster the hydroxylation of proline the fewer residues of lysine will be hydroxylated. However, this can only be part of the story, if at all, since the hydroxylation of lysine is dependent, at least in part, on the local triplet sequence (Kivirikko et al., 1973). In addition, blockage of proline hydroxylation by incorporation of the analog, dehydroproline, is paralleled by simultaneous inhibition of lysine hydroxylation (Rosenbloom and Prockop, 1971). There are many gaps still to be filled, and some confusing contradictions to be resolved (Jimenez and Rosenbloom, 1974), but the story is fascinating and may lead to pharmacological methods for controlling collagen metabolism in disease states.

Analogs

An intriguing approach to pharmacological manipulation of collagen biosynthesis and deposition has been made by the administration of proline analogs which are incorporated by the cell into the collagen polypeptide chains; the list includes azetidine-2-carboxylic acid, cis-4-fluoroproline, 3,4-dehydroproline, and cis-4-hydroxyproline (Uitto et al., 1972; Harsch et al., 1972). All four compounds are incorporated into the α chains, resulting in an early shutdown of collagen secretion accompanied by backup of underhydroxylated, nonhelical collagen chains within the cell (Jimenez and Rosenbloom, 1974). After several hours of synthesis of the abnormal protein, the rate of synthesis itself is slowed. This may be due to a direct toxic effect on the synthesizing apparatus or simply back inhibition by the clogging of the biosynthetic and secretory apparatus with heavy loads of accumulating abnormal protein. The use of both *cis*-hydroxyproline and dehydrolysine is a more effective inhibitor of collagen metabolism than either analog alone, and Jimenez and Rosenbloom (1974) speculated that the incorporated lysine analog in some way inhibits hydroxylation of proline.

It is surprising that *cis*-4-hydroxyproline is readily incorporated into the polypeptide chain (Rosenbloom and Prockop, 1971) since *trans*-4-hydroxyproline cannot be incorporated into collagen in any detectable amount and, in fact, binds only slightly to tRNA (Urivetsky *et al.*, 1966). Apparently proline tRNA will not accept the trans form of hydroxyproline. The insertion of the analog probably is not biologically important since the molecule is aborted, and Mother Nature may not be worried about being "wasteful" in multicellular animals. On the other hand, she may hate to lose a regulatory mechanism. The incorporation of the trans form may be prohibited (teleologically speaking) since posttranslational hydroxylation seems to provide an important type of control over collagen that would be lost if hydroxyproline were directly incorporated.

In vivo experiments utilizing azetidine-2-carboxylic acid and *cis*-hydroxyproline indicate selective blockage of collagen metabolism; at the dosages used there is relatively little interference with metabolism of other proteins. The former compound has been used to evaluate the role of collagen in morphogenetic processes such as lobulation of lung rudiments in embryonic explants (Alescio, 1973). It would appear that the early effect of the analog is interference with collagen formation, which in turn inhibits normal morphogenesis of the organ. Later, there is interference with growth suggesting an effect of azetidine beyond that on collagen production alone.

Surgeons are now exploring the possibilities of using some of these analogs, particularly cis-hydroxyproline, in tendon repair, to interfere specifically with scarring and adhesions (Bora et al., 1972). There is serious consideration of the use of such analogs in the control of a variety of local and systemic fibroses.

Procollagen

Although much has been learned about intracellular biosynthesis and processing of the constituent α chains, and about fibril formation from tropocollagen in the extracellular space, there has been much puzzlement about the way the α chains associate to form the triple helix, how the helical molecules are packaged and secreted, and what keeps them from polymerizing to fibrils at random—if indeed this is a spontaneous process? Schmitt (1960) had predicted that physiological fibrillogenesis would probably follow a route similar to that of the fibrinogen–fibrin system, requiring the enzymatic removal of a specific terminal peptide from the monomer before polymerization could occur. Eleven years later Speakman (1971) proposed the existence of additional peptide extensions attached distally to the NH_2-terminal telopeptides, which would function as a possible "registration" mechanism to permit the correct alignment of the three newly synthesized α chains via disulfide bond formation. The discovery of a "transport" form of collagen, in triple helical form but of higher molecular weight than tropocollagen, by Layman, McGoodwin, and Martin (1971) in the media of cultures of human skin fibroblasts, and by Bellamy and Bornstein (1971) in the homogenates of rat calvaria, quickly led to substantiation of both hypotheses via a single mechanism. The molecule was reported to have extension "nonhelical" peptides of the order of 20,000 molecular weight, covalently attached to the NH_2-terminal end of each of the three α chains (see Fig. 10). The amino acid composition is not characteristic of collagen, containing only 3% glycine, 0.2% hydroxyproline, about 1% proline, and in addition, six residues per thousand of half cystine, and a detectable amount of tryptophan (von der Mark and Bornstein, 1973). The presence of cysteine residues in the extensions had previously been reported by Burgeson *et al.* (1972), who considered them to be in disulfide linkage holding together three α chains.

This molecule is considered to be a precursor of tropocollagen requiring enzymatic excision of the extra peptides in order to convert it to the latter form. This could readily be accomplished *in vitro* by treatment of the "procollagen" with pepsin at low temperature. Bellamy and Bornstein (1971) determined a molecular weight of about 120,000 for the constituent polypeptide chains of procollagen as compared with about 95,000 for those of tropocollagen. Shortly thereafter, Dehm *et al.* (1972) were able to precipitate procollagen from chick embryo tendon cells in the form of segment long-spacing crystallites, which in the electron microscope revealed an extension of about 130 Å at the NH$_2$-terminal end of the molecule. This, however, would not account for a molecular weight of 20,000–25,000 estimated by the difference between that of pro-α and α chains (von der Mark and Bornstein, 1973). Either the molecular weight measurements were inaccurate, or the peptide extensions are compact, coiled, or bent back on themselves, or portions had been deleted in the preparation for electron microscopy. Monson and Bornstein (1973) now report that the previously used acid extraction procedures had indeed removed a portion of the extension peptides and that neutral salt extraction including a "cocktail" of proteinase inhibitors permitted recovery of a larger procollagen molecule. There are some indications that the extension peptides may be even larger for certain procollagens, such as that of basement membranes (Grant *et al.*, 1972). Fessler's laboratory (Burgeson *et al.*, 1972; Fessler *et al.*, 1973) first reported the presence in fibroblast culture medium of disulfide-linked, triple-stranded procollagen containing incorporated labeled cysteine. This was confirmed almost simultaneously by Dehm *et al.* (1972), Smith *et al.* (1972), and Goldberg *et al.* (1972). All groups found that the additional procollagen peptide extensions on three adjacent chains were linked by disulfide bonds concluding that they are probably responsible for the initial lining up of the three polypeptides during or after their synthesis within the cell. Goldberg et al. (1972; Goldberg and Scherr, 1973) confirmed the molecular weight of the pro-α1 and pro-α2 chains of the procollagen molecule and provided further evidence that in human diploid fibroblast cultures collagen is secreted as a disulfide-stabilized procollagen trimer consisting of two pro-α1 chains and one pro-α2 chain. This molecule is subsequently converted to typical native tropocollagen by extracellular enzymatic excision of the NH_2-terminal peptide extensions. The timing of disulfide bond and triple helix formation may be different for different cell types although in all cases it occurs within the cell (Harwood et al., 1974). Molecular sieve and ion exchange chromatography, acrylamide gel electrophoresis and isotope incorporation analyses played key roles in all these studies.

An important link in this chain of events is the excision mechanism as described elsewhere in this presentation. Lenaers et al. (1971) independently, and before procollagen was described in normal tissue cultures, demonstrated the presence of a protease in extracts of normal calf skin capable of excising the peptide extensions from the abnormally long collagen molecules produced in large amounts in the skin of genetically defective cattle. Lapiere et al. (1971) isolated and characterized this enzyme, now called procollagen peptidase (Fig. 10, E1), which subsequently was obtained from extracts of rat and chick calvaria (Bornstein et al., 1972). Layman and Ross (1973) have found the enzyme in the culture media of confluent normal human fibroblasts, but not in homogenates of the cell layer, a finding indicative that the enzyme functions extracellularly. It is not detectable during the lag phase of growth, a pattern similar to that for lysyl oxidase (Layman et al. 1972) and prolyl hydroxylase (Gribble et al., 1969). In the latter instance, an inactive precursor is activated around the time of cell confluence (McGee et al., 1971), and Layman and Ross suggested that procollagen peptidase may also be regulated in this manner.

By means of CNBr peptide cleavage, low temperature pepsin digestion, or digestion of the helical regions with bacterial collagenase, it was possible to separate and isolate the extension peptides in quantities sufficient for amino acid analysis and molecular weight measurements. Sequence studies are now underway in several laboratories. Antisera to pro-α chains have been produced, which appear to be specifically directed to the NH_2-terminal extension peptides as demonstrated by radioimmunoassay and inhibition type experiments using unlabeled pro-α1 chains and isolated extension peptides (von der Mark et al., 1973).

All the evidence now indicates that intracellular synthesis of α chains begins with this nonhelical, noncollagen type peptide consisting of about 200 residues including cysteine and tryptophan (Fig. 10). Since α chains derived from tropocollagen will not normally reassociate in triple helical form at neutral pH and 37°, it is possible that the disulfide bond association between three extension peptides on three different pro-α chains facilitates the self-assembly process of the triple helix under physiologic intracellular conditions.

It is also possible that structural specificity of the propeptides is responsible for arranging α1 and α2 chains in skin and bone collagen in the 2:1 ratio. We also begin to see something of the manner in which the patterns of deposition of collagen fibrils may be controlled by procollagen peptidase during morphogenesis. The observations of Kallman and Grobstein(1965)—to the effect that collagen synthesized in embryonic organ mesenchyme, placed transfilter to epithelium, may diffuse relatively long distances through the Millipore filter without precipitation and then polymerize to fibrils just beneath the epithelium—may now be explained. Procollagen remains in molecular dispersion under physiologic conditions and rapidly forms striated fibrils when enzymatically transformed to tropocollagen.

Dermatosparaxis

Much of the excitement generated by the discovery of procollagen may be attributed to the simultaneous discovery of a genetic disease of collagen in cattle. Newborn calves carrying the defective genes have extremely fragile skin in which the electron microscope revealed large numbers of flat, twisted unbanded collagen fibrils in disordered patterns (Lenaers et al., 1971). Extracts of skin removed relatively little collagen, all of which, however was abnormal in that it contained α chains characterized by 10% higher molecular weight and the presence of cysteine (Lenaers et al., 1971). Electron microscopy of long-spacing crystallites revealed an additional band at the NH$_2$-terminal end of the segment (Stark *et al.*, 1971), the crystallite looking essentially identical to the SLS produced from the normal pro-collagen (Dehm *et al.*, 1972). Dermatosparaxic collagen when incubated with simple saline extracts of normal bovine skin was converted to typical tropocollagen molecules, which readily polymerized *in vitro* to form the usual striated collagen fibrils (Lenaers *et al.*, 1971). The Belgian workers (Lapiere *et al.*, 1971) then isolated and characterized the enzyme, now known as procollagen peptidase from normal skin extracts, demonstrating its ability to cleave the nonhelical peptide extensions from the NH$_2$-terminal ends of the dermatosparaxic collagen. The skin of the diseased animals contained little or no active enzyme, thus the genetic defect was not an intrinsic abnormality in collagen structure itself, but rather the absence of a normal enzyme responsible for an essential post-translational modification of the newly synthesized protein. Tissue fibrils produced by dermatosparaxic cells were organized in an abnormal pattern apparently resulting in weakening of the tissue structure. Bailey and Lapiere (1973) have observed a marked decrease in the aldimine-type intermolecular cross-linking of dermatosparaxic skin fibrils. After removal of the extension peptides, the collagen will then polyermize normally as striated fibrils and, *in vitro,* become cross-linked in the normal manner. Thus, the precursor aldehydes of the cross-links are present in normal amounts, but the extra propeptides prevent normal quarter-stagger aggregation of the molecule. As Tanzer (1967, 1968) showed for normal collagen in any arrangement other than quarter-stagger, intermolecular cross-links will not be made.

Very recently Lichtenstein *et al.* (1973) have described the human counterpart of dermatosparaxis in three patients suffering from a clinically diagnosed form of Ehlers-Danlos disease. These patients have increased amounts of procollagen and near absent procollagen peptidase.

Thus, the simultaneous and independent discoveries of an abnormal collagen in genetically defective animals and of procollagen in cultures and extracts of normal tissues converged and produced a "great leap forward" in our understanding of collagen metabolism and "The Heritable Disorders of Connective Tissue" (McKusick).

V. OSTEOLATHYRISM, CROSS-LINKING, AND BIRTH DEFECTS

Medical students are frequently reminded of those significant advances in fundamental science sparked by the observations of the clinician. It can justly be claimed that part of the credit for stimulating recent rapid advances in collagen biology, and also of the beginning of understanding of the pathogenesis of heritable collagen disease, might go to an orthopedic surgeon, Ignacio Ponseti, whose interest in skeletal deformities led him to compare human kyphoscoliosis with experimental osteolathyrism (Ponseti and Baird, 1952; Ponseti and Shepard, 1954). See reviews by Selye (1957), Tanzer (1965), and Levene (1973). Having been intrigued by Ponseti's account of lathyrism at a Gordon Conference on Bone, I made a note to look at this condition some day. I ordered the active principle, β-aminopropionitrile (βAPN) for the shelf, and forgot about it. Being determined to embark on an embryological problem, C. I. Levene, a pathologist postdoctoral fellow, and I began a study of the mechanism of joint-space formation in the early chick embryo limb by implanting compounds which might block collagen synthesis but not that of hyaluronic acid. Repeated failure led us to look further in the stockroom for other reagents and βAPN fell into our hands.

The original observations on osteolathyrism (Geiger's Ph.D. thesis) were reported by Geiger et al. (1933), who were trying to duplicate in the rat the human neurological disorder, neurolathyrism. This nutritional disease, still endemic in many parts of the world is a result of inclusion in the diet of various species of the hardy *Lathyrus* plant which grow well during periods of drought and famine. Having at hand only the American variety, *Lathyrus odoratus,* these workers were surprised to find that instead of producing neurological disease in their rats, feeding the ground meal from the plant resulted in severe skeletal deformities, avulsed tendons, slipped epiphyses, and frequently death resulting from rupture of the aorta. Ponseti and colleagues (1952, 1954) provided careful description of the skeletal abnormalities (Fig. 11). In the mid-1950's the active principle was isolated from the sweet pea, crystallized and identified as β(N-γ-L-glu-

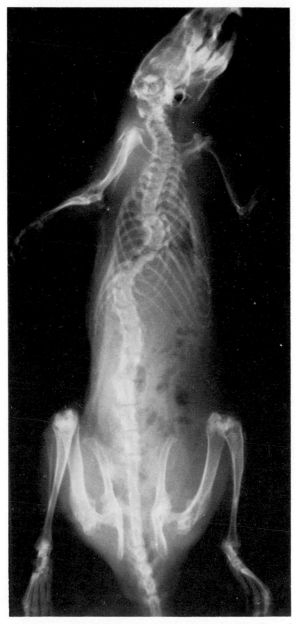

FIG. 11. X-Ray picture of lathyritic rat. Note severe distortion of the spinal column. (Courtesy of Dr. I. Ponseti.)

tamyl)aminopropionitrile (Dupuy and Lee, 1954; McKay *et al.*, 1954; Dasler, 1954; Schilling and Strong, 1954, 1955), and the synthesized fumarate or HCl derivative of the active portion, β-aminopropionitrile (βAPN) soon became commercially available in large quantities.

Levene and I were struck by the dramatic tensile strength changes and skeletal deformities produced in the living embryos by the lathyrogen, and we decided to shift the emphasis of our studies. Histological and histochemical examination of bones and soft tissues of these animals plus the usual elementary analyses for water, collagen, mucopolysaccharides, and protein, revealed no useful information. Some serious reflection, however, on what we knew of the properties of the major structural element imparting tensile strength to the tissues, namely collagen, and its extractability in cold neutral salt solutions led us to design a simple experiment to determine whether something was amiss in the collagen fibrillar organization. Cold neutral saline extracts of bone and skin of the lathyritic animals removed considerable amounts of the tissue collagen in molecular dispersion, in contrast with the nearly complete insolubility of the collagen of untreated embryos. We were able to correlate progressive loss of tensile strength with increasing extractability of collagen as a function of time after administration of the lathyrogen (Levene and Gross, 1959). Collagen was synthesized at an apparently normal rate and deposited in the tissues in the typical fibrillar form (van den Hooff *et al.*, 1959); however, on lowering the temperature in the presence of salt solution even at physiologic ionic strength, these fibrils would dissolve in the extracting medium, a behavior totally unlike that of the fibrils of control embryos. Only collagen newly synthesized in the presence of lathyrogens was soluble (Smiley *et al.*, 1962), not the older fibrils as we originally thought (Levene and Gross, 1959; Tanzer and Gross, 1964).

Amino acid composition, molecular dimensions, and stability of the purified extracted lathyritic collagen revealed no obvious alterations in molecular structure; however, the fibrils formed by warming a cold neutral salt solution of lathyritic collagen to 37° were abnormal in that they would promptly redissolve on cooling, even after an incubation period as long as three weeks

(Gross, 1963a). This is in contrast with the behavior of normal collagen which became progressively insoluble with time (Gross, 1958). This failure of maturation substantiated our original deduction of a subtle molecular defect preventing intermolecular cross-linking.

We postulated that the lathyrogen might bind onto the collagen at some critical position, thereby blocking cross-link formation; treatment with isotopically labeled β-aminopropionitrile failed to substantiate this hypothesis since the isolated lathyritic collagen had essentially no bound radioactivity (Orloff and Gross, 1963). By allowing lathyritic and normal collagen to react with 2,4,-dinitrophenylhydrazine, Levene (1961) concluded that there were aldehyde groups on normal collagen which were diminished in the lathyritic state [confirmed more specifically by Bornstein and Piez (1966) and Rojkind and Juarez (1966)]. Gallop and colleagues (Rojkind *et al.*, 1966) then documented the presence of aldehydes in collagen molecules both qualitatively and quantitatively and postulated that these compounds might be active cross-linking precursors. Observing the interaction of normal collagen in solution with thiosemicarbazide, a lathyrogenic agent which binds firmly to aldehydes, Tanzer and associates (1966) proposed that aldehydes were involved in intermolecular cross-linking of collagen *in vitro* and suggested that cross-links could be formed as Schiff bases between aldehydes and the ϵ-amino group of lysine.

At about the same time Bornstein, Kang, and Piez (1966) at the NIH sequenced the NH_2-terminal nonhelical regions of the normal rat skin collagen molecule (isolated α chains) and found that the lysine residue located at the fifth position from the end (Fig. 12) had been oxidatively deaminated to the aldehyde, α-aminoadipic acid-δ-semialdehyde (allysine). They proposed that the covalent intramolecular cross-link between the component α chains was produced by aldol condensation of two adjacent aldehydes (Fig. 13). The resultant α, β unsaturated aldehyde was later deduced to be a precursor of an *inter*molecular cross-link termed the "post-histidine peak" from its chromatographic elution position (Kang *et al.*, 1969; Franzblau *et al.*, 1970; Kang and Gross, 1970). See Fig. 14, which schematizes the likely arrangements of intermolecular cross-links.

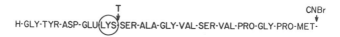

α2 CHAIN

```
         C              T                                    CNBr
         ↓              ↓                                     ↓
H·GLU·TYR·SER·ASP(LYS)GLY·VAL·SER·ALA·GLY·PRO·GLY·PRO·MET⁻
```

α1 CHAIN

```
                       T                                    CNBr
                       ↓                                     ↓
H·GLY·TYR·ASP·GLU(LYS)SER·ALA·GLY·VAL·SER·VAL·PRO·GLY·PRO·MET⁻
```

FIG. 12. Amino acid sequences of the NH₂-terminal peptide (telopeptide) of rat skin α1 and α2 chains, showing the position of the critical lysine residue that is converted to an aldehyde (allysine), which is the precursor of cross-links. From Bornstein, Kang, and Piez (1966).

It was apparent that oxidative deamination of the critical lysine residue occurs after the collagen molecule had been completely synthesized and secreted into the extracellular space, since a portion of the molecules extracted from fresh connective tissues in cold physiological saline did not carry aldehydes. Lathyritic neutral extractable collagen did not have the critical allysine (aldehydic) residue required for cross-linking. Pinnell and Martin (1968) and Siegel and Martin (1970) searched for, found, and characterized the enzyme, lysyl oxidase, responsible for converting the specific lysine residue to an aldehyde and also discovered that the lathyrogen βAPN functions by inhibiting this enzyme. Of considerable interest is the indication that the enzyme functions much more efficiently on collagen fibrils than on collagen molecules in solution (Siegel and Martin, personal communication). Are native type fibrils (640 Å axial period) required, or will any aggregate in the solid state, including amorphous fibrils, be equally effective substrates?

There is as yet relatively little information regarding physiologic control of cross-linking. Shoshan et al. (1972) have observed that hypophysectomy in rats interferes with cross-linking of collagen in Millipore chambers implanted in the rat abdominal cavity, suggesting hormonal control over lysyl oxidase. Ascorbic acid deficiency diminishes cross-linking of collagen by cells in

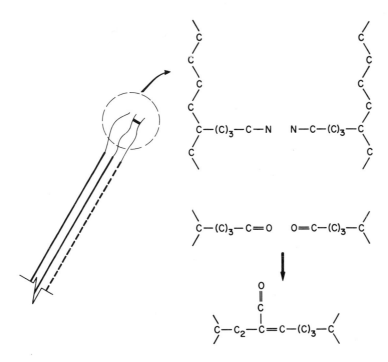

FIG. 13. Formation of intramolecular cross-links: Schematic representation of the amino terminal end of the triple-stranded molecule with a cross-link between one α1 and one α2 chain in the telopeptide region in the circle. On the right are two adjacent schematized amino terminal peptides with the critical lysines on each chain in close proximity. The enzyme lysyl oxidase oxidatively deaminates these two residues to produce two aldehydes (allysine) illustrated below the first arrow, which then condense spontaneously to form an aldol cross-link, the secondary aldehyde of which is available to produce an intermolecular cross-link with a reactive group on an adjacent molecule.

culture (Levene *et al.*, 1972), probably because it is required for hydroxylation of both lysine and proline.

Thus, the early observations on osteolathyrism laid the essential groundwork for the elucidation of the collagen cross-linking mechanism. Of interest from the vantage point of 1973 is the fact that this first and best understood phenotype of human skeletal birth defects is a disease of post-translational modification of a structure protein—not a primary structure defect as in the

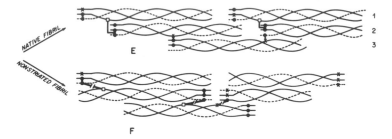

FIG. 14. Representation of intermolecular cross-linking: In the native fibrils (E), in which the molecules all face in the same direction and overlap each other in a quarter-staggered array, intermolecular cross-links may form between allysine (●) and lysine or hydroxylysine (×) forming the compounds lysinonorleucine, or hydroxylysinonorleucine, or between the aldol and another reactive group (□). In nonstriated fibrils (F), where there is only a random order of parallel molecules, allysine or aldol cannot undergo further interaction since appropriate reactive groups are not sterically apposed. This diagram is modified from Piez (1969) and Kang and Gross (1970).

hemoglobinopathies. The pathogenesis of this experimental prototype disease is almost completely understood, from changes in tissue properties, to the molecular defect to the biochemical mechanism; only the route to the gross deformities remains to be revealed.

A by-product of these studies on lathyrism was the provision of a technique for enabling the extraction of non cross-linked, newly synthesized collagen both *in vivo* and in cell and tissue culture, a tool which has facilitated subsequent investigations of the biosynthesis and postsynthetic processing and maturation of collagen.

Cross-linking

Since 1966 there have been a plethora of studies on the isolation, characterization, and localization of collagen cross-links and the changes which occur as a function of age, hormone activity, and disease. Rojkind *et al.* (1966) identified aldehydes in collagen, and Tanzer and colleagues (1966) postulated their involvement in intermolecular cross-linking via Schiff base formation with a neighboring amino group on an adjacent molecule. Blumenfeld and Gallop (1966) introduced the use of tritiated borohydride for tagging free aldehydes in collagen, and Tanzer (1967,

1968) used this labeled reducing agent for simultaneously stabilizing and tagging Schiff bases in collagen, which made possible identification and semiquantitation of intermolecular cross-links and their precursors (see reviews by Traub and Piez, 1971; Tanzer, 1973). The best evidence to date indicates that the allysine or hydroxyallysine residue in the NH_2 and COOH terminal peptides of the molecule, plus the secondary aldehyde in the aldol condensation product, are the precursors of Schiff bases formed with lysine or hydroxylysine residues probably located at a number of specific sites along the helical body of the molecule. Perhaps the most interesting aspect of Tanzer's early studies (1967, 1968) was the observation that intermolecular cross-links would not form unless the molecules were reconstituted in quarter-stagger array, forming the native type cross-striated fibril.

The actual cross-link compounds (Table I) which have been isolated and characterized both chemically and by mass spectros-

TABLE I

COLLAGEN CROSS-LINKS[a]

Cross-link	Origin	Comments
α,β-Unsaturated "aldol"		
$NH_2-CH-COOH$ $\quad\mid$ $(CH_2)_3$ $\quad\mid$ HC $\quad\parallel$ $O=C-C$ $\mid\quad\mid$ $H\ (CH_2)_2$ $\qquad\mid$ $NH_2-CH-COOH$	Aldol condensation product of two α-aminoadipic acid δ-semialdehydes	Found only near NH_2-terminal of collagen chains, acting as an intramolecular cross-link; present in elastin
Lysinonorleucine		
$NH_2-CH-COOH$ $\quad\mid$ $(CH_2)_4$ $\quad\mid$ NH $\quad\mid$ $(CH_2)_4$ $\quad\mid$ $NH_2-CH-COOH$	Reduced Schiff base product of lysine and α-aminoadipic acid δ-semialdehyde	Common to both collagen and elastin

(Continued)

TABLE I (*Continued*)

Cross-link	Origin	Comments

Hydroxylysinonorleucine

$$NH_2-CH-COOH$$
$$(CH_2)_4$$
$$NH$$
$$CH_2$$
$$CHOH$$
$$(CH_2)_2$$
$$NH_2-CH-COOH$$

Reduced Schiff base product of either lysine and δ-hydroxy, α-aminoadipic acid δ-semialdehyde, or hydroxylysine and α-aminoadipic acid δ-semialdehyde

Abundant in most collagens

Dihydroxylysinonorleucine

$$NH_2-CH-COOH$$
$$(CH_2)_2$$
$$CHOH$$
$$CH_2$$
$$NH$$
$$CH_2$$
$$CHOH$$
$$(CH_2)_2$$
$$NH_2-CH-COOH$$

Reduced Schiff base product of hydroxylysine and δ-hydroxy-α-aminoadipic acid δ-semialdehyde

Most abundant in mineralized collagens

N^ϵ-*Glucitol-lysine, N^ϵ-mannitol-lysine*

$$NH_2-CH-COOH$$
$$(CH_2)_4$$
$$NH$$
$$CH_2$$
$$(CHOH)_4$$
$$CH_2OH$$

Reduced Schiff base product of lysine and either glucose or mannose

Origin unknown; present in "older" connective tissues

N^ϵ-*Hexosylhydroxylysine*

$$NH_2-CH-COOH$$
$$(CH_2)_2$$
$$CHOH$$
$$CH_2$$
$$NH$$
$$CH_2$$
$$(CHOH)_4$$
$$CH_2OH$$

Reduced Schiff base product of hydroxylysine and a hexose

Origin partially from collagen; present in connective tissues which contain polysaccharides

[a] From Tanzer (1973). Copyright 1973 by the American Association for the Advancement of Science.

TABLE I (*Continued*)

Cross-link	Origin	Comments

Hydroxymerodesmosine
 	
NH$_2$—CH—COOH
    (CH$_2$)$_3$
    CH
    ‖
CHOH—CH$_2$—NH—CH$_2$—C
(CH$_2$)$_2$ (CH$_2$)$_2$
NH$_2$—CH—COOH NH$_2$—CH—COOH
	Reduced Schiff base product of unsaturated "aldol" and hydroxylysine	Analogous to merodesmosine of elastin

Aldol-histidine NH$_2$ H$_2$ CH—C NH$_2$—CH—COOH COOH (CH$_2$)$_3$ N=N—HC CH$_2$OH—CH (CH$_2$)$_2$ NH$_2$—CH—COOH	Michael addition product of unsaturated "aldol" and histidine, isolated after reduction	Abundant only in cow skin collagen
Histidino-hydroxymerodesmosine NH$_2$ H$_2$ CH—C NH$_2$—CH—COOH COOH (CH$_2$)$_3$ N=N—HC CHOH—CH$_2$—NH—CH$_2$—CH (CH$_2$)$_2$ (CH$_2$)$_2$ NH$_2$—CH—COOH NH$_2$—CH—COOH	Reduced Schiff base product of aldolhistidine and hydroxylysine	Abundant in most collagens, isolated as two isomeric forms

copy, and about which there is essentially complete agreement, are lysinonorleucine (from elastin, Franzblau *et al.*, 1965; from collagen, Tanzer and Mechanic, 1970; Kang *et al.*, 1970), hydroxylysinonorleucine (Bailey and Peach, 1968), and hydroxylysinohydroxynorleucine (Mechanic and Tanzer, 1970; Mechanic *et al.* 1971). Of importance is the fact that Bensusan (1972) isolated and identified the same compounds by complete enzymatic hydrolysis of calf skin collagen. Again, using the sodium borohydride reduction and labeling methods, Tanzer and colleagues (1973) have detected a histidine derivative of the aldol condensa-

tion product, termed aldol-histidine, and another more compli-
cated molecule also involving a histidine residue, termed histidi-
nohydroxymerodesmosine, which is simply the aldol-histidine
cross-link to which is attached another hydroxylysine residue from
a third chain (Table I). Although these last two compounds
have been identified and well characterized by mass spectroscopy,
their existence *in vivo* has been disputed by Robins and Bailey
(1973b), who consider them to be an artifact of the borohydride
reduction procedure. This controversey needs settling.

Of interest is the fact that these compounds must be in the
relatively unstable Schiff base form in order to be detected by
sodium borotritide labeling and therefore should be precursors
of more stable cross-links; aldimines are dissociable at low pH
and under strong denaturing conditions. Their detection in the
reduced stable form requires direct isolation and characterization,
which at present is difficult because of their very low concentration. Using isotope dilution techniques (see review by Tanzer,
1973), it was concluded that 25–50% of hydroxylysinonorleucine
and dehydrohydroxylysinohydroxynorleucine become reduced *in
vivo*. A similar spontaneous reduction was observed in *in vitro*
aged reconstituted fibrils. On the other hand, Robins *et al.* (1973)
have found no evidence for reduced cross-links in bovine collagen
even though there is a clear loss with age of the less stable aldimine compounds, and they claim that the aldimine bond must
be stabilized to a nonreducible form by some reaction other than
reduction. In confirmation, Eyre and Glimcher (1973a,b) found
no evidence for natural reduction of dehydrohydroxylysinohydroxynorleucine.

It is well known that embryonic tissues, such as chick and
rat skin, are highly insoluble, as are the collagens of mature bone
and cartilage. It would appear that the predominant cross-link
in these embryonic tissues is dehydrohydroxylysinohydroxynorleucine (Bailey and Robins, 1972), as in bone, and this compound
stabilizes readily by spontaneous rearrangement to a keto amine,
or enaminol form, as suggested by Robins and Bailey (1973a),
Tanzer (1973), and Eyre and Glimcher (1973a). It should be
recalled that Tanzer (1968) once proposed that local polypeptide
conformation might contribute substantially to the stability of

otherwise unstable Schiff base type bonds in collagen. The exact nature of the highly stable intermolecular cross-links which make most collagen so insoluble is still an undecided issue, although their intermediates seem to have been well characterized. Eyre and Glimcher (1973c) have reported the isolation of a cross-link compound from chick bone collagen which binds at a COOH-terminal telopeptide of one α chain to a region near the NH_2-terminus within the helical region (α1-CB6) of another α-chain presumably on an adjacent molecule. This borohydride reduced cross-link, dehydrohydroxylysinohydroxynorleucine, appears to contain the disaccharide, galactosyl glucose. Eyre and Glimcher (1973c) have also isolated this same glycosylated cross-link compound from the collagen of an invertebrate, the echinoderm, *Thyone briareus*. They imply that the NH_2-terminal glycosylated hydroxylysine on CNBr peptide, α1-CB5 is a precursor of that particular cross-link compound. Although Tanzer (1973) includes glycosylated compounds in his table of cross-links, neither he nor Robins and Bailey (1972) believe that the sugars are directly involved in cross-linking.

The importance of cross-links becomes more apparent as the deforming skeletal birth defects are explored in greater depth with new knowledge and more powerful biochemical tools. Aging changes in collagen (Robins *et al.*, 1973) and questions of the reversibility of fibrotic tissue changes in human disease may hinge significantly on cross-linking.

Malformations

For most proteins, including enzymes, secondary structure and function are completely determined by amino acid sequence of polypeptide chains. With the exception of catalytic removal of extra peptides necessary for activating certain proteins, such as fibrinogen, proinsulin, proparathyroid hormone, some of the digestive enzymes, the post-translational methylation of histidine and lysine in myosin (Huszar, 1972), and phosphorylation and methylation of chromatin proteins, there appears to be little modification after peptide bond formation. Collagen is an outstanding exception in that there are at least six post-translational enzymatic alterations of the primary structure and at least three spontaneous intrachain and intermolecular interactions involving conformational changes and covalent bond formation before the protein is functional (Fig. 10). These alterations have a profound effect on the structure, properties, and biological behavior of this protein. In the past several years three heritable diseases of collagen have been discovered, all involving post-translational events.

Pinnell et al. (1972) reported the amino acid analysis of the dermal collagen from skin biopsies of two young siblings with skeletal and soft tissue malformations resembling Ehlers-Danlos disease—increasing scoliosis since birth, joint laxity and repeated dislocations, hyperextensibility of the skin and numerous thin scars. There was a marked deficiency in hydroxylysine (5% of normal) but not abnormalities of the other amino acids, including hydroxyproline. Hydroxylysine content of collagen in other cases of classic Ehlers-Danlos and Marfan's syndrome were normal. The collagen of the skin of these two children was more soluble in denaturing solvents than that of matched controls, which is consistent with deficiency in cross-linking between collagen molecules in the fibrils. Eyre and Glimcher (1972) reported a marked reduction in borohydride reducible cross-links in skin, tendon, and bone of the two patients with hydroxylysine-deficient collagen, particularly dehydrohydroxylysinohydroxynorleucine, and also a considerable deficit in the "post-histidine" peak, another intermolecular cross-link compound involving hydroxylysine. They also noted that the defect appears to be limited to type I collagens. Cultures of cells from skin biopsies of these children (Krane et al., 1972) revealed a marked deficiency in lysyl hydroxylase activity (Fig. 10, E_3) which could reflect either an actual lack of the enzyme, or a tight association with an inhibitor, or the production of mutant, inactive protein. McKusick now considers this condition to be one of a number of variants of Ehlers-Danlos syndrome.

In another genetic disease of man, homocysteinuria, also characterized by widespread skeletal deformities, including kyphoscoliosis, laxity of the joints, pigeon breast, osteoporosis, ectopia lentis, and diffuse vascular disease, there is also a failure of collagen cross-linking, based, however, on an entirely different type of defect. Here collagen is attacked as an innocent bystander by an abnormal metabolite which happens to be capable of binding aldehydes. The genetic defect is a deficiency in the enzyme, cystathionine synthetase, which catalyzes the conversion of homocysteine to cystathionine. Homocysteine behaves much like penicillamine (Deshmukh and Nimni, 1969) in that it can bind the aldehyde group in allysine (Fig. 15), blocking cross-link formation (Kang and Trelstad, 1973). The collagen in these patients is excessively soluble and diminished in its content of reducible cross-link compounds. In addition, homocysteine will inhibit insolubilization of collagen in an *in vitro* system in a manner similar to penicillamine. Since homocysteine does not often accumulate to readily detectable levels in blood or tissue of these patients, one might assume that it is actively bound by the tissues and that even low levels are enough to cause trouble. However, further documentation by actually demonstrating the presence of homocysteine in collagen produced by the cultured cells of patients with this metabolic disease would help to strengthen the case. In this situation, where the abnormality is not directly related to the normal metabolic processing of collagen, caution is necessary. For example, McCully (1972) believes that the key pathogenetic defect is abnormal mucopolysaccharide production due to excessive sulfation. However, the idea of accidental involvement of collagen

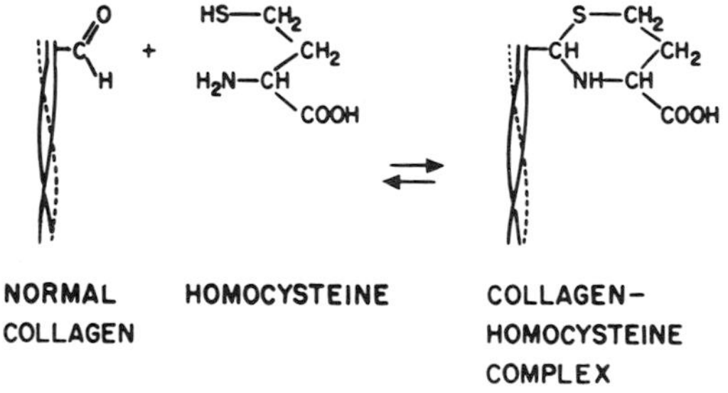

FIG. 15. Mechanism proposed for mode of action of homocysteine analogous to that for penicillamine. From Kang and Trelstad (1973).

with an unrelated metabolite is interesting and should be pursued. The third known heritable defect involving post-translational modification of collagen is another clinical variant of Ehlers-Danlos disease, the pathogenesis of which appears to be identical with that of dermatosparaxis in cattle, discussed earlier. As in the animal prototype, there is an abnormal amount of procollagen in the connective tissues, associated with deficiency in the enzyme procollagen peptidase measured in cell culture (Lichtenstein *et al.*, 1973). These patients also display hyperextensibility of the skin, excessive joint flexibility, and multiple joint dislocations, particularly of the hips. In this situation interference with the formation of normal collagen fibrils reduces the normal tissue tensile strength and distorts the normal structural organization. There are some differences between the animal and human diseases in their clinical manifestations in that the most prominent aspect of the cattle disorder is very fragile skin and little skeletal deformity whereas the reverse is true in the human disease.

Thus, we have three birth defects of collagen, all manifesting very similar clinical features, such as severe skeletal deformities, principally involving the spinal column, hyperextensibility, and fragility of the connective tissues, most readily manifested as dislocations of the joints but also seen in the skin, eyes, and vascular system. In each of the three cases the final molecular lesion is similar, involving inadequate intermolecular cross-linking; however, the biochemical mechanisms leading to it are different in each instance, reflecting the failure of three different post-translational modifications of the collagen molecule two enzymatic and a third chemical. It is possible that amino acid sequence abnormalities will eventually be found that also will interfere with fibril formation or cross-linking. It is, however, likely that any primary structure defect which leads to serious interference with triple helix formation or stability would be lethal in that the malformed protein could not leave the cell.

One might also visualize partial blocks in the biosynthetic mechanism, which would simply result in diminished amounts of collagen in the tissue, or a defective enzymatic removal mechanism, which might lead to excessive amounts of collagen. Other interesting possibilities might involve failure or mistiming in the transition of one type of collagen to another, or their maldistribution.

VI. How Tadpoles Lose Their Tails: Biological Degradation

In 1961 at Woods Hole, Marcus Singer stimulated my interest in the mechanism of limb regeneration. A review of the literature suggested that removal of intercellular matrix between the distal cells of the amputation stump and the failure to form a dermal scar were essential features of the development of a regeneration blastema (Butler and Puckett, 1940; Chalkley, 1959). This critical phase of "dedifferentiation" and removal of the intercellular substances requires enzymes capable of degrading collagen and the interfibrillar ground substance. The metamorphosing anuran tadpole seemed a more suitable subject for a search for degradative enzymes than the salamander since, in frogs, during early stages of metamorphosis amputated limbs are capable of regeneration, but subsequent to developing joint function these limbs no longer regenerate but form scars characteristic of healing in mammalian amputations. The enzymes responsible for tail resorption in anuran metamorphosis should at least be related to those doing the same job in limb regeneration.

Neutral saline extracts of tadpole tails and other tissues from both premetamorphic and metamorphosing animals failed to yield an enzyme capable of degrading native collagen at neutral pH and physiologic temperatures. After considering the possibility that at any one time the enzyme concentration might be below detection levels and that it might be bound to tissue collagen, I turned to a short-term culture system where the enzyme might escape from the explant and accumulate over a period of time to concentrations high enough to visibly degrade a reconstituted collagen substrate. Within 24 hours at 37° and neutral pH clear areas of lysis in the fibrillar substrate appeared around live, sterile fragments of certain tadpole tissues (Fig. 16). Luckily, we had not been set up at the time for tissue culture and had no serum or embryo extract at hand, otherwise we never would have found

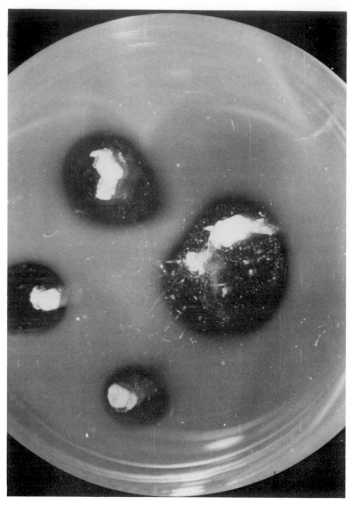

FIG. 16.   Lysis of collagen gel by explants of living tadpole tissue. Opalescent area is intact gel. Black regions around explants are areas of lysis.

the enzyme, since both these usual ingredients of tissue culture media contain potent collagenase inhibitors. My former colleague Charles Lapiere and I then embarked upon a systematic study of the collagenolytic process in cultures of tadpole tail tissues, demonstrating its enzymatic nature, establishing a quantitative assay for the activity in tissue explants and showing that living cells were required for production of the enzyme (Gross and Lapiere, 1962; Lapiere and Gross, 1963). Subsequent studies (Eisen and Gross, 1965) revealed that exposure to puromycin prevented lysis of the collagen substrate, adding further support for the idea that the enzyme was produced *de novo* by living cells. It was unlikely that lysosomal storage and release was involved. Only specific tissues had collagenolytic activity, namely, back and tail skin, gill and gut, i.e., those which consisted of relatively large amounts of connective tissue and which underwent dramatic structural alterations during metamorphosis (Gross, 1964a; Usuku and Gross, 1965). These active tissues were obtained from nonmetamorphosing tadpoles; the presence or absence of thyroxine had little significant effect on their collagenolytic properties in culture, and histologically the explants appeared to undergo spontaneous metamorphosis.

Primary cultures of large amounts of tail fin and back skin floating on filter paper discs in amphibian Ringer solutions accumulated relatively large amounts of enzymatic activity in the medium which could be isolated, purified, and characterized with regard to optimal requirements for enzymatic function, inhibitors, and mode of action on the collagen substrate. We devised a simple, sensitive and quantitative assay, relying on the measurement of soluble radioactive breakdown products from reconstituted ^{14}C-labeled collagen fibrils which now is in general use (Lapiere and Gross, 1963; Nagai et al., 1966). Measurable enzymes appeared in the culture medium after 2 or 3 days at 37°, could be isolated as two distinct peaks of different molecular weight on a molecular sieve column (Harper and Gross, 1970), had a pH optimum of 7.6–7.8, was irreversibly inactivated below pH 4, and was inhibited by serum (Nagai et al., 1966), by EDTA (reversibly), and cysteine (irreversibly), but not by diisopropylfluorophosphate (DFP) (Lapiere and Gross, 1963) or phenylmethylsulfonyl fluoride (PMSF) (Harper and Gross, unpublished). The active serum inhibitors appear to be α-2-macroglobulin and α-1 antitryptic factor (Eisen et al., 1970), although there now appears to be some doubt about the latter (Nagai, 1973; Sakamoto et al. 1972; Berman et al., 1973).

The enzyme attacks native collagen either in neutral solution or in the native or reconstituted fibrillar form at temperatures below that required for denaturation of substrate. The purified enzyme makes a single cleavage through the triple helical molecule at a locus three-fourths the distance from the NH_2-terminal end producing two fragments still in the helical conformation, the longer fragment termed TC^A, the smaller one called TC^B (Fig. 17) (Gross and Nagai, 1965; Kang *et al.*, 1966; Sakai and Gross, 1967). The cleavage site may be located on the SLS crystallite between bands 41 and 42 (Fig. 2) and in the sequence of the $\alpha1$ chain at the peptide bond between glycine residue No. 572 and isoleucine No. 573 (Fig. 9). In the $\alpha2$ chain the Gly-Leu bond, probably immediately adjacent to Gly-Ile in $\alpha1$ is also cleaved, however, the sequence of $\alpha2$ is not yet known. There is nothing obviously unique about the sequence around the cleavage site in the $\alpha1$ chain, yet two other Gly-Ile sequences elsewhere (in $\alpha1$-CB8 and $\alpha1$-CB6) are not attacked. We are now analyzing some general properties, such as distribution of bulky side chains and the relative helical stability of different types of triplets, in a search for low structural stability of the cleavage site. Because the enzyme operates much more efficiently on triple helical molecules than on the isolated nonhelical α chain (McCroskery *et al.*, 1973; Harris and McCroskery, 1974), we suspect that local

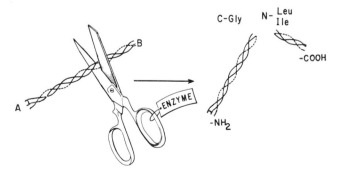

FIG. 17. The site of cleavage in the collagen molecule by the animal collagenases: The "A" and "B" ends of the molecule are the NH_2 and COOH termini, respectively. Liberated "C" and "N" terminal residues at cleavage site are shown at right.

helical conformation around the cleavage site is essential for enzyme-substrate binding.

We know from electron microscopy and sequence studies of the NH_2-terminal end of the one-fourth length fragment, TC^B that two different animal collagenases, one from the tadpole and the second from the rabbit V2 ascites cell carcinoma (Harris et al., 1972) cleave the collagen substrate at precisely the same peptide bond (Gross et al., in preparation). Collagens from all mammalian and amphibian tissues examined to date are cleaved by these enzymes at the same locus, as shown by electron microscopy although sequence analysis is still limited to that mentioned above. In several specific instances, however, namely the collagenases from post partum rat uterus (Jeffrey and Gross, 1970), rat skin (Tokoro et al., 1972), regenerating newt limb (Dresden and Gross, 1970) and the crab hepatopancreas (Eisen et al., 1971), the semipurified enzyme seems to cleave two additional small peptide fragments from the COOH-terminal end of the cleavage site, leaving 67 and 62% of the TC^A fragment intact. Whether this represents the action of contaminating enzymes rather than the pure collagenase itself is at present unknown.

Using the tissue culture techniques and assay procedures devised for the tadpole tissues, collagenases have now been detected, isolated, and characterized from a wide variety of animal tissues in which collagen degradation occurs in vivo (Table II) (for recent reviews see Perez-Tamayo, 1973 and Harris and Krane, 1974). The cell source of collagenase is variable among the different species and tissues. It was well established by Eisen and Gross (1965) that the tadpole tail epithelium actively produced collagenase whereas the mesenchyme cells did not. It was thought at first that intact human skin epidermis was the most active source of the enzyme, but more detailed studies indicated the major sources of the enzyme to be the upper papillary region of the dermis with only minimal activity produced by the epidermis and essentially none from mid and lower dermis (Eisen, 1969). However, in healing wounds (Grillo and Gross, 1967; Eisen, 1969; Donoff et al., 1971), both epithelium and mesenchymal cells are actively producing collagenases which appear to differ in molecular weight and susceptibility to cysteine inhibition, at

TABLE II

SOURCES OF ANIMAL COLLAGENASES

Amphibian	
Tail fin, body skin, gut, and gill	Tadpole (*R. catesbeiana*)
Regenerating limb	Newt (*Triturus viridescens*)
Mammalian	
Bone	Human, rodent, goat, chick
Skin	Human, rodent, chick embryo
Skin wounds (epithelium and granulation tissue)	Human and rodent
Postpartum uterus	Rodent
Granuloma (carageenin)	Rodent
Cholesteatoma	Human
Cornea (epithelia and stromal cells)	Human and rodent
Synovial tissue	Human, rheumatoid arthritis
Rheumatoid nodules	Human, rheumatoid arthritis
Gingiva	Human and rodent
Intestinal tissue	Human and rodent
Reticuloendothelium	Kupffer cells of rat liver
Tumors	Human and rodent
Leukocytes (PMN)	Human and rodent
Macrophages	Rodent peritoneal exudates
Invertebrates	
Hepatopancreas	Crab
Whole body	Planarian

least in rabbit skin wounds (Donoff *et al.,* 1971). It is now evident that a wide range of mesenchymal cells can produce collagenase. Of interest is the general experience that only primary tissue cultures have been capable of producing the enzyme, but recently Werb and Burleigh (1974) have reported production of active enzyme by rabbit synovial cells in continuous culture for at least six passages.

Although the mode of action of all the animal collagenases are similar, there are significant species differences among them. Molecular weight varies from 25,000 to 100,000, there are charge differences, differences in sensitivity, and response to inhibitors or lack of immunologic cross reactivity between most species except those close to each other in an evolutionary sense (see Perez-Tamayo, 1973).

A question of some considerable importance relating to the physiologic significance of this group of animal collagenases has been raised concerning their ability to cleave insoluble collagen fibrils, of which the greatest bulk of most tissue collagens is composed. Leibovich and Weiss (1971) have reported that "polymeric" collagen (insoluble in "all" nondenaturing agents) is not cleaved by purified synovial tissue collagenase unless it is first attacked by other proteases, presumably by lysosomal hydrolases at low pH. They argue that this initial unspecific cleavage is necessary to remove the cross-linked telopeptide regions before the collagenases can function. Harper and Gross (unpublished) using some of Leibovich and Weiss's substrate (generously provided by them) have observed 50% degradation by semipurified tadpole collagenases under the identical conditions of Leibovich and Weiss. Prior cleavage of telopeptide regions by contaminating proteases is ruled out by the fact that there is no evidence for disappearance of β components on disc electrophoresis of the reaction products (Gross and Nagai, 1965). The experiments of Harris et al. (1970) and Harris and McCroskery (1974) demonstrated that rheumatoid synovial tissue collagenase is capable of degrading insoluble cartilage collagen in the tissue. Of interest are the observations of Harris and Farrell (1972) that formaldehyde cross-linking of collagen markedly diminishes the rate of fibril cleavage by synovial collagenase at a fixed temperature, but that a rapid increment in rate occurs at and slightly above 37°C, apparently requiring a somewhat higher temperature characteristic of that for an inflamed joint (Harris and McCroskery, 1974). The recent report (Robertson and Miller, 1972) suggesting that cartilage collagen is not susceptible to degradation by animal collagenases (from leukocytes and inflamed gingiva) has not been substantiated for the collagenases of bone (Glimcher, personal communication), rheumatoid synovial tissue (Harris and Krane, 1972; Wooley et al., 1972), or tadpole (Harper and Gross, unpublished; Nagai, 1973) or cornea (Davison and Berman, 1973). It would appear that the reaction rate with this substrate is slower than that with skin collagens but proceeds in the same manner, producing the same reaction products.

How, then is an insoluble fibril degraded? The physiologic

significance of this limited cleavage by collagenase became apparent when Sakai and Gross (1967) found that the two helical fragments were soluble in physiologic saline at body temperature, in contrast with the insolubility of the intact molecules under these conditions. Mammalian collagen in fibril form, even when uncross-linked, denatures at about 58°C (Gross, 1964b); the soluble reaction products, however, denature at about 5° below body temperature, becoming susceptible to degradation by any nonspecific protease (Sakai and Gross, 1967). One can visualize the enzyme first attacking collagen molecules at the surface of the fibril which may be cross-linked through their NH_2 and COOH terminal peptides to their neighbors. The single cleavage loosens the two fragments which then drift (dissolve) away into the surrounding medium, still connected to the fibril by their ends. They will then spontaneously denature and become susceptible to further degradation by either extra- or intracellular neutral proteases (Fig. 18).

Although it has been proposed that lysosomal acid hydrolases

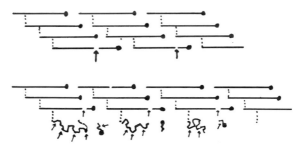

FIG. 18. Proposed mechanism for collagenolytic degradation of insoluble fibrils: Tropocollagen molecules are shown in the characteristic quarter-stagger arrangement within the fibril and a single covalent intermolecular cross-link is placed between each molecule (short, dotted vertical line). The arrows in the top frame point to the locus of initial attack by the enzyme. The small fragment spontaneously floats away from the fibril and denatures at body temperature. The larger fragment while still attached by its intermolecular cross-link to its neighbors will also diffuse away and denature spontaneously, as illustrated in the second frame. The denatured dangling or free fragments are readily susceptible to complete proteolysis by another set of specific or nonspecific proteases possibly present in the extracellular fluids or within macrophages, which may engulf the damaged fibrils.

digest collagen, there is no evidence that these enzymes can do anything more than cleave the nonhelical telopeptides under physiologic conditions. This in itself would not solubilize the fibrils at neutral pH and body temperature nor alter the denaturation temperature. Milsom *et al.* (1972) observed some fragmentation and partial dissolution of human skin polymeric (insoluble) collagen by a crude lysosomal fraction at acid pH (the enzyme is active between pH 3.5 and 5) and 3.7, as seen by electron microscopy. The result is not unexpected since pepsin will do essentially the same thing under these unphysiologic denaturing conditions (Gross, 1953). They propose that the lysosomal acid hydrolases prepare the fibrils for digestion by the neutral collagenases, a proposition which I find unnecessary to invoke. It was reported that the tadpole collagenase could cleave denatured collagen at a number of different peptide bonds (Nagai *et al.,* 1966), but at only one locus in the native helical structure; it is now apparent that these enzymes when highly purified do not effectively attack gelatin (denatured α chains) (McCroskery *et al.* 1973; Gross *et al.,* unpublished) and, when they do, they make a single cleavage at the usual site. It is my guess that effective enzyme binding to the substrate requires the triple helical structure, that the peptide bond is in some as yet not recognized way, determined by the local substrate sequence. Harris and Krane (1972) separated a neutral peptidase from collagenase in the culture medium of rheumatoid synovia, which degraded gelatin to low molecular weight peptides. This enzyme had no collagenolytic activity, but was inactivated by the same inhibitors as was the collagenase. The collagenolytic process does appear, now, to involve at least several different enzymes operating at neutral pH; the collagenase makes the initial specific and critical cleavage which prepares the molecule for subsequent proteolytic attack by arranging for its spontaneous denaturation.

There has always been some question as to the physiologic significance of the animal collagenases, if they could only be produced in tissue culture. Our original assumption (Gross and Lapiere, 1962) was that the enzyme was made de novo as required, and accumulated over a period of time in the culture medium, therefore not enough was present in the tissue at any one time to extract in detectable amounts. We also speculated on the possibilities that it might be inhibited in the tissue, that it might be present as a zymogen awaiting activation or that it might be bound to the tissue collagen (Lapiere and Gross, 1963), since this occurs with bacterial collagenase. There were some few exceptions to the requirement for tissue culture; active enzyme has been obtained from extracts of human leukocytes (Lazarus et al., 1968), rheumatoid synovial fluid (Harris et al., 1969) and frog hepatopancreas (Eisen et al. 1973). In recent years a number of different laboratories have succeeded in extracting at least small amounts of collagenase from tissue which we thought always required culture. Eisen et al. (1971) found collagenolytic activity in saline extracts of human skin, suggesting that the enzyme was normally present in the tissue but bound by the serum inhibitors, α-1 antitryptic factor and the $\alpha2$ macroglobulin. The complexes formed thereby, were separated by molecular sieve chromatography. However, Abe and Nagai (1972) have found that $\alpha2$ macroglobulin combines very firmly with the enzyme, requiring 3 M KSCN to separate the two proteins, and then only partially.

The suggestion that collagenase might be bound to its fibrillar substrate *in vivo,* and therefore not readily accessible to extraction, has been documented by the observations of Ryan and Woessner (1971), who allowed homogenates of involuting rat uterus to incubate at 37° and neutral pH, after which free enzyme could be found in the supernatant fluid after centrifugation. The mechanism here is probably degradation of the substrate by bound collagenase, followed by liberation of the enzyme. Nagai and Hori (1972) were able to accomplish the same thing with homogenized tadpole skin, rat skin, and human rheumatoid synovial tissue; the amount of enzyme extractable from tadpole back skin accounted for 10–20% of that produced in tissue cultures. Active collagenase was obtained from demineralized chick bones by extractions with cold 1 M NaCl (Sakamoto et al., 1973a). Jeffrey et al. (1971a) in a study of rat uterus collagenase state that "the enzymes are not stored in the tissue in appreciable amounts as evidenced by the fact that far higher levels of enzyme activity are present in the medium of cultures of small amounts of tissue than in direct extracts of large amounts of fresh tissue." The extractability of active collagenase from human granulocytes has been well established (Lazarus *et al.*, 1968, 1972; Ohlsson and Olsson, 1973; Kruze and Wojtecka, 1972; Oronsky *et al.*, 1973), and recently collagenolytic enzymes have been extracted from rabbit ascites cell tumor (Harris *et al.*, 1972), from Kupffer cells of rat liver (Fujiwara *et al.*, 1973) and from human platelets (Chesney *et al.*, 1974).

Because we were goaded by one of our biochemical colleagues (Dr. Donald Comb), who was not happy about the *de novo* enzyme synthesis idea, we set about to search for a zymogen. Having prepared an antibody to purified tadpole collagenase, we looked for and found cross reacting protein in tissue extract by immunodiffusion (Harper *et al.*, 1970). This protein could be isolated and purified to electrophoretic homogeneity under the same conditions used for the active enzyme. By SDS gel electrophoresis it migrated as a single band with molecular weight of 110,000 as compared with 100,000 for the enzyme. However, it required activation before it could be considered a zymogen. This could not be accomplished by trypsin, chymotrypsin, or plasmin; however, the third-day culture medium (from which collagenase was removed by adsorption to fibrous collagen) transformed the inactive protein to active collagenase (Table III), which had all the characteristics of the known enzyme (Harper *et al.*, 1971). We also found that the active enzyme could be adsorbed to fibrous collagen and the procollagenase could not, a distinction that proved useful for separating the two and for assay purposes. Using a simple, efficient "immunodisplacement" assay for measuring enzymatically inactive cross-reacting protein, developed by McGee and Udenfriend (1972) for proline hydroxylase, we could measure the zymogen content of tissue fluids and extracts. The zymogen competitively and reproducibly displaced the enzyme from its antibody. A systematic, quantitative examination of the temporal relationships of the appearance of zymogen, enzyme, and activator in the media of tadpole tail fin and back skin cultures by assaying the daily consecutive harvest for all three indicated the presence of maximum amounts of zymogen from day 1 through 3, after which it diminished progressively (Fig. 19).

414   JEROME GROSS

TABLE III

EFFECT OF TEMPERATURE AND TIME ON
ZYMOGEN ACTIVATION

Incubation[a]	Cpm released	
(min)	27°C	37°C
15	0	0
30	80	320
60	260	660

[a] The reaction mixture consisted of 0.1 ml
of zymogen, containing 162 μg of protein
and 0.1 ml of "activator," containing 1425 μg
of protein; these reactants were mixed and
incubated under the conditions indicated
prior to addition to labeled collagen fibrils
(total cpm/tube 1500). Control tubes containing 180 μg of peak I enzyme or 1425 μg
of "activator" were treated similarly; under
all conditions tested, the former released approximately 620 and 25 cpm of solubilized
collagen, respectively. From Harper, Bloch,
and Gross (1971).

Neither active enzyme nor activator could be found until day
3 at which time it rapidly increased in a roughly reciprocal relationship with the diminution of procollagenase (Harper and
Gross, 1972). Harper and I (unpublished), in cultures of normal
human skin from several areas, have found the same pattern of
appearance of cross-reacting proteins, enzyme, and activator in
the media as a function of days of incubation. Preliminary examination of two keloids indicate abnormally low levels of activator
factors. We are now bending our efforts to an examination of the
nature of the activating substances (Harper and Gross, 1973).

Procollagenases have been found in bone culture media by Vaes
(1972a,b) and in leukocyte homogenates (Kruze and Wojtecka,
1972; Oronsky et al., 1973). Bone zymogen activation seems

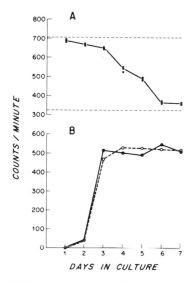

FIG. 19. Relationship between amounts of zymogen, active collagenase, and activator in the culture media of tadpole tail tissue culture as a function of days of incubation. (A) Zymogen concentration reported in counts per minute of immunologically displaced enzyme activity. (B) Collagenolytic activity (●———●) and activating activity (○———○) in medium as a function of time. From Harper and Gross (1972).

to require limited hydrolysis by proteases such as trypsin or chymotrypsin, or some other factor in the media which then transforms the zymogen (MW 105,000) to the active enzyme (MW 85,000). Purified liver lysosomes are said to have the same effect (Vaes, 1972b). The leukocyte zymogen is activated by a factor present in rheumatoid synovial fluid, itself not a collagenase (Kruze and Wojtecka, 1972; Oronsky et al., 1973) and is not present in normal or osteoarthritic fluids. With further purification of the components of the activator system and the preparation of specific antisera, it should be possible to localize and measure these elements of the regulatory process under various conditions of pharmacologic and hormonal inhibition and stimulation.

Looking at the pathogenesis of fibrotic states from a point of view other than that of increased collagen synthesis, namely, the possibility that the degradative side of normal metabolism might be slowed or blocked at a later stage by the presence of natural collagenase inhibitors, such as the $\alpha 2$ macroglobulin of serum, there is a distinct possibility that dilated and leaky blood vessels in hypertrophic scars (J. Burke, personal communication) may be a major factor in increasing the level of serum inhibitors. in the extravascular tissues. Even minor inhibition of the degradative side of turnover could tilt the scales in favor of accumulation. In collaboration with our colleagues in the Shriners Burns Institute and the Pediatrics Department at this hospital we are exploring this avenue.

Looking now at the question of tissue dissolution, the old hypothesis that mechanical pressure by a growing mass of dead tissue can result in bone destruction was the subject of critical evaluation by a surgical resident on the Ear, Nose, and Throat Service at this hospital while working as a member of our laboratory. Chronic middle ear infections not infrequently give rise to a growing mass of dead tissue in the inner ear which is associated with progressive bone destruction, frequently resulting in loss of hearing and occasionally in brain abcesses or destruction of the facial nerve. Abramson cultured tissues obtained during radical mastoidectomy, observing the production of active collagenase by the thin layer of epithelium scraped from the surface of autolyzing bone and none by the associated mass of dead tissue, the cholesteatoma (Abramson and Gross, 1971). It seemed quite unlikely to us that simple mechanical pressure could result in bone destruction since one can squeeze a dead bone indefinitely without causing resorption. Clearly, living cells are needed and living cells mean enzymatic processes. We concluded that the thin layer of endothelium in close contact with the bone of the middle ear causes resorption through the release of collagenolytic enzymes. If this is true, surgery would be successful if the endothelium as well as the inert tissue mass is completely removed permitting the growth of a thick layer of granulation tissue which subsequently turns into a protective scar. The possibility that invasive tumors include collagenolytic enzymes as part of their attack armamentarium is not unreasonable since certain neoplasms have been found to be active producers of collagenase (Riley and Peacock, 1967; Dresden et al. 1972; Hashimoto et al. 1972, 1973; Yamanishi et al. 1973; Harris et al. 1972).

The possibility of manipulating the degradative side of collagenase metabolism via pharmacologic agents and the endocrine system provides us with a potential therapeutic tool and also another probe to help understand the pathogenesis of fibrosis and autolysis. There are a number of biologically important substances known to stimulate cultured tissues to initiate or increase their production of collagenase; colchicine on rheumatoid synovial tissue (Harris and Krane, 1971), parathyroid hormone (Walker et al. 1964) and heparin (Sakamoto et al. 1973) on bone, bacterial toxins (Wahl et al. 1974a) and lymphocyte extracts (Wahl et al. 1974b) on macrophages, and dexamethazone on corneal fibroblasts (Hook et al. 1973). The use of known chemical inhibitors of collagenase in the treatment of corneal ulceration has shown some promise in that repeated application of cysteine and/or EDTA to animal and human eyes severely burned with alkali has prevented the usual sequellae of perforation of the eye ball in statistically significant numbers of cases (Brown and Weller, 1970; Slansky et al. 1970; Dohlman and Slansky, 1972). However, there are technical problems and some indication of toxic response to cysteine and EDTA (Sugar and Waltman, 1973). It seemed to us that a more fruitful approach might be the direct inhibition of production of the enzyme via a hormonal mechanism. Jeffrey et al. (1971a) reported that progesterone at physiologic levels prevented the production of active collagenase in uterine tissue cultures. We found a similar action of the hormone on tadpole tail fin cultures (unpublished work). Dr. David Newsome (ophthalmology resident at the Massachusetts Eye and Ear Infirmary and member of this laboratory) and I in preliminary experiments have been able to prevent perforation in rabbit corneas severely burned with alkali by the application of a single subconjunctival depot of medroxyprogesterone. If further experimentation confirms these early results the way is opened to more effective treatment of a variety of chronic collagenolytic disorders.

Finally we return to the starting point of these studies on animal collagenases, namely the postulated presence of lytic mechanisms of extracellular macromolecules in the regenerating newt limb. We succeeded in demonstrating, as predicted, the appearance of collagenolytic activity in the amputation stump at maximal levels just beneath the blastema, the enzyme appearing during the stage of dedifferentiation and persisting until morphogenesis in the blastema begins. As the new limb took shape collagenase activity rapidly diminished and disappeared (Grillo *et al.* 1968; Dresden and Gross, 1970). We look forward to the impact of such new information and further experimentation on our understanding of, and ability to manipulate, the regenerative process.

VII. SUMMARY

The emerging pattern of collagen formation and organization into a functional tissue is a fascinating series of interactions between polypeptide chains involving conformational changes and alteration in states of aggregation. The amino acid sequence endows the α chains with a morphogenetic potential realized through a post-synthetic succession of specific enzymatic alterations and self-assembly mechanisms which are regulated in feedback manner by the changes in state.

The attainment of a complex helical conformation necessitates a post-translational change in primary structure accomplished by a specific enzyme, prolyl hydroxylase, which requires its substrate to be in random form; further hydroxylation is inhibited by the consequent, spontaneously developing helix. Secretion of the molecule requires the triple helical condition, thus hydroxylation of proline is essential for this cellular process as well as for molecular stability. Normal organization of the molecules into a cross-striated fibril in the intercellular space must await the specific enzymatic removal of an amino terminal peptide appendage essential, earlier, for aligning the three polypeptide chains at the time of their synthesis. The major functional property of the newly formed fibril, its tensile strength, is now imparted by another specific enzyme which modifies a single (or very few) strategically located lysine or hydroxylysine residue(s), producing reactive precursors of covalent crosslinks. The latter then form spontaneously between molecules only when they are arrayed in the proper steric relationship with each other. The functions of post-translational hydroxylation and glycosylation of lysine are still not fully understood, but may, at least in part, be related to cross-linking and perhaps to the calcification mechanism.

The increasing list of collagen types, each a different gene product, the accumulating evidence for orderly transitions from one to another during the course of embryonic development, and their differential assignment to different tissues open new vistas in approaching the relationship between primary structure and physiologic function.

Insoluble fibrils, once formed, may be destined to last the lifetime of the animal, or they may be rapidly removed to make way for a different form of scaffolding required for further growth or changing function. Collagenase, the specific enzyme needed for initiating the dismantling process, preferentially functions on intact triple helical molecules, and its localized subtle attack within the molecule prepares its substrate for further demolition by other, possibly less specific, enzymes. It is quite likely that the animal collagenases are regulated through a complex activating mechanism and perhaps their action is modulated by serum or tissue inhibitors. The manner in which degradation is synchronized with collagen biosynthesis and extracellular deposition should shed important light on the morphogenetic process.

Interference at any stage in this chain of events can result in malformation or malfunction. In those few genetic diseases of collagen about which we know a little, the last step of the pathogenetic chain seems to be interference with cross-linking, although arrived at via different routes. No doubt there are other final common pathways to collagen abnormalities which significantly affect the form and function of the organism.

VIII. WHERE TO FROM HERE?

What goes into making a nose? What mechanisms are at work in the development in culture of a femur from a blob of "unorganized" embryonic tissue?

Ultimately we need to know the pathways whereby genes manipulate morphogenesis through a continuous chain of command progressing through the various levels of organization from cell, to tissue, to organ, to animal. Analysis of the regulation of transcription and translation moves at a rapid pace, but there are few clues presently available to indicate the organizing factors functioning from the cell surface outward. Intracellular control mechanisms switch on and off the various specific biosynthetic processes for structural elements and enzymes, determining when, where, and how they will be deposited, ordered, or dismantled. But how do different cell types coordinate their activities so that, for example, the femur becomes clearly differentiated morphologically from the tibia.

From an experimental point of view, one may reduce the general problem to a predictable series of operational questions. How do the cells communicate with each other over long distances, determining when they will move, where they will move to, and what they will do when they get there? Are all cells in a developing structure in contact with each other via continuous threads of cytoplasm? Are there highly localized, permissive chemical gradients between groups of cells which specifically influence their behavior? Are there specific cell "pheromones" which delineate pathways of migration? Are there specific groups of extracellular macromolecules, such as the various glycosaminoglycans, involved in determining aspects of cell behavior? Specifically, do the various types of extracellular macromolecules and their organizational pattern influence the behavior of nonmesenchymal cell types? There are beginning indications that glycosaminoglycans and collagens may play active and permissive roles in early morphogenesis of embryonic organ anlage, particularly influencing the organization of epithelia. What are the biochemical mechanisms involved in these interactions?

Does the matrix play a role in regulating growth? Does the production of matrix by both epithelial and mesenchymal cells function, under certain circumstances, as a feedback inhibition control in slowing cell proliferation and perhaps blocking cell communication at a time when it should be cut off? Do such factors play a role in determining organ size and contour? Do basement membranes function as mechanical or selective diffusion barriers, devised in part for such purposes?

What are the factors regulating the distribution and organization of collagen fibrils within a tissue, which can result in the remarkable plywood-like order of collagen fibrils of the cornea, or in the continuous parallel arrays of fibrils in tendon, or in the more random structure of mammalian dermis? These different patterns determine important properties such as tensile strength, elasticity, transparency, and gross morphology. Directly related to this type of organization is the question of regulation of individual fibril size. Since the type of fibrillar organization and the uniformity of fibrillar size frequently extend over large areas, encompassing the domains of many cells, the need for precise intercellular coordination of collagen synthesis, and secretion and regulation of fibrogenesis is apparent. This intercellular control probably involves synchronously pulsed processes to account for morphologic continuities and discontinuities.

Nearly all of our efforts are, at present, at the molecular and cellular levels, where, in the light of present knowledge and techniques, it is easier to obtain answers. The going gets more difficult as we approach the more complex hierarchies of tissue organization; however, this is where the future action lies and where new ideas are badly needed.

With continued effective commitments to fundamental basic research and training by governmental and private agencies the answers to these questions may come sooner than any of us would care to predict.

ACKNOWLEDGMENTS

This lecture was given with warm memories of three good friends who contributed greatly to this subject and to me, the late Professors William T. Astbury, Karl H. Gustavson, and Paul Klemperer. I particularly wish to acknowledge my debt to and affection for the late Dr. Walter Bauer, who, as Chief of the Medical Services at the Massachusetts General Hospital, year in and year out supported basic research with deeds. I owe more than I can acknowledge to my colleagues and also to the granting agencies, principally the National Institutes of Health, The American Heart Association, the National Foundation—March of Dimes, and Hoffmann-La Roche, Inc., for providing long-term research support. This is publication No. 626 of the Robert W. Lovett Memorial Group for the Study of Diseases Causing Deformities.

REFERENCES

Abe, S., and Nagai, Y. (1972). *Biochim. Biophys. Acta* **278**, 125.

Abramson, M., and Gross, J. (1971). *Ann. Otol. Rhinol. Laryngol.* **80**, 177.

Aguilar, J. H., Jacobs, H. G., Butler, W. T., and Cunningham, L. W. (1973). *J. Biol. Chem.* **248**, 5106.

Alescio, T. (1973). *J. Embryol. Exp. Morphol.* **29**, 439.

Bailey, A. J., and Lapiere, C. M. (1973). *Eur. J. Biochem.* **34**, 91.
Bailey, A. J., and Peach, C. M. (1968). *Biochem. Biophys. Res. Commun.* **33**, 812.
Bailey, A. J., and Robins, S. P. (1972). *FEBS Lett.* **21**, 330.
Batisell, G. A. (1920/21). *Ann. J. Anat.* **28**, 447.
Baitsell, G. A. (1925). *Quart. J. Microsc. Sci.* **69**, 571.
Balian, G., Click, E. M., and Bornstein, P. (1971). *Biochemistry* **10**, 4470.
Balian, G., Click, E. M., Hermodson, M. A., and Bornstein, P. (1972). *Biochemistry* **11**, 3798.
Banfield, W., Lee, C. R., and Lee, C. F. (1973). *Arch. Pathol.* **95**, 262.
Bear, R. S. (1942). *J. Amer. Chem. Soc.* **64**, 727.
Bear, R. S. (1944). *J. Amer. Chem. Soc.* **66**, 1297.
Bear, R. S. (1952). *Advan. Protein Chem.* **7**, 69.
Bellamy, G., and Bornstein, P. (1971). *Proc. Nat. Acad. Sci. U.S.* **68**, 1138.
Benveniste, K., Wilczek, J., and Stern, R. (1973). *Nature (London)* **246**, 303.
Bensusan, H. B. (1972). *Biochim. Biophys. Acta* **285**, 447.
Berg, R. A., and Prockop, D. J. (1973a). *Biochemistry* **12**, 3395.
Berg, R. A., and Prockop, D. J. (1973b). *Biochem. Biophys. Res. Commun.* **52**, 115.
Berman, M. B., Barber, J. C., Talamo, R. C., and Langley, C. E. (1973a). *Invest. Ophthalmol.* **12**, 759.
Berman, M. B., Kerza-Kwiatecki, A. P., and Davison, P. F. (1973b). *Exp. Eye Res.* **15**, 367.
Bernfield, M. R., and Wessells, N. R. (1970). *Develop. Biol.* Suppl. 4, 195.
Blumenfeld, O. O., and Gallop, P. M. (1966). *Proc. Nat. Acad. Sci.* **56**, 1260.
Boedtker, H., and Doty, P. (1956). *J. Amer. Chem. Soc.* **78**, 4267.
Bora, F. W., Jr., Lane, J. M., and Prockop, D. J. (1972). *J. Bone Joint Surg. Amer. Vol.* **54**, 1501.
Bornstein, P. (1967). *Biochemistry* **6**, 3082.
Bornstein, P., and Piez, K. A. (1965). *Science* **148**, 1353.
Bornstein, P., and Piez, K. A. (1966). *Biochemistry* **5**, 340.
Bornstein, P., Kang, A. H., and Piez, K. A. (1966). *Proc. Nat. Acad. Sci. U.S.* **55**, 417.
Bornstein, P., Ehrlich, P., and Wyke, A. W. (1972). *Science* **175**, 544.
Bosmann, H. B., and Eyler, E. H. (1968). *Biochem. Biophys. Res. Commun.* **30**, 89.
Bruns, R. R., and Gross, J. (1973). *Biochemistry* **12**, 808.
Bruns, R. R., and Gross, J. (1974). *Biopolymers,* **13**, 931.
Bruns, R. R., Trelstad, R. L., and Gross, J. (1973). *Science* **181**, 269.
Brown, S. I., and Weller, C. A. (1970). *Arch. Ophthalmol.* **83**, 352.
Burgeson, R. E., Wyke, A. W., and Fessler, A. (1972). *Biochem. Biophys. Res. Commun.* **48**, 892.
Butler, E. J., and Puckett, W. O. (1940). *J. Exp. Zool.* **84**, 223.
Butler, W. T. (1970). *Biochemistry* **9**, 40.
Butler, W. T., and Ponds, S. L. (1971). *Biochemistry* **10**, 2076.

Butler, W. T., Piez, K. A., and Bornstein, P. (1967). *Biochemistry* 6, 3771.

Cardinale, G. J., and Udenfriend, S. (1974). *Advan. Enzymol.,* in press.

Chalkley, D. T. (1959). *In* "Regeneration of Vertebrates" (C. S. Thornton, ed.), p. 34. Univ. of Chicago Press, Chicago, Illinois.

Chapman, J. A. (1974). *Connect. Tissue Res.,* in press.

Chung, E., and Miller, E. J. (1974). *Science* 183, 1200.

Chesney, C., McI., Harper, E., and Colman, R. W. (1974). *J. Clin. Invest.,* 53, 1647.

Dasler, W. (1954). *Science* 120, 307.

Davison, P. F., and Berman, M. (1973). *Connect. Tissue Res.* 2, 57.

Dehm, P., Jimenez, S. A., Olsen, D. R., and Prockop, D. J. (1972). *Proc. Nat. Acad. Sci. U.S.* 69, 60.

Deshmukh, R., and Nimni, M. E. (1969). *J. Biol. Chem.* 244, 1787.

Deshmukh, R., and Nimni, M. E. (1972). *Biochem. Biophys, Res. Commun.* 46, 175.

Diegelman, R. F., Bernstein, L., and Peterkofsky, B. (1973). *J. Biol. Chem.* 248, 6514.

Dintzis, H. M. (1961). *Proc. Nat. Acad. Sci. U.S.* 47, 247.

Dodson, J. W., and Hay, E. D. (1971). *Exp. Cell Res.* 65, 215.

Dohlman, C. H., and Slansky, H. H. (1972). *In* "Contemporary Ophthalmology" (J. G. Bellows, ed.), p. 57. Williams & Wilkins, Baltimore, Maryland.

Donoff, R. B., McLennan, J., and Grillo, H. C. (1971). *Biochim. Biophys. Acta* 266, 639.

Doyle, B. B., Traub, W., Lorenzi, G. P., and Blout, E. R. (1971). *Biochemistry* 10, 3052.

Dresden, M. H., and Gross, J. (1970). *Develop. Biol.* 22, 129.

Dresden, M. H., Heilman, S. A., and Schmidt, J. D. (1972). *Cancer Res.* 32, 993.

Dupuy, H. P., and Lee, J. G. (1954). *J. Amer. Pharm. Ass.* 43, 61.

Eisen, A. Z. (1969). *J. Invest. Dermatol.* 52, 442.

Eisen, A. Z., and Gross, J. (1965). *Develop. Biol.* 12, 408.

Eisen, A. Z., Bloch, K. J., and Sakai, T. (1970). *J. Lab. Clin. Invest.* 75, 258.

Eisen, A. Z., Bauer, E. A., and Jeffrey, J. J. (1971). *Proc. Nat. Acad. Sci. U.S.* 68, 248.

Eisen, A. Z., Henderson, K. O., Jeffrey, J. J., and Bradshaw, R. A. (1973). *Biochemistry* 12, 1814.

Evanson, J. M. (1970). *In* "Chemistry and Molecular Biology of the Matrix" (E. A. Balazs, ed.), Vol. 3, p. 1637. Academic Press, New York.

Eyre, D. R., and Glimcher, M. J., (1972). *Proc. Nat. Acad. Sci. U.S.* 69, 2594.

Eyre, D. R., and Glimcher, M. J. (1973a). *Biochem. J.* 135, 393.

Eyre, D. R., and Glimcher, M. J. (1973b). *Biochem. Biophys. Res. Commun.* 52, 663.

Eyre, D. R., and Glimcher, M. J. (1973c). *Proc. Soc. Exp. Biol. Med.* 144, 400.

424   JEROME GROSS

Fernandez-Madrid, F. (1967). *J. Cell Biol.* **33**, 27.

Fessler, L. I., Burgeson, R. E., Morris, N. P., and Fessler, J. H. (1973). *Proc. Nat. Acad. Sci. U.S.* **70**, 2993.

Fietzek, P. P., Rexrodt, F. W., Wendt, P., Stark, M., and Kuhn, K. (1972a). *Eur. J. Biochem.* **30**, 163.

Fietzek, P. P., Wendt, P., Kell, I., and Kuhn, K. (1972b). *FEBS Lett.* **26**, 74.

Fietzek, P. P., Rexrodt, F. W., Hopper, K., and Kuhn, K. (1973). *Eur. J. Biochem.* **38**, 396.

Franzblau, C., Sinex, F. M., Faris, B., and Lampidis, R. (1965). *Biochem. Biophys. Res. Commun.* **21**, 575.

Franzblau, C., Kang, A. H., and Faris, B. (1970). *Biochem. Biophys. Res. Commun.* **40**, 437.

Fujiwara, K., Sakai, T., Oda, T., and Igarashi, S. (1973). *Biochem. Biophys. Res. Commun.* **54**, 531.

Gallop, P. M., Blumenfeld, O. O., and Seifter, S. (1972). *Annu. Rev. Biochem.* **41**, 617.

Geiger, B. J., Steenbock, J., and Parsons, H. T. (1933). *J. Nutr.* **6**, 427.

Giersberg, H. (1921). *Biol. Zentrbl.* **41**, 145.

Goldberg, B. (1974). *Proc. Nat. Acad. Sci. U.S.*, in press.

Goldberg, B., and Green, H. (1967). *J. Mol. Biol.* **26**, 1.

Goldberg, B., and Scherr, C. J. (1973). *Proc. Nat. Acad. Sci. U.S.* **70**, 361.

Goldberg, B., Epstein, E. H., Jr., and Scherr, C. J. (1972). *Proc. Nat. Acad. Sci. U.S.* **69**, 3665.

Grant, M. E., and Prockop, D. J. (1972). *New Engl. J. Med.* **286**, 194.

Grant, M. E., Kefalides, N. A., and Prockop, D. J. (1972). *J. Biol. Chem.* **247**, 3545.

Gribble, T. J., Comstock, J. P., and Udenfriend, S. (1969). *Arch. Biochem. Biophys.* **129**, 308.

Grillo, H. C., and Gross, J. (1967). *Develop. Biol.* **15**, 300.

Grillo, H. C., Lapiere, C. M., Dresden, M. H., and Gross, J. (1968). *Develop. Biol.* **17**, 571.

Gross, E., and Witkop, B. (1961). *J. Amer. Chem. Soc.* **83**, 510.

Gross, J. (1953). *Ann. N.Y. Acad. Sci.* **56**, 674.

Gross, J. (1956). *J. Biophys. Biochem. Cytol.* **2**, 261.

Gross, J. (1958). *J. Exp. Med.* **108**, 215.

Gross, J. (1961). *Sci. Amer.* **204**, 120.

Gross, J. (1963a). *Biochim. Biophys. Acta* **71**, 249.

Gross, J. (1963b). In "Comparative Biochemistry, A Comprehensive Treatise" (M. Florkin and H. S. Mason, eds.), p. 307. Academic Press, New York.

Gross, J. (1964a). *Medicine* **43**, 291.

Gross, J. (1964b). *Science* **143**, 960.

Gross, J., and Lapiere, C. M. (1962). *Proc. Nat. Acad. Sci. U.S.* **48**, 1014.

Gross, J., and Nagai, Y. (1965). *Proc. Nat. Acad. Sci. U.S.* **54**, 1197.

Gross, J., Highberger, J. H., and Schmitt, F. O. (1954). *Proc. Nat. Acad. Sci. U.S.* **40**, 697.

Gross, J., Highberger, J. H., and Schmitt, F. O. (1955). *Proc. Nat. Acad. Sci. U.S.* **41**, 1.

Gross, J., Hooper, E., Harris, Jr., E. D., McCroskery, P. A., Highberger, J. H., Corbett, C. M., and Kang, A. H., in preparation.

Gustavson, K. H. (1954). *Acta. Chem. Scand.* **8**, 1298.

Gustavson, K. H. (1957). *In* "Connective Tissue; a Symposium" (R. E. Tunbridge, ed.), p. 185. Blackwell, Oxford.

Harkness, R. D., Marko, A. N., Muir, H. M., and Neuberger, A. (1954). *Biochem. J.* **56**, 558.

Harper, E., and Gross, J. (1970). *Biochim. Biophys. Acta* **198**, 286.

Harper, E., and Gross, J. (1972). *Biochem. Biophys. Res. Commun.* **48**, 1147.

Harper, E., and Gross, J. (1973). *Fed. Proc., Fed. Amer. Soc. Exp. Biol.* **32**, 614 (Abstract).

Harper, E., Bloch, K. J., and Gross, J. (1970). *Progr. Amer. Rheum. Ass.* **28**, 33 (Abstract).

Harper, E., Bloch, K. J., and Gross, J. (1971). *Biochemistry* **10**, 3035.

Harris, E. D., Jr. (1972) *J. Clin. Invest.* **51**, 2973.

Harris, E. D., and Farrell, M. E. (1972). *Biochim. Biophys. Acta* **278**, 133.

Harris, E. D., Jr., and Krane, S. M. (1971). *Arthritis Rheum.* **14**, 669.

Harris, E. D., Jr., and Krane, S. M. (1972). *Biochim. Biophys. Acta* **258**, 566.

Harris, E. D., Jr., and Krane, S. M. (1974). *N. Engl. J. Med.*, in press.

Harris, E. D., Jr., and McCroskery, P. A. (1974). *N. Engl. J. Med.* **291**, 1.

Harris, E. D., Jr., DiBona, D. R., and Krane, S. M. (1969). *J. Clin. Invest.* **48**, 2104.

Harris, E. D., Jr., DiBona, E. D., and Krane, S. M. (1970). *Trans. Ass. Amer. Phys.* **83**, 267.

Harris, E. D., Jr., Faulkner, C. S., and Wood, S. (1972 *Biochem. Biophys. Res. Commun.* **48**, 1247.

Harsch, M., Murphy, L., and Rosenbloom, J. (1972). *FEBS Lett.* **26**, 48.

Harwood, R., Grant, M. E., and Jackson, D. S. (1974). *Biochem. Biophys. Res. Commun.*, in press.

Hashimoto, K., Yamanishi, Y., and Dabbous, M. K. (1972). *Cancer Res.* **32**, 2561.

Hashimoto, K., Yamanishi, Y., Maeyens, E., Dabbous, M. K., and Ranzaki, T. (1973). *Cancer Res.* **33**, 2790.

Hauschka, S. D., and Konigsberg, I. R. (1966). *Proc. Nat. Acad. Sci. U.S.* **55**, 119.

Hauschka, S. D., and White, N. K. (1971). *Excerpta Med. Found. Int. Congr. Ser. No.* **240**, 53.

Hay, E. D., and Dodson, J. W. (1973). *J. Cell. Biol.* **57**, 190.

Hay, E. D., and Revel, J. P. (1969). *In* "Monographs in Developmental Biology" (A. Wolski and P. A. Chen, eds.), p. 1. Karger, Basel.

Highberger, J. H., Gross, J., and Schmitt, F. O. (1950). *J. Amer. Chem. Soc.* **72**, 3321.

Highberger, J. H., Gross, J., and Schmitt, F. O. (1951). *Proc. Nat. Acad. Sci. U.S.* **37**, 286.

Hodge, A. J., and Petruska, J. A. (1963). In "Aspects of Protein Structure" (G. N. Ramachandran, ed.), p. 289. Academic Press, New York.

Hodge, A. J., and Schmitt, F. O. (1960). *Proc. Nat. Acad. Sci. U.S.* **46**, 186.

Hook, R. M., Hook, C. W., and Brown, S. I. (1973). *Invest. Ophthalmol.* **12**, 771.

Hulmes, J. S., Miller, A., Darry, D. A. D., Piez, K. A., and Wardhead-Galloway, J. (1973). *J. Mol. Biol.* **79**, 137.

Hurych, J., and Chvapil, M. (1965). *Biochim. Biophys. Acta* **97**, 361.

Huszar, G. (1972). *Nature (London) New Biol.* **240**, 260.

Hutton, J. J., Tappel, A. L., and Udenfriend, S. (1967). *Arch. Biochem. Biophys.* **118**, 231.

Igarashi, S., Kang, A. H., and Gross, J. (1970). *Biochem. Biophys. Res. Commun.* **38**, 697.

Igarashi, S., Trelstad, R. L., and Kang, A. H. (1973). *Biochim. Biophys. Acta* **295**, 514.

Jackson, D. S., and Bentley, T. B. (1960). *J. Biophys. Biochem. Cytol.* **7**, 37.

Jackson, D. S., and Fessler, J. H. (1955). *Nature (London)* **176**, 169.

Jeffrey, J. J., Coffrey, R. J., and Eisen, A. Z. (1971a). *Biochim. Biophys. Acta* **252**, 136.

Jeffrey, J. J., Coffey, R. J., and Eisen, A. Z. (1971b). *Biochim. Biophys. Acta* **252**, 143.

Jeffrey, J. J., and Gross, J. (1970). *Biochemistry* **9**, 268.

Jimenez, S. A., and Rosenbloom, J. (1974). *Arch. Biochem. Biophys.,* in press.

Jimenez, S. A., Harsch, M., and Rosenbloom, J. (1973). *Biochem. Biophys. Res. Commun.* **52**, 106.

Kallman, F., and Grobstein, C. (1965). *Develop. Biol.* **11**, 169.

Kang, A. H., and Gross, J. (1970). *Proc. Nat. Acad. Sci. U.S.* **67**, 1307.

Kang, A. H., and Trelstad, R. L. (1973). *J. Clin. Invest.* **52**, 2571.

Kang, A. H., Nagai, Y., Piez, K. A., and Gross, J. (1966). *Biochemistry* **5**, 509.

Kang, A. H., Bornstein, P., and Piez, K. A. (1967). *Biochemistry* **7**, 788.

Kang, A. H., Farris, B., and Franzblau, C. (1969). *Biochem. Biophys. Res. Commun.* **36**, 345.

Kang, A. H., Faris, B., and Franzblau, C. (1970). *Biochem. Biophys. Res. Commun.* **39**, 175.

Katzman, R., and Kang, A. H. (1972). *J. Biol. Chem.* **247**, 5486.

Kefalides, N. A. (1971a). *Int. Rev. Exp. Pathol.* **10**, 1.

Kefalides, N. A. (1971b). *Biochim. Biophys. Res. Commun.* **45**, 226.

Kefalides, N. A. (1973). *Annu. Rev. Connect. Tissue Res.* **6**, 63.

Kerwar, S. S., Cardinale, G. J., Kohn, L. D., Spears, C. L., and Stassen, F. L. H. (1973). *Proc. Nat. Acad. Sci. U.S.* **70**, 1378.

Kivirikko, K. I., and Prockop, D. J. (1967). *Arch. Biochem. Biophys.* **118**, 611.

Kivirikko, K. I., and Prockop, D. J. (1972). *Biochim. Biophys. Acta* **258**, 366.

Kivirikko, K. I., Shudo, R., Sakakibara, S., and Prockop, D. J. (1972). *Biochemistry* **11**, 122.

Kivirikko, K. I., Ryhanen, L., Anttinen, H., Bornstein, P., and Prockop, D. J. (1973). *Biochemistry* **12**, 4966.

Klemperer, P. (1953). *Harvey Lect.* **49**, p. 100.

Klemperer, P. (1961). *Amer. Rev. Resp. Dis.* **83**, 331.

Klemperer, P., Pollack, H. D., and Baehr, G. (1942). *J. Amer. Med. Ass.* **119**, 331.

Klinge, F. (1933). *Ergeb. Allg. Pathol. Pathol. Anat.* **27**, 1.

Krane, S. M., Pinnell, S. R., and Erbe, R. W. (1972). *Proc. Nat. Acad. Sci. U.S.* **69**, 2899.

Kratky, O., and Sekora, A. (1943). *J. Makromol. Chem.* **1**, 113.

Kruze, D., and Wojtecka, E. (1972). *Biophys. Biochem. Acta* **285**, 436.

Lapiere, C. M., and Gross, J. (1963). In "Mechanisms of Hard Tissue Destruction," Publ. No. 75, Amer. Ass. Advanc. Sci., Washington, D.C., p. 663.

Lapiere, C. M., Lenaers, A., and Kohn, L. D. (1971). *Proc. Nat. Acad. Sci. U.S.* **68**, 3054.

Layman, D. L., and Ross, R. (1973). *Arch. Biochem. Biophys.* **157**, 451.

Layman, D. L., McGoodwin, E. B., and Martin, G. R. (1971). *Proc. Nat. Acad. Sci. U.S.* **68**, 454.

Layman, D. L., Narayanian, A. S., and Martin, G. R. (1972). *Arch. Biochem. Biophys.* **149**, 97.

Lazarides, E. L., and Lukens, L. N. (1971). *Nature (London) New Biol.* **232**, 37.

Lazarides, E. L., Lukens, L. N., and Infante, A. A. (1971). *J. Mol. Biol.* **58**, 831.

Lazarus, G. S., Daniels, J. R., Brown, R. S., Bladen, H. A., and Fullmer, H. M. (1968). *J. Clin. Invest.* **47**, 2622.

Lazarus, G. S., Daniels, J. R., Lian, J., and Burleigh, M. C. (1972). *Amer. J. Pathol.* **68**, 565.

Lazlo, F., and Olsen, B. R. (1969). *Eur. J. Biochem.* **11**, 140.

Lenaers, A., Ansay, M., Nusgens, D. V., and Lapiere, C. M. (1971). *Eur. J. Biochem.* **23**, 533.

Levene, C. I. (1961). *J. Exp. Med.* **114**, 295.

Levene, C. I. (1973). In "Molecular Pathology of Connective Tissues" (R. Perez-Tamayo and M. Rojkind, eds.), p. 175. Dekker, New York.

Levene, C. I., and Gross, J. (1959). *J. Exp. Med.* **110**, 771.

Levene, C. I., Shoshan, S., and Bates, C. J. (1972). *Biochim. Biophys. Acta* **257**, 384.

Levitt, D., and Dorfman, A. (1974). *Curr. Top. Develop. Biol.* in press.

Lichtenstein, J. R., Martin, G. R., Kohn, L. D., Byers, P. H., and McKusick, V. A. (1973). *Science* **182**, 298.

Leibovich, S. J., and Weiss, J. B. (1971). *Biochim. Biophys. Acta* **251**, 109.

Linsenmayer, T. F., Trelstad, R. L., Toole, B. P., and Gross, J. (1973a). *Biochem. Biophys. Res. Commun.* **52**, 870.

Linsenmayer, T. F., Trelstad, R. L., and Gross, J. (1973b). *Biochem. Biophys. Res. Commun.* **53**, 39.

Linsenmayer, T. F., Toole, B. P., and Trelstad, R. L. (1973c). *Develop. Biol.* **35**, 232.

McCroskery, P. A., Wood, S., Jr., and Harris, E. D., Jr. (1973). *Science* **182**, 70.

McCully, K. S. (1972). *Amer. J. Pathol.* **66**, 83.

McGee, J. O., and Udenfriend, S. (1972). *Biochem. Biophys. Res. Commun.* **46**, 1646.

McGee, J. O., Largness, U., and Udenfriend, S. (1971). *Proc. Nat. Acad. Sci. U.S.* **68**, 1585.

McKay, G. F., Lalich, J. J., Schilling, E. D., and Strong, F. M. (1954). *Arch. Biochem. Biophys.* **52**, 313.

Manner, G., Kretsinger, R. H., Gould, B. S., and Rich, A. (1967). *Biochim. Biophys. Acta* **134**, 411.

Mechanic, G. (1972). *Biochem. Biophys. Res. Commun.* **47**, 267.

Mechanic, G., and Tanzer, M. L. (1970). *Biochem. Biophys. Res. Commun.* **41**, 1597.

Mechanic, G., Gallop, P. M., and Tanzer, M. L. (1971). *Biochem. Biophys. Res. Commun.* **45**, 644.

Miller, E. J. (1971). *Biochemistry* **10**, 1652.

Miller, E. J. (1972). *Biochemistry* **11**, 4903.

Miller, E. J., and Lunde, L. G. (1973). *Biochemistry* **12**, 3153.

Miller, E. J., and Matukas, V. J. (1969). *Proc. Nat. Acad. Sci. U.S.* **64**, 1264.

Miller, E. J., Woodall, D. L., and Vail, M. S. (1973). *J. Biol. Chem.* **24**, 1666.

Miller, R. L. (1971). *Arch. Biochem. Biophys.* **147**, 339.

Miller, R. L., and Udenfriend, S. (1970). *Arch. Biochem. Biophys.* **139**, 104.

Milsom, D. W., Stevens, F. S., Hunter, J. A., Thomas, H., and Jackson, D. S. (1972). *Connect. Tissue Res.* **1**, 251.

Monson, J. M., and Bornstein, P. (1973). *Proc. Nat. Acad. Sci.* **70**, 3521.

Murphy, L., and Rosenbloom, J. (1973). *Biochem. J.* **135**, 249.

Nagai, Y. (1973). *Mol. Cell. Biochem.* **1**, 137.

Nagai, Y., and Hori, H. (1972). *J. Biochem.* **72**, 1147.

Nagai, Y., Lapiere, C. M., and Gross, J. (1966). *Biochemistry* **5**, 3123.

Newsome, D. A., and Kenyon, K. R. (1973). *Develop. Biol.* **32**, 387.

Nold, J. (1973). Ph.D. Thesis Dissertation. Harvard University.

Nordwig, A., and Pfab, F. K. (1968). *Biochim. Biophys. Acta* **154**, 603.

Nordwig, A., Nowack, H., and Hieber-Rogall, F. (1973). *J. Mol. Evol.* **2**, 175.

Ohlsson, K., and Olsson, J. (1973). *Eur. J. Biochem.* **36**, 473.

Olsen, B. R., Berg, R. A., Kishida, Y., and Prockop, D. J. (1973). *Science* **182**, 825.

Orekhovitch, V. N., Tustanowski, A. A., Orekhovitch, K. D., and Plotnikova, N. E. (1948). *Biokhimiya* **13**, 55.

Orloff, S. D., and Gross, J. (1963). *J. Exp. Med.* **117**, 1009.

Oronsky, A. L., Perper, R. J., and Schroder, H. C. (1973). *Nature (London)* **246**, 417.

Perez-Tamayo, R. (1970). *Lab. Invest.* **22**, 137; **22**, 142.

Perez-Tamayo, R. (1973). In "Molecular Pathology of Connective Tissues" (R. Perez-Tamayo, and M. Rojkind, eds.), p. 323. Dekker, New York.

Perez-Tamayo, R., and Rojkind, M., eds. (1973). In "Molecular Pathology of Connective Tissues," p. 175. Dekker, New York.

Piez, K. A. (1965). *Biochemistry* **4**, 2590.

Piez, K. A. (1969). In "Aging of Connective and Skeletal Tissue," p. 33. Thule International Symposium, Nordiska Bokhandelns Forlag, Stockholm.

Piez, K. A., Lewis, M. S., Martin, G. R., and Gross, J. (1961). *Biochim. Biophys. Acta* **53**, 596.

Piez, K. A., Eigner, E. A., and Lewis, M. S. (1963). *Biochemistry* **2**, 58.

Piez, K. A., Bladen, A. J., Lane, J. M., Miller, E. J., Bornstein, P., Butler, W. T., and Kang, A. H. (1968). *Brookhaven Symp. Biol.* **21**, 345.

Pinnell, S. R., and Martin, G. R. (1968). *Proc. Nat. Acad. Sci. U.S.* **61**, 708.

Pinnell, S. R., Fox, R., and Krane, S. M. (1971). *Biochim. Biophys. Acta* **229**, 119.

Pinnell, S. R., Krane, S. M., Kenzora, J. E., and Glimcher, M. J. (1972). *N. Engl. J. Med.* **286**, 1013.

Ponseti, I. V., and Baird, W. A. (1952). *Amer. J. Pathol.* **28**, 1059.

Ponseti, I. V., and Shephard, R. S. (1954). *J. Bone Joint Surg. Amer. Vol.* **36**, 1031.

Popenoe, E. H., and Aronson, R. B. (1972). *Biochim. Biophys. Acta* **258**, 380.

Prockop, D. J., and Juva, K. (1965). *Proc. Nat. Acad. Sci. U.S.* **53**, 61.

Ramachandran, G. N., and Kartha, G. (1954). *Nature (London)* **174**, 269.

Ramachandran, G. N., and Kartha, G. (1956). *Nature (London)* **176**, 593; **177**, 710.

Rauterberg, J., and Kühn, K. (1969). *FEBS Lett.* **1**, 230.

Rauterberg, J., and Kühn, K. (1971). *Eur. J. Biochem.* **19**, 398.

Rauterberg, J., Fietzig, P. P., Rexrodt, F. W., Becker, U., Stark, M., and Kühn, K. (1972). *FEBS Lett.* **21**, 75.

Rhoads, R. E., and Udenfriend, S. (1969). *Arch. Biochem. Biophys.* **133**, 108.

Rhoads, R. E., Udenfriend, S., and Bornstein, P. (1971). *J. Biol. Chem.* **246**, 4138.

Rich, A., and Crick, F. H. C. (1955). *Nature (London)* **176**, 915.

Riley, W. B., and Peacock, E. E., Jr. (1967). *Proc. Soc. Exp. Biol. Med.* **124**, 207.

Robertson, P. B., and Miller, E. J. (1972). *Biochim. Biophys. Acta* **289**, 247.

Robins, S. P., and Bailey, A. J. (1972). *Biochem. Biophys. Res. Commun.* **48**, 76.

Robins, S. P., and Bailey, A. J. (1973a). *Biochem. J.* **135**, 657.

Robins, S. P., and Bailey, A. J. (1973b). *FEBS Lett.* **33**, 167.

Robins, S. P., Shimokomaki, M., and Bailey, A. J. (1973). *Biochem. J.* **131**, 771.

Rojkind, M., and Juarez, H. (1966). *Biochem. Biophys. Res. Commun.* **25**, 481.

Rojkind, M., Blumenfeld, O. O., and Gallop, P. M. (1966). *J. Biol. Chem.* **241**, 1530.

Rosenbloom, J., and Prockop, D. J. (1971). *J. Biol. Chem.* **246**, 1549.

Ryan, J. N., and Woessner, J. F., Jr. (1971). *Biochem. Biophys. Res. Commun.* **44**, 144.

Sakai, T., and Gross, J. (1967). *Biochemistry* **6**, 518.

Sakamoto, S., Goldhaber, P., and Glimcher, M. J. (1972). *Calcif. Tissue Res.* **10**, 280.

Sakamoto, S., Goldhaber, P., and Glimcher, M. J. (1973a). *Calcif. Tissue Res.* **12**, 247.

Sakamoto, S., Sakamoto, M., Goldhaber, P., and Glimcher, M. J. (1973b). *Biochem. Biophys. Res. Commun.* **53**, 1102.

Schilling, E. D., and Strong, F. M. (1954). *J. Amer. Chem. Soc.* **76**, 2848.

Schilling, E. D., and Strong, F. M. (1955). *J. Amer. Chem. Soc.* **77**, 2845.

Schiltz, J. R., Mayne, R., and Holtzer, H. (1973). *Differentiation* **1**, 97.

Schmitt, F. O. (1945). *Harvey Lect.* **40**, 249.

Schmitt, F. O. (1960). *Bull. N.Y. Acad. Med.* **36**, 725.

Schmitt, F. O., Hall, C. E., Jakus, M. A. (1942). *J. Cell. Comp. Physiol.* **20**, 11.

Schmitt, F. O., Gross, J., and Highberger, J. H. (1953). *Proc. Nat. Acad. Sci. U.S.* **39**, 459.

Schmitt, F. O., Gross, J., and Highberger, J. H. (1955). *Exp. Cell Res.,* Suppl. 3, 326.

Selye, H. (1957). *Rev. Can. Biol.* **16**, 1.

Shoshan, S., Finkelstein, S., Kushner, W., and Weinseb, M. (1972). *J. Connect. Tissue Res.* **1**, 47.

Siegel, R. C., and Martin, G. R. (1970). *J. Biol. Chem.* **245**, 1653.

Slansky, H. H., Berman, M. B., Dohlman, C. H., and Rose, J. (1970). *Ann. Ophthalnol.* **1**, 357.

Slavkin, H. C. (1972). "The Comparative Molecular Biology of Extracellular Matrices," Academic Press, New York.

Smiley, J. D., Yeager, H., and Ziff, M. (1962). *J. Exp. Med.* **116**, 45.

Smith, B. D., Byers, P. H., and Martin, G. R. (1972). *Proc. Nat. Acad. Sci. U.S.* **69**, 3260.

Smith, J. W. (1965). *Nature (London)* **205**, 356.

Smith, J. W. (1968). *Nature (London)* **219**, 157.

Speakman, P. T. (1971). *Nature (London)* **229**, 241.

Spiro, R. G. (1969). *J. Biol. Chem.* **244**, 602.

Spiro, R. G. (1972). *N. Eng. J. Med.* **288**, 1337.

Spiro, R. G., and Spiro, M. J. (1971). *J. Biol. Chem.* **246**, 4919.

Stark, M., Lenaers, A., Lapiere, C. M., and Kuhn, K. (1971). *FEBS Lett.* **18**, 225.

Stark, M., Miller, E. J., and Kuhn, K. (1972). *Eur. J. Biochem.* **27**, 192.

Stetten, M. R. (1949). *J. Biol. Chem.* **181**, 31.

Stetten, M. R., and Schoenheimer, O. R. (1944). *J. Biol. Chem.* **153**, 113.

Strawich, E., and Nimni, M. E. (1971). *Biochemistry* **10**, 3905.

Sugar, A., and Waltman, S. R. (1973). *Invest. Ophthalmol.* **12**, 779.

Tanzer, M. L. (1965). *Int. Rev. Connect. Tissue Res.* **3**, 91.

Tanzer, M. L. (1967). *Biochim. Biophys. Acta* **133**, 584.

Tanzer, M. L. (1968). *J. Biol. Chem.* **243**, 4045.

Tanzer, M. L. (1973). *Science* **180**, 561.

Tanzer, M. L., and Gross, J. (1964). *J. Exp. Med.* **119**, 275.

Tanzer, M. L., and Mechanic, G. (1970). *Biochem. Biophys. Res. Commun.* **39**, 183.

Tanzer, M. L., Monroe, E. D., and Gross, J. (1966). *Biochemistry* **5**, 1919.

Tanzer, M. L., Housley, T., Berube, L., Fairweather, R., Franzblau, C., and Gallop, P. M. (1973). *J. Biol. Chem.* **248**, 393.

Tokoro, Y., Eisen, A. Z., and Jeffrey, J. J. (1972). *Biochim. Biophys. Acta* **258**, 289.

Toole, B. P., Kang, A. H., Trelstad, R. L., and Gross, J. (1972). *Biochem. J.* **127**, 715.

Traub, W., and Piez, K. A. (1971). *Advan. Protein Chem.* **25**, 243.

Trelstad, R. L. (1974). *Biochem. Biophys. Res. Commun.*, **57**, 717.

Trelstad, R. L., and Kang, A. H. (1974). *Exp. Eye Res.*, **18**, 395.

Trelstad, R. L., Kang, A. H., Igarashi, S., and Gross, J. (1970). *Biochemistry* **9**, 1.

Trelstad, R. L., Kang, A. H., Toole, B. P., and Gross, J. (1972). *J. Biol. Chem.* **247**, 6469.

Trelstad, R. L., Kang, A. H., Cohen, A. M., and Hay, E. D. (1973). *Science* **179**, 295.

Trelstad, R. L., Hayashi, K., and Toole, B. P. (1974). *J. Cell Biol.*, in press.

Uitto, J., Dehm, P., and Prockcop, D. J. (1972). *Biochim. Biophys. Acta* **278**, 601.

Urivetzeky, M., Frei, J. M., and Meilmam, E. (1966). *Arch. Biochem. Biophys.* **117**, 224.

Usuku, G., and Gross, J. (1965). *Develop. Biol.* **11**, 352.

Vaes, G. (1972a). *FEBS Lett.* **28,** 198.

Vaes, G. (1972b). *Biochem. J.* **126,** 275.

van den Hoof, A., Levene, C. I., and Gross, J. (1959). *J. Exp. Med.* **110,** 1017.

Veis, A., Anesey, J., and Mussell, S. (1967). *Nature (London)* **215,** 931.

von der Mark, K., and Bornstein, P. (1973). *J. Biochem.* **248,** 285.

von Ebner, V. (1897). *Z. Wiss. Zool.* **62,** 469.

Vuust, J., and Piez, K. A. (1970). *J. Biol. Chem.* **245,** 6201.

Vuust, J., and Piez, K. A. (1972). *J. Biol. Chem.* **247,** 856.

Wahl, L. M., Wahl, S. M., Martin, G. R., and Mergenhagen, S. E. (1974a). *J. Reticuloendothel. Soc.,* in press.

Wahl, L. M., Wahl, S. M., Martin, G. R., and Mergenhagen, S. E. (1974b). *Fed. Proc., Fed. Amer. Soc. Exp. Biol.* **33,** 618.

Walker, D. G., Lapiere, C. M., and Gross, J. (1964). *Biochem. Biophys. Res. Commun.* **15,** 397.

Wendt, P., von der Mark, K., Rexrodt, F. W., and Kuhn, K. (1972). *Eur. J. Biochem.* **30,** 169.

Werb, J., and Burleigh, M. C. (1974). *Biochem. J.* **137,** 373.

Wolpers, C. (1943). *Klin. Wochenschr.* **22,** 624.

Wooley, D. E., Glanville, R. W., and Crossley, M. J. (1972). *Scand. J. Clin. Lab. Invest.* **29,** Suppl. 123, 37.

Yamanishi, Y., Maeyans, E., Dabbous, M., Ohyama, H., and Hashimoto, K. (1973). *Cancer Res.* **33,** 2507.

FORMER OFFICERS OF THE HARVEY SOCIETY

1905–1906

President: GRAHAM LUSK
Vice-President: SIMON FLEXNER
Treasurer: FREDERIC S. LEE
Secretary: GEORGE B. WALLACE

Council:
C. A. HERTER
S. J. MELTZER
EDWARD K. DUNHAM

1906–1907

President: GRAHAM LUSK
Vice-President: SIMON FLEXNER
Treasurer: FREDERIC S. LEE
Secretary: GEORGE B. WALLACE

Council:
C. A. HERTER
S. J. MELTZER
JAMES EWING

1907–1908

President: GRAHAM LUSK
Vice-President: JAMES EWING
Treasurer: EDWARD K. DUNHAM
Secretary: GEORGE B. WALLACE

Council:
SIMON FLEXNER
THEO. C. JANEWAY
PHILIP H. HISS, JR.

1908–1909

President: JAMES EWING
Vice-President: SIMON FLEXNER
Treasurer: EDWARD K. DUNHAM
Secretary: FRANCIS C. WOOD

Council:
GRAHAM LUSK
S. J. MELTZER
ADOLPH MEYER

1909–1910*

President: JAMES EWING
Vice-President: THEO. C. JANEWAY
Treasurer: EDWARD K. DUNHAM
Secretary: FRANCIS C. WOOD

Council:
GRAHAM LUSK
S. J. MELTZER
W. J. GIES

1910–1911

President: SIMON FLEXNER
Vice-President: JOHN HOWLAND
Treasurer: EDWARD K. DUNHAM
Secretary: HAVEN EMERSON

Council:
GRAHAM LUSK
S. J. MELTZER
JAMES EWING

---

* At the Annual Meeting of May 18, 1909, these officers were elected. In publishing the 1909–1910 volume their names were omitted, possibly because in that volume the custom of publishing the names of the incumbents of the current year was changed to publishing the names of the officers selected for the ensuing year.

1911–1912

President: S. J. MELTZER
Vice-President: FREDERIC S. LEE
Treasurer: EDWARD K. DUNHAM
Secretary: HAVEN EMERSON

Council:
GRAHAM LUSK
JAMES EWING
SIMON FLEXNER

1912–1913

President: FREDERIC S. LEE
Vice-President: WM. H. PARK
Treasurer: EDWARD K. DUNHAM
Secretary: HAVEN EMERSON

Council:
GRAHAM LUSK
S. J. MELTZER
WM. G. MACCALLUM

1913–1914

President: FREDERIC S. LEE
Vice-President: WM. G. MACCALLUM
Treasurer: EDWARD K. DUNHAM
Secretary: AUGUSTUS B. WADSWORTH

Council:
GRAHAM LUSK
WM. H. PARK
GEORGE B. WALLACE

1914–1915

President: WM. G. MACCALLUM
Vice-President: RUFUS I. COLE
Treasurer: EDWARD K. DUNHAM
Secretary: JOHN A. MANDEL

Council:
GRAHAM LUSK
FREDERIC S. LEE
W. T. LONGCOPE

1915–1916

President: GEORGE B. WALLACE*
Treasurer: EDWARD K. DUNHAM
Secretary: ROBERT A. LAMBERT

Council:
GRAHAM LUSK
RUFUS I. COLE
NELLIS B. FOSTER

1916–1917

President: GEORGE B. WALLACE
Vice-President: RUFUS I. COLE
Treasurer: EDWARD K. DUNHAM
Secretary: ROBERT A. LAMBERT

Council:
GRAHAM LUSK†
W. T. LONGCOPE
S. R. BENEDICT
HANS ZINSSER

1917–1918

President: EDWARD K. DUNHAM
Vice-President: RUFUS I. COLE
Treasurer: F. H. PIKE
Secretary: A. M. PAPPENHEIMER

Council:
GRAHAM LUSK
GEORGE B. WALLACE
FREDERIC S. LEE
PEYTON ROUS

* Dr. William G. MacCallum resigned after election. On Doctor Lusk's motion Doctor George B. Wallace was made President—no Vice-President was appointed.
† Doctor Lusk was made Honorary permanent Counsellor.

1918–1919

President: GRAHAM LUSK
Vice-President: RUFUS I. COLE
Treasurer: F. H. PIKE
Secretary: K. M. VOGEL

Council:
GRAHAM LUSK
JAMES W. JOBLING
FREDERIC S. LEE
JOHN AUER

1919–1920

President: WARFIELD T. LONGCOPE
Vice-President: S. R. BENEDICT
Treasurer: F. H. PIKE
Secretary: K. M. VOGEL

Council:
GRAHAM LUSK
HANS ZINSSER
FREDERIC S. LEE
GEORGE B. WALLACE

1920–1921*

President: WARFIELD T. LONGCOPE
Vice-President: S. R. BENEDICT
Treasurer: A. M. PAPPENHEIMER
Secretary: HOMER F. SWIFT

Council:
GRAHAM LUSK
FREDERIC S. LEE
HANS ZINSSER
GEORGE B. WALLACE

1921–1922

President: RUFUS I. COLE
Vice-President: S. R. BENEDICT
Treasurer: A. M. PAPPENHEIMER
Secretary: HOMER F. SWIFT

Council:
GRAHAM LUSK
HANS ZINSSER
H. C. JACKSON
W. T. LONGCOPE

1922–1923

President: RUFUS I. COLE
Vice-President: HANS ZINSSER
Treasurer: CHARLES C. LIEB
Secretary: HOMER F. SWIFT

Council:
GRAHAM LUSK
W. T. LONGCOPE
H. C. JACKSON
S. R. BENEDICT

1923–1924

President: EUGENE F. DUBOIS
Vice-President: HOMER F. SWIFT
Treasurer: CHARLES C. LIEB
Secretary: GEORGE M. MACKENZIE

Council:
GRAHAM LUSK
ALPHONSE R. DOCHEZ
DAVID MARINE
PEYTON ROUS

---

* These officers were elected at the Annual Meeting of May 21, 1920 but were omitted in the publication of the 1919–1920 volume.

1924–1925

President: EUGENE F. DuBois
Vice-President: PEYTON ROUS
Treasurer: CHARLES C. LIEB
Secretary: GEORGE M. MACKENZIE

Council:
GRAHAM LUSK
RUFUS COLE
HAVEN EMERSON
WM. H. PARK

1925–1926

President: HOMER F. SWIFT
Vice-President: H. B. WILLIAMS
Treasurer: HAVEN EMERSON
Secretary: GEORGE M. MACKENZIE

Council:
GRAHAM LUSK
EUGENE F. DuBois
WALTER W. PALMER
H. D. SENIOR

1926–1927

President: WALTER W. PALMER
Vice-President: WM. H. PARK
Treasurer: HAVEN EMERSON
Secretary: GEORGE M. MACKENZIE

Council:
GRAHAM LUSK
HOMER F. SWIFT
A. R. DOCHEZ
ROBERT CHAMBERS

1927–1928

President: DONALD D. VAN SLYKE
Vice-President: JAMES W. JOBLING
Treasurer: HAVEN EMERSON
Secretary: CARL A. L. BINGER

Council:
GRAHAM LUSK
RUSSEL L. CECIL
WARD J. MACNEAL
DAVID MARINE

1928–1929

President: PEYTON ROUS
Vice-President: HORATIO B. WILLIAMS
Treasurer: HAVEN EMERSON
Secretary: PHILIP D. MCMASTER

Council:
GRAHAM LUSK
ROBERT CHAMBERS
ALFRED F. HESS
H. D. SENIOR

1929–1930

President: G. CANBY ROBINSON
Vice-President: ALFRED F. HESS
Treasurer: HAVEN EMERSON
Secretary: DAYTON J. EDWARDS

Council:
GRAHAM LUSK
ALFRED E. COHN
A. M. PAPPENHEIMER
H. D. SENIOR

1930–1931

President: ALFRED E. COHN
Vice-President: J. G. HOPKINS
Treasurer: HAVEN EMERSON
Secretary: DAYTON J. EDWARDS

Council:
GRAHAM LUSK
O. T. AVERY
A. M. PAPPENHEIMER
S. R. DETWILER

1931–1932

President: J. W. JOBLING
Vice President: HOMER W. SMITH
Treasurer: HAVEN EMERSON
Secretary: DAYTON J. EDWARDS

Council:
GRAHAM LUSK
S. R. DETWILER
THOMAS M. RIVERS
RANDOLPH WEST

1932–1933

President: ALFRED F. HESS
Vice-President: HAVEN EMERSON
Treasurer: THOMAS M. RIVERS
Secretary: EDGAR STILLMAN

Council:
GRAHAM LUSK
HANS T. CLARKE
WALTER W. PALMER
HOMER W. SMITH

1933–1934

President: ALFRED HESS*
Vice-President: ROBERT K. CANNAN
Treasurer: THOMAS M. RIVERS
Secretary: EDGAR STILLMAN

Council:
STANLEY R. BENEDICT
ROBERT F. LOEB
WADE H. BROWN

1934–1935

President: ROBERT K. CANNAN
Vice-President: EUGENE L. OPIE
Treasurer: THOMAS M. RIVERS
Secretary: RANDOLPH H. WEST

Council:
HERBERT S. GASSER
B. S. OPPENHEIMER
PHILIP E. SMITH

1935–1936

President: ROBERT K. CANNAN
Vice-President: EUGENE L. OPIE
Treasurer: THOMAS M. RIVERS
Secretary: RANDOLPH H. WEST

Council:
ROBERT F. LOEB
HOMER W. SMITH
DAVID MARINE

1936–1937

President: EUGENE L. OPIE
Vice-President: PHILIP E. SMITH
Treasurer: THOMAS M. RIVERS
Secretary: McKEEN CATTELL

Council:
GEORGE B. WALLACE
MARTIN H. DAWSON
JAMES B. MURPHY

1937–1938

President: EUGENE L. OPIE
Vice-President: PHILIP E. SMITH
Treasurer: THOMAS M. RIVERS
Secretary: McKEEN CATTELL

Council:
GEORGE B. WALLACE
MARTIN H. DAWSON
HERBERT S. GASSER

* Dr. Hess died December 5, 1933.

1938–1939

President: PHILIP E. SMITH
Vice-President: HERBERT S. GASSER
Treasurer: KENNETH GOODNER
Secretary: MCKEEN CATTELL

Council:
HANS T. CLARKE
JAMES D. HARDY
WILLIAM S. TILLETT

1939–1940

President: PHILIP E. SMITH
Vice-President: HERBERT S. GASSER
Treasurer: KENNETH GOODNER
Secretary: THOMAS FRANCIS, JR.

Council:
HANS T. CLARKE
N. CHANDLER FOOT
WILLIAM S. TILLETT

1940–1941

President: HERBERT S. GASSER
Vice-President: HOMER W. SMITH
Treasurer: KENNETH GOODNER
Secretary: THOMAS FRANCIS, JR.

Council:
N. CHANDLER FOOT
VINCENT DU VIGNEAUD
MICHAEL HEIDELBERGER

1941–1942

President: HERBERT S. GASSER
Vice-President: HOMER W. SMITH
Treasurer: KENNETH GOODNER
Secretary: JOSEPH C. HINSEY

Council:
HARRY S. MUSTARD
HAROLD G. WOLFF
MICHAEL HEIDELBERGER

1942–1943

President: HANS T. CLARKE
Vice-President: THOMAS M. RIVERS
Treasurer: KENNETH GOODNER
Secretary: JOSEPH C. HINSEY

Council:
ROBERT F. LOEB
HAROLD G. WOLFF
WILLIAM C. VON GLAHN

1943–1944

President: HANS T. CLARKE
Vice-President: THOMAS M. RIVERS
Treasurer: COLIN M. MACLEOD
Secretary: JOSEPH C. HINSEY

Council:
ROBERT F. LOEB
WILLIAM C. VON GLAHN
WADE W. OLIVER

1944–1945

President: ROBERT CHAMBERS
Vice-President: VINCENT DU VIGNEAUD
Treasurer: COLIN M. MACLEOD
Secretary: JOSEPH C. HINSEY

Council:
WADE W. OLIVER
MICHAEL HEIDELBERGER
PHILIP D. MCMASTER

1945–1946

President: ROBERT CHAMBERS
Vice-President: VINCENT DU VIGNEAUD
Treasurer: COLIN M. MACLEOD
Secretary: EDGAR G. MILLER, JR.

Council:
PHILIP D. MCMASTER
EARL T. ENGLE
FRED W. STEWART

1946–1947

President: VINCENT DU VIGNEAUD
Vice-President: WADE W. OLIVER
Treasurer: COLIN M. MACLEOD
Secretary: EDGAR G. MILLER, JR.

Council:
EARL T. ENGLE
HAROLD G. WOLFF
L. EMMETT HOLT, JR.

1947–1948

President: VINCENT DU VIGNEAUD
Vice-President: WADE W. OLIVER
Treasurer: HARRY B. VAN DYKE
Secretary: MACLYN MCCARTY

Council:
PAUL KLEMPERER
L. EMMETT HOLT, JR.
HAROLD G. WOLFF

1948–1949

President: WADE W. OLIVER
Vice-President: ROBERT F. LOEB
Treasurer: HARRY B. VAN DYKE
Secretary: MACLYN MCCARTY

Council:
PAUL KLEMPERER
SEVERO OCHOA
HAROLD L. TEMPLE

1949–1950

President: WADE W. OLIVER
Vice-President: ROBERT F. LOEB
Treasurer: JAMES B. HAMILTON
Secretary: MACLYN MCCARTY

Council:
WILLIAM S. TILLETT
SEVERO OCHOA
HAROLD L. TEMPLE

1950–1951

President: ROBERT F. LOEB
Vice-President: MICHAEL HEIDELBERGER
Treasurer: JAMES B. HAMILTON
Secretary: LUDWIG W. EICHNA

Council:
WILLIAM S. TILLETT
A. M. PAPPENHEIMER, JR.
DAVID P. BARR

1951–1952

President: RENÉ J. DUBOS
Vice-President: MICHAEL HEIDELBERGER
Treasurer: JAMES B. HAMILTON
Secretary: LUDWIG W. EICHNA

Council:
DAVID P. BARR
ROBERT F. PITTS
A. M. PAPPENHEIMER, JR.

1952–1953

President: MICHAEL HEIDELBERGER
Vice-President: SEVERO OCHOA
Treasurer: CHANDLER MCC. BROOKS
Secretary: HENRY D. LAUSON

Council:
ROBERT F. PITTS
JEAN OLIVER
ALEXANDER B. GUTMAN

1953–1954

President: SEVERO OCHOA
Vice-President: DAVID P. BARR
Treasurer: CHANDLER MCC. BROOKS
Secretary: HENRY D. LAUSON

Council:
JEAN OLIVER
ALEXANDER B. GUTMAN
ROLLIN D. HOTCHKISS

1954–1955

President: DAVID P. BARR
Vice-President: COLIN M. MACLEOD
Treasurer: CHANDLER McC. BROOKS
Secretary: HENRY D. LAUSON

Council:
ALEXANDER B. GUTMAN
ROLLIN D. HOTCHKISS
DAVID SHEMIN

1955–1956

President: COLIN M. MACLEOD
Vice-President: FRANK L. HORSFALL, JR.
Treasurer: CHANDLER McC. BROOKS
Secretary: RULON W. RAWSON

Council:
ROLLIN D. HOTCHKISS
DAVID SHEMIN
ROBERT F. WATSON

1956–1957

President: FRANK L. HORSFALL, JR.
Vice-President: WILLIAM S. TILLETT
Treasurer: CHANDLER McC. BROOKS
Secretary: RULON W. RAWSON

Council:
DAVID SHEMIN
ROBERT F. WATSON
ABRAHAM WHITE

1957–1958

President: WILLIAM S. TILLETT
Vice-President: ROLLIN D. HOTCHKISS
Treasurer: CHANDLER McC. BROOKS
Secretary: H. SHERWOOD LAWRENCE

Council:
ROBERT F. WATSON
ABRAHAM WHITE
JOHN V. TAGGART

1958–1959

President: ROLLIN D. HOTCHKISS
Vice-President: ANDRE COURNAND
Treasurer: CHANDLER McC. BROOKS
Secretary: H. SHERWOOD LAWRENCE

Council:
ABRAHAM WHITE
JOHN V. TAGGART
WALSH McDERMOTT

1959–1960

President: ANDRE COURNAND
Vice-President: ROBERT F. PITTS
Treasurer: EDWARD J. HEHRE
Secretary: H. SHERWOOD LAWRENCE

Council:
JOHN V. TAGGART
WALSH McDERMOTT
ROBERT F. FURCHGOTT

1960–1961

President: ROBERT F. PITTS
Vice-President: DICKINSON W. RICHARDS
Treasurer: EDWARD J. HEHRE
Secretary: ALEXANDER G. BEARN

Council:
WALSH McDERMOTT
ROBERT F. FURCHGOTT
LUDWIG W. EICHNA

1961–1962

President: DICKINSON W. RICHARDS
Vice-President: PAUL WEISS
Treasurer: I. HERBERT SCHEINBERG
Secretary: ALEXANDER G. BEARN

Council:
ROBERT F. FURCHGOTT
LUDWIG W. EICHNA
EFRAIM RACKER

1962–1963

President: PAUL WEISS
Vice-President: ALEXANDER B. GUTMAN
Treasurer: I. HERBERT SCHEINBERG
Secretary: ALEXANDER G. BEARN

Council:
LUDWIG W. EICHNA
EFRAIM RACKER
ROGER L. GREIF

1963–1964

President: ALEXANDER B. GUTMAN
Vice-President: EDWARD L. TATUM
Treasurer: SAUL J. FARBER
Secretary: ALEXANDER G. BEARN

Council:
EFRAIM RACKER
ROGER L. GREIF
IRVING M. LONDON

1964–1965

President: EDWARD TATUM
Vice-President: CHANDLER McC. BROOKS
Treasurer: SAUL J. FARBER
Secretary: RALPH L. ENGLE, JR.

Council:
ROGER L. GREIF
LEWIS THOMAS
IRVING M. LONDON

1965–1966

President: CHANDLER McC. BROOKS
Vice-President: ABRAHAM WHITE
Treasurer: SAUL J. FARBER
Secretary: RALPH L. ENGLE, JR.

Council:
IRVING M. LONDON
LEWIS THOMAS
GEORGE K. HIRST

1966–1967

President: ABRAHAM WHITE
Vice-President: RACHMIEL LEVINE
Treasurer: SAUL J. FARBER
Secretary: RALPH L. ENGLE, JR.

Council:
LEWIS THOMAS
GEORGE K. HIRST
DAVID NACHMANSOHN

1967–1968

President: RACHMIEL LEVINE
Vice-President: SAUL J. FARBER
Treasurer: PAUL A. MARKS
Secretary: RALPH L. ENGLE, JR.

Council:
GEORGE K. HIRST
DAVID NACHMANSOHN
MARTIN SONENBERG

1968–1969

President: SAUL J. FARBER
Vice-President: JOHN V. TAGGART
Treasurer: PAUL A. MARKS
Secretary: ELLIOTT F. OSSERMAN

Council:
DAVID NACHMANSOHN
MARTIN SONENBERG
HOWARD EDER

1969–1970

President: JOHN V. TAGGART
Vice-President: BERNARD L. HORECKER
Treasurer: PAUL A. MARKS
Secretary: ELLIOTT F. OSSERMAN

Council:
MARTIN SONENBERG
HOWARD A. EDER
SAUL J. FARBER

1970–1971

President: BERNARD L. HORECKER
Vice-President: MACLYN MCCARTY
Treasurer: EDWARD C. FRANKLIN
Secretary: ELLIOTT F. OSSERMAN

Council:
HOWARD A. EDER
SAUL J. FARBER
SOLOMON A. BERSON

1971–1972

President: MACLYN MCCARTY
Vice-President: ALEXANDER BEARN
Treasurer: EDWARD C. FRANKLIN
Secretary: ELLIOTT F. OSSERMAN

Council:
SAUL J. FARBER
SOLOMON A. BERSON*
HARRY EAGLE

* Dr. Berson died on April 10, 1972 during his term of office as Councillor.

CUMULATIVE AUTHOR INDEX*

DR. JOHN J. ABEL, 1923–24 (d)
PROF. J. D. ADAMI, 1906–07 (d)
DR. ROGER ADAMS, 1941–42 (d)
DR. THOMAS ADDIS, 1927–28 (d)
DR. E. D. ADRIAN, 1931–32 (h)
DR. FULLER ALBRIGHT, 1942–43 (h)
DR. FRANZ ALEXANDER, 1930–31 (h)
DR. FREDERICK ALLEN, 1916–17 (a)
DR. JOHN F. ANDERSON, 1908–09 (d)
DR. R. J. ANDERSON, 1939–40 (d)
DR. CHRISTOPHER H. ANDREWS, 1961–62 (h)
DR. CHRISTIAN B. ANFINSEN, 1965–66 (h)
PROF. G. V. ANREP, 1934–35 (h)
DR. CHARLES ARMSTRONG, 1940–41 (d)
DR. LUDWIG ASCHOFF, 1923–24 (d)
DR. LEON ASHER, 1922–23 (h)
DR. W. T. ASTBURY, 1950–51 (h)
DR. EDWIN ASTWOOD, 1944–45 (h)
DR. JOSEPH C. AUB, 1928–29 (h)
DR. JULIUS AXELROD, 1971–72 (h)
DR. E. R. BALDWIN, 1914–15 (d)
PROF. JOSEPH BARCROFT, 1921–22 (d)
DR. PHILIP BARD, 1921–22 (h)
DR. H. A. BARKER, 1949–50 (h)
PROF. LEWELLYS BARKER, 1905–06 (d)
DR. JULIUS BAUER, 1932–33 (d)
PROF. WILLIAM M. BAYLISS, 1921–22 (d)
DR. FRANK BEACH, 1947–48 (h)
DR. GEORGE W. BEADLE, 1944–45 (h)
DR. ALBERT BEHNKE, 1941–42 (h)
DR. BARUJ BENACERRAF, 1971–72 (a)
PROF. F. G. BENEDICT, 1906–07 (d)
DR. STANLEY BENEDICT, 1915–16 (d)
PROF. R. R. BENSLEY, 1914–15 (d)
DR. SEYMOUR BENZER, 1960–61 (h)
DR. PAUL BERG, 1971–72 (h)

DR. MAX BERGMANN, 1935–36 (d)
DR. ROBERT W. BERLINER, 1958–59 (h)
DR. SOLOMON A. BERSON, 1966–67 (a)
DR. MARCEL C. BESSIS, 1962–63 (h)
DR. C. H. BEST, 1940–41 (h)
DR. A. BIEDL, 1923–24 (h)
DR. RUPERT E. BILLINGHAM, 1966–67 (h)
DR. RICHARD J. BING, 1954–55 (a)
DR. JOHN J. BITTNER, 1946–47 (d)
PROF. FRANCIS G. BLAKE, 1934–35 (d)
DR. ALFRED BLALOCK, 1945–46 (d)
DR. KONRAD BLOCH, 1952–53 (a)
DR. WALTER R. BLOOR, 1923–24 (d)
DR. DAVID BODIAN, 1956–57 (h)
DR. JAMES BONNER, 1952–53 (h)
DR. JULES BORDET, 1920–21 (h)
DR. WILLIAM T. BOVIE, 1922–23 (d)
DR. EDWARD A. BOYSE, 1971–72 (h)
DR. STANLEY E. BRADLEY, 1959–60 (a)
DR. ARMIN C. BRAUN, 1960–61 (h)
PROF. F. BREMER, (h)†
PROF. T. G. BRODIE, 1909–10 (d)
DR. DETLEV W. BRONK, 1933–34 (h)
DR. B. BROUWER, 1925–26 (d)
DR. WADE H. BROWN, 1928–29 (d)
DR. JOHN M. BUCHANAN, 1959–60 (h)
DR. JOHN CAIRNS, 1970–1971 (h)
PROF. A. CALMETTE, 1908–09 (d)
DR. MELVIN CALVIN, 1950–51 (h)
PROF. WALTER B. CANNON, 1911–12 (d)
PROF. A. J. CARLSON, 1915–16 (d)
DR. WILLIAM B. CASTLE, 1934–35 (h)
PROF. W. E. CASTLE, 1910–11 (d)
DR. I. L. CHAIKOFF, 1951–52 (d)

*(h), honorary; (a), active; (d) deceased.
† Did not present lecture because of World War II.

Dr. Rita Levi-Montalcini, 1964–65 (h)
Dr. Sam Z. Levine, 1946–47 (d)
Dr. Howard B. Lewis, 1940–41 (d)
Dr. Paul A. Lewis, 1916–17 (d)
Prof. Thomas Lewis, 1914–15 (d)
Dr. Warren H. Lewis, 1925–26, 1935–36 (d)
Dr. Choh Hao Li, 1950–51 (h)
Dr. K. Lindstrom-Lang, 1938–39 (d)
Dr. Karl P. Link, 1943–44 (h)
Dr. Fritz Lipmann, 1948–49 (a)
Dr. C. C. Little, 1921–22 (d)
Prof. Jacques Loeb, 1910–11, 1920–21 (d)
Dr. Leo Loeb, 1940–41 (d)
Dr. Robert F. Loeb, 1941–42 (a)
Prof. A. S. Loevenhart, 1914–15 (d)
Dr. Otto Loewi, 1932–33 (d)
Dr. E. S. London, 1927–28 (h)
Dr. Irving M. London, 1960–61 (a)
Dr. C. N. H. Long, 1936–37 (h)
Dr. Esmond R. Long, 1929–30 (h)
Prof. Warfield T. Longcope, 1915–16 (d)
Dr. Rafael Lorente de Nó, 1946–47 (a)
Prof. Konrad Lorenz, 1959–60 (h)
Dr. William D. Lotspeich, 1960–61 (d)
Dr. Oliver H. Lowry, 1962–63 (a)
Dr. Einar Lundsgaard, 1937–38 (d)
Dr. S. E. Luria, 1964–65 (h)
Dr. Graham Lusk, 1908–09, 1929–30 (d)
Dr. Andre Lwoff, 1954–55 (h)
Dr. Feodor Lynen, 1952–53 (h)
Dr. A. B. Macallum, 1908–09 (d)
Dr. W. G. MacCallum, 1908–09 (d)
Prof. J. J. R. MacLeod, 1913–14 (d)
Dr. William deB. MacNider, 1928–29 (d)
Dr. Thorvald Madsen, 1924–25, 1936–37 (d)
Dr. E. Margoliash, 1970–71 (h)

Prof. A. Magnus-Levy, 1909–10 (d)
Dr. H. W. Magoun, 1951–52 (h)
Dr. F. B. Mallory, 1912–13 (d)
Dr. Frank C. Mann, 1927–28 (d)
Dr. David Marine, 1923–24 (d)
Dr. Clement L. Markert, 1963–64 (h)
Dr. Paul A. Marks, 1970–71 (a)
Dr. Guy Marrian, 1938–39 (h)
Prof. W. McKim Marriott, 1919–20 (d)
Dr. E. K. Marshall, Jr., 1929–30 (d)
Dr. Daniel Mazia, 1957–58 (h)
Dr. Maclyn McCarty, 1969–70 (a)
Prof. E. V. McCollum, 1916–17 (d)
Dr. Walsh McDermott, 1967–68 (a)
Dr. W. D. McElroy, 1955–56 (h)
Dr. Philip D. McMaster, 1941–42 (a)
Dr. P. B. Medawar, 1956–57 (h)
Dr. Walter J. Meek, 1940–41 (d)
Prof. Alton Meister, 1967–68 (h)
Dr. S. J. Meltzer, 1906–07 (d)
Prof. Lafayette B. Mendel, 1905–06, 1914–15 (d)
Dr. R. Bruce Merrifield, 1971–72 (h)
Prof. Adolph Meyer, 1909–10 (d)
Prof. Hans Meyer, 1905–06 (d)
Dr. Karl Meyer, 1955–56 (a)
Dr. K. F. Meyer, 1939–40 (h)
Dr. Otto Meyerhof, 1922–23 (d)
Dr. Leonor Michaelis, 1926–27 (d)
Dr. William S. Miller, 1924–25 (d)
Prof. Charles S. Minot, 1905–06 (d)
Dr. George R. Minot, 1927–28 (d)
Dr. A. E. Mirsky, 1950–51 (a)
Dr. Jacques Monod, 1961–62 (h)
Dr. Carl V. Moore, 1958–59 (h)
Dr. Francis D. Moore, 1956–57 (h)
Dr. Stanford Moore, 1956–57 (a)
Prof. T. H. Morgan, 1905–06 (d)
Dr. Giuseppe Moruzzi, 1962–63 (h)

ACTIVE MEMBERS

Dr. Liese L. Abel
Dr. Harold Abramson*
Dr. Ruth Gail Abramson
Dr. Frederic J. Agate
Dr. Edward H. Ahrens
Dr. Philip Aisen
Dr. Salah Al-Askari
Dr. Anthony A. Albanese
Dr. Michael Harris Alderman
Dr. Benjamin Alexander
Dr. Robert Alexander
Dr. Emma Gates Allen
Dr. Fred H. Allen, Jr.
Dr. Jona Allerhand
Dr. Fred Allison, Jr.
Dr. Norman R. Alpert
Dr. Aaron A. Alter
Dr. Norman Altszuler
Dr. Burton M. Altura
Dr. J. Burns Amberson*
Dr. Richard P. Ames
Dr. A. F. Anderson*
Dr. Charles Anderson
Dr. Helen M. Anderson
Dr. Rubert S. Anderson*
Dr. Giuseppe A. Andres
Dr. Muriel M. Andrews
Dr. Alfred Angrist*
Dr. Henry Aranow, Jr.
Dr. Reginald M. Archibald
Dr. Diana C. Argyros
Dr. Irwin M. Arias
Dr. Donald Armstrong
Dr. Philip B. Armstrong*
Dr. Aaron Arnold
Dr. Robert B. Aronson
Dr. Paul W. Aschner*
Dr. Amir Askari

Dr. Muvaffak A. Atamer
Dr. Dana W. Atchley*
Dr. Kimball Chase Atwood
Dr. Joseph T. August
Dr. Peter A. M. Auld
Dr. Felice B. Aull
Dr. Robert Austrian
Dr. D. Robert Axelrod
Dr. Stephen M. Ayres
Dr. L. Fred Ayvazian
Dr. Henry A. Azar
Dr. Mortimer E. Bader
Dr. Richard A. Bader
Dr. George Baehr*
Dr. Silvio Baez
Dr. John C. Baiardi
Dr. Robert D. Baird*
Mrs. Katherine J. Baker
Dr. Sulamita Balagura
Dr. David S. Baldwin
Dr. Horace S. Baldwin*
Dr. M. Earl Balis
Dr. S. Banerjee
Dr. Nils Ulrich Bang
Dr. Arthur Bank
Dr. Norman Bank
Dr. Alvan L. Barach*
Dr. Michael Barany
Dr. W. H. Barber*
Dr. Marion Barclay
Dr. S. B. Barker*
Dr. Lane Barksdale
Dr. Peter Barland
Dr. W. A. Barnes
Dr. Harry Baron
Dr. Howard Baron
Dr. Jeremiah A. Barondess
Dr. David P. Barr*
Dr. Bruce A. Barron

* Life member.

450

Dr. Guy T. Barry
Dr. Herbert J. Bartelstone
Dr. C. Andrew L. Bassett
Dr. Bruce Batchelor
Dr. Jeanne Bateman*
Dr. Jack R. Battisto
Dr. Stephen G. Baum
Dr. Leona Baumgartner*
Dr. Eliot F. Beach
Dr. Joseph W. Beard*
Dr. Alexander G. Bearn
Dr. Carl Becker
Dr. David Becker
Dr. E. Lovell Becker
Dr. Frederick F. Becker
Dr. William H. Becker
Dr. Paul B. Beeson*
Dr. Jeannette Allen Behre
Dr. Richard E. Behrman
Dr. Sam M. Beiser
Dr. Julius Belford
Dr. A. L. Loomis Bell
Dr. Bertrand Bell
Dr. Fritz Karl Beller
Dr. Baruj Benacerraf
Dr. Morris Bender*
Dr. Aaron Bendich
Dr. Bernard Benjamin*
Dr. Bry Benjamin
Dr. Ivan L. Bennett
Dr. Thomas P. Bennett
Dr. Harvey L. Benovitz
Dr. Gordon Benson
Dr. Benjamin N. Berg*
Dr. Kåre Berg
Dr. Stanley S. Bergen
Dr. Adolph Berger
Dr. Eugene Y. Berger
Dr. Lawrence Berger
Dr. Ingemar Berggård
Dr. Edward H. Bergofsky
Dr. James Berkman
Dr. Alice R. Bernheim*
Dr. Alan W. Bernheimer

Dr. Harriet Bernheimer
Dr. Leslie Bernstein
Dr. Stanley Bernstein
Dr. Carl A. Berntsen
Dr. George Packer Berry*
Dr. John F. Bertles
Dr. Otto A. Bessey*
Dr. Joseph J. Betheil
Dr. Richard E. Bettigole
Dr. Margaret Bevans
Dr. Sherman Beychok
Dr. Edward Bien
Dr. John T. Bigger, Jr.
Dr. R. J. Bing
Dr. Carl A. L. Binger*
Dr. Francis Binkley
Dr. Robert M. Bird
Dr. Charles Birnberg
Dr. LeClair Bissell
Dr. Mark W. Bitensky
Dr. Maurice M. Black
Dr. William A. Blanc
Dr. Kenneth C. Blanchard*
Dr. David H. Blankenhorn
Dr. Sheldon P. Blau
Dr. Richard W. Blide
Dr. Hubert Bloch
Dr. Konrad E. Bloch
Dr. Barry Bloom
Dr. Oscar Bodansky*
Dr. Diethelm Boehme
Dr. Bruce I. Bogart
Dr. Victor Bokisch
Dr. Richard J. Bonforte
Dr. Roy W. Bonsnes
Dr. Robert M. Bookchin
Dr. A. Bookman*
Dr. Max Bovarnick
Dr. John Z. Bowers
Dr. Barbara H. Bowman
Dr. Linn J. Boyd*
Dr. Richard C. Bozian
Dr. Norman Brachfield

* Life member.

Dr. Stanley Bradley
Dr. Thomas B. Bradley
Dr. J. Leonard Brandt
Dr. Jo Anne Brasel
Dr. Goodwin Breinin
Dr. Esther Breslow
Dr. Robin Briehl
Dr. Stanley A. Briller
Dr. Anne E. Briscoe
Dr. William Briscoe
Dr. Susan Broder
Dr. Bernard Brodie
Dr. Felix Bronner
Dr. Chandler McC. Brooks
Dr. Dana C. Brooks
Dr. Vernon B. Brooks
Dr. D. E. S. Brown*
Dr. John Lyman Brown
Dr. Howard C. Bruenn*
Dr. Joseph Brumlik
Dr. J. Marion Bryant
Dr. J. Robert Buchanan
Dr. John L. Buchanan
Dr. Thomas M. Buchanan
Dr. Nancy M. Buckley
Dr. Joseph A. Buda
Dr. Elmer D. Bueker
Dr. George E. Burch
Dr. Joseph H. Burchenal
Dr. Richard Burger
Dr. Dean Burk*
Dr. Edward R. Burka
Dr. E. A. Burkhardt*
Dr. John J. Burns
Dr. Earl O. Butcher*
Dr. Vincent P. Butler, Jr.
Dr. Joel N. Buxbaum
Dr. Roy Cacciaguida
Dr. Abbie Knowlton Calder
Dr. Peter T. B. Caldwell
Dr. Lawrence A. Caliguiri
Dr. Xenophon C. Callas
Dr. Berry Campbell
Dr. Virginia C. Canale

Dr. Robert E. Canfield
Dr. Paul Jude Cannon
Dr. Guilio L. Cantoni
Dr. Charles R. Cantor
Dr. Eric T. Carlson
Dr. Peter Wagner Carmel
Dr. Fred Carpenter
Dr. Malcolm B. Carpenter
Dr. Hugh J. Carroll
Dr. Steven Carson
Dr. Anne C. Carter
Dr. Sidney Carter
Dr. J. Casals-Ariet*
Dr. Albert E. Casey*
Dr. Joan I. Casey
Dr. William D. Cash
Dr. McKeen Cattell*
Dr. William Caveness
Dr. Peter P. Cervoni
Dr. R. W. Chambers
Dr. Philip C. Chan
Dr. W. Y. Chan
Dr. J. P. Chandler*
Dr. Merrill W. Chase*
Dr. Norman E. Chase
Dr. Herbert Chasis*
Dr. Kirk C. S. Chen
Dr. Theodore Chenkin
Dr. Norman L. Chernik
Dr. Shu Chien
Dr. C. Gardner Child
Dr. Francis P. Chinard
Dr. Purnell W. Choppin
Dr. Charles L. Christian
Dr. Ronald V. Christie*
Dr. Judith K. Christman
Dr. Nicholas P. Christy
Dr. Jacob Churg
Dr. Louis J. Cizek
Dr. Duncan W. Clark
Dr. Delphine H. Clarke
Dr. Frank H. Clarke
Dr. Albert Claude*
Dr. Hartwig Cleve

* Life member.

Dr. E. E. Cliffton
Dr. Leighton E. Cluff
Dr. Jaime B. Coelho
Dr. Bernard Cohen
Dr. Michael I. Cohen
Dr. Sidney Q. Cohlan
Dr. Cal K. Cohn
Dr. Mildred Cohn
Dr. Zanvil A. Cohn
Dr. Henry Colcher
Dr. Morton Coleman
Dr. Spencer L. Commerford
Dr. Richard M. Compans
Dr. Neal J. Conan, Jr.
Dr. Lawrence A. Cone
Dr. Stephen C. Connolly
Dr. James H. Conover
Dr. Jean L. Cook
Dr. John S. Cook
Dr. Stuart D. Cook
Dr. George Cooper
Dr. Norman S. Cooper
Dr. Jack M. Cooperman
Dr. W. M. Copenhaver*
Dr. George N. Cornell
Dr. George Corner*
Dr. Armand F. Cortese
Dr. Richard Costello
Dr. Lucien J. Cote
Dr. George Cotzias
Dr. Andre Cournand*
Dr. W. P. Covell*
Dr. David Cowen
Dr. Herold R. Cox*
Dr. Rody P. Cox
Dr. George Craft
Dr. Francis N. Craig
Dr. Elizabeth Crawford
Dr. B. B. Crohn*
Dr. Richard J. Cross
Dr. Bruce Cunningham
Dr. Dorothy J. Cunningham
Dr. Edward C. Curnen

Dr. Mary G. McCrea Curnen
Dr. T. J. Curphey*
Dr. Samuel W. Cushman
Dr. Samuel Dales
Dr. Marie Maynard Daly
Dr. Raymond Damadian
Dr. Joseph Dancis
Dr. Betty S. Danes
Dr. Farrington Daniels, Jr.
Dr. R. C. Darling
Dr. James E. Darnell, Jr.
Dr. Fred M. Davenport
Dr. John David
Dr. Leo M. Davidoff*
Dr. Murray Davidson
Dr. Jean Davignon
Dr. Bernard D. Davis
Dr. Robert P. Davis
Dr. Emerson Day
Dr. Peter G. Dayton
Dr. Norman Deane
Dr. Robert H. De Bellis
Dr. Paul F. de Gara*
Dr. Thomas J. Degnan
Dr. A. C. DeGraff*
Dr. John E. Deitrick*
Dr. C. E. de la Chapelle*
Dr. Nicholas Delhias
Dr. R. J. Dellenback
Dr. Felix E. Demartini
Dr. Quentin B. Deming
Dr. Felix de Narvaez
Dr. Carolyn R. Denning
Dr. Miriam de Salegue
Dr. Ralph A. Deterling, Jr.
Dr. Wolf-Dietrich Dettbarn
Dr. Ingrith J. Deyrup
Dr. Herbert S. Diamond
Dr. Leroy S. Dietrich
Dr. George W. Dietz, Jr.
Dr. Mario Di Girolamo
Dr. Alexander B. Dimich
Dr. Peter Dineen
Dr. J. R. Di Palma

* Life member.

Dr. Nicholas Di Salvo
Dr. P. A. Di Sant'Agnese
Dr. Zacharias Dische
Dr. Charles A. Doan*
Dr. William Dock*
Dr. Alvin M. Donnenfeld
Dr. Philip J. Dorman
Dr. Louis B. Dotti*
Dr. Joseph C. Dougherty
Dr. Gordon W. Douglas
Dr. Steven D. Douglas
Dr. Charles V. Dowling
Dr. Alan W. Downie*
Dr. Cora Downs*
Dr. Arnold Drapkin
Dr. Paul Dreizen
Dr. David T. Dresdale
Dr. René J. Dubos*
Dr. Allan Dumont
Dr. John H. Dunnington*
Dr. Vincent Du Vigneaud*
Dr. Murray Dworetzky
Dr. D. Dziewiatkowski
Dr. Harry Eagle
Dr. Lila W. Easley
Dr. Paul Ebert
Dr. Gerald M. Edelman
Dr. Chester M. Edelmann, Jr.
Dr. Howard A. Eder
Dr. Adrian L. E. Edwards
Dr. Richard M. Effros
Dr. Hans J. Eggers
Dr. Kathryn H. Ehlers
Dr. Klaus Eichmann
Dr. Ludwig W. Eichna
Dr. Max Eisenberg
Dr. William J. Eisenmenger
Dr. Robert P. Eisinger
Dr. Borje Ejrup
Dr. Stuart D. Elliott
Dr. John T. Ellis
Dr. Rose-Ruth Tarr Ellison
Dr. Peter Elsbach
Dr. Samuel K. Elster

Dr. Charles A. Ely
Dr. Kendall Emerson, Jr.*
Dr. George Emmanuel
Dr. Morris Engelman
Dr. Mary Allen Engle
Dr. Ralph L. Engle, Jr.
Dr. Yale Enson
Dr. Leonard Epifano
Dr. Frederick H. Epstein
Dr. Joseph A. Epstein
Dr. Bernard F. Erlanger
Dr. Normon H. Ertel
Dr. Solomon Estren
Dr. Hugh E. Evans
Dr. John Evans
Dr. Henry E. Evert
Dr. Elaine Eyster
Dr. John Fabianek
Dr. Stanley Fahn
Dr. Saul J. Farber
Dr. Mehdi Farhangi
Dr. Peter B. Farnsworth
Dr. John W. Farquhar
Dr. Lee E. Farr*
Dr. Don W. Fawcett
Dr. Aaron Feder
Dr. Martha E. Fedorko
Dr. Muriel F. Feigelson
Dr. Philip Feigelson
Dr. Maurice Feinstein
Dr. Daniel Feldman
Dr. Elaine B. Feldman
Dr. Colin Fell
Dr. Bernard N. Fields
Dr. Ronald R. Fieve
Dr. Laurence Finberg
Dr. Charles W. Findlay, Jr.
Dr. Bruno Fingerhut
Dr. Louis M. Fink
Dr. Stanley R. Finke
Dr. John T. Finkenstaedt
Dr. Edward E. Fischel
Dr. Vincent A. Fischetti
Dr. Arthur Fishberg*

* Life member.

DR. SAUL FISHER
DR. ALFRED P. FISHMAN
DR. PATRICK J. FITZGERALD
DR. MARTIN FITZPATRICK
DR. CHARLES FLOOD*
DR. ALFRED FLORMAN
DR. JORDI FOLCH-PI*
DR. CONRAD T. O. FONG
DR. VINCENT FONTANA
DR. FRANK W. FOOTE, JR.
DR. JOSEPH FORTNER
DR. ARTHUR C. FOX
DR. CHARLES L. FOX, JR.
DR. LEWIS M. FRAAD
DR. CHARLES W. FRANK
DR. HARRY MEYER FRANKEL
DR. EDWARD C. FRANKLIN
DR. RICHARD C. FRANSON
DR. ANDREW G. FRANTZ
DR. AARON D. FREEDMAN
DR. MICHAEL L. FREEDMAN
DR. ALVIN FREIMAN
DR. MATTHEW JAY FREUND
DR. RICHARD H. FREYBERG
DR. HENRY CLAY FRICK, II
DR. ARNOLD J. FRIEDHOF
DR. RALPH FRIEDLANDER
DR. ELI A. FRIEDMAN
DR. S. MARVIN FRIEDMAN
DR. CHARLOTTE FRIEND
DR. GEORGE W. FRIMPTER
DR. WILLIAM FRISELL
DR. HARRY FRITTS
DR. JOSEPH S. FRUTON*
DR. FRITZ F. FUCHS
DR. MILDRED FULOP
DR. ROBERT F. FURCHGOTT*
DR. J. FURTH*
DR. PALMER H. FUTCHER
DR. JACQUES L. GABRILOVE
DR. MORTON GALDSTON
DR. THOMAS F. GALLAGHER
DR. NICHOLAS F. GANG
DR. HENRY GANS

DR. G. GAIL GARDNER
DR. WILLIAM A. GARDNER*
DR. MARTIN GARDY
DR. LAWRENCE GARTNER
DR. NANCY E. GARY
DR. MARIO GAUDINO
DR. MALCOLM GEFTER
DR. WALTON B. GEIGER
DR. JACK GELLER
DR. LESTER M. GELLER
DR. DOROTHY S. GENGHOF
DR. DONALD GERBER
DR. JAMES L. GERMAN, III
DR. HERBERT GERSHBERG
DR. E. C. GERST
DR. MENARD GERTLER
DR. MELVIN GERTNER
DR. NORMAN R. GEVIRTZ
DR. NIMAI GHOSH
DR. STANLEY GIANNELLI, JR.
DR. LEWIS I. GIDEZ
DR. GERHARD H. GIEBISCH
DR. HARRIET S. GILBERT
DR. HELENA GILDER
DR. ALFRED GILMAN
DR. SID GILMAN
DR. CHARLES GILVARG
DR. H. EARL GINN
DR. HAROLD S. GINSBERG
DR. ISAAC F. GITTLEMAN
DR. SHELDON GLABMAN
DR. PHILIP R. GLADE
DR. HERMAN GLADSTONE
DR. WARREN GLASER
DR. GEORGE B. JERZY GLASS
DR. EPHRAIM GLASSMANN
DR. VINCENT V. GLAVIANO
DR. FRANK GLENN*
DR. SEYMOUR M. GLICK
DR. MARVIN L. GLIEDMAN
DR. DAVID L. GLOBUS
DR. MARTIN J. GLYNN, JR.
DR. DAVID J. GOCKE
DR. GABRIEL C. GODMAN

* Life member.

Dr. Walther F. Goebel*
Dr. Robert B. Golbey
Dr. Allen M. Gold
Dr. Harry Gold*
Dr. Allan R. Goldberg
Dr. Burton Goldberg
Dr. Henry P. Goldberg
Dr. Ross Golden*
Dr. Anna Goldfeder
Dr. Martin G. Goldner
Dr. Roberta M. Goldring
Dr. William Goldring*
Dr. Edward I. Goldsmith
Dr. Eli D. Goldsmith*
Dr. Jack Goldstein
Dr. Marvin H. Goldstein
Dr. Julius Golubow
Dr. Peter John Gomatos
Dr. Robert A. Good
Dr. Robert Goodhart
Dr. DeWitt S. Goodman
Dr. Laurance D. Goodwin
Dr. Norman L. Gootman
Dr. Albert S. Gordon
Dr. Alvin J. Gordon
Dr. Harry H. Gordon*
Dr. Irving Gordon
Dr. Fred Gorstein
Dr. Emil Claus Gotschlich
Dr. Eugene Gottfried
Dr. Dicran Goulian, Jr.
Dr. Arthur W. Grace*
Dr. Irving Graef*
Dr. William R. Grafe
Dr. Samuel Graff*
Dr. Frank A. Graig
Dr. Jose Luis Granda
Dr. Lester Grant
Dr. Arthur I. Grayzel
Dr. Jack Peter Green
Dr. Robert H. Green
Dr. Saul Green
Dr. Lowell M. Greenbaum
Dr. Elias L. Greene

Dr. Lewis J. Greene
Dr. Olga Greengard
Dr. Ezra M. Greenspan
Dr. Isidor Greenwald*
Dr. John R. Gregg
Dr. Gregory Gregariadis
Dr. John D. Gregory
Dr. Roger I. Greif
Dr. Ira Greifer
Dr. Joel Grinker
Dr. Arthur Grishman
Dr. William R. Griswold
Dr. David Grob
Dr. Howard S. Grob
Dr. Arthur P. Grollman
Dr. Milton M. Gross
Dr. Paul Gross*
Dr. Ruth T. Gross
Dr. Lionel Grossbard
Dr. Carlo E. S. Grossi
Dr. Melvin Grumbach
Dr. Dezider Grunberger
Dr. Harry Grundfest*
Dr. Alan B. Gruskin
Dr. Richard S. Gubner
Dr. Peter Guida
Dr. Guido Guidotti
Dr. Connie M. Guion*
Dr. Stephen J. Gulotta
Dr. Alexander B. Gutman*
Dr. Sidney Gutstein
Dr. David V. Habif
Dr. Susan Jane Hadley
Dr. Hanspaul Hagenmaier
Dr. Jack W. C. Hagstrom
Dr. Richard G. Hahn*
Dr. Seymour P. Halbert
Dr. Bernard H. Hall
Dr. David Hamerman
Dr. James B. Hamilton
Dr. Leonard Hamilton
Dr. Paul B. Hamilton
Dr. Warner S. Hammond
Dr. Chester W. Hampel*

* Life member.

Dr. Roger P. Hand
Dr. Eugene S. Handler
Dr. Evelyn E. Handler
Dr. Leonard C. Harber
Dr. James D. Hardy*
Dr. Kendrick Hare*
Dr. Ken Harewood
Dr. Joseph Harkavy*
Dr. Peter Cahners Harpel
Dr. Albert H. Harris*
Dr. Ruth C. Harris
Dr. Benjamin Harrow*
Dr. Una Hart
Dr. Donald H. Harter
Dr. ReJane Harvey
Dr. Rudy Haschemeyer
Dr. George A. Hashim
Dr. Sam A. Hashim
Dr. George M. Hass*
Dr. William K. Hass
Dr. A. Baird Hastings*
Dr. A. Daniel Hauser
Dr. Louis Hausman*
Dr. Teru Hayashi
Dr. Arthur H. Hayes
Dr. Richard M. Hays
Dr. Robert M. Heggie*
Dr. Edward J. Hehre
Dr. Michael Heidelberger*
Dr. Henry Heinemann
Dr. William Carroll Heird
Dr. Leon Hellman
Dr. Milton Helpern
Dr. Lawrence Helson
Dr. Walter L. Henley
Dr. Philip H. Henneman
Dr. Victor Herbert
Dr. Robert M. Herbst*
Dr. Morris Herman*
Dr. Frederic P. Herter
Dr. Robert B. Hiatt
Dr. Margaret Hilgartner
Dr. Charles H. Hill
Dr. James G. Hilton

Dr. Lawrence E. Hinkle, Jr.
Dr. Joseph C. Hinsey*
Dr. Christophe H. W. Hirs
Dr. Jacob Hirsch
Dr. James G. Hirsch
Dr. Jules Hirsch
Dr. Robert L. Hirsch
Dr. Erich Hirschberg
Dr. Kurt Hirschhorn
Dr. George K. Hirst*
Dr. Paul Hochstein
Dr. Paul F. A. Hoefer*
Dr. Thomas I. Hoen*
Dr. Joseph Hoffman
Dr. Lee Hoffman
Dr. Alan F. Hofmann
Dr. Frederick G. Hofmann
Dr. Duncan A. Holaday
Dr. Raymond F. Holden*
Dr. Charles S. Hollander
Dr. Vincent Hollander
Dr. J. H. Holmes
Dr. L. Emmett Holt, Jr.*
Dr. Erich Holtzman
Dr. Donald A. Holub
Dr. Robert S. Holzman
Dr. Edward W. Hook
Dr. Bernard L. Horecker
Dr. William H. Horner
Dr. Marshall S. Horwitz
Dr. Verne D. Hospelhorn
Dr. Rollin D. Hotchkiss*
Dr. S. S. Hotta
Dr. Michael Luray Howe
Dr. Paul E. Howe*
Dr. Howard H. T. Hsu
Dr. Konrad Chang Hsu
Dr. Mon-Tuan Huang
Dr. William N. Hubbard, Jr.
Dr. L. E. Hummel*
Dr. George H. Humphreys*
Dr. Jerard Hurwitz
Dr. Dorris Hutchinson
Dr. Thomas H. Hutteroth

* Life member.

Dr. Michale Iacobellis
Dr. Anthony R. Imondi
Dr. Harry L. Ioachim
Dr. Henry D. Isenberg
Dr. Raymond S. Jackson
Dr. Richard W. Jackson*
Dr. Jerry C. Jacobs
Dr. Ernst R. Jaffe
Dr. Herbert Jaffe
Dr. S. Jakowska
Dr. George James
Dr. James D. Jamieson
Dr. Aaron Janoff
Dr. Alfonso H. Janoski
Dr. Henry D. Janowitz
Dr. Saul Jarcho*
Dr. Jamshid Javid
Dr. Norman B. Javitt
Dr. Graham H. Jeffries
Dr. Frode Jensen
Dr. Alan J. Johnson
Dr. Dorothy D. Johnson
Dr. Walter D. Johnson, Jr.
Dr. Barbara Johnston
Dr. Kenneth H. Johnston
Dr. Thomas Jones
Dr. Alan S. Josephson
Dr. Austin L. Joyner*
Dr. Elvin A. Kabat*
Dr. Lawrence J. Kagen
Dr. Melvin Kahn
Dr. Thomas Kahn
Dr. Alfred J. Kaltman
Dr. William Kammerer
Dr. Yoshinobu Kanno
Dr. Thomas G. Kantor
Dr. F. F. Kao
Dr. Barry H. Kaplan
Dr. David Kaplan
Dr. Attallah Kappas
Dr. Alan E. Kark
Dr. Arthur Karlin
Dr. Simon Karpatkin
Dr. Maxwell Karshan*

Dr. Arnold M. Katz
Dr. Michael Katz
Dr. Robert Katzman
Dr. George L. Kauer, Jr.
Dr. M. Ralph Kaufmann
Dr. Seymour Kaufmann
Dr. Hans Kaunitz
Dr. Herbert J. Kayden
Dr. Donald Kaye
Dr. Gordon I. Kaye
Dr. B. H. Kean
Dr. Aaron Kellner
Dr. Muriel Kerr
Dr. Lee Kesner
Dr. Richard H. Kessler
Dr. Walter R. Kessler
Dr. Andre C. Kibrick*
Dr. John G. Kidd*
Dr. Edwin D. Kilbourne
Dr. Margaret Kilcoyne
Dr. Thomas Killip
Dr. Charles W. Kim
Dr. Giho Kim
Dr. Anne C. Kimball
Dr. Daniel Kimberg
Dr. Thomas J. Kindt
Dr. Barry G. King*
Dr. Donald West King
Dr. Glenn C. King*
Dr. Mary Elizabeth King
Dr. Lawrence C. Kingsland, Jr.
Dr. David W. Kinne
Dr. John M. Kinney
Dr. R. A. Kinsella*
Dr. Esben Kirk
Dr. D. M. Kirschenbaum
Dr. David Klapper
Dr. Bernard Klein
Dr. Abraham M. Kleinman
Dr. A. K. Kleinschmidt
Dr. Percy Klingenstein*
Dr. Jerome L. Knittle
Dr. W. Eugene Knox
Dr. Joseph A. Kochen

* Life member.

Dr. Shaul Kochwa
Dr. Samuel Saburo Koide
Dr. Kiyomi Koizumi
Dr. M. J. Kopac*
Dr. Levy Kopelovich
Dr. Arthur Kornberg
Dr. Peter Kornfeld
Dr. Leonard Korngold
Dr. Irvin M. Korr*
Dr. Nechama S. Kossower
Dr. Charles E. Kossmann*
Dr. Arthur Kowalsky
Dr. O. Dhodanand Kowlessar
Dr. Philip Kozinn
Dr. Irwin H. Krakoff
Dr. Lawrence R. Krakoff
Dr. Benjamin Kramer*
Dr. Alvan Krasna
Dr. Stephen J. Kraus
Dr. Richard M. Krause
Dr. Norman Kretchmer
Dr. Howard P. Krieger
Dr. Isidore Krimsky
Dr. Robert A. Kritzler
Dr. Robert Schild Krooth
Dr. Stephen Krop
Dr. Saul Krugman
Dr. Edward J. Kuchinskas
Dr. Friedrich Kueppers
Dr. I. Newton Kugelmass*
Dr. William J. Kuhns
Dr. Henry G. Kunkel
Dr. Sherman Kupfer
Dr. Herbert S. Kupperman
Dr. Marvin Kuschner
Dr. Henn Kutt
Dr. David M. Kydd
Dr. John S. LaDue
Dr. Chun-Yen Lai
Dr. Michael Lake*
Dr. Michael Lamm
Dr. R. C. Lancefield*
Dr. Robert Landesman
Dr. M. Daniel Lane

Dr. William B. Langan
Dr. Gertrude Lange
Dr. Kurt Lange
Dr. Glen A. Langer
Dr. Louis Langman*
Dr. Philip Lanzkowsky
Dr. John H. Laragh
Dr. Daniel L. Larson
Dr. Etienne Y. Lasfargues
Dr. Sigmund E. Lasker
Dr. Richard P. Lasser
Dr. Raffaelle Lattes
Dr. John Lattimer
Dr. Henry D. Lauson
Dr. George I. Lavin*
Dr. Leroy S. Lavine
Dr. Christine Lawrence
Dr. H. S. Lawrence
Dr. Walter Lawrence, Jr.
Dr. Richard W. Lawton
Dr. Robert W. Leader
Dr. Stanley L. Lee
Dr. Sylvia Lee-Huang
Dr. Robert S. Lees
Dr. Albert M. Lefkovits
Dr. David Lehr
Dr. Gerard M. Lehrer
Miss Grace Leidy
Dr. Edgar Leifer
Dr. Louis Leiter
Dr. Edwin H. Lennette*
Dr. E. Carwile LeRoy
Dr. Stephen H. Leslie
Dr. Gerson J. Lesnick
Dr. Harry Le Veen
Dr. Stanley M. Levenson
Dr. Arthur H. Levere
Dr. Richard D. Levere
Dr. Harold A. Levey
Dr. Robert Levi
Dr. Aaron R. Levin
Dr. Louis Levin*
Dr. Philip Levine*
Dr. Rachmiel Levine

* Life member.

DR. ROBERT A. LEVINE
DR. CYRUS LEVINTHAL
DR. MARVIN F. LEVITT
DR. BARNET M. LEVY
DR. HARVEY M. LEVY
DR. HYMAN LEVY
DR. LESTER LEVY
DR. MILTON LEVY*
DR. ROBERT L. LEVY*
DR. ARTHUR LEWIS
DR. JAMES L. LEWIS
DR. N. D. C. LEWIS*
DR. MARJORIE LEWISOHN
DR. ALLYN B. LEY
DR. KOIBONG LI
DR. HERBERT C. LICHTMAN
DR. CHARLES S. LIEBER
DR. SEYMOUR LIEBERMAN
DR. FREDERICK M. LIEBMAN
DR. MARTIN R. LIEBOWITZ
DR. FANNIE LIEBSON
DR. PHILIP D. LIEF
DR. ASA L. LINCOLN*
DR. EDITH M. LINCOLN*
DR. GEOFFREY C. LINDER*
DR. ALFRED S. C. LING
DR. GEORGE LIPKIN
DR. MARTIN LIPKIN
DR. FRITZ LIPMANN*
DR. M. B. LIPSETT
DR. IRIS F. LITT
DR. JULIUS LITTMAN
DR. STEPHEN D. LITWIN
DR. GEORGE LIU
DR. TEH-YUNG LIU
DR. ARTHUR LIVERMORE
DR. DAVID P. C. LLOYD*
DR. JOSEPH LoBUE
DR. MICHAEL D. LOCKSHIN
DR. JOHN N. LOEB
DR. ROBERT F. LOEB*
DR. WERNER R. LOEWENSTEIN
DR. IRVING M. LONDON
DR. MORRIS LONDON

DR. L. G. LONGSWORTH*
DR. WILLIAM F. LOOMIS
DR. R. LORENTE DE NÓ*
DR. DONALD B. LOURIA
DR. BARBARA W. LOW
DR. JEROME LOWENSTEIN
DR. OLIVER H. LOWRY
DR. BERTRAM A. LOWY
DR. FRED V. LUCAS
DR. JEAN M. LUCAS-LENARD
DR. E. HUGH LUCKEY
DR. A. LEONARD LUHBY
DR. DANIEL S. LUKAS
DR. CLARA J. LYNCH*
DR. HAROLD LYONS
DR. GEORGE I. LYTHCOTT
DR. FERDINAND F. MCALLISTER
DR. KENNETH MCALPIN*
DR. MARSH MCCALL
DR. W. S. MCCANN*
DR. KENNETH S. MCCARTY
DR. MACLYN MCCARTY
DR. WALTER S. MCCLELLAN*
DR. ROBERT MCCLUSKY
DR. DAVID J. MCCONNELL
DR. JAMES E. MCCORMACK
DR. W. W. MCCRORY
DR. DONOVAN J. MCCUNE*
DR. WALSH MCDERMOTT
DR. FLETCHER MCDOWELL
DR. CURRIER MCEWEN*
DR. PAUL R. MCHUGH
DR. RAWLE MCINTOSH
DR. RUSTIN MCINTOSH*
DR. COSMO G. MACKENZIE*
DR. JOHN MACLEOD*
DR. ROBERT G. MCKITTRICK
DR. EDMUND F. MCNALLY
MISS HELEN MCNAMARA
DR. JAMES J. MCSHARRY
DR. CHARLES K. MCSHERRY
DR. THOMAS MAACK
DR. NICHOLAS T. MACRIS
DR. MELVILLE G. MAGIDA

* Life member.

Dr. T. P. Magill*
Dr. Jacob V. Maizel, Jr.
Dr. Ole J. W. Malm
Dr. Benjamin Mandel
Dr. William M. Manger
Dr. Mart Mannik
Dr. James M. Manning
Dr. Wladyslaw Manski
Dr. Karl Maramorosch
Dr. Carlos Marchena
Dr. Aaron J. Marcus
Dr. Cyril Carlisle Marcus
Dr. Donald M. Marcus
Dr. Philip I. Marcus
Dr. Stewart L. Marcus
Dr. Morton Marks
Dr. Paul A. Marks
Dr. Donald J. Marsh
Dr. Douglas A. Marsland*
Dr. Daniel S. Martin
Dr. Kirby Martin*
Dr. Richard L. Masland
Dr. Richard C. Mason
Dr. Arthur M. Master*
Dr. Edmund B. Masurovsky
Dr. James A. L. Mathers
Dr. Robert Matz
Dr. Paul H. Maurer
Dr. Evelyn A. Mauss
Dr. Morton H. Maxwell
Dr. Klaus Mayer
Dr. Aubre de L. Maynard
Dr. E. W. Maynert
Dr. Rajarshi Mazumder
Dr. Abraham Mazur
Dr. Valentino Mazzia
Dr. Edward Meilman
Dr. Gilbert W. Mellin
Dr. Robert B. Mellins
Dr. Ismael Mena
Dr. Milton Mendlowitz
Dr. Walter L. Mersheimer
Dr. Clarence G. Merskey
Dr. William Metcalf

Dr. Karl Meyer*
Dr. Leo M. Meyer
Dr. Alexander J. Michie
Dr. Catherine Michie
Dr. Gardner Middlebrook
Dr. G. Burroughs Mider*
Dr. Peter O. Milch
Dr. A. T. Milhorat*
Dr. David K. Miller*
Dr. Frederick Miller
Dr. John A. P. Millett*
Dr. C. Richard Minick
Dr. George S. Mirick
Dr. Alfred E. Mirsky*
Dr. Ormond G. Mitchell
Dr. William F. Mitty, Jr.
Dr. Walter Modell*
Dr. Carl Monder
Dr. William L. Money
Dr. Dan H. Moore
Dr. John A. Moore
Dr. Norman S. Moore*
Dr. Stanford Moore
Dr. Anatol G. Morrell
Dr. Augusto Moreno
Dr. Gilda Morillo-Cucci
Dr. Akiro Morishima
Dr. Robert S. Morison*
Dr. Thomas Quinlan Morris
Dr. Alan N. Morrison
Dr. Jane H. Morse
Dr. Stephen I. Morse
Dr. Norman Moscowitz
Dr. Michale W. Mosesson
Dr. Melvin L. Moss
Dr. Harry Most*
Dr. Isabel M. Mountain*
Dr. Walter E. Mountcastle
Dr. Arden W. Moyer
Dr. Richard W. Moyer
Dr. R. S. Muckenfuss*
Dr. Stuart Mudd*
Dr. G. H. Mudge
Dr. John V. Mueller

* Life member.

Dr. Hans J. Müller-Eberhard
Dr. Ursula Müller-Eberhard
Dr. John H. Mulholland*
Dr. M. G. Mulinos*
Dr. Otto H. Muller*
Dr. George E. Murphy
Dr. James S. Murphy
Dr. M. Lois Murphy
Dr. Carl Muschenheim*
Dr. W. P. Laird Myers
Dr. Martin S. Nachbar
Dr. Ralph L. Nachman
Dr. David D. Nachmansohn*
Dr. Gabriel G. Nahas
Dr. Tatsuji Namba
Dr. William Nastuk
Dr. Samuel Natelson
Dr. Gerald Nathenson
Dr. M. Nathenson
Dr. Stanley G. Nathenson
Dr. Clayton L. Natta
Dr. Enid A. Neidle
Dr. Norton Nelson
Dr. Harold C. Neu
Dr. Maria M. New
Dr. Walter Newman
Miss Eleanor B. Newton*
Dr. Shih-hsun Ngai
Dr. Warren W. Nichols
Dr. John F. Nicholson
Dr. John L. Nickerson*
Dr. Giorgio L. Nicolis
Dr. Julian Niemetz
Dr. Ross Nigrelli*
Dr. Jerome Nisselbaum
Dr. Charles Noback*
Dr. W. C. Noble*
Dr. M. R. Nocenti
Dr. Hymie L. Nossel
Dr. Richard Novick
Dr. Alex B. Novikoff
Dr. Ruth Nussenzweig
Dr. Victor Nussenzweig
Dr. Irwin Nydick

Dr. William B. Ober
Dr. Manuel Ochoa, Jr.
Dr. Severo Ochoa*
Dr. Herbert F. Oettgen
Dr. Michiko Okamoto
Dr. Arthur J. Okinaka
Dr. William M. O'Leary
Dr. Eng Bee Ong
Dr. Stanley Opler
Dr. Jack H. Oppenheimer
Dr. Peter Orahovats
Dr. Irwin Oreskes
Dr. Marian Orlowski
Dr. Ernest V. Orsi
Dr. Louis G. Ortega
Dr. Eduardo Orti
Dr. Priscilla J. Ortiz
Dr. Elliott F. Osserman
Dr. Elena I. R. Ottolenghi
Dr. Zoltan Ovary
Dr. M. D. Overholzer*
Dr. Norbert I. A. Overweg
Dr. Geraldine Pace
Dr. George H. Paff*
Dr. Irvine H. Page*
Dr. George Paladf
Dr. Photini S. Papageorgiou
Dr. Paul S. Papavasiliou
Dr. George D. Pappas
Dr. A. M. Pappenheimer, Jr.
Dr. John R. Pappenheimer
Dr. E. M. Papper
Dr. Jean Papps
Dr. Frank S. Parker
Dr. Raymond C. Parker*
Dr. Gary Aiken Parks
Dr. Robert J. Parsons*
Dr. Pedro Pasik
Dr. Tauba Pasik
Dr. Pierluigi Patriarca
Dr. Philip Y. Patterson
Dr. Elsa Paulsen
Dr. Mary Ann Payne
Dr. O. H. Pearson

* Life member.

Dr. Edmund D. Pellegrino
Dr. Abraham Penner
Dr. James M. Perel
Dr. George A. Perera
Dr. Eli Perlman
Dr. Gertrude Perlmann
Dr. James H. Pert
Dr. Demetrius Pertsemlidis
Dr. Mary Petermann*
Dr. Malcolm L. Peterson
Dr. Frederick S. Philips
Dr. Robert A. Philips*
Dr. Lennart Philipson
Dr. Emanuel T. Phillips
Dr. Mildred Phillips
Dr. Julia M. Phillips-Quagliata
Dr. E. Converse Pierce, II
Dr. John G. Pierce
Dr. Cynthia H. Pierce-Chase
Dr. Lou Ann Pilkington
Dr. Joseph B. Pincus
Dr. Johanna Pindyck
Dr. Kermit L. Pines
Dr. Margaret Pittman*
Dr. Robert F. Pitts*
Dr. Calvin F. Plimpton
Dr. Charles M. Plotz
Dr. Fred Plum
Dr. Norman H. Plummer*
Dr. Beatriz G. T. Pogo
Dr. Alan Paul Poland
Dr. William Pollack
Dr. Eric H. Pollaczek
Dr. Marcel W. Pons
Dr. Edwin A. Popenoe
Dr. J. W. Poppell
Dr. Hans Popper
Dr. Keith R. Porter
Dr. Jerome G. Porush
Dr. Jerome B. Posner
Dr. Joseph Post
Dr. Edward L. Pratt
Dr. Rudolf Preisig
Dr. John B. Price, Jr.

Dr. Marshall P. Primack
Dr. R. B. Pringle
Dr. Philip H Prose
Dr. John F. Prudden
Dr. Lawrence Prutkin
Dr. Charles B. Pryles
Dr. Maynard E. Pullman
Dr. Dominick P. Purpura
Dr. Franco Quagliata
Dr. Paul G. Quie
Dr. Michel Rabinovitch
Dr. Julian Rachele
Dr. Efraim Racker
Dr. Bertha Radar
Dr. C. A. Ragan, Jr.
Dr. Morris L. Rakieten*
Dr. Henry T. Randall
Dr. Helen M. Ranney
Dr. Felix T. Rapaport
Dr. Howard G. Rapaport
Dr. Fred Rapp
Dr. Maurice M. Rapport
Dr. Sarah Ratner*
Dr. Aaron R. Rausen
Dr. Rulon W. Rawson
Dr. Bronson S. Ray*
Dr. George G. Reader
Dr. Walter Redisch
Dr. Colvin Manuel Redman
Dr. S. Frank Redo
Dr. George Reed
Dr. Gabrielle H. Reem
Dr. Carl Reich
Dr. Edward Reich
Dr. Franz Reichsman
Dr. Christine Reilly
Dr. Joseph F. Reilly
Dr. Leopold Reiner
Dr. Donald J. Reis
Dr. Charlotte Ressler
Dr. Paul Reznikoff*
Dr. Goetz W. Richter
Dr. Maurice N. Richter*
Dr. Ronald F. Rieder

* Life member.

DR. HAROLD RIFKIN
DR. ROBERT R. RIGGIO
DR. WALTER F. RIKER, JR.
DR. CONRAD M. RILEY
DR. VERNON RILEY
DR. DAVID ALLEN RINGLE
DR. HARRIS RIPPS
DR. RICHARD S. RIVLIN
DR. ELLIOTT ROBBINS
DR. WILLIAM C. ROBBINS
DR. CARLETON W. ROBERTS
DR. JAY ROBERTS
DR. KATHLEEN E. ROBERTS
DR. RICHARD B. ROBERTS
DR. ALAN G. ROBINSON
DR. WILLIAM G. ROBINSON
DR. DUDLEY F. ROCHESTER
DR. OLGA M. ROCHOVANSKY
DR. MORRIS ROCKSTEIN
DR. MURIEL ROGER
DR. WILLIAM M. ROGERS*
DR. BERNARD ROGOFF
DR. IDA PAULINE ROLF*
DR. PAUL D. ROSAHN*
DR. MARIE C. ROSATI
DR. HARRY M. ROSE*
DR. HERBERT G. ROSE
DR. THEODORE ROSEBURY*
DR. DAVID M. ROSEMAN
DR. GERALD ROSEN
DR. JOHN F. ROSEN
DR. ORA ROSEN
DR. MURRAY D. ROSENBERG
DR. PHILIP ROSENBERG
DR. ISADORE ROSENFIELD
DR. HERBERT S. ROSENKRANZ
DR. WILLIAM S. ROSENTHAL
DR. WILLIAM ROSNER
DR. HERBERT ROSS
DR. EUGENE F. ROTH
DR. ALAN B. ROTHBALLER
DR. SIDNEY ROTHBARD
DR. EDMUND O. ROTHSCHILD
DR. M. A. ROTHSCHILD

DR. J. ROTSTEIN
DR. BRUCE ROWE
DR. LEWIS P. ROWLAND
DR. PAUL ROYCE
DR. ALBERT L. RUBIN
DR. BENJAMIN A. RUBIN
DR. RONALD P. RUBIN
DR. WALTER RUBIN
DR. DANIEL RUDMAN
DR. MARIA A. RUDZINSKA
DR. PAUL RUEGESEGGAR
DR. GEORGE D. RUGGIERI
DR. MARK G. RUSH
DR. HENRY I. RUSSEK
DR. DAVID D. RUTSTEIN
DR. DAVID SABATINI
DR. F. B. ST. JOHN*
DR. STANLEY WALTER SAJDERA
DR. LESTER B. SALANS
DR. GERALD SALEN
DR. LETTY G. M. SALENTIJN
DR. LEE SALK
DR. MILTON R. J. SALTON
DR. PAUL SAMUEL
DR. HERBERT SAMUELS
DR. STANLEY SAMUELS
DR. JOHN SANDSON
DR. B. J. SANGER*
DR. SHIGERU SASSA
DR. JUSSI J. SAUKKONEN
DR. ARTHUR SAWITSKY
DR. PHILIP N. SAWYER
DR. WILBUR H. SAWYER
DR. BRIJ SAXENA
DR. DAVID SCHACHTER
DR. RUSSELL W. SCHAEDLER
DR. MORRIS SCHAEFFER
DR. FENTON SCHAFFNER
DR. MATTHEW D. SCHARFF
DR. JOSEPH SCHATTNER
DR. FREDERICK G. SCHECHTER
DR. ANDREAS S. SCHEID
DR. I. HERBERT SCHEINBERG
DR. ISAAC SCHENKEIN

* Life member.

Dr. Barbara M. Scher
Dr. Lawrence Scherr
Dr. Gerald Schiffman
Dr. Fred J. Schilling
Dr. E. B. Schlesinger
Dr. R. W. Schlesinger
Dr. Jeffrey Schlom
Dr. Donald H. Schmidt
Dr. Willard C. Schmidt
Dr. Howard A. Schneider
Dr. J. B. Schorr
Dr. Paul Schreibman
Dr. Henry A. Schroeder*
Dr. Ernest Schwartz
Dr. Gabriel Schwartz
Dr. Irving L. Schwartz
Dr. James H. Schwartz
Dr. Morton K. Schwartz
Dr. David Schwimmer
Dr. John J. Sciarra
Dr. John Martin Scott
Dr. T. F. McNair Scott*
Dr. William Addison Scott
Dr. John C. Scott-Baker
Dr. John Scudder*
Dr. Beatrice C. Seegal*
Dr. David Seegal*
Dr. Mildred S. Seelig
Dr. Barry M. Segal
Dr. Sheldon J. Segal
Dr. George Seiden
Dr. Samuel Seifter
Dr. Stephen J. Seligman
Dr. Ewald Selkurt
Dr. Fabio Sereni
Dr. Aura.E. Severinghaus*
Dr. Robert E. Shank
Dr. James A. Shannon*
Dr. Harvey C. Shapiro
Dr. Herman S. Shapiro
Dr. L. L. Shapiro*
Dr. Lucille Shapiro
Dr. William R. Shapiro
Dr. Lewis Inman Sharp*

Dr. Joyce C. Shaver
Dr. Elliott Shaw
Dr. David Shemin
Dr. Paul Sherlock
Dr. Raymond Lionel Sherman
Dr. Sol Sherry
Dr. Maurice E. Shils
Dr. Bong-Sop Shim
Dr. W. C. Shoemaker
Dr. Sheppard Siegal
Dr. Charles D. Siegel
Dr. George Siegel
Dr. Morris Siegel*
Dr. Philip Siekevitz
Dr. Ernest B. Sigg
Dr. Selma Silagi
Dr. Robert Silber
Dr. Maximillian Silbermann*
Dr. Lous E. Siltzbach
Dr. Lawrence Silver
Dr. Richard T. Silver
Dr. Morris Silverman
Dr. William A. Silverman
Dr. Emanuel Silverstein
Dr. Martin E. Silverstein
Dr. Samuel C. Silverstein
Dr. Michael Simberkoff
Dr. Eric J. Simon
Dr. Norman Simon
Dr. Kai Lennart Simons
Dr. Joe L. Simpson
Dr. Melvin V. Simpson
Dr. Gregory Siskind
Dr. William R. Sistrom
Dr. Anneliese L. Sitarz
Dr. Vladimir P. Skipski
Dr. Lawrence E. Skogerson
Dr. Robert J. Slater
Dr. Daniel N. Slatkin
Dr. George K. Smelser*
Dr. Frank Rees Smith
Dr. James P. Smith
Dr. M. De Forest Smith*
Dr. Elizabeth M. Smithwick

* Life member.

Dr. I. Snapper*
Dr. Edna Sobel
Dr. Louis Soffer*
Dr. Richard Luber Soffer
Dr. Arthur Sohval
Dr. Leon Sokoloff
Dr. Samuel Solomon
Dr. Alex C. Solowey
Dr. Martin Sonenberg
Dr. Chull Sung Song
Dr. Sun K. Song
Dr. Chester M. Southam
Dr. Hamilton Southworth
Dr. Paul Spear
Dr. Abraham Spector
Dr. Francis Speer*
Dr. Robert Sisson Spiers
Dr. Frank C. Spencer
Dr. Sol Spiegelman
Dr. Morton Spivack
Dr. David Sprinson
Dr. Norton Spritz
Dr. Katherine Sprunt
Dr. P. R. Srinivasan
Dr. Frank G. Standaert
Dr. Neal H. Steigbigel
Dr. Richard M. Stein
Dr. William Stein
Dr. Philip R. Steinmetz
Dr. Herman Steinberg
Dr. Kurt H. Stenzel
Dr. Kenneth Sterling
Dr. Joseph R. Stern
Dr. Marvin Stern
Dr. Stephen Sternberg
Dr. Irmin Sternlieb
Dr. C. A. Stetson, Jr.
Dr. De Witt Stetten, Jr.
Dr. Fred W. Stewart*
Dr. Harold J. Stewart*
Dr. John M. Stewart
Dr. W. B. Stewart
Dr. Walter A. Stewart*
Dr. C. Chester Stock

Dr. Walter Stoeckenius
Dr. Herbert Carl Stoerk
Dr. Peter E. Stokes
Dr. Daniel J. Stone
Dr. Fritz Streuli
Dr. William T. Stubenbord
Dr. Jackson H. Stuckey
Dr. Horace W. Stunkard*
Dr. John Y. Sugg*
Dr. W. James Sullivan
Dr. Martin I. Surks
Dr. Marcy Sussman
Dr. Emanuel Suter
Dr. Joseph G. Sweeting
Dr. Roy C. Swingle
Dr. Margaret Prince Sykes
Dr. Wlodzimierz Szer
Dr. Milton Tabachnick
Dr. John Taggart
Dr. Tadasu Takumaru
Dr. Igor Tamm
Dr. Donald F. Tapley
Dr. Suresh S. Tate
Dr. Edward Lawrie Tatum
Dr. Robert N. Taub
Dr. Harry Taube
Dr. Sheldon B. Taubman
Dr. Howard Taylor, Jr.*
Dr. Constantin V. Teodoru
Dr. Robert D. Terry
Dr. Gail A. Theis
Dr. Lewis Thomas
Dr. David D. Thompson
Dr. Gerald E. Thomson
Dr. Neils A. Thorn
Dr. David A. Tice
Dr. William S. Tillett*
Dr. Edward Tolstoi*
Dr. Helene W. Toolan
Dr. William A. Triebel
Dr. George L. Tritsch
Dr. Walter Troll
Dr. R. C. Truex
Dr. Orestes Tsolas

* Life member.

Dr. DAN TUCKER
Dr. GERARD M. TURINO
Dr. LOUIS B. TURNER
Dr. ROBERT A. TURNER
Dr. GRAY H. TWOMBLY*
Dr. SIDNEY UDENFRIEND
Dr. JOHNATHAN W. UHR
Dr. JOHN E. ULTMANN
Dr. PAUL N. UNGER
Dr. HARRY E. UNGERLEIDER*
Dr. ARTHUR CANFIELD UPTON
Dr. MORTON URIVETZKY
Dr. CARLO VALENTI
Dr. FRED VALENTINE
Dr. PARKER VANAMEE
Dr. WILLIAM G. VAN DER KLOOT
Dr. MARIO VASSALLE
Dr. EDWARD F. VASTOLA
Dr. ELLIOT S. VESELL
Dr. CARMINE T. VICALE
Dr. WOLF VISHNIAC
Dr. F. STEPHEN VOGEL
Dr. HENRY J. VOGEL
Dr. ALFRED VOGL
Dr. MÖGENS VOLKERT
Dr. SPYROS M. VRATSANOS
Dr. IRVING H. WAGMAN
Dr. BERNARD M. WAGNER
Dr. STANLEY WALLACH
Dr. LILA A. WALLIS
Dr. RODERICH WALTER
Dr. S. C. WANG
Dr. LEWIS W. WANNAMAKER
Dr. GEORGE E. WANTZ
Dr. BETTINA WARBURG*
Dr. ROBERT C. WARNER
Dr. LOUIS R. WASSERMAN
Dr. ALICE M. WATERHOUSE*
Dr. ROBERT F. WATSON
Dr. SAMUEL WAXMAN
Dr. ANNEMARIE WEBER
Dr. BRUCE WEBSTER*
Dr. JEROME P. WEBSTER*
Dr. RENE WEGRIA

Dr. RICHARD WEIL, III
Dr. VIRGINIA L. WEIMAR
Dr. LEO WEINER
Dr. HERBERT WEINFELD
Dr. I. BERNARD WEINSTEIN
Dr. LEONARD H. WEINSTEIN
Dr. STEPHEN W. WEINSTEIN
Dr. IRWIN M. WEINSTOCK
Dr. JOHN M. WEIR
Dr. ABNER I. WEISMAN
Dr. HARVEY J. WEISS
Dr. JULIUS H. WEISS
Dr. PAUL A. WEISS
Dr. HERBERT WEISSBACH
Dr. BERNARD WEISSMAN
Dr. NORMAN WEISSMAN
Dr. GERALD WEISSMANN
Mrs. JULIA T. WELD*
Dr. DANIEL WELLNER
Dr. GERHARDT WERNER
Dr. SIDNEY C. WERNER*
Dr. ARTHUR R. WERTHEIM
Dr. W. CLARKE WESCOE
Dr. C. D. WEST
Dr. JOSEPH P. WHALEN
Dr. HENRY O. WHEELER
Dr. FREDERICK E. WHEELOCK
Dr. ABRAHAM WHITE
Dr. ABRAHAM G. WHITE
Dr. JOHN C. WHITSELL, II
Dr. EDKHART WIEDEMAN
Dr. NORMAN WIKLER
Dr. HERBERT B. WILCOX, JR.
Dr. M. HENRY WILLIAMS
Dr. JOHN WILSON
Dr. VICTOR J. WILSON
Dr. SIDNEY J. WINAWER
Dr. ERICH E. WINDHAGER
Dr. MYRON WINICK
Dr. ASHER WINKELSTEIN
Dr. ROBERT M. WINTERS
Dr. JONATHAN WITTENBERG
Dr. HERBERT WOHL

* Life member.

DR. ABNER WOLF*
DR. GEORGE A. WOLF
DR. JULIUS WOLF
DR. ROBERT L. WOLF
DR. STEWART G. WOLF, JR.
DR. JAMES A. WOLFF
DR. HARVEY WOLINSKY
DR. SANDRA R. WOLMAN
DR. HARRISON F. WOOD
DR. HENRY N. WOOD
DR. JOHN A. WOOD
DR. JOHN L. WOOD
DR. JAMES M. WOODRUFF
DR. KENNETH R. WOODS
DR. MELVIN H. WORTH, JR.
DR. WALTER D. WOSILAIT
DR. IRVING S. WRIGHT
DR. MELVIN D. YAHR
DR. SEHCHI YASUMURA

DR. CHESTER L. YNTEMA*
DR. BRUCE YOUNG
DR. FULI YU
DR. TASAI-FAN YU
DR. JOHN B. ZABRISKIE
DR. GEORGE A. ZAK
DR. RALPH ZALUSKY
DR. ESMAIL D. ZANJANI
DR. VRATISLAV ZBUZEK
DR. JAMES E. ZIEGLER, JR.
DR. HARRY M. ZIMMERMAN
DR. NORTON ZINDER
DR. ARTHUR ZITRIN
DR. BURTON L. ZOHMAN
DR. OLGA ZONERAICH
DR. SAMUEL ZONERAICH
DR. JOSEPH ZUBIN*
DR. MARJORIE B. ZUCKER
DR. BENJAMIN W. ZWEIFACH

* Life member.

DECEASED MEMBERS

T. J. ABBOTT
ISIDOR ABRAHAMSON
MARK H. ADAMS
ISAAC ADLER
DAVID ADELERSBERG
ANDREW J. AKELAITUS
F. H. ALBEE
HARRY L. ALEXANDER
SAMUEL ALEXANDER
F. M. ALLEN
ALF S. ALVING
H. L. AMOSS
DOROTHY H. ANDERSON
W. B. ANDERTON
WM. DEWITT ANDRUS
HERMAN ANFANGER
W. PARKER ANSLOW, JR.
WILLIAM ANTOPOL
VIRGINIA APGAR
R. T. ATKINS
HUGH AUCHINCLOSS
JOHN AUER
J. HAROLD AUSTIN
O. T. AVERY
HALSEY BAGG
C. V. BAILEY
HAROLD C. BAILEY
PEARCE BAILEY
ELEANOR DEF. BALDWIN
CLARENCE G. BANDLER
BOLTON BANGS
W. HALSEY BARKER
F. H. BARTLETT
LOUIS BAUMAN
W. W. BEATTIE
CARL BECK
WILLIAM H. BECKMAN
EDWIN BEER
RHODA W. BENHAM
A. A. BERG

MAX BERGMANN
CHARLES M. BERRY
SOLOMON A. BERSON
HERMANN M. BIGGS
FRANCIS G. BLAKE
N. R. BLATHERWICK
SIDNEY BLUMENTHAL
ERNEST P. BOAS
AARON BODANSKY
CHARLES F. BOLDUAN
RICHARD WALKER BOLLING
RALPH H. BOOTS
J. B. BORDEN
DAVID BOVAIRD
SAMUEL BRADBURY
ERWIN BRAND
A. BRASLAU
S. M. BRICKNER
NATHAN E. BRILL
J. J. BRONFENBRENNER
HARLOW BROOKS
F. TILDEN BROWN
SAMUEL A. BROWN
WADE H. BROWN
MAURICE BRUGER
JOSEPH D. BRYANT
SUE BUCKINGHAM
JACOB BUCKSTEIN
LEO BUERGER
HENRY G. BUGBEE
FREDERICK C. BULLOCK
JESSE H. M. BULLOWA
JOSEPH L. BUNIM
CLAUDE A. BURRETT
GLENWORTH R. BUTLER
GEORGE F. CAHILL
W. E. CALDWELL
WM. F. CAMPBELL
ALEXIS CARREL
HERBERT S. CARTER

John R. Carty
L. Casamajor
Russell L. Cecil
William H. Chambers
Harry A. Charipper
John W. Churchman
W. LeGros Clark
Hans T. Clarke
F. Morris Class
A. F. Coca
Martin Cohen
Alfred E. Cohn
L. G. Cole
Rufus Cole
Charles F. Collins
Harvey S. Collins
Robert A. Cooke
Otis M. Cope
A. Curtis Corcoran
James A. Corscaden
Pol N. Coryllos
Frank Co-Tui
Edwin B. Cragin
Lyman C. Craig
Floyd M. Crandall
G. W. Crary
Glenn E. Cullen
John G. Curtis
Edward Cussler
H. D. Dakin
C. Darlington
William Darrach
Martin H. Dawson
Richard C. de Bodo
H. J. Devel, Jr.
Smith O. Dexter, Jr.
Henry D. Diamond
Joseph S. Diamond
Paul A. Dineen
Konrad Dobriner
Blake F. Donaldson
Edwin J. Doty
Henry Doubilet
W. K. Draper
Alexander Duane
E. F. DuBois

Theodore Dunham
C. B. Dunlap
F. Duran-Reynals
Walter H. Eddy
Wilhelm E. Ehrich
Max Einhorn
Robert Elman
C. A. Elsberg
W. J. Elser
A. Elywyn
Haven Emerson
Earl T. Engle
Albert A. Epstein
Lowell Ashton Erf
Samuel M. Evans
James Ewing
Gioacchino Failla
K. G. Falk
L. W. Famulener
Morris S. Fine
Maurice Fishberg
Simon Flexner
Austin Flint
Rolfe Floyd
Joseph E. Flynn
Ellen B. Foot
N. Chandler Foot
Joseph Fraenkel
Edward Francis
Thomas Francis, Jr.
Robert T. Frank
Virginia K. Frantz
Rowland G. Freeman
Webb Freundenthal
Wolff Freundenthal
E. D. Friedman
Lewis F. Frissell
H. Dawson Furniss
C. Z. Garside
Herbert S. Gasser
F. L. Gates
F. P. Gay
Samuel H. Geist
Bertram M. Gesner
H. R. Geyelin
William J. Gies

J. H. GLOBUS
S. GOLDSCHMIDT
S. S. GOLDWATER
KENNETH GOODNER
FREDERICK GOODRIDGE
MALCOLM GOODRIDGE
N. W. GREEN
HARRY S. N. GREENE
MAGNUS I. GREGERSEN
LOUISE GREGORY
MENAS S. GREGORY
LOUIS GROSS
EMIL GRUENING
FREDERICK GUDERNATSCH
H. V. GUILE
JOHN H. HALL
JOHN W. HALL
ROBERT H. HALSEY
FRANKLIN M. HANGER
LAWRENCE W. HANLON
MEYER M. HARRIS
R. STUART HART
FRANK HARTLEY
ROBERT A. HATCHER
HANS O. HATERIUS
H. A. HAUBOLD
JAMES A. HAWKINS
SELIG HECHT
GEORGE HELLER
CARL M. HERGET
W. W. HERRICK
GEORGE J. HEUER
HOWARD H. HINES
CHARLES L. HOAGLAND
AUGUST HOCH
EUGENE HODENPYL
GEORGE M. HOGEBOOM
ARTHUR L. HOLLAND
FRANKLIN HOLLANDER
A. W. HOLLIS
J. G. HOPKINS
HENRY HORN
HERBERT I. HOROWITZ
FRANK HORSFALL, JR.
HUBERT S. HOWE
STEPHEN HUDACK

JOHN H. HUDDLESTON
F. B. HUMPHREYS
II. M. IMDODEN
MOSES L. ISAACS
BENJAMIN JABLONS
LEOPOLD JACHES
HOLMES C. JACKSON
ABRAHAM JACOBI
WALTER A. JACOBS
GEORGE W. JACOBY
A. G. JACQUES
JOSEPH JAILER
WALTER B. JAMES
EDWARD G. JANEWAY
H. H. JANEWAY
JAMES W. JOBLING
SCOTT JOHNSON
WILLIAM C. JOHNSON
NORMAN JOLLIFFE
DON R. JOSEPH
LOUIS JULIANELLE
FREDERICK KAMMERER
DAVID KARNOPSKY
HAIG H. KASABACH
LUDWIG KAST
JACOB KAUFMANN
F. L. KEAYS
EDWARD C. KENDALL
FOSTER KENNEDY
LEO KESSEL
BEN WITT KEY
E. L. KEYES
GEORGE KING
FRANCIS P. KINNICUTT
D. B. KIRBY
STUART F. KITCHEN
HERBERT M. KLEIN
I. S. KLEINER
PAUL KLEMPERER
WALTER C. KLOTZ
ARNOLD KNAPP
HERMANN KNAPP
YALE KNEELAND, JR.
SEYMOUR KORKES
ARTHUR F. KRAETZER
MILTON LURIE KRAMER

CHARLES KRUMWIEDE
L. O. KUNKEL
ANN G. KUTTNER
RAPHAEL KURZROK
WILLIAM S. LADD
ALBERT R. LAMB
ADRIAN V. S. LAMBERT
ALEXANDER LAMBERT
ROBERT A. LAMBERT
S. W. LAMBERT
ERNEST W. LAMPE
CARNEY LANDIS
GUSTAV LANGMANN
H. CLAIRE LAWLER
BURTON J. LEE
EGBERT LeFEVRA
E. S. L'ESPERANCE
P. A. LEVENE
MICHAEL LEVINE
SAM Z. LEVINE
CHARLES H. LEWIS
JACQUES M. LEWIS
EMANUEL LIBMAN
CHARLES C. LIEB
FRANK L. LIGENZOWSKI
WRAY LLOYD
JOHN S. LOCKWOOD
JACQUES LOEB
LEO LOEB
ROBERT O. LOEBEL
LEO LOEWE
ALFONSO A. LOMBARDI
C. N. LONG
PERRIN LONG
WARFIELD T. LONGCOPE
RAY R. LOSEY
ROSE LUBSCHEZ
SIGMUND LUSTGARTEN
JOHN D. LYTTLE
W. G. MACCALLUM
DUNCAN A. MACINNES
GEORGE M. MACKENZIE
THOMAS T. MACKIE
COLIN M. MACLEOD
WARD J. MACNEAL
F. B. MALLORY

A. R. MANDEL
JOHN A. MANDEL
F. S. MANDELBAUM
MORRIS MANGES
GEORGE MANNHEIMER
DAVID MARINE
W. B. MARPLE
WALTON MARTIN
HOWARD MASON
HUNTER MCALPIN
CHARLES MCBURNEY
GERTRUDE S. MCCANN
W. S. MCCANN
W. ROSS MCCARTY
J. F. MCGRATH
EARL B. MCKINLEY
FRANKLIN C. MCLEAN
PHILIP D. MCMASTER
GEORGE MCNAUGHTON
EDWARD S. MCSWEENY
FRANK S. MEARA
W. J. MEEK
VICTOR MELTZER
ADOLF MEYER
ALFRED MEYER
MICHAEL MICAILOVSKY
HENRY MILCH
EDGAR G. MILLER
GEORGE N. MILLER
SAMUEL CHARLES MILLER
H. C. MOLOY
CARL MOORE
ROBERT A. MOORE
C. V. MORRILL
A. V. MOSCHCOWITZ
ELI MOSCHCOWITZ
ABRAHAM MOSS
JOHN P. MUNN
EQUINN W. MUNNELL
EDWARD MUNTWYLER
J. R. MURLIN
JAMES B. MURPHY
CLAY RAY MURRAY
V. C. MYERS
JAMES F. NAGLE
JAMES NEILL

CARL NEUBERG
SELIAN NEUHOF
ISAAC NEUWIRTH
WALTER L. NILES
CHARLES V. NOBACK
JOSE F. NONIDEZ
VAN HORNE NORRIE
CHARLES NORRIS
JOHN H. NORTHROP
NATHANIEL READ NORTON
FRANCIS W. O'CONNOR
CHARLES T. OLCOTT
PETER K. OLITSKY
EUGENE L. OPIE
B. S. OPPENHEIMER
HANS OPPENHEIMER
KERMIT E. OSSERMAN
SADAO OTANI
JOHN OVERMAN
RALPH S. OVERMAN
BERYL H. PAIGE
ARTHUR PALMER
WALTER W. PALMER
GEORGE W. PAPANICOLAOU
A. M. PAPPENHEIMER
WILLIAM H. PARK
STEWART PATON
JOHN M. PEARCE
LOUISE PEARCE
CHARLES H. PECK
JAMES PEDERSEN
E. J. PELLINI
DAVID PERLA
E. COOPER PERSON
J. P. PETERS
FREDERICK PETERSON
GODFREY R. PISEK
HARRY PLOTZ
MILTON PLOTZ
G. R. POGUE
ALBERT POLICARD
WILLIAM M. POLK
ABOU D. POLLACK
F. L. POLLACK
SIGMUND POLLITZER
NATHANIEL B. POTTER

THOMAS D. PRICE
T. M. PRUDDEN
EDWARD QUINTARD
FRANCIS M. RACKEMANN
GEOFFREY W. RAKE
C. C. RANSOM
BRET RATNER
GEORGE B. RAY
R. G. REESE
JULES REDISH
BIRDSEY RENSHAW
C. P. RHOADS
A. N. RICHARDS
D. W. RICHARDS
HENRY B. RICHARDSON
OSCAR RIDDLE
AUSTEN FOX RIGGS
JOHN L. RIKER
SEYMOUR RINZLER
DAVID RITTENBERG
THOMAS M. RIVERS
ANDREW R. ROBINSON
FRANK H. ROBINSON
W. STANTON ROOT
MARTIN ROSENTHAL
NATHAN ROSENTHAL
M. A. ROTHSCHILD
PEYTON ROUS
WILFRED F. RUGGIERO
F. J. RYAN
GEORGE H. RYDER
FLORENCE R. SABIN
BERNARD SACHS
WM. P. ST. LAWRENCE
WILLIAM A. SALANT
T. W. SALMON
BENJAMIN SALZER
E. F. SAMPSON
HAROLD E. SANTEE
WILBUR A. SAWYER
REGINALD H. SAYRE
HERBERT W. SCHMITZ
RUDOLPH SCHOENHEIMER
LOUIS C. SCHROEDER
HERMAN VON W. SCHULTE
E. L. SCOTT

H. SHAPIRO
HARRY H. SHAPIRO
GEORGE Y. SHINOWARA
EPHRAIM SHORR
HAROLD SHORR
WILLIAM K. SIMPSON
M. J. SITTENFIELD
J. E. SMADEL
A. ALEXANDER SMITH
CARL H. SMITH
HOMER W. SMITH
R. GARFIELD SNYDER
J. W. STEPHENSON
KURT G. STERN
GEORGE D. STEWART
H. A. STEWART
E. G. STILLMAN
RALPH G. STILLMAN
L. A. STIMSON
C. R. STOCKARD
GEORGE H. STUECK, JR.
ARTHUR M. SUTHERLAND
JOHN E. SUTTON
PAUL C. SWENSON
HOMER F. SWIFT
SAM SWITZER
JEROME T. SYVERTON
L. JAMES TALBOT
STERLING P. TAYLOR, JR.
OSCAR TEAGUE
J. DE CASTRO TEIXEIRA
EDWARD E. TERRELL
JOHN S. THACHER
ALLEN M. THOMAS
GILES W. THOMAS
W. HANNA THOMPSON
KARL J. THOMPSON
EDGAR W. TODD
WISNER R. TOWNSEND
THEODORE T. TSALTAS
JAMES D. TRASK, JR.
H. F. TRAUT
NORMAN TREVES
FOLKE TUDVAD
JOSEPH C. TURNER
KENNETH B. TURNER

CORNELIUS J. TYSON
EDWARD UHLENHUTH
F. T. VAN BEUREN, JR.
PHILIP VAN INGEN
R. VAN SANTVOORD
DONALD D. VAN SLYKE
H. N. VERMILYE
KARL VOGEL
WILLIAM C. VON GLAHN
HARRY SOBOTKA
F. P. SOLLEY
H. J. SPENCER
J. BENTLEY SQUIER, JR.
W. C. STADIE
NORBERT STADTMÜLLER
HENRICUS J. STANDER
DANIEL STATS
J. MURRAY STEELE
RICHARD STEIN
ANTONIO STELLA
AUGUSTUS WADSWORTH
HEINRICH B. WAELSCH
H. F. WALKER
GEORGE B. WALLACE
WILBUR WARD
JAMES S. WATERMAN
JANET WATSON
LESLIE T. WEBSTER
R. W. WEBSTER
WEBB W. WEEKS
RICHARD WEIL
LOUIS WEISFUSE
SARA WELT
JOHN R. WEST
RANDOLPH WEST
GEORGE W. WHEELER
JOHN M. WHEELER
J. S. WHEELWRIGHT
DANIEL WIDELOCK
CARL J. WIGGERS
HERBERT B. WILCOX
H. B. WILLIAMS
ARMINE T. WILSON
MARGARET B. WILSON
PHILIP D. WILSON
JOSEPH E. WINTERS

DAN H. WITT
HAROLD G. WOLFF
I. OGDEN WOODRUFF
D. WAYNE WOOLLEY
HERMAN WORTIS
S. BERNARD WORTIS
ARTHUR M. WRIGHT

JONATHAN WRIGHT
WALTER H. WRIGHT
JOHN H WYCKOFF
L. ZECHMEISTER
FREDERICK D. ZEMAN
H. F. L. ZIEGEL
HANS ZINSSER

B 5
C 6
D 7
E 8
F 9
G 0
H 1
I 2
J 3